3 5046 00324 2353

SO-AUI-200

Study Guide Plus

for

Henslin

Sociology
A Down-to-Earth Approach

Ninth Edition

prepared by

Jessica Herrmeyer
Hawkeye Community College

PEARSON

Boston   New York   San Francisco
Mexico City   Montreal   Toronto   London   Madrid   Munich   Paris
Hong Kong   Singapore   Tokyo   Cape Town   Sydney

SANTA MONICA COLLEGE LIBRARY

Copyright © 2008 Pearson Education, Inc.

All rights reserved. No part of the material protected by this copyright notice may be reproduced or utilized in any form or by any means, electronic or mechanical, including photocopying, recording, or by any information storage and retrieval system, without written permission from the copyright owner.

To obtain permission(s) to use material from this work, please submit a written request to Allyn and Bacon, Permissions Department, 75 Arlington Street, Boston, MA 02116 or fax your request to 617-848-7320.

ISBN-13: 978-0-205-57039-3
ISBN-10:   0-205-57039-9

Printed in the United States of America

10 9 8 7 6 5 4 3 2   11 10 09 08

Contents

CHAPTER 1
THE SOCIOLOGICAL PERSPECTIVE

CHAPTER SUMMARY

- Sociology offers a perspective—a view of the world—that stresses that people's social experiences underlie their behavior. For C. Wright Mills, this is the interaction of biography and history.

- Sociology is the scientific study of society and human behavior, and, as such, is one of the social sciences, which study human behavior, in contrast to the natural sciences, which focus on explaining events in our natural environment.

- Sociology emerged during the upheavals of the Industrial Revolution. Early sociologists such as Auguste Comte, Herbert Spencer, Karl Marx, Emile Durkheim, Max Weber, and Harriet Martineau focused on how the sweeping social changes brought about by the Industrial Revolution affected human behavior.

- Sociologists agree that sociological research should be value free but disagree concerning the proper purposes and uses of social research. Some believe its purpose should be only to advance the understanding of human behavior; others feel that its goal should be to investigate harmful social arrangements and reform society.

- Weber believed that in order the understand others' behavior, sociologists must try to see the world from their perspective (*Verstehen*). Durkheim stressed the importance of uncovering the objective social conditions that influence behavior (social facts).

- In the early years of sociology, only a few wealthy women received an advanced education. Harriet Martineau was an Englishwoman who wrote about social life in Great Britain and the United States and published a book titled *Society in America*.

- In North America, departments of sociology began to be established at the end of the nineteenth century. In the early years, the contributions of women and minorities were largely ignored.

- Pure sociology is research whose only purpose is to make discoveries, while applied sociology is the use of sociology to solve social problems in settings ranging from the workplace to the family.

- A theory is a general statement about how sets of facts are related to one another. Because no one theory encompasses all of reality, sociologists use three primary theoretical frameworks: (1) symbolic interactionism, concentrating on how people use symbols to develop and share their views of the world, usually focuses on the micro level; (2) functional analysis, stressing that society is made up of various interrelated parts which, when working properly, contribute to the stability of society, focuses on the macro level;

and (3) conflict theory, emphasizing that social life is based on a competitive struggle to gain control over scarce resources, also focuses on the macro level.

- Sociology today is coming closer to its roots of applying sociological knowledge to social change, and two major trends are applied sociology and globalization. This latter trend is likely to broaden the scope of sociological inquiry beyond its traditional concentration on U.S. society.

LEARNING OBJECTIVES
After reading Chapter 1, you should be able to:

1. Explain the sociological perspective: what it is, what it offers, and why C. Wright Mills referred to it as "the intersection of biography (the individual) and history (the social factors that influence the individual)." (4)
2. Know what is meant by social location and how it helps people define themselves and helps others define them. (4)
3. Understand how sociology is applicable to the growing global world. (5)
4. Identify, understand, and make distinctions between the natural sciences and the social sciences. (5-6)
5. Identify and explain the goals of science. (7)
6. Understand how sociology views and studies human behavior and how its particular areas of focus are similar to—and different from—each of the other social sciences. (5-6)
7. Discuss the social changes—and the changing social conditions—which fostered the development of sociology as a distinct academic discipline in the middle of the nineteenth century. (8-10)
8. Identify and critique the sociological contributions of the following mid-to-late nineteenth and early twentieth century European sociologists: Auguste Comte, Herbert Spencer, Karl Marx, Emile Durkheim, Max Weber, and Harriet Martineau. (10-17)
9. Understand how and why levels of social integration may affect rates of suicide and how Emile Durkheim's nineteenth century study of suicide helped demonstrate how social forces affect people's behaviors. (12-13)
10. Explain the role of values in social research as prescribed by Max Weber, and the ensuing controversies over whether sociological research can be and/or should be value free.(14)
11. Distinguish between "*Verstehen*," as envisioned by Max Weber, and "social facts," as defined by Emile Durkheim; explain how, despite their differences, both can be used together in social research. (15-16)
12. Discuss why there were so few women sociologists in the nineteenth and early twentieth century, and how the contributions of women sociologists during this time period were received and evaluated by their male counterparts. (16-17)
13. Trace the history of sociology in North America from the late 1800s to the present time, identifying the specific sociological contributions of the following American sociologists: Jane Addams, W.E.B. Du Bois, Talcott Parsons, and C. Wright Mills. (18-22)
14. Understand the historical tensions and ongoing debates in North American sociology between social reform and social analysis, and discuss how the sociological contributions of Jane Addams, W.E.B. Du Bois, Talcott Parsons, and C. Wright Mills fit into the tensions and debates. (18-22)

15. Discuss the current state of American sociology as it relates to the debate between social reform and social analysis and the role applied sociology plays in this debate. (21-22)
16. Explain what applied sociologist do, the careers that applied sociologists may have, and how some applications of sociology such as capturing Saddam Hussein or the study of job discrimination are examples of applied sociology. (21-23, 32)
17. Define what is meant by theory and explain why it is an important part of sociology. (22-23)
18. Identify the three major theoretical perspectives in sociology—symbolic interactionism, functional analysis, and conflict theory—and describe the particular level of analysis, characteristics, viewpoints, and concerns that are associated within each. (23-31)
19. Apply each of the three sociological perspectives to a contemporary issue such as the increasing rates of divorce in America. (30)
20. Understand the changing directions in sociology. (31-33)
21. Explain why the American Sociological Association is promoting public sociology. (32)
22. Describe the current trends that are shaping the future of sociology in the United States, and how globalization, in particular, may expand American sociology's horizons in the twenty-first century. (31-33)

CHAPTER OUTLINE

I. **The Sociological Perspective**
   A. This perspective is important because it provides a different way of looking at familiar worlds. It allows us to gain a new vision of social life.
   B. This perspective stresses the broader social context of behavior by looking at individuals' social location—employment, income, education, gender, age, and race—and by considering external influences—people's experiences—which are internalized and become part of a person's thinking and motivations. We are thus able to see the links between what people do and the social settings that shape their behavior.
   C. This perspective enables us to analyze and understand both the forces that contribute to the emergence and growth of the global village and our unique experiences in our own smaller corners of this village.

II. **Sociology and the Other Sciences**
   A. Science is the systematic methods used to obtain knowledge and the knowledge obtained by those methods. It can be divided into the natural sciences and the social sciences. Sociology is defined as "the scientific study of society and human behavior."
   B. The natural sciences attempt to comprehend, explain, and predict events in our natural environment.
   C. Social sciences attempt to objectively study the social world. Like the natural sciences, the social sciences are divided into specialized fields based on their subject matter.
      1. Anthropology is the sister discipline of sociology and attempts to understand culture (a people's total way of life) by focusing primarily on tribal people. This is giving way, though, to study of groups in industrialized settings.
      2. Economics analyzes the production, distribution, and allocation of the material goods and services of a society.

3. Political science focuses on politics or government.
4. Psychology concentrates on processes that occur within the individual.
5. Sociology is similar to the other social sciences in some ways, but is distinct because it looks at all social institutions, focuses on industrialized societies, and looks at external factors which influence people.

D. All sciences have certain goals.
  1. The first goal is to explain *why* something happens.
  2. The second goal is to make generalizations by looking for patterns, recurring characteristics, or events.
  3. The third goal is to predict what will happen in the future, given current knowledge.

E. To achieve these goals, scientists must move beyond common sense and rely on conclusions based on systematic study.

III. The Origins of Sociology

A. Sociology developed in the middle of the nineteenth century when European social observers began to use scientific methods to test their ideas. The following four factors led to its development:
  1. The social upheaval in Europe as a result of the Industrial Revolution, which led to changes in the way people lived their lives;
  2. The political revolutions in America and France, which encouraged people to rethink their ideas about social life;
  3. The development of imperialism; as the Europeans conquered other nations, they came in contact with different cultures and began to ask why cultures varied;
  4. The success of the natural sciences created a desire to apply scientific methods to find answers for the questions being raised about the social world.

B. Auguste Comte coined the term "sociology" and suggested the use of positivism—applying the scientific approach to the social world—but he did not utilize this approach himself. Comte believed that this new science should not only discover sociological principles, but apply them to social reform.

C. Herbert Spencer viewed societies as evolutionary, coined the term "the survival of the fittest," and became known for social Darwinism. Spencer was convinced that no one should intervene in the evolution of society and that attempts at social reform were wrong.

D. Karl Marx, whose ideas about social classes and class struggle between the bourgeoisie and the proletariat was the foundation of the conflict perspective, believed that class conflict was the key to human history. Marx believed that conflict and struggle would end only with a revolution by the working class.

E. Emile Durkheim played an important role in the development of sociology.
  1. One of his primary goals was to get sociology recognized as a separate academic discipline.
  2. He was interested in understanding the social factors that influence individual behavior; he studied suicide rates among different groups and concluded that social integration—the degree to which people are tied to their social group—was a key social factor in suicide.

3. Durkheim's third concern was that social research be practical; sociologists should not only diagnose the causes of social problems but develop solutions for them.

F. Max Weber was one of the most influential of all sociologists, raising issues that remain controversial today. Disagreeing with Karl Marx, Weber defined religion as a central force in social change (i.e., Protestantism encourages greater economic development and was the central factor in the rise of capitalism in some countries).

1. The Protestant belief system encouraged its members to embrace change.
2. Protestants sought "signs" that they were in God's favor; financial success became a major sign. The more money they made, the more secure they were about their religious standing.
3. Weber called this behavior the *Protestant ethic*; he called their readiness to invest capital in order to make more money the *spirit of capitalism.*

IV. Values in Sociological Research

A. Weber advocated that sociological research should be value free (personal values or biases should not influence it) and objective (totally neutral).
   1. Sociologists agree that objectivity is a proper goal, but acknowledge that no one can escape values entirely.
   2. Replication is when a study is repeated to see if the same results are found. It is one means to avoid the distortions that values can cause.
B. Although sociologists may agree that research should be objective, the proper purposes and uses of sociology are argued among sociologists. Some take the position that the proper role of sociology is to advance understanding of social life, while others believe that it is the responsibility of sociologists to explore the harmful social arrangements of society.
C. On one side are those who say that understanding social behavior is sociology's proper goal and that the knowledge gained through research belongs to the scientific community, to be used by anyone for any purpose. The other side is those who say the goal of sociological research should be to investigate harmful social conditions and lead the way in reforming society.

V. *Verstehen* and Social Facts

A. Weber argued that sociologists should use *Verstehen* ("to grasp by insight") in order to see beyond the social facts to the subjective meanings that people attach to their own behavior.
B. Durkheim believed that social facts, patterns of behavior that characterize a social group, reflect underlying conditions of society and should be used to interpret other social facts.
C. Social facts and *Verstehen* fit together because they reinforce each other; sociologists use *Verstehen* in order to interpret social facts.

VI. Sexism in Early Sociology

A. In the early years of sociology, the field was dominated by men because rigidly defined social roles prevented most women from pursuing an education.

14. Social facts and *Verstehen*: (15)
    a. have no relationship to each other.
    b. have been disproved.
    c. go hand-in-hand.
    d. were both concepts developed by Durkheim.

15. Which of the following statements about the experiences of North American women in sociology is *incorrect*? (16)
    a. In the early years of sociology, the situation of women in North America was similar to that of European women—they were largely excluded and their work ignored.
    b. Unlike the situation in Europe, many North American women found that there were few barriers and they were able to train in sociology and receive faculty appointments.
    c. Many early women sociologists in North America turned to social activism.
    d. Many male sociologists who worked as professors denied female sociologists the title of sociologist, preferring to call them social workers.

16. Jane Addams won the Nobel Prize for: (18)
    a. her literary work, *Society in America.*
    b. her contributions to the founding of the NAACP.
    c. her role in the British Revolution.
    d. working on behalf of poor immigrants.

17. Which of the following North American sociologists wrote extensively on race relations, experienced prejudice and discrimination personally and professionally, and helped found the NAACP? (18-20)
    a. Wright Mills
    b. Talcott Parsons
    c. W. E. B. Du Bois
    d. Jane Addams

18. Sociologists who research social problems for government commissions or agencies are: (21)
    a. politically correct.
    b. basic sociologists.
    c. applied sociologists.
    d. pure sociologists.

19. Which of the following is not an accurate description of a theory? (23)
    a. a general statement about how some parts of the world fit together
    b. using objective, systematic observations
    c. formula of concepts that explain how two or more "facts" are related to one another
    d. an explanation of social phenomenon

20. The theoretical perspective that views society as composed of symbols that we use to establish meaning, develop our views of the world, and communicate with one another is: (23-24)
    a. functionalism.
    b. symbolic interactionism.
    c. dramaturgical theory.
    d. conflict theory.

21. According to Robert Merton, an action that has an unintended consequence that can hurt a system's equilibrium is a: (26)
    a. manifest function.
    b. latent function.
    c. dysfunction.
    d. latent dysfunction.

22. Industrialization and urbanization have undermined the traditional purposes of the family, according to theorists using _____ analysis. (27)
    a. conflict
    b. exchange
    c. symbolic interaction
    d. functional

23. Karl Marx first asserted that _____ was inherent in all relations that have authority. (29)
    a. conflict
    b. symbolic interaction
    c. nonverbal interaction
    d. subjective meaning

24. Which sociologist noted that conflict is most likely to develop among people who are in close relationships? (29)
    a. Karl Marx
    b. Lewis Coser
    c. Herbert Spencer
    d. Robert Edgerton

25. Conflict theorists might explain the high rate of divorce by looking at: (30)
    a. the changing meanings associated with marriage and divorce.
    b. society's basic inequalities between males and females.
    c. changes that have weakened the family unit.
    d. the loss of family functions which held a husband and wife together.

26. Which theorists focus on the macro level of analysis? (30)
    a. functionalists and conflict theorists
    b. functionalists and symbolic interactionists
    c. conflict theorists and symbolic interactionists
    d. functionalists only

27. According to your text, which theoretical perspective is best for studying human behavior? (31)
    a. the functionalist perspective
    b. the symbolic interactionist perspective
    c. the conflict perspective
    d. a combination of all of the above

28. The first phase of sociology in the United States was characterized by: (31)
    a. a concern with establishing sociology as a social science.
    b. a focus on establishing sociology as a respectable field of knowledge.
    c. an interest in using sociological knowledge to improve social life and change society.
    d. a broad acceptance of women and racial minorities within the discipline.

29. What did Devah Pager find from her research on whether prison records made a difference in getting a job? (32)
    a. That having a prison record did not make a difference in terms of getting a job.
    b. That gender played a significant role in who got offered a job.
    c. That white men with a prison record were more likely to be offered a job than African American men with a clean record.
    d. That white women with a record were less likely to get a job than a white male with a prison record.

30. What trend does the author of your text suggest is likely to transform the scope and focus of U.S. sociology in the future? (33)
    a. race, class, and gender inequalities
    b. cultural diversity
    c. technology
    d. globalization

TRUE-FALSE QUESTIONS

1. _____The sociological perspective helps us understand that people's social experiences underlie what they feel and do. (4)
2. _____Social location is where people are located in history and society. (4)
3. _____The natural sciences try to subjectively understand the world of nature. (6)
4. _____Like anthropologists, sociologists study culture and are interested in group structure and belief systems. (6)
5. _____Sociologists believe that internal mechanisms are very important in explaining an individual's thinking and motivations. (6-7)

6. _____Positivism refers to sociologists, attempts to see the good in society. (10)
7. _____Historically, the success of the natural sciences led to the search for answers to the social world as well. (10)
8. _____Herbert Spencer believed that human societies evolve like those of animal species. (10)
9. _____Karl Marx thought that a classless society eventually would exist. (11)
10. _____Durkheim found that social integration is a key social factor in studying suicide. (12)
11. _____Weber concluded that class conflict was the key factor in the rise of capitalism. (14)
12. _____According to Weber, subjective meanings are important in understanding human behavior. (15)
13. _____By applying *Verstehen*, we can better understand why there are more weddings in June and more babies born on Tuesdays. (15-16)
14. _____Harriet Martineau was widely recognized for her pioneering studies of social life in Great Britain and the United States. (17)
15. _____Du Bois battles racism as both a sociologist and a journalist. (19)
16. _____Symbolic interactionists primarily analyze how our definitions of ourselves and others underlie our behaviors. (23-25)
17. _____According to functionalists, the family has lost all of its traditional purposes. (27)
18. _____All conflict theorists focus on conflict between the bourgeoisie and the proletariat. (29)
19. _____Symbolic interactionism and conflict theories use macro-level analysis. (30)
20. _____Globalization is likely to broaden sociological horizons, refocusing research and theory away from its concentration on U.S. society. (33)

FILL-IN-THE-BLANK QUESTIONS

1. The _____ stresses the social contexts in which people are immersed and that influence their lives. (4)
2. _____ refers to the corners in life that people occupy because of where they are located in society. (4)
3. A_____ is a statement that goes beyond the individual case and is applied to a broad group or situation. (7)
4. Using objective, systematic observations to test theories is known as the _____. (10)
5. Comte stressed that sociology would not only discover social principles, but also would apply these to social _____. (10)
6. _____ is used to uncover bias in research by repeating a study in order to compare results with original findings. (14)
7. _____ analysis is a theoretical framework in which society is viewed as composed of various parts, each with a function that contributes to society's equilibrium.(26)
8. If an action is intended to help some part of a system, it is a _____ function. (26)

9. Lewis Coser pointed out that _____ is most likely to develop among people who are in close relationships. (29)
10. Feminist stress that men and women should have _____ rights. (29)
11. Conflict theorists see _____ as reflecting society's basic inequalities between male and females. (29)
12. Functionalists and conflict theorists focus on the _____ level; that is they examine large-scale patterns of society. (30)
13. Symbolic interactionsists focus on _____, what people do when they are in one another's presence. (30)
14. A tension between social reform and _____ has always run through sociology. (31)
15. _____ is the breaking down of national boundaries because of advances in communication, trade, and travel. (33)

MATCH THESE SOCIAL SCIENTISTS WITH THEIR CONTRIBUTIONS

_____	1. Auguste Comte	a. known as the "father of sociology"
_____	2. Herbert Spencer	b. wrote "Society in America" addressing American social life
_____	3. Karl Marx	c. this person studied suicide and social isolation
_____	4. C. Wright Mills	d. argued that the engine of human history is class conflict between the "halves" and "have nots"
_____	5. Emile Durkheim	e. argued that religion was the key force of social change and the rise of Capitalism
_____	6. Harriet Martineau	f. awarded the Nobel Prize for work establishing the Hull House
_____	7. Charles Horton Cooley	g. one of the founders of the NAACP
_____	8. W. E. B. Du Bois	h. developed concept of Social Darwinism, stated that societies evolve from lower to higher forms
_____	9. Max Weber	i. urged sociologists to go back to social reform
_____	10. Jane Addams	j. founder of symbolic interactionism

ESSAY QUESTIONS

1. Explain what the sociological perspective encompasses and then, using that perspective, discuss the forces that shaped the discipline of sociology.

2. Emile Durkheim studied European society at a time when it was undergoing major social upheaval as a result of the industrial revolution. In this first chapter, you are introduced to some of his major contributions—his work on suicide and his conclusions about social integration and anomie. Summarize what his contributions were and then consider how they are still useful for understanding social life today.

3. The textbook notes that *Verstehen* and social facts go hand in hand; explain how this is so. Assume that you have been asked to carry out research to find out more about why growing numbers of women and children are homeless and what particular problems they face. Discuss how you could use both *Verstehen* and social facts in your study.

4. Explain why, since the very beginning of society, there has been a continuing tension between analyzing society and working toward reforming society.

5. Explain what Weber meant when he said that sociology should be value free. Do you think this is possible? How do values play a role in determining the purpose and use of sociology?

CHAPTER 2
CULTURE

CHAPTER SUMMARY

- Culture is universal; all human groups create a design for living that includes both material and nonmaterial culture. Ideal culture, a group's ideal norms and values, exist alongside its real culture, the actual behavior that often falls short of the cultural ideals.

- All people perceive and evaluate the world through the lens of their own culture. People are naturally ethnocentric; that is, they use their own culture as a standard against which to judge other cultures. In comparison, cultural relativism tries to understand other peoples within the framework of their own culture.

- The central components of nonmaterial culture are symbols—anything to which people attach meaning and use to communicate with one another. Included in nonmaterial culture are gestures, language, values, norms, sanctions, folkways, and mores. Language is essential for culture because it allows us to move beyond the present, sharing with others our past experiences and our future plans. According to the Sapir-Whorf hypothesis, language not only expresses our thinking and perceptions but actually shapes them.

- All groups have values and norms and use positive and negative sanctions to show approval or disapproval of those who do or don't follow the norms.

- A subculture is a group whose values and behaviors set it apart from the general culture; a counterculture holds values that stand in opposition to the dominant culture.

- Although the U.S. is a pluralistic society made up of many groups, each with its own set of values, certain core values dominate. Some values cluster together to form a larger whole. Core values that contradict one another indicate areas of social tension and are likely to become points of social change.

- Cultural universals are values, norms or other cultural traits that are found in all cultures.

- No animals have language in the sociological sense of the term. However, different experiments suggest that some animals have a limited capacity to learn language.

- Cultural lag refers to a condition in which a group's nonmaterial culture lags behind its changing technology. Today's technology in travel and communication makes cultural diffusion occur more rapidly around the globe than in the past, resulting in some degree of cultural leveling, a process by which cultures become similar to one another.

LEARNING OBJECTIVES

After reading Chapter 2, you should be able to:

1. Understand what is meant by the term culture and list the principles surrounding culture. (38-41)
2. Distinguish between material and nonmaterial culture. (38)
3. Know what is meant by cultural shock, provide examples of situations that may result in cultural shock, and explain how cultural shock forces people to challenge their own cultural assumptions. (39)
4. Define ethnocentrism and cultural relativism, offer examples of both, and list their positive and negative consequences. (39-41)
5. List the components of symbolic culture. (44-50)
6. Define—and differentiate between—gestures and language. (44-48)
7. Explain why language is the basis of culture, including why it is critical to human life and essential for cultural development. (45-48)
8. Understand the Sapir-Whorf hypothesis and provide examples of how language not only reflects and expresses thinking, perceptions, and experiences, but also shapes and influences them. (48)
9. Define values, norms, sanctions, folkways, mores, and taboos; provide examples of each; and discuss their sociological significance. (48-50)
10. Compare, contrast, and offer examples of dominant cultures, subcultures, and countercultures. (51-52)
11. List the core values in American society as identified by Robin Williams and supplemented by James Henslin. (53)
12. Explain what is meant by value clusters and value contradictions, and offer examples of some value clusters and value contradictions in American society. (56)
13. Understand how value contradictions can affect social change. (56-57)
14. Discuss the differences between "ideal" and "real" culture. (58-59)
15. Define and identify some cultural universals and discuss how carrying out universal human activities may differ from one group to another. (59)
16. List some current "new technologies" and talk about how they are changing social behaviors and relationships in the United States and around the world. (60)
17. Define and discuss cultural lag and cultural change. (61)
18. Discuss the role that technology has played in cultural diffusion, and cultural leveling. (61-62)

CHAPTER OUTLINE

I. **What is Culture?**
    A. Culture is defined as the language, beliefs, values, norms, behaviors, and even material objects passed from one generation to the next.
        1. Material culture is things such as jewelry, art, buildings, weapons, machines, clothing, hairstyles, etc.

        2.   Nonmaterial culture is a group's ways of thinking (beliefs, values, and assumptions) and common patterns of behavior (language, gestures, and other forms of interaction).

B.   Culture provides a taken-for-granted orientation to life.

        1.   We assume that our own culture is normal or natural; in fact, it is not natural, but is learned. It penetrates our lives so deeply that it is taken for granted and provides the lens through which we perceive and evaluate things.

        2.   It provides implicit instructions that tell us what we ought to do and a moral imperative that defines what we think is right and wrong.

        3.   Coming into contact with a radically different culture produces "culture shock," challenging our basic assumptions.

        4.   A consequence of internalizing culture is ethnocentrism, using our own culture (and assuming it to be good, right, and superior) to judge other cultures. It is functional when it creates in-group solidarity, but can be dysfunctional if it leads to discrimination against those who are different.

C.   Cultural relativism consists of trying to appreciate other groups' ways of life in the context in which they exist, without judging them as superior or inferior to our own way of life.

        1.   Because we tend to use our own culture as the standard, cultural relativism presents a challenge to ordinary thinking.

        2.   At the same time, this view helps us appreciate other ways of life.

        3.   Robert Edgerton suggests developing a scale for evaluating cultures on their "quality of life". He argues that those cultural practices that result in exploitation *should* be judged as morally inferior to those that enhance people's lives.

II. Components of Symbolic Culture

A.   Sociologists sometimes refer to nonmaterial culture as symbolic culture.

        1.   A central component of culture is the symbol—something to which people attach meaning and use in communications.

        2.   Symbols include gestures, language, values, norms, sanctions, folkways, and mores.

B.   Gestures, or using one's body to communicate with others, are shorthand means of communication.

        1.   People in every culture use gestures, although the gestures and the meanings differ; confusion or offense can result because of misunderstandings over the meaning of a gesture or misuse of a gesture.

        2.   There is disagreement over whether there are any universal gestures. They tend to vary considerably around the world.

        3.   Because some gestures are so closely associated with emotional messages, the gestures themselves can elicit emotions.

C.   Language consists of a system of symbols that can be put together in an infinite number of ways in order to communicate abstract thought. Each word is a symbol to which a culture attaches a particular meaning. It is important because it is the primary means of communication between people.

1.   It allows human experiences to be cumulative; each generation builds on the body of significant experiences passed on to it by the previous generation, thus freeing people to move beyond immediate experiences.

2.   It allows for a social or shared past, and we are able to discuss past events with others.

3.   It allows for a social or shared future. Language allows us to plan future activities with one another.

4.   It allows the exchange of perspectives (i.e., ideas about events and experiences).

5.   It allows people to engage in complex, shared, goal-directed behavior.

6.   The Sapir-Whorf hypothesis states that our thinking and perception are not only expressed by language but are actually shaped by language because we are taught not only words but also a particular way of thinking and perceiving. Rather than objects and events forcing themselves onto our consciousness, our very language determines our consciousness.

D.   Culture includes values, norms, and sanctions.

1.   Values are the standards by which people define good and bad, beautiful and ugly. Every group develops values and expectations regarding the right way to reflect them.

2.   Norms are the expectations, or rules of behavior, that develop out of a group's values.

3.   Sanctions are the positive or negative reactions to the way in which people follow norms. Positive sanctions (a money reward, a prize, a smile, or even a handshake) are expressions of approval; negative sanctions (a fine, a frown, or harsh words) denote disapproval for breaking a norm.

4.   To relieve the pressure of having to strictly follow the norms, some cultures have moral holidays—specified times when people are allowed to break the norms and not worry about being sanctioned. Mardi Gras is an example of a moral holiday in our society.

5.   Some societies have moral holiday places; locations where norms are expected to be broken. An example would be red light districts where prostitution is allowed.

E.   Norms vary in terms of their importance to a culture.

1.   Folkways are norms that are not strictly enforced, such as passing on the left side of the sidewalk. They may only result in a person getting a dirty look.

2.   Mores are norms that are believed to be essential to core values; we insist on conformity to these core values. A person who steals, rapes, and kills has violated some of society's most important mores.

3.   Norms that one group considers to be folkways may be viewed as mores by another group. A male walking down the street with the upper half of his body uncovered may be violating a folkway; a female doing the same thing may be violating a mores.

4.   Taboos are norms so strongly ingrained that even the thought of them is greeted with revulsion. Eating human flesh and having sex with one's parents are examples of such behavior.

III. Many Cultural Worlds: Subcultures and Countercultures

A. Subcultures are groups whose values and related behaviors are so distinct that they set their members off from the dominant culture.

    1. Each subculture is a world within the larger world of the dominant culture, and has a distinctive way of looking at life, but remains compatible with the dominant culture.

    2. U.S. society contains tens of thousands of subcultures. Some are quite broad (teenagers), while others are narrow (body builders). Some ethnic groups form subcultures, as do certain occupational groups.

B. Countercultures are groups whose values set their members in opposition to the dominant culture.

    1. Although usually associated with negative behavior, some countercultures are not.

    2. Countercultures are often perceived as a threat by the dominant culture because they challenge the culture's values; for this reason the dominant culture will move against a particular counterculture in order to affirm its own core values. For example, the Mormons in the 1800's challenged the dominant culture's core value of monogamy.

IV. Values in U.S. Society

A. Identifying core values in U.S. society is difficult because it is a pluralistic society with many different religious, racial, ethnic, and special interest groups.

    1. Sociologist Robin Williams identified twelve core values: achievement and success (especially, doing better than others); individualism (success due to individual effort); activity and work; efficiency and practicality; science and technology (using science to control nature); progress; material comfort; humanitarianism (helpfulness, personal kindness, philanthropy); freedom; democracy; equality (especially of opportunity); racism, and group superiority.

    2. Henslin updated Williams's list by adding education; religiosity (belief in a Supreme Being and following some set of matching precepts); and romantic love.

B. Values are not independent units; value clusters are made up of related core values that come together to form a larger whole. In the value cluster surrounding success, for example, we find hard work, education, efficiency, material comfort, and individualism all bound together.

C. Some values conflict with each other. There cannot be full expressions of democracy, equality, racism, and sexism at the same time. These are value contradictions; as society changes some values are challenged and undergo modification.

D. A cluster that is emerging in response to fundamental changes in U.S. society is made up of the values of leisure, self-fulfillment, physical fitness, and youthfulness. Another emerging value is concern for the environment.

    1. Valuing leisure is reflected in the huge recreation industry that exists today.

    2. Self-fulfillment is expressed through the human potential movement and the popularity of self-help books and talk shows.

3. While physical fitness is not a new value, it is emphasized more today, as evidenced by the interest in health foods, weight and diet, and the growth in the number of health club/physical fitness centers.

4. There is today a new sense of urgency in being young, perhaps because of the presence of aging baby boomers who are trying to deny their biological fate.

5. Our history suggests a lack of concern for the environment; it was generally viewed as a challenge to be overcome. However, today there is a genuine concern for protecting the environment.

E. Core values do not change without meeting strong resistance.

1. Change is seen as a threat to the established way of life, something that will undermine people's present and their future.

2. Today's clash in values is often so severe that the term "culture wars" has been coined to refer to it.

F. Values and their supporting beliefs may blind people to other social circumstances. Success stories blind many people in the United States to the dire consequences of family poverty, lack of education, and dead-end jobs.

G. Ideal culture refers to the ideal values and norms of a people. What people actually do usually falls short of this ideal, and sociologists refer to the norms and values that people actually follow as real culture.

V. Cultural Universals

A. Although there are universal human activities, there is no universally accepted way of doing any of them.

1. Anthropologist George Murdock concluded that all human groups have certain cultural universals: customs about courtship, cooking, marriage, funerals, games, laws, music, myths, incest taboos, and toilet training are present in all cultures.

2. Even so, the specific customs differ from one group to another. By way of example, there is no universal form of the family, no universal way of disposing of the dead, and even methods of toilet training differ from one culture to another. Even incest is defined differently from group to group.

B. Sociobiologists argue that, as a result of natural selection, the basic cause of human behavior is biology.

1. Just as physical characteristics and instinctual behavior of animals is the result of natural selection (i.e., those genetic traits that aid in survival tend to become common to a species while those that do not tend to disappear), so is human behavior.

2. Edward Wilson has argued that religion, competition and cooperation, slavery and genocide, war and peace, envy and altruism, can all be explained in terms of genetic programming.

3. Most sociologists reject this claim. Unlike other species, humans are capable of reasoning and abstract thought; they can consider alternatives, reflect on outcomes, and make choices.

VI. Technology in the Global Village
    A.   Central to a group's material culture is its technology. In its simplest sense, technology can be equated with tools. In its broadest sense, technology also includes the skills or procedures necessary to make and use those tools.
        1.   The emerging technologies of an era that make a major impact on human life are referred to as new technologies. The printing press and the computer are both examples of new technologies.
        2.   The sociological significance of technology is that it sets the framework for the nonmaterial culture, influencing the way people think and how they relate to one another.
    B.   Not all parts of culture change at the same pace; *cultural lag* was William Ogburn's term for situations where the material culture changes first and the nonmaterial culture lags behind.
    C.   Although for most of human history cultures had little contact with one another, there has always been some contact with other groups, resulting in groups learning from one another.
        1.   This transmission of cultural characteristics is cultural diffusion; it is more likely to produce changes in material culture than the nonmaterial culture.
        2.   Cultural diffusion occurs more rapidly today, given the technology.
        3.   Travel and communication unite the world to such an extent that there almost is no "other side of the world" anymore. For example, Japan, no longer a purely Eastern culture, has adapted Western economic production, forms of dress, music, and so on. This leads to cultural leveling, when cultures become similar to one another.

KEY TERMS
After studying the chapter, review the definition for each of the following terms.

counterculture: a group whose values, beliefs, and related behaviors place its members in opposition to the values of the broader culture (52)
cultural diffusion: the spread of cultural characteristics from one group to another (61)
cultural lag: William Ogburn's term for human behavior lagging behind technological innovations (61)
cultural leveling: the process by which cultures become similar to one another, and especially when Western industrial culture is imported and diffused into industrializing nations (62)
cultural relativism: not judging a culture, but trying to understand it on its own terms (41)
cultural universal: a value, norm, or other cultural trait that is found in every group (56)
culture: the language, beliefs, values, norms, behaviors, and even material objects that are passed from one generation to the next (38)
culture shock: the disorientation that people experience when they come in contact with a fundamentally different culture and can no longer depend on their taken-for-granted assumptions about life (39)
ethnocentrism: the use of one's own culture as a yardstick for judging the ways of other individuals or societies, generally leading to a negative evaluation of their values, norms, and behaviors (39)

folkways: norms that are not strictly enforced (50)

gestures: the ways in which people use their bodies to communicate with one another (44)

ideal culture: the ideal values and norms of a people, the goals held out for them (58)

language: a system of symbols that can be combined in an infinite number of ways and represent not only objects but abstract thought (45)

material culture: the material objects that distinguish a group of people, such as their art, buildings, weapons, utensils, machines, hairstyles, clothing, and jewelry (38)

mores: norms that are strictly enforced because they are thought essential to core values (50)

negative sanction: an expression of disapproval for breaking a norm, ranging from a mild, informal reaction such as a frown to a formal prison sentence or an execution (48)

new technology: the emerging technologies of an era that have a significant impact on social life (60)

nonmaterial culture: a group's ways of thinking (including its beliefs, values, and other assumptions about the world) and of doing (its common patterns of behavior, including language and other forms of interaction) (38)

norms: the expectations, or rules of behavior, that reflect and enforce values (48)

pluralistic society: a society made up of many different groups (52)

positive sanction: a reward given for following norms, ranging from a smile to a prize (48)

real culture: the norms and values that people actually follow (59)

sanctions: expressions of approval or disapproval given to people for upholding or violating norms (48)

Sapir-Whorf hypothesis: Edward Sapir and Benjamin Whorf's hypothesis that language creates ways of thinking and perceiving (48)

sociobiology: a framework of thought that views human behavior as the result of natural selection and considers biological characteristics to be the fundamental cause of human behavior (59)

subculture: the values and related behaviors of a group that distinguish its members from the larger culture; a world within a world (51)

symbol: something to which people attach meaning and then use to communicate with others (44)

symbolic culture: another term for nonmaterial culture (44)

taboo: a norm so strong that it brings revulsion if it is violated (50)

technology: in its narrow sense, tools; its broader sense, the skills or procedures necessary to make and use those tools (60)

value clusters: a series of interrelated values that together form a larger whole (56)

value contradictions: values that conflict with one another; to follow the one means to come into conflict with the other (56)

values: the standards by which people define what is desirable or undesirable, good or bad, beautiful or ugly (48)

KEY PEOPLE

Review the major theoretical contributions or findings of these people.

Peter Conrad: He notes that not all homosexuals have the Xq28, "gay gene", and some people who have this gene are not homosexual. This gene does not determine behavior, and social causes should be examined. (60)

Charles Darwin: Darwin studied the principles on which natural selection occurred. (59)

Robert Edgerton: Edgerton attacks the concept of cultural relativism, suggesting that because some cultures endanger their people's health, happiness, or survival, there should be a scale to evaluate cultures on their "quality of life." (42)

Douglas Massey: This sociologist has studied the impact that immigration is having on Miami, predicting that the city will become the first "truly bilingual" city. (47)

George Murdock: Murdock was an anthropologist who sought to determine which cultural values, norms, or traits, if any, were found universally across the globe. (59)

William Ogburn: Ogburn coined the term "cultural lag." (61)

Edward Sapir and Benjamin Whorf: These two anthropologists argued that language not only reflects thoughts and perceptions, but actually shapes the way people think and perceive the world. (48)

JoEllen Shively: This sociologist's research demonstrated that Native Americans' identification with cowboys in Westerns was based on the symbolism of the West as a free, natural way of life. She discovered that they think of themselves as the real cowboys. (56)

William Sumner: Sumner developed the concept of ethnocentrism. (39)

Robin Williams: He identified twelve core U.S. values. (53)

Edward Wilson: Wilson is an insect specialist who claims that human behavior is also the result of natural selection. (59)

Eviatar Zerubavel: This sociologist offers an example of how language shapes our perceptions of the world (the *Sapir-Whorf hypothesis*). He notes that in his native Hebrew, there is no distinction made between the two forms of fruit spread—jams and jellies. It was only when he learned English that he was able to "see" the differences that were so obvious to English speakers. (48)

STUDENT APPLICATION PROJECTS

This is your opportunity to apply the sociological perspective to the world around you. The projects in this section refer to material introduced in this chapter of your text. These projects help you apply the sociological perspective "down to your earth...down to your daily life."

1. Over a period of two or three days observe various gestures that people use to communicate. List the various gestures. Are these gestures confusing to people as they try to communicate with one another? Are there easily shared meanings of the various gestures?

2. U.S. society contains thousands of subcultures and countercultures. Think of an example of each and identify the values they hold that distinguish them from, and in the case of the counterculture, place them in opposition to, the dominant society. Then explain how one could apply cultural relativism to understand each culture on its own terms.

3. Think about the text's various discussions about values, core values, and emerging values. Further, think about yourself, your parent(s), and your grandparent(s). Do different generations view values and the priority of certain values differently? Or are certain values universal across generations in the United States. Provide illustrations from your own family.

4. As noted in the text, there are various new technologies emerging and they have a significant impact on our culture and our lives. Choose two new technologies that you currently use and explore the positive and negative effects these technologies have on society. For each technology, list three positive and three negative effects. Overall, do you think culture will "catch up" to the newest technological developments? Explain your answer.

SELF-TEST
MULTIPLE CHOICE QUESTIONS

1. Which of the following would you use to describe a group's ways of thinking and doing, including language and other forms of interaction? (38)
    a. material culture
    b. nonmaterial culture
    c. ideological culture
    d. values

2. Which of the following is not part of material culture? (38)
    a. weapons and machines
    b. clothing
    c. value of individualism
    d. hairstyles

3. Which of these statements regarding culture is *not* true? (40-41)
    a. People generally are aware of the effects of their own culture.
    b. Culture touches almost every aspect of who and what a person is.
    c. At birth, people do not possess culture.
    d. Culture is the lens through which we perceive and evaluate what is going on around us.

4. In the textbook the author describes his feeling of disorientation while in Morocco. Which of the following best describes what he was feeling? (39)
    a. cultural diffusion
    b. cultural leveling
    c. cultural relativism
    d. cultural shock

5. An American thinks citizens of another country are barbarians if they like to attend bullfights. Which of the following concepts best describes this reaction? (39)
    a. cultural shock
    b. cultural relativism
    c. ethnocentrism
    d. cultural lag

6. Which of the following statements about cultural relativism is *incorrect*? (41)
    a. Cultural relativism does present a challenge to our ordinary thinking.
    b. None of us can be entirely successful at practicing cultural relativism.
    c. Robert Edgerton argues that we should accept other cultures according to their customs and values.
    d. Cultural relativism is an attempt to appreciate other ways of life.

7. Which of the following statements about gestures is *correct*? (44-45)
    a. Gestures are studied by anthropologists but not sociologists.
    b. Gestures are universal.
    c. Gestures always facilitate communication between people.
    d. Gestures can lead to misunderstandings and embarrassment.

8. Which of the following makes it possible for people to share a past, future, and common view of the world? (46)
    a. language
    b. cultural universals
    c. gestures
    d. computers

9. Sociologist Eviatar Zerubavel gives a good example when he states that his native language of Hebrew does not have separate words for jam and jelly. What is this an example of? (48)
    a. sociobiology
    b. the Davis-Moore theory
    c. the Sapir-Whorf hypothesis
    d. the Linguistic perspective

10. Every group develops expectations about the right ways to reflect its values. These expectations are: (48)
    a. ideal culture.
    b. real culture.
    c. norms.
    d. moral standards.

11. A monetary reward, a prize, a hug, or a pat on the back are all examples of: (48)
    a. norms.
    b. values.
    c. positive sanctions.
    d. negative sanctions.

12. Moral holidays are: (49)
    a. times when people can break the norms and not be sanctioned.
    b. often center around people getting drunk and being rowdy.
    c. celebrations like Mardi Gras.
    d. locations where norms are expected to be broken.

13. As you are shopping at a crowded mall, you absentmindedly forget to hold the door open for an elderly woman coming through behind you. The consequence is that the door slams in her face. Which of the following cultural components has been violated as a result of your behavior? (50)
    a. taboos
    b. mores
    c. values
    d. folkways

14. Which of the following statements about mores is *correct*? (50)
    a. Mores are essential to our core values and require conformity.
    b. Mores are norms that are not strictly enforced.
    c. Mores state that a person should not try to pass you on the left side of the sidewalk.
    d. Mores are less important in contemporary societies.

15. The author of your text cites eating human flesh as an example of: (50)
    a. folkways.
    b. mores.
    c. taboos.
    d. a behavior that is universally sanctioned.

16. Subcultures: (51)
    a. are a world within a world.
    b. have values and related behaviors that set their members apart from the dominant culture.
    c. include occupational groups.
    d. are all of the above.

17. The Hell's Angels are an example of a: (52)
    a. motorcycle enthusiast group.
    b. perverted people.
    c. counterculture.
    d. subculture.

18. U.S. society is made up of many different groups. Which of the following terms would a sociologist use to describe this type of society? (52)
    a. a melting pot
    b. a pluralist society
    c. a conflicted society
    d. a counterculture

19. Which of the following is not a value identified by sociologist Robin Williams in the 1960's? (53)
    a. achievement and success
    b. individualism
    c. romantic love
    d. progress

20. According to the author of your text, a new value cluster is emerging in the United States. Which of the following combination of core values make up this new value cluster? (57)
    a. achievement and success, activity and work, material comfort
    b. individualism, freedom, democracy, equality
    c. leisure, self-fulfillment, physical fitness, youngness
    d. youngness, self-fulfillment, romantic love, material comfort

21. Which of the following reflects conditions under which value contradictions can occur? (56)
    a. A value, such as the one that stresses group superiority, comes into direct conflict with other values, such as democracy and equality.
    b. Societies have very little social change.
    c. A series of interrelated values bind together to form a larger whole.
    d. Values blind people to many social circumstances.

22. The term *culture wars* refers to: (58)
    a. intense conflict between different cultures.
    b. intense conflict between subcultures and countercultures.
    c. wars fought because of ethnocentrism.
    d. the contemporary clash in core values in U.S. society.

23. Which of the following statements about ideal culture is correct? (58)
    a. Ideal culture is a value, norm, or other cultural trait that is found in every group.
    b. Ideal culture reflects the values and norms which people in a culture attempt to hold.
    c. Ideal culture is the norms people follow when they know they are being watched.
    d. Ideal culture is not a sociological concept.

24. Which of the following is *not* a cultural universal identified by George Murdock? (59)
    a. toilet training
    b. discipline
    c. courtship
    d. music

25. What is the perspective that views human behavior as the result of natural selection and considers biological characteristics to be the fundamental cause of human behavior? (56-59)
    a. natural science
    b. social science
    c. anthropology
    d. sociobiology

26. Edward Wilson, an insect specialist, claims that human behavior is the result of_____. (59)
    a. socialization
    b. natural selection
    c. genetics
    d. DNA

27. What would the printing press or the computer be considered? (60)
    a. inventive technologies
    b. diffused technologies
    c. examples of cultural leveling
    d. new technologies

28. There are computer tests that outperform physicians in diagnosing and prescribing treatment, yet most of us still visit doctors and rely on their judgement. What does this situation reflect? (61)
    a. resistance to new technologies
    b. cultural diffusion
    c. the social construction of technology
    d. cultural lag

29. Today bagels, woks, and hammocks are all a part of U.S. culture. The adoption of these objects illustrates which of the following processes or concepts? (61)
    a. cultural leveling
    b. nonmaterial culture
    c. cultural diffusion
    d. cultural universals

30. Coca-Cola is found in almost every country in the world. This is an example of: (62)
    a. cultural sharing.
    b. cultural leveling.
    c. enrichment of local cultures through contact with U.S. material culture.
    d. culture shock.

TRUE-FALSE QUESTIONS

1. _____Culture consists primarily of nonmaterial objects that are passed from one generation to another. (38)
2. _____Culture has little to do with people's ideas of right and wrong. (40)
3. _____No one can be entirely successful at practicing cultural relativism. (40)
4. _____Robert Edgerton is a strong critic of cultural relativism, arguing that cultures should be rated on the basis of their "quality of life." (41)
5. _____The gesture of nodding the head up and down to indicate "yes" is universal. (44)
6. _____Without language, humans could still successfully plan future events. (46)
7. _____Sanctions are positive or negative reactions to the ways people follow norms. (48)
8. _____While folkways may change across cultures, mores are universally the same. (50)
9. _____Motorcycle enthusiasts who emphasize personal freedom and speed, while maintaining values of success, form part of a counterculture. (51-52)
10. _____Racism and group superiority are core values in U.S. society. (53)
11. _____In her research, JoEllen Shively found that Native Americans identify with cowboys. (56)
12. _____Concern for the environment has always been a core value in U.S. society. (57)
13. _____It is not common for some values to conflict with one another. (56)
14. _____Today's clash in values is so severe it is referred to as a culture war. (58)
15. _____Although certain activities are present in all cultures, the specific customs differ from one group to another. (59)
16. _____Most sociologists do not agree with sociobiology. (59-60)
17. _____Edward Wilson argues that human behavior is different from animal behavior. (59-60)
18. _____Although new technologies may affect material culture, including the way things are done in a society, they have only minimal impact on nonmaterial culture, including the way people think and what they value. (60)
19. _____According to William Ogburn, a group's material culture usually changes first, with the nonmaterial culture lagging behind. (61)
20. _____Because of cultural leveling, the piñatas in Mexico are no longer donkeys but Mickey Mouse. (62)

FILL-IN-THE-BLANK QUESTIONS

1. The material objects that distinguish a group of people, such as their art, building, weapons, utensils, machines, hairstyles, clothing, and jewelry are known as _____. (38)
2. When Sue experiences disorientation from moving from the U.S. to Africa, this is known as _____. (39)
3. Trying to understand a culture on its own terms is the concept of _____. (41)
4. A _____ is something to which people attach meaning and then use to communicate with others. (44)

5. _____ are ways in which people use their body to communicate with one another. (44)
6. The Sapir-Whorf hypothesis says _____ has embedded in it ways of looking at the world. (48)
7. Expectations, or rules of behavior, that develop out of a group's values, are _____. (48)
8. Norms, that are not strictly enforced, are _____. (48)
9. _____ groups have values and norms that place it in opposition to the dominant culture. (52)
10. _____ are a series of interrelated values that together form a larger whole. (56)
11. Leisure time is becoming an emerging _____. (57)
12. Sociologists call the norms and values that people actually follow _____. (59)
13. Emerging technologies that have a significant impact on social life are referred to as _____. (60)
14. William Ogburn used the term_____ to refer to a situation in which nonmaterial culture takes a period of time to adjust to changes in the material culture. (61)
15. The process in which cultures become similar to one another is _____. (62)

MATCH THESE SOCIAL SCIENTISTS WITH THEIR CONTRIBUTIONS

_____	1. Edward Sapir and Benjamin Whorf	a.	*Stated Miami is truly bilingual*
_____	2. Robin Williams	b.	*introduced the concept of cultural lag*
_____	3. George Murdock	c.	*looked for cultural universals*
_____	4. Douglas Massey	d.	*principles of natural selection*
_____	5. Robert Edgerton	e.	*studied Native Americans' identification with Westerns*
_____	6. Edward Wilson	f.	*stated that language shapes perceptions of reality*
_____	7. William Sumner	g.	*believed natural selection produces human behavior*
_____	8. Charles Darwin	h.	*criticized aspects of cultural relativism*
_____	9. William Ogburn	i.	*noted core values of U.S. society*
_____	10. JoEllen Shively	j.	*developed the concept of ethnocentrism*

ESSAY QUESTIONS

1. Explain cultural relativism and discuss both the advantages and disadvantages of practicing it.

2. As the author points out, the United States is a pluralistic society, made up of many different groups. Having read this chapter about culture, discuss some of the things that are gained by living in such a society, as well as some of the problems that are created.

3. Consider the degree to which the real culture of the United States falls short of the ideal culture. Provide concrete examples to support your essay.

4. Thinking about William Ogburn's term cultural lag, explain why college students still attend traditional classes in the classroom when the technology is available to take classes over the Internet.

CHAPTER 3
SOCIALIZATION

CHAPTER SUMMARY

- Scientists have attempted to determine how much of people's characteristics come from heredity and how much from the social environment. One way to examine this is through identical twins who have been reared apart. Observations of feral, isolated, and institutionalized children also help to answer this question, as well as the Harlow's research on deprived monkeys. These studies have concluded that language and intimate interaction are essential to the development of human characteristics.

- Humans are born with the *capacity* to develop a self, but this self must be socially constructed through social interaction. Charles H. Cooley, George H. Mead, Jean Piaget, Sigmund Freud and Lawrence Kohlberg provide insights into the social development of human beings. The work of Cooley and Mead demonstrates that the self is created through our interactions with others. Piaget identified four stages in the development of our ability to reason: (1) sensorimotor; (2) preoperational; (3) concrete operational; and (4) formal operational. Freud defined the personality in terms of the id, ego, and superego; personality developed as the inborn desires (id) clashed with social constraints (superego); the ego develops to balance the id and the superego. Kohlberg focused on stages of moral development: (1) amoral, (2) preconventional, (3) conventional, and (4) postconventional.

- Socialization influences not only *how* we express our emotions, but *what* emotions we feel. These vary based on gender, culture, social class, and relationships.

- Gender socialization is a primary means of controlling human behavior, and social institutions reinforce a society's ideals of sex-linked behaviors. Gender messages in the family, from peers, and in the mass media are very powerful influences in reinforcing gender roles.

- The main agents of socialization—family, the neighborhood, religion, day care, school, peer groups, the mass media, sports, and the workplace—together contribute to our socialization, enabling us to become full-fledged members of society.

- Resocialization is the process of learning new norms, values, attitudes and behaviors. Intense resocialization takes place in total institutions. Most resocialization is voluntary, but some is involuntary.

- Socialization, which begins at birth, continues throughout the life course; at each stage the individual must adjust to a new set of social expectations. Life course patterns vary by social location such as history, gender, race-ethnicity, and social class, as well as by individual experiences such as health and age at marriage.

- Although socialization lays down the basic self and is modified by our social location, humans are not robots but rational beings who consider options and make choices.

LEARNING OBJECTIVES
After reading Chapter 3, you should be able to:

1. Discuss the ongoing debate over what most determines human behavior: "nature" (heredity) or "nurture" (social environment), and cite the evidence that best supports one position or the other. (66-70)

2. Discuss how studies of feral, isolated, and institutionalized children prove that social contact and interaction is essential for healthy human development. (66-69)

3. Identify key findings from Margaret and Harry Harlow's research on deprived monkeys and discuss how this research can be extrapolated to human beings. (69-70)

4. Explain Charles Horton Cooley's theory on the looking glass self. (70)

5. Discuss the stages that George Herbert Mead has identified in role taking. (71)

6. Explain Jean Piaget's research on the development of reasoning and identify what happens in each stage. (72-73)

7. Explain Freud's view on the development of personality and the sociologist's view of Freud's theory. (73-75)

8. Differentiate between Kohlberg and Gilligan's theory on the development of morality. (75-76)

9. Talk about how socialization is not only critical to the development of the mind, but also to the development of emotions—affecting not only how people express their emotions, but also what particular emotions they may feel. (76-77)

10. Know what is meant by gender socialization and how the family, media, and other agents of socialization *teach* children, from the time of their birth, to act masculine or feminine based on their gender. (78-81)

11. Describe some of the "gender messages" in the family and mass media and discuss how these messages may contribute to social inequality between men and women. (78-81)

12. List the major agents of socialization in American society, and talk about how each of these teach—and influence—people's attitudes, behaviors, and other orientations toward life. (81-87)

13. Define the term resocialization and provide examples of situations that may necessitate resocialization. (87-88)

14. Discuss how different settings, including total institutions, may go about the task of resocializing individuals. (88)

15. Understand why socialization is a lifelong process and summarize the needs, expectations, and responsibilities that typically accompany different stages of life. (88-92)

16. Identify changes that have occurred within society that have impacted how the stages of the life course have changed over time. (88-92)

17. Discuss why human beings are not prisoners of socialization while providing examples of how people can—and do—exercise a considerable degree of freedom over which agents of socialization to follow and which cultural messages to accept—or not accept—from those agents of socialization. (93)

CHAPTER OUTLINE

I. **What Is Human Nature?**
A. For centuries, people have tried to find an answer to the question of what is human about human nature. Studies of identical twins who have been reared apart help answer the question.
B. Feral (wild) children, who may have been raised by wild animals, have occasionally been found living in the woods. These stories lead one to wonder what humans would be like if left untouched by society.
C. Isolated children may show what humans might be like if secluded from society at an early age. Isabelle is a case in point. Although initially believed to be retarded, a surprising thing happened when she was given intensive language training. She began to acquire language and in only two years she had reached the normal intellectual level for her age. Without language there can be no culture or shared way of living.
D. Institutionalized children show that traits such as intelligence, cooperative behavior, and friendliness are the result of early close relations with other humans. Research with children reared in orphanages and cases like Genie, the 13½-year-old who had been kept locked in a small room for years, demonstrate the importance of early interaction for human development.
E. The Harlow's studies of monkeys reared in isolation have reached similar results. They concluded that if isolated for longer than six months, the more difficult adjustment becomes.
F. Babies do not "naturally" develop into human adults; although their bodies grow, human interaction is required for them to acquire the traits we consider normal for human beings. The process by which we learn the ways of our society, through interaction with others, is socialization.

II. **Socialization into Self, Mind, and Emotions**
A. Charles H. Cooley (1864-1929) concluded that human development is socially created—that our sense of self develops from interaction with others. He coined the term "looking-glass self" to describe this process.
   1. According to Cooley, this process contains three steps: (1) we imagine how we look to others; (2) we interpret others' reactions (how they evaluate us); and (3) we develop a self-concept.
   2. A favorable reflection in the "social mirror" leads to a positive self-concept, while a negative reflection leads to a negative self-concept.
   3. Even if we misjudge others' reactions, the misjudgments become part of our self-concept.
   4. This development process is an ongoing, lifelong process.
B. George H. Mead (1863-1931) agreed with Cooley but added that play is critical to the development of a self. In play, we learn to take the role of others—to understand and anticipate how others feel and think.
   1. Mead concluded that children are first able to take only the role of significant others (parents or siblings, for example); as the self develops, children internalize the expectations of other people, and eventually the entire group. Mead referred

to the norms, values, attitudes and expectations of people "in general" as the generalized other.

2. According to Mead, the development of the self goes through stages: (1) imitation (children initially can only mimic the gestures and words of others); (2) play (beginning at age three, children play the roles of specific people, such as a firefighter or the Lone Ranger); and (3) games (in the first years of school, children become involved in organized team games and must learn the role of each member of the team).

3. He distinguished the "I" from the "me" in development of the self: the "I" component is the subjective, active, spontaneous, creative part of the social self (for instance, "I shoved him"), while the "me" component is the objective part—attitudes internalized from interactions with others (for instance, "He shoved me").

4. Mead concluded that not only the self, but also the mind is a social product. We cannot think without symbols, and it is our society that gives us our symbols by giving us our language.

C. After years of research, Jean Piaget (1896-1980) concluded that there are four stages in the development of cognitive skills.

1. The sensorimotor stage (0-2 years): Understanding is limited to direct contact with the environment (touching, listening, seeing).

2. The preoperational stage (2-7 years): Children develop the ability to use symbols (especially language), which allow them to experience things without direct contact.

3. The concrete operational stage (7-12 years): Reasoning abilities become much more developed. Children now can understand numbers, causation, and speed, but have difficulty with abstract concepts such as truth.

4. The formal operational stage (12+ years): Children become capable of abstract thinking, and can use rules to solve abstract problems ("If X is true, why doesn't Y follow?").

D. Conclusions that Cooley, Mead, and Piaget came to regarding the self and reasoning appear to be universal. However, there is not consensus about the universality of Piaget's four stages of cognitive development.

1. Some adults never appear to reach the fourth stage, whether due to particular social experiences or to biology.

2. The content of what we learn varies from one culture to another; with very different experiences and the thinking processes that revolve around these experiences, we cannot assume that the developmental sequences will be the same for everyone.

E. Sigmund Freud (1856-1939) believed that personality consists of three elements: the id, ego, and superego.

1. The id inherited drives for self-gratification, demands fulfillment of basic needs such as attention, safety, food, and sex.

2. The ego balances between the needs of the id and the demands of society.

3. The superego, the social conscience we have internalized from social groups, gives us feelings of guilt or shame when we break rules, and feelings of pride and self-satisfaction when we follow them.

4. Sociologists object to Freud's view that inborn and unconscious motivations are the primary reasons for human behavior, for this view denies the central tenet of sociology—that social factors shape people's behaviors.

5. Feminist sociologists have been especially critical of Freud. According to Freud, females are inferior, castrated males.

F. Psychologist Lawrence Kohlberg concluded that humans go through a sequence of stages in the development of morality.

1. The amoral stage: the child does not distinguish between right and wrong.

2. The preconventional stage: the child follows the rules in order to stay out of trouble.

3. The conventional stage: the child follows the norms and values of society.

4. The postcoventional stage: the child reflects on abstract principles of right and wrong, using these principles to judge behavior.

G. Carol Gilligan studied differences between males and females in how they view morality.

1. Gilligan disagreed with Kohlberg's conclusions because they did not match her own experience and he only used boys in his studies.

2. She found that females tend to evaluate morality in terms of personal relationships and how their actions will affect others.

3. Males think in terms of abstract principles of right and wrong.

4. Other researchers tested Gilligan's conclusions and found no gender differences. Based on subsequent work, Gilligan no longer supports her original position.

5. Although it appears that the looking-glass self, role taking, and the social mind are universal phenomena,

H. Emotions are not simply the result of biology; they also depend on socialization within a particular society.

1. Anthropologist Paul Ekman concluded that everyone experiences six basic emotions: anger, disgust, fear, happiness, sadness, and surprise.

2. The expression of emotions varies according to gender, social class, culture, and relationships.

3. Socialization not only leads to different ways of expressing emotions but also to expressing what we feel.

I. Most socialization is meant to turn us into conforming members of society. We do some things and not others as a result of socialization. When we contemplate an action, we know the emotion (good or bad) that would result; thus society sets up controls on our behavior.

III. Socialization into Gender

A. By expecting different behaviors from people because they are male or female, society nudges boys and girls in separate directions from an early age, and this foundation carries over into adulthood.

B. Parents begin the process; researchers have concluded that in our society, mothers unconsciously reward their female children for being passive and dependent and their male children for being active and independent.

C. The mass media reinforce society's expectations of gender in many ways:

1. Ads perpetuate stereotypes by portraying males as dominant and rugged and females as sexy and submissive.
2. On television, male characters outnumber females and are more likely to be portrayed in higher-status positions.
3. Males are much more likely than females to play video games; we have no studies of how these games affect their players' ideas of gender.
4. Sociologist Melissa Milkie concluded that males use media images to discover who they are and what is expected of them as males.
5. We are not simply passive consumers of media images; we select those that are significant to our situation and use them to help us construct our understanding of the world.

IV. Agents of Socialization

A. Our experiences in the family have a lifelong impact on us, laying down a basic sense of self, motivation, values, and beliefs.
   1. Parents—often unaware of what they are doing—send subtle messages to their children about society's expectations for them as males or females.
   2. Research by Melvin Kohn suggests that there are social class and occupational differences in child rearing. The main concern of working-class parents is their children's outward conformity while middle-class parents show greater concern for the motivations for their children's behavior. The type of job held by the parent is also a factor: the more closely supervised the job is, the more likely the parent is to insist on outward conformity.
B. The neighborhood has an impact on children's development. Some neighborhoods are better places for children to grow up than others. For example, residents of more affluent neighborhood watch out for children more than do residents of poorer neighborhoods.
C. Religion plays a major role in the socialization of most Americans, even if they are not raised in a religious family. Religion especially influences morality, but it also influences ideas about what dress, speech, and manners are appropriate.
D. With more mothers today working for wages, day care is now a significant agent of socialization.
   1. One national study that followed 1300 children, in ten cities, from infancy into kindergarten found that the more hours per week that a child spends in day care, the weaker the bonds between mother and child and the greater the child's behavior problems.
   2. Children who spent less time in day care were more affectionate to their mothers and more cooperative.
   3. This pattern held regardless of the quality of day care, the family's social class, or whether the child is a boy or girl.
   4. We do not know how to explain these patterns. It could be that children who spend many hours in day care do not have their emotional needs met or that mothers who put their children in day care for more hours are less sensitive to their children in the first place.

5. These same researchers also found that the more hours children spend in day care, the higher they score on language tests. This was especially true for children in low income or abusive homes.

E. Schools serve many manifest (intended) functions for society, including teaching the skills and values thought to be appropriate. Schools also have several latent (unintended) functions.

1. At school, children are placed outside the direct control of friends/relatives and exposed to new values and ways of looking at the world. They learn *universality*, or that the same rules apply to everyone.

2. Schools also have a *hidden curriculum*—values not explicitly taught but inherent in school activities. For example, the wording of stories may carry messages about patriotism and democracy; by teaching that our economic system is just, schools may teach children to believe problems such as poverty are never caused by oppression and exploitation.

3. Schools also have a corridor curriculum—where students are taught by one another outside of the classroom. Unfortunately, these are often not positive values.

4. Conflict theorists note that schools teach children to take their place in the work force. Children of the wealthy go to private schools, where they acquire the skills and values appropriate to their eventual higher position, while children of working class parents attend public schools, where they are rarely placed in college prep classes.

F. One of the most significant aspects of education is that it exposes children to peer groups. A peer group is a group of people of roughly the same age who share common interests. Next to the family, peer groups are the most powerful socializing force in society.

1. Research by Patricia and Peter Adler document how elementary age children separated themselves by sex and developed their own worlds and norms. They found that popular boys were athletic, cool, and tough. Popular girls depended on family background, physical appearance, and the ability to attract popular boys.

2. It is almost impossible to go against a peer group, whose cardinal rule is to conform or be rejected. As a result, the standards of peer groups tend to dominate our lives.

G. Sports are also powerful socializing agents; children are taught not only physical skills, but also values. Boys often learn that masculinity is related to success in sports—the more successful a boy is in a sport, the more masculine he is considered, and the more he is accepted.

H. The workplace is a major agent of socialization for adults; from jobs, we learn not only skills, but also matching attitudes and values. We may engage in anticipatory socialization, learning to play a role before actually entering it, and enabling us to gradually identify with the role.

V. Resocialization

A. Resocialization refers to the process of learning new norms, values, attitudes and behaviors. Resocialization in its most common form occurs each time we learn something contrary to our previous experiences, such as going to work in a new job. It can be an intense experience, although it does not have to be.

B. Erving Goffman used the term *total institution* to refer to places such as boot camps, prisons, concentration camps, or some mental hospitals, religious cults, and boarding schools—places where people are cut off from the rest of society and are under almost total control of agents of the institution.

    1. A person entering the institution is greeted with a degradation ceremony, which may include fingerprinting, shaving the head, banning personal items, and being forced to strip and wear a uniform. In this way, his current identity is stripped away and a new identity is created.

    2. Total institutions are quite effective in isolating people from outside influences and information; supervising their activities; suppressing previous roles, statuses, and norms and replacing them with new rules and values; and controlling rewards and punishments.

VI. Socialization Through the Life Course

A. Socialization occurs throughout a person's entire lifetime and can be broken up into different stages.

B. Childhood (birth to 12): In earlier times, children were seen as miniature adults who served an apprenticeship. To keep them in line, they were beaten and subjected to psychological torture. Industrialization changed the way we see children. The current view is that children are tender and innocent, and parents should guide the physical, emotional, and social development of their children while providing them with care, comfort, and protection.

C. Adolescence (13-17): Adolescence is a social invention. Economic changes resulting from the Industrial Revolution brought about material surpluses that allowed millions of teenagers to remain outside the labor force, while at the same time, increasing the demand for education. Biologically equipped for both work and marriage but denied both, adolescents suffer inner turmoil and develop their own standards of clothing, hairstyles, language, music, and other claims to separate identities.

D. Transitional Adulthood (18-29): Adult responsibilities are postponed through extended education such as college. Even after college, many young people are returning to live with parents in order to live cheaply and establish their careers.

E. The Middle Years (30-65): This can be separated into two periods.

    1. Early Middle Years (30-49): People are more sure of themselves and their goals in life than before, but severe jolts such as divorce or being fired can occur. For U.S. women, it can be a trying period, as they try to "have it all"—job, family, and everything else.

    2. Later Middle Years (50-65): A different view of life emerges, including trying to evaluate the past and coming to terms with what lies ahead. Individuals may feel they are not likely to get much farther in life, while health and mortality become concerns. However, for most people it is the most comfortable period in their entire lives.

F. Older years (65 and beyond): This can also be separated into two periods.

    1. The Early Older Years: Improvements in nutrition, public health, and medical care delay the onset of old age. For many, this period is an extension of middle

years. Those who still work or are socially active are unlikely to see themselves as old.

2. The Later Older Years: Growing frailty and illness, and eventually death marks this period.

G. The social significance of the life course is how it is shaped by social factors—the period in which the person is born and lives his or her life, as well as social location—social class, gender, and race.

VII. Are We Prisoners of Socialization?

A. Sociologists do not think of people as little robots who simply are the result of their exposure to socializing agents. Although socialization is powerful and profoundly affects us all, we have a self, and the self is dynamic. Each of us uses his or her own mind to reason and make choices.

B. In this way, each of us is actively involved even in the social construction of the self. Our experiences have an impact on us, but we are not doomed to keep our orientations if we do not like them. We can choose to change our experiences by exposing ourselves to other groups and ideas.

KEY TERMS
After studying the chapter, review the definition for each of the following terms.

agents of socialization: people or groups that affect our self-concept, attitudes, or other orientations towards life (81)

anticipatory socialization: because one anticipates a future role, one learns part of it now (87)

degradation ceremony: a term coined by Harold Garfinkel to describe an attempt to remake the self by stripping away an individual's self-identity and stamping a new identity in its place (88)

ego: Freud's term for a balancing force between the id and the demands of society (73)

feral children: children assumed to have been raised by animals, in the wilderness, isolated from other humans (67)

gender role: the behaviors and attitudes considered appropriate because one is male or female (80)

gender socialization: the ways in which society sets children onto different courses in life because they are male or female (78)

generalized other: the norms, values, attitudes, and expectations of people "in general"; the child's ability to take the role of the generalized other is a significant step in the development of a self (71)

id: Freud's term for our inborn basic drives (73)

latent function: unintended beneficial consequences of people's actions (84)

life course: the stages of our life as we go from birth to death (88)

looking-glass self: a term coined by Charles Horton Cooley to refer to the process by which our self develops through internalizing others' reactions to us (70)

manifest function: the intended consequences of people's actions designed to help some part of the social system (84)

mass media: forms of communication, such as radio, newspapers, and television, that are directed to mass audiences (80)

peer group: a group of individuals roughly the same age linked by common interests (80)

resocialization: process of learning new norms, values, attitudes, and behaviors (87)

self: the unique human capacity of being able to see ourselves "from the outside"; the picture we gain of how others see us (70)

significant other: an individual who significantly influences someone else's life (71)

social environment: the entire human environment, including direct contact with others (66)

social inequality: a social condition in which privileges and obligations are given to some but denied to others (81)

socialization: the process by which people learn the characteristics of their group—the attitudes, values, and actions thought appropriate for them (70)

superego: Freud's term for the conscience, the internalized norms and values of our social groups (74)

taking the role of the other: putting oneself in someone else's shoes; understanding how someone else feels and thinks and thus anticipating how that person will act (71)

total institution: a place in which people are cut off from the rest of society and are almost totally controlled by the officials who run the place (88)

transitional adulthood: a term that refers to a period following high school when young adults have not yet taken on the responsibilities ordinarily associated with adulthood; also called adultolescence (91)

KEY PEOPLE
Review the major theoretical contributions or findings of these people.

Patricia and Peter Adler: These sociologists have documented how peer groups socialize children into gender-appropriate behavior. (86)

Charles Horton Cooley: Cooley studied the development of the self, coining the term "the looking-glass self." (70)

Donna Eder: She studied conversations between middle school girls and examined how girls reinforce what they think is appropriate for females. (80)

Paul Ekman: This anthropologist studied emotions in several countries and concluded that people everywhere experience six basic emotions—anger, disgust, fear, happiness, sadness, and surprise. (76-77)

Sigmund Freud: Freud developed a theory of personality development that took into consideration inborn drives (id), the internalized norms and values of one's society (superego), and the individual's ability to balance the two competing forces (ego). (73,75)

Carol Gilligan: Gilligan was uncomfortable with Kohlberg's conclusions regarding the development of morality because they did not match her own experiences and Kohlberg used only boys in his studies. She studied gender differences in morality, concluding that men and women use different criteria in evaluating morality. (75-76)

Erving Goffman: Goffman studied the process of resocialization in total institutions. (88)

Susan Goldberg and Michael Lewis: Two psychologists studied how parents' unconscious expectations about gender behavior are communicated to their young children. (78-79)

Harry and Margaret Harlow: These psychologists studied the behavior of monkeys raised in isolation and found that the length of time they were isolated affected their ability to overcome its effects. (69)

Lawrence Kohlberg: This psychologist studied the development of morality, concluding that individuals go through a sequence of developmental stages. (75)

Melvin Kohn: Kohn has done extensive research on the social class differences in child-rearing between working-class and middle-class parents. (83)

George Herbert Mead: Mead emphasized the importance of play in the development of the self, noting that children learn to take on the role of the other and eventually learn to perceive themselves as others do. (71-72)

Melissa Milkie: This sociologist studied how adolescent boys used media images to discover who they are as males. (80)

Michael Messner: He notes that girls are more likely to construct their identities on meaningful relationships whereas the identity for boys develops out of competitive success. (87)

Jean Piaget: Piaget studied the development of reasoning skills in children and identified four stages. (72-73)

H. M. Skeels and H. B. Dye: These psychologists studied how close social interaction affected the social and intellectual development of institutionalized children. (67-68)

STUDENT APPLICATION PROJECTS

This is your opportunity to apply the sociological perspective to the world around you. The projects in this section refer to material introduced in this chapter of your text. These projects help you apply the sociological perspective "down to your earth...down to your daily life."

1. Cooley said that our sense of self develops from our interactions with others. He called this process the "looking-glass self". Think about your daily interactions and explain how these three steps are a part of your everyday life.

2. Watch one afternoon and one evening of television. (Some people might say you ought not to be encouraged to do this!) Note the time of the day or evening, what day or night of the week it is, and the type of program (soap opera, or sit-com, etc.). What are the images of men and women on the programs? Refer to gender, age/aging, and social class. Log your observations, and relate them to your text's discussions of socialization.

3. Think about the agents of socialization that you have experienced in your life. Which one has been the most influential? Explain why. Which agent do you think was more important for your parents? Explain why.

4. Think about yourself, your family, and the different generations. Perhaps you could interview a parent and grandparent. Ask them to describe what life was like for them at your age and what society was like(norms, technology, etc.). Discuss the similarities and differences as they have moved through stages of the life course and examine what challenges each generation faces.

SELF-TEST

MULTIPLE CHOICE QUESTIONS

1. Which of the following statements best describes feral children? (67)
    a. After their parents supposedly abandoned them, they were reared by someone else.
    b. They supposedly were abandoned by their parents and then reared by animals.
    c. They are viewed as significant for our understanding of human nature by most social scientists.
    d. They quickly recovered from their experiences of deprivation once they were rescued.

2. From the case of Isabelle, it is possible to conclude that: (67)
    a. humans have no natural language.
    b. Isabelle was retarded.
    c. a person who has been isolated cannot progress through normal learning stages.
    d. all of the above.

3. What conclusions can be made from Skeels and Dye's study of institutionalized children? (68)
    a. Mental retardation was biological.
    b. Early physical contact did little to change the intelligence levels of these children.
    c. The absence of stimulating social interaction was the basic cause of low intelligence among these children, not some biological incapacity.
    d. Children who are cared for by a mentally retarded adult will "learn" to be retarded, while those who are cared for by professional staff will not

4. What do studies of isolated rhesus monkeys demonstrate? (70)
    a. The monkeys were able to adjust to monkey life after a time.
    b. They instinctively knew how to enter into "monkey interaction" with other monkeys.
    c. They knew how to engage in sexual intercourse.
    d. The monkeys were not able to adjust fully to monkey life and did not know instinctively how to enter into interaction with other monkeys.

5. Which of the following is not an element of the looking-glass self? (70)
    a. we imagine how we appear to those around us
    b. we interpret others' reactions
    c. we develop a self-concept
    d. we form opinions about others based on our self-concept

6. According to Mead's theory, at what stage do children pretend to take the roles of specific people? (71)
    a. imitation
    b. game
    c. play
    d. generalized other

7. To Mead, what is the "I"? (72)
    a. It is the self as subject.
    b. It is the self as object.
    c. It is the same as the id.
    d. It represents the passive robot aspect of human behavior.

8. According to Mead, which of the following is a product of society? (72)
    a. language
    b. the mind
    c. the self
    d. all three are products of society

9. According to Piaget, at what stage are children capable of abstract thinking? (72)
    a. sensorimotor
    b. preoperational
    c. concrete operational
    d. formal operational

10. Using Piaget's theory, at which stage of cognitive development are children likely to become "young philosophers," able to talk about abstract concepts, come to conclusions based on general principles, and use rules to solve abstract problems? (72-73)
    a. sensorimotor
    b. preoperational
    c. concrete operational
    d. formal operational

11. What is the term Freud used to describe our inborn drives for self-gratification? (73)
    a. id
    b. superego
    c. ego
    d. libido

12. Larry is 8 years old. He tries very hard to be nice to his younger sister because he knows that his mother gets very upset when the two of them fight and hit each other. According to Lawrence Kohlberg, which stage of moral development is reflected in Larry's behavior? (75)
    a. amoral
    b. preconventional
    c. conventional
    d. postconventional

13. Which of the four stages of moral development are most people unlikely to ever reach, according to Kohlberg? (75)
    a. amoral
    b. preconventional
    c. conventional
    d. postconventional

14. Gilligan's early research suggests that women evaluate morality in terms of: (76)
    a. abstract principles.
    b. a code of ethics.
    c. personal relationships.
    d. concrete values.

15. Which of the following statements about emotions is *correct*? (76)
    a. People around the world feel the same emotions and express them in the same way.
    b. How we express emotions depends on our culture and our social location.
    c. For the most part, emotions are the result of biology.
    d. Socialization has little to do with emotions.

16. According to this chapter, what is one of the most effective ways in which society sets controls over our behavior? (77)
    a. hiring police officers and other law enforcement officials
    b. defining those who do not abide by the rules as "deviants"
    c. socializing us into self and emotions
    d. using the media effectively

17. _____ refers to the ways in which society sets children onto different courses for life purely because they are male or female? (78)
    a. sex socialization
    b. gender socialization
    c. masculinization and feminization
    d. brainwashing

18. What conclusions did psychologists Susan Goldberg and Michael Lewis reach after observing mothers with their six-month-old infants in a laboratory setting? (79)
    a. The mothers kept their male children closer to them.
    b. They kept their male and female children about the same distance from them.
    c. They touched and spoke more to their sons.
    d. They unconsciously rewarded daughters for being passive and dependent.

19. Which of the following statements reflects Melissa Milkie's research findings? (80)
    a. Young males actively used media images to help them understand what was expected of them as males in our society.
    b. Young males avoided talking about male images in television and movies because they wanted to avoid being labeled a "weenie."
    c. Young females are passive consumers of media images, rather than active ones.
    d. Young males were very similar to young females in how they used media images as role models for "cool" behavior.

20. What do middle-class parents try to develop in their children, according to Melvin Kohn? (83)
    a. outward conformity
    b. neatness and cleanliness
    c. curiosity, self-expression, and self-control
    d. obedience to rules

21. Melvin Kohn suggests that the key to understanding social class differences in child rearing is: (83)
    a. the income level of the parents.
    b. the type of job the parents' have.
    c. the amount of education the parents have.
    d. the parents' access to expert advice on how to raise children.

22. Which of the following statements is *false* regarding religion in the U.S.? (84)
    a. Religious teaching has become a substitute for what parents teach.
    b. Religion is a key component in teaching ideas of right or wrong.
    c. Sixty-five percent of Americans belong to a local congregation.
    d. During a typical week, two or five Americans attend a religious service.

23. Which of the following statements summarizes the research findings on the impact that day care has on preschool children? (84)
    a. The number of hours a child spends in day care does not seem to matter in terms of their observed behavior.
    b. The more hours per week a child spends in day care, the weaker the bond is between mother and child.
    c. The more hours per week a child spends in day care, the more social the child.
    d. The more hours per week a child spends in day care, the more prepared the child is to learn once he/she gets to primary school.

24. When students teach one another values and behaviors outside of the classroom, this is known as: (84-86)
    a. following a formal curriculum.
    b. teaching a corridor curriculum.
    c. fulfilling the hidden curriculum.
    d. satisfying a latent function of education.

25. What conclusions can be drawn about peer groups and academic achievement from Adler and Adler's research? (86)
    a. Both boys and girls avoid doing well academically.
    b. Boys want to do well academically in order to boost their standing in the peer group, but girls avoid being labeled as smart, because it will hurt their image.
    c. Both boys and girls believe that good grades will translate into greater popularity among their respective peer groups.
    d. For boys, to do well academically is to lose popularity, while for girls, getting good grades increases social standing.

26. According to Michael Messner, sports encourage boys to develop: (87)
    a. a love of physical fitness.
    b. a competitive spirit.
    c. instrumental relationships.
    d. a keen appreciate for teamwork.

27. Under which of the following conditions is resocialization likely to occur? (88)
    a. When we take a new job.
    b. If we were to join a cult.
    c. When we are sent to military boot camp.
    d. All of the above would involve resocialization.

28. Which of the following statements about total institutions is *incorrect*? (88)
    a. They suppress preexisting statuses so that the inmates will learn that previous roles mean nothing and that the only thing that counts is their current role.
    b. They are not very effective in stripping away people's personal freedom.
    c. They are isolated, with barriers to keep inmates in and keep outsiders from interfering.
    d. They suppress the norms of the "outside world," replacing them with their own values, rules and interpretations.

29. Which stage of the lifecourse was recently added to postindustrial societies to reflect a period of extended youth? (91)
    a. childhood
    b. adolescence
    c. transitional adulthood
    d. pre-adolescence

30. Which stage of the life course poses a special challenge for women? (92)
    a. early middle years
    b. later middle years
    c. early older years
    d. later older years

TRUE-FALSE QUESTIONS

1. _____Language is the key to human development. (67)
2. _____Studies of institutionalized children demonstrate that some of the characteristics that we take for granted as being "human" traits result from our basic instincts. (67-68)
3. _____The Harlow's found that when monkeys were frightened they ran to the wire frame "mother" with the bottle. (69)
4. _____Charles H. Cooley introduced the concept of the generalized other to sociology. (70)
5. _____According to Freud, the ego is the balancing force between the id and the demands of society that suppress it. (73-74)
6. _____Kohlberg assumed female subjects were not necessary because the results of research with boys would apply to girls as well. (75)
7. _____Since emotions are natural human responses, socialization has very little to do with how we feel. (76)
8. _____Much of our socialization is intended to turn us into conforming members of society. (77)
9. _____Parents may give their sons and daughters different toys to play with, but they do not have different expectations about how they will behave or the kind of play in which they engage. (78)
10. _____Advertisements have made a concerted effort to not perpetuate gender stereotypes by portraying males as dominant and rugged and females as sexy and submissive. (80-81)
11. _____The first agent of socialization to have a major impact on us is our peer group. (83)
12. _____The benefits of day care depend in part on the child's background. (84)
13. _____A latent function of education is transmitting the skills and values appropriate for earning a living. (84)
14. _____Next to the family, the peer group is the most powerful socializing force in society. (86)
15. _____Work gives us the opportunity to learn anticipatory socialization, learning to play a role before entering it. (87)
16. _____Total institutions are very effective in stripping away people's personal freedom. (88)
17. _____Adolescence is a social creation in industrialized societies. (91)
18. _____Divorce and losing jobs are common during the older years. (92)
19. _____Industrialization brought with it a delay in the onset of old age. (92)
20. _____Most sociologists believe that people cannot help what they do, think, or feel, for everything is simply a result of their exposure to socialization. (93)

FILL-IN-THE-BLANK QUESTIONS

1. Without _____, people have no mechanism for developing thought. (67)
2. The Harlow experiments with _____ support what we know about children raised in isolation. (69)
3. Charles H. Cooley coined the term _____ to describe the process by which a sense of self develops. (70)
4. To put yourself in someone else's shoes is to learn how to _____. (71)
5. Mead used the term _____ to refer to our perception of how people in general think of us. (71)
6. In the _____ stage of Piaget's model of reasoning, children develop the ability to use symbols. (72)
7. One of the main findings of the sociologist Kohn was that socialization depends on a family's _____. (83)
8. By influencing values, _____ becomes a key component in people's ideas of right and wrong. (83)
9. The process of learning new norms, values, attitudes, and behaviors to match new life situations is _____. (87)
10. An attempt to remake the self by stripping away the individual's current identity and stamping a new one in its place is a _____. (88)
11. Childhood, adolescence, transitional adulthood, the middle years, and the older years are all stages in the _____. (88)
12. The life course *stage* between childhood and transitional adulthood is _____. (91)
13. The stage of the life course that poses a special challenge for United States women is _____. (91)
14. In pre-industrial societies, *old age* was thought to begin around age _____. (92)
15. Because individuals are not robots, their _____ is difficult to predict. (93)

MATCH THESE SOCIAL SCIENTISTS WITH THEIR CONTRIBUTIONS

_____ 1. Melvin Kohn

a. *concluded that people everywhere experience six basic emotions*

_____ 2. Erving Goffman

_____ 3. Melissa Milkie

b. *conducted studies of isolated rhesus monkeys*

c. *Studies adolescent boys' use of media images*

_____ 4. Paul Ekman

d. *studied gender differences in moral development*

_____ 5. Jean Piaget

_____ 6. Harry and Margaret Harlow

e. *studied total institutions*

f. *found social class differences in child rearing*

_____ 7. H.M. Skeels and H.B. Dye

g. *carried out research on the Ik of Uganda*

_____ 8. Lawrence Kohlberg

h. *studied institutionalized children*

_____ 9. Carol Gilligan

i. *discovered that there are four stages in cognitive development*

_____ 10. Colin Turnbull

j. *studied the development of morality*

ESSAY QUESTIONS

1. Explain what is necessary in order for us to develop into full human beings.

2. Why do sociologists argue that socialization is a process and not a product?

3. The family, the media, and peers all influence our gender socialization. Discuss why gender roles tend to remain unchanged from one generation to the next.

4. As the text points out, the stages of the life course are influenced by the biological clock, but they also reflect broader social factors. Identify the stages of the life course and indicate how social factors have contributed to the definition of each of these stages.

5. Do you think that it is possible that society in the United States would ever be like that of the Ik? Please explain.

CHAPTER 4
SOCIAL STRUCTURE AND SOCIAL INTERACTION

CHAPTER SUMMARY

- There are two levels of sociological analysis: macrosociology investigates the large-scale features of social structure, while microsociology focuses on social interaction. Functional and conflict theorists tend to use a macrosociological approach, while symbolic interactionists are more likely to use a macrosociological approach.

- The term social structure refers to a society's framework, which forms an envelope around us and sets limits on our behavior. The individual's location in the social structure affects his or her perceptions, attitudes, and behaviors. Culture, social class, social status (both ascribed and achieved), roles, groups, and institutions are the major components of the social structure.

- Social institutions are the organized and standard means that a society develops to meet its basic needs. Functionalists view social institutions as established ways of meeting universal group needs; however, conflict theorists see social institutions as the primary means by which the elite maintains its privileged position.

- Over time, social structure undergoes changes. Sometimes this change is very dramatic, as illustrated by Durkheim's concepts of mechanical and organic solidarity and Tönnies' constructs of *Gemeinschaft* and *Gesellschaft*.

- In contrast to functionalist and conflict theorists who, as macrosociologists, focus on the "big picture," symbolic interactionists tend to be microsociologists, looking at social interaction in everyday life. They examine how people look at things and how that, in turn, affects their behavior.

- Stereotypes, assumptions made about others based on their visible characteristics, guide our behavior toward them; in turn, their behavior then reinforces our stereotypes.

- Symbolic interactionists note that each of us is surrounded by a "personal bubble" that we carefully protect. The size of the bubble varies from one culture to another. Americans have four different "distance zones": intimate, personal, social, and public.

- The dramaturgical analysis provided by Erving Goffman analyzes everyday life in terms of the stage. At the core of this approach is the analysis of the impressions we attempt to make on others by using *sign-vehicles* (setting, appearance, and manner), *teamwork*, and *face-saving behavior*.

- Ethnomethodologists try to uncover the background assumptions which provide us with basic ideas about the way life is. The social construction of reality refers to how we each create a view, or understanding, of our world.

- Both macrosociology and microsociology are needed to understand human behavior because we must grasp both social structure and social interaction.

LEARNING OBJECTIVES
After reading Chapter 4, you should be able to:

1. Differentiate between the macrosociological and microsociological approach to studying social life, and indicate which of the approaches is most likely to be used by functionalists, conflict theorists, and symbolic interactionists. (98)
2. Define social structure, list its major components, and discuss how it guides people's behaviors. (99-100)
3. Understand the concepts of culture, social class, social status, roles, groups, and social institutions. (100-103)
4. Differentiate between ascribed, achieved, and master status. (101-102)
5. Identify the social institutions common to industrial and postindustrial societies and summarize their basic features. (104-106)
6. Understand the role of the media as an emerging institution. (104)
7. Discuss the disagreement between functionalists and conflict theorists over the purposes for, and effects of, social institutions. (106)
8. Understand why social structure is not static and how structural changes can significantly alter the way a society is organized. (107)
9. Differentiate between Emile Durkheim's concepts of mechanical and organic solidarity and Ferdinand Tönnies' constructs of *Gemeinschaft* and *Gesellschaft*, and discuss why they continue to be relevant. (108)
10. Define stereotypes and explain their significance. (111)
11. Talk about the various ways different cultures perceive and use personal space, touching, and eye contact. (110-113)
12. Differentiate between role conflict, role exit and role strain, and provide examples of each. (114)
13. Know the key components of dramaturgy and discuss how people try to control other people's impressions of them through sign-vehicles, teamwork, and face-saving behavior. (113-114)
14. Understand how and why ethnomethodologists examine different ways people use background assumptions to make sense out of everyday life. (118-119)
15. Explain what is meant by the "social construction of reality" and how it is related to the "Thomas theorem." (119-120)
16. Know why both macrosociology and microsociology are essential to understanding social life. (121-124)

CHAPTER OUTLINE

I. **Levels of Sociological Analysis**
   A. Macrosociology places the focus on large-scale features of social structure by investigating large-scale social forces and the effects they have on entire societies and the groups within them. It is utilized by functionalist and conflict theorists.
   B. Microsociology places the emphasis on social interaction, or what people do when they come together and symbolic interactionism uses this level of analysis.
   C. Each yields distinctive perspectives, and both are needed to gain a more complete understanding of social life.

II. **The Macrosociological Perspective: Social Structure**
   A. Social structure is defined as the patterned relationships between people that persist over time. Behaviors and attitudes are determined by our location in the social structure. Components of social structure are culture, social class, social status, roles, groups, and institutions.
   B. Culture refers to a group's language, beliefs, values, behaviors, and gestures. It includes the material objects used by a group, and determines what kind of people we will become.
   C. Social class is based on income, education, and occupational prestige. Large numbers of people who have similar amounts of income and education and who work at jobs that are roughly comparable in prestige make up a social class.
   D. Social status refers to the positions that an individual occupies. A status may carry a great deal of prestige (judge or astronaut), or very little (gas station attendant or cook in a fast-food restaurant).
      1. Status set refers to all the statuses or positions that an individual occupies.
      2. Ascribed statuses are positions an individual either inherits at birth or receives involuntarily later in life. Examples include race, sex, and social class of parents.
      3. Achieved statuses are positions that are earned, accomplished, or involve at least some effort or activity on the individual's part. Examples include becoming a college president or a bank robber.
      4. Each status provides guidelines for how we are to act and feel.
      5. Status symbols are signs that people use who want others to recognize that they occupy a certain status. For example, wedding rings that are worn, fancy cars, living in expensive homes, etc.
      6. A master status—such as being male or female—cuts across the other statuses that an individual occupies. Status inconsistency is a contradiction or mismatch between statuses. A disability can become a master status for some. This condition can override other statuses and determines others' perception of this person.
   E. Roles are the behaviors, obligations, and privileges attached to a status. The individual occupies a status, but plays a role. Roles are an essential component

of culture because they lay out what is expected of people, and as individuals perform their roles, those roles mesh together to form the society.

F. A group consists of people who regularly and consciously interact with one another and typically share similar values, norms, and expectations. When we belong to a group we give up to others at least some control over our lives.

   1. The control depends on the relationship and amount of interaction that we have with that group.

III. Social Institutions

A. Social institutions are society's standard ways of meeting its basic needs.

   1. The family, religion, law, politics, economics, education, science, medicine, and the military all are social institutions.

   2. In industrialized societies, social institutions tend to be more formal and in nonliterate societies, more informal.

   3. Each institution has its own groups, status, values, and norms.

B. Social institutions are sociologically significant because they set limits and provide guidelines for our behavior.

C. The mass media is an emerging social institution; it influences our attitudes toward social issues, other people, and even our self-concept. Of interest is who controls the mass media. Functionalists would say that the mass media represent the varied interests of the many groups that make up the nation, while conflict theorists would see that the interests of the political elite are represented.

D. The functionalists and conflict theorists differ in how they see social institutions.

   1. Functionalists view social institutions as established ways of meeting group needs (or functional requisites), such as replacing members; socializing new members; producing and distributing goods and services; preserving order; and providing a sense of purpose.

   2. Conflict theorists look at social institutions as the primary means by which the elite maintains its privileged position.

E. Changes in social structure occur as culture changes because of evolving values, new technologies, innovative ideas, and globalization.

F. Many sociologists have tried to find an answer to the question of what holds society together.

   1. Emile Durkheim found the key to social cohesion, the degree to which members of a society feel united by shared values and other social bonds, in the concepts of mechanical solidarity and organic solidarity. Mechanical solidarity is a collective consciousness that people experience as a result of performing the same or similar tasks, while organic solidarity is a collective consciousness based on the interdependence brought about by an increasingly specialized division of labor—that is, how people divide up tasks.

   2. Ferdinand Tönnies analyzed how intimate community *(Gemeinschaft)* was being replaced by impersonal associations *(Gesellschaft)*. *Gemeinschaft* is a society in which life is intimate; a community in which

everyone knows everyone else and people share a sense of togetherness and *Gesellschaft* is a society dominated by impersonal relationships, individual accomplishments, and self-interest.

3. These concepts are still relevant today, helping us understand contemporary events such as the rise of Islamic fundamentalism.

IV. The Microsociological Perspective: Social Interaction in Everyday Life

A. The microsociological approach places emphasis on face-to-face social interaction, or what people do when they are in the presence of one another.

B. Symbolic interactionists are interested in the symbols that people use to define their worlds, how people look at things, and how that affects their behavior. Included within this perspective are studies of stereotypes, personal space, and touching.

1. Stereotypes are used in everyday life. First impressions are shaped by the assumptions one person makes about another person's sex, race, age, and physical appearance. Such assumptions affect one's ideas about the person and how one acts toward that person. Stereotypes tend to be self-fulfilling—that is, they bring out the very kinds of behavior that fit the stereotype. They even have an impact on what we accomplish. People can also resist stereotypes and change outcomes.

2. Personal space refers to the physical space that surrounds us and that we claim as our own. The amount of personal space varies from one culture to another. Anthropologist Edward Hall found that Americans use four different distance zones: (1) Intimate distance (about 18 inches from the body) for lovemaking, wrestling, comforting, and protecting; (2) Personal distance (from 18 inches to 4 feet) for friends, acquaintances, and ordinary conversations; (3) Social distance (from 4 feet to 12 feet) for impersonal or formal relationships such as job interviews; and (4) Public distance (beyond 12 feet) for even more formal relationships such as separating dignitaries and public speakers from the general public.

3. From our culture, we learn rules about touching. Both the frequency and the meaning of touching vary from one culture to the next. Men and women react differently to being touched.

4. We protect our personal space by controlling eye contact.

C. Dramaturgy is an analysis of how we present ourselves in everyday life.

1. Dramaturgy is the name given to an approach pioneered by Erving Goffman. Social life is analyzed in terms of drama or the stage.

2. According to Goffman, socialization prepares people for learning to perform on the stage of everyday life. *Front stage* is where performances are given (wherever lines are delivered). *Back stage* is where people rest from their performances, discuss their presentations, and plan future performances.

3. *Role performance* is the particular emphasis or interpretation that an individual gives a role, the person's "style." *Role conflict* occurs when the expectations attached to one role are incompatible with the expectations

of another role—in other words, conflict between roles. *Role strain* refers to conflicts that someone feels within a role.

4. *Impression management* is the person's efforts to manage the impressions that others receive of her or him.

5. We tend to become the roles we play. Some roles become part of our self-concept. For some, when leaving a role such as a marriage, police work, the military, the role can become so intertwined that leaving it can threaten a person's identity.

6. Three types of *sign-vehicles* are used to communicate information about the self: (1) social setting—where the action unfolds, which includes scenery (furnishings used to communicate messages); (2) appearance—how a person looks when he or she plays his or her role, and this includes props which decorate the person; and (3) manner—the attitudes demonstrated as an individual plays her or his roles.

7. Teamwork, which is when two or more players work together to make sure a performance goes off as planned, shows that we are adept players.

8. When a performance doesn't come off, we engage in face-saving behavior, or ignoring flaws in someone's performance, which Goffman defines as tact.

9. A face-saving technique that might be used is *studied nonobservance* in which a behavior might be completely ignored in order that neither person will face embarrassment.

10. Impression management also occurs with families, businesses, colleges and even the government.

D. Ethnomethodology involves the discovery of rules concerning our views of the world and how people ought to act.

1. Ethnomethodologists try to undercover people's background assumptions, which form the basic core of one's reality, and provide basic rules concerning our view of the world and of how people ought to act.

2. Harold Garfinkel founded the ethnomethodological approach. He conducted experiments asking subjects to pretend that they did not understand the basic rules of social life in order to uncover others' reactions and break background assumptions.

E. The social construction of reality refers to what people define as real because of their background assumptions and life experiences.

1. Symbolic interactionists believe that people define their own reality and then live within those definitions.

2. The Thomas theorem (by sociologist W. I. Thomas and Dorothy S. Thomas) states, "If people define situations as real, they are real in their consequences."

3. Therefore, our behavior does not depend on the objective existence of something, but on our subjective interpretation or our definition of reality.

4. James Henslin and Mae Biggs conducted research to show that when physicians are performing gynecological exams they will socially construct reality so that the vaginal exams become nonsexual.

V. The Need for Both Macrosociology and Microsociology

A. To understand human behavior, it is necessary to grasp both social structure (macrosociology) and social interaction (microsociology).

B. Both are necessary to understand social life fully because each adds to our knowledge of human experience.

KEY TERMS

After studying the chapter, review the definition for each of the following terms.

achieved statuses: positions that are earned, accomplished, or involve at least some effort or activity on the individual's part (101)

ascribed statuses: positions an individual either inherits at birth or receives involuntarily later in life (101)

back stage: where people rest from their performances, discuss their presentations, and plan future performances (113)

background assumptions: deeply embedded common understandings of how the world operates and how people ought to act (118)

body language: the ways in which people use their bodies to give messages to other, much of which is done subconsciously (113)

division of labor: the splitting of a group's or society's tasks into specialties (107)

dramaturgy: an approach, pioneered by Erving Goffman, analyzing social life in terms of drama or the stage; also called *dramaturgical analysis* (113)

ethnomethodology: the study of how people use background assumptions to make sense of life (118)

face-saving behavior: techniques used to salvage a performance that is going sour (115)

front stage: where performances are given (113)

functional requisites: the major tasks that a society must fulfill if it is to survive (106)

Gemeinschaft: a type of society in which life is intimate; a community in which everyone knows everyone else and people share a sense of togetherness (108)

Gesellschaft: a type of society dominated by impersonal relationships, individual accomplishments, and self-interests (108)

group: people who have something in common and who believe that what they have in common is significant; also called a social group (103)

impression management: people's efforts to control the impressions that others receive of them (113)

macrosociology: analysis of social life that focuses on broad features of society, such as social class and the relationships of groups to one another; usually used by functionalist and conflict theorists (98)

master status: a status that cuts across the other statuses that an individual occupies (102)

mechanical solidarity: Durkheim's term for the unity (a shared consciousness) that people feel as a result of performing the same or similar tasks (107)

microsociology: analysis of social life focusing on social interaction; an approach usually used by symbolic interactionists (98)

organic solidarity: the interdependence that results from the division of labor–people needing others to fulfill their jobs (107)

role: the behaviors, obligations, and privileges attached to a status (103)

role conflict: conflict that someone feels *between* roles because the expectations attached to one role are incompatible with the expectations of another role (114)

role performance: the ways in which someone performs a role within the limits that the role provides; showing a particular "style" or "personality" (114)

role strain: conflicts that someone feels *within* a role (114)

sign-vehicles: the term used by Goffman to refer to how people use social setting, appearance, and manner to communicate information about the self (115)

social class: according to Weber, a large group of people who rank close to one another in wealth, power and prestige; according to Marx, one of two groups: capitalists who own the means or production or workers who sell their labor (101)

social construction of reality (the): the process by which people use their background assumptions and life experiences to define what is real (120)

social institution: the organized, usual, or standard ways by which society meets its basic needs (104)

social integration: the degree to which members of a group or society feel united by shared values and other social bonds; also known as social cohesion (107)

social interaction: people's interaction with one another (98)

social structure: the framework that surrounds us, consisting of the relationships of people and groups to one another, which give direction to and set limits on behavior (99)

status: the position that someone occupies in society or a social group (101)

status inconsistency (or discrepancy): ranking high on some dimensions of social class and low on others (102)

status set: all of the statuses or positions that an individual occupies (101)

status symbols: items used to identify a status (101)

stereotype: assumptions of what people are like, whether true or false (111)

teamwork: the collaboration of two or more persons to manage impressions jointly (115)

Thomas theorem: William I. and Dorothy S. Thomas' classic formulation of the definition of the situation: "If people define situations as real, they are real in their consequences." (119)

KEY PEOPLE
Review the major theoretical contributions or findings of these people.

Elijah Anderson: In a series of books, Anderson has studied the lives of inner city residents (*Streetwise* and *Code of the Streets*) and suggests that their world is organized around the same norms and beliefs that characterize our wider society. (98)

William Chambliss: Chambliss used macro- and microsociology to study high school gangs and found that social structure and interaction explained the patterns of behavior in these groups. (121)

Emile Durkheim: Durkheim identified mechanical and organic solidarity as the keys to social cohesion. As societies get larger, they divide up work and this division of labor makes people depend on one another. (107)

Helen Ebaugh: Ebaugh interviewed people who were no longer performing a role that had once been central in their lives—people whose marriages had ended, people who had left jobs and careers as police officers, military personnel, or religious orders. Since these roles were so critical, she found that many of them struggled to define their very identity as a result of the loss of these roles. (117)

Harold Garfinkel: Garfinkel is the founder of ethnomethodology; he conducted experiments in order to uncover people's background assumptions. (118-119)

Erving Goffman: Goffman developed dramaturgy, the perspective within symbolic interactionism that views social life as a drama on the stage. (113-116)

Edward Hall: This anthropologist found that personal space varied from one culture to another and that North Americans use four different "distance zones." (110-112)

James Henslin and Mae Biggs: The author of your text, along with gynecological nurse Biggs, researched how doctors and patients constructed the social reality of vaginal examinations in order to define these exams as nonsexual. (120-121)

Elliot Liebow: This sociologist studied street-corner men and found that their lives are not disorganized, but influenced by the same norms and beliefs of the larger society. (98)

Mark Snyder: Snyder carried out research in order to test whether stereotypes are self-fulfilling; he found that subjects were influenced to behave in a particular way based on their stereotypes. (111)

W. I. Thomas and Dorothy S. Thomas: These sociologists said that "If people define situations as real, they are real in their consequences." (119-120)

Ferdinand Tönnies: Tönnies analyzed different types of societies that existed before and after industrialization. He used the terms *Gemeinschaft* and *Gesellschaft* to describe the two types of societies. (108)

STUDENT APPLICATION PROJECTS

This is your opportunity to apply the sociological perspective to the world around you. The projects in this section refer to material introduced in this chapter of your text. These projects help you to apply the sociological perspective "down to earth...down to your daily life."

1. Once you have finished reading this chapter, try and analyze the statuses, roles, and so on in your own life. How does when and where you were born affect your life? What are your current statuses and roles? What kinds of role conflict or role strain have you experienced in these roles? Do you think your situation would be different if you had a different ascribed status? For example, would your situation different if you had been born a member of the opposite sex?

2. Think about the type of community you grew up in and the social relationships that existed there. Which of Durkheim's types of solidarity would best describe your hometown. Explain. Does your hometown seem more like a Gemeinschaft or Gesellschaft society? Explain.

3. What are some things you do on a daily basis to practice impression management? Have you ever had a case where your attempts to manage impressions backfired? Explain. What types of face-saving behavior did you use afterwards? Explain.

4. Think about the background assumptions that you hold. What are the advantages to having background assumptions and having others follow through with those assumptions? Are there situations where there might be disadvantages to having background assumptions? Why is it so important to us that others hold the same background assumptions.

SELF-TEST

After completing this self-test, check your answers against the Answer Key beginning on of this Study Guide and against the text on the page(s) indicated in parentheses.

MULTIPLE CHOICE QUESTIONS

1. Which of the following statements does *not* applies to macrosociology? (98)
    a.   It focuses on social interaction.
    b.   It investigates large-scale social forces.
    c.   It focuses on broad features of social structure.
    d.   It is used by functionalists and conflict theorists.

2. Which level of analysis do sociologists use to study individuals? (98)
    a.   dramaturgy
    b.   ethnomethodology
    c.   macrosociology
    d.   microsociology

3. You want to research the perceptions that different social classes have of each other in the United States. Which would you use? (98)
    a.   macrosociology
    b.   microsociology
    c.   functionalism
    d.   conflict perspective

4. Which of the following statements about social structure is *incorrect*? (99)
    a.   The sociological significance of social structure is that it guides our behavior.
    b.   People learn their behaviors and attitudes because of their location in the social structure.
    c.   An individual's behaviors and attitudes are due to biology (one's race or sex, for instance) as much as it is due to his/her location in the social structure.
    d.   The social structure, or the framework of society, exists before we are born and will continue to exist after we die.

5. Social Class is based on all the following except: (101)
    a.   income.
    b.   education.
    c.   occupational prestige.
    d.   age.

6. Sociologists use the term status to refer to the _____ that someone occupies. (101)
   a. social class
   b. prestige
   c. role
   d. position

7. A person is simultaneously a daughter, a wife, and a mother. All together, these make up a what? (101)
   a. social status
   b. social class
   c. status position
   d. status set

8. Which of the following describe an individual's race, gender, and inherited social class? (101)
   a. ascribed statuses
   b. achieved statuses
   c. status inconsistencies
   d. status incongruities

9. Once you finish your education, you will move into some kind of occupation or profession—that is, perhaps one based on your educational training. This job or career you will eventually hold is considered a(n): (101)
   a. voluntary membership.
   b. involuntary membership.
   c. ascribed status.
   d. achieved status.

10. Wedding rings, military uniforms, and clerical collars are all examples of: (101)
    a. social stigma.
    b. social class.
    c. status symbols.
    d. achieved statuses.

11. Which of the following statements regarding status symbols is *incorrect*? (101)
    a. Status symbols are signs that identify a status.
    b. Status symbols often are used to show that people have "made it."
    c. Status symbols are always positive signs or people would not wear them.
    d. Status symbols are used by people to announce their statuses to others.

12. Master statuses are: (102)
    a. ascribed.
    b. achieved.
    c. both ascribed and achieved.
    d. neither ascribed or achieved.

13. Under what conditions is status inconsistency most likely to occur? (102)
    a. When a contradiction or mismatch between statuses exists.
    b. When we know what to expect of other people.
    c. When a person wears too many status symbols at once.
    d. When a society has few clearly defined master statuses.

14. What do we call the behaviors, obligations, and privileges attached to statuses? (103)
    a. status sets
    b. master statuses
    c. status differentiations
    d. roles

15. A _____ consists of people who perceive themselves as belonging together and regularly interact with one another. (103)
    a. group
    b. role
    c. status
    d. status set

16. Which of the following is *false* about social institutions: (104)
    a. education is informally structured.
    b. they tend to be more formal.
    c. they include economics and science.
    d. they have their own statuses, values, and norms.

17. According to _____, social institutions are used by the elite for its own advantage. (104)
    a. functionalists
    b. conflict theorists
    c. symbolic interactionists
    d. dramaturgists

18. Which of the following would be found in a society characterized by organic solidarity? (107)
    a. A highly specialized division of labor.
    b. Members who are interdependent on one another.
    c. A high degree of impersonal relationships.
    d. All of the above.

19. What type of society is described as an "intimate community" where everyone knows everyone else and members conform because they are sensitive to others' opinions and want to avoid gossip? (108)
    a. *Gemeinschaft*
    b. *Gesellschaft*
    c. mechanical society
    d. organic society

20. Which of the following statements about stereotypes is *incorrect*? (110)
    a. When you first meet someone, the assumptions you have about certain social characteristics have a tendency to shape your first impressions of that person.
    b. Stereotypes are unlikely to be self-fulfilling.
    c. Stereotypes can have an impact on what we are able to accomplish because they influence how others' behave toward us.
    d. People are able to resist stereotypes and change outcomes.

21. Hall observed that North Americans used different distance zones. The "zone" that marks the impersonal or formal relationship is: (112)
    a. social distance zone.
    b. the intimate zone.
    c. the personal distance zone.
    d. the public distance zone.

22. According to Goffman, where do we go when we want to be ourselves? (113)
    a. front stage
    b. back stage
    c. on stage
    d. off stage

23. Susan is a college student who takes classes in the evening after work. One day her boss asks her to move from working days to working evenings; he wants her to work the same hours as she is supposed to be in class. In this situation, what is Susan experiencing? (114)
    a. role strain
    b. role performance
    c. role demands
    d. role conflict

24. The professor poses a question in class. You know the answer and want to raise your hand but are afraid that if you do, you will show up the other students in the class. What are you experiencing in this situation? (114)
    a. role strain
    b. role conflict
    c. role distance
    d. role performance

25. Which of the following statements applies to social setting, appearance, and manner? (115)
    a. They are less important than role performance for impression management.
    b. They are sign-vehicles used by individuals for managing impressions.
    c. They are more important for females than males.
    d. They are techniques for saving face when a performance fails.

26. If you went to your doctor's office and he/she started cutting your hair this would be an example of violating: (115)
    a. face-saving behavior.
    b. impression management.
    c. a master status.
    d. background assumption.

27. He encouraged his students to act as though they did not understand the basic rules of social life. (118)
    a. Harold Garfinkel
    b. Erving Goffman
    c. Edward Hall
    d. W. I. Thomas

28. The research done by James Henslin and Mae Biggs demonstrated: (120)
    a. background assumptions are so deeply embedded in our consciousness that it is virtually impossible for sociologists to ever determine what they are.
    b. the social construction of reality regarding vaginal examinations.
    c. people use common sense understandings to make sense out of their lives when visiting their doctors
    d. people are comfortable when interchanging roles.

29. Within which sociological perspective would you place the Thomas theorem? (119)
    a. functionalism
    b. conflict theory
    c. symbolic interactionism
    d. exchange theory

30. What did the research on the Saints and the Roughnecks demonstrate? (121)
    a. Social class is unimportant when it comes to encounters with teachers, police, and the general community.
    b. The reputations that the boys acquired as teenagers disappeared once they reached adulthood.
    c. The Saints were significantly less delinquent than the Roughnecks because they came from more solid middle-class families.
    d. To understand what happened to the boys in the study, William Chambliss analyzed both the social structure and the patterns of social interaction that characterized their lives.

TRUE-FALSE QUESTIONS

1. _____Social structure has little impact on our ideas, beliefs, and behaviors. (98)
2. _____A person's ideas, attitudes, and behaviors largely depend on his or her social class. (101)
3. _____To sociologists, the terms "social class" and "social status" mean the same thing. (101)
4. _____Being a teenager is an example of an achieved status. (101)
5. _____The purpose of status symbols is to tell the world that you've made it to a particular place in society. (101)
6. _____Being male or female is not considered a master status. (102)
7. _____You occupy a status, but you play a role. (103)
8. _____Groups that we belong to generally don't have that much control over many aspects of our behavior. (101)
9. _____Sociologists have identified five basic social institutions in contemporary societies. (103)
10. _____The mass media is an emerging social institution. (104)
11. _____Conflict theorists view social institutions as working harmoniously for the common good. (106)
12. _____The Amish are an example of a *Gemeinschaft* society.. (109)
13. _____We have a tendency to make assumptions about a person based on his or her visible features; these stereotypes may affect how we act toward that person. (110)
14. _____The amount of personal space people prefer varies from one culture to another. (112)
15. _____Researchers have found that lower-status individuals tend to touch more, because touching is a way of claiming more status. (112)
16. _____According to the dramaturgy, we use impression management in our back stages. (113)
17. _____The same setting will rarely serve as both a back and a front stage. (113)
18. _____Role conflict is a conflict that someone feels within a role. (114)
19. _____Studied non-observance is a form of face-saving behavior. (115)
20. _____Sociologists have determined that both macrosociological perspectives are sufficient for understanding human behavior. (121)

FILL-IN-THE-BLANK QUESTIONS

1. _____ places the focus on broad features of society. (98)
2. _____ is what people do when they are in the presence of one another. (98)
3. The down-to-earth sociology box on football mirrors social _____. (100)
4. Income, educated, and occupational prestige indicate _____. (101)
5. A _____ is one that cuts across the other statuses you hold. (101)

6. _____ are the behaviors, obligations, and privileges attached to a status. (103)
7. _____ view social institutions as working together to meet universal needs. (104)
8. _____ is the degree to which members of a society feel united by shared values and other bonds. (107)
9. As societies get larger, their _____ becomes more specialized. (107)
10. Ferdinand Tönnies used the term _____ to refer to societies dominated by impersonal relations, individual accomplishments, and self interest. (108)
11. Hall and Hall found that North Americans use _____(#) different personal distance zones. (110)
12. When two or more people collaborate to manage impressions jointly, this is referred to as _____. (113)
13. Goffman called the techniques that we use to salvage a performance that is going bad as _____. (115)
14. _____ is the study of how people use their background assumptions to make sense of life. (118)
15. The Thomas Theorum states, "If people define situations as real, they are real in their _____. (119)

MATCH THESE SOCIAL SCIENTISTS WITH THEIR CONTRIBUTIONS

_____ 1. James Henslin and Mae Biggs
_____ 2. Ferdinand Tönnies
_____ 3. Erving Goffman
_____ 4. Harold Garfinkel
_____ 5. William Chambliss
_____ 6. Edward Hall
_____ 7. Elijah Anderson
_____ 8. Elliot Leibow
_____ 9. Mark Snyder
_____ 10. W. I. Thomas

a. *developed dramaturgy*
b. *researched the social construction of reality regarding vaginal exams*
c. *used macro- and microsociology to study high school gangs*
d. *studied the lives of inner city residents*
e. *described Gemeinschaft and Gesellschaft societies.*
f. *studied street-corner men*
g. *known for the statement, "If people define situations as real, they are real in their consequences."*
h. *an anthropologists who did research on personal space*
i. *carried out research to discover whether or not stereotypes are self-fulfilling*
j. *founder of ethnomethodology*

ESSAY QUESTIONS

1. Choose a research topic and discuss how you approach this topic using both macrosociological and microsociological approaches.

2. The concept of a social structure is often difficult to grasp. Yet the social structure is a central organizing feature of social life. Identify the ways in which it takes shape in our society and in our lives.

3. Today we can see many examples of people wanting to recreate a simpler way of life. Using Tönnies' framework, analyze this tendency.

4. Assume that you have been asked to give a presentation to your sociology class on Goffman's dramaturgy approach. Describe what information you would want to include in such a presentation.

5. Differentiate between role conflict, role exit, and role strain and give examples.

CHAPTER 5
HOW SOCIOLOGISTS DO RESEARCH

CHAPTER SUMMARY

- Sociologists conduct research about almost every area of human behavior. The choice of research topics depends on the sociologist's interests, the availability of subjects, the appropriateness of methods, and ethical considerations.

- Sociological research is needed because common sense ideas are often incorrect and based on limited information.

- Eight basic steps are included in scientific research: (1) selecting a topic, (2) defining the problem, (3) reviewing the literature, (4) formulating a hypothesis, (5) choosing a research method, (6) collecting the data, (7) analyzing the results, and (8) sharing the results.

- Sociologists use six research methods (or research designs) for gathering data: (1) surveys, (2) participant observations, (3) secondary analysis, (4) documents, (5) unobtrusive measures, and (6) experiments. The choice of a research method depends on the research questions to be answered, the researcher's access to potential subjects, the resources available, the researcher's background and training, and ethical considerations.

- In the past, sociologists used to ignore the world of women, although that is no longer the case. However, in some kinds of research, the gender of the researcher can affect the findings.

- Ethics are of concern to sociologists, who are committed to openness, honesty, truth, and protecting subjects.

- Research and theory are related to one another. Theory is used to generate research questions and interpret the data that are collected; when research findings don't match what is expected, theories are modified.

LEARNING OBJECTIVES
After reading Chapter 5, you should be able to:

1. Talk about what areas of human behavior and aspect of social life are valid topics for sociological research. (128)
2. Explain why there is a need for sociological research. (128)
3. List and describe the eight basic steps for conducting scientific research. (128-130)
4. Know and discuss the six research methods that sociologists use, the tools that they employ, and the strengths and limitations of each. (131-141)
5. Cite the four primary factors that determine which research method or methods a sociologist uses to conduct his or her research. (141)
6. Define, describe, and discuss the significance of the following terms associated with the research process: hypothesis, variable, independent variable, dependent variable,

correlation, spurious correlation, operational definitions, validity, reliability, causation, replication, and generalizability. (129-139)

7. Define, describe, and discuss the significance of the following terms associated with the six research methods: survey, population, sample, random sample, stratified random sample, questionnaires, self-administered questionnaires, interview, interviewer bias, structured interviews, closed-ended questions, unstructured interviews, open-ended questions, rapport, participant observation, secondary analysis, documents, unobtrusive measures, experiment, experimental group, and control group. (131-141)

8. Understand the Hawthorne effect and explain about its significance. (140)

9. Distinguish between quantitative and qualitative research methods. (141)

10. Discuss the role that gender can and often does play in sociological research. (144)

11. Know the ethical guidelines that sociologists are expected to follow and discuss the ethical issues raised in Mario Brajuha's and Laud Humphrey's research. (145-146)

12. Discuss how and why research and theory need to work together in order to fully explore and understand human behavior. (146-148)

CHAPTER OUTLINE

I. What is a Valid Sociological Topic?
A. Sociologists research just about every area of human behavior at both the macro and micro levels.
B. No aspect of human behavior is ineligible for research, whether it is routine or unusual, respectable or reprehensible.

II. Common Sense and the Need for Sociological Research
A. Common sense cannot be relied on as a source of knowledge because it is often based on limited information.
B. To move beyond common sense and understand what is really going on, it is necessary to do sociological research.

III. A Research Model
A. Selecting a topic is guided by sociological curiosity, interest in a particular topic, research funding from governmental or private sources, and pressing social issues.
B. Defining the problem involves specifying what the researcher wants to learn about the topic.
C. Reviewing the literature uncovers existing knowledge about the problem, helps narrow down the problem by learning what areas need to be researched, and provides ideas about what questions to ask.
D. Formulating a hypothesis involves stating the expected relationship between variables, based on predictions from a theory. Hypotheses need operational definitions, or precise ways to measure the variables.
E. Choosing a research method is influenced by the research topic and the questions that need to be answered.
F. Collecting the data involves concerns over validity, the extent to which operational definitions measure what was intended, and reliability, the extent to which data

produce consistent results. Inadequate operational definitions and sampling hurt reliability.

G. Analyzing the results involves the use of either qualitative or quantitative techniques to analyze data. Computers have become powerful tools in data analysis because they reduce large amounts of data to basic patterns, take the drudgery out of analyzing data, allow the use of a variety of statistical tests, and give the researcher more time to interpret the results.

H. By writing up and publishing the results, the findings are available for replication. That is, others can repeat your study to see if they come up with similar findings.

IV. Research Methods

A. Surveys involve collecting data by having people answer a series of questions.

   1. The first step is to determine a population (the target group to be studied) and select a sample (individuals from within the target population who are intended to represent the population to be studied). Random samples are those where everyone in the target population has the same chance of being included in the study. A stratified random sample is a sample of specific subgroups (e.g. freshmen, sophomores, juniors) of the target population (a college or university) in which everyone in the subgroup has an equal chance of being included in the study.

   2. The respondents (people who respond to a survey) must be allowed to express their own ideas so that the findings will not be biased.

   3. The questionnaires can be administered either by asking respondents to complete the survey themselves (self-administered questionnaires) or by asking respondents the questions directly (interviews). The researcher must consider the effects that interviewers have on respondents that can lead to biased answers (interviewer bias) and whether to make the questions structured (closed-ended questions in which the answers are provided) or unstructured (open-ended questions which people answer in their own words).

   4. It is important to establish rapport, or a feeling of trust between researchers and subjects.

B. In participant observation, the researcher participates in a research setting while observing what happens in that setting.

   1. Generalizability, which is the extent to which the findings from one group (or sample) can be generalized or applied to other groups (or populations), is a problem in participant observation studies.

   2. Results of participant observation studies can stimulate hypotheses and theories that can be tested in other settings, using other research methods.

C. Secondary analysis, which is the analysis of data already collected by other researchers, is used when resources are limited and/or existing data may provide excellent sources of information. However, because the researcher did not directly carry out the research, he or she cannot be sure that the data were systematically gathered, accurately recorded, and biases avoided.

D. Documents, or written sources, may be obtained from many sources, including books, newspapers, police reports, and records kept by various organizations.

E.   Unobtrusive measures involve observing social behavior of people who do not know they are being studied.

F.   Experiments are especially useful in determining causal relationships.

1.   Experiments involve independent (factors that cause a change in something) and dependent variables (factors that are changed).

2.   Experiments require an experimental group (subjects exposed to the independent variable) and a control group (subjects not exposed to the independent variable).

G.   Deciding which method to use involves four primary factors.

1.   The researcher must consider resources like time and available money.

2.   Access to subjects is important; the sample may be physically inaccessible to the researcher, thereby influencing the choice of methods.

3.   The researcher takes into consideration the purpose of the research, choosing the method that will be most suitable for obtaining answers to the questions posed.

4.   The researcher's background or training also influences the choice of methods. Those trained in use of quantitative research methods (emphasis placed on precise measurement and the use of statistics and numbers) are likely to choose surveys, while those trained in use of qualitative research methods (emphasis placed on describing and interpreting people's behavior) lean toward participant observation.

V.   Gender in Sociological Research

A.   Because gender can be a significant factor in social research, researchers take steps to prevent it from biasing their findings.

B.   Gender can also be an obstacle to doing research, particularly when the gender of the researcher is different from that of the research subjects and the topic under investigation is a sensitive one.

C.   There are also questions regarding the degree to which findings from a sample made up exclusively of one gender can be generalized to the other.

VI.   Ethics in Sociological Research

A.   Ethics are of fundamental concern to sociologists when it comes to doing research.

B.   Ethical considerations include being open, honest, and truthful; not harming the subject in the course of conducting the research; protecting the anonymity of the research subjects; and not misrepresenting themselves to the research subjects.

C.   The Brajuha research demonstrates the lengths sociologists will go to in order to protect the anonymity of research subjects, while the Humphreys research illustrates questionable research ethics.

VII. How Research and Theory Work Together

A.   Sociologists combine research and theory in different ways. Theory is used to interpret data (i.e. functionalism, symbolic interaction and conflict theory provide frameworks for interpreting research findings) and to generate research. Research helps to generate theory.

B.   Real life situations often force researchers to conduct research in ways that fall short of the ideal.

KEY TERMS

After studying the chapter, review the definition for each of the following terms.

closed-ended questions: questions followed by a list of possible answers to be selected by the respondent (136)

control group: the group of subjects not exposed to the independent variable in the study (138)

dependent variable: a factor that is changed by an independent variable (138)

documents: in its narrow sense, written sources that provide data; in its extended sense, archival material of any sort, including photographs, movies, CD's, DVD's, and so on (137)

experiment: the use of control and experimental groups and dependent and independent variables to test causation (138)

experimental group: the group of subjects exposed to the independent variable in a study (138)

generalizability: the extent to which the findings from one group (or sample) can be generalized or applied to other groups (or populations) (137)

hypothesis: a statement of the expected relationship between variables according to predictions from a theory (129)

independent variable: a factor that causes a change in another variable, called the dependent variable (138)

interview: direct questioning of respondents (135)

interviewer bias: effect that interviewers have on respondents that lead to biased answers (135)

open-ended questions: questions that respondents are able to answer in their own words (136)

operational definition: the way in which a variable in a hypothesis is measured (130)

participant observation (or fieldwork): research in which the researcher *participates* in a research setting while *observing* what is happening in that setting (136)

population: the target group to be studied (131)

qualitative research method: research in which the emphasis is placed on observing, describing, and interpreting people's behavior (141)

quantitative research method: research in which the emphasis is placed on precise measurement, the use of statistics and numbers (141)

questionnaires: a list of questions to be asked (135)

random sample: a sample in which everyone in the target population has the same chance of being included in the study (132)

rapport: a feeling of trust between researchers and the subjects that they are studying (136)

reliability: the extent to which data produce consistent or dependable results (130)

replication: repeating a study in order to test its findings (130)

research method (or research design): one of six procedures sociologists used to collect data: surveys, participant observation, secondary analysis, documents, unobtrusive measures, and experiments (130)

respondents: the people who respond to a survey, either in interviews or self-administered questionnaires (133)

sample: the individuals intended to represent the population to be studied (131)

secondary analysis: the analysis of data already collected by other researchers (137)

self-administered questionnaire: questionnaires filled out by respondents (135)

stratified random sample: a sample from select subgroups of the target population in which everyone in these subgroups has an equal chance of being included in the research study (133)

structured interviews: interviews that use closed-ended questions (136)

survey: the collection of data by having people answer a series of questions (131)

unobtrusive measures: the various ways of observing people who do not know they are being studied (140)

unstructured interviews: interviews that use open-ended questions (136)

validity: the extent to which an operational definition measures what it was intended to measure (130)

variable: a factor thought to be significant for human behavior, which varies or changes from one case to another (129)

KEY PEOPLE
Review the major theoretical contributions or findings of these people.

Chloe Bird and Patricia Rieker: These sociologists caution against assuming that research findings that apply to one gender apply to the other. Because women's and men's lives differ significantly, doing research on only one half of humanity will lead to incomplete research. (144)

Mario Brajuha: During an investigation into a restaurant fire, officials subpoenaed notes taken by this sociologist in connection with his research on restaurant work. He was threatened with jail. (145-146)

Laud Humphreys: This sociologist carried out doctoral research on homosexual activity but ran into problems when he misrepresented himself to his research subjects. Although he earned his doctorate degree, he was fired from his position because of his questionable ethics. (146)

Elton Mayo: Mayo is famous for his research at the Western Electric Company Hawthorne plant during the 1920s. He found that workers' productivity changed in directions that had not been originally hypothesized. He concluded that workers adjusted their productivity because they knew they were being observed. This phenomenon came to be known as the *Hawthorne effect.* (140)

C. Wright Mills: Mills argued that research without theory is of little value, simply a collection of unrelated "facts," and theory that is unconnected to research is abstract and empty, unlikely to represent the way life really is. (146)

Peter Rossi: Rossi produced a controversial piece of research related to counting of the homeless, which revealed that the average number of homeless on any given night was far less than homeless advocates had been stating. (142-144)

Diana Scully and Joseph Marolla: These two sociologists interviewed convicted rapists in prison and found that rapists are not sick or overwhelmed by uncontrollable urges, but rather, are men who have learned to view rape as appropriate in various circumstances. (144-148)

STUDENT APPLICATION PROJECTS

This is your opportunity to apply the sociological perspective to the world around you. The projects in this section refer to material introduced in this chapter of your text. These projects help you to apply the sociological perspective "down to earth...down to your daily life."

1. Think back to the last time you participated in a survey (phone, web, or mail). Did you really want to participate in the survey? Why or Why not? What problems did you notice with the survey? Do you think most people are compelled to give socially acceptable answers in a survey? Explain. Finally, discuss to what extent you think surveys are a good way to do research.

2. If you were a researcher, identify a couple of settings in which you could use the participant observation method. What would be the positives in using this method and what concerns might you have in using such a method?

3. Why is marketing research controversial in sociology? Explain. What are the pros and cons of marketing research? What do you think about marketing research?

4. Imagine you are conducting research on physical abuse in the home involving children between the ages of 2 and 10. Identify three ethical issues you would face and what you might do to address these issues.

SELF-TEST

MULTIPLE CHOICE QUESTIONS

1. A researcher doing a macro level study would choose _____ as a topic. (128)
   a. waiting in public places
   b. race relations
   c. interactions between people on street corners
   d. meat packers at work

2. Sociologists believe that research is necessary because: (128)
   a. common sense ideas may or may not be true.
   b. they want to move beyond guesswork.
   c. researchers want to know what really is going on.
   d. All of the above.

3. _____ steps are involved in scientific research. (128)
   a. Four
   b. Six
   c. Eight
   d. Ten

4. Which of the following is *not* a reason why researchers review the literature? (129)
   a. To help them narrow down the problem by pinpointing particular areas to examine.
   b. To develop ideas about how to do their own research.
   c. To insure that their research findings will confirm their hypotheses.
   d. To determine whether the problem has been addressed already.

5. A relationship between or among variables is predicted: (129)
   a. by a hypothesis.
   b. by use of operational definitions.
   c. when the researcher selects the topic to be studied.
   d. when the researcher is analyzing the results.

6. Why is validity important in the research process? (130)
   a. Because the researcher wants to make sure his research will be published.
   b. Because the researcher wants to be sure that his operational definitions are really measuring what they are intended to measure.
   c. Because the researcher is ethically bound to produce valid results.
   d. Because validity is what distinguishes scientific research from common sense.

7. Reliability refers to: (130)
   a. the extent to which operational definitions measure what they are intended to measure.
   b. the extent to which data produce consistent results from one study to the next.
   c. the integrity of the researcher.
   d. the ways in which the variables in a hypothesis are measured.

8. In analyzing data gathered by participant observation, a researcher is likely to choose: (130)
   a. computer analysis.
   b. quantitative analysis.
   c. qualitative analysis.
   d. statistical analysis.

9. Why are computers valuable in quantitative analysis? (130)
   a. Sociologists can analyze huge amounts of information and identify basic patterns.
   b. Computer software programs take much of the drudgery out of data analysis.
   c. Researchers can try various statistical tests to see which prove the most valuable for analyzing their data.
   d. All of the above.

10. Replication: (130)
    a. is the extent to which operational definitions measure what they were intended to measure.
    b. is the examination of a source to identify its themes.
    c. is the repetition of research by others in order to test its findings.
    d. is copying the work of some other researcher.

11. Based on Table 5.2 in your text, all of the following are ways to measure "average" *except*: (133)
    a. medial.
    b. mean.
    c. median.
    d. mode.

12. Which of the following is *not* a method for gathering data? (131-140)
    a. ethnomethodology
    b. surveys
    c. unobtrusive measures
    d. secondary analysis

13. A sample is defined as: (131)
    a. people available to be studied.
    b. a partial representation of the target group.
    c. the individuals intended to represent the population to be studied.
    d. specific subgroups of the population who have volunteered to participate.

14. You have decided to compare the experiences of freshmen and seniors. You identify students in the two classes you are interested in studying, and then you select a certain number from each group, making sure that each person has an equal chance of being selected. Which of the following sampling methods have you used? (133)
    a. target sampling
    b. random sampling
    c. stratified random sampling
    d. random subsampling

15. Sometimes when a researcher is asking questions of a respondent face-to-face or over the telephone, the person may feel compelled to give "socially acceptable" answers. This outcome is due to: (135)
    a. asking open-ended questions.
    b. rapport between the respondent and researcher.
    c. interviewer bias.
    d. interviewee bias.

16. Why might a researcher "load the dice" in designing a research project? (134)
    a. The researcher doesn't know any better.
    b. The researcher may have a vested interest in the outcome of the research.
    c. The researcher is short on time and money but still wants to get the desired results.
    d. All of the above.

17. You have been hired to do a survey of a community's views on a proposed anti-crime program. With only a small budget, you need to contact at least 70 percent of the residents living in the affected areas within the next month. Which method are you most likely to choose? (133-135)
    a. participant observation
    b. self-administered questionnaires
    c. interviews
    d. structured interviews

18. The advantage of structured interviews is that: (135)
    a. they use open-ended questions to get in-depth responses.
    b. they are faster to administer and make it easier for answers to be coded.
    c. they make it possible to test hypotheses about cause and effect relationships.
    d. none of the above.

19. Problems that must be dealt with in conducting participant observation include: (136)
    a. the researcher's personal characteristics.
    b. developing rapport with respondents.
    c. generalizability.
    d. all of the above.

20. The analysis of data already collected by other researchers is referred to as: (137)
    a. surveying the literature.
    b. use of documents.
    c. secondary analysis.
    d. replication.

21. Sources such as newspapers, diaries, bank records, police reports, household accounts, and immigration files are all considered: (137)
    a. unreliable data sources.
    b. documents that provide useful information for investigating social life.
    c. useful for doing quantitative research but not valid when doing qualitative analysis.
    d. of limited validity because it would be difficult to replicate the study.

22. To study patterns of alcohol consumption in different neighborhoods, you decide to go through the recycling bins and count the beer, wine, and liquor bottles. You would be using: (139)
    a. participant observation.
    b. experimental methods.
    c. unobtrusive methods.
    d. qualitative methods.

23. Which method will a researcher use if he or she is interested in determining causal relationships? (137)
    a. an experiment
    b. survey research
    c. participant observation
    d. none of the above

24. In an experiment, the group not exposed to the independent variable in the study is: (138)
    a. the guinea pig group.
    b. the control group.
    c. the experimental group.
    d. the maintenance group.

25. The change in behavior that occurs when subjects know they are being studied is: (140)
    a. the Hawthorne effect.
    b. the Humphreys effect.
    c. the unobtrusive effect.
    d. the obtrusive effect.

26. When you analyze your data you find that men who abuse women are often drunk at the time the abuse takes place. How do sociologists refer to the simultaneous presence of both alcohol and abuse? (138)
    a. simulation
    b. correlation
    c. association
    d. intervening variable

27. Surveys are more likely to be used by researchers trained in: (141)
    a. social psychology.
    b. ethnomethodology.
    c. quantitative research methods.
    d. qualitative research methods.

28. Why is it important to consider gender in planning and conducting research? (144)
    a. the gender of the interviewer might produce interviewer bias.
    b. it cannot be assumed that men and women experience the social work in the same way, so both need to be studied in order to have a complete picture.
    c. gender is a significant factor in social life.
    d. all of the above.

29. Research ethics require: (145)
    a. openness.
    b. that a researcher not falsify results or plagiarize someone else's work.
    c. that research subjects should not be harmed by the research.
    d. all of the above.

30. Which of the following statements best describes the relationship between theory and research? (146)
    a. Research is really more important than theory, since it is research that proves or disproves common sense.
    b. Research and theory are both important, since research without theory is simply facts and theory without research is abstract and empty.
    c. Theory is really more important than research, since it is theory that provides the explanations for why people do what they do.
    d. Research should always follow theory, since theory is more important to sociology than research.

TRUE-FALSE QUESTIONS

1. _____ Date rape is an acceptable topic for sociological research. (128)
2. _____ After selecting a topic, the next step in the research model is defining the problem. (128)
3. _____ An operational definition refers to the precise ways in which researchers measure their variables. (130)

4. _____In general, researchers give higher priority to reliability than validity. (130)
5. _____Reliability is the extent to which data produce consistent results. (130)
6. _____Validity is important in order to test the findings from a study. (130)
7. _____Computers are valuable to research sociologists because they can store a great deal of information very efficiently. (130)
8. _____One of the first steps in conducting survey research is to determine a population. (131)
9. _____In survey research, it is undesirable for respondents to express their own opinions. (133)
10. _____The wording of questionnaires can affect research results. (135)
11. _____Structured interviews always use closed-ended questions. (135)
12. _____Establishing rapport is extremely important in participant observation. (136)
13. _____Secondary analysis and use of documents mean the same thing in terms of research methods. (137)
14. _____It is always unethical to observe social behavior in people when they do not know they are being studied. (140)
15. _____The purpose of an experiment is to identify causal relationships. (138)
16. _____Before a researcher can conclude that a cause-effect relationship exists, it is necessary to rule out possible spurious corrections. (138)
17. _____Quantitative research methods emphasize precise measurement, the use of statistics and numbers. (141)
18. _____Research done on one gender can be applied to the other gender. (144)
19. _____Research conducted by sociologists must meet professional ethical criteria. (145)
20. _____The research by Scully and Marolla demonstrate that research must be done under ideal conditions in order for the findings to be valid. (147)

FILL-IN-THE-BLANK QUESTIONS

1. A statement about the relationship between variables according to predictions from a theory is known as a _____. (128)
2. After you gather data, it is time to _____ them. (130)
3. The _____is the target group you intend to study. (131)
4. There are _____ways to measure the average. (133)
5. The best sample is a _____sample. (133)
6. A survey researcher needs to make sure questions are _____. (135)
7. In order to research topics like domestic violence, it is important that the researcher establish _____with respondents. (136)
8. A sociologists who is studying the trash left behind in garbage cans, is most likely engaging in the _____ method. (137)
9. The _____ variable causes a change in another variable. (138)
10. Sociologists trained in quantitative research methods are most likely to use the _____ method. (141)
11. Peter Rossi and his associates attempted to count the _____ in Chicago. (142-143)
12. Sometimes in research, one's gender can lead to _____ bias. (144)

13. _____ disguised himself and mislead his subjects while conducting research. (145)
14. C. Wright Mills argued that you cannot have research without _____. (146)
15. Systematic research and the application of theory take us beyond _____. (146)

MATCH THESE CONCEPTS WITH THEIR DEFINITIONS

_____ 1. Hawthorne effect   a. *observation of people who don't know they are being studied*

_____ 2. population   b. *behavior change due to subject's awareness of being studied*

_____ 3. control group   c. *the interviewer's effect on respondents that leads to biased answers*

_____ 4. interviewer bias   d. *the way in which a researcher measures a variable*

_____ 5. replication   e. *written sources*

_____ 6. secondary analysis   f. *the target group to be studied*

_____ 7. documents   g. *the analysis of data already collected by other researchers*

_____ 8. independent variable   h. *the group of subjects who are exposed to the independent variable*

_____ 9. operational definition   i. *repeating a study to see if the same results are obtained*

_____ 10. unobtrusive measures   j. *a factor that causes a change in another variable*

ESSAY QUESTIONS

1. Choose a topic and explain how you would go through the different steps in the research model.

2. Discuss some of the things that can go wrong in the process of doing research and provide suggestions on how to overcome such problems.

3. The author of your text discussed six different research methods. Pick a research topic of interest to you and discuss how you might try to investigate this topic using these different methods. In your answer, consider how a particular method may or may not be suitable for the topic under consideration.

4. Explain why ethical guidelines are necessary when conducting social science research.

5. Discuss the relationship between theory and research and why common sense is not enough.

CHAPTER 6
SOCIETIES TO SOCIAL NETWORKS

CHAPTER SUMMARY

- Groups are the essence of life in society. We become who we are by our membership in groups. Essential features of group are that members have a sense of belonging and interact with one another. Society is the largest and most complex group that sociologists study.

- On the way to postindustrial society, humans passed through four types of societies, each due to a social revolution that was linked to new technology. The societies that have existed are (1) hunting and gathering; (2) pastoral and horticultural, the result of the domestication revolution; (3) agricultural, the result of the invention of the plow; and (4) industrial, the result of the Industrial Revolution. Today's postindustrial society, based on information, services, and technology, has emerged with the invention of the computer chip. A distinctive level and pattern of social inequality has characterized each type of society. Another new type of society, the bioeconomic society, may be emerging.

- The following types of groups exist within society: primary groups, secondary groups, in-groups and out-groups, reference groups, and social networks. Changed technology has given birth to a new type of group—the electronic community.

- Group dynamics concern the ways in which individuals affect groups and groups affect individuals. Group size is a significant aspect of group dynamics. As a group grows larger, it becomes more stable but the intensity or intimacy of the group decreases.

- Leaders can be either instrumental (task-oriented) or expressive (socioemotional); both are essential for the functioning of the group. The three main leadership styles are authoritarian, democratic, and laissez-faire.

- The Asch experiment demonstrates the influence peer groups have over their members, while the Milgram experiment shows how powerfully people are influenced by authority. Groupthink, which occurs when political leaders become cut off from information that does not support their opinion, poses a serious threat to society's well-being.

LEARNING OBJECTIVES
After reading Chapter 6, you should be able to:

1. Know the essential features of a group and why groups are said to be the essence of life in society. (152)
2. Identify the five types of societies that have developed in the course of human history, understand how they evolved, and cite their distinct forms of social division, social labor, and social inequality. (153-157)

3. Name the four technological innovations most responsible for the social transformations of society and explain their respective roles in those transformations. (153-157)

4. Discuss how recent advances in human genetics, such as cloning and bioengineering, may be transforming society. (157-158)

5. Distinguish between the terms "aggregate," "category," and "group." (159)

6. Describe the social characteristics, relationships, and/or functions that are associated with primary groups, secondary groups, in-groups and out-groups, reference groups, social networks, and electronic communities. (159-165)

7. Know what is meant by "group dynamics" and the effect of group size on the stability and intimacy within the group. (165-168)

8. Describe how group size can affect attitudes, behavior, and willingness to help. (167)

9. Identify and compare the two types of group leaders and the three types of group leadership styles that are commonly found within groups. (168-170)

10. Discuss the methodology, findings, and implications of the Asch experiment and the Milgram experiment as they relate, respectively, to peer pressure and obedience to authority. (170-171)

11. Define the term "groupthink," explain why it is dangerous, and discuss what can—and should—be done to prevent it. (173-174)

CHAPTER OUTLINE

I. Societies and Their Transformation

    A. Groups are the essence of life in society; the groups to which we belong help determine our goals and values, how we feel about ourselves, and even how we feel about life itself.

    B. An essential element of a social group is that its members have something in common and they believe that what they have in common makes a difference.

    C. Society, which consists of people who share a culture and a territory, is the largest and most complex group that sociologists study. As society changes, so does the nature and types of its groups.

    D. The first societies were hunting and gathering societies.

        1. Their survival depended on hunting animals and gathering plants. Since an area could only support a limited number of people who obtained food this way, the groups were small in size and nomadic, moving elsewhere when the supply of food ran out.

        2. They had few social divisions beyond that based on sex. There was usually a shaman, an individual thought to be able to influence spiritual forces, but their status was generally not much higher than that of everyone else.

        3. The family was the basic unit—distributing food, educating the children, nursing the sick, etc.

        4. Since what they gathered was perishable, they did not accumulate possessions. Of all societies, they were the most egalitarian.

    E. Hunting and gathering societies were transformed into pastoral (characterized by the pasturing of animals) and horticultural (characterized by the growing of plants) societies as a result of the domestication revolution.

1. The domestication of plants and animals is called the first social revolution, although the process was extremely gradual.

2. The resulting societies created food surpluses that allowed for increased population size and some specialized division of labor.

3. Increased trade and interaction between groups developed, and people began to accumulate objects they considered valuable.

4. As families or clans acquired more goods than others, feuds and wars erupted.

5. Leaders began to accumulate more of these possessions than other people did, and to pass these advantages along to their descendants. As a result, simple equality began to give way to inequality.

F. The agricultural revolution (the second social revolution) occurred with the invention of the plow about 5,000 to 6,000 years ago. Pastoral and horticultural societies were transformed into agricultural societies.

1. Since plows pulled by animals were used instead of hoes and digging sticks, a much larger food surplus was produced. This allowed people to engage in activities other than farming.

2. Sometimes referred to as the dawn of civilization, this period produced the wheel, writing, and numbers. Cities developed, and groups were distinguished by their greater or lesser possessions. An elite gained control of the surplus resources.

3. Social inequalities became a fundamental feature of social life. Those with greater resources surrounded themselves with armed men to protect their possessions and growing privileges. They began to levy taxes on their "subjects." This concentration of resources and power, along with the oppression of the powerless, was the forerunner of the state.

4. Females became subjugated to males. Elise Boulding suggests that this change occurred because men were in charge of plowing and the cattle.

G. The Industrial Revolution (the third social revolution) began in 1765, when the steam engine was first used to run machinery in Great Britain. Agricultural societies were transformed into industrial societies.

1. The industrial societies developed and harnessed many mechanical power sources, resulting in a dramatic shift from agriculture to manufacturing as the major sources of power, wealth, and prestige.

2. Initially, social inequality increased greatly, as did the size of the population. The individuals who first utilized the new technology accumulated great wealth, controlling the means of production and dictating the conditions under which people could work for them. A huge surplus of labor developed, as masses of people were thrown off the land their ancestors had farmed.

3. Initially denied the right to unionize or strike, workers eventually won their demands for better living conditions. The consequence was that wealth spread to larger segments of society.

4. As industrialization continued, the pattern of growing inequality was reversed. Indicators of greater equality include better housing, a vast increase in consumer goods, the abolition of slavery, and more representative political systems.

H. Industrial societies are being transformed into postindustrial societies; these social changes are linked to the new technology of the microchip.

1.   Postindustrial societies are moving away from production and manufacturing to service industries. The basic component of this new society is information.
2.   The United States was the first country to have more than 50 percent of its work force employed in service industries. Australia, New Zealand, western Europe, and Japan soon followed.
3.   Social analysts are suggesting that we are witnessing a fourth social revolution because our way of life has been radically transformed by the microchip.

I.   Some social analysts believe that another new type of society, called a biotech society, is emerging.
1.   Its origins go back to either the identification of the double-helix structure of DNA or the decoding of the human genome. Its chief characteristic will be an economy that centers around the application of genetic structures.
2.   Biotechnology is already replacing botany and biochemistry is replacing chemistry.
3.   It is not clear whether this is a society that will replace postindustrial society or simply be another aspect of this information-based society. Regardless, we can look forward to revolutionary changes in health care and maybe even the human species.

J.   As society is transformed, so are we. These changes even affect the way we think about ourselves and the way we live our lives. Not all societies go through all the stages; many societies today reflect a mixture of the different types.

II.   Groups Within Society

A.   Groups are viewed as a buffer between individuals and society.
1.   Durkheim believed that small groups serve as a sort of lifeline that helps prevent anomie.
2.   Sociologists distinguish between aggregates, categories, and groups. An aggregate is made up of individuals who temporarily share the same physical space but do not have a sense of belonging together. A category is a collection of people who have similar characteristics. Unlike groups, the individuals who make up aggregates or categories do not interact with one another or take each other into account.

B.   Sociologist Charles H. Cooley used the term "primary group" to refer to groups characterized by cooperative, intimate, long-term, face-to-face relationships.
1.   The group becomes part of the individual's identity and the lens through which to view life.
2.   It is essential to an individual's psychological well-being, as humans have an intense need for associations that promote feelings of self-esteem.

C.   Secondary groups are larger, relatively temporary, more anonymous, formal, and impersonal than primary groups, and are based on some interest or activity.
1.   Members are likely to interact on the basis of specific roles, such as president, manager, worker, or student.
2.   In industrial societies, secondary groups have multiplied and become essential to our welfare.

3. Secondary groups tend to break down into primary groups within the larger group, such as friendship cliques at school or work. The primary group serves as a buffer between the individual and the needs of the secondary group.

D. Groups toward which individuals feel loyalty are called in-groups, while those toward which they feel antagonisms are called out-groups.

    1. The division is significant sociologically because in-groups provide a sense of identification or belonging, which often produce rivalries between groups.

    2. In-group membership leads to discrimination; given our loyalty, we favor members of our in-group. Sociologist Robert K. Merton identified a double standard produced by this: the behaviors by members of an in-group are seen as virtues, while the same behaviors by members of an out-group are viewed as vices.

    3. Dividing the world into "we" and "them" can sometimes lead to acts directed against an out-group.

E. Reference groups are the groups we use as standards to evaluate ourselves, whether or not we actually belong to those groups.

    1. They exert great influence over our behavior; people may change their clothing, hair style, speech, and other characteristics to match what the reference group would expect of them.

    2. Having two reference groups that clearly conflict with each other can produce intense internal conflict.

F. Social networks consist of people linked by various social ties. Clusters, or factions that form within large groups, are called cliques. Cliques, family, friends, and acquaintances can all be bases for social networks.

    1. Interaction takes place within social networks that connect us to the larger society.

    2. One of the ways in which people are expanding their social networks is through facebooking, an electronic way to meet "friends."

    3. Stanley Milgram did an experiment that demonstrated how small our social world really is; he found that social networks are so interrelated that almost everyone in the United States is connected by just six links

    4. One reason why it is so difficult to overcome social inequality is because our social networks contribute to inequality.

G. In the 1990s, due to technology, an entirely new type of human group made its appearance—the electronic community.

    1. Through the Internet, people around the world interact with one another in news groups.

    2. While most news groups are a new and interesting way of communicating, some meet our definition of a group because the people who use them have established relationships and think of themselves as belonging together.

III. Group Dynamics

A. How individuals affect groups and groups affect individuals is known as group dynamics.

    1. The study of group dynamics focuses on group size, leadership, conformity, and decision making.

2.   Sociologists recognize a small group as one that is small enough for everyone in it to interact directly with all the other members.

B.   As Georg Simmel (1858-1918) noted, the size of the group is significant for its dynamics.

1.   A dyad is a social group containing two members. It is the smallest and most fragile of all human groupings. Marriages and love affairs are examples: if one member loses interest, the dyad collapses.

2.   A triad is a group of three persons—a married couple with a first child, for example. Triads are stronger than dyads but are still extremely unstable. It is not uncommon for coalitions to form in which there is alignment of some members of the group against another. Often, one member becomes an arbitrator or mediator because he or she always tries to settle disagreements between the other two members of the group.

3.   As more members are added to a group, intensity decreases and stability increases, for there are more linkages between more people within the group. The groups develop a more formal structure to accomplish their goals, for instance by having a president, treasurer, and so on. This structure enables groups to survive over time.

4.   Research by Darley and Latané found that as groups grow larger, they tend to break into smaller groups, people are less willing to take individual responsibility (diffusion of responsibility), and they interact more formally toward one another.

C.   A leader may be defined as someone who influences the behavior of others.

1.   There are two types of group leaders. Instrumental (task-oriented) leaders are those who try to keep the group moving toward its goals, reminding the members of what they are trying to accomplish. Expressive (socioemotional) leaders are those who are less likely to be recognized as leaders but help with the group's morale. These leaders may have to minimize the friction that instrumental leaders necessarily create.

2.   There are three types of leadership styles. Authoritarian leaders are those who give orders and frequently do not explain why they praise or condemn a person's work. Democratic leaders are those who try to gain a consensus by explaining proposed actions, suggesting alternative approaches, and giving "facts" as the basis for their evaluation of the members' work. Laissez-faire leaders are those who are very passive and give the group almost total freedom to do as it wishes.

3.   Psychologists Ronald Lippitt and Ralph White discovered that the leadership styles produced different results when used on small groups of young boys. Under authoritarian leaders the boys became either aggressive or apathetic; under democratic leaders they were more personal and friendly; and under laissez-faire leaders they asked more questions, made fewer decisions, and were notable for their lack of achievement.

4.   Different situations require different leadership styles.

5.   Sociologists would disagree that people are born to be leaders. Rather, they find that people with certain characteristics are more likely to become leaders—those who represent the group's values, are seen as capable of leading the group out of crisis, are more talkative, express determination and self-confidence, are taller or are judged better looking.

D. A study by Dr. Solomon Asch indicates that people are strongly influenced by peer pressure. Asch was interested in seeing whether individuals would resist the temptation to change a correct response to an incorrect response because of peer pressure.

    1. Asch held cards up in front of small groups of people and asked which sets of cards matched; one at a time, they were supposed to respond aloud. All but one of the group members was a confederate, having been told in advance by the researcher how to answer the question.

    2. After two trials in which everyone answered correctly, the confederates intentionally answered incorrectly, as they had previously been instructed to do.

    3. Of the fifty people tested, 33 percent ended up giving the incorrect answers at least half of the time, even though they knew the answers were wrong; only 25 percent always gave the right answer despite the peer pressure.

E. Dr. Stanley Milgram sought to determine why otherwise "good people" apparently participated in the Nazis' slaughter of Jews and others.

    1. He conducted experiments in which one person (the "teacher") was instructed to administer an electric shock to the other person (the "learner") for each wrong answer given to certain questions and to increase the voltage of the shock after each wrong answer.

    2. In fact, the "learner" was playing a role, intentionally giving wrong answers, but only pretending to be receiving an electrical shock.

    3. Since a person in apparent authority (scientist, white coat, university laboratory) continually stated that the experiment had to go on, most of the "teachers" gave in to that authority and continued to administer the "shocks" even when they appeared to produce extreme pain.

    4. The scientific community was disturbed not only by Milgram's findings, but also by his methods. Associations of social researchers accordingly adopted codes of ethics to require that subjects be informed of the nature and purpose of social research, and almost all deception was banned.

F. Sociologist Irving Janis coined the word "groupthink" to refer to situations in which a group of people think alike and any suggestion of alternative thinking becomes a sign of disloyalty. Even moral judgments are put aside for the perceived welfare of the group.

    1. The Asch and Milgram experiments demonstrate how groupthink can develop.

    2. U.S. history provides examples of governmental groupthink: presidents and their inner circles have committed themselves to a single course of action (e.g., refusal to believe the Japanese might attack Pearl Harbor; continuing and expanding the war in Vietnam; and the Watergate scandal) even when objective evidence showed the course to be wrong. The leaders became cut off from information that did not coincide with their own opinions.

    3. Groupthink can be prevented only by insuring that leaders regularly are exposed to individuals who have views conflicting with those of the inner circle.

KEY TERMS

After studying the chapter, review the definition for each of the following terms.

aggregate: individuals who temporarily share the same physical space but do not see themselves as belonging together (159)

agricultural revolution: the second social revolution, based on the invention of the plow, which led to agricultural society (155)

agricultural society: a society based on large-scale agriculture, dependent on plows drawn by animals (155)

authoritarian leader: a leader who leads by giving orders (169)

biotech society: an economy that centers around the application of genetics—human genetics for medicine, and plant and animal genetics for the production of food (157)

category: people who have similar characteristics (159)

clique: a cluster of people within a larger group who choose to interact with one another; an internal faction (163)

coalition: the alignment of some members of a group against others (166)

democratic leader: a leader who leads by trying to reach a consensus (165)

domestication revolution: the first social revolution, based on the domestication of plants and animals, which led to pastoral and horticultural societies (154)

dyad: the smallest possible group, consisting of two persons (165)

electronic community: individuals who regularly interact with one another on the Internet and who think of themselves as belonging together (165)

expressive leader: an individual who increases harmony and minimizes conflict in a group; also known as a socioemotional leader (169)

group: people who have something in common and who believe that what they have in common is significant; also called a social group (152)

group dynamics: the ways in which individuals affect groups and groups affect individuals (165)

groupthink: Irving Janis's term for a narrowing of thought by a group of people, leading to the perception that there is only one correct answer, in which to even suggest alternatives becomes a sign of disloyalty (173)

horticultural society: a society based on cultivating plants by the use of hand tools (154)

hunting and gathering society: a human group dependent on hunting and gathering for its survival (153)

Industrial Revolution: the third social revolution, occurring when machines powered by fuels replaced most animal and human power (155)

industrial society: a society based on the harnessing of machines powered by fuels (156)

in-groups: groups toward which one feels loyalty (161)

instrumental leader: an individual who tries to keep the group moving toward its goals; also known as a task-oriented leader (169)

laissez-faire leader: an individual who leads by being highly permissive (169)

leader: someone who influences other people (168)

leadership styles: ways in which people express their leadership (169)

networking: using one's social networks for some gain (165)

out-groups: groups toward which one feels antagonism (161)

pastoral society: a society based on the pasturing of animals (154)

postindustrial society: a society based on information, services, and high technology, rather than on raw materials and manufacturing (156)

primary group: a group characterized by intimate, long-term, face-to-face association, and cooperation (159)

reference group: Herbert Hyman's term for the groups we use as standards to evaluate ourselves (162)

secondary group: compared with a primary group, a larger, relatively temporary, more anonymous, formal, and impersonal group based on some interest or activity, whose members are likely to interact on the basis of specific roles (159)

shaman: the healing specialist or intermediary with the spirit world in a tribal society (153)

small group: a group small enough for everyone to interact directly with all the other members (165)

social network: the social ties radiating outward from the self that link people together (162)

society: people who share a culture and a territory (152)

triad: a group of three persons (166)

KEY PEOPLE
Review the major theoretical contributions or findings of these people.

Solomon Asch: Asch is famous for his research on conformity to peer pressure. (170-171)

Herbert Blumer: He describes an industrial society as one in which goods are no longer produced by the brute force of humans or animals but by machines powered by fuels. (156)

Elise Boulding: This sociologist hypothesized that women's status in agricultural societies declined sharply once men were put in charge of plowing and the cattle. (155)

Charles H. Cooley: It was Cooley who noted the central role of primary groups in the development of one's sense of self. (159)

John Darley and Bibb Latané: These researchers investigated how group size affects members' attitudes and behaviors. They found that as the group grew, individuals' sense of responsibility diminished, their interactions became more formal, and the larger group tends to break down into small ones. (168)

Emile Durkheim: Durkheim viewed the small group as a buffer between the individual and society, helping to prevent anomie. (159)

Lloyd Howells and Selwyn Becker: These social psychologists found that factors such as location within a group underlie people's choices of leaders. (169)

Irving Janis: Janis coined the term "groupthink" to refer to the tunnel vision that a group of people sometimes develop. (173)

Ronald Lippitt and Ralph White: These social psychologists carried out a classic study on leadership styles and found that the style of leadership affected the behavior of group members. (169)

Robert Merton: Merton observed that the traits of in-groups become viewed as virtues, while those same traits in out-groups are seen as vices. (161)

Stanley Milgram: Milgram's research has contributed greatly to sociological knowledge of group life. He did research on social networks and individual conformity to group pressure. (163-165,171-173)

Georg Simmel: This early sociologist was one of the first to note the significance of group size; he used the terms dyad and triad to describe small groups. (165-166)

STUDENT APPLICATION PROJECTS

This is your opportunity to apply the sociological perspective to the world around you. The projects in this section refer to material introduced in this chapter of your text. These projects help you to apply the sociological perspective "down to earth...down to your daily life."

1. Do you think a new bioeconomic society is developing? Why or why not? What concerns do you have about biotechnology?

2. Do you have a reference group that you use or have used to evaluate your life? How important is this reference group to you? Explain.

3. Do you use facebooking as a way to expand your social network? How do you see this as positively or negatively affecting how people in society interact with one another?

4. Do you believe that Milgram's "small world phenomenon" has any validity given the work done by Kleinfeld? Can you think of occasions when you proclaimed "it's a small world?

SELF-TEST

MULTIPLE CHOICE QUESTIONS

1.   What term is used to describe people who interact with one another and think of themselves as belonging together? (152)
     a.   assembly
     b.   aggregate
     c.   category
     d.   group

2.   What is the largest and most complex group that sociologists study? (152)
     a.   the global community
     b.   a society
     c.   a nation-state
     d.   a secondary group

3.   Which of the following is *not* a characteristic of hunting and gathering societies? (153)
     a.   They have the fewest social divisions.
     b.   A shaman is usually part of this society.
     c.   They consist of 50-100 members.
     d.   tTey accumulate few personal possessions.

4.   Of all types of societies, which is the simplest? (153)
     a.   hunting and gathering societies
     b.   horticultural societies
     c.   agricultural societies
     d.   industrial societies

5.   On what are pastoral societies based? (154)
     a.   the cultivation of plants
     b.   the pasturing of animals
     c.   the invention of the plow
     d.   large-scale agriculture

6.   Which of the following was a consequence of the domestication revolution? (155)
     a.   human groups became larger
     b.   a food surplus was created
     c.   the division of labor became more specialized
     d.   all of the above

7.   The plow's invention ushered in a new type of society called: (155)
     a.   pastoral society.
     b.   farming society.
     c.   agricultural society.
     d.   agrarian society.

8. In an industrial society, which of the following was an indicator of increasing equality? (156)
   a. better housing
   b. the abolition of slavery
   c. a move toward more representative political systems
   d. all of the above

9. On what is postindustrial society based? (156)
   a. information, services, and high technology
   b. emphasis on raw materials
   c. the production of new products
   d. all of the above

10. Which was the first country to have more than 50 percent of its work force in the service sector? (157)
    a. Japan
    b. the United States
    c. Australia
    d. Great Britain

11. A society in which the economy centers around the application of human genetics for medicine and plant genetics for the production of food is: (158)
    a. associated with the identification of the double-helix structure of DNA.
    b. the decoding of the human genome in 2000.
    c. representing a new type of society or simply another aspect of postindustrial society.
    d. all of the above.

12. According to Emile Durkheim, what is the value of small groups? (159)
    a. They promote diversity.
    b. They generate change.
    c. They prevent anomie.
    d. They encourage conformity.

13. Which term describes people who have similar characteristics? (159)
    a. group
    b. aggregate
    c. category
    d. society

14. An aggregate is: (159)
    a.   a set of individuals who interact in an anonymous, formal, and rather impersonal fashion.
    b.   a set of individuals who share a common identity and interact with one another.
    c.   a set of individuals who temporarily share the same physical space but do not see themselves as belonging together.
    d.   a set of individuals toward whom we feel antagonisms.

15. According to Cooley, which are essential to an individual's psychological well-being? (159)
    a.   primary groups
    b.   secondary groups
    c.   therapy groups
    d.   interpersonal groups

16. Secondary groups: (159)
    a.   have members who are likely to interact on the basis of specific roles.
    b.   are characteristic of industrial societies.
    c.   are essential to the functioning of contemporary societies.
    d.   all of the above.

17. How do sociologists refer to groups that provide a sense of identification or belonging? (161)
    a.   personal groups
    b.   in-groups
    c.   my-group
    d.   homeboys' groups

18. What are some of the consequences of in-group membership? (161)
    a.   discrimination
    b.   hatred
    c.   killing
    d.   all of the above

19. If Sue wanted a promotion to a supervisory position, managers in her company would serve as which type of group to her? (162)
    a.   primary
    b.   secondary
    c.   reference
    d.   aggregate

20. What term describes the social ties radiating out from the self, linking people together? (162)
    a.   social networks
    b.   reference groups
    c.   cliques
    d.   inner-circles

21. In which ways are some college students finding new ways to meet friends electronically? (164)
    a. through cliques
    b. facebooking
    c. telecommuting
    d. facesaving

22. Dyads: (165)
    a. are the most intense or intimate of all human groups.
    b. require continuing active participation and commitment of both members.
    c. are the most unstable of social groups.
    d. all of the above.

23. Which of the following is *not* a characteristic of a triad? (166)
    a. The introduction of a third person into a dyad reduces the intensity of the interactions.
    b. A triad is inherently unstable because coalitions can form.
    c. One of the members of the group often acts as an arbitrator or mediator.
    d. The continuation of the group depends on the success of the arbitrator in settling disputes.

24. A diffusion of responsibility occurs: (168)
    a. when someone does not identify with a reference group.
    b. when someone feels excluded from a coalition.
    c. when a group is larger than a dyad and each member feels that someone else will act.
    d. when the leadership is authoritarian.

25. An expressive leader: (169)
    a. tries to keep the group moving toward its goals.
    b. is also known as a task-oriented leader.
    c. increases harmony and minimizes conflict in a group.
    d. is the director of the drama club.

26. According to Lippitt and White, which type of leader is *best* for most situations? (169)
    a. authoritarian
    b. democratic
    c. laissez-faire
    d. instrumental

27. According to sociologists, leaders tend to have certain characteristics that may include: (169)
    a. how they are more outgoing.
    b. that they tend to be taller and are judged better-looking than others.
    c. where they sit in a group.
    d. all of the above.

28. Of the 50 people that Solomon Asch tested, what percentage stuck to their guns and always gave the right answer? (171)
    a. 25 percent
    b. 33 percent
    c. 40 percent
    d. 53 percent

29. What did the Milgram experiment demonstrate? (172)
    a. that people who know they are being studied will behave differently as a result
    b. that peer groups have an awesome influence over their members
    c. that people are strongly influenced by authority
    d. that political leaders can become isolated

30. According to the author of the text, what is the key to preventing groupthink? (174)
    a. making sure that the membership of groups is constantly changing
    b. having decisions made by the widest possible audience, rather than committees acting alone
    c. making sure that the results of social science research and the information gathered by media reporters is widely circulated
    d. making sure that committees represent a diversity of interests

TRUE-FALSE QUESTIONS

1. _____ Society is the largest and most complex group that sociologists study. (152)
2. _____ The domestication of animals and plants was the first social revolution. (153)
3. _____ According to Elise Boulding, women's status in agricultural societies increased with the development of metals that were then attached to plows. (155)
4. _____ Industrial societies were brought about by the invention of the plow. (156)
5. _____ Social inequality increased during the first stage of industrialization, while social equality increased as industrialization progressed. (156)
6. _____ Japan was the first country to have more than 50 percent of its work force employed in service industries. (156)
7. _____ The basic component of the postindustrial society is information. (157)
8. _____ Anomie is most likely to occur in the absence of ties to primary groups. (159)
9. _____ Members of primary groups are likely to interact on the basis of specific roles. (159)
10. _____ Robert Merton observed that traits of our in-groups tend to be viewed as virtues, while those same traits are seen as vices when found among members of out-groups. (161)
11. _____ Reference groups are the groups we use as standards to evaluate ourselves. (162)
12. _____ A person has to be a member of his or her reference groups. (162)
13. _____ Research by Stanley Milgram demonstrates how small our social world really is. (163)
14. _____ Networking refers to the conscious use or even cultivation of networks for some gain. (162)
15. _____ Dyads are the most intimate and stable of all group sizes. (165)
16. _____ As a small group grows larger, its intensity decreases and its stability increases. (168)

17. _____Researchers have demonstrated that group size is a factor in determining whether strangers will help one another when a problem arises. (168)
18. _____Sociologically speaking, a leader is one who is officially appointed or elected to be the "leader." (168)
19. _____The laissez-faire leadership style often leads to fewer results and decisions being made. (169)
20. _____ The Columbia space shuttle disaster is an example of groupthink. (173)

FILL-IN-THE-BLANK QUESTIONS

1. _____ groups tend to be more formal and impersonal. (152)
2. _____ societies are based on the cultivation of plants by the use of hand tools. (153)
3. Emile Durkheim wondered what could be done to prevent _____ in society. (154)
4. The _____ gives us our basic orientation to life. (159)
5. Groups toward which we feel loyalty are called _____. (159)
6. A _____ group provides a yardstick to evaluate ourselves. (162)
7. A clique is synonymous with the term internal _____. (163)
8. A group of individuals who interact with one another on the Internet may be members of an _____ community. (165)
9. A _____ is the alignment of some members of a group against others. (166)
10. Instrumental leaders tend to be _____ oriented. (169)
11. A _____ leader leads giving orders. (169)
12. Milgram found that it took an average of _____ jumps for letters to reach designated individuals in his "small world phenomenon" experiment. (172)
13. As group size increases, stability _____and intimacy _____. (168)
14. Irving Janis coined the term _____. (173)
15. Groupthink refers to the collective _____ vision that groups sometimes develop. (173)

MATCH THESE SOCIAL SCIENTISTS WITH THEIR CONTRIBUTIONS

_____	1. Irving Janis	a.	*primary groups*
_____	2. Georg Simmel	b.	*obedience to authority*
_____	3. Emile Durkheim	c.	*dyads*
_____	4. Stanley Milgram	d.	*classic study on leadership styles*
_____	5. Solomon Asch	e.	*leadership role influenced by seating in group*
_____	6. Charles H. Cooley	f.	*noted that women's status changed with the invention of the plow*
_____	7. Robert K. Merton	g.	*small groups and anomie*
_____	8. Ronald Lippitt & Ralph White	h.	*groupthink*
_____	9. Elise Boulding	i.	*conformity to peer pressure*
_____	10. Lloyd Howells & Selwyn Becker	j.	*in-group prejudice leads to double standard*

ESSAY QUESTIONS

1. After summarizing the fundamental social changes that resulted from each of the different social revolutions, evaluate the degree to which the new technology of the microchip is contributing to a similar level of fundamental change.

2. Durkheim was among the first sociologists to argue that small groups stand as a buffer between the individual and the larger society. The author of your text notes that secondary groups today have become essential to our welfare, yet they fail to satisfy our deep needs for intimate association. In this essay, consider how it is possible that they are essential for our welfare if they fail to satisfy essential human needs.

3. Explain the three different leadership styles and suggest reasons why the democratic leader is the best style of leader for most situations.

4. Explore the factors that influence the emergence of groupthink and consider strategies for minimizing the development of this collective tunnel vision.

5. Discuss how the size of the group affects attitudes and behavior.

CHAPTER 7
BUREAUCRACY AND FORMAL ORGANIZATIONS

CHAPTER SUMMARY

- The rationalization of society refers to a major transformation in the way people think—from a desire to protect time-honored ways to a concern with efficiency and practical results. Max Weber traced the rationalization of society to Protestantism, while Marx attributed it to capitalism.

- As a result of the emphasis on rationality, formal organizations—secondary groups designed to achieve explicit objectives—have proliferated. Their most common form is a bureaucracy, characterized by Weber as having a hierarchy of authority, a division of labor, written rules, written communications, and impersonality. Weber's characteristics of bureaucracy are an "ideal type" that may not accurately describe any real organization.

- The dysfunctions of bureaucracies include alienation, red tape, the lack of communication between units, goal displacement, and incompetence. In Weber's view, the impersonality of bureaucracies tends to produce alienation among workers. In Marx's view, workers experience alienation when they lose control of the work process and are cut off from the finished product of their labor.

- In the United States voluntary associations (groups made up of volunteers who organize on the basis of some mutual interest) also have proliferated. Voluntary associations play an important role in society, furthering interests, offering people an identity and a sense of purpose, and govern and maintain social order. Additionally, some voluntary organizations provide functions such as mediating between the individual and government, bringing people into the political mainstream, and paving the way for social change. The iron law of oligarchy—the tendency of formal organizations to be dominated by a small, self-perpetuating elite—is a problem in voluntary associations.

- The concept of corporate culture refers to the organization's traditions, values, and unwritten norms. Much of this culture is invisible. It can affect its members, either negatively or positively, depending on the members' available opportunities to achieve.

- Greater emphasis is now being placed on humanizing work settings to develop human potential. Included among the attempts that humanize the work place are quality circles, work teams, corporate day care, and employee stock ownership plans. Conflict theorists see this as yet another way for employers to manipulate workers.

- The Japanese corporate model provides a contrast to the American corporate model, although the reality of life in the Japanese corporation is at variance with the model that is generally presented.

LEARNING OBJECTIVES
After reading Chapter 7, you should be able to:

1. Define the rationalization of society and discuss its ramifications. (178)
2. Differentiate between the views of Karl Marx and Max Weber on what led to the rationalization of society. (178-180)
3. List and discuss the characteristics of bureaucracies. (181-183)
4. Explain the difference between "ideal" and "real" bureaucracy. (183-184)
5. Cite and discuss examples of the dysfunctions of bureaucracies. (184-187)
6. Know how bureaucracies perpetuate themselves. (187)
7. Explain the sociological significance of bureaucracies. (188)
8. Contrast bureaucracies with voluntary organizations. (188)
9. Discuss the functions of voluntary organizations. (189)
10. Explain the problem of oligarchy within voluntary associations. (190)
11. Understand the hidden corporate culture and its ramifications on women and minority employees. (192-193)
12. Describe and evaluate the different steps many corporations have taken to humanize their work settings and maximize the potential of their employees. (193-194)
13. Discuss the conflict perspective's critique of corporate attempts to humanize the work setting. (195)
14. Explain the role technology currently plays in the control of workers and how that role may soon be expanding. (195-196)
15. Know the differences between the Japanese and American corporate models and how those differences include both myths and realities. (196-198)

CHAPTER OUTLINE

I. **The Rationalization of Society**
   A. Rationality, the acceptance of rules, efficiency, and practical results as the right way to approach human affairs, is a characteristic of industrial societies.
   B. Historically, the traditional orientation to life is based on the idea that the past is the best guide for the present; however, this orientation stands in the way of industrialization.
      1. Capitalism requires a shift in people's thinking, away from the idea that "This is the way we've always done it," to "Let's find the most efficient way to do it."
      2. Personal relationships are replaced by impersonal, short-term contracts.
      3. The "bottom line" becomes the primary concern.
   C. Marx said that the development of capitalism caused people to change their way of thinking, not the other way around. Because capitalism was more efficient, produced things in greater abundance, and yielded high profits, people changed their ideas.
   D. Weber believed that religion held the key to understanding the development of capitalism.
      1. He noted that capitalism emerged first in predominantly Protestant countries.

2. In *The Protestant Ethic and the Spirit of Capitalism* Weber proposed that a set of behaviors rooted in Protestantism led to the development of capitalist activity and the rationalization of society.

3. Weber argued that because of the Calvinistic belief in predestination, people wanted to show they were among the chosen of God. Financial success in life became a sign of God's approval; however, money was not to be spent on oneself. Rather, the investment of profits became an outlet for their excess money, while the success of those investments became a further sign of God's approval.

4. Because capitalism demanded rationalization (the careful calculation of practical results), traditional ways of doing things, if not efficient, must be replaced, for what counts are the results.

E. No one has yet been able to establish which view is correct. Consequently, the two continue to exist side by side within sociology.

II. Formal Organizations and Bureaucracy

A. Formal organizations, secondary groups designed to achieve explicit objectives, have become a central feature of contemporary life.

B. Early examples of formal organization were guilds and the army. With industrialization, secondary groups became more common. Formal organizations, especially as they increase in size, tend to develop into bureaucracies.

C. Max Weber identified the essential characteristics of bureaucracies, which help these organizations reach their goals, as well as grow and endure. These include the following:
   1. a hierarchy where assignments flow downward and accountability flows upward.
   2. a division of labor.
   3. written rules.
   4. written communications and records.
   5. impersonality.

D. Weber's characteristics of bureaucracy describe an ideal type—a composite of characteristics based on many specific examples. The real nature of bureaucracy often differs from its ideal image.

E. Weber's model only accounts for some of the characteristics of bureaucracies. Dysfunctions can also be identified.
   1. Red tape, or the strict adherence to rules, results in nothing getting accomplished.
   2. A lack of communication between units means that they are sometimes working at cross purposes; sometimes one unit "undoes" what another unit has accomplished because the two fail to inform one another what each is doing.
   3. Bureaucratic alienation, a feeling of powerlessness and normlessness, occurs when workers are assigned to repetitive tasks in order for the corporation to achieve efficient production, thereby cutting them off from the product of one's labor.

4.   To resist alienation, workers form primary groups within the larger secondary organization, relating to one another not just as workers, but as people who value one another.

5.   The alienated bureaucrat is one who feels trapped in the job, does not take initiative, will not do anything beyond what she or he is absolutely required to do, and uses rules to justify doing as little as possible.

6.   Bureaucratic incompetence is reflected in the Peter Principle—members of an organization are promoted for good work until they reach their level of incompetence. If this principle were generally true then bureaucracies would be staffed by incompetents and would fail. In reality, bureaucracies are highly successful.

F.   Goal displacement occurs when an organization adopts new goals after the original goals have been achieved and there is no longer any reason for it to continue.

    1.   The March of Dimes is an example of this.

    2.   It was originally formed to fight polio, but when that threat was eliminated, the professional staff found a new cause, birth defects.

    3.   With the possibility of birth defects some day being eliminated as our knowledge of the human genes expands, the organization has adopted a new slogan—breakthroughs for babies—which is vague enough to ensure their perpetual existence.

G.   To the sociologist, bureaucracies are significant because they represent a fundamental change in how people relate to one another. Prior to this rationalization, work focused on human needs, such as making sure than everyone had an opportunity to earn a living; with rationalization, the focus shifts to efficiency in performing tasks and improving the bottom line.

III. Voluntary Associations

A.   Voluntary associations are groups made up of volunteers who have organized on the basis of some mutual interest.

B.   All voluntary associations have one or more of the following functions:

    1.   to advance the particular interests they represent (e.g., youth in Scouting programs).

    2.   to offer people an identity and, for some, a sense of purpose in life.

    3.   to help govern the nation and maintain social order (e.g., Red Cross disaster aid).

C.   Some voluntary associations have the following functions:

    1.   to mediate between the government and the individual.

    2.   to train people in organizational skills so they can climb the occupational ladder.

    3.   to help bring disadvantaged groups into the political mainstream.

    4.   to challenge society's definitions of what is "normal" and socially acceptable.

D.   Voluntary associations represent no single interest or purpose. The idea of mutual interest is characteristic of all voluntary associations; a shared interest in some view or activity is the tie that binds members together.

    1.   The motivation for joining a group differs widely among its members, from the expression of strong convictions to the cultivation of personal contacts.

2. Because of this, membership turnover tends to be high.

E. Within voluntary associations is an inner core of individuals who stand firmly behind the group's goals and are committed to maintaining the organization. Robert Michels used the term "iron law of oligarchy" to refer to the tendency of this inner core to dominate the organization by becoming a small, self-perpetuating elite.

1. Some are disturbed because when an oligarchy develops, many people are subsequently excluded from leadership because they don't reflect the inner circle's values or background.

2. If the oligarchy gets too far out of line with the membership, it runs the risk of rebellion by the grassroots.

IV. Working for the Corporation

A. Rosabeth Moss Kanter's organizational research demonstrates that the corporate culture contains hidden values that create a self-fulfilling prophecy that affects people's careers.

1. The elite have an image of who is most likely to succeed. Those whose backgrounds are similar to the elite and who look like the elite are singled out and provided with better access to information, networking, and "fast track" positions. Workers who are given opportunities to advance tend to outperform others and are more committed.

2. Those who are judged outsiders and experience few opportunities think poorly of themselves, are less committed, and work below their potential.

3. The hidden values of the corporate culture that create this self-fulfilling prophecy are largely invisible.

B. These same values also contribute to the iron law of oligarchy.

1. The top leadership reproduces itself by favoring people who "look" like its members—that is, white and male.

2. Because females and minorities do not match the stereotype of a corporate leader, they may by treated differently. They may experience "showcasing" or being put in highly visible positions with little power so that the company is in compliance with affirmative action. These positions are often "slow-track" positions where promotions are slow because accomplishments in these areas seldom come to the attention of top management.

C. Morale is influenced by the level one achieves in an organization; the higher people go, the higher their morale.

D. A significant part of bureaucracies lies below the surface and is largely invisible. Because of this, workers ascribe differences in behavior and attitudes to individual personalities rather that the corporate structure of culture.

V. Humanizing the Corporate Culture

A. Weber believed that bureaucracies would eventually dominate social life because of their efficiency and capacity to replace themselves.

B. Humanizing a work setting refers to efforts to organize the workplace in such a way that it develops rather than impedes human potential.

1. More humane work settings are ones in which (1) access to opportunities is based on ability and contributions rather than personal characteristics; (2)

             power is more equally distributed; and (3) rules are less rigid and decision making more open.

      2.   There is nothing inherent in bureaucracies that makes them insensitive to people's needs or prevents them from becoming more humane.

  C.   Corporate attempts to make work organizations more humane include the following:

      1.   work teams; within these groups workers are able to establish primary relationships with other workers so that their identities are tied up with their group; the group's success becomes the individual's success.

      2.   corporate day care facilities at work; these ease the strain on parents, leading to reduced turnover, less absenteeism, and shorter maternity leaves.

      3.   employee stock ownership where employees own some stock; this does not mean that working conditions and employee-management relations are friction-free because profitability still is the key.

      4.   quality circles; these are small groups of workers and a manager or two who meet regularly to try and improve the quality of the work setting and the product. This is an example of a business fad.

      5.   The cooperative is an alternative to bureaucracy; these are collectives owned by members who collectively make decisions, determine goals, evaluate resources, set salaries, and assign work tasks. The economic results of cooperatives have been mixed; some are more profitable than private organizations, some are less.

  D.   Conflict theorists point out that the basic relationship between workers and owners is confrontational regardless of how the work organization is structured. Their basic interests are fundamentally opposed to each other.

VI. Technology and the Control of Workers

  A.   While the computer has the capacity to improve the quality of people's lives, it also holds the potential of severe abuse.

      1.   Computers allow managers to increase surveillance without face-to-face supervision.

      2.   Computers can create the "maximum-security workplace," potentially keeping track of every movement a worker makes while on the job. Some worry that it is only a short step from this type of workplace to the "maximum-security society."

VII. U.S. and Japanese Corporations

  A.   William Ouchi lists five ways in which this model differs from the U.S. system:

      1.   Hiring and promotion: The Japanese model features a team approach; a starting cohort of workers gets the same salary, is rotated through the organization, and develops intense loyalty to one another and the organization. In the U.S. model, employees are hired on the basis of what the individual can contribute; the emphasis is on competition; and individual loyalty is to the individual him- or herself, not to the company.

      2.   Lifetime security: The Japanese model takes lifetime security for granted; the company is loyal to the employee and expects the employee to be loyal to the company. In the U.S. model, lifetime security is unusual; continued

employment is based on good and/or bad economic conditions; and workers are expected to look out for themselves.

3. Almost total involvement: Work is like a marriage in Japan, in that the company and the employee are committed to each other. In the U.S., the work relationship is highly specific; fulfill your job obligations and the rest of your time is your private life, separate from the firm.

4. Broad training: In Japan, workers move from one job to another within the corporation. In the U.S., employees are expected to perform one job well and then be promoted to a job with more responsibility.

5. Decision-making by consensus: In Japan, decision-making occurs after lengthy deliberations in which each person to be affected by a decision is included in the process. In the U.S., the individual responsible for the unit does as much consulting as she or he thinks necessary and then makes the decision.

6. Much of the Japanese corporate model appears to be a myth and does not reflect Japanese corporate life today.

KEY TERMS
After studying the chapter, review the definition for each of the following terms.

alienation: Marx's term for the experience of workers' being cut off from the product of their labor which results in a sense of powerlessness and normlessness (186)

bureaucracy: a formal organization with a hierarchy of authority; a clear division of labor; emphasis on written rules, communications, and records; and impersonality of positions (181)

capitalism: an economic system characteristized by private ownership and the pursuit of profit (180)

corporate culture: the orientations that characterize corporate work settings (191)

formal organization: a secondary group designed to achieve explicit objectives (181)

goal displacement: a goal displaced by another goal; in this context, the adoption of new goals by an organization; also known as *goal replacement* (187)

humanizing a work setting: organizing a workplace in such a way that it develops rather than impedes human potential (193)

iron law of oligarchy (the): Robert Michels's phrase for the tendency of formal organizations to be dominated by a small, self-perpetuating elite (190)

McDonaldization of society (the): the process by which ordinary aspects of life are rationalized and efficiency comes to rule such things as food production (184)

Peter Principle: a bureaucratic "law," according to which the members of an organization are promoted for good work until they reach their level of incompetence, the level at which they can no longer do good work (187)

rationality: using rules, efficiency, and practical results as the right way to approach human affairs (178)

rationalization of society: a widespread acceptance of rationality and a social organization built around this idea (179)

self-fulfilling prophecy: Robert Merton's term for a false assertion that becomes true simply because it was predicted (191)

traditional orientation: the idea, characteristic of tribal, peasant, and feudal societies, that the past is the best guide for the present (178)

voluntary association: a group made up of volunteers who have organized on the basis of some mutual interest (188)

KEY PEOPLE
Review the major theoretical contributions or findings of these people.

Peter Evans and James Rauch: These sociologists examined government bureaucracies in 35 developing nations and found that those with centralized bureaucracies in which workers are hired on the basis of merit were more prosperous than those that lacked such organization. (187)

Elaine Fox and George Arquitt: These sociologists studied local posts of the Veterans of Foreign Wars (VFW) and found three types of members and evidence of the iron law of oligarchy. (190)

Rosabeth Moss Kanter: Kanter studied the hidden corporate culture and found that for the most part it continually reproduces itself by promoting those workers who fit the elite's stereotypical views. (191)

Gary Marx: Marx has written about the "maximum-security" workplace, given the increased use of computers to control workers. (196)

Karl Marx: Marx believed that the emergence of rationality was due to capitalism. Capitalism changed the way people thought about life, rather than people's orientation to life producing capitalism. (179-180)

Robert Michels: Michels first used the term "the iron law of oligarchy" to describe the tendency for the leaders of an organization to become entrenched. (190)

William Ouchi: Ouchi studied the characteristics of the Japanese corporation. (196)

George Ritzer: Ritzer coined the term the "McDonaldization of society" to describe the increasing rationalization of modern social life. (184)

David Sills: Sills studied goal displacement in the March of Dimes; he also identified four additional functions that some voluntary groups perform. (189)

Alexis de Tocqueville: This Frenchman traveled across the United States in the 1830s in order to observe the customs of the new nation. He commented on the tendency of Americans to join voluntary associations. (188)

Max Weber: Weber studied the rationalization of society by investigating the link between Protestantism and capitalism and identifying the characteristics of bureaucracy. (180-184)

STUDENT APPLICATION PROJECTS

This is your opportunity to apply the sociological perspective to the world around you. The projects in this section refer to material introduced in this chapter of your text. These projects help you to apply the sociological perspective "down to earth...down to your daily life."

1. Find an organizational chart of your college or university. What characteristics of a bureaucracy does this organizational chart show? Explain. What dysfunctions of a bureaucracy have you experienced at your school or university? What do you think should be done to reduce these dysfunctions?

2. Think of your past work experiences. Did any of your places of employment exhibit dysfunctions associated with bureaucracies? If so, which dysfunctions were present and how did they affect you?

3. List the voluntary organizations that you have participated in over your lifetime. Why did you join each of these organizations? Which volunteer organization has had the greatest impact on your life? Explain.

4. Compare and contrast the United States vs. Japanese corporate systems. Which country would you prefer to be employed? Explain.

SELF-TEST
MULTIPLE CHOICE QUESTIONS

1. What is rationality? (178)
    a. the idea that the past is the best guide for the present
    b. making excuses for bureaucratic incompetence
    c. accepting rules, efficiency, and practical results as the way to approach human affairs
    d. None of the above.

2. The idea that the past is the best guide for the present is referred to as: (178)
    a. traditional orientation.
    b. modern orientation.
    c. status quo.
    d. rationalization.

3. What was one of the major obstacles to industrialization? (178)
    a. the medieval church
    b. a traditional orientation
    c. money lenders
    d. the traditional family

4. According to Karl Marx, what was the force behind rationality replacing the traditional orientation to life? (180)
    a. religion
    b. technology
    c. capitalism
    d. culture

5. According to Max Weber, capitalism: (180)
    a. is the investment of capital in the hopes of producing profit.
    b. became an outlet for the excess money of Calvinists.
    c. produced success for many that became a sign of God's approval.
    d. All of the above.

6. In reconciling Weber's and Marx's views on rationality, sociologists feel that: (181)
    a. Weber was most correct.
    b. Marx was most correct.
    c. Weber and Marx were both incorrect.
    d. no analyst has yet reconciled the opposing views to their satisfaction.

7. A secondary group designed to achieve explicit objectives is the sociological definition of: (181)
    a. a social institution.
    b. a formal organization.
    c. a rationalized system.
    d. none of the above.

8. All of the following are characteristics of bureaucracy, *except*: (181-183)
   a. a division of labor.
   b. a hierarchy with assignments flowing upward and accountability flowing downward.
   c. written rules, communications, and records.
   d. impersonality.

9. Which characteristic of a bureaucracy believes that the office, not the individual who holds the office, is important? (1783
   a. clear levels of organiaztion
   b. written rules
   c. impersonality
   d. written communications

10. George Ritzer used the term "the McDonaldization of society" to refer to: (184)
    a. the preference for McDonald's over Burger King.
    b. the spread of McDonald's world-wide.
    c. the increasing rationalization of daily living.
    d. All of the above.

11. What is the force behind "the McDonaldization of society"? (184)
    a. the desire to control the marketplace with uniform products
    b. the increased efficiency which contributes to lower prices
    c. the security that comes from knowing the product
    d. corporate greed

12. Dysfunctions of bureaucracies include: (184-187)
    a. alienation.
    b. bureaucratic incompetence.
    c. red tape.
    d. All of the above.

13. As a worker in a large corporation, Linda is often unhappy. At work she feels that no one appreciates her and that the work she does is boring and repetitive. Which of the following best describes Linda's situation? (187)
    a. bureaucratic incompetence
    b. alienation
    c. goal displacement
    d. goal frustration

14. How do workers resist alienation? (187)
    a. by forming primary groups
    b. by praising each other and expressing sympathy when something goes wrong
    c. by putting pictures and personal items in their work areas
    d. all of the above.

15. According to your text, what is the alienated bureaucrat likely to do? (187)
    a. quit his or her job once unhappiness and dissatisfaction set in
    b. seek counseling to overcome the problem
    c. not do anything for the organization beyond what he or she is required to do
    d. return to school for further training in order to move up in the organization

16. Which of the following is true about the Peter Principle: (187)
    a. states that each employee of a bureaucracy is promoted to his or her level of competence.
    b. states that each employee of a bureaucracy is promoted to his or her level of incompetence.
    c. is generally true and explains why so many bureaucracies fail.
    d. was first stated by Max Weber.

17. When does goal displacement occur? (187)
    a. when a bureaucrat is unable to see the goals of the organization and to function as a cooperative, integrated part of the whole.
    b. when goals conflict with one another.
    c. when an organization adopts new goals
    d. when members of an organization are promoted until they reach their level of incompetence.

18. The sociological significance of bureaucracy is that it: (188)
    a. has always existed as a way of organizing human activity.
    b. reflects the best way of organizing work.
    c. is more dysfunctional than functional.
    d. represents a fundamental change in the way people relate to one another.

19. Voluntary associations: (188)
    a. are groups made up of volunteers who organize on the basis of some mutual interest.
    b. include political parties, unions, professional associations, and churches.
    c. have been an important part of American life.
    d. all of the above.

20. Why do people in the United States belong to voluntary associations? (188)
    a. they meet people's basic needs
    b. people are required to belong to these organizations
    c. people don't have anything to do other than work
    d. they take the place of government agencies

21. Which of the following did David Sills identify as functions that some voluntary associations perform? (189)
    a. to serve as a mediator between the government and the individual
    b. to provided training in organizational skills
    c. to pave the way for social change
    d. all of the above.

22. What is the term that describes the tendency for organizations to be dominated by a small, self-perpetuating elite? (190)
    a. the Peter Principle
    b. bureaucratic engorgement
    c. the iron law of oligarchy
    d. the corporate power struggle

23. According to Rosabeth Moss Kanter, what is the nature of the corporate culture? (191)
    a. it contains "hidden values"
    b. the people with the best qualifications typically will rise to the top of an organization
    c. the employees who work the hardest and are the most cooperative have the greatest likelihood of being promoted
    d. all of the above.

24. Pepsi executives a good example of: (191)
    a. modeling diversity training in the workplace.
    b. promoting primarily within the organization.
    c. maintaining "hidden values" within the corporation.
    d. none of the above.

25. What does it mean to humanize a work setting? (193)
    a. employees bring plants, pictures, and other personal items to the office
    b. having a period of time in which workers visit with each other, tell jokes, and get to know each other more personally
    c. purchasing furniture that is more comfortable for employees
    d. organizing a workplace so that human potential is developed rather than impeded

26. Research on the costs and benefits of employer-financed day care demonstrated that: (194)
    a. such a benefit is costly to the employer because of strict government regulations that must be met.
    b. such a benefit cuts into stockholders' dividends by eating up profits.
    c. few employees took advantage of the benefit.
    d. such a benefit can save the employer money by reducing turnover and absenteeism.

27. Business practices are subject to fads and _____ are an excellent example. (195)
    a. quality circles
    b. cooperatives
    c. collectives
    d. corporate day care

28. Which of the following reflects the views of conflict theorists? (195)
    a. Quality circles, employee stock ownership, and small work groups are excellent ways to solve the problems encountered in bureaucracies.
    b. The interests of workers and owners both may be met by humanizing the work setting.
    c. The interests of workers and owners are fundamentally opposed and, in the final analysis, workers are always exploited.
    d. There is less conflict in the Japanese corporate model than in the U.S. model.

29. Computers in the workplace: (196)
    a. have reduced drudgery of the work.
    b. could lead to more surveillance of workers by managers.
    c. may be the first step towards a society in which every move a citizen makes is recorded.
    d. all of the above.

30. Which of the following statements best describes the Japanese workers' access to lifetime job security? (196)
    a. Almost all Japanese workers enjoy lifetime job security
    b. About one half of Japanese workers, who are employed in small firms, have lifetime job security.
    c. Lifetime job security is elusive, and only about one-third of workers have it.
    d. Lifetime job security is restricted to top management only.

TRUE-FALSE QUESTIONS

1. _____ Rationality involves the acceptance of rules, efficiency, and practical results as the right way to approach human affairs. (178)
2. _____ Traditional orientation is based on the idea that the present is the best guide for the future. (178)
3. _____ Marx argued that rationality was the result of economics. (180)
4. _____ Max Weber believed that the growth of capitalism contributed to the rise of the Protestant ethic. (180)
5. _____ Calvinists believed that thrift was a virtue and that money should not be spent on the luxuries of life. (180)
6. _____ Either primary or secondary groups can be formal organizations. (181)
7. _____ Weber identified five essential characteristics of bureaucracy. (181-183)
8. _____ Most colleges and universities do not have written systems of accountability for faculty members. (182)
9. _____ In a bureaucracy, each worker is a replaceable unit. (183)
10. _____ The characteristics of bureaucracy identified by Max Weber are ideal types. (183)
11. _____ Marx coined the term alienation to describe the feelings of workers that they are often treated more like objects than people. (186)
12. _____ According to conflict theorists, workers can successfully resist becoming alienated if they work at it. (186)
13. _____ The Peter Principle has been proven to be true. (187)

14. _____Voluntary associations are made up of volunteers who have organized on the basis of some mutual interest. (188)
15. _____Voluntary associations may help some individuals climb the occupational ladder. (189)
16. _____The iron law of oligarchy was defined by Robert Michels. (190)
17. _____Corporate daycare, employee stock ownership, and small work teams are three ways companies have been attempting to humanize the work force. (194)
18. _____Conflict theorists believe that bureaucracies exploit workers regardless of the way in which work is set up. (195)
19. _____ The Japanese corporate model emphasizes teamwork and lifetime security. (196)
20. _____In real life, the Japanese corporate model works much the way that it is described. (196)

FILL-IN-THE-BLANK QUESTIONS

1. Until recently, people were immersed in a _____ orientation to life. (178)
2. Karl Marx was one of the first to note how tradition had given way to _____. (179)
3. In his study of capitalism, Max Weber studied the teachings of _____. (180)
4. In a bureaucracy, there is a _____ of labor. (181)
5. As with culture, a bureaucracy often differs from its _____ image. (181)
6. The process by which ordinary aspects of life are rationalized and efficiency comes to rule such things as food preparation is known as the _____ of society. (184)
7. _____ is the term used by Marx to describe the experience of being cut off from the product of one's labor. (186)
8. If _____ were generally true, then organizations would not be successful. (187)
9. People join volunteer groups who organize on the basis of some_____. (188)
10. The _____ refers to how organizations come to be dominated by a small, self-perpetuating elite. (190)
11. Rosabeth Moss Kaunter stressed that corporate culture contains _____ values. (191)
12. _____ teams are used by one of five U.S. Companies. (194)
13. The conflict perspective points out that the basic relationship between workers and owners is always _____. (195)
14. According to William Ouchi, work is like a _____ in Japan. (196)
15. Peering beneath the surface reveals that the reality of the Japanese corporation differs from the _____. (198)

MATCH THESE SOCIAL SCIENTISTS WITH THEIR CONTRIBUTIONS

_____	1. Max Weber	a. *the iron law of oligarchy*
_____	2. Robert Michels	b. *early observer of U.S. society who noted the presence of voluntary associations*
_____	3. William Ouchi	c. *goal displacement in the March of Dimes*
_____	4. Karl Marx	d. *exploitation of workers by capitalists*
_____	5. Rosabeth Moss	e. *the McDonaldization of society*

Kanter
_____	6.	George Ritzer	f. *development of the "maximum-security" workplace*
_____	7.	Alexis de Tocqueville	g. *hidden values in the corporate culture*
_____	8.	Fox & Arquitt	h. *rationalization of society*
_____	9.	Gary Marx	i. *problems of oligarchy in the VFW*
_____	10.	David Sills	j. *Japanese corporate model*

ESSAY QUESTIONS

1. Explain what sociologists mean by the expression "rationalization of society" and discuss why this change has occurred.

2. Explain "hidden values" within the workplace and why this continues in contemporary organizations.

3. Define the iron law of oligarchy and discuss why this problem occurs in voluntary associations.

4. This chapter provides discussion of strategies to humanize the work place. After identifying some of these strategies, consider the conflict perspective on these types of initiatives.

5. Evaluate whether the use of technology to control workers is an inevitable aspect of bureaucracy.

CHAPTER 8
DEVIANCE AND SOCIAL CONTROL

CHAPTER SUMMARY

- Deviance, which refers to violations of social norms, is relative; what people consider deviant varies from one culture to another and from group to group within a society. It is not the act itself but the reaction to the act that makes something deviant. To explain deviance, biologists and psychologists look for reasons within people, such as genetic predispositions or personality disorders, while sociologists look for explanations in social relationships.

- Symbolic interactionists use differential association theory, control theory, and labeling theory to analyze how group membership influences people's behaviors and views of the world. There are several different strategies, or techniques of neutralization, that people who commit deviant acts use in order to continue to think of themselves as conformists.

- Functionalists state that deviance is functional, using strain theory and illegitimate opportunity structures to argue that widespread socialization into norms of material success accounts for much of the crime committed by the poor.

- Conflict theorists argue that the group in power imposes its definitions on other groups—that is, the ruling class directs the criminal justice system against the working class, which commits highly visible property crimes, while it diverts its own criminal activities awaw from the criminal justice system.

- In reacting to criminal deviance, the U.S. has adopted a "get-tough" policy, imprisoning millions of people. African Americans make up a disproportionate number of U.S. prisoners.

- The conclusions of both symbolic interactionists and conflict theorists cast doubts on the accuracy of official crime statistics.

- Society may deal with deviance by medicalizing it and calling it mental illness. Thomas Szasz disagrees with this approach by claiming that deviance is just problem behavior, not mental illness.

- With deviance inevitable, the larger issues are how to protect people from deviant behaviors that are harmful to their own welfare, to tolerate those that are not, and to develop systems of fairer treatment for deviants.

LEARNING OBJECTIVES
After reading Chapter 8, you should be able to:

1. Define "deviance" and understand why, from a sociological perspective, deviance is relative. (204)
2. Know why human groups need norms to exist and, consequently, develop a system of social control for enforcing norms. (204-205)
3. Describe some of the sanctions human groups use to enforce norms, including shaming and degradation ceremonies. (206)
4. Differentiate between biological, psychological, and sociological explanations of why people violate norms. (208)
5. Discuss deviance from the symbolic interactionist perspective—describing and applying the various components of differential association theory, control theory, and labeling theory. (209-213)
6. List and discuss the five techniques of neutralization. (212)
7. Understand, from the functionalist perspective, what functions deviance fulfills for society. (213-214)
8. Explain strain theory and discuss the four deviant paths in response to strain. (215)
9. Describe the different ways street crime and white-collar crime are perceived by the public and treated by the criminal justice system. (216)
10. Talk about the role power plays in defining and punishing deviance while discussing, from the conflict perspective, how the criminal justice system legitimates and perpetuates social inequality. (220)
11. Discuss the reasons for, and implications of, "get tough" policies on crime in the United States. (223)
12. Discuss the decline in crime and the recidivism rate. (224)
13. Explain gender, social class and racial and ethnic biases in the death penalty. (225-227)
14. Explain why crime statistics may be misleading and should be interpreted with caution. (229)
15. Know what is meant by the medicalization of deviance and why some sociologists view mental illness as more of a social, rather than biological, condition. (230-231)
16. Explain why the United States needs to develop a fairer and more humane approach to dealing with deviance. (232)

CHAPTER OUTLINE

I. **What is Deviance?**
   A. Sociologists use the term deviance to refer to a violation of norms.
      1. According to sociologist Howard S. Becker, it is not the act itself that makes an action deviant, but rather how society reacts to it.
      2. Because different groups have different norms, what is deviant to some is not deviant to others. This is true even for criminal deviance, the violation of rules that have been written into law.
      3. Deviants are people who violate rules, whether the infraction is minor (jaywalking) or serious (murder). When sociologists study deviance they are nonjudgmental; they are not judging whether the behavior is good or bad, just

that it is viewed negatively by people within the social group. To sociologists, all people are deviants because everyone violates rules from time to time.

    4. Erving Goffman used "stigma" to refer to attributes that discredit one's claim to a "normal" identity; a stigma (e.g., blindness, mental handicaps, facial birthmarks) defines a person's master status, superceding all other statuses the person occupies.

B. Norms make social life possible by making behavior predictable and without norms, social chaos would exist. The reason deviance is seen as threatening is because it undermines predictability. Thus, social control (the formal and informal means of enforcing norms) is necessary for social life.

C. When a norm is violated, sanctions are imposed.

    1. Sanctions can be either negative or positive.

    2. Negative sanctions, which reflect disapproval of a particular behavior, range from frowns and gossip for breaking a folkway to imprisonment and capital punishment for breaking a more.

    3. Positive sanctions, from smiles to formal awards, are used to reward conformity.

    4. Most sanctions are informal.

D. Shaming is another sanction and is particularly effective when used by members of a primary group or in a small community.

    1. Shaming can be the centerpiece of public ritual, marking the violator as deviant for all the world to see.

    2. Harold Garfinkel used the term *degradation ceremony* to describe formal attempts to label someone as an outsider.

E. Comparisons can be made between biological, psychological, and sociological explanations of deviance.

    1. Psychologists and sociobiologists explain deviance by looking within individuals; sociologists look outside the individual.

    2. Biological explanations focus on genetic predisposition, including factors such as intelligence; the "XYY" theory (an extra Y chromosome in men leads to crime); or body type (squarish, muscular persons are more likely to commit street crimes).

    3. Psychological explanations focus on personality disorders (e.g., "bad toilet training," "suffocating mothers," and so on). Yet these do not necessarily result in the presence or absence of specific forms of deviance in a person.

    4. Sociological explanations search outside the individual: crime is a violation of norms written into law and each society has its own laws against certain types of behavior. But social influences such as socialization, subcultural group memberships, or social class (people's relative standing in terms of education, occupation, income and wealth) may "recruit" some people to break norms.

II. The Symbolic Interaction Perspective

A. Differential association is Edwin Sutherland's term to indicate that those who associate with groups oriented toward deviant activities learn an "excess of definitions" of deviance and thus are more likely to engage in deviant activities.

    1. The key to differential association is the learning of ideas and attitudes favorable to following the law or breaking it. Some groups teach members to violate norms

(e.g., families involved in crime may set their children on a lawbreaking path; some friends and neighborhoods tend to encourage deviant behavior; even subcultures contain particular attitudes about deviance and conformity that are learned by their members).

2. Symbolic interactionists stress that people are not mere pawns; individuals help produce their own orientation to life and their choice of association helps shape the self.

B. According to control theory, everyone is propelled towards deviance, but a system of controls work against these motivations to deviate.

1. Walter Reckless described two complementary systems of control. Inner controls are our capacity to withstand temptations toward deviance and internalized morality, integrity, fear of punishment, and the desire to be good. Outer controls involve groups (e.g. family, friends, the police) that influence us not to deviate.

2. Travis Hirschi noted that strong bonds to society, based on attachments, commitments, involvements, and beliefs, lead to more effective inner controls.

C. Labeling theory is the view that the labels people are given affect their own and others' perceptions of them, thus channeling their behavior either into deviance or conformity.

1. Gresham Sykes and David Matza use the term "techniques of neutralization" to describe the strategies deviants employ to resist society's label. These are (1) denial of responsibility ("I didn't do it"); (2) denial of injury ("Who really got hurt?"); (3) denial of a victim ("She deserved it"); (4) condemnation of the condemners ("Who are you to talk?"); and (5) appeal to higher loyalty ("I had to help my friends").

2. Sometimes an individual's deviant acts begin casually and he or she gradually slides into more serious deviance.

3. Most people resist being labeled deviant, but some revel in a deviant identity (e.g., motorcycle gangs who are proud of getting in trouble, laughing at death, and so on).

4. William J. Chambliss's study of the Saints (troubled boys from respectable middle class families) and the Roughnecks (boys from working class families who hang out on the streets) provides an excellent illustration of labeling theory how labels given to people affect how others perceive them and how they perceive themselves, thus channeling their behavior into deviance or conformity. The study showed how labels open and close doors of opportunity for the individuals involved.

III. The Functionalist Perspective

A. Emile Durkheim stated that deviance, including crime, is functional, for it contributes to social order.

1. Deviance clarifies moral boundaries (a group's ideas about how people should act and think) and affirms norms.

2. Deviance promotes social unity (by reacting to deviants, group members develop a "we" feeling and collectively affirm the rightness of their own ways).

3. Deviance promotes social change (if boundary violations gain enough support, they become new, acceptable behaviors).

B. Robert Merton developed strain theory to analyze what happens when people are socialized to desire cultural goals but denied the institutionalized means to reach them.

1. Merton used "anomie" (Durkheim's term) to refer to the strain people experience when they are blocked in their attempts to achieve those goals.

2. The most common reaction to cultural goals and institutionalized means is conformity (using lawful means to seek goals society sets).

3. He identified four types of deviant responses to anomie: innovation (using illegitimate means to achieve them); ritualism (giving up on achieving cultural goals but clinging to conventional rules of conduct); retreatism (rejecting cultural goals, dropping out); and rebellion (seeking to replace society's goals).

4. According to strain theory, deviants are not pathogenic individuals but the products of society.

C. Sociologists Richard Cloward and Lloyd Ohlin developed illegitimate opportunity theory to explain why social classes have distinct styles of crime.

1. They suggest that these differences are due to differential access to institutionalized means.

2. Illegitimate opportunity structures are opportunities for crimes such as robbery, burglary, and drug dealing, that are woven into the texture of life. These structures may result when legitimate structures fail.

3. For the urban poor, there are opportunities to make money through "hustles" such as robbery, burglary, drug dealing, prostitution, pimping, gambling, and other crimes. The "hustler" is a role model because he or she is one of the few who comes closest to the cultural goals of success.

4. White-collar crime (crimes that people of respectable and high social status commit in the course of their occupations) results from an illegitimate opportunity structure among higher classes. Such crimes exist in greater numbers than commonly perceived, and can be very costly, possibly totaling several hundred billion dollars a year. They can involve physical harm and sometimes death; for instance, unsafe working conditions kill about 100,000 Americans each year, or about five times the number of people killed by street crime.

D. There have been some recent changes in the nature of crime; one of which is the growing ranks of female offenders. As women have become more involved in the professions and the corporate world, they too have been enticed by illegitimate opportunities.

IV. The Conflict Perspective

A. The state's machinery of social control favors the interests of the wealthy and powerful; this group determines the laws whose enforcement is essential for maintaining its power.

B. The criminal justice system directs its energies against violations by the working class; it tends to overlook the harm done by the owners of corporations, though flagrant violations are prosecuted. The publicity given this level of white-collar crime helps stabilize the system by providing evidence of fairness.

C.   The law is an instrument of oppression, a tool designed to maintain the powerful in privileged positions and keep the powerless from rebelling and overthrowing the social order. When members of the working class get out of line, they are arrested, tried and imprisoned in the criminal justice system.

V. Reactions to Deviance

A.   Imprisonment, which follows a degradation ceremony (public trial/pronouncement that the person is unfit to live among law-abiding people), is an increasingly popular reaction to crime but fails to teach inmates to stay away from crime.

    1.   The United States has the dubious distinction of having not only more prisoners than any other nation, but also a larger percentage of its population in prison.

    2.   African Americans are disproportionately represented among the prison population.

    3.   For about the past twenty years, the United States has followed a "get tough" policy. The "three strikes and you're out" laws have become common. Unfortunately, these laws have had some unintended consequences.

    4.   The recidivism rate (the proportion of persons who are rearrested) in the United States is high. For those sentenced to prison for crimes of violence, within just three years of their release, 62 percent are rearrested, and 52 percent are back in prison.

B.   The death penalty is the most extreme and controversial measure the state can take. Many argue that there are biases in the use of the death penalty. These biases reflect regional, gender, social class, as well as racial and ethnic biases.

C.   The definition of behavior as deviant varies across societies, groups, and time periods. The emergence of hate crime legislation in the United States is an example of this.

D.   Caution is needed when interpreting official crime statistics because the reactions of authorities are influenced by the social class of the offender.<NOTE:this sentence doesn't make sense to me; I'm not sure how to rewrite it!>

    1.   Crime statistics are a human creation, produced within a specific social and political context for some particular purpose.

    2.   Police discretion—deciding whether to arrest someone or to ignore a situation—is a routine part of police work. Crime statistics reflect this and many other biases.

E.   Medicalization of deviance is the view of deviance as a symptom of some underlying illness that needs to be treated by physicians.

    1.   Thomas Szasz argues that mental illness is simply problem behaviors: some forms of "mental" illnesses have organic causes (e.g., depression caused by a chemical imbalance in the brain); while others are responses to troubles with various coping devices.

    2.   Szasz's analysis suggests that social experiences, and not some illness of the mind, underlie bizarre behaviors.

    3.   Being mentally ill can sometimes lead to other problems like homelessness; but being homeless can lead to unusual and unacceptable ways of thinking that are defined by the wider society as mental illness.

F.   With deviance inevitable, one measure of a society is how it treats its deviants.

1. The larger issues are how to protect people from deviant behaviors that are harmful to their welfare, to tolerate those that are not, and to develop systems of fairer treatment for deviants.

KEY TERMS

After studying the chapter, review the definition for each of the following terms.

capital punishment: the death penalty (225)

capitalist class: the wealthy who own the means of production and buy the labor of the working class (220)

control theory: the idea that two control systems, inner and outer, work against our tendencies to deviate (210)

corporate crime: crimes committed by executives in order to benefit the corporation (216)

crime: the violation of norms that are written into law (204)

criminal justice system: the system of police, courts, and prisons set up to deal with people who are accused of having committed a crime (219)

cultural goals: the legitimate objectives held out to the members of a society (215)

degradation ceremonies: rituals designed to strip an individual of his or her identity as a group member; for example, a court martial or the defrocking of a priest (206)

deviance: the violation of rules or norms (204)

differential association: Edwin Sutherland's term to indicate that associating with some groups results in learning an "excess of definitions" of deviance, and, by extension, in a greater likelihood that one will become deviant (209)

genetic predispositions: inborn tendencies, in this context, to commit deviant acts (208)

hate crime: crimes to which more severe penalties are attached because they are motivated by hatred (dislike, animosity) of someone's race-ethnicity, religion, sexual orientation, disability, or national origin (229)

illegitimate opportunity structures: opportunities for crimes woven into the texture of life (216)

institutionalized means: approved ways of reaching cultural goals (215)

labeling theory: the view, developed by symbolic interactionists, that the labels people are given affect their own and others' perceptions of them, thus channeling their behavior either into deviance or into conformity (211)

marginal working class: the most desperate members of the working class, who have few skills, little job security, and are often unemployed (220)

medicalization of deviance: to make deviance a medical matter, a symptom of some underlying illness that needs to be treated by physicians (230)

negative sanction: an expression of disapproval for breaking a norm (206)

personality disorders: the view that a personality disturbance of some sort causes an individual to violate social norms (208)

police discretion: the practice of the police, in the normal course of their duties, to either arrest someone for an offense or overlook the matter (229)

positive sanction: a reward or positive reaction for approved behavior, for conformity (206)

recidivism rate: the proportion of persons who are rearrested (224)

serial murder: the killing of several victims in three or more separate events (226)

social control: a group's formal and informal means of enforcing norms (205)

social order: a group's usual and customary social arrangements, on which its members depend and on which they base their lives (205)

stigma: "blemishes" that discredit a person's claim to a "normal" identity (204)

strain theory: Robert Merton's term for the strain engendered when a society socializes large numbers of people to desire a cultural goal (such as success) but withholds from many the approved means to reach that goal; one adaptation to the strain is crime, the choice of an innovative means (one outside the approved system) to attain the cultural goal (215)

street crime: crimes such as mugging, rape, and burglary (208)

techniques of neutralization: ways of thinking or rationalizing that help people deflect society's norms (211)

white-collar crime: Edwin Sutherland's term for crimes committed by people of respectable and high social status in the course of their occupations; for example, bribery of public officials, securities violations, embezzlement, false advertising, and price fixing (216)

working class: those who sell their labor to the capitalist class (220)

KEY PEOPLE

Review the major theoretical contributions or findings of these people.

Howard Becker: Becker observed that an act is not deviant in and of itself, but only when there is a reaction to it. (204)

William Chambliss: Chambliss demonstrated the power of the label in his study of two youth gangs—the Saints and the Roughnecks. (212-213)

Richard Cloward and Lloyd Ohlin: These sociologists identified the illegitimate opportunity structures that are woven into the texture of life in urban slums and provide an alternative set of opportunities for slum residents when legitimate ones are blocked. (214-216)

Emile Durkheim: Durkheim noted that deviance is functional for society. (213)

Robert Edgerton: This anthropologist's studies document how different human groups react to similar behaviors, demonstrating that what is deviant in one context is not in another. (205)

Harold Garfinkel: Garfinkel used the term degradation ceremonies to describe formal attempts to mark an individual with the status of an outsider. (206)

Erving Goffman: Goffman wrote about the role of stigma in the definition of who and what is deviant. (204)

Travis Hirschi: Hirschi studied the strength of the bonds an individual has to society in order to understand the effectiveness of inner controls. (211)

Ruth Horowitz: This sociologist conducted participant observation in a Chicano neighborhood in Chicago. She found that attitudes about honor, which were common among residents, helped to propel young men into deviance. (210)

Martin Sánchez Jankowski: Jankowski studied gangs and identified traits that characterize gang members and the functions that gangs play in urban neighborhoods. (217)

Robert Merton: Merton developed strain theory to explain patterns of deviance within a society. (215)

Donald Partington: This lawyer examined executions for rape and attempted rape in Virginia between 1908 and 1963 and found that only Black men were executed for these crimes during those years. (227)

Walter Reckless: Reckless developed control theory, suggesting that our behavior is controlled by two different systems, one external (outer controls like the police, family and friends) and the other internal (inner controls like our conscience, religious principles, and ideas of right and wrong). (210)

Edwin Sutherland: Sutherland not only developed differential association theory, but was the first to study and give a name to crimes that occur among the middle class in the course of their work—white collar crime. (209-216)

Gresham Sykes and David Matza: These sociologists studied the different strategies delinquent boys use to deflect society's norms—techniques of neutralization. (211)

Thomas Szasz: Szasz argued that mental illness represents the medicalization of deviance. (230)

Mark Watson: Watson studied motorcycle gangs and found that these people actively embraced the deviant label. (212)

STUDENT APPLICATION PROJECTS

This is your opportunity to apply the sociological perspective to the world around you. The projects in this section refer to material introduced in this chapter of your text. These projects help you to apply the sociological perspective "down to earth...down to your daily life."

1. In thinking about contemporary U.S. society, what broader social changes have contributed to the passage of hate crime legislation? What are some problems associated with enforcement of these laws? Do you agree that we need such legislation? Why or why not?

2. Choose three evenings this week to watch the evening news. How many crimes were covered in the news? List each one and briefly summarize the crimes covered. Of those reported, were any of them white-collar crimes? Why do you think the news media is less likely to cover white-collar crime on the nightly news? Do you think white-collar crime should be covered more in the media? Why or why not?

3. Identify as many acts as you can that would be considered deviant in the United States, but would not be considered a crime. Was this easy or difficult to do? What acts would be deviant 30-40 years ago, but would not be considered deviant today? Explain what happens to deviant acts over time and what accounts for this change.

4. Consider the issue of the medicalization of deviance when applied to murder as a deviant behavior. Identify what you think would be the main arguments on each side of the debate. Do you agree with one side more than the other? Explain.

SELF-TEST

MULTIPLE CHOICE QUESTIONS

1. In sociology, to what does the term deviance refer? (204)
    a.   behavior that sociologists believe is bad enough to warrant being punished by society
    b.   all violations of social rules
    c.   the violation of serious rules
    d.   crime

2. Why is deviance often seen as threatening? (204)
    a.   because it is always harmful to society
    b.   because it undermines the predictability of social life
    c.   because it costs society a great deal of money
    d.   because it is bad

3. Of what are frowns, gossip, and crossing people off guest lists all examples? (206)
    a.   retribution
    b.   degradation ceremonies
    c.   negative sanctions
    d.   institutionalized means to achieve goals

4. Most negative sanctions are: (206)
    a.   very punitive.
    b.   universally the same.
    c.   generally informal.
    d.   all of the above.

5. According to Erving Goffman, what is the function of stigma? (204)
    a.   to punish the person because she or he violates the norms
    b.   to reward society for conforming to the norms
    c.   to identify the person who violates the norm as deviant
    d.   to regulate behavior

6. A court martial where the guilty officer is publicly stripped of his rank is an example of: (206)
    a.   degradation ceremonies.
    b.   humiliation ceremonies.
    c.   stigmatization.
    d.   deinstitutionalization.

7. Differential association theory is based on the: (209)
    a.   functionalist perspective.
    b.   conflict perspective.
    c.   symbolic interactionist perspective.
    d.   psychological perspective.

8. According to differential association theory, why does someone become a deviant? (209)
    a. because of genetic predispositions
    b. because of personality disorders
    c. because of a lack of opportunities to engage in conventional activities
    d. because he learns to deviate from or conform to society's norms

9. The idea that two control systems, inner and outer, work against our tendencies toward deviance is called: (210)
    a. conflict theory.
    b. differential association theory.
    c. control theory.
    d. strain theory.

10. According to Travis Hirschi, what is it that determines the effectiveness of our inner controls? (210)
    a. our social class background
    b. our gender
    c. our bonds to society
    d. our age

11. Which of the following is *not* one of the ways of neutralizing deviance? (211)
    a. appeal to higher loyalties
    b. denial of responsibility
    c. denial of deviant labels
    d. denial of injury and of a victim

12. What does William Chambliss's study of the Saints and the Roughnecks suggest? (212)
    a. Labels are easy to cast off once a person gets away from the group doing the labeling.
    b. People often live up to the labels that a community gives them.
    c. People often rebel against the labels given them and lead a completely different life.
    d. Sociological research on labeling has produced few conclusions.

13. For Chambliss, what factors influence whether people are seen as deviant? (212)
    a. social class
    b. the visibility of offenders
    c. styles of interaction
    d. all of the above.

14. Which perspective stresses that deviance promotes social unity and social change? (213-214)
    a. functionalist
    b. conflict
    c. symbolic interactionist
    d. differential association

15. Which of the following is/are example(s) of *institutionalized means*? (215)
    a. getting an education
    b. getting a good job
    c. working hard
    d. all of the above.

16. All of the following are responses to anomie as identified by Robert Merton, *except*: (215)
    a. ritualism.
    b. rebellion.
    c. retreatism.
    d. recidivism.

17. According to strain theory, who gives up pursuit of success by abusing alcohol or drugs? (215)
    a. rebels
    b. retreatists
    c. neurotics
    d. ritualists

18. Steve lives in a neighborhood with high crime rates and poor schools. He believes he will never make it to college. He decides to quit school and sell drugs for a local drug dealer. He is quickly making a lot of money. He buys new clothes and a new car. Steve's behavior reflects which of Merton's deviant paths? (215)
    a. innovation
    b. ritualism
    c. retreatism
    d. rebellion

19. The illegitimate opportunity structures theory is based on: (216)
    a. the conflict perspective.
    b. the symbolic interactionist perspective.
    c. the exchange perspective.
    d. the functionalist perspective.

20. What are crimes committed by high-status people in the course of their occupations called? (216)
    a. upper-class crime
    b. crimes of respectability
    c. white-collar crime
    d. tuxedo crime

21. Sears defrauded the poor of more than $100 million. This is an example of: (216)
    a. good business practices.
    b. innovation.
    c. corporate crime.
    d. negative sanctions.

22. How much does corporate crime cost us as a society? (217)
    a. $400 billion/year
    b. $600 billion/year
    c. $700 billion/year
    d. $800 billion/year

23. Which country today has the largest percentage of its population in prison? (219)
    a. Cuba
    b. United States
    c. Russia
    d. China

24. Which racial/ethnic group is disproportionately represented among the prison population of the United States? (223)
    a. whites
    b. Latinos
    c. African Americans
    d. Native Americans

25. What of the following statements about the recidivism rate in the United States is *correct*? (224)
    a. As a result of the U.S. government's "get-tough" policy in recent years, there has been a sharp drop in the recidivism rate.
    b. About one-half of all recidivists have been convicted of violent crimes.
    c. Approximately two-thirds of all released prisoners will be rearrested within a year.
    d. It is estimated that slightly more than one-half of all prisoners have served time in the past.

26. Who is disproportionately at risk of being put to death under the death penalty? (227)
    a. whites
    b. African Americans
    c. Latinos
    d. Asian Americans

27. According to statistics on hate crimes, which group is most likely to be victimized? (229)
    a. African Americans
    b. whites
    c. Latinos
    d. Asian Americans

28. Hate crimes consist of: (229)
    a. crime because of someone's race
    b. crime because of someone's sexual orientation
    c. crime because of someone's disability
    d. all of the above.

29. The medicalization of deviance refers to: (230)
    a. the castration of sex offenders.
    b. use of lethal injections for the death penalty.
    c. viewing deviance as a medical matter.
    d. all of the above.

30. With deviance inevitable, the author of your textbook suggests that one measure of a society is: (232)
    a. how low the overall rates of deviance are.
    b. what types of deviance there is.
    c. what gets defined as deviance and what doesn't.
    d. how deviants are treated.

TRUE-FALSE QUESTIONS

1. _____Across all cultures, certain acts are considered to be deviant by everyone. (204)
2. _____According to your text, a college student cheating on an exam and a mugger lurking on a dark street have nothing at all in common. (204)
3. _____To be considered deviant, a person does not even have to do anything. (204)
4. _____Social control includes both formal and informal means of enforcing norms. (205)
5. _____All sanctions are negative. (206)
6. _____Sociologists search for explanations of deviance among factors outside the individual. (208)
7. _____According to differential association theory, the source of deviant behavior may be found in a person's socialization, or social learning. (209)
8. _____Symbolic interactionists stress that we are mere pawns in the hands of others. (209)
9. _____Sykes and Matza identified five techniques of neutralization. (211-212)
10. _____Outlaw bikers hold the conventional world in contempt and are proud of getting into trouble. (212)
11. _____In the study by Chambliss, the Saints and the Roughnecks both turned out largely as their labels would have predicted. (213)
12. _____The functionalist perspective states that deviance contributes to the social order. (213)
13. _____According to strain theory, everyone has a chance to get ahead in society, but some people prefer to use illegal means to achieve their goals. (215)
14. _____According to strain theory, some people experience greater pressures to deviate from society's norms because of their social location. (215)
15. _____Illegitimate opportunity structures are readily available in urban slums. (216)
16. _____White-collar crime is not as costly as street crime. (216)
17. _____Both functionalists and conflict theorists agree that the criminal justice system functions for the well-being of all citizens. (216)
18. _____Researchers have found that the U.S. recidivism rate is as high as 75 percent. (225)
19. _____Police discretion is a routine part of police work. (220)
20. _____Official statistics are accurate counts of the crimes committed in our society. (222)

FILL-IN-THE-BLANK QUESTIONS

1. Sociologists use the term _____ to refer to any violation of a norm. (204)
2. Expressions of disapproval of deviance are called _____ sanctions. (206)
3. Psychologists focus on abnormalities within the _____. (208)
5. Sociologists search for factors about deviance_____ of the individual. (208)
6. Researchers have found that delinquents are more likely to come from _____ that get into trouble with the law. (209)
7. Travis Hirschi noted that the stronger our bonds are with society, the more effective our _____ controls are. (211)
8. Skyes and Matza found that there are five techniques to _____ one can use to deflect society's norms. (211-212)
9. According to the functionalist perspective, deviance promotes social _____. (213)
10. An innovator _____ cultural goals and rejects institutionalized means. (215)
11. According to Robert Merton, people who experience social strain, are likely to feel _____, a sense of normlessness. (215)
12. Martha Stewart is an example of someone who committed _____ crime. (216)
13. A major change in the nature of crime is the growing number of _____ offenders. (223)
14. _____ was a well-intended law that had unintended consequences. (225)
15. In the United States, the _____ rate—the percentage of former prisoners who are rearrested—is extremely high. (224)
16. Thomas Szasz argued that mental illnesses are simply _____ behaviors. (230)

MATCH THESE SOCIAL SCIENTISTS WITH THEIR CONTRIBUTIONS

_____	1. Edwin Sutherland	a. *strain theory*
_____	2. Robert Merton	b. *embracing the deviant label*
_____	3. Erving Goffman	c. *degradation ceremonies*
_____	4. Thomas Szasz	d. *white-collar crime*
_____	5. Howard Becker	e. *definition of deviance*
_____	6. William Chambliss	f. *effects of labeling*
_____	7. Gresham Sykes & David Matza	g. *importance of stigma*
_____	8. Travis Hirschi	h. *techniques of neutralization*
_____	9. Harold Garfinkel	i. *myth of mental illness*
_____	10. Mark Watson	j. *inner controls*

ESSAY QUESTIONS

1. Discuss how the different sociological perspectives could be combined to provide a more complete picture of deviance.

2. Explain how forms of deviance such as street gangs can be both functional and dysfunctional at the same time.

3. Using any one of the different sociological perspectives, develop an explanation for why white-collar crime is generally treated as less serious crime in our society.

4. Discuss the "get tough" policy that the United States has followed and how successful that has been.

5. Obesity could be viewed as deviance because it is a condition that violates our cultural norms regarding appearance. Develop an explanation for how this type of deviance is increasingly subject to medicalization.

CHAPTER 9
GLOBAL STRATIFICATION

CHAPTER SUMMARY

- Social stratification is a system in which people are divided into layers according to their relative power, property, and prestige. The nations of the world, as well as people within a nation, are stratified into groups based on relative power, prestige, and property. In every society men, as a group, are placed above women as a group.

- Four major systems of social stratification include (1) slavery—owning other people; (2) caste—lifelong status determined by birth; (3) estate—feudal society divided into nobility, clergy, and commoners; and (4) class—based on possession of money or material possessions. Class systems are characteristic of industrialized societies. Gender discrimination cuts across all forms of social stratification.

- Early sociologists disagreed about the meaning of social class in industrialized nations. Karl Marx argued that a person's relationship to the means of production was the only factor determining social class. Max Weber argued that three elements—property, prestige, and power—dictate an individual's standing in society.

- Various arguments have been developed to explain the universal presence of stratification. Kingsley Davis and Wilbert Moore argued that society must offer rewards in order to assure that important social positions are filled by the most competent people. Gaetano Mosca believed that society will be stratified by power and this is inevitable. Conflict theorists see that stratification is the consequence of group struggles for scarce resources. Modern conflict sociologists examine how groups within the same class compete for larger pieces of the pie.

- Gerhard Lenski combined the functional and conflict perspectives to explain the historical evolution of stratification systems.

- To maintain stratification within a nation, the ruling class controls ideas and information, technology, and the police and military.

- In Britain, the most striking features of the class system are differences in speech and accent and differences in education. In the former Soviet Union, communism resulted in one set of social classes being replaced by another.

- The model of global stratification presented in this text divides nations into three groups: the "Most Industrialized," the "Industrializing," and the "Least Industrialized" Nations. The oil-rich nations are an exception.

- The major theories explaining the origins of global stratification are colonialism, world system theory, and the culture of poverty. Most sociologists agree with colonialism and the world system theory.

- International stratification is maintained through neocolonialism, the ongoing dominance of the Least Industrialized Nations by the Most Industrialized Nations, and multinational corporations which operate across national boundaries. The new technology gives advantage to the world's Most Industrialized Nations.

- Global stratification affects each individual's life chances.

LEARNING OBJECTIVES

After reading Chapter 9, you should be able to:

1. Define social stratification and explain why it is sociologically significant. (237)
2. Describe and provide examples of the four major systems of social stratification. (237-242)
3. Discuss the relationship between gender and social stratification. (242)
4. Describe the major points of disagreement between Karl Marx and Max Weber regarding the meaning of social class in industrialized societies. (243-244)
5. According to the functionalist view articulated by Kingsley Davis and Wilbert Moore, list the functions that social stratification provides for society. (245-246)
6. List and discuss Melvin Tumin's counter-arguments to the functionalist view of social stratification. (245)
7. Discuss the conflict perspective of social stratification as it relates to class conflict and scarce resources. (251)
8. Discuss and evaluate Gerhard Lenski's attempt to synthesize the functionalist and conflict perspectives on social stratification. (247-248)
9. Expalin how ideology rather than force is more effective for the elite classes in maintaining social stratification. (248-249)
10. Compare the social stratification systems in Great Britain and the former Soviet Union to the social stratification system in the United States. (249-250)
11. Identify the major characteristics associated with the Most Industrialized Nations, Industrializing Nations, and Least Industrialized Nations. (250-254)
12. Discuss why modifications may be necessary in classifying nations into level of industrialization. (255)
13. Describe and evaluate the major theories pertaining to the origins and maintenance of global stratification. (258-263)

CHAPTER OUTLINE

I. Systems of Social Stratification
   A. Social stratification is a system in which large groups of people are divided into layers according to their relative power, property, and prestige.
   B. Stratification exists within a society and between nations and affects our life chances and orientations to life.
   C. Slavery is a form of social stratification in which some people own other people.
      1. Initially, slavery was based on debt, punishment for violation of the law, or defeat in battle.

2. Gerda Lerner notes that women were the first people enslaved through warfare. They were valued for sexual purposes, reproduction, and their labor.

3. Slavery could be temporary or permanent and was not necessarily passed on to one's children. Typically, slaves owned no property and had no power; this was not universally true, however.

4. The first form of slavery in the New World was bonded labor or indentured service—a contractual system in which someone voluntarily sold his or her services for a specified period of time; at the end of that time the individual was freed.

5. Given the shortage of indentured servants, American colonists first tried to enslave Indians and then turned to Africans, who were being brought to North and South America by the British, Dutch, English, Portuguese, and Spanish.

6. When American slave owners found it was profitable to own slaves for life, they developed beliefs to justify what they wanted and to make slavery inheritable (i.e., the slaves' children could be sold, bartered, or traded). The practice of slavery was written into law.

7. There is some debate as to whether or not slavery is still practiced in certain parts of the world today. Although denied by their governments, accusations have been made that the slave trade has been revived in Sudan and Mauritania.

D. In a caste system, status is determined by birth and is life-long.

1. Ascribed status is the basis of a caste system. Caste societies try to make certain that boundaries between castes remain firm by practicing endogamy (marriage within their own group) and developing rules about ritual pollution (teaching that contact with inferior castes contaminates the superior caste).

2. Although abolished by the Indian government in 1949, the caste system remains part of everyday life in India, as it has for almost 3,000 years. This system is based on religion and is made up of four main castes which are subdivided into thousands of specialized subcastes or *jati*. The lowest caste, the Dalit, are known as the "untouchables." If higher castes are contaminated by "the untouchables" *abolution* (washing rituals) are required.

3. South Africa's caste system was called apartheid and based on the separation of the races. By law there were four different racial castes, and the law specified where people could live, work, and go to school based on their caste. While this system has been dismantled by the government following decades of international protest, its legacy continues to haunt South Africa. Whites still dominate and the blacks remain uneducated and poor. Political violence has been replaced by street crime.

4. An American racial caste system developed in the United States when slavery ended. Even in the earlier parts of this century, all whites were considered higher than all African Americans and separate accommodations were maintained for the races in the South.

E. During the Middle Ages, Europe developed the estate stratification system consisting of three groups, or estates.

1. The *first estate* was made up of the nobility, who ruled the land.

2. The *second estate* consisted of the clergy, who not only owned vast tracts of land and collected taxes from commoners, but also set its seal of approval on rulers.

Members of the mobility practiced primogeniture, allowing only firstborn sons to inherit land so that their vast land holdings wouldn't be divided into small chunks.

3.   The *third estate* was made up of commoners, known as serfs. They were born into this estate and had few opportunities to move up.

4.   Women belonged to the estate of their husbands.

F.   A class system is a form of social stratification based primarily on the possession of money or material possessions.

1.   Initial social class position is based on that of one's parents (ascribed status).

2.   With relatively fluid boundaries, a class system allows for social mobility, or movement up or down the social class ladder, based on achieved status.

G.   No matter what system a society may use to divide people into different layers, gender is always an essential part of those distinctions within each layer. On the basis of gender, people are sorted into categories and given differential access to rewards. Social distinctions have always favored males. In every society men's earnings are higher than women's and most of the worlds illiterate are women.

II.   What Determines Social Class?

A.   According to Karl Marx, social class is determined by one's relationship to the means of production—the tools, factories, land, and investment capital used to produce wealth.

1.   The bourgeoisie (capitalists) own the means of production; the proletariat (workers) works for those who own the means of production.

2.   While Marx recognized the existence of other groups—farmers and peasants, a lumpenproletariat, and self-employed professionals—he did not consider these groups social classes because they lacked class consciousness.

3.   As capital becomes more concentrated, the two classes will become increasingly more hostile to one another.

4.   Class consciousness, or an awareness of a common identity based on position in the means of production, will develop; it is the essential basis of the unity of workers, according to Marx.

5.   Marx believed that the workers would revolt against the capitalists, take control of the means of production, and usher in a classless society. However, the workers' unity and revolution are held back by false class consciousness—the mistaken identification of workers with the interests of capitalists.

B.   Unlike Marx, Max Weber did not believe that property was the sole basis of a person's position in the stratification system but rather that property, prestige, and power determine social class.

1.   Property (or wealth) is an essential element; however, powerful people, like managers of corporations, control the means of production, even though they do not own them.

2.   Prestige may be derived from ownership of property; however, it also may be based on other factors such as athletic skills.

3.   Power is the ability to control others, even over their objections.

III. Why is Social Stratification Universal?

A. According to the functionalist view expressed by Kingsley Davis and Wilbert Moore, stratification is inevitable for the following four reasons:

1. Society must make certain that its important positions are filled. Some positions are more important than others, the more important positions need to be filled by the more qualified people, and these people must be offered greater rewards.

B. Melvin Tumin was the first to present a number of criticisms to the Davis and Moore thesis.

1. He asked how the importance of a position is measured (e.g., "Is a surgeon really more important to society than a garbage collector?"). Rewards cannot be used to measure the importance of a job; there must be some independent measure of importance.

2. He noted that if stratification worked as Davis and Moore describe it, society would be a meritocracy, a form of social stratification in which all positions are awarded on the basis of merit, but it does not work this way (e.g., the best predictor of college entrance is family income, not ability).

3. Finally, he noted that stratification is dysfunctional to many people, thus not functional.

C. Conflict theorists stress that conflict, not function, is the basis of social stratification. Every society has only limited resources to go around, and in every society, groups struggle with one another for those resources.

1. Gaetano Mosca argued that it is inevitable that society will be stratified by power. Society cannot exist unless it is organized; thus, there must be politics to get the work of society done. Political organization results in inequalities of power because some people take leadership positions and others follow. It is human nature to be self-centered; thus, people in positions of power use their positions to bring greater rewards to themselves.

2. Marx believed that human history is the history of class struggle; those in power use society's resources to benefit themselves and oppress others. He predicted that workers would one day revolt against their oppressors.

3. Modern conflict theorists stress that conflict between capitalists and workers is not the only important conflict in contemporary society, but rather, groups within the same class compete for scarce resources, resulting in conflict between many groups (e.g., young vs. old; women vs. men).

D. Gerhard Lenski offered a synthesis between functionalist and conflict theories.

1. Functionalists are right when it comes to societies that have only basic resources and do not accumulate wealth, such as hunting and gathering societies.

2. Conflict theorists are right when it comes to societies with a surplus. In such societies humans pursue self-interests and struggle to control those surpluses. This leads to the emergence of a small elite who then builds inequality into the society, resulting in a full-blown system of social stratification.

IV. How Do Elites Maintain Stratification?

A. Social stratification is maintained within a nation by elites who control ideas and information, and use force to do so.

1. In Medieval Europe, the divine right of kings ideology was developed to control the commoners. This ideology says that the king's authority comes from God and therefore he and his representatives must be obeyed. This was more effective than coercion since it breeds hostility and lays the ground for rebellion.
2. Elites also control information in order to maintain their position of power. Fear is a common tactic among dictators.
3. Technology, especially monitoring devices, helps the elite maintain its position. For example, the U.S. has distributed fake news reports to be broadcast to the nation.

B. Underlying the maintenance of stratification is control of social institutions such as the legal establishment, the police, and the military.

V. Comparative Social Stratification

A. Great Britain's class system can be divided into upper, middle, and lower classes. A little over half of the population is in the lower or working class, close to half of the population is in the middle class, and only about 1 percent is in the upper class. Language and speech patterns are important class indicators. Education is the primary way the class system is perpetuated from one generation to the next.

B. The ideal of communism, a classless society, was never realized in the former Soviet Union. Before the Communist revolution, the elite was based on inherited wealth; afterward, it consisted of top party officials, a relatively small middle class, and a massive lower class of peasants and unskilled workers. How recent reforms will affect the stratification system is yet to be seen, but a class of newly rich individuals is emerging. Some of these had political connections; others had the foresight and initiative to take advantage of the changes.

VI. Global Stratification: Three Worlds

A. Until the 1980s, a simple model was used, consisting of the First World (industrialized, capitalistic nations), Second World (communist nations), and Third World (any nations that didn't fit the other categories). A more neutral way of categorizing nations is to use terms related to a nation's level of industrialization: "Most Industrialized," "Industrializing," and "Least Industrialized."

B. The Most Industrialized Nations (U.S., Canada, Great Britain, France, Germany, Switzerland, other countries of Western Europe, Japan, Australia, New Zealand) are capitalistic, although variations exist in economic systems.
1. These nations have only 16 percent of the world's population, but have 31 percent of the world's land.
2. The poor in these nations live better/longer than the average citizens of the Least Industrialized Nations.

C. The Industrializing Nations include the former Soviet Union and its satellites in Eastern Europe.
1. The dividing line between these nations and the Most Industrialized Nations is soft; consequently, it is difficult to classify some nations.
2. These nations account for 16 percent of the world's population and 20 percent of the land.

3. The people of these nations have considerably lower income and a lower standard of living than people in the Most Industrialized Nations; while their access to electricity, indoor plumbing, and other material goods is more limited than those in the Most Industrialized Nations, it is higher than those in the Least Industrialized Nations.

D. In the Least Industrialized Nations of the world, most people live on farms or in villages with low standards of living.
   1. These nations account for 49 percent of the earth's land and 68 percent of the world's population.
   2. These nations are characterized by high birth rates and rapidly growing populations (placing even greater burdens on limited facilities).
   3. Most people in these nations live on less than $1,000 per year.

E. Classifying the nations of the world into these three categories creates certain problems.
   1. How much industrialization does a nation need in order to be classified as Most Industrialized or Industrializing?
   2. Does the fact that some nations have become "postindustrial" mean that a separate classification needs to be created?
   3. While the oil-rich nations of the world are immensely wealthy, they are not industrialized. How are they classified?

VII. How Did the World's Nations Become Stratified?

A. The theory of colonialism focuses on how the first nations to industrialize got the jump on the rest of the world.
   1. With profits generated by the Industrial Revolution, industrialized nations built powerful armaments and fast ships and invaded weaker nations, making colonies of them and exploiting their labor/natural resources. European nations tended to focus on Africa, while the United States concentrated on Central and South America.
   2. Powerful European nations would claim a colony and then send in their representatives to run the government, while the United States chose to plant a corporate flag, and let the corporations dominate the territory's government.
   3. Colonialism shaped many of the Least Industrialized Nations. Often, the Most Industrialized Nations created states that disregarded tribal or cultural considerations.

B. According to world system theory as espoused by Immanuel Wallerstein, countries are politically and economically tied together.
   1. There are four groups of interconnected nations: (1) core nations, where capitalism first developed; (2) semi-periphery (Mediterranean area), who are highly dependent on trade with core nations; (3) periphery (eastern Europe), who are mainly limited to selling cash crops to core nations, with limited economic development; and (4) external areas (most of Africa/Asia) left out of the growth of capitalism, with few economic ties to the core nations.
   2. A capitalist world economy (capitalist dominance) results from relentless expansion; even external area nations are drawn into this commercial web.

3. Globalization (the extensive interconnections among nations resulting from the expansion of capitalism) has been speeded up because new technological forms of communication and transportation now exist. The consequence is that no nation is able to live in isolation.

C. John Kenneth Galbraith argued that some nations remained poor because they were crippled by a culture of poverty, a way of life based on traditional values and religious beliefs that perpetuated poverty from one generation to the next and kept some of the Least Industrialized Nations from developing.

D. Most sociologists prefer colonialism and world system theory.
1. The culture of poverty theory places the blame on the victim, focusing on the characteristics of poor nations rather than the structural arrangements that benefit some nations (the Most Industrialized Nations) at the expense of others (the Least Industrialized Nations).
2. Each theory only partially explains global stratification.

VIII. Maintaining Global Stratification

A. Neocolonialism is the economic and political dominance of the Least Industrialized Nations by the Most Industrialized Nations.
1. Michael Harrington asserts that the Most Industrialized Nations control the Least Industrialized Nations because they control markets, set prices, and so on.
2. The Most Industrialized Nations determine how much they will pay for the natural resources and raw materials they buy from the Least Industrialized Nations; they also move hazardous industries to the Least Industrialized Nations.
3. The Most Industrialized Nations sell weapons and manufactured goods to the Least Industrialized Nations on credit, turning these countries into eternal debtors. They use resources to pay off the debt, thereby preventing the countries from developing their own industrial capacity.

B. Multinational corporations contribute to the exploitation of the Least Industrialized Nations.
1. Some exploit the Least Industrialized Nations directly by controlling national and local politics, running them as a fiefdom.
2. The Most Industrialized Nations are primary beneficiaries of profits made in the Least Industrialized Nations.
3. They often work closely with the elite of the Least Industrialized Nations, sometimes in informal partnerships that are mutually beneficial.
4. In some situations, multinational corporations may bring prosperity to the Least Industrialized Nations because new factories provide salaries and opportunities that otherwise would not exist for workers in those countries.

C. The new technology favors the Most Industrialized Nations, enabling them to maintain their global domination.
1. The profits of multinational corporations can be invested in developing and acquiring the latest technology, thereby generating even greater profits.
2. Many of the Least Industrialized Nations do not have the resources to invest in new technology, creating an even greater global gap between the levels of industrialization.

D.   Global stratification has a profound impact on each person's life including their access to materials possessions, education, and even the likely age at which they will die.

KEY TERMS
After studying the chapter, review the definition for each of the following terms.

apartheid: the separation of races as was practiced in South Africa (241)

bonded labor or indentured service: a contractual system in which someone sells his or her body (services) for a specified period of time (an arrangement very close to slavery, except that it is voluntarily entered into) (238)

bourgeoisie: Karl Marx's term for the people who own the means of production (243)

caste system: a form of social stratification in which one's status is determined by birth and is lifelong (240)

class consciousness: Marx's term for awareness of a common identity based on one's position in the means of production (244)

class system: a form of social stratification based primarily on the possession of money or material possessions (242)

colonialism: the process by which one nation takes over another nation, usually for the purpose of exploiting its labor and natural resources (258)

culture of poverty: the assumption that the values and behaviors of the poor make them fundamentally different from other people; that these factors are largely responsible for their poverty; and that parents perpetuate poverty across generations by passing these characteristics to their children (261)

divine right of kings: the idea that the king's authority comes directly from God (248)

endogamy: marriage within one's own group (240)

estate stratification system: the stratification system of medieval Europe, consisting of three groups or estates; the nobility, the clergy, and commoners (242)

false class consciousness: Marx's term to refer to workers identifying with the interests of capitalists (244)

globalization of the capitalism: (investing to make profits) becoming the globe's dominant economic system (259)

ideology: beliefs about the way things ought to be that justify social arrangements (238)

means of production: the tools, factories, land, and investment capital used to produce wealth (243)

meritocracy: a form of social stratification in which all positions are awarded on the basis of merit (246)

multinational corporations: companies that operate across many national boundaries; also called transnational corporations (262)

neocolonialism: the economic and political dominance of the Least Industrialized Nations by the Most Industrialized Nations (261)

proletariat: Karl Marx's term for the people who work for those who own the means of production (243)

slavery: a form of social stratification in which some people own other people (237)

social mobility: movement up or down the social class ladder (242)

social stratification: the division of large numbers of people into layers according to their relative power, property, and prestige; applies to both nations and to people within a nation, society, or other group (237)

world system theory: economic and political connections that tie the world's countries together (259)

KEY PEOPLE

Review the major theoretical contributions or findings of these people.

Kingsley Davis and Wilbert Moore: According to these functionalists, inequality is universal because it motivates the most qualified members of society to strive for the most important social positions. (245-246)

W. E. B. Du Bois: This sociologist wrote about slavery in the United States, noting that over time the South became committed to keeping African Americans in slavery and killing those who rebelled against this institution. (238)

John Kenneth Galbraith: This economist argued that the Least Industrialized Nations remain poor because their own culture holds them back. (261)

Michael Harrington: Harrington saw that colonialism has been replaced by neocolonialism. (261)

Martha Huggins: This sociologist investigated poverty in Brazil. (254-255)

Gerhard Lenski: Lenski offered a synthesis of functionalist and conflict views of stratification which focused on the surpluses that groups accumulate. (247-248)

Gerda Lerner: This historian noted that women were usually the first enslaved by war and conquest. (237)

Oscar Lewis: This anthropologist was among the first to write about the culture of poverty. (261)

Karl Marx: Marx concluded that social class depended exclusively on the means of production; an individual's social class was determined by whether or not he owned the means of production. (243-244,247)

Gaetano Mosca: Mosca argued that every society is inevitably stratified by power. (247)

Melvin Tumin: Tumin was the first to offer a criticism of the functionalist view on stratification. (246)

Immanuel Wallerstein: This historian proposed a world system theory to explain global stratification. (259)

Max Weber: Weber argued that social class was based on three components: property, prestige, and power. (244-245)

STUDENT APPLICATION PROJECTS

This is your opportunity to apply the sociological perspective to the world around you. The projects in this section refer to material introduced in this chapter of your text. These projects help you to apply the sociological perspective "down to earth...down to your daily life."

1. Why do you think social stratification is universal? What role do you think technology plays in continuing social stratification in the United States? What technological gadgets do you currently own? What ones would you like to own? Do you think having access to a computer gives a college student an advantage over college students who do not have access to a computer? Explain.

2. What role do you play in perpetuating global stratification? Go home and look at the tags on the back of five shirts hanging in your closet. List the countries where your shirts were assembled. How many of them are Least Industrialized Nations? What do you pay for your shirts? What do you think workers in those countries get paid? What does this example have to do with world systems theory? Explain.

3. Why do you think multinational corporations are assembling goods in less developed countries? Do you think this trend will continue? Why or why not?

4. Examining society today, do you agree or disagree with Davis and Moore's explanation that social inequality and social stratification is universal?

SELF-TEST

<u>**MULTIPLE CHOICE QUESTIONS**</u>

1. What is the division of large numbers of people into layers according to their relative power, property, and prestige? (231)
   a. social distinction
   b. social stratification
   c. social distance
   d. social diversification

2. What is a form of social stratification in which some people own other people? (231)
   a. a caste system
   b. slavery
   c. a class system
   d. apartheid

3. Slavery in the United States: (232)
   a. started as indentured service.
   b. was based on the ideology of racism that justified importing slaves from Africa.
   c. became inheritable.
   d. all of the above.

4. Where is the best example of a caste system found? (234)
   a. the United States
   b. South America
   c. India
   d. South Africa

5. In which type of stratification system is endogamy most likely to be found? (234)
   a. class system
   b. caste system
   c. meritocracy
   d. socialist system

6. The South African system of social stratification known as apartheid: (235)
   a. was a caste system containing four different racial categories.
   b. was enforced by law.
   c. was brought down as a result of international pressure.
   d. all of the above.

7. In the system that existed during the Middle Ages, who was in the *second estate*? (235)
   a. nobility
   b. military leaders
   c. the clergy
   d. commoners

8. Which of the following characterizes class systems? (236)
   a. social mobility
   b. geographic mobility
   c. distribution of social standings belonging to an extended network of relatives
   d. fixed boundaries between layers of the stratification system

9. Which of the following statements is *correct*? (236)
   a. While men generally earn more than women, there are a small but growing number of countries where women earn more than men.
   b. About 60 percent of the world's illiterate are females.
   c. Gender is no longer an important basis for stratifying people.
   d. Gender was an important basis for stratifying people in caste and estate systems, but not in slavery or class systems.

10. According to Marx, on what does social class depend? (237)
    a. wealth, power, and prestige
    b. the means of production
    c. where one is born in the social stratification system
    d. what a person achieves during his or her lifetime

11. According to Max Weber, what determines social class? (238)
    a. one's property, prestige, and power
    b. one's relationship to the means of production
    c. one's tasks and how important they are to society
    d. one's political power

12. Which of these statements is consistent with the functionalist view of stratification? (239)
    a. Stratification is dysfunctional for society.
    b. Stratification is the outcome of conflict between different social classes.
    c. Stratification will disappear in societies that are characterized by a meritocracy.
    d. Stratification is an inevitable feature of social organization.

13. Which of these is *not* one of Tumin's criticisms of the functionalist theory of stratification? (239)
    a. The importance of a social position cannot be measured by the rewards it carries.
    b. The functionalists ignore the impact of family background.
    c. Stratification is not functional for everyone.
    d. The functionalists focus too much on the status and power and not enough on income.

14. A form of social stratification in which positions are awarded based on merit is called a(n): (239)
    a. meritocratic system.
    b. egalitarian system.
    c. socialistic system.
    d. democratic system.

15. Gaetano Mosca argued that every society will be stratified by: (240)
    a. wealth.
    b. class.
    c. individuals' relation to the mean of production.
    d. power.

16. According to contemporary conflict theorists, the basis of social stratification is: (240)
    a. functional necessity in society.
    b. conflict over limited resources.
    c. ascribed statuses.
    d. the way in which individuals perceive their social class position.

17. According to Gerhard Lenski, the key to reconciling the various explanations of stratification is: (241)
    a. whether or not a social group has a surplus.
    b. the degree to which there is universal education.
    c. the type of division of labor that characterizes the society.
    d. the size of the population.

18. The key to maintaining national stratification is: (241-242)
    a. having a strong police force and military to demand compliance.
    b. control of social institutions.
    c. control of information.
    d. all of the above.

19. The British perpetuate their class system from one generation to the next by: (243)
    a. emphasis on material possessions such as clothes and cars.
    b. religion.
    c. education.
    d. encouraging people in all classes to marry others within their own class.

20. In the former Soviet Union, the system of stratification was based on: (243)
    a. occupation.
    b. trade union membership.
    c. Communist party membership.
    d. education.

21. In the global system of stratification presented in your textbook, where would the former Soviet Union and its satellites in eastern Europe be placed? (244)
    a. the Most Industrialized Nations
    b. the Industrializing Nations
    c. the Least Industrialized Nations
    d. none of the above.

22. Why is it difficult to know how to classify some nations into a global system of stratification? (248)
    a. It is difficult because the lines that separate the three levels—Most Industrialized, Industrializing, and Least Industrialized—are soft.
    b. Some nations have moved beyond industrialization, becoming "postindustrial" nations.
    c. Some nations have not yet industrialized but are still extremely wealthy.
    d. All of the above reflect problems with classifying nations into a global system.

23. Which of the following statement(s) is true about the Least Industrialized Nations. (248)
    a. most people live on less than $1000 a year
    b. these nations account for 68 percent of the Earth's land
    c. about 5% of their population belongs to the elite class
    d. none of the above

24. In what way did U.S. colonialism differ from that of European nations? (249)
    a. The United States restricted its invasions to Asian nations like the Philippines or Hawaii.
    b. The United States usually chose to plant corporate flags rather than national flags.
    c. Colonialism undertaken by the United States was on a much larger scale than that of other industrialized nations.
    d. The United States was always sensitive to the cultural and religious differences of its colonies.

25. According to world system theory, all of the following are groups of interconnected nations, *except*: (249)
    a. core nations.
    b. nations on the semiperiphery.
    c. nations on the periphery.
    d. nations in the internal area that have extensive connections with the core nations.

26. The culture of poverty theory was used to analyze global stratification by: (253)
    a. Immanuel Wallerstein.
    b. Max Weber.
    c. John Kenneth Galbraith.
    d. Karl Marx.

27. Why do most sociologists reject the culture of poverty theory in trying to explain global stratification? (254)
    a. because it was developed by an economist, not a sociologist
    b. because it is outdated
    c. because focuses on culture rather than social structure
    d. because it places the blame for poverty on the poor nations themselves, rather than focusing on the international arrangements that benefit some at the expense of others

28. Neocolonialism refers to: (254)
    a. recent efforts by the Most Industrialized Nations to colonize the Least Industrialized Nations.
    b. the economic policies of the Most Industrialized Nations that are designed to control the markets of the Least Industrialized Nations.
    c. programs like the Peace Corps that attempt to teach residents of the Least Industrialized Nations the skills necessary to survive in an industrial society.
    d. the economic policy of the Least Industrialized Nations in which they hold the Most Industrialized Nations hostage by controlling access to national resources like oil.

29. According to the neocolonialist argument, why do so many of the Least Industrialized Nations remain poor? (254)
    a. The Most Industrialized Nations set the prices they will pay for these nations' raw materials and natural resources.
    b. The Most Industrialized Nations sell these nations weapons and manufactured goods on credit.
    c. The capital needed to develop the industrial capacity of these nations is used to pay off their debts to the Most Industrialized Nations.
    d. All of the above.

30. Which of the following countries have been able to enter the race for global domination because of technology and outsourced labor? (255)
    a. Korea and India
    b. China and India
    c. Russia and Yugoslavia
    d. Hungary and Hong Kong

TRUE-FALSE QUESTIONS

1. _____Social stratification refers only to individuals. (231)
2. _____Throughout history, slavery has always been based on racism. (231)
3. _____The first form of slavery in the New World was indentured service. (232)
4. _____A caste system is a form of social stratification in which individual status is determined by birth and is lifelong. (234)
5. _____A class system is based primarily on money or material possessions. (236)
6. _____Gender discrimination cuts across all systems of social stratification. (236)
7. _____According to Karl Marx, the means of production is the only factor in determining social class. (237)
8. _____According to Max Weber, class standing is a combination of power, prestige, and property. (238)
9. _____Colin Powell's power derived from his position as the secretary of state. (238)
10. _____Functionalists believe that people should be rewarded for their unique abilities and that the type of position they hold in society is not important. (239)
11. _____All conflict theorists focus on conflicts that occur between social classes. (240)

12. _____According to conflict theorists, the oppressed often support laws even when the laws operate against their own interests. (240)

13. _____Gerhard Lenski said that the functionalist view of stratification was most appropriate when studying societies with a surplus of wealth. (241)

14. _____The idea of the divine right of kings is an example of how the ruling elite use ideas to maintain stratification. (241)

15. _____In maintaining stratification, elites find that technology is not particularly useful, because everyone can access technology. (241-242)

16. _____Kuwait, with its wealth, is an example of the challenge of classifying nations as least, most, and industrializing. (248)

17. _____Most European nations rejected colonialism as a strategy for gaining access to cheap raw materials. (249)

18. _____The expansion of capitalism resulted in a capitalist world economy dominated by the core nations. (249)

19. _____The culture of poverty thesis is generally preferred by sociologists as an explanation of global stratification. (253)

20. _____Neocolonialism is the economic and political dominance of the Least Industrialized Nations by the Most Industrialized Nations. (254)

FILL-IN-THE-BLANK QUESTIONS

1. _____ is a form of social stratification in which some people own other people. (231)

2. A gray area between a contract and slavery is _____ service. (232)

3. In a _____system, status is determined by birth. (234)

4. In an estate system, women belonged to the estate of their _____. (236)

5. In every society in the world, _____ is a basis for social stratification. (236)

6. Karl Marx argued that workers suffer from _____, workers mistakenly thinking of themselves as capitalists. (237)

7. Great Britain would be classified as a _____nation. (244)

8. The divine right of kings was an _____ that made the king God's direct representative on earth. (241)

9. _____ is the primary way by which the British perpetuate their class system. (243)

10. The _____ theory focuses on how the countries that industrialized first got the jump on the rest of the world. (249)

11. Immanuel Wallerstein calls those countries that industrialized first the _____ nations. (249)

12. Assembly-for-export plants on the Mexican-United States border are known as _____. (252)

13. John Kenneth Galbraith claimed that the _____ of the Least Industrialized Nations held them back. (253)

14. Neocolonialism theory argues that keeping least industrialized countries in _____ makes them submit to trading terms dictated by the neocolonialists. (254)

15. Multinational corporations try to work closely with the _____ of Least Industrialized Nations. (255)

MATCH THESE SOCIAL SCIENTISTS WITH THEIR CONTRIBUTIONS

_____ 1. W.E. Du Bois
_____ 2. Kingsley Davis & Wilbert Moore
_____ 3. Gaetano Mosca
_____ 4. Immanuel Wallerstein
_____ 5. Michael Harrington
_____ 6. John Kenneth Galbraith
_____ 7. Martha Huggins
_____ 8. Melvin Tumin
_____ 9. Gerhard Lenski
_____ 10. Gerda Lerner

a. *women were the first to be enslaved by war*
b. *criticism of functional view of stratification*
c. *stressed culture of poverty*
d. *false consciousness*
e. *stated functionalist view of stratification*
f. *wrote about slavery in the United States*
g. *synthesis of functionalist and conflict views*
h. *studied poverty in Brazil*
i. *neocolonialism*
j. *world system theory*

ESSAY QUESTIONS

1. Compare Marx's theory of stratification with Weber's theory. Discuss why Weber's is more widely accepted by sociologists.

2. Using the different theories presented in this chapter, answer the question, "Why is stratification universal?"

3. Consider why ideology is a more effective way of maintaining stratification than brute force.

4. Compare and contrast the three theories of global stratification.

CHAPTER 10
SOCIAL CLASS IN THE UNITED STATES

CHAPTER SUMMARY

- Most sociologists have adopted Weber's definition of social class as a large group of people who rank closely to one another in terms of wealth, power, and prestige. Wealth consists of property and income; power is defined as the ability to carry out one's will despite the resistance of others; and prestige is a measure of the regard or respect accorded an individual or social position.

- Status refers to social ranking. Most people are status consistent, meaning that they rank high or low on all three dimensions of social class. People who rank high on some dimensions and low on others are status inconsistent. The frustration of status inconsistency tends to produce political radicalism.

- Sociologists use two models to portray the social class structure. Erik Wright developed a four class model based on the ideas of Karl Marx. Dennis Gilbert and Joseph Kahl developed a six class model based on the ideas of Max Weber.

- Social class leaves no aspect of life untouched. Class membership affects physical and mental health, family life, child rearing, educational attainment, religious affiliation, political participation and contact with crime and the criminal justice system.

- In studying the mobility of individuals within society, sociologists look at intergenerational mobility (individual changes in social class from one generation to the next), exchange mobility (the movement of large numbers of people from one class to another), and structural mobility (the social and economic changes that affect the social class position of large numbers of people).

- Poverty is unequally distributed in the United States. Minorities, children, female-headed households, and the rural poor are more likely to be poor. Sociologists generally focus on structural factors, such as employment opportunities, in explaining poverty. Sociologists argue that life orientations are a consequence, not the cause, of people's position in the class structure.

- The Horatio Alger myth encourages people to strive to get ahead, and blames failures on individual shortcomings.

LEARNING OBJECTIVES
After reading Chapter 10, you should be able to:

1. Define social class, describe its various components, and discuss the debate between different theorists over those components. (268)

2. Differentiate between wealth, power, and prestige and explain how each are distributed in the United States. (268-273)
3. Discuss the relationship between occupations and prestige. (272-273)
4. Define status inconsistency and discuss its implications. (274)
5. Compare Erik Wright's and Karl Marx's model of social class. (274-276)
6. Describe each of the six classes in Gilbert and Kahl's model of social class. (276-279)
7. Using Gilbert and Kahl's model, describe social class in the automobile industry. (278)
8. Know the consequences of social class on physical health, mental health, family life, education, religion, politics, and crime. (280-284)
9. Understand the relationship between social class and the changing economy. (284)
10. Describe—and distinguish between—the three types of social mobility. (284-286)
11. Talk about women and social mobility. (285)
12. Discuss the role of statistics when examining social mobility. (285-286)
13. Discuss the pain that either upward or downward social mobility can bring. (286)
14. Discuss the myths associated with the poor and how those myths can be dispelled. (288)
15. Know how the United States government defines poverty and the implications of that definition. (286)
16. Identify the major characteristics of the poor in the United States. (289-290)
17. Describe how race and poverty are related in children. (291)
18. Describe how long poverty might last. (292)
19. Compare structural to individual explanations of poverty in the United States. (292)
20. Talk about recent changes in welfare policy in the United States and the controversies associated with those changes. (293-294)
21. Discuss the advantages or disadvantages of deferred gratification. (294)
22. Identify the social functions of the Horatio Alger myth and discuss the myth's sociological implications. (294-295)

CHAPTER OUTLINE

I.   **What Is Social Class?**
     A. Sociologists do not have a clear-cut definition of social class.
     B. Most agree with Weber that social class can be defined as a large group of people who rank close to each other in wealth, power, and prestige.
     C. Wealth consists of property (what we own) and income (money we receive). Wealth and income are not always the same; a person may own much property yet have little income, or vice versa. Usually, however, wealth and income go together.
         1. Ownership of property (real estate, stocks and bonds, and so on) is not distributed evenly: 10 percent of the U.S. population owns 70 percent of the wealth, and the wealthiest 1 percent of Americans own one third of all of the U.S. assets.
         2. Income is also distributed disproportionately: the top 20 percent of U.S. residents have 47 percent of the income; the bottom 20 percent receives 4.2 percent. Each one-fifth of the U.S. population receives approximately the same proportion of national income today as it did in 1935; those changes that have occurred reflect growing inequality.

3.   Apart from the very rich, the most affluent group in U.S. society is the executive officers of the largest corporations. Their median income (including salaries, bonuses, and stock options) is $3 million a year.

D.   Power is the ability to carry out your will despite resistance.

E.   Mills coined the term the "power elite," to refer to those who are the big decision makers in U.S. society. This group shares the same ideologies and values, belong to the same clubs, and reinforce each other's world view.

F.   Domhoff believes that no major decision in the U.S. government is made without the approval of this power elite.

G.   Prestige is the respect or regard given to various occupations and accomplishments.

    1.   Occupations are the primary source of prestige, although some people gain prestige through inventions, feats, or doing good for others. Occupations with the highest prestige pay more, require more education, entail more abstract thought, and offer greater autonomy.

    2.   For prestige to be valuable, people must acknowledge it. The elite traditionally have made rules to emphasize their higher status.

    3.   Status symbols, which vary according to social class, are ways of displaying prestige. In the United States they include designer label clothing, expensive cars, prestigious addresses, and attending particular schools.

H.   Status inconsistency is the term used to describe the situation of people who have a mixture of high and low rankings in the three components of social class (wealth, power, and prestige).

    1.   Most people are status consistent; they rank at the same level in all three components. People who are status inconsistent want others to act toward them on the basis of their highest status, but others tend to judge them on the basis of their lowest status.

    2.   Sociologist Gerhard Lenski determined that people suffering the frustrations of status inconsistency are more likely to be radical and approve political action aimed against higher status groups.

    3.   Status inconsistency is common for lottery winners whose wealth is vastly greater than either their education or occupational status.

II.   Sociological Models of Social Class

A.   The number of classes that exist in an industrial society is a matter of debate, but there are two main models, one based on Marx and the other on Weber.

B.   Sociologist Erik Wright realized that not everyone falls into Marx's two broad classes (capitalists and workers), which were based on a person's relationship to the means of production. For instance, although executives, managers, and supervisors would fall into Marx's category of workers, they act more like capitalists.

    1.   Wright resolved this problem by regarding some people as simultaneously members of more than one class, which he called contradictory class locations.

    2.   Wright identified four classes: capitalists (owners of large enterprises); petty bourgeoisie (owners of small businesses); managers (employees who have authority over others); and workers.

C. Using the model originally developed by Weber, sociologists Dennis Gilbert and Joseph Kahl created a model to describe class structure in the United States and other capitalist countries.
1. The capitalist class (1 percent of the population) is composed of investors, heirs, and a few executives; it is divided into "old" money and "new" money. The children of "new" money move into the old money class by attending the right schools and marrying "old" money.
2. The upper-middle class (15 percent of the population) is composed of professionals and upper managers, almost all of whom have attended college or university and frequently have postgraduate degrees. This class is the one most shaped by education.
3. The lower-middle class (34 percent of the population) is composed of lower managers, craftspeople and foremen. They have at least a high-school education.
4. The working class (30 percent of the population) is composed of factory workers and low-paid white collar workers. Most have high-school educations.
5. The working poor (16 percent of the population) is composed of relatively unskilled blue-collar and white-collar workers, and those with temporary and seasonal jobs. If they graduated from high school, they probably did not do well in school.
6. The underclass (4 percent of the population) is concentrated in the inner cities and has little connection with the job market. Welfare is their main support.
7. The homeless are so far down the class structure that their position must be considered even lower than the underclass. They are the "fallout" of industrialization, especially the postindustrial developments that have led to a decline in the demand for unskilled labor.

D. The automobile industry illustrates the social class ladder as described by Gilbert and Kahl.
1. The Ford family and Ford executives represent both the upper and lower levels of the capitalist class.
2. Owners of Ford dealerships are members of the upper middle class, while a salesperson employed there is drawn from the lower middle class.
3. Mechanics who repair Ford automobiles are members of the working class. The working poor are presented by the "detail" workers.
4. If the agency employs day laborers to mow the lawn or clean the lot, they would come from the underclass.

III. Consequences of Social Class

A. The lower a person's social class, the more likely that person is to die at an earlier age than people in higher classes; this is true at all ages. Social class shapes our lifestyles, which affects our health. And since medical care is expensive, the higher classes receive better medical care, despite government aid to the poor; the result is a two-tiered system of medical care. Additionally, life is better for those in higher social classes. They have fewer problems and more resources to deal with the ones that they do have.

B. Mental health is worse for the lower classes because of stresses associated with their class position. Those higher in the class system are better able to afford vacations, psychiatrists, and counselors; their class position gives them greater control over their lives, which is a key to good mental health.

C. Social class also plays a role in family life.
   1. Children of the capitalist class are under great pressure to select the right mate in order to assure the continuity of the family line. Parents in this social class play a large role in mate selection.
   2. Marriages are more likely to fail in the lower social classes given the challenges of inadequate income; the children of the poor are therefore more likely to live in single-parent households.
   3. Child rearing varies by class, with each class raising its children with attitudes and behaviors suited to the kinds of occupations they will eventually hold. Lower class families teach children to defer to authority, as is required in their jobs. Higher class families encourage freedom, creativity, and self-expression, as is found in their jobs.
D. Education levels increase as one moves up the social class ladder. The change occurs not only in terms of the amount of education obtained, but also in terms of the type of education, with the capitalist class bypassing public schools in favor of exclusive private schools, where its children are trained to take a commanding role in society.
E. All aspects of religious orientation follow class lines. Social classes tend to cluster around different denominations. Lower classes are attracted to spontaneous worship services and louder music, as found with Baptists, while higher classes prefer more restrained worship services such as those in the Methodist religion.
F. Political views and involvement are influenced by social class.
   1. The rich and the poor take divergent political paths, with people in lower social classes more likely to vote Democrat, while those in higher classes vote Republican; the parties are seen as promoting different class interests.
   2. People in the working class are more likely to be liberal on economic issues (more government spending) and more conservative on social issues (opposition to abortion).
   3. Political participation is not equal: the higher classes are more likely to vote and get involved in politics than those in lower social classes.
G. The criminal justice system is not blind to class either.
   1. The white-collar crimes of the more privileged classes are more likely to be dealt with outside of the criminal justice system, while the street crimes of the lower classes are dealt with by the police and courts.
   2. Members of the lower classes are more likely to be arrested, to be on probation, parole, or in jail, and, more crimes occur in lower class neighborhoods.
H. The new technology does not affect social classes in the same way.
   1. The higher one is on the social class ladder, the more likely they are to benefit from technology. For the capitalist class, the new technology is a means to extensive, worldwide profits.
   2. The upper-middle class also benefits because the new technology enables them to achieve in their chosen professions, and their education prepares them to take a leading role in managing the new global system.
   3. Below these top two classes, technology creates more uncertainty, which increases as you move down the ladder. Those at the bottom have few

technological skills and face the real possibility of losing their jobs because of technological change.

IV. Social Mobility

A. There are three basic types of social mobility: intergenerational, structural, and exchange.

    1. Intergenerational mobility is the change that family members make in their social class from one generation to the next. As a result of individual effort, a person can rise from one level to another; in the event of individual failure, the reverse can be true.

    2. Structural mobility involves social changes that affect large numbers of people. By way of example, when computers were invented, many opportunities opened up for people to switch from blue-collar to white-collar work. While individual effort played a role, the major reason for the change in position was structural.

    3. Exchange mobility is movement of people up and down the social class system, where, on balance, the system remains the same. The term refers to general, overall movement of large numbers of people that leaves the class system basically untouched.

B. Women have been largely ignored in studies of occupational mobility. Studies of social mobility among men indicate that about one half of sons have moved beyond their fathers; about one third have stayed the same; and about one sixth have fallen down the ladder.

    1. As structural changes in the U.S. economy creates opportunities for women to move up the social class ladder, studies of their mobility patterns have appeared.

    2. One study indicated that women who did move up were encouraged by their parents to postpone marriage and get an education.

C. Statistics can be used either positively or negatively to explain social mobility, depending on the purpose.

    1. It appears that about one-third of the poorest 10 percent and one-third of the richest 10 percent of children end up in the same social class as their parents.

D. The costs of social mobility include risking the loss of one's roots.

    1. A study of British women who had achieved middle class status through education or marriage found that these women were caught between two worlds—the one they were brought up in and their current one.

    2. An American study found that among working class families in which the adult children had achieved upward social mobility (because parental sacrifices enabled them to get an education), the parent-adult child relationship was marked by estrangement, lack of communication, and bitterness.

V. Poverty

A. The U.S. government classifies the poverty line as families whose incomes are less than three times a low-cost food budget.

    1. This official measure is grossly inadequate since it inflates the amount of money that is spent on food. It is also the same across the country, even though the cost of living is higher in some states than in others.

2. Any modification of this measure instantly adds or subtracts millions of people with significant consequences.

B. Certain social groups are disproportionately represented among the poor population.

   1. The poor tend to be clustered in the south, a pattern that has existed for about 100 years. The poverty rate for the rural poor is higher than the national average. While they show the same racial and ethnic characteristics as the nation as a whole, they are less likely to be on welfare or to be single parents, are less skilled and educated, and find that only lower-paying jobs are available to them.

   2. Race is a major factor. Racial minorities are much more likely to be poor: 10 percent of whites and 26 percent of Latinos and 24 percent of African Americans live in poverty.

   3. The chances of being poor decrease as the amount of education increases.

   4. The gender of the person who heads a family is another major predictor of whether or not a family is poor. Most poor families are headed by women. The major causes of this phenomenon, called the feminization of poverty, are divorce, births to unwed mothers, and the lower wages paid to women.

   5. Although the percentage of poor people over age 65 is practically the same as their overall percentage, elderly Hispanic Americans and African Americans are almost three times more likely to be poor than elderly white Americans.

   6. The elderly are less likely than the general population to be poor.

C. Children are more likely to live in poverty than are adults or the elderly. This holds true regardless of race, but poverty is much greater among minority children.

D. In the 1960s, it was suggested that the poor get trapped in a "culture of poverty" as a result of having values and behaviors that make them "fundamentally different" from other U.S. residents.

   1. National statistics indicate that most poverty is short term, lasting one or less years. Only 12 percent of the poor live in poverty for five or more years.

   2. Since the number of people who live in poverty remains fairly constant, this means that as many people move into poverty as move out of it.

E. In trying to explain poverty, the choice is between focusing on individual explanations or on social structural explanations.

   1. Sociologists look to such factors as inequalities in education; access to learning job skills; racial, ethnic, age, and gender discrimination; and large-scale economic change to explain the patterns of poverty in society.

   2. The other explanation is individualistic, focusing on the characteristics of individuals that are assumed to contribute to their own poverty.

F. In 1996, federal welfare reform was enacted. There are now caps on welfare assistance and recipients are required to look for work.

   1. In the aftermath of this reform, welfare rolls dropped. However, this does not mean that these people are working; they may not be on welfare any longer because they have reached their limit.

   2. Conflict theorists argue that the purpose of the welfare system is to maintain an army of reserve workers. In times of economic expansion, welfare requirements are tightened, forcing workers into the job market. When recession hits, welfare rules are relaxed.

3. Two out of five people who left welfare also moved out of poverty. Three out of five are still in poverty or back on welfare. A third, who were forced off welfare, have no jobs.

G. Because the poor don't see the future as different from the past, they find it difficult to defer gratification—that is, give up things now for the sake of greater gains in the future. Sociologists argue that the behaviors of the poor are not the cause of their poverty but rather a result of their poverty.

H. Because there are real-life examples of people from humble origins who climbed far up the social ladder, most U.S. residents (including minorities and the working poor) believe that they have a chance of getting ahead.

1. The Horatio Alger myth is obviously a statistical impossibility. Despite this, functionalists stress that this belief is functional for society because it encourages people to compete for higher positions, while placing the blame for failure squarely on the individual.

2. As Marx and Weber both noted, social class affects our ideas of life and our proper place in society. At the same time, the dominant ideology often blinds us to these effects in our own lives.

KEY TERMS
After studying the chapter, review the definition for each of the following terms.

anomie: Durkheim's term for a condition of society in which people become detached from the norms that usually guide their behavior (275)

contradictory class location: Erik Wright's term for a position in the class structure that generates contradictory interests (276)

culture of poverty: the assumption that the values and behaviors of the poor make them fundamentally different from other people; that these factors are largely responsible for their poverty; and that parents perpetuate poverty across generations by passing these characteristics on to their children (292)

deferred gratification: forgoing something in the present in the hope of achieving greater gains in the future (294)

downward social mobility: movement down the social class ladder (284)

exchange mobility: about the same numbers of people moving up and down the social class ladder such that, on balance, the social class system shows little change (285)

feminization of poverty: a trend in U.S. poverty whereby most poor families are headed by women (290)

Horatio Alger myth: the belief that due to limitless possibilities anyone can get ahead if he or she tries hard enough (295)

income: money received, usually from a job, business, or assets (268)

intergenerational mobility: the change that family members make in social class from one generation to the next (284)

poverty line: the official measure of poverty; calculated to include those whose incomes are less than three times a low-cost food budget (286)

power: the ability to carry out your will, even over the resistance of others (271)

power elite: C. Wright Mills' term for the top people in U.S. corporations, military, and politics, who make the nation's major decisions (271)

prestige: respect or regard (272)

property: material possessions (268)

social class: according to Weber, a large group of people who rank close to one another in wealth, power, and prestige; according to Marx, one of two groups: capitalists who own the means of production and workers who sell their labor (268)

status: the position that someone occupies in society or a social group (274)

status consistency: ranking high or low on all three dimensions of social class (274)

status inconsistency: ranking high on some dimensions of social class and low on others; also known as *status discrepancy* (274)

structural mobility: movement up or down the social class ladder that is due to changes in the structure of society, not to individual efforts (285)

underclass: a small group of people for whom poverty persists year after year and across generations (279)

upward social mobility: movement up the social class ladder (284)

wealth: the total value of everything someone owns, minus the debts (268)

KEY PEOPLE

Review the major theoretical contributions or findings of these people.

William Domhoff: Drawing upon the work of C. Wright Mills, Domhoff states that the power elite is so powerful that no major decisions in the U.S. government is made without its approval. (271)

Dennis Gilbert and Joseph Kahl: These sociologists developed a more contemporary stratification model based on Max Weber's work. (278)

Ray Gold: In research on status inconsistency, Gold studied tenant reactions to janitors who earned more than they did. He found that the tenants acted "snooty" to the janitors, and the janitors took pleasure in knowing the intimate details of the tenants' lives. (274)

Daniel Hellinger and Dennis Judd: These sociologists identified the average citizen's belief that he/she exercises political power through the voting process as the "democratic façade" that conceals the real source of power in the United States. (271)

Elizabeth Higgenbotham and Lynn Weber: These sociologists studied the mobility patterns for women. They found that those women who experienced upward mobility were most likely to have strong parental support to defer marriage and get an education. (285)

Melvin Kohn: Kohn studied social class differences in child-rearing patterns. (282)

Steph Lawler: This sociologist interviewed British women who had achieved upward mobility through education or marriage. (286)

Elliot Liebow: Back in 1967, this sociologist studied black street-corner men. He noted that their circumstances made it difficult for them to save for the future, since whatever funds they had were needed to survive in the present. (294)

Gerhard Lenski: Lenski noted that everyone wants to maximize their status, but that others often judge an individual on the basis of his lowest status despite the individual's efforts to be judged on the basis of his highest status. (274)

Karl Marx: Marx believed that there were only two social classes—the capitalists and the workers. Membership is based on a person's relationship to the means of production. (274)

C. Wright Mills: Mills used the term "power elite" to describe the top decision-makers in the nation. (271)

Richard Sennett and Jonathan Cobb: Sennett and Cobb studied the impact that a child's upward mobility had on his relationship with his parents. They found that the parents' sacrifices in order to afford the educational costs for their children were rarely appreciated; with increased education the child grew distant from the parents' world. (268)

Max Weber: Weber developed the definition of social class that is used by most sociologists. He noted that social class is made up of a large group of people who rank close to one another in terms of wealth, power, and prestige. (268,276)

Erik Wright: Wright proposed an updated version of Marx's theory of stratification. (276)

STUDENT APPLICATION PROJECTS

This is your opportunity to apply the sociological perspective to the world around you. The projects in this section refer to material introduced in this chapter of your text. These projects help you to apply the sociological perspective "down to earth...down to your daily life."

1. What social class were your parents? What social class are you now? How did your social class impact your choice of a college or university? Explain. Do you think your college educational experiences will lead to a change in your social class? Why?

2. What images come to mind when you hear the word poverty? List these images. Did your list include images of children without food, clothing, or shelter? Why do many social analysts argue that it is time to stop blaming the victim? What do you think needs to happen to reduce the negative effects of childhood poverty?

3. Choose two social classes and do some research beyond what is in your textbook. How is life different for people in these classes in terms of jobs or careers, family life, health, leisure time, etc?

4. Sociologists use income, education, and occupational prestige to measure social class. The resulting six categories of social classes are presented in Figure 10.5 on page 277. These three elements used by sociologists may not be the best means of classification for all members of society. If you were to create your own model of the U.S. social class ladder, what elements would you use to classify individuals? Why do you believe that these elements would be appropriate, and how might they provide a better understanding of social stratification in the U.S.?

SELF-TEST

MULTIPLE CHOICE QUESTIONS

1. According to your text, on what do most sociologists agree concerning social class? (268)
   a. it has a clear-cut, accepted definition in sociology.
   b. it is best defined by the two classes as set out by Marx.
   c. it is best defined by Weber's dimensions of social class.
   d. it has no clear-cut, accepted definition and thus is used differently by all sociologists.

2. What percent of the nation's families own 70 percent of the wealth in the United States? (268)
   a. 1%
   b. 5%
   c. 10%
   d. 20%

3. According to Paul Samuelson, if an income pyramid were made out of a child's blocks that were 1 1/2" tall, how far off the ground would the typical American be? (268)
   a. 2 ft.
   b. 6 ft.
   c. 8 ft.
   d. 12 ft.

4. Which of the following statements best describes changes in the distribution of U.S. income? (271)
   a. The income distribution has remained virtually unchanged across time.
   b. The percentage of income going to the richest 20 percent of U.S. families has declined while the percentage going to the poorest 20 percent has increased.
   c. The percentage of income going to the middle income groups has increased at the expense of groups at both the top and bottom of the income scale.
   d. The percentage of income going to the richest 20 percent of U.S. families has increased while the percentage going to the poorest 20 percent has decreased.

5. What term do Hellinger and Judd use to describe the myth that the average citizen exercises power when he or she votes for representatives to Congress or the U.S. president? (271)
   a. democratic charade
   b. popular façade
   c. democratic façade
   d. political power myth

6. What term did Mills use to refer to decision makers at the top of society? (271)
   a. the decision elite
   b. the power elite
   c. the power corps
   d. the power brokers

7. Which of the statements regarding the jobs that have the most prestige is *not* true? (273)
   a. they pay more
   b. they require more education
   c. they require special talent or skills
   d. they offer greater autonomy

8. Based on his research, what did Ray Gold discover about status inconsistency? (274)
   a. College professors tend to be politically radical.
   b. Most people ignore their own inconsistent status while focusing on others.
   c. Tenants related to the inconsistent status of the apartment building janitors by acting "snooty" toward them.
   d. Status inconsistency is a very uncommon situation because most people try to be placed in approximately the same place in all three dimensions of stratification.

9. How did Erik Wright update Marx's class categories in response to criticisms that they were too broad? (276)
   a. He divided each of the two classes into three subclasses, making six classes in all.
   b. He created an open scale in which people place themselves into classes.
   c. He recommended listing people's different associations and then classifying them on the basis of their most important one.
   d. He recognized that people can be members of more than one class at the same time.

10. According to Gilbert and Kahl, the members of which social class can attribute their location in the class system to having a college or postgraduate education? (276)
    a. the capitalist class
    b. the upper middle class
    c. the lower middle class
    d. the working class

11. According to Gilbert and Kahl, all of the following describe the working class, *except*: (271)
    a. most are employed in relatively unskilled blue-collar and white-collar jobs.
    b. most have attended college for one or two years.
    c. most hope to get ahead by achieving seniority on the job.
    d. about 30 percent of the population belong to this class.

12. Which of the following statements best describes the place of the homeless in our system today? (279)
    a. They are on the lowest rung with little or no chance of climbing anywhere.
    b. They are the "fallout" of our developing postindustrial economy.
    c. In another era, they would have had plenty of work as unskilled laborer.
    d. All of the above.

13. According to your text, the typical mechanic in a Ford dealership would be in the: (280)
    a. upper-middle class.
    b. lower-middle class.
    c. working class.
    d. underclass.

14. What factor or factors explain the social class difference in death rates? (281)
    a. two-tiered system of medical care
    b. lifestyle differences
    c. unequal access to medical care
    d. all of the above

15. Which of the following statements about social class differences in mental health is *correct*? (281)
    a. The rich have less control over their wealth, since it is invested in the stock market, so they worry more about becoming poor.
    b. The poor have less job security and lower wages than the nonpoor, which contribute to higher levels of stress.
    c. The rich experience more divorce and alcoholism, which can undermine their mental health.
    d. The middle class is squeezed by higher and higher taxes, which produces feelings of discontent and poor mental health.

16. According to Melvin Kohn, lower-class parents are concerned that their children are: (282)
    a. creative.
    b. independent.
    c. conformists.
    d. all of the above.

17. Which class tends to bypass public schools entirely, in favor of exclusive private schools? (283)
    a. capitalist
    b. upper-middle
    c. middle
    d. all of the above

18. Which class tends to be conservative on social issues but liberal on economic ones? (284)
    a. upper class
    b. middle class
    c. lower class
    d. working class

19. What types of criminal activities are most likely to be handled outside of the criminal justice system? (284)
    a. street crime
    b. organized crime
    c. white-collar crime
    d. petty crimes

20. Members of the _____ class are more likely to be robbed, burglarized, or murdered. (284)
    a. upper
    b. middle
    c. lower
    d. none of the above

21. Which class or classes benefit from technological changes and the globalization of capital? (284)
    a. working class and the working poor
    b. upper and lower middle classes
    c. lower middle and working classes
    d. capitalist and upper middle classes

22. A homeless person whose father was a physician has experienced: (284)
    a. exchange mobility.
    b. structural mobility.
    c. upward mobility.
    d. downward mobility.

23. Higgenbotham and Weber found that for career women from working class backgrounds: (285)
    a. intergenerational mobility was greater for sons than for daughters.
    b. upwardly mobile women achieved higher positions despite their parent's reservations.
    c. upwardly mobile women achieved higher class positions because of parental encouragement that began when they were just little girls.
    d. any upward mobility was due entirely to structural changes in the economy rather than individual effort or parental influences.

24. What did sociologists Steph Lawler discover about social mobility? (285)
    a. It was much more painful moving down the social class ladder than up.
    b. Moving up or down the social class ladder had no affect on individuals.
    c. It was just as painful to move up the social class ladder as down.
    d. None of the above.

25. What was the greatest challenge faced by African Americans who experienced upward social mobility? (287)
    a. adjusting to whites as a primary reference group
    b. adapting to new jobs and being the supervisor
    c. moving into exclusive white neighborhoods
    d. leaving behind one's racial-ethnic group

26. The measure of poverty that is based on a figure three times a low-cost food budget is the: (286)
    a. adjusted income level.
    b. the welfare distribution scale.
    c. the poverty line.
    d. the welfare line.

27. In the United States, which group has poverty rates that are lower than the national average? (289)
    a. women
    b. racial minorities
    c. the elderly
    d. children

28. In trying to explain poverty, sociologists are most likely to stress: (292)
    a. individual characteristics that are assumed to contribute to poverty.
    b. features of the social structure that contribute to poverty.
    c. decisions made by the poor that prevent them from ever moving out of poverty.
    d. that poverty is intergenerational, so that most people who are born poor will remain poor.

29. Why is it difficult for the poor to practice deferred gratification? (294)
    a. because they need all their resources to survive in the present
    b. because they lack proper values
    c. because they only care about living in the present
    d. because they are weak and can't save

30. The Horatio Alger myth: (295)
    a. is beneficial for society, according to the functionalists.
    b. reduces pressures on the social system.
    c. motivates people to try harder to succeed because anything is possible.
    d. all of the above.

TRUE-FALSE QUESTIONS

1. _____Within sociology, there is a clear-cut, widely accepted definition of social class. (268)
2. _____Wealth and income are the same thing. (268)
3. _____The richest 1 percent of U.S. families are worth more than the entire bottom 90 percent of Americans. (270)
4. _____Apart from the very rich, the most affluent group in U.S. society consists of the chief executive officers of the nation's largest corporations. (271)
5. _____Occupational prestige rankings vary widely across countries and over time. (272)
6. _____College professors typically are an example of status inconsistency. (274)
7. _____ Lottery winners often find themselves experiencing status inconsistency. (274)
8. _____According to Gilbert and Kahl, the capitalist class has the ability to shape the consciousness of the nation. (276)
9. _____The distinctions between lower-middle class and working class are more blurred than those between other classes. (279)
10. _____The underclass is concentrated in the inner city with few ties to the job market. (279)
11. _____The working class are functionally illiterate, finding it difficult to even read the want ads. (279)
12. _____Social class affects a person's chances of living and dying. (280)
13. _____Marriages of the poor are more likely to fail and their children to group up in broken homes. (282)
14. _____Members of the lower classes are more likely to be on probation, on parole, or in jail than members of the upper classes. (284)
15. _____Structural mobility refers to social and economic changes that affect the status of large numbers of people. (284)
16. _____Exchange mobility leaves the class system basically untouched. (285)
17. _____Half of sons passed up the social class of their father. (286)
18. _____Whites have higher rates of poverty than ethnic/racial minorities simply because there are so many more whites in the U.S. population. (286)
19. _____The majority of the poor live below the poverty line for more than five years. (286)
20. _____Sociological explanations of poverty tend to focus on structural features of society more than on any particular characteristics of poor individuals. (292)

FILL-IN-THE-BLANK QUESTIONS

1. _____ consists of property and income. (268)
2. 68% of the total net worth of all U.S. families is owned by ____ % of U.S. families. (268)
3. C. Wright Mills coined the term _____ to refer to those who make the big decisions in U.S. Society. (271)
4. _____ class location is Erik Wright's term for a position in the class structure that generates contradictory interests. (276)
5. Only about ____% of the U.S. population occupies the top rung of the class ladder. (277)
6. Of all the classes, the upper middle class is the one most shaped by _____. (278)
7. On the lowest rung, the _____ have no change of climbing up the social class ladder. (279)

8. Social class is so significant that it affects our chances of living and _____. (280-281)

9. Lower classes experience higher rates of marital friction and _____. (282)

10. The working class is more liberal on _____ issues and more conservative on _____ issues. (279)

11. _____ is the change that family members make in social class from one generation to another. (284)

12. To determine who is poor, the United States government uses a _____. (284)

13. The majority of the poor in the United States are clustered in the _____. (289)

14. _____ of poverty is the trend in the U.S. whereby most poor families are headed by women. (290)

15. Conflict theorists believe that the purpose of welfare is to maintain a _____. (293)

MATCH THESE SOCIAL SCIENTISTS WITH THEIR CONTRIBUTIONS

_____ 1. Gerhard Lenski   a. *studied tenant reactions to janitors' higher status*

_____ 2. Hellinger and Judd   b. *difficulty for street corner men to defer gratification*

_____ 3. Erik Wright   c. *hidden costs of mobility*

_____ 4. Gilbert & Kahl   d. *status inconsistency*

_____ 5. Daniel Moynihan   e. *updated Marx's model*

_____ 6. Sennett & Cobb   f. *childhood poverty and the breakdown of the family*

_____ 7. Elliot Liebow   g. *upward mobility of British women*

_____ 8. Higgenbotham & Weber   h. *women's patterns of social mobility*

_____ 9. Steph Lawler   i. *democratic facade*

_____ 10. Ray Gold   j. *updated Weber's model*

ESSAY QUESTIONS

1. Identify the three dimensions of social class and discuss some of the consequences of social class.

2. Discuss why you think women have been largely ignored in studies of mobility.

3. Describe which groups are at greater risks of poverty and then suggest ways in which poverty can be reduced by targeting these populations.

4. Explore why individual explanation of poverty are easier for the average American to accept than structural explanations.

5. Discuss the Horatio Alger myth and whether or not it is functional for society.

CHAPTER 11
SEX AND GENDER

CHAPTER SUMMARY

- Gender stratification refers to unequal access to power, property, and prestige on the basis of sex. Each society establishes a structure that, on the basis of sex and gender, opens and closes access to privileges. Sex refers to biological distinctions between males and females; gender refers to behaviors and attitudes thought to be socially acceptable for males and females.

- In the "nature versus nurture" debate, almost all sociologists take the side of nurture. In recent years the door to biology has opened somewhat. Studies that have been done indicate that human behavior is not either nature or nurture, but a combination of the two working together. This could be an interesting and controversial area of future sociological research.

- The dominant theory to explain the status of women as a minority group focuses on the physical limitations imposed by childbirth. Women assumed tasks associated with the home while men went out for periods of time to hunt large animals. Men were able to acquire possessions and gain prestige.

- George Murdock found a pattern of sex-typed activities among premodern societies, with greater prestige given to those performed by males. Patriarchy, or male dominance, appears to be universal.

- Gender discrimination also happens at a global level. The gender gaps occur in education, politics, pay, and violence against women.

- Although feminist movements in the United States have battled to eliminate some of the most blatant forms of gender discrimination, there are still many areas of inequality. For example, bias exists in health care where women may not receive the same treatment and seriousness to symptoms that are given to male patients. More females than males now attend college, but both generally end up in gender-biased academic fields, although there are some signs of change today. Two indicators of gender inequality in everyday life are the general devaluation of femininity and the male dominance of conversation.

- In the workplace women's problems include discrimination in pay, the glass ceiling, being controlled along gender lines, and sexual harassment.

- Traditional gender patterns still exist in regard to violent behavior. Female circumcision is a special case of violence against women.

- Women's traditional roles as homemakers and child care providers used to keep them out of politics, but today the trend is toward greater political equality.

■ As females come to play a larger role in decision-making processes of U.S. social institutions, stereotypes and role models will be broken. It is possible that a new concept of the human personality—that is, one that allows males and females to pursue their individual interests unfettered by gender—might occur.

LEARNING OBJECTIVES
After reading Chapter 11, you should be able to:

1. Define gender stratification and distinguish between sex and gender. (2300)
2. Understand the controversy over what most accounts for gender differences in behavior, biology or culture; cite the evidence that best supports each side of the argument; and explain the dominant sociological position in the debate. (300-303)
3. Describe studies that have added evidence to the biological side of the nature-nurture debate thereby leading more sociologists to acknowledge the role of biological factors in human behavior. (303-304)
4. Describe the global nature of gender inequality and provide concrete examples of global gender discrimination. (305-306)
5. Evaluate the different theories as to the origins of patriarchy. (306-308)
6. Describe how gender and work are related. (308-309)
7. In addition to work, discuss other aspects of global gender discrimination. (309-312)
8. Define feminism. (312)
9. Describe the three "waves" of the women's movement in the United States. (314)
10. Discuss and provide examples of gender inequality in healthcare and education (315-318)
11. Describe the different forms of gender inequality in everyday life, including the general devaluation of femininity. (319-320)
12. Discuss gender relations in the workplace, including the pay gap, the cracking glass ceiling, the glass escalator, the division of workers, and sexual harassment. (320-324)
13. Explain why and how violence against women continues to be a significant social problem in the United States. (325-328)
14. Discuss why women are underrepresented in American politics and what can, and is, being done about it. (328-329)
15. Describe future scenarios of gender definitions and relations in the United States. (329)

CHAPTER OUTLINE

I.   **Issues of Sex and Gender**
   A.   Gender stratification refers to men's and women's unequal access to power, prestige, and property.
      1.   Gender is especially significant because it is a master status, cutting across all aspects of social life.
      2.   No matter what we attain in our lifetime, we carry the label male and female with us; this label guides our behavior and serves as a basis of power and privilege.
   B.   Sex and gender reflect different bases.

1. Sex is biological characteristics distinguishing males and females, including primary sex organs (organs related to reproduction) and secondary sex organs (physical distinctions not related to reproduction).

2. Gender is a social characteristic which varies from one society to another and refers to what the group considers proper for its males and females.

3. The sociological significance of gender is that it is the means by which society controls its members; it sorts us, on the basis of sex, into different life experiences.

C. Some researchers argue that biological factors (two X chromosomes in females, one X and one Y in males) result in differences in conduct, with men being more aggressive and domineering and women being more comforting and nurturing.

1. Larry Summers, the President of Harvard, made a controversial statement when he said that the reason there are fewer female engineers and scientists is due to innate differences between men and women. That is, biological not sociological factors account for the difference. His statement was met with anger by his colleagues at Harvard, as well as by those at other organizations.

D. The dominant sociological position is that social factors explain why we do what we do. People in every society determine what the physical differences separating men and women mean to them.

1. Children learn these contrasting explanations of life and then take the positions that society assigns to them on the basis of their sex.

2. Sociologists argue that if biology is the primary factor in human behavior, then women the world over would all behave the same way, as would men. In fact, ideas of gender vary greatly from one culture to another.

E. The door, however, to biological factors being involved in human behavior is being acknowledged by some sociologists. Real-life cases provide support for the argument that men's and women's behavior is influenced by biology.

1. Alice Rossi suggested that women are better prepared biologically for "mothering" than are men: nature provides biological predispositions that are overlaid with culture.

2. A medical accident led to a young boy being reassigned to the female sex. Reared as a female, the child behaved like a girl; however, by adolescence she was unhappy and having a difficult time adjusting to being a female. In adolescence, the child underwent medical procedures to once again become a male.

3. A study of Vietnam veterans found that the men who had higher levels of testosterone tended to be more aggressive and to have more problems.

II. Gender Inequality in Global Perspective

A. Around the world, gender is *the* primary division between people. Because society sets up barriers to deny women equal access, they are referred to as a minority even though they outnumber men.

B. The major theory of the origin of patriarchy points to social consequences of human reproduction.

1. Since life was short and women were tied to reproductive roles, they assumed tasks around the home.

2. Men took over hunting of large animals and left the home base for extended periods of time. This enabled men to make contact with other tribes, trade with those other groups, and wage war and gain prestige by returning home with prisoners of war or with large animals to feed the tribe; little prestige was given to women's more routine tasks.

C. After reviewing the historical record, historian and feminist Gerda Lerner has concluded that women as a group have never held decision-making power over men as a group. This was true even in the earliest known societies, in which there was much less gender discrimination.

D. George Murdock, who surveyed 324 premodern societies, found activities to be sex typed in all of them; activities considered female in one society may be male in another. There is nothing about anatomy that requires this.

E. Universally, greater prestige is given to male activities regardless of what they are. If caring for cattle is men's work, it carries high prestige; if it is women's work, it has less prestige.

F. Globally, gender discrimination occurs in the areas of education, politics, paid employment, and violence against women.

III. Gender Inequality In the United States

A. A society's culture and institutions both justify and maintain its customary forms of gender inequality.

B. Until the twentieth century, U.S. women did not have the right to vote, hold property, make legal contracts, or serve on a jury.

1. Males did not willingly surrender their privileges; rather, greater political rights for women resulted from a prolonged and bitter struggle waged by a "first wave" of feminists in the nineteenth and early twentieth centuries.

2. This movement was divided into radical and conservative branches. The radical branch wanted to reform all social institutions, while the conservative branch concentrated only on winning the vote for women. After 1920 and the achievement of suffrage for women, the movement dissolved.

3. A "second wave" of feminism began in the 1960s. As more women gained an education and began to work outside the home, they compared their wages and working conditions to those of men. As awareness of gender inequalities grew, protest and struggle emerged. The goals of this second wave of feminism are broad, from changing work roles to changing policies on violence against women.

4. The second wave of feminism was also characterized by two branches, one conservative and the other liberal, each of which has had different goals and different tactics.

5. A "third wave" is now emerging. Three main aspects are apparent. The first involves a greater focus on women in the Least Industrialized Nations. The second is a criticism of the values that dominate work and society. The third is the removal of barriers to women's love and sexual pleasure.

6. While women enjoy more rights today, gender inequality still continues to play a central role in social life.

C. There is growing evidence of sexual discrimination in health care.

1. Studies showed that women are twice as likely to die after coronary bypass surgery than are men. Physicians had not taken the complaints of chest pain as seriously in female patients as they had males. As a result, women received surgery later, after the disease had a chance to progress, thereby reducing their chance for survival.

2. Surgeons were also likely to recommend more radical surgeries to their female patients on their reproductive system than necessary.

D. There is evidence of educational gains made by women; more females than males are enrolled in U.S. colleges and universities, females earn 56 percent of all bachelor's degrees, women complete bachelor's degrees faster than men, and the proportion of professional degrees earned by women has increased sharply. Despite these gains, some old practices and patterns persist.

1. Women's sports are still underfunded because they are not considered as important as men's sports.

2. There is still the matter of gender tracking. In college, males and females are channeled into different fields; 81 percent of engineering degrees are awarded to males, while 88 percent of library science degrees are awarded to women.

3. In graduate school, the proportion of females enrolled in programs decreases with each passing year.

4. There is gender stratification in both the rank and pay within higher educational institutions. Women professors are less likely to be in the higher ranks of academia, are paid less than their male counterparts, and are less likely to be taken seriously.

E. Patterns of gender discrimination continue to exist in everyday life.

1. Females' capacities, interests, attitudes, and contributions are not taken as seriously as those of males'. For example, the worst insult that can be thrown at a male is that he is a sissy or that he does things like a girl.

2. Patterns of conversation reflect inequalities between men and women. Men are more likely than women to interrupt a conversation and control a change in topics.

IV. Gender Inequality in the Workplace

A. One of the chief characteristics of the U.S. work force is the steady growth in the number of women who work outside the home for wages.

1. Today nearly one in every two women is employed.

2. Men earn more than women, even when their educational achievement is the same. U.S. women who work full time average only 68 percent of what men are paid. All industrialized nations have a pay gap.

3. Studies have found an association between height and income. Taller men (over 6 ft tall) made more money than shorter men. Taller females also earn more than shorter women.

4. Researchers found that half of the gender pay gap is due to women choosing lower-paying careers. The other half is due to gender discrimination and the "child penalty"—women losing work experience while they care for their children.

5. On average, men started out with higher salaries than women after graduating from college.

6. Of the top 500 corporations, only eight are headed by women. The best chance to be CEO of the largest U.S. corporations is to have a name such as John, Robert, James, William, or Charles. One of the few women to head a Fortune 500 company had a man's name: Carleton Fiorina of Hewlett-Packard.

B. The "glass ceiling" describes an invisible barrier that women face while trying to reach the executive suites.

1. Researchers find that women are not in positions such as marketing, sales, and production, the ones from which top executives are recruited. Rather, they are steered into human resources and public relations; their work is not appreciated to the same degree because it does not bring in profits.

2. Another explanation for the situation is that women lack mentors; male executives are reluctant to mentor them because they fear the gossip and sexual harassment charges if they get too close to female subordinates or because they see women as weak.

3. There are cracks in the glass ceiling as women learn to play by "men's rules" and develop a style with which men feel comfortable. In the background of about three-fourths of these women is a supportive husband who shares household duties and adapts his career to the needs of his executive wife.

4. Christine Williams found that men who go into nontraditional fields do not encounter a glass ceiling; rather they find a "glass escalator"—they move up more quickly than female coworkers.

C. Conflict theorists examine how capitalists exploit gender divisions among workers in order to control them.

1. For example, uniform colors are based on gender with men wearing one color and women another.

2. Having women think of themselves as women workers rather just as workers makes them easier to control. These women were less likely to file a complaint when their bosses flirted with them.

D. Until the 1970s, women did not draw a connection between unwanted sexual advances on the job and their subordinate positions at work.

1. As women began to discuss the problem, they named it *sexual harassment* and came to see such unwanted sexual advances by men in powerful positions as a structural problem. The change in perception resulted from reinterpreting women's experiences, giving them a name.

2. The meaning of the term is vague; court cases are the basis for determining what is and is not sexual harassment.

3. Sexual harassment is an abuse of power that is structured into relationships of inequality in the workplace.

4. Sexual harassment and rape are common in the military. Three-fourths of women who had been raped did not report their assault. We will have to wait and see what will be done to put adequate reforms into place.

V. Gender and Violence

A. Most victims of violence are females.

1.   Each year almost 7 of every 10,000 American women age 12 and older is raped. This figure is seriously underreported and it is more likely that the accurate total is three times this rate.
2.   Most victims are between the ages of 12-24 years old and know their attacker.
3.   An aspect of rape that is usually overlooked is the rape of men in prison; it is estimated that between 15 and 20 percent of men in prison are raped.
4.   Date rape (sexual assault in which the assailant is acquainted with the victim) is not an isolated event. Most go unreported because the victim feels partially responsible, since she knows the person and was with him voluntarily.
5.   Males are more likely than females to commit murder and be the victim of murder.
6.   Other forms of violence against women include battering, spousal abuse, incest and female circumcision.
7.   Although women are less likely than men to kill, when they do, judges are more likely to be lenient on them. More research is required to understand why this pattern exists.

B.   Feminists use symbolic interactionism to understand violence against women. They stress that U.S. culture promotes violence by males. It teaches men to associate power, dominance, strength, virility, and superiority with masculinity. Men use violence to try and maintain a higher status.

C.   To solve violence, we must first break the link between violence and masculinity.

VI. The Changing Face of Politics

A.   Despite the gains U.S. women have made in recent elections, they continue to be underrepresented in political office, especially in higher office.
1.   Reasons for this include the fact that women have been underrepresented in law and business, the careers from which most politicians are drawn; they have not seen themselves as a voting block who need political action to overcome discrimination; they have generally found the roles of mother and politician incompatible; and men have rarely incorporated women into the centers of decision making or presented them as viable candidates.
2.   There are signs that this pattern is changing. More women are going into law and business; child care is now more likely to be seen as a mutual responsibility; and in some areas of the country, party leaders are searching for qualified candidates who can win regardless of their gender.

B.   Trends in the 1990s indicate that women will participate in political life in far greater numbers than in the past

VII. Glimpsing the Future—With Hope

A.   As women play a fuller role in decision-making processes, further structural obstacles to women's participation in society will give way.

B.   As gender stereotypes are abandoned, both males and females will be free to feel and express their needs and emotions, something that present arrangements deny them.

KEY TERMS
After studying the chapter, review the definition for each of the following terms.

feminism: the philosophy that men and women should be politically, economically, and socially equal; an organized activity on behalf of this principle (312)

gender: the social characteristics that a society considers proper for its males and females; masculinity or femininity (300)

gender stratification: males' and females' unequal access to power, prestige, and property on the basis of their sex (300)

glass ceiling: the mostly invisible barrier that keeps women from advancing to the top levels of work (323)

glass escalator: the mostly invisible accelerators that push men into higher-level positions, more desirable work assignments, and higher salaries (324)

matriarchy: a society in which women as a group dominate men as a group (303)

patriarchy: a society in which men dominate women; authority is vested in males (303)

sex: biological characteristics that distinguish females and males, consisting of primary and secondary sex characteristics (300)

sexual harassment: the abuse of one's position of authority to force unwanted sexual demands on someone (324)

KEY PEOPLE
Review the major theoretical contributions or findings of these people.

Janet Chafetz: Chafetz studied the second wave of feminism in the 1960s, noting that as large numbers of women began to work in the economy, they began to compare their working conditions with those of men. (305,314)

Donna Eder: This sociologist discovered that junior high boys call one another "girl" when they don't hit each other hard enough during a football game. (319)

Frederick Engels: Engels was a colleague of Karl Marx and wrote a book about the origins of the family in which he argued that male dominance developed with the origin of private property. (308)

Sue Fisher: She discovered that surgeons were recommending total hysterectomies to female patients when they were not necessary. (316)

Cynthia Fuchs Epstein: Epstein is a proponent of the view that differences between males' and females' behavior is solely the result of social factors such as socialization and social control. (302)

Douglas Foley: This sociologist's study of sports lends support to the view that things feminine are generally devalued. (319)

Janet Giele and Judith Lorber: As stereotypes are broken, men and women will have the opportunity to express needs and emotions than was previously acceptable. (329)

Steven Goldberg: This sociologist's view is that the differences between males and females are not due to environment but to inborn differences that direct the emotions and behaviors of the two genders. (303)

Barbara Grosz: A professor at Harvard who experienced that female professors are not taken as seriously as male professors. (318)

Marvin Harris: This anthropologist suggested that male dominance grew out of the greater strength that men had which made them better suited for the hand-to-hand combat of tribal societies; women became the reward to entice men into battle. (308)

Karen Horsfeld: Companies that divide their workers along gender lines find it easier to control their female workers. Females were less likely to file complaints when their bosses flirted with them. (324)

Alison Jaggar: As society changes, we may see a greater appreciation for sexual differences and gender equality can become a background condition for living in society rather than a goal to strive for. (329)

Gerda Lerner: While acknowledging that in all societies women—as a group—have never had decision-making power over men, Lerner suggested that patriarchy may have had different origins in different places around the globe. (305,308)

George Murdock: This anthropologist surveyed 324 premodern societies around the world and found that in all of them, activities were sex typed. (308)

Alice Rossi: This feminist sociologist has suggested that women are better prepared biologically for "mothering" than are men. (302)

Diana Scully: She learned that surgeons "sell" unnecessary female operations to women in order to keep themselves in business. (316)

Jean Stockard and Miriam Johnson: These sociologists observed boys playing basketball and heard them exchange insults that reflect a disrespect and devaluation of women. (319)

Samuel Stouffer: In his classic study of combat soldiers during World War II, Stouffer noted the general devaluation of things associated with women. (319)

Larry Summers: President of Harvard university that suggest that women's inborn characteristics make them less qualified to succeed in being engineers and scientists. (306)

Christine Williams: Williams found that men in nontraditional careers and occupations often experience a glass escalator—moving more quickly than women into desirable work assignments, higher-level positions, and larger salaries. (323)

STUDENT APPLICATION PROJECTS

This is your opportunity to apply the sociological perspective to the world around you. The projects in this section refer to material introduced in this chapter of your text. These projects help you apply the sociological perspective "down to your earth...down to your daily life."

1. Interview a few women that you know who are in the paid work force. Have they experienced any kind of gender discrimination on the job? Have them describe any challenges that they have faced getting to their current position, especially if they are in a supervisory or management position.

2. Are your earnings/income (future or current) affected by your gender? Why or why not? Will having a family someday have an impact on your earnings? Why? Do you know people who have experienced less income and less job opportunities due to their gender? Explain. Overall, do you expect the gender gap to continue in the United States? Explain. Do you expect it to continue in the world? Explain.

3. What do you think...do United States audiences find violence against women entertaining or even amusing? Do a study of your own: Watch television for one week, at various times of the day, evening, and late night. Note the name of the program you are watching and the date and time. What images of women are portrayed in these programs? Write two to three sentences for each program. At the weeks' conclusion, answer the following questions: What images of women and violence did you observe? What images do you think movies and television portray about women and violence? How do you react to these images? Do you think these images impact society in any way? Explain.

4. We receive gender messages that promote inequality from the day we are born. Visit the local library and randomly select ten children's books. Read through them and identify the gender messages that are expressed. Be sure not to miss those presented in the illustrations. If possible, select some of your favorite books from childhood and explore how gender messages present in these books have impacted you and/or your life.

SELF-TEST

MULTIPLE CHOICE QUESTIONS

1. The term gender _____ refers to unequal access to property, power, and prestige on the basis of sex. (300)
    a. stratification
    b. socialization
    c. stereotyping
    d. roles

2. To what does the term "sex" refer? (300)
    a. the social characteristics that a society considers proper for its males and females
    b. the biological characteristics that distinguish females and males
    c. masculinity and femininity
    d. all of the above

3. Which of the following statements about gender is *incorrect*? (300)
    a. There is not a lot of variation in gender roles around the world.
    b. Gender is a social, not a biological, characteristic.
    c. Gender consists of whatever a group considers proper for its males and females.
    d. The sociological significance of gender is that it is a device by which society controls its members.

4. Patriarchy: (307)
    a. is a society in which men dominate women.
    b. has existed throughout history.
    c. is universal.
    d. all of the above.

5. If biology is the principal factor in human behavior, what would we find around the world? (302)
    a. things would be just like they are
    b. men and women would be much more like each other than they currently are
    c. women would be one sort of person and men another
    d. none of the above

6. The study of Vietnam Veterans discussed in this chapter is an indication of how sociologists are slowly becoming open to consider _____ factors in human behavior. (304)
    a. gender
    b. testosterone
    c. biological
    d. psychological

7.   Which minority group represents that largest segment of the U.S. population? (306)
        a.   African Americans
        b.   Latinos
        c.   Women
        d.   Children

8.   The major theory of the origin of patriarchy points to: (307)
        a.   the social consequences of human reproduction.
        b.   men's greediness.
        c.   women's willingness to give up power and control in return for protection.
        d.   men's greater strength enabled them to overpower women.

9.   _____ surveyed information on tribal societies and found that all of them have sex-linked activities and give greater prestige to male activities. (308)
        a.   George Murdock
        b.   W.E.B. Du Bois
        c.   Jane Adams
        d.   Max Weber

10.   In regard to the prestige of work: (308)
        a.   greater prestige is given to activities that are considered to be of great importance to a society, regardless of whether they are performed by females or males.
        b.   greater prestige goes to female activities that males cannot do, like pregnancy and lactation.
        c.   greater prestige is given to male activities.
        d.   none of the above.

11.   Which statement concerning global discrimination is *incorrect*? (309)
        a.   Of about 1 billion adults around the world who cannot read, two-thirds are women.
        b.   The United States leads the world in the number of women who hold public office.
        c.   Around the globe, women average less pay than men.
        d.   A global human rights issue has become violence against women.

12.   Which of the following is true about female circumcision? (313)
        a.   it is still practiced in some parts of the world today
        b.   feminists believe this is done to control female sexuality
        c.   fourteen African countries have banned female circumcision
        d.   all of the above

13.   Women won the right to vote in what year? (314)
        a.   1920
        b.   1918
        c.   1890
        d.   1945

14. A "second wave" of protest and struggle against gender inequalities: (314)
    a. occurred when women began to compare their working conditions with those of men.
    b. began in the 1960s.
    c. had as its goals everything from changing work roles to changing policies on violence against women.
    d. all of the above.

15. A possible "third wave" of feminism is now emerging. What is the focus of this wave? (314)
    a. widespread legal reforms to guarantee equality
    b. greater compensation for victims of sexual harassment
    c. broadening the values that underlie work and other social institutions
    d. inclusion of women's contributions to our history

16. Research has found that who is more likely to die after coronary bypass surgery? (315)
    a. men
    b. women
    c. men and women have equal rates
    d. researchers aren't sure since only men have been studies

17. Gender inequality in education: (315)
    a. has virtually disappeared today.
    b. is allowed by law.
    c. is perpetuated by the use of sex to sort students into different academic disciplines.
    d. disappears by the time men and women enter graduate school.

18. Researchers who have studied conversation patterns between men and women conclude that: (319)
    a. women talk more and interrupt men more frequently than the other way around.
    b. men and women are social equals when it comes to everyday conversation.
    c. even in everyday conversation, the talk between a man and a woman reflects social inequality.
    d. men interrupt more in conversations, but women control the topics that are discussed.

19. The pay gap between men and women: (320)
    a. is found primarily among those with less than a high-school education.
    b. is found primarily among those with college and graduate education.
    c. is found at all educational levels.
    d. largely has disappeared.

20.   The glass ceiling: (323)
    a.   keeps both men and women out of nontraditional occupations.
    b.   has largely been shattered by today's generation of business women.
    c.   refers to the invisible barrier that keeps women from reaching the executive suite.
    d.   All of the above.

21.   Which of the following is *not* a reason for women's absence from core corporate positions? (323)
    a.   The male corporate culture stereotypes potential leaders as people who look like themselves; women are seen as better at providing "support."
    b.   Women do not seek out opportunities for advancement and do not spend enough time networking with powerful executives.
    c.   Women lack mentors who take an interest in them and teach them the ropes.
    d.   Women are generally steered away from jobs that are stepping stones to top corporate office; instead they are recruited for jobs in human resources and public relations.

22.   The glass escalator: (324)
    a.   is a term used by Christine Williams in her research on men employed in traditional female occupations like nursing, elementary school teaching, and social work.
    b.   refers to a situation where men accelerated into higher-level positions, were given more desirable work assignments, and paid higher wages than female co-workers.
    c.   is driven by the stereotype that because someone is a male, he is more capable.
    d.   all of the above.

23.   Which theorists believe that capitalists divide workers along gender lines to control them? (324)
    a.   conflict
    b.   functionalist
    c.   symbolic interactionism
    d.   none of the above

24.   Which of the following statements about sexual harassment is *incorrect*? (324)
    a.   it is no longer exclusively a female problem.
    b.   it is rooted in the structure of the workplace rather than individual relationships.
    c.   it involves a person in authority using the position to force unwanted sex on subordinates.
    d.   male victims of sexual harassment receive more sympathy than female victims.

25.   The pattern of date rape shows: (326)
    a.   that it is not an isolated event.
    b.   most go unreported.
    c.   it is difficult to prosecute.
    d.   all of the above.

26.   Women who are convicted of killing another person: (327)
        a.   are generally given stiffer penalties than men.
        b.   usually have a history of interpersonal violence.
        c.   are more likely to be given probation than is a man.
        d.   are placed in minimum security prisons because they are not considered a risk to society.

27.   Which of the following is *not* among feminist explanations for gender violence? (327)
        a.   higher testosterone levels in males
        b.   males reassert their declining power and status
        c.   the association of strength and virility with violence
        d.   cultural traditions that are patriarchal

28.   Women have been underrepresented in politics because: (328)
        a.   they are not really interested in pursuing political careers.
        b.   they are not viewed as serious candidates by the voters.
        c.   their roles as mothers and wives are incompatible with political roles.
        d.   they lack the proper educational backgrounds.

29.   What is it that keeps most males and females locked into fairly rigid gender roles? (329)
        a.   social structural obstacles
        b.   socialization
        c.   stereotypes
        d.   all of the above

30.   What is most likely to break the stereotypes locking us into traditional gender activities? (329)
        a.   stricter laws
        b.   equal pay
        c.   increased female participation in the decision-making processes of social institutions
        d.   increased male participation in nurturing activities

TRUE-FALSE QUESTIONS

1.   _____Gender refers to biological distinctions between males and females. (300)
2.   _____The study of the medical accident with identical twins cited in the text supports the view of the role of biology in human behavior. (303)
3.   _____Matriarchy, or male dominance, appears to be universal. (303)
4.   _____Research by a number of social scientists has established that there was great variability in terms of the amount of prestige accorded to male and female activities. (308)
5.   _____ Women have come to having equal representation in the political system in Sweden. (309)
6.   _____Although female circumcision was once common in parts of Africa and southeast Asia, it is quite rare today. (313)

7. _____In the United States, women's political rights were gained only after a prolonged and bitter struggle. (314)
8. _____In the second wave of the U.S. women's movement, the liberal wing of the movement had a radical wing, while the conservative faction did not. (314)
9. _____An alarming number of unnecessary hysterectomies in women is an example of gender discrimination in health care. (315)
10. _____Today, women and men have equal levels of achievement in higher education. (315)
11. _____Women are less likely to hold the rank of full professor in colleges and universities, and if they do, they are likely to get paid less than male counterparts. (317)
12. _____In a study of World War II combat soldiers, Samuel Stouffer reported that officers used feminine terms as insults to motivate soldiers. (319)
13. _____Women are more likely to interrupt a conversation and control topics. (319)
14. _____For college graduates, the lifetime pay gap runs over a million dollars in favor of men. (320)
15. _____The "glass ceiling" has a more negative impact on women than on men in corporations and the professions. (323)
16. _____The "glass escalator" refers to the opportunities that women have to advance quickly in traditional male occupations. (324)
17. _____Once sexual harassment was defined as a problem, women saw some of their experiences in a different light. (324)
18. _____In the United States, males kill at about the same rate as females. (327)
19. _____Women are the typical victims of family violence. (327)
20. _____The only reason there are not more women in public office is because men keep them out. (328)

FILL-IN-THE-BLANK QUESTIONS

1. Gender is a _____ status; it cuts across all aspects of social life. (300)
2. Gender consists of what behaviors and attitudes a _____ considers proper for males and females. (300)
3. _____ is a society in which women as a group dominate men as a group. (303)
4. In his study of 324 societies around the world, George Murdock found that in all of them activities are _____. (308)
5. Most sociologists take the nature side in the nature vs. nurture debate over behaviors of males and females. (302)
6. The philosophy that men and women should be equal is known as _____. (304)
7. All waves of feminism have had both liberal and _____ branches. (314)
8. Throughout the United States, even when women become full professors, they average less pay than _____ who are full professors. (320)
9. Research on the devaluation of things feminine shows that _____ is valued more highly, for it represents strength and success. (320)
10. _____ percent of workers in the U.S. workforce are female. (320)
11. Women who work full time average only _____ % of what men are paid. (321)
12. A female fire fighter is likely to experience the glass _____. (323)
13. A male elementary teacher is likely to experience the glass _____. (324)

14. Central to sexual harassment is the abuse of _____. (324)
15. _____ women have served in the United States Senate. (328)

MATCH THESE SOCIAL SCIENTISTS WITH THEIR CONTRIBUTIONS

_____	1. Janet Chafetz	a.	*experienced that female professors were taken less seriously than their male counterparts*
_____	2. Alice Rossi	b.	*men in nontraditional occupations often experience a glass escalator*
_____	3. Giele and Lorber	c.	*male dominance grew out of the greater strength that men had*
_____	4. Christine Williams	d.	*study supports the view that things feminine are generally devalued*
_____	5. Gerda Lerner	e.	*In the future, men and women will be more expressive of needs and emotions*
_____	6. Barbara Grosz	f.	*Companies divide their workers along gender lines*
_____	7. Samuel Stouffer	g.	*women are better prepared biologically for "mothering" than are men*
_____	8. Marvin Harris	h.	*patriarchy may have had different origins around the globe*
_____	9. Karen Horsfeld	i.	*noted the devaluation of things associated with women among soldiers*
_____	10. Douglas Foley	j.	*studied the second wave of feminism in the 1960s*

ESSAY QUESTIONS

1. Summarize the sociobiology argument concerning behavioral differences between men and women. Explain which position most closely reflects your own: biological, sociological, or sociobiological.

2. Compare and contrast the two waves of the feminist movement in this country by identifying the forces that contributed to both waves.

3. Discuss gender tracking and how that perpetuates inequality in education and the workforce.

4. Discuss why women are so often the victims of violence.

5. As most of the legal barriers to women's full participation in society have been eliminated, it is commonly assumed that women have gained equality. Given what you have learned in this chapter, consider whether this is the case.

CHAPTER 12
RACE AND ETHNICITY

CHAPTER SUMMARY

- Race is a complex and often misunderstood concept. Race is a reality in the sense that inherited physical characteristics distinguish one group from another. However, race is a myth in the sense of one race being superior to another and of there being pure races. Race is so arbitrary that scientists cannot agree upon how many races there are. The *idea* of race is a powerful reality in our everyday lives. Race refers to inherited biological characteristics, while ethnicity refers to cultural ones. Ethnicity includes foods, clothing, language, music etc.

- A minority group is defined as one singled out for unequal treatment by members of the dominant group. Both race and ethnicity can be a basis for unequal treatment. The extent of ethnic identification depends on the relative size of the group, its power, broad physical characteristics, and the amount of discrimination. Ethnic work is the process of constructing an ethnic identity.

- Prejudice refers to an attitude and discrimination to unfair treatment. Individual discrimination is the negative treatment of one person by another, while institutional discrimination is discrimination built into society's social institutions. Prejudice can be learned based on the association with certain groups.

- Psychological theories explain the origin of prejudice in terms of stress frustration that gets directed toward scapegoats and also in terms of the development of authoritarian personalities. Functionalists emphasize how different social environments affect levels of prejudice. Conflict theorists look at the exploitation of racial-ethnic divisions by those in power, and symbolic interactionists stress how labels create selective perception and self-fulfilling prophecies.

- Dominant groups typically practice one of five policies toward minority groups: genocide, population transfer, internal colonialism, segregation, assimilation, or pluralism. We can see many examples throughout history both in the U.S. and globally that demonstrate these patterns of intergroup relations.

- The major ethnic groups in the United States, ranked from largest to smallest, are European Americans, Latinos, African Americans, Asian Americans, and Native Americans.

- Each minority group faces different issues. African Americans are increasingly divided into middle and lower classes, each with very different experiences. Latinos are divided by country of origin. The well-being of Asian Americans also varies by country of origin. For Native Americans, the issues are poverty, nationhood, and settling treaty obligations.

- The primary issues that dominate race-ethnic relations today are immigration, affirmative action, and how to develop a truly multicultural society.

LEARNING OBJECTIVES
After reading Chapter 12, you should be able to:

1. Explain how the concept of race is both a reality and a myth. (334-335)
2. Distinguish between race and ethnicity. (335-337)
3. Describe the characteristics of minority groups and dominant groups. (338-339)
4. Know what is meant by ethnic identity and the four factors that heighten or reduce it. (339)
5. Differentiate between prejudice and discrimination. (340)
6. Describe how prejudice can be learned through association with different groups and through the internalizing of dominant norms (340-341)
7. Distinguish between individual discrimination and institutional discrimination. (341)
8. Understand the psychological and sociological theories of prejudice. (343-345)
9. List the six patterns of intergroup relations that develop between minority and dominant groups and provide examples for each. (345-348)
10. Understand the racial breakdown of racial-ethnic groups in the United States. (349-350)
11. Compare and contrast the experiences of White Europeans, Latinos, African Americans, Asian Americans, and Native Americans in the United States. (351-364)
12. Disucss the major issues—and debates—currently dominating race and ethnic relations in the United States including immigration and affirmative action. (365-367)
13. State how the United States can move toward a multicultural society. (367)

CHAPTER OUTLINE

I. Laying a Sociological Foundation
   A. Race, a group with inherited physical characteristics that distinguish it from another group, is both a myth and a reality.
      1. It is a reality in the sense that humans come in different colors and shapes.
      2. It is a myth that any race is superior to others. Throughout history, there are examples in which this myth was put into practice. Examples include the holocaust, the massacre in Rwanda, and the "ethnic cleansing" in Bosnia.
      3. It is a myth because there are no pure races; what we call "races" are social classifications, not biological categories. The mapping of the human genome shows that humans are strikingly homogenous.
      4. The classification of race is complex. Some scientists have classified humans into two "races" while others have found as many as two thousand.
      5. The myth of race makes a difference for social life because people believe these ideas are real and they act on their beliefs.
   B. Race and ethnicity are often confused due to the cultural differences people see and the way they define race. The terms ethnicity and ethnic refer to cultural characteristics that distinguish a people.
   C. Minority groups are people singled out for unequal treatment and who regard themselves as objects of collective discrimination.
      1. They are not necessarily in the numerical minority. Sociologists refer to those who do the discriminating as the dominant group; they have greater power, more

privileges, and higher social status. The dominant group attributes its privileged position to its superiority, not to discrimination.

2. A group becomes a minority through the expansion of political boundaries by another group. Another way for a group to become a minority is by migration into a territory, either voluntarily or involuntarily.

D. Some people feel an intense sense of ethnic identity while others feel very little.

1. An individual's sense of ethnic identity is influenced by the relative size and power of the ethnic group, its appearance, and the level of discrimination aimed at the group. If a group is relatively small, has little power, has a distinctive appearance, and is an object of discrimination, its members will have a heightened sense of ethnic identity.

2. Ethnic work refers to how ethnicity is constructed and includes enhancing and maintaining a group's distinctiveness or attempting to recover ethnic heritage. In the United States, millions of Americans are engaged in ethnic work, which has challenged the notion that our nation should be a melting pot, with most groups quietly blending into a sort of ethnic stew.

II. Prejudice and Discrimination

A. Prejudice and discrimination exist in societies throughout the world.

1. Discrimination is unfair treatment directed toward someone. When based on race, it is known as racism. It also can be based on many other features such as weight, age, sex, sexual preference, disability, religion, or politics.

2. Prejudice is prejudging of some sort, usually in a negative way.

3. Sociologist found that some people learned prejudice after association with certain groups. Racism was not the cause for joining a racist group but the result of their membership in that group.

4. It has been found that prejudice against one racial-ethnic group leads to prejudice against others.

5. People can learn to be prejudiced against their own groups by internalizing the norms of the dominant group.

6. Psychologist found through the "implicit association test" that we hold biased perceptions of racial groups through the ethnic maps that we have learned in our culture.

B. Sociologists distinguish between individual discrimination (negative treatment of one person by another) and institutional discrimination (negative treatment of a minority group that is built into society's institutions).

1. Race-ethnicity is a significant factor in getting a mortgage or a car loan. Researchers found that even when two mortgage applicants were identical in terms of credit histories, African Americans and Latinos were 60 percent more likely than whites to be rejected.

2. In terms of health care, researchers compared the age, sex, race, and income of heart patients and found that whites were more likely than minorities to be given coronary bypass surgery or receive knee replacements.

III. Theories of Prejudice

A. Psychological Perspectives

1. According to John Dollard, prejudice results from frustration: people unable to strike out at the real source of their frustration find scapegoats to unfairly blame.

2. According to Theodor Adorno, highly prejudiced people are insecure, intolerant people who long for the firm boundaries established by strong authority; he called this complex of personality traits the authoritarian personality.

3. Subsequent studies have generally concluded that people who are older, less educated, less intelligent and from a lower social class are more likely to be authoritarian.

B. Sociological Perspectives

1. To functionalists, the social environment can be deliberately arranged to generate either positive or negative feelings about people. Prejudice is functional in that it creates in-group solidarity and out-group antagonism, but dysfunctional because it destroys human relationships. Functionalists do not justify what they discover but simply identify the functions and dysfunctions of human action.

2. To conflict theorists, the ruling class systematically pits group against group; by splitting workers along racial-ethnic lines they benefit because solidarity among the workers is weakened. The higher unemployment rates of minorities create a reserve labor force from which owners can draw when they need to expand production temporarily. The existence of the reserve labor force is a constant threat to white workers, who modify their demands rather than lose their jobs to unemployment. Racial-ethnic divisions at work are also encouraged and exploited. This weakens workers' bargaining power.

3. To symbolic interactionists, the labels we learn color our perceptions, leading to selective perception—we see certain things and are blind to others. Racial and ethnic labels are especially powerful because they are shorthand for emotionally laden stereotypes. Symbolic interactionists stress that we learn our prejudices in interactions with others. These stereotypes not only justify prejudice and discrimination, but also lead to a self-fulfilling prophecy—stereotypical behavior in those who are stereotyped.

IV. Global Patterns of Intergroup Relations

A. Genocide is the actual or attempted systematic annihilation of a race or ethnic group that is labeled as less than fully human. The Holocaust, and the U.S. government's treatment of Native Americans are examples. Labels that dehumanize others help people compartmentalize; they can separate their acts from their sense of being good and moral people.

B. Population transfer is involuntary movement of a minority group. Indirect transfer involves making life so unbearable that members of a minority then leave; direct transfer involves forced expulsion. A combination of genocide and population transfer occurred in Bosnia, in former Yugoslavia, as Serbs engaged in the wholesale slaughter of Muslims and Croats, with survivors forced to flee the area.

C. Internal colonialism is a society's policy of exploiting a minority by using social institutions to deny it access to full benefits. Slavery is an extreme example, as well as South Africa's system of apartheid.

D. Segregation is the formal separation of groups that accompanies internal colonialism. Dominant groups maintain social distance from minorities yet still exploit their labor.

E. Assimilation is the process by which a minority is absorbed into the mainstream. Forced assimilation occurs when the dominant group prohibits the minority from using its own religion, language, or customs. Permissive assimilation is when the minority adopts the dominant group's patterns in its own way and/or at its own speed.

F. Multiculturalism, also called pluralism, permits or encourages ethnic variation. Switzerland is an excellent example of multiculturalism. The French, Italians, Germans, and Romansh have kept their own languages and live in political and economic unity.

V. Race and Ethnic Relations in the United States
   A. Racial and ethnic terms that are used in the United States are controversial.
      1. White Americans comprise 68 percent of the U.S. population with racial and ethnic minorities comprising the other 31 percent.
      2. Minority groups tend to be clustered in geographic areas so that the distribution of dominant and minority groups among the states rarely comes close to the national average.
   B. White Anglo-Saxon Protestants (WASPs) established the basic social institutions in the United States when they settled the original colonies.
      1. WASPs were very ethnocentric and viewed immigrants from other European countries as inferior. Subsequent immigrants were expected to speak English and adopt other Anglo-Saxon ways of life.
      2. White ethnics are white immigrants to the United States whose culture differs from that of WASPs. They include the Irish, Germans, Poles, Jews, and Italians. They were initially discriminated against by WASPs who felt that something was wrong with people with different customs.
      3. The institutional and cultural dominance of Western Europeans set the stage for current ethnic relations.
   C. The terms Latino and Hispanic do not refer to a race, but to different ethnic groups. Latinos may be black, white, or Native American.
      1. When Europeans first arrived on this continent, Latinos had already established settlements in Florida and New Mexico.
      2. Today, Latinos are the largest minority group in the United States. About twenty-five million trace their origins to Mexico, three million to Puerto Rico, one million to Cuba, and almost five million from Central or South America. While most are legal residents, large numbers have entered the United States illegally and avoid contact with public officials.
      3. The migration of Mexicans across the U.S. border has become a major social issue. A group called the Minutemen, who organized through the internet, are volunteers who offered to patrol the border.
      4. Concentrated in four states (California, Texas, New York, and Florida), these immigrants are causing major demographic shifts.
      5. The Spanish language distinguishes them from other minorities; perhaps half are unable to speak English without difficulty. This is a major obstacle to getting well-paid jobs. Some Anglos perceive the growing use of Spanish as a threat and

have initiated an "English only" movement; they have succeeded in getting states to consider making English their official language.

6. Divisions of social class and country of national origin prevent political unity.

7. Compared with non-Latino whites, Latinos are worse off on all indicators of well-being. The country of origin is significant, with Cuban Americans scoring much higher on indicators of well-being and Puerto Rican Americans scoring the lowest.

8. People from South American and Cuba attain more education than those coming from elsewhere.

D. African Americans face a legacy of racism.

1. In 1955, African Americans in Montgomery, Alabama, using civil disobedience tactics advocated by Martin Luther King, Jr., protested laws believed to be unjust. This led to the civil rights movement that challenged existing patterns of racial segregation throughout the South.

2. The 1964 Civil Rights Act and 1965 Voting Rights Act heightened expectations for African Americans that better social conditions would follow these gains. Frustration over the pace of change led to urban riots and passage of the 1968 Civil Rights Act.

3. Since then, African Americans have made political and economic progress. For example, African Americans have quadrupled their membership in the U.S. House of Representatives in the past 30 years, and enrollment in colleges continues to increase. Half of all African American families make more than $35,000 a year.

4. Despite these gains, however, African Americans continue to lag behind in politics, economics, and education. In 2004 Barack Obama became the first African American man to be elected to the Senate. Currently, African Americans average 61 percent of whites' incomes; only 17 percent of African Americans have graduated from college; and African American males are more than five times as likely to be homicide victims as are white males.

5. According to William Wilson, social class (not race) is the major determinant of quality of life. The African American community today is composed of a middle class who took advantage of the opportunities created by civil rights legislation and advanced economically, living in good housing, having well-paid jobs, and sending their children to good schools. It is also composed of a large group of poorly educated and unskilled African Americans who were left behind as opportunities for unskilled labor declined and now find themselves living in poverty, facing violent crime and dead-end jobs, sending their children to lesser schools.

6. Others argue that discrimination on the basis of race persists, despite gains made by some African Americans. African Americans are still paid less than white Americans for the same job.

7. Racism still continues to be a part of life. Researchers found that resumes that had white sounding names received 50 percent more callbacks than those having more black sounding names. In addition, voices that sounded like a white voice were more likely to receive callbacks about rental apartment availability.

8.   African American women are in a double bind situation. They are discriminated against because of their race-ethnicity and for being a woman.

E.   Asian Americans have long faced discrimination in the United States.

1.   Chinese immigrants were drawn here by the gold strikes in the West and the need for unskilled workers to build the railroads. In 1882, Congress passed the Chinese Exclusion Act, suspending all Chinese immigration for 10 years.

2.   When the Japanese arrived, they met spillover bigotry, a stereotype that lumped all Asians together, depicted them negatively. After the attack on Pearl Harbor in World War II, hostilities toward Japanese Americans increased; many were imprisoned in "relocation camps."

3.   On the average, Asian Americans have a higher annual income and lower unemployment rates than other racial-ethnic groups. Those most likely to be in poverty, though, come from Southeast Asia.

4.   The success of Asian Americans can be traced to three factors: (1) a close family life, (2) educational achievement, and (3) assimilation into the mainstream.

5.   Asian American children are the most likely to grow up with two parents. They have very high rates of college graduation. And the high intermarriage rate of Japanese Americans has enabled them to assimilate into mainstream culture.

6.   Asian Americans are becoming more prominent in politics. Hawaii has elected several Asian American governors and sent several Asian American senators to Washington. In 1996, Gary Locke was elected governor of Washington.

F.   Due to the influence of old movie westerns, many Americans tend to hold stereotypes of Native Americans as uncivilized savages; as a single group of people subdivided into separate bands.

1.   In reality, however, Native Americans represent a diverse group of people with a variety of cultures and languages. Although originally numbering between five and ten million, their numbers were reduced to a low of 500,000 due to a lack of immunity to European diseases and warfare. Today there are about 2 million Native Americans who speak about 150 different languages.

2.   At first, relations between European settlers and the Native Americans were peaceful. However, as the number of settlers increased, tensions increased. Because they stood in the way of expansion, many were slaughtered. Government policy shifted to population transfer, with Native Americans confined to reservations.

3.   Today, they are an invisible minority. Almost half live in three states: Oklahoma, California, and Arizona; most other Americans are hardly aware of them. They have the highest rates of suicide and lower life expectancy of any U.S. minority. These negative conditions are the result of Anglo domination.

4.   In the 1960s Native Americans won a series of legal victories that restored their control over the land and their right to determine economic policy. Many Native Americans have opened businesses on their land, ranging from industrial parks to casinos. Today many Native Americans are interested in recovering and honoring their own traditions.

5.   Pan-Indianism emphasizes elements that run through all Native American cultures, in order to develop self-identification that goes beyond any particular tribe.

VI. Looking Toward the Future

    A.   Central to this country's history, immigration and the fear of its consequences is once again an issue facing the United States as it moves into the next century. The concern has been that "too many" immigrants will alter the character of the United States, undermining basic institutions and contributing to the breakdown of society.

        1.   In some states, such as California, the racial-ethnic minorities constitute a majority.

        2.   There is fear that Spanish speakers will threaten the primacy of the English language and that immigrants will take jobs away from native-born Americans.

    B.   Another central concern is the role of affirmative action. Liberals argue that this policy is the most direct way in which to level the playing field of economic opportunity, while conservatives believe that such practices result in reverse discrimination.

        1.   One of the most controversial rulings was *Proposition 209.* This amendment to the California state constitution banned preferences to minorities and women in hiring, promotion, and college admission.

        2.   A ruling by the court in a case about the University of Michigan admission process has continued to make this a challenging topic regarding the role of affirmative action

    C.   In order for the United States to become a multicultural society, people must respect differences and be willing to work together without any one group dominating others and racial categories need to be seen as an irrelevant system of categorization.

KEY TERMS

After studying the chapter, review the definition for each of the following terms.

assimilation: the process of being absorbed into the mainstream culture (348)

authoritarian personality: Theodor Adorno's term for people who are prejudiced and rank high on scales of conformity, intolerance, insecurity, respect for authority, and submissiveness to superiors (343)

compartmentalize: to separate acts from feelings or attitudes (347)

discrimination: an act of unfair treatment directed against an individual or a group (340)

dominant group: the group with the most power, greatest privileges, and highest social status (338)

ethnic cleansing: a policy of population elimination, including forcible expulsion and genocide (348)

ethnic work: activities designed to discover, enhance, or maintain ethnic and racial identification (339)

ethnicity (and ethnic): having distinctive cultural characteristics (335)

genocide: the systematic annihilation or attempted annihilation of people because of their presumed race or ethnic group (334)

individual discrimination: the negative treatment of one person by another on the basis of that person's perceived characteristics (341)

institutional discrimination: negative treatment of a minority group that is built into a society's institutions; also called *systemic discrimination* (341)

internal colonialism: the policy of economically exploiting a minority group (348)

melting pot: the view that Americans of various backgrounds would blend into a sort of ethnic stew (339)

minority group: people who are singled out for unequal treatment, and who regard themselves as objects of collective discrimination (338)

multiculturalism (also called pluralism): a philosophy or political policy that permits or encourages ethnic difference (348)

pan-Indianism: a movement that focuses on common elements in the cultures of Native Americans in order to develop a cross-tribal self-identity and to work toward the welfare of all Native Americans (364)

population transfer: forcing a minority group to move (347)

prejudice: an *attitude* or prejudging, usually in a negative way (340)

race: inherited physical characteristics that distinguish one group from another (334)

racism: prejudice and discrimination on the basis of race (340)

reserve labor force: the unemployed; unemployed workers who are thought of as being "in reserve"—capitalists take them "out of reserve" (put them back to work) during times of high production and lay them off (put them back in reserve) when they are no longer needed (344)

rising expectations: the sense that better conditions are soon to follow, which, when unfulfilled, increases frustration (357)

scapegoat: an individual or group unfairly blamed for someone else's troubles (343)

segregation: the policy of keeping racial or ethnic groups apart (348)

selective perception: seeing certain features of an object or situation, but remaining blind to others (345)

split-labor market: workers are split along racial, ethnic, gender, age or any other lines; this split is exploited by owners to weaken the bargaining power of workers (344)

WASP: a white Anglo-Saxon Protestant; narrowly, an American of English descent; broadly, an American of western European ancestry (351)

white ethnics: white immigrants to the United States whose culture differs from that of WASPs (351)

KEY PEOPLE
Review the major theoretical contributions or findings of these people.

Theodor Adorno: Adorno identified the authoritarian personality type. (343)

Kathleen Blee: Blee interviewed women who were members of the KKK and Aryan Nation and found that their racism was not the cause of their joining, but the result of their membership in those groups. (340)

Ashley Doane: Doane identified four factors that affect an individual's sense of ethnic identity. (339)

John Dollard: This psychologist first suggested that prejudice is the result of frustration, and that scapegoats become the targets for their frustration. (343)

Rapheal Ezekiel: This sociologist did participant observation of neo-Nazis and the Ku Klux Klan in order to examine racism from inside racist organizations. (341)

Anthony Greenwald and Mahzarin Banaji: These psychologists created the "Implicit Association Test". They found that we learn the ethnic maps of our culture and a route to biased perception. (340)

Eugene Hartley: His study found that prejudice does not depend on negative experiences with others. Those who are prejudice against racial-ethnic groups are likely prejudice against others. (340)

Douglas Massey: This sociologists conducted research with students on race and the real estate industry. He found that white students' experiences were significantly different from those of African-American students, with the latter less likely to get a call back from an agent, less likely to be told an apartment was available, and more likely to pay an application fee. (360)

Peggy McIntosh: Being white is a taken-for-granted background assumption of U.S. society. (352)

Ashley Montagu: This physical anthropologist pointed out that some scientists have classified humans into only two races while others have identified as many as two thousand. (335)

Alejandro Portes and Rueben Rumbaut: These sociologists looked at the impact that immigration has had on our country, pointing out that there has always been an anti-immigrant sentiment present. (365)

Muzafer and Carolyn Sherif: The Sherifs researched the functions of prejudice and found that it builds in-group solidarity. (344)

W. I. and Dorothy Thomas: The Thomases observed that once people define a situation as real, it is real in its consequences. (335)

William Wilson: Wilson is known for his work on racial discrimination, in which he argues that class is a more important factor than race in explaining patterns of inequality. (359)

Louis Wirth: Wirth offered a sociological definition of minority group. (338)

STUDENT APPLICATION PROJECTS

This is your opportunity to apply the sociological perspective to the world around you. The projects in this section refer to material introduced in this chapter of your text. These projects help you apply the sociological perspective "down to your earth...down to your daily life."

1. Does your family have a great sense of ethnicity? Why or why not? Do you engage in any activities (food, clothing, music, celebrations) that are related to your ethnic heritage? If so, explain. Overall, do you think more Americans are searching for their ethnic heritage? Why?

2. What are your thoughts about affirmative action in the workplace? What are the advantages and disadvantages?

3. Should race be a factor in college admissions? Why or why not? What do you think should be done to insure that everyone has equal educational opportunity in the United States? What should colleges base admissions on? Are grades and SAT or ACT tests good measures? What factors do you think should be important? Why?

SELF-TEST

MULTIPLE CHOICE QUESTIONS

1. Race: (334)
    a. means having distinctive cultural characteristics.
    b. means having inherited physical characteristics that distinguish one group from another.
    c. means people who are singled out for unequal treatment.
    d. is relatively easy to determine.

2. People often confuse race and ethnicity because: (334)
    a. they dislike people who are different from themselves.
    b. of the cultural differences people see and the way they define race.
    c. they are unaware of the fact that race is cultural and ethnicity is biological.
    d. all of the above.

3. A minority group: (338)
    a. is discriminated against because of physical or cultural differences.
    b. is discriminated against because of personality factors.
    c. does not always experience discrimination.
    d. all of the above.

4. To what does the dominant group in a society almost always consider its position to be due? (338)
    a. its own innate superiority
    b. its ability to oppress minority group members
    c. its ability to control political power
    d. all of the above

5. Which of the following factors affects a group's sense of ethnic identity? (339)
    a. the amount of power the group has
    b. the size of the group
    c. the degree to which the group's physical appearance differs from the mainstream
    d. all of the above

6. Many people today are tracing their family lines. This is an example of: (339)
    a. ethnic identity.
    b. ethnic enclaves.
    c. ethnic work.
    d. ethnic pride.

7. Which of the following is the best description of a melting pot? (339)
   a. a society in which groups quietly blend into a sort of ethnic stew
   b. a society in which each ethnicity maintains its distinctiveness
   c. a society where everyone adapts to the dominant group's ways
   d. none of the above

8. Prejudice and discrimination: (340)
   a. are less prevalent in the United States than in other societies.
   b. are more prevalent in the United States than in other societies.
   c. appear to characterize every society, regardless of size.
   d. appear to characterize only large societies.

9. Prejudice: (340)
   a. is an attitude.
   b. may be positive or negative.
   c. is often the basis for discrimination.
   d. all of the above.

10. From her interviews with women in the KKK and Aryan Nation, what did , Kathleen Blee conclude? (340)
    a. these women are basically ignorant people who want to stir up problems.
    b. these women did extensive research on the group prior to membership
    c. these women joined because it matched their racist beliefs
    d. racism was a result of membership in the group not the cause of joining the group

11. Discrimination that is woven into the fabric of society is refers to as: (341)
    a. cultural discrimination.
    b. societal discrimination.
    c. individual discrimination.
    d. institutional discrimination.

12. Negative treatment on the basis of personal characteristics is: (341)
    a. individual discrimination.
    b. individual prejudice.
    c. institutional discrimination.
    d. institutional prejudice.

13. What do the findings of research on patterns of mortgage lending confirm? (342)
    a. discrimination is the result of individual bankers' decisions.
    b. decisions to reject loans reflect sound banking practices.
    c. while African Americans and Latinos were rejected more often than whites, the rate was not significant.
    d. discrimination is built into the country's financial institutions.

14. According to John Dollard, what is the source of prejudice? (343)
    a. the authoritarian personality
    b. frustration
    c. a split-labor market
    d. selective perception

15. Why do functionalists consider prejudice functional for some groups? (344)
    a. it is a useful weapon in maintaining social divisions.
    b. it contributes to the creation of scapegoats.
    c. it helps to create solidarity within the group by fostering antagonisms directed against other groups.
    d. it affects how members of one group perceive members of other groups.

16. According to conflict theorists, prejudice: (344)
    a. benefits capitalists by splitting workers along racial or ethnic lines.
    b. contributes to the exploitation of workers, thus producing a split-labor market.
    c. keeps workers from demanding higher wages and better working conditions.
    d. all of the above.

17. Which sociological perspective stresses how labels create selective perception and self-fulfilling prophecies? (345)
    a. symbolic interactionism
    b. functionalism
    c. conflict perspective
    d. feminism

18. Genocide: (347)
    a. occurred when Hitler attempted to destroy all Jews.
    b. is the systematic annihilation of a race or ethnic group.
    c. often requires the cooperation of ordinary citizens.
    d. all of the above.

19. The process of expelling a minority from a country or a particular area is called: (347)
    a. population redistribution.
    b. direct population transfer.
    c. indirect population transfer.
    d. expelled population transfer.

20. A society's policy of exploiting a minority group, using social institutions to deny the minority access to the society's full benefits is referred to as: (348)
    a. segregation.
    b. pluralism.
    c. internal colonialism.
    d. genocide.

21. Separating people on the basis of their racial and ethnic identity and then maintaining social distance is know as (348)
    a. genocide.
    b. population transfer.
    c. ethnic cleansing.
    d. segregation.

22. The process of being absorbed into the mainstream culture is: (348)
    a. pluralism.
    b. assimilation.
    c. cultural submersion.
    d. internal colonialism.

23. What is the challenge in the U.S. when trying to classify people into racial-ethnic groups? (349)
    a. basic terms can be controversial
    b. racial terms might include some, but exclude other groups
    c. racial-ethnic identity is fluid
    d. all of the above

24. Which of the following statements about WASPs is *incorrect*? (351)
    a. they embraced whites from other European nations, helping them assimilate
    b. they took power and determined the national agenda, controlling the destiny of the nation
    c. the term refers to White Anglo-Saxon Protestants whose ancestors came from England
    d. they were highly ethnocentric and viewed other immigrants as inferior

25. According to your text, Latinos are distinguished from other ethnic minorities in the United States by: (352-355)
    a. the Spanish language.
    b. the fact that virtually all Latinos entered the United States illegally.
    c. the short length of time Latinos have been in the United States.
    d. all of the above.

26. According to William Wilson, what was it that created new opportunities for middle-class African Americans to move up the social class ladder? (359)
    a. economic prosperity
    b. organized religion
    c. civil rights legislation
    d. technological advances

27. Which of the following statements about reparations is *incorrect*? (359)
   a. It is widely accepted that blacks deserve compensation for slavery, the only disagreement is what form that compensation should take.
   b. It has been argued that the greater wealth of today's white Americans is built on centuries of unpaid labor of black slaves.
   c. Reparations are a form of back wages.
   d. Most of today's white population descended from people who immigrated to the U.S. after slavery ended and therefore had nothing to do with slavery.

28. Which of the following statements about the experiences of Asian Americans is *incorrect*? (360-362)
   a. Much of the hostility directed toward Japanese Americans was due to Pearl Harbor.
   b. Asian Americans are becoming more prominent in politics.
   c. The view that Asian Americans have been successful in this country is basically correct.
   d. Most Asian Americans grow up in tight-knit families.

29. The overarching issue for minorities is overcoming _____. (364)
   a. discrimination
   b. poverty
   c. assimilation
   d. ethnic work

30. What is a difference between the earlier wave of immigration at the turn of the last century and the current wave? (365)
   a. the current wave is much smaller.
   b. the current wave is more global in content.
   c. the current wave is experiencing a more welcoming environment.
   d. all of the above.

TRUE-FALSE QUESTIONS

1. _____Scientists generally agree on just how many races there are in the world. (334)
2. _____Sociologists often use the terms race and ethnicity interchangeably. (334)
3. _____Either physical or cultural differences can be a basis of unequal treatment in societies. (334)
4. _____Groups are determined a minority based on the percentage of the population they represent. (338)
5. _____Sociologists believe that race depends on biological characteristics (343)
6. _____Discrimination is an attitude, and prejudice is an action. (340)
7. _____Prejudice is so extensive that people can show prejudice against groups that don't even exist. (340)
8. _____Ethnic work depends on the degree to which an individual has an ethnic identity. (339)

9. _____Some members of minority groups internalize the dominant norms and show prejudice against their own group. (340)
10. _____Sociological theories of prejudice stress the authoritarian personality and frustration displaced toward scapegoats. (343)
11. _____Sociologists believe that individual discrimination is an adequate explanation for discrimination in the United States. (343)
12. _____Research shows that African Americans and Latinos are 60 percent more likely than whites to be rejected for mortgages, all other factors being similar. (342)
13. _____According to research, even mild levels of frustration can lead to higher levels of prejudice. (343)
14. _____Adorno's research suggests that people of lower social class are more likely to be authoritarian. (343)
15. _____Functionalists focus on the role of the capitalist class in exploiting racism and ethnic inequalities. (337)
16. _____Symbolic interactionists stress that the labels we use encourage us to see things selectively. (345)
17. _____Genocide often relies on labeling and compartmentalization. (347)
18. _____Segregation allows the dominant group to exploit the labor of the minority while maintaining social distance. (348)
19. _____Asian Americans are referred to as the invisible minority in America. (362)
20. _____Affirmative action has worked exceptionally well in the U.S. (365)

FILL-IN-THE-BLANK QUESTIONS

1. The mapping of the human genome systems shows that humans are strikingly _____. (334)
2. _____ is both a reality and a myth. (334)
3. _____ are singled out for unequal treatment and regard themselves as objects of collective discrimination. (338)
4. We can use the term _____ to refer to the way people construct their ethnicity. (339)
5. Many analysts are using the term _____ rather than melting pot when referring to the American ethnic experience. (339)
6. In her research on women who joined organizations like the KKK and the Aryan Nation, Blee found that their intense racism was not the cause of their joining, but the _____ of their membership. (340)
7. Discrimination does not have to be _____. (342)
8. Gender and _____ also provide common bases for scapegoating. (343)
9. According to the text, last century's two most notorious examples of genocide occurred in Germany and _____. (347)
10. _____ are the largest minority group in the United States. (350)
11. African-Americans have _____ their membership in the U.S. House of Representatives in the past 30 years. (357)
12. _____ experienced spillover bigotry when they immigrated to the U.S. (361)
13. Native Americans can truly be called the _____. (362)

14. A highly controversial issue among Native Americans is _____. (363)
15. _____in the state of California challenged affirmative action. (365)

MATCH THESE SOCIAL SCIENTISTS WITH THEIR CONTRIBUTIONS

_____	1. Theodor Adorno	a.	*measured racial attitudes of white students*
_____	2. Ashley Doane	b.	*argues that class is more important than race in explaining inequality*
_____	3. John Dollard	c.	*observed that defining a situation as real, makes it real in its consequences*
_____	4. Raphael Ezekiel	d.	*identified the authoritarian personality type*
_____	5. Louis Wirth	e.	*people can be prejudiced against people that they have never met*
_____	6. William Gray	f.	*identified four factors that affect an individual's sense of ethnic identity*
_____	7. Donald Muir	g.	*suggested that prejudice is the result of frustration*
_____	8. William Wilson	h.	*self-segregation on college campuses*
_____	9. Eugene Hartley	i.	*offered a sociological definition of minority group*
_____	10. W. I. Thomas	j.	*studied racism in neo-Nazis and KKK organizations*

ESSAY QUESTIONS

1. Explain how race and ethnicity differ.

2. Using the experiences of different racial and ethnic groups in the United States, identify and discuss the six patterns of intergroup relations.

3. Explore how both psychological and sociological theories can be used together to gain a deeper understanding of prejudice and discrimination.

4. Discuss the difference between individual and institutional discrimination and give examples of both.

5. What would have to change in our society in order for us to truly be a multicultural society?

CHAPTER 13
THE ELDERLY

CHAPTER SUMMARY

- There are no universal attitudes, beliefs or policies regarding the aged; they range from exclusion and killing to integration and honor. Today there is a trend for people to live longer. Attitudes toward the elderly are rooted in society and differ from one social group to another.

- Industrialization is a worldwide trend. As countries industrialize, more of its people are able to live longer and reach old age. This is known as the graying of the globe. All countries will face issues regarding care of the elderly.

- In the United States, the rising proportion of older people in the population is referred to as the "graying of America." Because of this trend, the cost of health care for the elderly has become a social issue, and sentiment about the elderly seems to be shifting.

- The symbolic interaction perspective identifies four factors that influence when people label themselves as "old": biological changes, biographical events, gender age, and cultural timetables. Culture is important in determining how individuals experience aging. Ageism is based on stereotypes that are influenced by the mass media.

- The functional perspective analyzes the withdrawal of the elderly from positions of responsibility. Disengagement, activity, and continuity theories are functional theories of how people adjust to growing old.

- Conflict theorists study the competition for scarce resources by rival interest groups (e.g., how different age cohorts may be on a collision course regarding Social Security, Medicare, and Medicaid).

- Elderly women are most likely to be alone and to be poor. About 5 percent of the elderly live in nursing homes. Problems of dependency for the elderly include inadequate and understaffed nursing homes, elder abuse, and poverty. Poverty in old age has been greatly reduced through government programs.

- Industrialization has changed the individual's experience with death. The process of dying involves denial, anger, negotiation, depression, and acceptance. Hospices, a recent cultural device, are intended to provide dignity in death, to reduce the emotional and physical burden on relatives, to reduce costs, and to make people comfortable during the living-dying interval. Suicide increases with age and shows sharply different patterns by sex and race.

- With technological advances, it may be possible to increase the human life span. It is possible that as body parts wear out, they will simply be replaced. There are many questions that could be asked regarding what society would be like if citizens lived to 150 or 200 years old.

LEARNING OBJECTIVES
After reading Chapter 13, you should be able to:

1. Understand what is meant by the "social construction of aging" and how it affects the way societies define and treat their elderly members. (372)
2. Explain the effects of industrialization on life expectancy, population demographics, and the distribution of resources. (372-373)
3. Describe and illustrate the "graying of America." (374-376)
4. Understand the regional, gender, racial, and ethnic differences of aging in the United States. (374-376)
5. Understand the global perspective of life expectancy in various countries of the world. (375)
6. Describe the various components of the symbolic interactionist perspective on aging, how it has changed over time, and the influence that the mass media plays. (376-378)
7. Describe the functionalist perspective on aging and the theories put forth about people's adjustment to aging which includes disengagement theory, activity theory, and continuity theory. (380-382)
8. Describe the conflict perspective on aging and some of the controversy surrounding these issues including social security and health care costs. (382-387)
9. Know the major organizations in the United States that protect and promote the political interests of the elderly. (387)
10. Describe and discuss some of the problems that many elderly people in the United States encounter, including social isolation and understaffed nursing homes. (388-392)
11. Describe the role that technology can play in nursing homes. (388-391)
12. Understand elder abuse and poverty among the elder including the role of gender and ethnicity. (391-392)
13. Know how industrialization and medical advances have affecting the sociology of death and dying in the United States. (392)
14. Identify the five stages of death that people go through when dying. (393)
15. Talk about how hospices protect the health and interests of elderly people in the United States, as well as humanize the processes of death and dying. (393)
16. Describe some of the social factors that may affect elderly suicide rates in the United States. (394)
17. Describe how adjustment to death is different for expected vs. unexpected deaths. (394)
18. Discuss the affect of technological breakthroughs on increasing the life span of humans. (395-396)

CHAPTER OUTLINE

I. Aging in Global Perspective

A. Every society must deal with the problem of people growing old; as the proportion of the population that is old increases, those decisions become more complex and the tensions between the generations grow deeper.

B. How a society views the aged and attitudes about aging are socially constructed; thus, the aging process depends on culture, not on biology.

    1. The Tiwi got rid of the old, decrepit females in their society by "covering them up". That is, they dug a hole, put the old woman in the hole, and covered her with dirt all the way with only her head showing. Returning in a day or two they found that she had died.

    2. The Abkasians, on the other hand, pay high respects to their elderly. They may be the longest-living people in the world, with many claiming to live past 100.

    3. The main factors that appear to account for their long lives are diet, lifelong physical activity, and a highly developed sense of community.

C. As a country industrializes, more of its people reach older ages.

    1. This reflects the higher standard of living, better public health measures, and successes in fighting deadly diseases.

    2. As the proportion of elderly increases, so does the bill that younger citizens must pay in order to provide for their needs. Among industrialized nations, this bill has become a major social issue. In the Least Industrialized Nations, families are expected to take care of their own elderly, with no help from the government.

D. In the United States, the "graying of America" refers to the proportion of older people in the U.S. population.

    1. Today, almost 13 percent of the population has achieved age 65; there are almost seven million more elderly Americans than teenagers.

    2. Because the proportion of non-whites in the United States is growing, the number of minority elderly is also increasing; differences in cultural attitudes about aging, types of family relationships, work histories, and health practices will be important areas of sociological investigation in the coming years.

    3. While life expectancy (the number of years that an average person at any age, including newborns, can expect to live) has increased, the life span (maximum length of life) has not.

    4. Life expectancy is highest in the most industrialized countries and lowest in developing countries.

II. The Symbolic Interactionist Perspective

A. There are several factors that push people to apply the label of "old".

    1. Biology changes how a person looks and feels; the person adopts the role of "old" (acts the way old people are thought to act) on experiencing these changes.

    2. Personal history (an injury that limits mobility) or biography (becoming a grandmother at an early age) may affect self-concept regarding age.

    3. Gender age also plays a part. The relative value that culture places on men's ages is less than that of women's ages.

4. When a particular society defines a person as "old," the person is likely to feel "old." These timetables are not fixed; groups sometimes adjust expectations about the onset of old age.

B. Aging is relative; when it begins and what it means varies from culture to culture.
1. For the traditional Native American, the signal for old age is more often the inability to perform productive social roles rather than any particular birthday.
2. The Tiwi tribe is a gerontocracy (a society run by the elderly) where older men are so entrenched in power that they control all of the wealth and all of the women.
3. To grow old in traditional Eskimo society meant voluntary death. Eskimo society was so precarious that a person no longer able to pull his or her own weight was expected to simply go off and die.

C. Robert Butler coined the term ageism to refer to prejudice, discrimination, and hostility directed at people because of their age.
1. With the coming of industrialization, the traditional bases of respect for the elderly eroded. The distinctiveness of age was lost and new ideas of morality made the opinions of the elderly outmoded. The meaning of old age was transformed—from usefulness to uselessness, from wisdom to foolishness, from an asset to a liability.
2. The meaning of old age is being transformed with the increasing wealth of the U.S. elderly and the coming of age of the Baby Boom generation. The Baby Boom generation, given their vast numbers and economic clout, are likely to positively affect our images of the elderly.
3. The mass media communicates messages about the aged, influencing our ideas about the elderly.

III. The Functionalist Perspective
A. Functionalists examine age from the standpoint of how those people who are retiring and those who will replace them in the work force make mutual adjustments.
B. Elaine Cumming and William Henry developed disengagement theory to explain how society prevents disruption to society when the elderly retire.
1. The elderly are rewarded in some way (pensions) for giving up positions rather than waiting until they become incompetent or die; this allows for a smooth transition of positions.
2. For many, disengagement begins during middle age, long before retirement. While not immediately disengaging, the individual begins to assign priority to certain goals and tasks.
3. This theory is criticized because it assumes that the elderly disengage and then sink into oblivion.
4. Dorothy Jerrome, a critic of disengagement theory, found in her research that the elderly exchange one set of roles for another; the new roles, which center around friendship, are no less satisfying than the earlier roles.
5. The nature of retirement has also been changing; more often, workers slow down rather than simply stop working. Many never "retire" but simply cut back.
C. According to activity theory older people who maintain a high level of activity tend to be more satisfied with life than those who do not.

     1.   Most research findings support the hypothesis that more active people are more satisfied people.

     2.   Contradictory findings from a number of different studies suggest that counting the number of activities is too simplistic. Rather, researchers need to take into account what activities mean to people.

  D. Continuity theory focuses on how people continue their roles in order to adjust to change. Over the course of our lives, we develop various strategies for coping with life. When confronted with old age, people continue to use these coping strategies.

     1.   People from higher social classes have greater resources to cope with the challenges of old age, and consequently adjust better.

     2.   People who have multiple roles—wife, mother, worker, friend—are better equipped to handle the loss of a role than are people who do not.

     3.   Critics claim that this theory is too broad; it is seen as a collection of loosely connected ideas with no specific application to the elderly.

IV. The Conflict Perspective

  A. Conflict theorists examine social life as a struggle between groups for scarce resources. Social Security legislation is an example of that struggle.

     1.   In the 1920s and 1930s, two-thirds of all citizens over 65 had no savings and could not support themselves. Francis Townsend enrolled one-third of all Americans over 65 in clubs that sought a national sales tax to finance a monthly pension for all Americans over age 65. To avoid supporting the plan without appearing to be opposed to old-age pensions, Social Security was enacted by Congress.

     2.   Initially the legislation required workers to retire at 65. But for decades, the elderly protested this ruling. Finally, in 1986, Congress eliminated mandatory retirement. Today, almost 90 percent of Americans retire by age 65, but they do so voluntarily.

     3.   Conflict theorists state that Social Security was not a result of generosity, but rather of competition among interest groups.

  B. Since equilibrium is only a temporary balancing of social forces, some form of continuing conflict between the younger and the older appears inevitable.

     1.   The huge costs of Social Security have become a national concern. Conflict is inevitable, as proportionately fewer working people are forced to pay for the benefits received by an increasing number of senior citizens.

     2.   The poverty rate for the elderly has decreased and is less than the national average. The success of social security has contributed to this. Additionally, those 65 and older have the highest standard of living compared to any time in U.S. history.

     3.   Some argue that the needs of the elderly and children are on a collision course. Data indicate that as the number of elderly poor decreased, children in poverty increased. Also, the medical costs for the elderly have soared and some fear that health care for children will be shortchanged. It has been argued that the comparison is misleading because the money that went to the elderly did not come from money intended for the children. Framing the issue in this way is an

attempt to divide the working class and to force a choice between children in poverty and elderly.

C.	Empowering the elderly, some organizations today work to protect the gains the elderly have achieved over the years.

1.	The Gray Panthers was organized in the 1960s to encourage people of all ages to work for the welfare of both the elderly and the young. On the micro level, the goal is to develop positive self-concepts; on the macro level, the goal is to build a power base with which to challenge all institutions that oppress the poor, young and old alike.

2.	To protect their gains, older Americans organized the American Association of Retired Persons, with 35 million members. This association monitors proposed federal and state legislation and mobilizes its members to act on issues affecting their welfare.

## V.	Recurring Problems

A.	While the elderly are not as isolated as stereotypes would lead us to believe, there are differences between men and women. Women are especially likely to be isolated. Because of differences in mortality, most older males (71 percent) are married and live with their wives, while most older women do not (only 41 percent live with husbands).

1.	What this means is that women are much more likely to take care of frail husbands than husbands are to care for frail wives.

2.	Most patients in nursing homes are women.

B.	About 5 percent of Americans over 65 are in nursing homes at any one time; about one-half of elderly women and one-third of elderly men will spend some time in a nursing home.

1.	Nursing home residents are likely to be quite ill, over 85, widowed or never married and thus have no family to take care of them. Over 90 percent are in wheelchairs or use walkers.

2.	The quality of care varies, but even the better ones tend to strip away human dignity.

3.	Researchers have found that in nursing homes that are understaffed, the patients are more likely to have bedsores, be malnourished, underweight and dehydrated. Ninety percent of nursing homes are understaffed. Anywhere from 40 to 100 percent of nursing home staff quit each year.

4.	Compared with the elderly who have similar conditions and remain in the community, those who are placed in nursing homes tend to get sicker and to die sooner.

5.	Continuing to be active socially, including using computers and the Internet to connect with family and friends, helps the elderly overcome problems of isolation, depression and anomie.

6.	A new model in which the elderly are able to be in more home-like settings, can take care of themselves somewhat, and interact with staff and other residents has showed more positive results.

C.	Elder abuse is a significant problem. Most abusers are members of the elderly person's family. Some researchers say the abuse occurs when an individual feels obligated to take care of a person who is highly dependent and demanding, which can be very stressful.

D. A major fear of the elderly is that their money may not last as long as their life does.
   1. Women are about 60 percent more likely than men to be poor.
   2. Elderly African Americans and Latinos are two to three times as likely as whites to be poor.
   3. As a result of governmental programs, the elderly now are less likely than the average American to be poor.

VI. The Sociology of Death and Dying

A. In preindustrial societies, the sick were cared for and died at home. With the coming of modern medicine, dying was transformed into an event to be managed by professionals; most people never have personally seen anyone die.
   1. The process of dying has become strange to most people; we hide from the fact of death, we even construct a language of avoidance (e.g., a person is "gone" or "at peace now," rather than dead).
   2. New technology has produced "technological life." This is neither life nor death; the person is brain dead, but the body lives on.

B. Elisabeth Kübler-Ross identified the stages a person passes through when told that she or he has an incurable disease: (1) denial; (2) anger; (3) negotiation; (4) depression; and (5) acceptance. Kübler-Ross noted that not everyone experiences all of these stages and not everyone goes through them in order.

C. Elderly persons want to die with dignity in the comforting presence of friends and relatives. Due to advances in medical technology, most deaths in the U.S. occur after the age of 65.
   1. Hospitals are awkward places to die, surrounded by strangers in hospital garb in an organization that puts routine ahead of individual needs. Patients experience what sociologists call "institutional death."
   2. Hospices have emerged as a solution to these problems, providing greater dignity and comfort at less cost.
   3. Hospitals are dedicated to prolonging life, while hospices are dedicated to providing dignity in death and making people comfortable in the living-dying interval—that period of time between discovering that death is imminent and death itself.

D. Suicide has a social base. The overall rate remains about the same, as does the method. Males are more likely to take their lives than females. Suicides by young people receive a lot of publicity, but such deaths are in fact relatively rare. The suicide rate for young people is lower than that of all other groups.
   1. The highest suicide rate is for those age 85 and over.

E. When adjusting to death, family members may experience conflicting feelings. Adjusting to death can take anywhere between one to two years.
   1. When death is expected, family members find it less stressful. because they have been able to say their goodbyes to their loved one.
   2. Unexpected deaths bring greater shock because there was no opportunity to say goodbye or bring closure to the relationship.

VII. Looking Toward the Future
   A.   Biomedical science is exploring ways of stretching the human life span, enabling people to live longer and longer lives.
   B.   If this happens, it will raise all sorts of questions. How will these elderly contribute to society? How will society be able to support them? How will the life course be redefined to take into consideration the expansion of life? What will it mean to be elderly?

KEY TERMS
After studying the chapter, review the definition for each of the following terms.

activity theory: the view that satisfaction during old age is related to a person's amount and quality of activity (381)

age cohort: people born at roughly the same time who pass through the life course together (380)

ageism: prejudice, discrimination, and hostility directed against people because of their age; can be directed against any age group, including youth (377)

continuity theory: the focus on this theory is how people adjust to retirement by continuing aspects of their earlier lives (382)

dependency ratio: the number of workers required to support dependent persons—those 65 and older and those 15 and younger (385)

disengagement theory: the view that society prevents disruption by having the elderly vacate (or disengage from) their positions of responsibility so that the younger generation can step into their shoes (381)

gender age: the relative value placed on men's and women's ages (377)

graying of America: refers to the growing percentage of older people in the U.S. population (374)

hospice: a place (or services brought into someone's home) for the purpose of giving comfort and dignity to a dying person (393)

life expectancy: the number of years that an average person at any age, including newborns, can expect to live (374)

life span: the maximum length of life of a species; for human, the longest that a human has lived (376)

KEY PEOPLE
Review the major theoretical contributions or findings of these people.

Robert Butler: Butler coined the term "ageism" to refer to prejudice, discrimination, and hostility directed against people because of their age. (377)

Elaine Cumming and William Henry: These two developed disengagement theory to explain how society prevents disruption when the elderly vacate their positions of responsibility. (381)

Charles Hart: This anthropology graduate student carried out research on the Tiwi, a gerontocracy. (371-372)

Dorothy Jerrome: This anthropologist is critical of disengagement theory. She pointed out the implicit bias that exists when the elderly give up productive roles in society and slip into oblivion. (381)

Elisabeth Kübler-Ross: This psychologist found that coming face-to-face with one's own death sets in motion a five-stage process. (392)

Margaret Kuhn: Founded the Gray Panthers in 1970. This organization encourages all people to work for the welfare of the young and old. (387)

Meredith Minkler and Ann Robertson: Conflict sociologists who believe that the costs for services for the elderly do not have to come at the expense of children. The government can support both of these groups to relieve poverty. (387)

Karl Pillemer and Jill Suitor: These sociologists interviewed more than 200 caregivers of Alzheimer patients and found that the precipitating cause of elder abuse is stress from caring for a person who is dependent, demanding, and even violent. (391)

Alan Simpson: A senator who called the elderly "greedy geezers" who demand government handouts while "teeing off near their second homes in Florida". (384)

STUDENT APPLICATION PROJECTS

This is your opportunity to apply the sociological perspective to the world around you. The projects in this section refer to material introduced in this chapter of your text. These projects help you apply the sociological perspective "down to your earth...down to your daily life."

1. After reading about the Social Security system, list some of the problems with the current system. What do you think of the proposed recommendations for solving the crisis? Would you support them? Why or why not?

2. In this chapter you read about how the media shapes our image(s) of older people. Think about some of the people you know who are over 60 years of age. How does the reality of their lives fit with the images of older people that are presented in movies, advertisements, and television? Explain and compare.

3. What kind of life do you hope to have when you reach your senior years? Given the current conditions, what societal changes would need to take place for you to achieve your goals?

4. How will the given advances in technology, over the next 50 years, impact aging and the perception of the elderly in our society? What are the positive and negative aspects of these technological changes on aging?

SELF-TEST

MULTIPLE CHOICE QUESTIONS

1. The Abkhasians present an interesting example regarding aging because they: (372)
    a. live such short lives.
    b. live such long lives.
    c. have so many words in their language for "old people."
    d. quit working when they are quite young.

2. In 2000, what percentage of Americans were age 65 or older? (372-373)
    a. 5.5
    b. 12.4
    c. 18.7
    d. 22

3. The process by which older persons make up an increasing proportion of the United States' population is referred to as: (374)
    a. the aging process.
    b. the graying of America.
    c. the gentrification process.
    d. none of the above.

4. The number of years a person is likely to live is referred to as: (374)
    a. life span.
    b. life course.
    c. life expectancy.
    d. life history.

5. The relative value that a culture places on men's and women's ages is: (377)
    a. cultural aging.
    b. ageism.
    c. gender age.
    d. relative age.

6. Factors that may push people to apply the label of old to themselves include: (377)
    a. personal history or biography.
    b. cultural signals about when a person is old.
    c. biological factors.
    d. all of the above.

7. A society that is run by the elderly is called a(n): (378)
    a. elder state.
    b. meritocracy.
    c. gerontocracy.
    d. eldertocracy.

8. Which theoretical perspective claims that industrialization eroded the respect that the elderly used to receive? (378)
    a. symbolic interactionism
    b. functionalist
    c. conflict
    d. Sapir-Whorf

9. It has been suggested that _____ will have a positive effect on U.S. social images of the elderly in the years to come, given their numbers and economic clout. (378)
    a. Congress
    b. the Baby Boom generation
    c. Generation X
    d. seniors living on Social Security

10. The example of China demonstrates that: (379)
    a. there is changing sentiment about the elderly due to the effects of industrialization.
    b. increasing life span is tearing at the bonds between generations.
    c. the high status of the elderly is slowly being challenged.
    d. all of the above.

11. Some researchers believe that the process of disengagement begins: (381)
    a. when a person first starts a job.
    b. during middle age.
    c. at retirement.
    d. about one year after retirement.

12. The mass media: (378)
    a. communicate messages that reflect the currently devalued status of the elderly.
    b. tell us what people over 65 should be like.
    c. often treat the elderly in discourteous and unflattering terms.
    d. all of the above.

13. Which theory assumes that the more activities elderly people engage in, the more satisfying they find life? (381)
    a. disengagement theory
    b. activity theory
    c. continuity theory
    d. conflict theory

14. Continuity theory has been criticized because: (382)
    a. it is too broad.
    b. it is really just a collection of loosely connected ideas.
    c. it has no specific application to the elderly.
    d. all of the above.

15. Conflict theorists believe that retirement benefits are the result of: (382)
    a. generous hearts in Congress.
    b. a struggle between competing interest groups.
    c. many years of hard work by elderly Americans.
    d. none of the above.

16. Which aspect of the original Social Security legislation was challenged by the elderly for many years following its passage in 1934? (382)
    a. mandatory retirement at age 65
    b. survivor payments to orphaned children
    c. lack of coverage for nonworking spouses
    d. payments tied to income

17. As the population of the U.S. grays, there is concern that: (384)
    a. participation in the electoral process will decline because older citizens are less likely to vote.
    b. the ratio of working people to retired people will become smaller, making it more difficult to support programs like Social Security.
    c. there will be a shortage of affordable housing for widowed individuals living on a fixed income.
    d. all of the above.

18. Which of the following is *not* a problem associated with Social Security today? (385)
    a. The cash payments senior citizens receive are not tied to the money they invested in the fund.
    b. The money collected from workers for Social Security is used by the government to cover general operating expenses.
    c. The number of workers who pay into Social Security is shrinking while the number of retired who collect from Social Security is growing.
    d. Low payments have contributed to an increase in elderly poverty.

19. What is the goal of the Gray Panthers? (387)
    a. To protect the interests of the elderly at the expense of other age groups.
    b. To work for the welfare of both the old and the young.
    c. To win special concessions for senior citizens.
    d. The closure of nursing homes.

20. Isolation is a problem for many people over 65, especially for: (388)
    a. women.
    b. minorities.
    c. the disabled.
    d. immigrants.

21. Nursing homes: (388)
    a. are very expensive.
    b. have residents who are likely to be widowed or never married.
    c. tend to strip away human dignity.
    d. all of the above.

22. What percent of nursing homes are understaffed? (389)
    a. 20%
    b. 52%
    c. 74%
    d. 90%

23. Researchers have found that elder abuse: (391)
    a. occurs less frequently than one might think, given the level of abuse shown in the media.
    b. is fairly extensive.
    c. is most often caused by workers in nursing homes.
    d. is easy to study because the victims are so visible.

24. Who is most likely to abuse an elderly person? (391)
    a. nursing home staff
    b. paid caretakers in the elderly person's home
    c. an elderly person's spouse
    d. an elderly person's son- or daughter-in-law

25. Who is more likely to be poor? (392)
    a. elderly men
    b. elderly women
    c. white Americans
    d. single men

26. In what way(s) did industrialization alter the circumstances of dying? (392)
    a. Death is physically less painful today than in the past because of modern medicines.
    b. Death is emotionally easier for us to accept because we know more about the diseases that can kill us.
    c. Death has been transformed into an event that is managed by professionals in hospitals.
    d. Death is no longer feared because of greater scientific knowledge and new technologies.

27. What is the term to describe a form of existence that is neither life nor death—the brain is dead but the body lives on. (393)
    a. institutional death
    b. technological life
    c. technological fix
    d. living death

28. In preindustrial societies, the sick: (393)
    a. were taken care of at home.
    b. were taken care of in hospitals.
    c. were taken care of in hospices.
    d. did not live long enough to have to be taken care of by anyone.

29. Which of the following is not one of the 5 stages a person typically pass through on their way to dying, according to Elisabeth Kübler-Ross? (393)
    a. denial
    b. negotiation
    c. conformity
    d. acceptance

30. What is the term used initially to describe a place where a person can find comfort and dignity in dying, but later broadened to include services brought to one's home? (393)
    a. hospital outreach
    b. church
    c. hospice
    d. mobile health care

TRUE-FALSE QUESTIONS

1. _____When sociologists say that aging is socially constructed, what they mean is that attitudes about aging reflect cultural values rather than biological factors. (372)
2. _____Two-thirds of all people who have ever lived past age 50 in the history of the world are alive today. (373)
3. _____Today in the United States there are seven million more elderly Americans than there are teenagers. (374)
4. _____Life expectancy and life span describe the same thing. (374)
5. _____According to the symbolic interactionists, a person's perceptions of "old" and what it means to be old are influenced by stereotypes and societal definitions of age. (376)
6. _____ _____A gerontocracy is a society run by younger people on behalf of the elderly. (377)
7. _____In comparison to the colonial period in U.S. history, views about old age are much more positive today. (378)
8. _____In the United States today, the elderly are underrepresented on TV, in ads, and even in popular magazines. (381)
9. That older male news anchors are likely to be retained by news stations while female anchors of the same age are more likely to be transferred to less visible positions is an example of gender age. (381)
10. _____Disengagement theory is used to explain how society prevents disruption by having the elderly vacate their positions of responsibility. (381)
11. _____Dorothy Jerrome has suggested that the elderly do not disengage from productive social roles, but rather exchange one set of roles for another. (381)

12. _____Activity theorists believe that older people who maintain a high level of activity tend to be more satisfied with life than those who do not. (381)
13. _____According to conflict theorists, the passage of social security legislation is an example of the struggle between the young and old in society. (383)
14. _____Social security payments are currently running more than 700 times higher than they were in 1950. (384)
15. _____The AARP is a politically powerful organization. (387)
16. _____Elderly men are more likely to experience the isolation that widowhood brings. (388)
17. _____The elderly will exhibit gender roles that they learned in their younger years and carry those into old age. (389)
18. _____Elder abuse includes financial exploitation. (389)
19. _____America's elderly are more likely than the average American to live in poverty. (392)
20. _____Anger is the first stage in the death process. (393)

FILL-IN-THE-BLANK QUESTIONS

1. The _____ may be the longest living people in the world. (372)
2. _____ countries have the highest percentage of elderly. (372)
3. The _____ refers to the increasing percentage of older people in the U.S. population. (374)
4. _____ is the relative value that a culture places on men's and women's ages. (377)
5. _____ refers to prejudice, discrimination, and hostility directed against people because of their age. (378)
6. People who are born at roughly the same time and who pass through the life course together are referred to as _____. (379)
7. Activity theory assumes that the _____ activities elderly people engage in, the more likely they find life satisfying. (381)
8. The major criticism of continuity theory is that it is too _____. (382)
9. The original social security legislation required that people retire at age _____. (383)
10. One suggested proposal to solve the social security problem is to raise the retirement age to age _____. (385)
11. The _____ were founded by Margaret Kuhn in 1970. (387)
12. Most elderly are cared for by _____. (388)
13. Today's elderly are _____ likely than the average American to be poor. (392)
14. The last stage in the death process is _____. (393)
15. _____ may be able to stretch the human life span. (396)

MATCH THESE SOCIAL SCIENTISTS WITH THEIR CONTRIBUTIONS

_____ 1. Robert Butler   a. *founder of Gray Panthers*

_____ 2. Dorothy Jerrome   b. *found no evidence that the elderly gained at children's expense*

_____ 3. E. Kübler-Ross   c. *in two decades half of the population of Italy and Japan will be older than 50s*

_____ 4. Cerulo & Ruane   d. *carried out anthropological studies of the Tiwi*

_____ 5. Cumming & Henry   e. *elder abuse and Alzheimer patients*

_____ 6. Robertson & Minkler   f. *suggested that facing death sets in motion a five-stage process*

_____ 7. Pillemer & Suitor   g. *criticized disengagement theory for its implicit bias against the old*

_____ 8. Kinsella and Phillips   h. *coined "ageism" to refer to prejudice or discrimination based on age*

_____ 9. Maggie Kuhn   i. *use the term "technological lifespace" for life sustained by technology*

_____ 10. Charles Hart   j. *developed disengagement theory*

ESSAY QUESTIONS

1. Explain why sociologists say that aging is socially constructed.

2. Choose one of the three different perspectives and discuss how that perspective approaches the subject of aging. Consider both the strengths and weaknesses of the perspective you chose.

3. Discuss the impact that industrialization and technology has had on aging and dying.

4. People who come here from other parts of the world are often very critical of families that place their elderly family members in nursing homes. Assume that a friend of yours who comes from another part of the world asks you about your family's decision to move your grandparent into a nursing home. Develop an explanation that draws on the material presented in this chapter.

5. Discuss the five stages of death and what is being done to humanize the process of death and dying.

CHAPTER 14
THE ECONOMY

CHAPTER SUMMARY

- The earliest hunting and gathering societies were characterized by subsistence economies; economic systems became more complex as people discovered first how to domesticate and cultivate (horticultural and pastoral societies), then to farm (agricultural societies) and finally to manufacture (industrial societies). Currently we are in a postindustrial society and with the merger of biology and economics we may be on the verge of the emergence of biotech societies.

- In the least complex societies, people exchanged goods and services through barter. As societies and economies evolved, certain items were assigned uniform value and became the medium of exchange. Today we rely increasingly on electronic transfer of funds with credit, debit cards, and e-cash.

- The two major economic systems are capitalism, in which the means of production are privately owned, and socialism, in which the means of production are state owned. There are different forms of both capitalism (laissez-faire capitalism and welfare capitalism) and socialism (democratic socialism). In recent years each system has adopted features of the other.

- Functionalists state that work is a fundamental source of social solidarity; preindustrial societies foster mechanical solidarity while industrial societies, with their more complex division of labor, are characterized by organic solidarity. This process has continued and we are now developing a global division of labor.

- Conflict theorists focus on power, noting how global capitalism affects workers and owners. Corporations dominate modern capitalism; an inner circle—a group of leaders from the major corporations—are mutually interested in making certain that corporate capitalism is protected. The sociological significance of global capitalism is that the interests of the inner circle extend beyond national boundaries. Workers lose jobs, while the inner circle maintains its power and profits.

- Almost everyone today works in service jobs. A quiet revolution has occurred due to the dramatic increase in the number of married women who work for pay. The underground economy, economic activity that is not reported to the government, runs perhaps 10 to 15 percent of the regular economy. Initially, the amount of leisure time decreased as the economy changed from preindustrial to industrial; with unionization, workers gained back some of their leisure time. Workers in the U.S. work more hours per week than do workers of any other industrialized nation.

- Work will continue to be restructured as a result of downsizing, new technologies, and the expansion of global capitalism. Increased economic inequality between the rich and poor nations is possible. Lower level workers may face challenges as a result of downsizing and restructuring.

LEARNING OBJECTIVES
After reading Chapter 14, you should be able to:

1. Trace the transformation of economic systems through the evolutionary history of human society and, for each society, discuss the different levels of—and reasons for—social inequality. (400-401)
2. Discuss how the industrialization of society to its modern form impacts an individual's life (401)
3. Know what is meant by the "medium of exchange;" describe how it has evolved along with economic systems and explain how it reflects and contributes to a country's development. (403)
4. Describe the basic components of capitalism; differentiate between laissez-faire capitalism and welfare capitalism; understand how and why welfare capitalism developed in the United States. (405-406)
5. Identify the basic component of socialism, talk about its goals, and discuss why some countries have developed democratic socialism in response to some of its shortcomings. (406-407)
6. Describe the ideologies of capitalism and socialism, the criticisms of capitalism and socialism, and the convergence of capitalism and socialism. (407-408)
7. Know the functionalist view of the globalization of capitalism, including the functional aspects of work, corporations, and the global division of labor. (409-412)
8. Describe the inner circle of corporate capitalism and how, according to the conflict perspective, members of the inner circle consolidate their power and maximize their profits at the expense of workers. (413-418)
9. Discuss how the composition of the American work force has changed significantly over the past one hundred years. (418-419)
10. Know what is meant by—and the extent of—the underground economy in the United States. (422)
11. Talk about recent changes in the U.S. economy related to the buying power of paychecks, patterns in work and leisure, telecommuting, new technologies, and downsizing. (422-424)
12. Discuss the implications for the future of global capitalism including global trade and the impact of new technologies. (424-425)

CHAPTER OUTLINE

I. **The Transformation of Economic Systems**
    A. Market, or economy, is the mechanism by which values are established in order to exchange goods and services.
        1. The economy, which may be one of our most important social institutions, is the system of distribution of goods and services.
        2. The economy today, impersonal and global, is radically different from the past.
        3. The economy is essential to our welfare.
    B. As societies developed, a surplus emerged that fostered social inequality.

1. The earliest hunting and gathering societies had subsistence economies characterized by little trade with other groups, and a high degree of social equality.
2. In pastoral and horticultural economies, people created more dependable food supplies. As groups settled down in one location and grew in size, a specialized division of labor developed. This led to the production of a surplus and trade between groups, all of which fostered social inequality.
3. The invention of the plow paved way for agricultural societies. As more people were freed from food production, a more specialized division of labor developed and trade expanded. This brought even more social, political, and economic inequality.

C. The surplus (and greater inequality) grew in industrial societies. As the surplus increased, emphasis changed from production of goods to consumption. Thorstein Veblen referred to this as conspicuous consumption.

D. The "information explosion" and the global village are key elements of postindustrial society. According to Daniel Bell, postindustrial economies have six traits: (1) a large service sector that most work in; (2) a large surplus of goods; (3) extensive trade among nations; (4) a wide variety and amount of goods available to the average person; (5) an information explosion; and (6) a global village with instantaneous, worldwide communications.

E. We may be on the verge of yet another new type of society.
1. This new society is being ushered in by advances in biology, especially the deciphering of the human genome system in 2001.
2. While the specifics are still unknown, the marriage of biology and economics will yield even greater surplus and trade.
3. The new society may lead to longer and healthier lives.

F. Whenever society changes, there are implications for our lives. It impacts the type of work that those who live in the society will do.

G. Around the globe the consequences of the information explosion are uneven. Due to political and economic arrangements, some nations and individuals will prosper while others suffer.

II. The Transformation of the Medium of Exchange

A. A medium of exchange is the means by which people value and exchange goods and services.

B. One of the earliest mediums of exchange was barter, the direct exchange of one item for another. This was common in hunting and gathering and pastoral and horticultural societies.

C. In agricultural economies, people came to use gold and silver coins. Deposit receipts became common. Under this arrangement, the ownership of a specified amount of gold, bushels of wheat, or some other item was transferred from one person to another. Toward the end of this period, the receipts were formalized into currency (paper money). Currency represented stored value; no more could be issued than the amount of gold or silver the currency represented.

D. In industrial economies, bartering largely disappeared and gold was replaced by paper currency. The gold standard (a dollar represents a specified amount of gold) kept the number of dollars that could be issued to a specific limit. When "fiat money" came into existence, the currency no longer could be exchanged for gold or silver.

    1.   Even without a gold standard, the amount of paper money that can be issued is limited: prices increase if a government issues currency at a rate higher than the growth of its gross domestic product. Issuing more produces inflation: each unit of currency will purchase fewer goods and services.

    2.   Checking accounts and credit cards have become common in industrial economies, largely replacing currency.

  E.   In postindustrial economies, paper money is being replaced by checks, credit cards, and debit cards. The latest phase of evolution of money is e-cash, digital money stored on the user's local computer. E-cash can be encoded in e-mail and sent over the Internet.

III. World Economic Systems

  A.   Capitalism has three essential features: (1) the private ownership of the means of production; (2) market competition; and (3) the pursuit of profit.

    1.   Pure (laissez-faire) capitalism exists only when market forces are able to operate without interference from the government.

    2.   The United States today has welfare (or state) capitalism. Private citizens own the means of production and pursue profits, but do so within a vast system of laws (market restraints) that are designed to protect the public welfare. These laws include antimonopoly legislation which requires that companies must obtain federal approval before acquiring another company in the same industry.

    3.   Under welfare capitalism the government supports competition but establishes its own monopoly over "common good" items, e.g., those presumed essential for the common good of the citizens.

  B.   Socialism also has three essential features: (1) public ownership of the means of production; (2) central planning; and (3) the distribution of goods without a profit motive.

    1.   Under socialism, the government owns the means of production, and a central committee determines what the country needs instead of allowing market forces (supply and demand) to control production and prices. Socialism is designed to eliminate competition, to produce goods for the general welfare, and to distribute them according to people's needs, not their ability to pay.

    2.   Socialism does not exist in a pure form. Although the ideology of socialism calls for resources to be distributed according to need rather than position, socialist nations found it necessary to offer higher salaries for some jobs in order to entice people to take greater responsibilities.

    3.   Some nations (e.g., Sweden and Denmark) have adopted democratic or welfare socialism: both the state and individuals engage in production and distribution, although the state owns certain industries (steel, mining, forestry, telephones, television stations, and airlines) while retail stores, farms, and most service industries remain in private hands.

  C.   Capitalism and socialism represent distinct ideologies.

    1.   Capitalists believe that market forces should determine both products and prices, and that it is good for people to strive for profits.

2. Socialists believe that profit is immoral and represents excess value extracted from workers.

3. These two different ideologies produce contrasting pictures of how the world should be; consequently, each sees the other ideology as not only inherently evil but also as a system of exploitation.

D. The primary criticism of capitalism is that it leads to social inequality (a top layer of wealthy, powerful people, and a bottom layer of people who are unemployed or underemployed). Socialism has been criticized for not respecting individual rights, and for not being capable of producing much wealth (thus the greater equality of socialism actually amounts to almost everyone having an equal chance of being poor).

E. In recent years, fundamental changes have taken place in these two economic systems. Both systems have adopted features of the other.

1. That capitalism and socialism are growing more similar is known as convergence theory.

2. In Russia and China the standard of living lagged far behind the West; both economies were plagued by the production of shoddy goods and shortages. In the 1980s and 1990s, both reinstated market forces—private ownership of property became legal and the state auctioned off many of its industries. Making a profit was encouraged.

3. Over the years the United States has adopted many socialistic practices such as unemployment compensation, subsidized housing, welfare, minimum wage, and Social Security.

4. While leaders in both systems accept certain elements of the other, the reality is that the two remain far from "converged," and the struggles between them continue, although they are more muted than in the past. With the pullback of socialism around the world, capitalism in its many varieties has a strong lead.

IV. The Functionalist Perspective on the Globalization of Capitalism

A. The globalization of capitalism may be the most significant economic change in the past 100 years.

B. Work is functional for society; it binds people together.

1. Work is central to Durkheim's principles of mechanical solidarity (unity from being involved in similar occupations or activities) and organic solidarity (interdependence resulting from mutual need as each individual fulfills his job).

2. Today, organic solidarity has expanded far beyond anything Durkheim envisioned, creating interdependencies that span the globe. These global interdependencies suggest a new global division of labor, although we do not yet feel a sense of unity with one another and we are increasingly dependent on one another.

C. The corporation (joint ownership of a business enterprise, whose liabilities are separate from those of its owners) changed the face of capitalism.

1. Sociologists use the term corporate capitalism to refer to the contemporary domination of the economy by corporations.

2. One of the most significant aspects of large corporations is the separation of ownership and management, producing ownership of wealth without appreciable control, and control of wealth without appreciable ownership.

3. What makes the separation of ownership and management functional is profits. Managers are motivated to maximize profits because they will then benefit through stock options and bonuses.
4. A stockholders' revolt (stockholders of a corporation refuse to rubber stamp management decisions) is likely to occur if the profits do not meet expectations.

D. The world is divided into three primary trading blocs: North and South America dominated by the United States, Europe dominated by Germany, and Asia dominated by Japan but with China close behind.
1. Functionalists stress that this new global division benefits both the multinationals and the citizens of the world.
2. Free trade leads to greater competition, which drives the search for greater productivity. This in turn lowers prices and raises the standard of living.
3. Free trade can also be dysfunctional. When business moves to countries where labor costs are lower, workers in the countries from which the business came from will lose their jobs.

V. The Conflict Perspective on the Globalization of Capitalism

A. Conflict theorists stress that the important point of global interdependence is how the wealthy benefit at the expense of workers.
B. The multinationals are headed by an inner circle. This group, which competes with one another, is still united by a mutual interest in preserving capitalism.
1. Oligopolies, several large companies that dominate a single industry, dictate pricing, set the quality of their products, and protect the market. Often they use their wealth and connections for political purposes (e.g., favorable legislation giving them special tax breaks or protecting their industry from imports).
2. One of the most significant developments today is the merger of giant corporations from different nations. Merging reduces competition.
3. Consolidation of power is one of the primary goals of these corporations.
4. If they find hostility, some are not above plotting murder and overthrowing governments. In 1973, ITT plotted with the CIA to unseat Salvador Allende, the democratically elected president of Chile because he was a socialist; this action led to his assassination.
5. U.S. economic power is so integrated with politics that the inner circle can even get U.S. presidents to pitch their products.
6. The interests of the multinationals and the top political leaders have converged. Together they form a power elite.
C. Interlocking directorates occur when individuals serve as directors of several companies, concentrating power and minimizing competition.
D. As corporations have outgrown national boundaries, the result is the creation of multinational corporations, detached from the interests and values of their country of origin with no concern other than making a profit. They are becoming a primary political force in the world today.
E. Because of their detachment from national boundaries, the multinationals may be a force for global peace or they could create a New World Order dominated by a handful of corporate leaders.

VI. Work in U.S. Society

A. In our postindustrial society, there are changes in the type of work that workers do.

1. In the 1800s, most U.S. workers were farmers; today farmers represent only two percent of the workforce.

2. In 1940, about one-half of U.S. workers worked in blue-collar jobs; today, the changing technology has reduced the market for these jobs.

3. The dominant job today is white collar.

B. A major change in our society has been the increase in women who work outside of the home for wages. Almost one out of two workers is a woman.

1. Men and women are different in terms of how they experience work. Women seem more concerned than men with maintaining a balance between work and family life. Men seem to follow models of individualism and power while women may stress collaboration and helping.

2. How likely a woman is to work depends on several factors such as her education and marital status; race and ethnicity have little influence.

3. The quiet revolution refers to the continually increasing proportions of women in the labor force. This transformation affects consumer patterns, relations at work, self-concepts, and familial relationships.

C. The underground (informal and off-the-books) economy involves exchange of goods and services not reported to the government, including income from work done "on the side" and from illegal activities (e.g., drug dealing).

1. The drug networks are so huge that a million Americans are arrested each year for illegal drug activities.

2. The million or so undocumented workers who enter the United States each year are also part of the underground economy. Their employers disregard their fake Social Security cards or pay them in cash.

3. Estimates place the underground economy at 10 to 15 percent of the regular economy, which means it may run close to $1 trillion. As a result, the Internal Revenue Service (IRS) loses billions of dollars a year in uncollected or "lost" taxes.

D. Since 1970, increases in workers' paychecks have not kept up with inflation; consequently, workers are falling behind.

E. Different societies have had differing amounts of leisure (time not taken up by work or required activities such as eating/sleeping).

1. Early societies had a lot of time for leisure. Industrialization brought changes: bosses and machines then controlled people's time.

2. It is not the activity itself that makes something leisure, but rather its purpose (e.g., driving a car for pleasure or to work). Patterns of leisure change with the life course, with both the young and the old enjoying the most leisure, and parents with young children having the least.

3. Compared with early industrialization, workers today have far more leisure time (shorter work weeks, for example). In recent decades, the trend for more leisure has been reversed in the United States. U.S. workers now work the highest number of hours work per year compared to any other industrialized nation.

F. New technologies are enabling millions of workers to work from home; they commute electronically. This has had both positive and negative effects.

    G.   Corporations are able to save office space and workers avoid traffic jams and long commutes.

    H.   Managers are concerned over the lack of control of their workers. Workers fear that their careers will be hindered by being out of touch with office politics.

VII. Facing the Future: Implications of Global Capitalism
    A.   There is every indication that global trade will continue to increase beyond anything we have ever seen as multinational corporations continue to carve up the world into major trading blocs and push for reduction of tariffs.

        1.   The Most Industrialized Nations will continue to garner the lion's share of the world's wealth.

        2.   A major concern is that economic inequality will increase between the richer and poorer nations.

    B.   Computer-driven production will continue to reduce the number of manufacturing jobs. While technology eliminates jobs, it also creates jobs. At the same time, those who bear the brunt of the change are low-level workers who live from paycheck to paycheck.

KEY TERMS
After studying the chapter, review the definition for each of the following terms.

barter: the direct exchange of one item for another (403)

capitalism: an economic system characterized by the private ownership of the means of production, the pursuit of profit, and market competition (405)

conspicuous consumption: Thorstein Veblen's term for a change from the Protestant ethic to an eagerness to show off wealth by the consumption of goods (401)

convergence theory: the view that as capitalist and socialist economic systems each adopt features of the other, a hybrid (or mixed) economic system will emerge (409)

corporate capitalism: the domination of the economic system by corporations (412)

corporation: the joint ownership of a business enterprise, whose liabilities and obligations are separate from those of the owners (412)

credit card: a device that allows its owner to purchase goods but be billed later (404)

currency: paper money (403)

debit card: a device that allows its owner to charge purchases against his or her bank account (404)

democratic socialism: a hybrid economic system in which capitalism is mixed with state ownership (407)

deposit receipts: a receipt stating that a certain amount of goods is on deposit in a warehouse or bank; the receipt is used as a form of money (403)

e-cash: digital money that is stored on computers (404)

economy: a system of distribution of goods and services (400)

fiat money: currency issued by a government that is not backed by stored value (403)

gold standard: paper money backed by gold (403)

gross domestic product (GDP): the amount of goods and services produced by a nation (403)

inflation: an increase in prices (403)

interlocking directorates: the same people serving on the board of directors of several companies (416)

laissez-faire capitalism: unrestrained manufacture and trade (literally, "hands off" capitalism) (405)

leisure: time not taken up by work or required activities (423)

market competition: the exchange of items between willing buyers and sellers (405)

market forces: the law of supply and demand (406)

market restraints: laws and regulations that limit the capacity to manufacture and sell products (405)

mechanical solidarity: Durkheim's term for the unity (or shared consciousness) that people feel as a result of performing the same or similar tasks (410)

medium of exchange: the means by which people value goods and services in order to make an exchange, for example, currency, gold, and silver (403)

money: any item (from sea shells to gold) that serves as a medium of exchange; today, currency is the most common form (403)

monopoly: the control of an entire industry by a single company (406)

multinational corporation: companies that operate across national boundaries; also called transnational corporations (413)

oligopoly: the control of an entire industry by several large companies (413)

organic solidarity: Durkheim's term for the interdependence that results from the division of labor; people depending on others to fulfill their jobs (411)

quiet revolution: the fundamental changes in society that occurred as a result of vast numbers of women entering the workforce (421)

socialism: an economic system characterized by public ownership of the means of prod-uction, central planning, and the distribution of goods without a profit motive (406)

stockholders' revolt: the refusal of a corporation's stockholders to rubber-stamp decisions made by its managers (412)

stored value: the backing of a currency by goods that are stored and held in reserve (403)

subsistence economy: a type of economy in which human groups live off the land with little or no surplus (400)

underground economy: exchanges of goods and services that are not reported to the government and thereby escape taxation (422)

welfare (state) capitalism: an economic system in which individuals own the means of production, but the state regulates many economic activities for the welfare of the population (405)

KEY PEOPLE
Review the major theoretical contributions or findings of these people.

Daniel Bell: Bell identified six characteristics of the postindustrial society. (401)

Emile Durkheim: Durkheim contributed the concepts of mechanical and organic solidarity to our understanding of social cohesion. (410-411)

Louis Gallambos: This historian of business has predicted that the new global business system will change the way everyone lives and works. (410)

Karl Marx: Marx was an outspoken critic of capitalism and wrote about the basis for profits under capitalism. (407)

Michael Useem: Using a conflict perspective, Useem studied the activities of the "inner circle" of corporate executives. (413)

Thorstein Veblen: Veblen created the term "conspicuous consumption" to refer to the eagerness to show off one's wealth through the elaborate consumption of material goods. (401)

STUDENT APPLICATION PROJECTS

This is your opportunity to apply the sociological perspective. The projects in this section refer to material introduced in this chapter of your text. These projects help you apply the sociological perspective "down to your earth...down to your daily life."

1. Do you think the United States will eventually become a paperless money society? Explain why or why not? What would be the conveniences and inconveniences of a paperless money society? Has your college or university adopted recent changes such a student card that acts as a debit card? If so, do you use it and why? If not, do you think your school will adopt such a card in the future? Explain. Overall, do you think debit cards instead of cash are a good idea? Why or why not?

2. List some ways people make extra income through the underground economy. Do you know people who make extra income through it? If so, explain. How large do you think the underground economy is in the United States? Do you think it is deviant to have a garage sale and not report the money? Why or why not? What parts of the underground economy are deviant and what parts are not? Give examples to support your position.

3. Your text states that compared with workers during early industrialization, today's workers have far more leisure. Estimate how much leisure time you have in a week. What type of activities do you engage in during this time? How much vacation time should a full time employee receive per year? Explain. Do you think Americans have enough leisure time compared to other industrialized countries in the world? Explain.

4. Can you think of examples in which the U.S. has programs or services that might be considered more socialist in nature? What would be the advantages and disadvantages of adopting more socialist practices in the United States?

SELF-TEST

MULTIPLE CHOICE QUESTIONS

1. What is an economy? (400)
    a.   it is a system of buying and selling
    b.   it is a system of producing and distributing goods and services
    c.   it means the movement of vast amounts of goods across international borders
    d.   all of the above

2. Which of the following characterize hunting and gathering societies? (400)
    a.   market economy
    b.   surplus economy
    c.   subsistence economy
    d.   maintenance economy

3. Which of the following took place in pastoral and horticultural economies? (400)
    a.   a subsistence economy existed
    b.   a more dependable food supply led to the development of a surplus
    c.   the plow was used extensively
    d.   extensive trade developed

4. Which of the following is *not* a feature of industrial economies? (400-401)
    a.   machines are powered by fuels
    b.   a surplus unlike anything the world had seen is created
    c.   the steam engine was invented and became the basis for the economy
    d.   a service sector developed and employed the majority of workers

5. What did Veblen label the lavishly wasteful spending of goods designed to enhance social prestige? (401)
    a.   prestigious consumption
    b.   wasteful consumption
    c.   conspicuous prestige
    d.   conspicuous consumption

6. Which is *not* a defining characteristic of postindustrial economies? (401)
    a.   a large surplus of goods
    b.   extensive trade among nations
    c.   machines powered by fuels
    d.   a "global village"

7. The author of your text suggests that a new type of society may be emerging. What two forces have combined to produce this new society? (401)
   a. biology and politics
   b. politics and economics
   c. biology and economics
   d. biology and religion

8. In what society was bartering a common medium of exchange: (403)
   a. postindustrial
   b. agricultural
   c. industrial
   d. pastoral and horticultural

9. In which type of society was money first used extensively? (403)
   a. agricultural
   b. industrial
   c. postindustrial
   d. pastoral and horticultural

10. In the past, the U.S. government maintained a policy whereby it would only issue as many paper dollars as it had gold stored in the vaults at Fort Knox. This policy was called: (403)
    a. the gold reserves.
    b. the cash standard.
    c. the gold standard.
    d. the Fort Knox standard.

11. What term describes the total goods and services that a nation produces? (403)
    a. the gross domestic product
    b. the net national product
    c. the national debt
    d. the medium of exchange

12. The debit card came into existence in the: (404)
    a. agricultural economy.
    b. industrial economy.
    c. postindustrial economy.
    d. none of the above.

13. Private ownership of the means of production is an essential feature of: (405)
    a. communism.
    b. socialism.
    c. democracy.
    d. capitalism.

14. The ownership of machines and factories by individuals who decide what to produce is: (404)
    a. state socialism.
    b. personal capitalism.
    c. private ownership of the means of production.
    d. public ownership of the means of production.

15. Which system has public ownership, central planning, and no profit motive? (406)
    a. democratic socialism
    b. socialism
    c. capitalism
    d. communism

16. For Marx, what is the amount of value created by workers' labor but withheld from them? (407)
    a. market prices
    b. profits
    c. labor costs
    d. overhead

17. The role of advertising in relation to the consumption of goods is to: (407)
    a. create discontent by presenting images that are impossible to attain.
    b. show us what we can really look like if we took the time and money to invest in ourselves.
    c. show us that there are guaranteed products that will improve our lives.
    d. none of the above.

18. The theory that capitalism and socialism grow more alike as they develop is: (408)
    a. unity theory.
    b. convergence theory.
    c. amalgamation theory.
    d. merger theory.

19. Which perspective views work as the tie that binds us together? (410)
    a. functionalist
    b. conflict
    c. symbolic interactionist
    d. ethnomethodological

20. As societies industrialize, they become based on: (410)
    a. mechanical solidarity.
    b. organic solidarity.
    c. social solidarity.
    d. none of the above.

21. Jointly owning an enterprise, with liabilities and obligations independent of its owners is: (410)
    a. an oligopoly.
    b. a monopoly.
    c. a corporation.
    d. an interlocking directorate.

22. A stockholders' revolt occurs when: (412)
    a. major stockholders dump their holdings in the open market.
    b. stockholders lead workers in a protest against company policies.
    c. stockholders refuse to rubber-stamp the recommendations made by management.
    d. people boycott the stocks of certain companies that are socially irresponsible.

23. Which of the following statements about Michael Useem's inner circle is *incorrect*? (413)
    a. Members of the inner circle are united by an interest in preserving capitalism.
    b. Relationships among members of the inner circle are always cooperative rather than competitive.
    c. Within their own country, they have close ties with political leaders who stand firmly for the private ownership of property.
    d. Globally, they promote the ideology of capitalism.

24. What is oligopoly? (413)
    a. the control of an entire industry by several large companies
    b. the control of an entire industry by a single company
    c. illegal in the United States
    d. none of the above

25. The elites who sit on the boards of directors of multiple companies are: (416)
    a. vertical integrators.
    b. interlocking trustees.
    c. interlocking directorates.
    d. oligopolies.

26. What term is used to describe the fundamental changes in society that follow the movement of vast numbers of women from the home to the work force? (419)
    a. the feminization of work
    b. the "mommy movement"
    c. the quiet revolution
    d. the backlash

27. The size of the underground economy (economic activity not reported to the government) runs about _____ percent of the regular economy. (422)
    a. 2
    b. 7
    c. 10
    d. 13

28. Which of the following statements about wages is *correct*? (422)
    a. The buying power of today's wages is greater than any time in the last 30 years.
    b. In current dollars, workers today are paid less than they were 30 years ago.
    c. The buying power of today's wages is actually less than it was 30 years ago.
    d. Both the buying power and current value of wages are greater today than they were 30 years ago.

29. When compared with workers in Western Europe, U.S. workers have _____ leisure time. (423)
    a. more
    b. less
    c. the same
    d. two hours more of

30. According to conflict theory, which group bears the brunt of technological change? (424)
    a. middle management
    b. top-level executives
    c. low-level workers
    d. laborers in the least industrialized nations

TRUE-FALSE QUESTIONS

1. _____Hunting and gathering societies were the first economies with a surplus. (400)
2. _____In pastoral and horticultural economies, some individuals were able for the first time in human history to develop their energies to tasks other than food production. (400)
3. _____In postindustrial societies people bartering for goods and services is a common practice. (401)
4. _____Industrial economies are based on information processing and providing services. (401)
5. _____The earliest medium of exchange was barter. (403)
6. _____The gold standard was a medium of exchange in industrial economies. (403)
7. _____Credit cards and debit cards are the same thing. (403)
8. _____Convergence theory refers to the notion that capitalism and socialism are growing similar. (405)
9. _____The United States government controls "common good" items. (405)
10. _____Socialists believe that profit is immoral. (406)
11. _____According to convergence theory, the world's nations are becoming increasingly more capitalistic. (408)
12. _____ Corporate capitalism is the domination of the economic system by giant corporations. (412)
13. _____In the transition to a postindustrial society, the number of farmers plum-meted, blue-collar work shrunk, and most people work at service jobs. (412)
14. _____Microsoft is the world's largest corporation. (413)

15. _____Oligopolies are formed when many different-size companies all compete within a single industry. (413)
16. _____The most common work today in the United States is white-collar employment. (418)
17. _____Researchers have found that both men and women workers are equally concerned with maintaining a balance between their work and family lives. (419)
18. _____The "quiet revolution" refers to the continually increasing proportions of women who have joined the ranks of paid labor. (419)
19. _____Industrialization increased the amount of leisure time workers had. (423)
20. _____The current technological revolution is making it possible for millions of workers to work from their homes; this trend is called *telecommuting*. (423)

FILL-IN-THE-BLANK QUESTIONS

1. The _____ multiplied food production, allowing agricultural societies to develop. (400)
2. Biotech societies are the merger between _____ and _____. (401)
3. The latest evolution of money is _____. (404)
4. The current form of U.S. capitalism i_____ or state capitalism. (405)
5. The Standard oil company at one time achieved a _____ of the oil industry by dictating prices to an entire nation. (406)
6. Sweden and Denmark developed democratic _____. (406)
7. That capitalism and socialism are growing similar is known as _____. (408)
8. A _____ is a business that is treated legally as person. (408)
9. Michael Useem notes that multinational corporations are headed by a group called the _____. (410)
10. _____ theorists stress how the elite consolidate their power through interlocking directorates. (413)
11. Today, almost one in _____ workers are women. (416)
12. The illegal immigrants who enter the U.S. to work are known as _____. (418)
13. Patterns of leisure change with the life course, following the _____. (421)
14. _____ allows workers to work from home while they commute electronically with their company. (423)
15. _____ production will continue to reduce the numbers of workers who are needed to make the goods we use. (424)

MATCH THESE CONCEPTS WITH THEIR DEFINITIONS

_____	1. barter	a. *purchases charged against bank account*
_____	2. democratic socialism	b. *currency issued by government and not backed by stored value*
_____	3. debit card	c. *control of an industry by several large companies*
_____	4. e-cash	d. *control of an industry by a single company*
_____	5. fiat money	e. *direct exchange of one item for another*
_____	6. market forces	f. *backing currency with goods that are held in reserve*
_____	7. oligopoly	g. *public ownership of the means of production*
_____	8. stored value	h. *laws of supply and demand*
_____	9. monopoly	i. *digital money stored on computers*
_____	10. socialism	j. *a hybrid economic system in which capitalism is mixed with state ownership*

ESSAY QUESTIONS

1. Discuss the advantages and disadvantages of both capitalism and socialism as ideologies and as economic systems.

2. Explain why functionalists believe that work is functional for society.

3. Take the perspective of a conflict theorist and explain the goals of corporate leaders and the strategies they use to achieve these goals.

4. Discuss what is meant by the underground economy and the extent to which it exists.

5. The chapter discusses several different economic trends that have been occurring in the second half of this century. Discuss the impact of each of the following: the movement of women into the economy, shrinking paychecks, changing patterns of work and leisure, and the emergence of the alternative office.

CHAPTER 15
POLITICS

CHAPTER SUMMARY

- The essential nature of politics is power, the ability to carry out one's will despite resistance; every group is political. *Micropolitics* is the term used to refer to the exercise of power in everyday life, while macropolitics refers to large-scale power, such as governing a nation.

- Authority refers to the legitimate use of power, while coercion is its illegitimate use. The state is a political entity that claims a monopoly on violence over a particular territory. Max Weber identified three types of authority: traditional, rational-legal, and charismatic. The orderly transfer of authority at the death, resignation, or incapacitation of a leader is critical for social stability.

- Three forms of government are monarchies (power is based on hereditary rule); democracies (power is given by the citizens); and dictatorships and oligarchies (power is seized by an individual or a small group).

- In the United States, with its winner-takes-all electoral system, political parties must appeal to the center, and minority parties make little headway. In contrast, many democracies in Europe have a system of proportional representation that encourages the formation of a coalitional government. Voting patterns in the United States consistently demonstrate that whites, the elderly, the rich, the employed, and the highly educated are most likely to vote. The more people are socially integrated and have a stake in the political system, the more likely they are to vote. Special interest groups, with their lobbyists and PACs, play a significant role in U.S. politics.

- Functionalists and conflict theorists have very different views on who rules the United States. According to the functionalists, no one group holds power; the outcome is that the competing interest groups balance one another (pluralism). According to conflict theorists, the United States is governed by a ruling class made up of members drawn from the elite (power elite).

- War is not an option for all human groups. Despite the massive costs in lives and property, war continues to be an option to pursue political objectives. Even though terrorism has been common through history, it is now a fact of life for Americans. The effect of war and exposure to brutality and killing often causes dehumanization of the enemy.

- The global expansion of communication, transportation, and trade, the widespread adoption of capitalism and the retreat of socialism, as well as the trend toward larger political unions suggest that a new international world order may be in the process of emerging. It is possible that this group could help bring about global peace. However, the resurgence of nationalism poses a roadblock to this new world order.

LEARNING OBJECTIVES
After reading Chapter 15, you should be able to:

1. Understand the relationship between power and politics and power and the state. (432)
2. Know the difference between authority and coercion, and explain why and how the state is able to claim a monopoly on the legitimate use of violence. (432-433)
3. Describe the three ideal types of authority identified by Max Weber and, for each type, explain how authority is transferred from one leader to another. (433-435)
4. Distinguish between—and identify the characteristics of—monarchies, democracies, dictatorships, and oligarchies. (436-439)
5. Discuss how the two major political parties in the United States are different from and similar to one another. (439-440)
6. Describe the differences between the democratic systems of the United States and Europe, and explain how these differences impact the role of minor political parties in each system. (440-441)
7. Identify the major voting patterns in the United States and discuss the reasons for voter alienation and voter apathy. (441-444)
8. Talk about the role that money plays in American politics and how lobbyists and special interest groups influence the political process. (444-445)
9. Compare and evaluate the competing views of functionalists and conflict theorists on the distribution of power in American politics. (446-447)
10. Discuss the causes, costs, and ramifications of war throughout human history, as well as the current threats involving nuclear, chemical, and biological weapons. (447-455)
11. Discuss terrorism and how it has more recently become a fact of life for Americans. (450-455)
12. Discuss war and its dehumanizing affect and identify the four characteristics of dehumanization. (449-450)
13. Evaluate the possibilities for—and the potential ramifications of—a new world order characterized by global political and economic unity. (255-258)

CHAPTER OUTLINE

I. **Micropolitics and Macropolitics**
   A. Politics refers to power relations wherever they exist.
   B. Power is the ability to carry out one's will despite resistance.
   C. Symbolic interactionists use the term micropolitics to refer to exercise of power in everyday life.
   D. Macropolitics is the exercise of large-scale power over a large group. Governments are examples of macropolitics.

II. **Power, Authority, and Violence**
   A. Authority is legitimate power that people accept as right, while coercion is power that people do not accept as just.
   B. The state claims a monopoly on legitimate force or the use of violence in society; violence is the ultimate foundation of political order.

1. Revolution (armed resistance to overthrow a government) is a rejection by the people of a government's claim to rule and of its monopoly on violence.
2. What some see as coercion, others see as authority.
3. A government that is viewed as legitimate is more stable than one that is not.

C. Traditional authority (based on custom) is prevalent in preliterate groups, where custom sets relationships. When society industrializes, traditional authority is undermined, but does not die out. For example, parental authority is traditional authority.

D. Rational-legal authority (based on written rules; also called bureaucratic authority) derives from the position an individual holds, not from the person. Everyone (no matter how high the office) is subject to the rules.

E. Charismatic authority (based on an individual's personal following) may pose a threat. Because this type of leader works outside the established political system and may threaten the established order, the authorities are often quick to oppose this type of leader.

F. Weber's three bases of authority—traditional, rational-legal, and charismatic—are ideal types representing composite characteristics found in real life examples. In rare instances, traditional and rational-legal leaders possess charismatic traits, but most authority is one type or another.

G. Orderly transfer of authority upon death, resignation, or incapacity of a leader is critical for stability. Succession is more of a problem with charismatic authority than with traditional or rational-legal authority because there are no rules for orderly succession with charismatic authority.

H. To deal with succession, some charismatic leaders will appoint a successor who may or may not be received favorably by the followers. Another strategy is to build an organization. This routinization of charisma refers to the transfer of authority from a charismatic leader to either traditional or rational-legal authority.

III. Types of Government

A. A monarchy is a government headed by a king or queen.
1. As cities developed, each city-state (an independent city whose power radiated outward, bringing adjacent areas under its rule) had its own monarchy.
2. As city-states warred with one another, the victors would extend their rule, eventually over an entire region. As the size of these regions grew, people began to identify with the region; over time this gave rise to the state.

B. A democracy is a government whose authority derives from the people.
1. The original American colonies were small and independent; after the American Revolution the colonies united and formed a democratic government.
2. The first democracy existed about 2,000 years ago in Athens. Members of some Native American tribes were able to elect chiefs; in some, women also voted and even held the position of chief.
3. Because of their small size, these groups were able to practice direct democracy (eligible voters meet to discuss issues and make decisions). Initially, the colonies and then the states practiced direct democracy because they were small. Representative democracy (when voters elect representatives to govern and make

decisions on their behalf) emerged as the U.S. population grew in size and spread out across the country, making direct democracy impossible.

4. It is possible that some form of direct democracy may re-emerge, given the new interactive communications technologies that make "electronic town meetings" possible.

5. Today, citizenship (people have basic rights by virtue of birth or residence) is taken for granted in the United States; this idea is quite new to the human scene. Universal citizenship (everyone having the same basic rights) came into practice very slowly and only through fierce struggle.

C. Dictatorship is government where power is seized and held by an individual; oligarchy results when a small group of individual seizes power. Dictators and oligarchies can be totalitarian (when the government exercises almost total control of a people).

IV. The U.S. Political System

A. The Democratic and Republican parties emerged by the time of the Civil War.

1. The Democrats are often associated with the poor and working class and the Republicans with people who are financially better off.

2. Each appeals to a broad membership and it is often difficult to distinguish conservative Democrats from liberal Republicans. It is easier, however, discern the extremes. In addition, those elected to Congress may cross party lines because although office holders support their party's philosophy, they do not necessarily support all of its specific proposals.

3. Despite their differences, however, both parties support fundamentals of U.S. society such as freedom of religion, free public education, a strong military, and capitalism.

4. Third parties do play a role in U.S. politics, although generally they receive little public support. Ross Perot's "United We Stand" party is one exception.

B. Not all democracies around the world are like ours.

1. U.S. elections are based on a winner-takes-all electoral system; most European countries use proportional representation (legislative seats divided according to the proportion of votes each political party received).

2. The U.S. system discourages minority parties; the proportional representation system encourages them. The United States has centrist parties, representing the center of political opinion. Noncentrist parties (representing marginal ideas) are more likely to develop in European systems with proportional representation.

3. Three main results follow from proportional representation: (1) minority parties can gain access to the media, which keep their issues alive; (2) minority parties can gain power beyond their numbers; and (3) the government may be unstable due to the breakdown of coalitions (a coalition occurs when a country's largest party aligns itself with one or more smaller parties to get required votes to make national decisions).

C. Voting Patterns

1. U.S. voting patterns are consistent: the percentage of people who vote increases with age; non-Hispanic whites are more likely to vote than African Americans, while Latinos are considerably less likely to vote than either; those with higher

levels of education are more likely to vote, as are people with higher levels of income; women are slightly more likely than men to vote.

2. The more that people feel they have a stake in the system, the more likely they are to vote. Those who have been rewarded by the system feel more socially integrated and perceive that elections directly affect their lives and the society in which they live.

3. People who gain less from the system in terms of education, income, and jobs are more likely to be alienated, they don't vote because they feel their vote won't count. Voter apathy is indifference/inaction to the political process. As a result of apathy, nearly one-half of eligible American voters do not vote for president and even more do not vote for members of Congress.

4. Today, we recognize a gender gap in voting. Men are split between Democratic and Republican candidates, while women are more likely to vote for Democratic candidates.

5. There is an even larger racial/ethnic gap in politics; few African Americans vote for a Republican presidential candidate.

D. Special-interest groups are people who think alike on a particular issue and can be mobilized for political action.

1. Lobbyists (paid to influence legislation on behalf of their clients) are employed by special interest groups and have become a major force in politics.

2. Political action committees (PACs) solicit and spend funds to influence legislation and bypass laws intended to limit the amount any individual, corporation, or group can give a candidate. PACs have become a powerful influence, bankrolling lobbyists and legislators, and the PACs with the most clout gain the ear of Congress.

3. A few PAC's represent broad social interests. Most stand for the financial interest of groups such as the dairy, oil, banking, and construction industries.

E. The high cost of elections contributes to the importance of lobbyists and PACs in Washington and state capitols.

1. An average candidate for the Senate will spend $5 million on the campaign. Once a candidate is elected, she or he owes people who helped with financing the campaign and wants to get reelected.

2. To finance a reelection campaign the average senator needs to raise over $2000 every day of their six year term.

3. The major criticism against lobbyists and PACs is that their money buys votes. Rather than representing the people who elected them, legislators end up supporting the special interests of groups able to help them stay in power.

V. Who Rules the United States?

A. According to the functionalists, the state was created because it fulfilled a basic social need.

1. People must find a balance between having no government (anarchy) and having a government that may be too repressive, turning against its own citizens.

2. The functionalists say that pluralism, the diffusion of power among interest groups, prevents anyone from gaining control of the government. Functionalists believe this helps keep the government from turning against its citizens.

3. To balance the interests of competing groups, the founders of the U.S. system of government created a system of checks and balances in which separation of powers among the three branches of government ensures that each is able to nullify the actions of the other two, thus preventing the domination by any single branch.

4. Our society is made up of many different groups representing special interests, including ethnic groups, women, farmers, factory workers, bankers, bosses, and the retired, to name a few. Since these groups need to negotiate and compromise with one another to meet their goals, conflict is minimized.

5. In this system, power is widely dispersed; as each group pursues its interests, it is balanced by others pursuing theirs.

B. According to the conflict perspective, lobbyists and even Congress are not at the center of decision making; rather, the power elite makes the decisions that direct the country and shake the world.

1. As stated by C. Wright Mills, the power elite (heads of leading corporations, powerful generals and admirals in the armed forces, and certain elite politicians) rule the United States. The corporate heads are the most powerful, so business interests come first, but all three view capitalism as essential to the welfare of the country.

2. According to William Domhoff, the ruling class (the wealthiest and most powerful individuals in the country) runs the United States. Its members control the United State's top corporations and foundations; presidential cabinet members and top ambassadors to the most powerful countries are chosen from this group.

3. The power elite is not a secret group. Their unity comes from the similarity of their backgrounds. All have attended prestigious schools, belong to exclusive clubs and are extremely wealthy.

C. While the functionalist and conflict views of power in U.S. society cannot be reconciled, it is possible to employ both. The middle level of C. Wright Mills model best reflects the functionalist view of competing interests holding each other at bay. At the top is an elite that follows its special interests, as conflict theorists suggest.

VI. War and Terrorism: Implementing Political Objectives

A. The state uses violence to protect citizens from individuals and groups, occasionally turning violence against other nations. War (armed conflict between nations or politically distinct groups) is often part of national policy.

B. War is not characteristic of all human groups, but simply one option for settling disputes.

C. At the same time, war is a fairly common occurrence; Pitirim Sorokin counted 967 wars between 500 B.C. and A.D. 1925, for an average of one war every two to three years. Since 1850, the United States has intervened militarily around the world more than 150 times, for an average of more than once a year.

D. Nicholas Timasheff identified three essential conditions of war.

1. An antagonistic situation exists, with two or more states confronting incompatible objectives.

2.   There is a cultural tradition of war; because war have been fought in the past, leaders see war as an option.

3.   A "fuel" heats the antagonistic situation to the boiling point, so that people move from thinking about war to engaging in it; Timasheff identified seven fuels: revenge; power; prestige; unity; position; ethnicity; and beliefs.

E.   Despite the fact that war is costly to society, it continues to be a common technique for pursuing political objectives.

1.   The cost in human life grows with industrialization and technological advances.

2.   War is also costly in terms of the money spent. The United States has spent $6 trillion on ten major wars.

F.   The Most Industrialized Nations lament regional conflicts that can quickly expand into larger wars; at the same time, they relentlessly pursue profits by selling powerful weapons to the Least Industrialized Nations; the United States is the chief merchant of death to the Least Industrialized Nations.

1.   Seeds of future wars are sown through arms deals involving conventional and nuclear weapons. Nations such as India, China, and North Korea possess nuclear weapons.

2.   The end of the Cold War in 1986 has reduced the threat of war as the United States and Russia began to cooperate with one another while still being leary of each other; they announced that they would no longer aim their missiles at each other's cities.

3.   The U.S. formed an organization called G-7. It consists of Canada, France, Germany, Great Britain, Italy, Japan, and the U.S. The purpose of the group was to perpetuate their global dominance, divide up the world's markets, and regulate global economic activity. In 2002, Russia was invited to become a member of this group. China has potential to also participate and this group will then be known as the G-9.

4.   Conflict continues to erupt with Iraq and Iran as the U.S. seeks to protect its interests in this oil-rich region.

G.   Today, terrorism has become a reality for Americans.

1.   Terrorism is the use of violence to create fear so that a group can meet its political objectives.

2.   Hatred between ethnic groups can serve as an impetus for terrorist activities.

3.   Suicide terrorism is one of the few options available to a weaker group that wants to retaliate against a powerful country. Examples include the attack on the World Trade Center and the Pentagon.

4.   The real danger is from nuclear, chemical, and biological weapons that could be unleashed against civilian populations.

H.   War has an effect on morality.

1.   Exposure to brutality and killing often causes dehumanization (reducing people to objects that do not deserve to be treated as humans).

2.   Characteristics of dehumanization include (1) increased emotional distance from others; (2) an emphasis on following procedures; (3) inability to resist pressures; and (4) a diminished sense of personal responsibility.

3.   Tamotsu Shibutani stressed that dehumanization is helped along by the tendency for prolonged conflicts to be transformed into a struggle between good and evil.

4. War exalts cruelty and killing and medals are given to glorify actions that otherwise would be condemned in other life contexts. The prisoner abuse at Abu Ghraib prison provides an excellent example of this.
5. Dehumanization does not always insulate the self from guilt; after the war ends, returning soldiers often find themselves disturbed by what they did during the war. Although most eventually adjust, some live with the guilt forever.

VII. A New World Order?
A. Today the embrace of capitalism and worldwide flow of information, capital, and goods has made national boundaries less meaningful. There are many examples of nations working together to solve mutual problems, such as the North American Free Trade Agreement (NAFTA), the European Union (EU), and the United Nations (UN).
B. The United Nations is striving to be the legislative body of the world. It operates a World Court and has a rudimentary army.
C. The resurgence of fierce nationalism represents a challenge to a new world order.
D. If global political and economic unity does come about, it is not clear what type of government will emerge. Under a benevolent government, there is tremendous potential for human welfare, but if a totalitarian government arises, the future could be bleak.

KEY TERMS
After studying the chapter, review the definition for each of the following terms.

anarchy: a condition of lawlessness or political disorder caused by the abuse or collapse of governmental authority (446)
authority: power that people consider legitimate, as rightly exercised over them; also called *legitimate power* (432)
centrist party: a political party that represents the center of political opinion (440)
charismatic authority: authority based on an individual's outstanding traits which attract followers (434)
checks and balances: the separation of powers among the three branches of U.S. government— legislative, executive and judicial—so that each is able to nullify the actions of the other two, thus preventing the domination by any single branch (446)
citizenship: the concept that birth (and residence) in a country impart basic rights (437)
city-state: an independent city whose power radiates outward, bringing the adjacent areas under its rule (436)
coalition government: a government in which a country's largest party aligns itself with one or more smaller parties (441)
coercion: power that people do not accept as rightly exercised over them; also called *illegitimate power* (432)
dehumanization: the act or process of reducing people to objects that do not deserve the treatment accorded humans (449)
democracy: a system of government in which authority derives from the people; the term comes from two Greek words that translate literally as "power to the people" (436)
dictatorship: a form of government in which power is seized by an individual (437)

direct democracy: a form of democracy in which the eligible voters meet together to discuss issues and make their decisions (437)

lobbyists: people who influence legislation on behalf of their clients (444)

macropolitics: the exercise of large-scale power, the government being the most common example (432)

micropolitics: the exercise of politics in everyday life, such as deciding who is going to do the housework or use the remote control (432)

monarchy: a form of government headed by a king or queen (436)

nationalism: a strong identity with a nation, accompanied by the desire for the nation to be dominant (456)

noncentrist party: a political party that represents marginal ideas (440)

oligarchy: a form of government in which power is held by a small group of individuals; the rule of the many by the few (438)

pluralism: the diffusion of power among many interest groups, preventing any single group from gaining control of the government (446)

political action committee (PAC): an organization formed by one or more special-interest groups to solicit and spend funds for the purpose of influencing legislation (445)

politics: the exercise of power and attempts to maintain or to change power relations (432)

power: the ability to carry out your will, even over the resistance of others (432)

power elite: C. Wright Mills term for the top people in U.S. corporations, military, and politics who make the nation's decisions (446)

proportional representation: an electoral system in which seats in a legislature are divided according to the proportion of votes each political party receives (440)

rational-legal authority: authority based on law or written rules and regulations; also called *bureaucratic authority* (434)

representative democracy: a form of democracy in which voters elect representatives to meet together to discuss issues, make decisions on their behalf (437)

revolution: armed resistance designed to overthrow a government (433)

routinization of charisma: the transfer of authority from a charismatic figure to either a traditional or a rational-legal form of authority (436)

ruling class: another term for the power elite (447)

special-interest group: a group of people who have a particular issue in common and who can be mobilized for political action (444)

state: a political entity that claims a monopoly on the use of violence in some particular territory; commonly known as a country (433)

terrorism: the use of violence or the threat of violence to produce fear in order to attain political objectives (450)

totalitarianism: a form of government that exerts almost total control over the people (438)

traditional authority: authority based on custom (433)

universal citizenship: the idea that everyone has the same basic rights by virtue of being born in a country (or by immigrating and becoming a naturalized citizen) (437)

voter apathy: indifference and inaction on the part of individuals or groups with respect to the political process (441)

war: armed conflict between nations or politically distinct groups (447)

KEY PEOPLE

Review the major theoretical contributions or findings of these people.

Peter Berger: Berger argued that violence is the ultimate foundation of any political order. (432-433)

William Domhoff: Like Mills, Domhoff saw that power resides in the hands of an elite few, which he referred to as the ruling class. He focused on the top one percent of Americans who belong to the super rich. (447)

C. Wright Mills: Mills suggested that power resides in the hands of an elite made up of the top leaders of the largest corporations, the most powerful generals of the armed forces, and certain elite politicians. (446-447)

Alejandro Portes and Ruben Rumbaut: These sociologists studied the process of assimilation of immigrants into American society, observing that the first step in the process is the group's developing a political organization to protect their ethnic interests. (442)

Tamotsu Shibutani: Shibutani noted that the process of dehumanization is helped along by the tendency for prolonged conflicts to be transformed into a struggle between good and evil. (450)

Pitirim Sorokin: Sorokin studied wars from 500 B.C. to A.D. 1925 and found that war was a fairly common experience. There had been 967 wars during this time span, for an average of a war every two or three years. (448)

Nicholas S. Timasheff: Timasheff identified three essential conditions of societies going to war—a cultural tradition of war, an antagonistic situation in which two or more countries have incompatible objectives, and a "fuel" that heats the situation to a boiling point so the line is crossed from thinking about war to actually waging it. (448)

Max Weber: Weber identified three different types of authority: traditional, rational-legal, and charismatic. (432-436)

STUDENT APPLICATION PROJECTS

This is your opportunity to apply the sociological perspective to the world around you. The projects in this section refer to material introduced in this chapter of your text. These projects help you apply the sociological perspective "down to your earth...down to your daily life."

1. Are you a registered voter? Why or why not? Do you think it is important for people to exercise their right to vote? Explain. Why do you think many people do not vote in the United States? Explain your answer.

2. Who do you think rules the United States? Do you agree with any particular perspective presented in this chapter? Explain.

3. What is meant by the new world order? Do you think the world is moving in this direction? Do you see this as a positive or negative change? Explain.

4. Do you think that the recent wars that the U.S. has chosen to engage in have been necessary? Were there other ways in which the conflict could have been resolved?

SELF-TEST

MULTIPLE CHOICE QUESTIONS

1. Which of the following relates to power? (432)
    a. the concept was defined by Max Weber
    b. it is the ability to carry out one's will in spite of resistance from others
    c. it is an inevitable part of everyday life
    d. all of the above

2. Governments, whether dictatorships or the elected forms, are examples of: (432)
    a. coercion.
    b. macropolitics.
    c. micropolitics.
    d. none of the above.

3. What is coercion? (432)
    a. legitimate authority
    b. power people do not accept as just
    c. micropolitics
    d. macropolitics

4. What did Peter Berger consider to be the ultimate foundation of any political order? (433)
    a. laws
    b. elections
    c. violence
    d. leaders

5. Revolutions: (433)
    a. are most likely to occur on the death of a charismatic leader.
    b. are a people's rejection of the government's claim to rule over them.
    c. occur only when economic conditions are bleak.
    d. all of the above.

6. Traditional authority: (433)
    a. is the hallmark of tribal groups.
    b. is based on custom.
    c. declines with industrialization.
    d. all of the above.

7. In which type of authority is power based on law and written procedures? (434)
    a. traditional
    b. rational-legal
    c. charismatic
    d. coercion

8. In the Middle Ages, soldiers followed Joan of Arc into battle because they saw her as a messenger of God, fighting on the side of justice and they accepted her leadership because of these appealing qualities. Her authority to lead would be considered: (434)
   a. traditional.
   b. rational-legal.
   c. charismatic.
   d. feminine.

9. John F. Kennedy: (435)
   a. was a rational-legal leader.
   b. was a charismatic leader.
   c. is an example of a leader who is difficult to classify in terms of ideal types.
   d. all of the above.

10. Which of the following is considered the least stable type of authority? (435)
    a. traditional
    b. rational-legal
    c. charismatic
    d. monarchy

11. Representative democracy: (437)
    a. is a form of democracy in which elected officials represent citizens' interests.
    b. is perhaps the greatest gift the United States has given the world.
    c. was considered revolutionary when it was first conceived.
    d. all of the above.

12. The idea that everyone has the same rights by virtue of being born in a country is: (437)
    a. direct democracy.
    b. universal citizenship.
    c. state citizenship.
    d. an ideal that has rarely been realized.

13. An individual who seizes power and imposes his will onto the people is known as a: (437)
    a. charismatic leader.
    b. dictator.
    c. totalitarian leader.
    d. monarch.

14. Which form of government exerts almost total control over the people? (438)
    a. monarchy
    b. dictatorship
    c. totalitarian regime
    d. oligarchy

15. The United States has: (440)
    a. centrist parties.
    b. noncentrist parties.
    c. proportional representation.
    d. none of the above.

16. Which of the following statements about political parties in the U.S. is *incorrect*? (440)
    a. Because both parties appeal to a broad membership, it is often difficult to distinguish one from the other, except at the extremes of both parties.
    b. Members of Congress maintain strict party allegiances and will never cross party lines to vote for legislation proposed by a member of the other party.
    c. Democrats and Republicans represent different slices of the center, firmly supporting fundamental principles of U.S. political philosophy.
    d. Because most Americans think a vote for a third party is a waste, third parties do very poorly in elections.

17. Which electoral system is most likely to encourage formation of minority political parties? (441)
    a. a winner-take-all system
    b. a proportional representation system
    c. direct democracy
    d. representative democracy

18. What do studies of voting patterns in the United States show? (441)
    a. Voting patterns are too inconsistent to draw meaningful conclusions.
    b. Voting varies by age, race/ethnicity, education, employment, income, and gender.
    c. Younger people are more likely to vote than older individuals.
    d. All of the above.

19. According to Portes and Rumbaut, on what basis do immigrants initially organize politically? (442)
    a. gender
    b. age
    c. social class
    d. race-ethnicity

20. Which of the following statements regarding participation in presidential elections today is *correct*? (443)
    a. Only about one-third of eligible voters actually vote.
    b. About one-half of eligible voters cast a ballot.
    c. About three-fourths of eligible voters participate in presidential elections today.
    d. Slightly less than two-thirds of eligible voters vote.

21. Lobbyists are: (444)
    a. people paid to influence legislation on behalf of their clients.
    b. bankrolled by political action committees.
    c. a major force in American politics.
    d. all of the above.

22. Functionalists see that _____ prevents groups from having total government control. (446)
    a. the existence of a powerful elite
    b. the presence of checks and balances
    c. the presence of many PACs to which politicians owe allegiance
    d. all of the above

23. Which perspective suggests that conflict is minimized as special-interest groups negotiate with one another and reach compromises? (446)
    a. functionalists
    b. conflict theorists
    c. symbolic interactionists
    d. political sociologists

24. Members of the power elite are drawn from: (446)
    a. the largest corporations.
    b. the armed forces.
    c. top political offices.
    d. all of the above.

25. According to conflict theorists, the ruling class is: (447)
    a. a group that meets together and agrees on specific matters.
    b. a group that tends to have complete unity on issues.
    c. made up of people whose backgrounds and orientations to life are so similar that they automatically share the same goals.
    d. a myth.

26. War is: (447)
    a. armed conflict between nations or politically distinct groups.
    b. universal.
    c. chosen for dealing with disagreements by all societies at one time or another.
    d. all of the above.

27. Which of the following is *not* one of the essential conditions of war identified by Nicholas Timasheff? (448)
    a. the existence of a strong, well-armed military force
    b. a cultural tradition of war
    c. an antagonistic situation in which two or more states confront incompatible objectives
    d. the presence of a "fuel" that heats the antagonistic situation to a boiling point

28. Which of the Most Industrialized Nations does the most business selling arms to other nations, and thereby sowing the seeds of possible future wars? (449)
    a. Sweden
    b. Great Britain
    c. France
    d. the United States

29. _____ is a cost of war where people no longer see others as worthy of human treatment, paving the way for torture and killing. (449)
    a. alienation
    b. dehumanization
    c. coercion
    d. nationalism

30. Which organization is striving to be the legislative body of the world? (455)
    a. CAFTA
    b. European United
    c. United Nations
    d. NAFTA

TRUE-FALSE QUESTIONS

1. _____In every group, large or small, some individuals have power over others. (432)
2. _____Coercion refers to legitimate power. (432)
3. _____The state claims a monopoly on violence within some designated territory. (433)
4. _____Even with industrialization, some forms of traditional authority go unchallenged. (433)
5. _____Rational-legal authority derives from the position that an individual holds, not from the person who holds the position. (434)
6. _____Because the authority of charismatic leaders is based on their personal ability to attract followers they pose no threat to the established political system. (434)
7. _____It is difficult to classify some leaders as having one specific type of authority. (434)
8. _____Routinization of charisma involves the transfer of authority from a charismatic leader to either traditional or rational-legal authority. (436)
9. _____Even in early societies that were small in size, there was a need for some form of political system. (437)
10. _____Direct democracy was impossible in the United States as its population grew in number and spread out. (437)
11. _____The concept of representative democracy based on citizenship was first developed in the United States. (437)
12. _____The idea of universal citizenship caught on quickly in the United States. (437)
13. _____The European system of democracy is not that different from our own. (428-440)
14. _____Voter turnout is higher among people who are more socially integrated. (441)
15. _____Most political action committees represent broad social interests such as environmental protection. (445)

16. _____Functionalists believe that pluralism prevents any one group from gaining control of the government and using it to oppress the people. (446)
17. _____Conflict theorists claim that no one group holds power in America; that the country's many competing interest groups balance each other. (447)
18. _____There were 937 documented wars in Europe between 500 B.C. to A.D. 1925. (448)
19. _____Because of technological advances in killing, the cost of war in terms of money spent and human lives lost has decreased. (449)
20. _____The globalization of capitalism and the trend toward regional economic and political unions may indicate that a world political system is developing. (451)
21.

FILL-IN-THE-BLANK QUESTIONS

1. _____ is the ability to get your own way even if others resist. (432)
2. The _____ is a political entity that claims a monopoly on violence over some territory. (433)
3. _____ authority is based on custom. (433)
4. Joan of Arc is an example of _____ authority. (435)
5. Because of their small size, tribes and cities were able to practice _____ democracy. (437)
6. The _____ holds the potential for transforming the way we vote and pass laws. (438)
7. _____ is almost total control of a people by the government. (439)
8. Most Europeans countries base their elections on a system of _____. (441)
9. Many people do not vote because of voter _____. (443)
10. The dairy industry is an example of a _____ group. (445)
11. The major criticism leveled against lobbyists and Political Action groups is that their _____ in effect buys votes. (445)
12. The system of _____ was designed to ensure that no one branch of government dominates. (446)
13. C. Wright Mills coined the phrase the _____. (447)
14. Sociologist William Domhoff uses the term _____ to refer to the power elite. (447)
15. _____ is the use of violence to create fear in an effort to bring about political objectives. (450)

MATCH THESE CONCEPTS WITH THEIR DEFINITIONS

_____ 1. anarchy
_____ 2. charismatic authority
_____ 3. democracy
_____ 4. dictatorship
_____ 5. monarchy
_____ 6. oligarchy
_____ 7. citizenship
_____ 8. pluralism
_____ 9. totalitarianism
_____ 10. traditional authority

a. *a form of government that exerts almost total control over people*

b. *a form of government headed by a king or queen*

c. *a form of government where power is held by a small group*

d. *birth and residence in a country imparts certain rights*

e. *authority based on an individual's outstanding traits*

f. *diffusion of power among many different groups*

g. *authority based on custom*

h. *system of government in which authority derives from the people*

i. *lawlessness caused by the abuse or collapse of authority*

j. *a government in which power is seized by an individual*

ESSAY QUESTIONS

1. Distinguish between macropolitics and micropolitics, explaining what each is and which perspectives are associated with each; provide your own examples to illustrate.

2. Compare and contrast the systems of democracy found in the United States and Europe, and discuss how some of the problems associated with our system, such as voter apathy, the power of political action committees, and the concentration of power, are related to our system.

3. Discuss the two major political parties in the United States. Explain their differences and similarities.

4. Discuss why wars happen.

CHAPTER 16
MARRIAGE AND FAMILY

CHAPTER SUMMARY

- Because there are so many cultural variations, family structure is hard to define. Nevertheless, family is defined broadly as two or more people who consider themselves related by blood, marriage, or adoption. Marriage and family patterns vary remarkably across cultures, but the four universal themes in marriage are mate selection, descent, inheritance, and authority.

- According to the functionalist perspective, the family is universal because it serves six essential functions: economic production, socialization of children, care of the sick and aged, recreation, sexual control, and reproduction. Conversely, isolation and emotional overload are the dysfunctions that result from the changes in the nuclear family. Conflict theorists focus on how marriage and the family help perpetuate inequalities. Symbolic interactionists focus on the contrasting experiences and perspectives of men and women that are played out in marriage, including the power struggle over housework.

- The family life cycle is analyzed in terms of love and courtship, marriage, childbirth, child rearing, and the family in later life. Within the United States, marriage follows predictable patterns of age, social class, race and religion, while childbirth and childbearing vary by social class.

- Family diversity in U.S. culture is based primarily on social class rather than racial and ethnic differences. One-parent families, childless families, blended families, and gay families represent some of the different types of families today.

- Trends in American families include postponement of first marriage, cohabitation, grandparents as parents, and the emergence of the "sandwich generation"—those who are caught between caring for their own children and caring for their elderly parents.

- Various studies have focused on problems in measuring divorce, children of divorce, ex-spouses, and remarriage. While time seems to heal most children's wounds over the divorce of their parents, research suggests that a minority carry the scars of divorce into adulthood. Men and women experience divorce differently: for men, this event often results in a weakening of their relationships with children; for women, it means a decline in their standard of living. Although most divorced people remarry, their rate of remarriage has slowed considerably.

- Violence and abuse—including child abuse, battering, marital rape, and incest—are the "dark side" of family life.

- Researchers have identified variables that help marriages and families last and be happy.

- The trends for the future include a continued increase in cohabitation, births to unmarried mothers, postponement of marriage, and parenting by grandparents. The continuing growth in the numbers of working wives will impact on marital balance of power.

LEARNING OBJECTIVES
After reading Chapter 16, you should be able to:

1. Explain why it is difficult to define precisely the term "family" and discuss some of the different ways that family systems can be organized and classified. (462)
2. Identify the common cultural themes that run through marriage and the family. (463-464)
3. Explain why the family is universal and list the basic societal needs that it fulfills. (464)
4. Contrast the functionalists, conflict, and symbolic interaction perspectives regarding marriage and family and provide examples that illustrate each of these perspectives. (464-468)
5. Identify the major elements of the family life cycle and discuss how each of these elements may be affected by age, education, social class, race and ethnicity, sex, and/or religion. (468-474)
6. Describe the distinctive characteristics of family life in African American, Latino, Asian American, and Native American families, and discuss the role that social class and culture play in affecting these distinctions. (474-477)
7. Discuss the characteristics and challenges that one-parent, childless, blended, gay and lesbian families in the United States may face. (478-780)
8. Identify the general patterns and trends in marriage and family life in the United States and discuss how these are reflected in postponement of marriage, cohabitation, single motherhood, grandparents as parents, the sandwich generation, divorce, grandchildren of divorce, absent fathers, and remarriage. (481-485)
9. Describe the different measures of divorce rates, the adverse effects of divorce on children, and the factors that most help children adjust to divorce in the United States. (485-490)
10. Describe the "dark side" of family life as it relates to battering, child abuse, marital rape, and incest. (491-493)
11. Identify the characteristics that most contribute to happy marriages and happy families. (493-494)
12. Talk about future patterns and trends in marriage and family life in the United States. (494)

CHAPTER OUTLINE

I. **Marriage and Family in Global Perspective**
   A. The term "family" is difficult to define because there are many types.
      1. In some societies men have more than one wife (polygyny) or women have more than one husband (polyandry).
      2. Many groups have various customs regarding marriage or family. For example, in the 1980's and 1990's several European countries legalized same-sex marriages. In 2003, so did Canada, as did the state of Massachusetts in 2004.
      3. In other societies, sexual relationships or the disciplining of a child do not characterize a family. As such, a broad definition of family is needed.

4. A family is a group of people who consider themselves related by blood, marriage, or adoption.

5. In contrast, a housing unit consists only of people who occupy the same dwelling.

6. A family is classified as nuclear (husband, wife, and children) or extended (a nuclear family plus other relatives like grandparents, aunts, uncles, and cousins).

7. The family of orientation is the family in which a person grows up, while the family of procreation is the family formed when a couple's first child is born. A person who is married but has not had a child is part of a couple, not a family.

8. Marriage is a group's approved mating arrangements, usually marked by a ritual to show the couple's new public status.

B. Common Cultural Themes do run through marriage and family.

1. Patterns of mate selection are established to govern who one can and cannot marry. Endogamy is the practice of marrying within one's own group, while exogamy is the practice of marrying outside of one's own group. The best example of exogamy is the incest taboo, which prohibits sex and marriage among designated relatives. Some norms of mate selection are written into law, others are informal.

2. Three major patterns of descent (tracing kinship over generations) are (a) bilateral (descent traced on both the mother's and the father's side); (b) patrilineal (descent traced only on the father's side); and (c) matrilineal (descent traced only on the mother's side).

3. Mate selection and descent are regulated in all societies in order to provide an orderly way of passing property, and other things, to the next generation. In a bilateral system, property passes to males and females; in a patrilineal system, property passes only to males; in a matrilineal system, property passes only to females.

4. Patriarchy is a social system in which men dominate women, and this runs through all societies. No historical records exist of a true matriarchy, a system in which women as a group dominate over men as a group. In an egalitarian social system, authority is more or less equally divided between men and women.

II. **Marriage and Family in Theoretical Perspective**

A. The functionalist perspective stresses how the family is related to other parts of society and how it contributes to the well-being of society.

1. The family is universal because it serves functions essential to the well-being of society: economic production, socialization of children, care of the sick and aged, recreation, sexual control, and reproduction.

2. The incest taboo (rules specifying which people are too closely related to have sex or marry) helps the family avoid role confusion and forces people to look outside the family for marriage partners, creating a network of support.

3. Unlike the extended family, the nuclear family has fewer people it can depend on for material and emotional support; thus, the members of a nuclear family are vulnerable to "emotional overload." The relative isolation of the nuclear family makes it easier for the "dark side" of families (incest and other types of abuse) to emerge.

B. Central to the conflict perspective is the struggle over scarce resources; in the family this struggle centers on housework, which is actually a struggle over the scarce resources of time, energy, and leisure.
　　1. Most men resist doing housework; consequently, working wives end up doing almost all of it. Wives who worked a 40 hour workweek did an average of 7 ½ more hours of work per week than their husbands.
　　2. Arlie Hochschild calls this additional work (after an 8-hour day at work) the "second shift". The result is that working wives feel deep discontent.
　　3. Although men are doing more work than in the past, they still feel that the "second shift" is the wife's responsibility. This can put a strain on the marriage.
　　4. Hochschild describes four strategies of resistance that men may engage in to get out of doing housework. These include waiting it out; playing dumb; needs reduction (man indicates that he doesn't mind wearing the unironed, wrinkled shirt; and substitute offerings (compliments wife on her ability to handle it all).

C. The symbolic interactionist perspective explores the different meaning that housework has for men and women and how each sex experiences marriage differently.
　　1. When men's and women's earning are about the same, men are more likely to share in the housework; if he gets laid off, his share decreases. When women earn more than their husbands, the men are least likely to do housework.
　　2. Understanding gender roles provides a key for explaining this; a wife's higher earnings tend to threaten a man's masculinity; doing "woman's work" is therefore a further threat.
　　3. Husbands who do more housework are less pleased with their marriage, but their wives are more pleased about it.

III. The Family Life Cycle
A. Romantic love is the idea of people being sexually attracted to one another and idealizing the other.
　　1. Research by Jankowiak and Fischer on 166 societies around the world found that the idea of romantic love existed in 88 percent, although its role was different in each.
　　2. It provides the ideological context in which Americans seek mates and form families.
　　3. Romantic love has two components: (1) emotional, a feeling of sexual attraction; and (2) cognitive, the feeling described as being "in love."

B. The social channels of love and marriage in the United States include age, education, social class, race, and religion.
　　1. Homogamy is the tendency of people with similar characteristics to marry one another and usually results from propinquity (spatial nearness).
　　2. Interracial marriage, which has increased sharply, is an exception to these social patterns. About 7 percent marry someone of another race, which totals about 4 million couples.
　　3. One of the most dramatic changes is marriages between African Americans and whites.

C. Contrary to what one might expect, parents are spending more time with their kids today than parents did in the 1970s and the 1980s.

       1.   This doesn't seem possible since more mothers are working outside of the home.

       2.   Parents have reduced the time they spend doing housework by buying more prepared meals or hiring cleaning services. Perhaps, they are also less fussy about how the house looks.

  D. As more mothers today are employed outside the home, child care has become an issue.

       1.   In comparing married couples and single mothers, child care arrangements appear to be quite similar. The main difference is the role played by the child's father while the mother is at work. For married couples, almost one of four children is cared for by the father, while for single mothers this arrangement occurs for about only one of fourteen children. Grandparents often help fill the child care gap left by absent fathers in single mother homes.

       2.   About one in six children is cared for in day care centers. Only a minority of U.S. day care centers offer high-quality care. The very low wages paid to day care workers seems to account for this. Two factors that seem to be associated with higher quality of care are: (1) fewer children per staff worker; and (2) staff training in early childhood development.

       3.   Nannies have become popular among upper middle-class parents. A recurring problem is tensions between parents and nanny.

       4.   According to Melvin Kohn, parents socialize children into the norms of their respective work worlds. Working-class parents want their children to conform to societal expectations. Middle-class parents are more concerned that their children develop curiosity, self-expression, and self-control.

  E. Later stages of family life bring both pleasures and problems.

       1.   The empty nest refers to a married couple's domestic situation after the last child has left home. The empty nest is not so empty anymore.

       2.   With prolonged education and a growing cost of establishing households, U.S. children are leaving home much later or are returning after having left.

       3.   42 percent of all 24- to 29-year-olds are living with their parents. These "adultolescents" face added issues with their parents regarding being independent and dependent.

       4.   Women are more likely than men to face the problem of adjusting to widowhood, for not only does the average woman live longer than a man but she has also usually married a man older than herself.

       5.   The survivor is faced with identity issues of who they are without their spouse. The adjustment is even more difficult when death is unexpected.

IV. Diversity in U.S. Families

  A. As with other groups, the family life of African Americans differs by social class.

       1.   The upper class is concerned with maintaining family lineage and preserving their privilege and wealth; the middle class focuses on achievement and respectability; poor African American families face the problems that poverty brings.

       2.   Poor men are likely to have few job skills and to be unemployed. As such, it is difficult to fulfill the cultural roles of husband and father. Poor families tend to

be headed by females and to have a higher rate of birth to single mothers. Divorce and desertion are also more common among the poor.

3.   Compared to other groups, African American families are the least likely to be headed by married couples and the most likely to be headed by women. The women are also more likely to marry men who are less educated than themselves.

B.   The effects of social class on families also apply to Latinos. In addition, families differ by country of origin.

1.   What really distinguishes Latino families is culture—especially the Spanish language, the Roman Catholic religion, and a strong family orientation, coupled with a disapproval of divorce.

2.   Machismo, the emphasis on male strength and dominance, use to be a characteristic of Latino families. Currently, machismo characterizes a small proportion of Latino husband-fathers.

C.   The structure of Asian American families is almost identical to that of white families.

1.   Because Asian Americans come from 20 different countries, family life varies considerably, reflecting these different cultures. The more recent the immigration, the closer the family life is to that of the country of origin.

2.   Bob Suzuki points out that while Chinese and Japanese American families have adopted the nuclear family pattern of the United States, they have also retained Confucian values that provide a distinct framework to family life: humanism, collectivity, self-discipline, hierarchy, respect for the elderly, moderation, and obligation.

3.   Asian Americans tend to be more permissive than Anglos in child rearing and more likely to use shame and guilt than physical punishment to control their children's behavior.

D.   For Native American families, the issue is whether to follow traditional values or to assimilate. The structure of Native American families is almost identical to that of Latinos; like others, these families differ by social class.

1.   Native American families are permissive with their children and avoid physical punishment.

2.   Elders play a much more active role in their children's families than they do in most U.S. families; they provide child care and teach and discipline children.

E.   There has been an increase in one-parent families.

1.   This is due to the high divorce rate and the sharp increase in births to unmarried women.

2.   The concern about one-parent families has more to with poverty than the fact that they are headed by a single parent. The reason for the poverty is that most are headed by women who earn less than men.

3.   Children from one-parent families are more likely to drop out of school, become delinquent, be poor as adults, divorce, and have children outside of marriage.

F.   Overall, about 19 percent of U.S. married couples never have children. Although somewhat influenced by race and ethnicity, in general, the more education a woman has, the more likely she is to expect to bear no children.

1.   The main reason couples choose not to have children is they want to be free to be able to change jobs or do spontaneous things; they want to avoid the expenses of

raising a child or the stresses associated with having children. Some do not like children, are in an unstable marriage, or feel they will be bored.

    2.   The proportion of couples who remain childless is likely to increase given that more education and careers are available to women; abortion is legal; advances have been made in contraception; cost of child rearing are so high; and the emphasis our society places on material things.

    3.   For many families, choice is not the reason they have no children; they are infertile. Some adopt, while others turn to new reproductive technologies.

G.   A blended family is one whose members were once part of other families (two divorced persons marry, bringing children into a new family unit). Blended families are increasing in number and often experience complicated family relationships.

H.   Many homosexual couples live in monogamous relationships that resemble heterosexual marriages in many respects.

    1.   In 1989, Denmark became the first country to legalize marriage between people of the same sex. Holland, Norway, and Sweden have since made same-sex marriages legal.

    2.   In 2004, Massachusetts became the first state to legalize same-sex marriages.

    3.   Gay and lesbian families are most likely to live in urban areas, with about half concentrated in just 20 cities. About one-fifth were previously married to heterosexuals.

    4.   Twenty-two percent of lesbian couples and five percent of gay couples have children from their heterosexual marriages.

    5.   Gay and lesbian couples also face the usual problems of heterosexual marriages: housework, money, careers, problems with relatives, and sexual adjustment. However, same-sex couples are more likely to break-up.

V.   Trends in U.S. Families

A.   The average age of American brides is the oldest it has been since records first were kept.

    1.   As a result, the age at which U.S. women have their first child is also the highest in U.S. history.

    2.   While many young people postpone marriage, they have not postponed the age at which they set up housekeeping with someone of the opposite sex.

B.   Cohabitation is living together as an unmarried couple, and has increased ten times over the last 30 years.

    1.   Sixty percent of the couples who marry today have lived together before marriage. Forty percent of children will spend some time in a cohabiting family.

    2.   Commitment is the essential difference between cohabitation and marriage: marriage assumes permanence; cohabiting assumes remaining together "as long as it works out."

    3.   Couples who cohabit before marriage are more likely to divorce than couples who did not live together before marriage. Many who live together feel pressure to marry and end up marrying a partner that they may not have chosen.

C.   As previously discussed, there has also been an increase in births to unmarried mothers.

1. Of the twelve industrialized nations for which data are available, all except Japan have experienced sharp increases in births to unmarried mothers; the U.S. rate falls in the middle of these nations.
2. Industrialization alone is too simple an explanation for this increase. To more fully understand this trend, future research must focus on customs and values embedded within a particular culture.

D. It is becoming more common for grandparents to raise their grandchildren.
1. About 4 percent of white children, 7 percent of Latino children, and 14 percent of white children are being reared by grandparents.
2. Often times, the parents are ill, homeless, addicted to drugs, or in prison.
3. Caring for grandchildren can bring great satisfaction. It can also bring stress in additional financial costs, the need to continue working when they were anticipating retirement and conflict with the parents of the children.

E. The "sandwich generation" refers to people who find themselves sandwiched between two generations, responsible for the care of their children and for their own aging parents. These people are typically between the ages of 40 and 55. Corporations have begun to offer some kind of elder care assistance to their employees, including seminars, referral services, and flexible work schedules.

VI. Divorce and Remarriage

A. There are problems measuring the extent of divorce in U.S. society.
1. Although the divorce rate is reported at 50 percent, this statistic is misleading because with rare exceptions, those who divorce do not come from the group who married that year.
2. An alternative is to compare the number of divorces in a given year to the entire group of married couples. The divorce rate for any given year is less than 2 percent of all married couples.
3. A third way calculates the percentage of all adult Americans who are divorced. People's race and ethnicity makes a difference in regards to the likelihood of divorce.
4. Another question to ask is the percentage of people who have ever been divorced. For women in their 50's forty percent have ever been divorced and for men in their 50's, 43 percent have been divorced at some point in their life.
5. Research has found that people who go to college, belong to a religion, wait to get married, and have children have a much better chance of their marriage lasting.
6. Working with co-workers of the opposite sex and working with people who are recently divorced increase one's risk for divorce.

B. Each year, more than one million children are in families affected by divorce. Divorce profoundly threatens a child's world.
1. Compared with children whose parents are not divorced, children from divorced families are more likely to experience emotional problems, more likely to be juvenile delinquents, less likely to complete high school, and more likely to divorce.
2. There is a debate between two psychological studies conducted by Judith Wallerstein and Mavis Hetherington. Wallerstein claims that divorce scars

children, causing depression and leaving them with insecurities that follow them into childhood. Hetherington's study found that 75 to 80 percent of the children of divorce function as well as children who are reared by both of their parents.

3. Several factors help children adjust to divorce: they adjust well if they experience little conflict, feel loved, live with the parent making a good adjustment, experience consistent family routines, and if the family has adequate money for its needs. Children also adjust better is a second adult can be counted on for support.

4. Adult children who come from a divorced family have a chance of a successful marriage if they marry someone whose parents did not divorce. Those couples where both husband and wife come from a divorced family are more likely to be marked by high distrust and conflict, leading to a higher chance of divorce.

C. Sociologists have found that the effects of divorce continue across generations; grandchildren of divorce have weaker ties to their parents, they don't go as far in school, and they have more marital discord with their spouses.

D. A new fathering pattern, known as serial fatherhood, is beginning to emerge. Divorced fathers tend to live with, support, and play an active fathering role with children of the woman to whom they are currently married or with whom they are currently living. Over time, contact with their children from a previous marriage diminishes. Only about one-sixth of children who live apart from their fathers see their dad as often as every week.

E. Women are more likely than men to feel that divorce gives them a new chance at life. The spouse who initiates the divorce usually gets over it and remarries sooner. Many divorced couples maintain contact with ex-spouses because of their children. Divorce often spells economic hardship for women, especially mothers of small children; the former husband's standard of living is likely to increase. The more education a woman has, the better prepared she is to survive financially after divorce.

F. Most divorced people eventually remarry, although the length of time between divorce and remarriage is longer today than in the past.

1. Most divorced people remarry other divorced people. Men are more likely to remarry than women; those who are most likely to remarry are mothers with small children and women who have not graduated from high school.

2. The divorce rate of remarried people without children is about the same as that of first marriages; remarriages in which children are present are more likely to end in divorce.

VII. Two Sides of Family Life

A. Spousal battering, child abuse, marital rape, and incest represent the dark side of family life.

1. Although wives are about as likely to attack their husbands as husbands are to attack their wives, it is generally the husband who lands the last and most damaging blow. Violence against women is related to the sexist structure of society and to our socialization.

2. Each year about 3 million U.S. children are reported to the authorities as victims of abuse or neglect; about 900,000 of these cases are substantiated.

3.   Marital rape is more common than previously thought. Between one-third and one-half of women who seek help at shelters for battered women are victims of marital rape. They are also less likely to report the rape.

4.   Rape victims include those in cohabiting and lesbian relationships.

5.   Incest is sexual relations between relatives, such as brothers and sisters or parents and children. It is most likely to occur in families that are socially isolated, and is more common than was previously thought. Uncles are the most common offenders; brother-sister incest is more common than father-child incest.

B.   A study of couples who had married fifteen years or longer reported these factors in making a relationship successful: thinking of their spouses as their best friend; liking their spouse as a person; having a commitment to the marriage and seeing it as sacred; agreeing with their spouse on aims and goals, believing that their spouse has grown more interesting; wanting the relationship to succeed; and laughing together.

1.   Sociologists have also found that marriages are happier when couples get along with their in-laws and when they do leisure activities together.

C.   While the statistics are important in order to gain a deeper understanding of the state of marriages and families in U.S. society, it is also important to remember that these are describing an overall pattern and not an individual case.

1.   The chances of having a successful marriage depend on each situation, especially the way people, *as individuals*, approach marriage.

2.   From a symbolic interactionist perspective, individuals create their own worlds, interpret experiences and act accordingly. If one thinks a marriage will fail, it increases the likelihood that it will. People tend to act according to their ideas, creating a self-fulfilling prophecy.

VIII.   The Future of Marriage and the Family

A.   In spite of problems, marriage will continue because it is functional. The vast proportion of Americans will continue to marry; many of those who divorce will remarry and "try again."

B.   It is likely that cohabitation, births to single mothers, age at first marriage, and parenting by grandparents will increase. More married women will join the work force and continue to gain marital power. Finally, more families will struggle with the twin demands of raising children and caring for aging parents.

C.   Individuals will continue to deal with the conflict between the bleak picture of marriage and family painted by the media and the rosy one painted by cultural myths. Sociologists can help correct these distortions through research.

KEY TERMS
After studying the chapter, review the definition for each of the following terms.

bilineal (system of descent): a system of reckoning descent that counts both the mother's and the father's side (464)

blended family: a family whose members were once part of other families (480)

cohabitation: unmarried couples living together in a sexual relationship (481)

egalitarian: authority more or less equally divided between people or groups, in this instance between a husband and wife (464)

empty nest: a married couple's domestic situation after the last child has left home (474)

endogamy: the practice of marrying within one's own group (463)

exogamy: the practice of marrying outside one's group (464)

extended family: a nuclear family plus other relatives, such as grandparents, uncles and aunts (462)

family: two or more people who consider themselves related by blood, marriage, or adoption (462)

family of orientation: the family in which a person grows up (462)

family of procreation: the family formed when a couple's first child is born (462)

homogamy: the tendency of people with similar characteristics to marry one another (470)

household: people who occupy the same housing unit (462)

incest: sexual relations between specified relatives, such as brothers and sisters or parents and children (493)

incest taboo: the rule that prohibits sex and marriage among designated relatives (464)

machismo: an emphasis on male strength and dominance (476)

marriage: a group's approved mating arrangements, usually marked by a ritual of some sort (463)

matriarchy: a society in which women as a group dominate men as a group (464)

matrilineal (system of descent): a system of reckoning descent that counts only the mother's side (464)

nuclear family: a family consisting of a husband, wife, and child(ren) (462)

patriarchy: a society or group in which men dominate women; authority is vested in males (464)

patrilineal (system of descent): a system of reckoning descent that counts only the father's side (464)

polyandry: a form of marriage in which women have more than one husband (462)

polygyny: a form of marriage in which men have more than one wife (462)

romantic love: feelings of erotic attraction accompanied by an idealization of the other (468)

serial fatherhood: a pattern of parenting in which a father, after divorce, reduces contact with his own children, serves as a father to the children of the woman he marries or lives with, then ignores these children, too, after moving in with or marrying another woman (490)

system of descent: how kinship is traced over the generations (464)

KEY PEOPLE

Review the major theoretical contributions or findings of these people.

Paul Amato and Jacob Cheadle: These sociologists were the first to study the grandchildren of divorced parents. They found that the effects of divorce continue across generations. (489)

Philip Blumstein and Pepper Schwartz: These sociologists interviewed same sex couples and found that they face the same problems as heterosexual couples. (480)

Urie Bronfenbrenner: This sociologist studied the impact of divorce on children and found that children adjust better if there is a second adult who can be counted on for support. (489)

Andrew Cherlin: Cherlin notes that our society has not yet developed adequate norms for remarriage. (491)

Donald Dutton and Arthur Aron: These researchers compared the sexual arousal levels of men who were in dangerous situations with men in safe situations. They found that the former were more sexually aroused than the latter. (470)

David Finkelhor and Kersti Yllo: These sociologists interviewed 10 percent of a representative sample of women from Boston who reported that their husbands used physical force to compel them to have sex. (493)

Lori Girshick: She interviewed lesbians who had been sexually assaulted by their partners. (493)

Mavis Hetherington: A psychologist who's research shows that 75-80 % of children of divorce function as well as children who are reared by both parents. (489)

Arlie Hochschild: Hochschild conducted research on families in which both parents are employed full-time in order to find out how household tasks are divided up. She found that women do more of the housework than their husbands, resulting in women putting in a *second shift* at home after their workday has ended. (495)

William Jankowiak andEdward Fischer: These anthropologists surveyed data on 166 societies and found that the majority of them contained the ideal of romantic love. (468)

Melvin Kohn: Kohn found that the type of work that parents do has an impact on how they rear their children. (473)

Jeanette and Robert Lauer: These sociologists interviewed 351 couples who had been married fifteen years or longer in order to find out what makes a marriage successful. (493)

Diana Russell: Russell found that incest victims who experience the most difficulty are those who have been victimized the most often over longer periods of time and whose incest was "more intrusive." (493)

William Sayres: He believes that the term family is so difficult to define because cultures organize members of family differently. (462)

Nicholas Stinnett: Stinnett studied 660 families from all regions of the United States and parts of South America in order to find out what are characteristics of happy families. (494)

Murray Straus: This sociologist has studied domestic violence and found that, while husbands and wives are equally likely to attack one another, men inflict more damage on women than the reverse. (491)

Bob Suzuki: This sociologist studied Chinese and Japanese American families and identified several distinctive characteristics of this type of family. (477)

Judith Wallerstein: A psychologist who claims that divorce has detrimental, long term effects on children. (488)

STUDENT APPLICATION PROJECTS

This is your opportunity to apply the sociological perspective. The projects in this section refer to material introduced in this chapter of your text. These projects help you apply the sociological perspective "down to your earth...down to your daily life."

1. Think about your nuclear family and your extended family. List the concepts of "marriage" and "family" that you see (or have seen). Have your family's "marriage" patterns stayed the same or changed over time? Has your family's structure stayed the same or changed over time? Explain.

2. Do you think the "second-shift" is a temporary problem or a long-range problem regarding family and marriage? How has the issue been dealt with in your family? How do you plan to resolve the potential issues caused by the "second shift" in your own marriage or family?

3. List the problems faced by American families. Given all the problems, do you think marriage and family are worth the effort? Why or why not?

4. What kinds of families do you think that we will have in the future? What will life be like for families and what challenges will they face?

SELF-TEST

MULTIPLE CHOICE QUESTIONS

1. Polyandry is: (462)
    a. a marriage in which a woman has more than one husband.
    b. a marriage in which a man has more than one wife.
    c. male control of a society or group.
    d. female control of a society or group.

2. A household differs from a family in which of the following ways? (462)
    a. it includes only those people who are related by blood
    b. it is a broader definition because it includes people who support the family, such as housekeepers and nannies
    c. it is only used by government agencies for statistical purposes
    d. it pertains only to people who occupy the same housing unit or living quarters

3. The family of orientation is: (462)
    a. the family formed when a couple's first child is born.
    b. the same thing as an extended family.
    c. the same as the family of procreation.
    d. a family in which a person grows up.

4. Endogamy is: (463)
    a. the practice of marrying outside one's group.
    b. the practice of marrying within one's own group.
    c. the practice of marrying someone within one's own family.
    d. none of the above.

5. In a matrilineal system: (464)
    a. descent is figured only on the mother's side.
    b. children are not considered related to their mother's relatives.
    c. descent is traced on both the mother's and the father's side.
    d. descent is figured only on the father's side.

6. In terms of authority within the family, an increasing number of U.S. families are: (464)
    a. matriarchal.
    b. patriarchal.
    c. egalitarian.
    d. without authority.

7. The incest taboo: (466)
    a. are rules specifying the degrees of kinship that prohibit sex or marriage.
    b. helps families avoid role confusion.
    c. facilitates the socialization of children.
    d. all of the above.

8. Which theoretical perspective looks at how weakened family functions increase divorce? (466)
    a. symbolic interactionism
    b. functionalism
    c. conflict theory
    d. feminism

9. Conflict theorists focus on inequality in marriages, especially unequal power between _____ and _____? (467)
    a. parents, children
    b. mothers, daughters
    c. fathers, sons
    d. husbands, wives

10. According to Arlie Hochschild, most men engage in strategies of resistance when it comes to doing housework. Which of the following is *not* one of the strategies she identified? (467)
    a. *playing dumb*—By withdrawing their mental attention from the task, men get credit for trying and being a good sport, but in such a way that they are not chosen the next time.
    b. *substitute labor*—By hiring someone else to do the work (a maid service, a lawn care company), they guarantee that the work gets done but that they're not the ones doing it.
    c. *waiting it out*—Some men never volunteer, thereby forcing their wives to ask them to do household chores. Wives sometimes don't ask, because they say it feels like "begging."
    d. *needs reduction*—The husband scales down his own housework "needs," forcing the wife to step in and do things herself because of her "greater need" to see them done right.

11. According to research findings, who of the following feels most threatened by doing housework, and consequently does the least? (467)
    a. men who earn significantly more money than their wives
    b. men who earn about the same amount of money as their wives
    c. men who earn less money than their wives
    d. men who are employed in occupations that are highly sex-typed as masculine

12. According to research by Dutton and Aron, what does love usually start with? (470)
    a. sexual attraction
    b. a commitment
    c. a cognitive awareness of our feelings
    d. a chance meeting

13. The tendency of people with similar characteristics to marry one another is: (470)
    a. propinquity.
    b. erotic selection.
    c. homogamy.
    d. heterogamy.

14. Families of the same _____ are likely to be similar, regardless of their race-ethnicity. (470)
    a. age
    b. social class
    c. region
    d. religion

15. In what ways do child care arrangements of married couples and single mothers differ? (471)
    a. Single mothers are more likely to leave their children home alone.
    b. Single mothers are much less likely to rely on the child's father for help.
    c. Single mothers are much more likely to rely on the child's father for help.
    d. Single mothers are more likely to enroll their children in poor-quality child care.

16. In comparing child-rearing styles of middle and working class parents, Kohn concluded that: (472)
    a. parents of all social classes socialize their children similarly.
    b. middle-class parents are more likely to use physical punishment.
    c. working-class parents are more likely to withdraw privileges or affection.
    d. none of the above.

17. What percent of 24- to 29–years-olds are living with their parents? (472)
    a. 25%
    b. 32%
    c. 40%
    d. 42%

18. A major concern of upper-class African American families is: (474)
    a. achievement and respectability.
    b. problems of poverty.
    c. family background of those whom their children marry.
    d. all of the above.

19. Machismo: (476)
    a. distinguishes Latino families from other groups.
    b. is an emphasis on male strength and dominance.
    c. is seen in some Chicano families where the man has a strong role in his family.
    d. all of the above.

20. In what ways do Native American families differ from most U.S. families? (477)
    a. there are more single parent families
    b. there is less nonmarital childbirth
    c. elders play a more active role in their children's families
    d. they have higher rates of divorce and marital instability

21. Since 1970, the number of children in the United States who live with both parents has: (478)
    a. remained stable.
    b. dropped.
    c. increased.
    d. has gone down and is now up again.

22. Children from one-parent families are more likely to: (478)
    a. drop out of school.
    b. become delinquent.
    c. be poor as adults.
    d. all of the above.

23. The three major changes that characterize U.S. families today include all of the following except: (480)
    a. postponement of first marriage.
    b. increase in cohabitation.
    c. increase in grandparents raising grandchildren.
    d. increase in interracial marriages.

24. In 2004, what state in the United States became the first to legalize same-sex marriages? (480)
    a. Hawaii
    b. California
    c. Vermont
    d. New York

25. Cohabitation: (481)
    a. is the condition of living together as an unmarried couple.
    b. has increased ten times in the past 30 years.
    c. has occurred before about half of all couples marry.
    d. all of the above.

26. The *sandwich generation* refers to: (485)
    a. stay-at-home moms who spend their days making sandwiches for their preschoolers.
    b. people who are sandwiched between two sets of family relations because of the increase in divorce today.
    c. young children who consume a lot of sandwiches and whose needs are often overlooked by parents whose time is stretched by work and household responsibilities.
    d. people who find themselves caught between two generations, simultaneously responsible for the care of their children and their aging parents.

27. Which of the following factors reduce someone's chance of divorce during the first 10 years of marriage? (485)
    a. getting married over the age of 25
    b. waiting to have a baby 7 months or longer after marriage
    c. having parents who are not divorced
    d. all of the above reduce risk of divorce

28. What did researchers find out about grandchildren of divorced parents? (489)
    a. this did not have any affect on them
    b. they have stronger ties with their parents
    c. they are more likely to have marital discord with their spouses
    d. most were college graduates

29. The growing numbers of women in the workforce are likely to continue to shift the balance of marital _____. (491)
    a. power
    b. happiness
    c. functions
    d. abuse

30. What trend(s) are likely to continue into the next century? (494)
    a. increase in cohabitation
    b. increase in age at first marriage
    c. more equality in the husband-wife relationship
    d. all of the above

TRUE-FALSE QUESTIONS

1. _____Marriage and cohabitation are mechanisms for governing mate selection, reckoning descent, and establishing inheritance and authority. (462)
2. _____The family of procreation is the family formed when the couple has their own child. (462)
3. _____Laws of endogamy in the United States prohibit interracial marriages. (463)
4. _____Today, family authority patterns in the United States are becoming more egalitarian. (464)

5. _____Functionalists believe that the incest taboo helps the family to avoid role confusion. (466)

6. _____Conflict theorists believe that one of the consequences of married women working for pay is a reshuffling of power in the home. (466)

7. _____Arlie Hochschild concluded that women are generally happy to work a second shift. (467)

8. _____According to Hochschild, it is important for a husband to express appreciation to his wife when she handles both work for wages and the second shift at home. (467)

9. _____Gender role is the key to understanding why men who get laid off from their jobs would decrease the amount of work they do around the house. (467)

10. _____Love, courtship, marriage, childbirth, child rearing, and the family in later life are all major elements of the family life cycle. (470)

11. _____Marital satisfaction increases after the birth of a child. (471)

12. _____Nannies have become a popular option for upper-middle-class parents. (471)

13. _____Researchers have found that the type of work that parents do has no impact on how they rear their children. (472)

14. _____Women are about as likely as men to face the problem of adjusting to widowhood. (473)

15. _____ The structure of Asian American families is almost identical to that of white families. (477)

16. _____Depending on what numbers you choose to compare, you can produce almost any divorce rate you wish, from 50 percent to less than 2 percent. (480)

17. _____Today's average first-time bride and groom are older than at any time in U.S. history. (480)

18. _____U.S. rate of births to unmarried women is the highest among a group of ten industrialized nations for which there are accurate data. (481)

19. _____Most divorced fathers do not maintain ongoing relationships with their children. (490)

20. 20._____According to research by Finkelhor and Yllo, one in ten women who were part of a representative sample reported that their husbands used physical force to compel them to have sex. (493)

FILL-IN-THE-BLANK QUESTIONS

1. The _____ forces people to look outside the family for marriage partners. (463)
2. There are no historical records of a true _____. (464)
3. Husbands who earn less than their wives do the _____ housework. (467)
4. Indian sociologists estimate that parents still arrange about _____ % of marriages. (469).
5. _____ occurs largely as a result of propinquity, or spatial nearness. (470)
6. The Roman Catholic religion and strong family orientation distinguish _____ families from others. (478)
7. Sociologists use the term _____ kin to refer to the stretching of kinship. (478)
8. The concern expressed over one-parent families may have more to do with _____ than with children being reared by one parent. (479)
9. _____ the first country to legalize marriage between people of the same sex. (480)
10. Postponing _____ is today's norm. (480)

11. _____ is the essential difference between cohabitation and marriage. (480)
12. It is becoming increasingly common for_____ to rear their grandchildren. (480)
13. The main reason for _____ families is that parents are incapable of caring for their children. (480)
14. Women are more likely than men to feel divorce is giving them a _____ in life. (490)
15. _____ is more likely to occur in families that are socially isolated. (494)

MATCH THESE SOCIAL SCIENTISTS WITH THEIR CONTRIBUTIONS

_____ 1. Judith Wallerstein
_____ 2. Urie Bronfenbrenner
_____ 3. Andrew Cherlin
_____ 4. Finkelhor & Yllo
_____ 5. Mavis Hetherington
_____ 6. Arlie Hochschild
_____ 7. Melvin Kohn

_____ 8. Jankowiak / Fischer
_____ 9. Diana Russell
_____ 10. Bob Suzuki

a. *divorce has long-term damaging effects*
b. *studied marital rape*
c. *found that societies had the ideal of romantic love*
d. *studied incest victims*
e. *75-80% of children of divorce will adjust well*
f. *children adjust better with a second adult around*
g. *identified distinctive characteristics of Asian-American families*
h. *noted lack of norms regarding remarriage*
i. *studied social class differences in child-rearing*
j. *identified the second shift*

ESSAY QUESTIONS

1. Discuss whether the family still provides a useful function.

2. Discuss what factors contribute to successful marriages and to happy families.

3. Identify the stages in the family life cycle, discussing what tasks are accomplished in each stage and what event marks the transition from one stage to the next.

4. Identify the trends among U.S. families today and explain the social forces that have contributed to each of them.

5. Discuss the impact that divorce has on family members—men, women and children.

CHAPTER 17
EDUCATION

CHAPTER SUMMARY

- In earlier societies, education consisted of informal learning and was synonymous with acculturation. Today, education is no longer the same as informal acculturation, for the term now refers to a group's formal system of teaching knowledge, values, and skills.

- In general, formal education reflects a nation's economy. It is more extensive in the most industrialized nations, such as Japan and very spotty in the least industrialized nations, such as Egypt.

- Functionalists emphasize the functions of education, including teaching knowledge and skills, transmitting cultural values, social integration, gatekeeping, and promoting personal and social change and mainstreaming. They note that education has replaced some traditional family functions and provides a host of other functions as well.

- Conflict theorists view education as a mechanism for maintaining social inequality and reproducing the social class system. Accordingly, they stress such matters as the way in which education reflects the social structure of society (the correspondence principle); unequal funding of schools; culturally biased IQ tests; the hidden curriculum; and the advantage of family background regardless of students' personal abilities.

- Symbolic interactionists examine classroom interaction. They study how teacher expectations cause a self-fulfilling prophecy, producing the very behavior that the teacher is expecting.

- Problems facing the current U.S. educational system include falling Scholastic Aptitude Test (SAT) scores, grade inflation, social promotion, functional illiteracy, and violence in schools. Suggestions for reform include implementing and maintaining a secure and safe learning environment, increasing academic standards and expectations, and implementing a school choice and site-based management program.

LEARNING OBJECTIVES
After reading Chapter 17, you should be able to:

1. Summarize the development of modern education and discuss the links between democracy, industrialization, and universal education. (500-502)
2. Compare the education systems of Japan, Russia, and Egypt, and discuss about how they represent the differences in education between Most Industrialized, Industrializing, and Least Industrialized Nations. (503-504)
3. From the functionalist perspective, identify and discuss the functions of education including: teaching knowledge and skills; cultural transmission of values; social integration; and gatekeeping. (505-508)

4. Discuss the family functions that have been replaced by the education system, as well as the other functions that it is fulfilling such as matchmaking; being a source of social networks; reducing the unemployment rate; and stabilizing society. (507-508)

5. From the conflict perspective, explain and discuss the different ways the education system reinforces basic social inequalities. This includes the hidden curriculum, use of IQ tests, funding of schools, the correspondence principle, and the effect of family background. (508-513)

6. From the symbolic interactionist perspective, cite the research into—and the implications of—the effects of teachers' expectations on students' performances. (513-515)

7. Identify the major problems that exist within the United States educational system and evaluate some of the potential solutions. (5015-521)

CHAPTER OUTLINE

I. The Development of Modern Education

A. In earlier societies, education was synonymous with acculturation (transmission of culture from one generation to the next), not with a separate institution.

    1. In societies where a sufficient surplus developed, a separate institution arose. Some individuals devoted themselves to teaching, while those who had leisure became their students. Education gradually came to refer to a group's *formal* system of teaching knowledge, values, and skills.

    2. During the Dark Ages, only the monks and a handful of the wealthy nobility could read and write.

    3. Industrialization created a need for the average citizen to be able to read, write, and work with figures due to the new machinery and new types of jobs.

B. In the years following the American Revolution, the founders of the Republic believed formal education should be the principal means for creating a uniform national culture.

    1. In the early 1800s, there was a jumble of schools administered by separate localities, with no coordination. Children of the wealthy attended private schools; children of the lower classes (and slaves) received no formal education.

    2. Horace Mann, a Massachusetts educator, proposed that "common schools", supported through taxes, be established throughout his state; the idea spread throughout the country.

    3. Industrialization and universal education occurred at the same time. Since the economy was undergoing fundamental change, political and civic leaders recognized the need for an educated work force. They also feared the influx of "foreign" values and looked on public education as a way to Americanize immigrants.

    4. Mandatory education laws requiring children to attend school to a specified age or to a particular grade level were enacted in all U.S. states by 1918.

    5. As industrialization progressed, education came to be seen as essential to the well-being of society; industrialized nations developed into credential societies.

    6. Today, a larger proportion of the population attends colleges and universities in the United States than in any other industrialized country in the world; 65 percent of all high-school graduates now enter college. One in six Americans has not

made it through high school. This leads to economic problems for most of them for the rest of their lives.

II.   Education in Global Perspective

A.   A central principle of education is that a nations' education reflects its culture. Education in the Most Industrialized Nations: Japan

1.   Japanese education reflects a group-centered ethic. Children in grade school work as a group, mastering the same skills/materials; cooperation and respect for elders (and positions of authority) are stressed.

2.   College admission procedures are based on test scores; only the top scorers are admitted, regardless of social class. However, the children from richer families are more likely to be admitted to college. It is likely that these families have spent more money on tutors to help their children prepare for the college entrance exams.

B.   Education in the Industrializing Nations: Russia

1.   After the Revolution of 1917, the new Soviet government insisted that socialist values dominate education; they saw education as a means to build support for the new political system.

2.   Universal education, including college, was free and math and natural sciences were stressed. Education was centralized, with schools across the nation following the same curriculum.

3.   Today, Russians are in the midst of "reinventing" education. Private, religious, and even foreign-run schools are operating, teachers are allowed to develop their own curriculum, and students are encouraged to think for themselves.

4.   The primary difficulty facing the post-Soviet educational system is the rapidly changing values and world views currently being experienced.

C.   Education in the Least Industrialized Nations: Egypt

1.   In the Least Industrialized Nations, most children do not get an education beyond a few years, either because their families see no reason for it or because they cannot afford it. Generally it is the wealthy who have the time and money and receive an education.

2.   Several centuries before the birth of Christ, Egypt was a world-renowned center of learning. Primary areas of study during this period were physics, astronomy, geometry, geography, mathematics, philosophy, and medicine. After defeat in war, education declined, never to rise to its former prominence.

3.   Today, the Egyptian constitution makes five years of grade school free and compulsory for all children; however, qualified teachers are few, classrooms are crowded, and education is highly limited. As a result, one-third of Egyptian men and over half of Egyptian women are illiterate. Those individuals that do receive a formal education attend grade school for five years, preparatory school for three years and high school for three years.

III.   The Functionalist Perspective: Providing Social Benefits

A.   Functionalists use the term *manifest function* to refer to the positive outcomes that are intended by human actions and *latent functions* to refer to positive outcomes that were not intended.

B. Education's most obvious manifest function is to teach knowledge and skills.
1. Increasingly, what often counts is not the learning, but the certification of learning.
2. A credential society is one in which employers use diplomas and degrees to determine job eligibility. The sheer size, urbanization and consequent anonymity of U.S. society is a major reason why credentials are required. Diplomas and degrees often serve as sorting devices for employers; because they do not know the individual personally, they depend on schools to weed out the capable from the incapable.
C. Another manifest function is cultural transmission of values. There are numerous ways in which cultural values like individualism, competition, and patriotism are transmitted—through the curriculum, the architecture of the schools, and the structure of the school day. Each country teaches its students that they live in the best country.
D. Schools facilitate social integration by molding students into a more cohesive unit and helping socialize them into mainstream culture. This forging of a national identity is to stabilize the political system. Today, children with disabilities are increasingly being integrated in regular social activities through the policy of inclusion or mainstreaming.
E. Gatekeeping—determining which people will enter which occupations—is another function of education. Tracking students into particular educational curricula supports gatekeeping and schools facilitate social placement; that is, funneling people into a society's various positions and holding out higher rewards for those who are willing up with years of rigorous education.
F. Over the years schools have expanded and have assumed some of the functions of the family, including child care, sex education, and birth control advice.
G. Other functions include (1) matchmaking (people finding a future spouse in school); (2) social networking; (3) reducing the unemployment rate (keeping unskilled individuals out of the labor market); and (4) stabilizing society (keeping people off the streets so that they aren't marching and protesting).

IV. The Conflict Perspective: Perpetuating Social Inequality
A. Conflict theorists see that the educational system is a tool used by those in the controlling sector of society to maintain their dominance.
B. The hidden curriculum refers to the unwritten rules of behavior and attitude (e.g., obedience to authority, conformity to cultural norms) taught in school in addition to the formal curriculum. Such values and work habits teach the middle and lower classes to support the status quo.
C. Conflict theorists criticize IQ (intelligence quotient) testing because they not only measure intelligence but also culturally acquired knowledge. By focusing on these factors, IQ tests reflect a cultural bias that favors the middle class and discriminates against minority and lower-class students.
D. Because public schools are largely financed by local property taxes, there are rich and poor school districts. Unequal funding stacks the deck against minorities and the poor.
E. The correspondence principle is how schools correspond to (or reflect) the social structure of society. The U.S. educational system is designed to turn students into dependable workers who will not question their bosses. It is also intended to produce innovators in thought and action who will still be loyal to the social system.

F. Based on research, family background affects the educational system. Those students, regardless of personal abilities, who come from more well-to-do families are not only more likely to go to college but also to attend the nation's most elite schools.

G. Schools not only reproduce social class inequalities, but also those based on race and ethnicity. Whites are more likely to complete high school, go to college, and get a degree than African Americans and Latinos. The education system helps pass privilege (or lack thereof) across generations.

V. **The Symbolic Interaction Perspective: Teacher Expectations**
A. Symbolic interactionists study face-to-face interaction inside the classroom. They have found that expectations of teachers are especially significant in determining what students learn.

B. The Rist research (participant observation in an African American grade school with an African American faculty) found tracking begins with teachers' perceptions.
1. After eight days, and without testing for ability, teachers divided the class into fast, average, and slow learners; social class was the basis for the assignments.
2. Rist found that social class was the underlying basis for assigning children to different groups.
3. Students from whom more was expected did the best; students in the slow group were ridiculed and disengaged themselves from classroom activities.
4. The labels applied in kindergarten tended to follow the child through school. What occurred was a self-fulfilling prophecy (Robert Merton's term for an originally false assertion that becomes true simply because it was predicted).

C. The Rosenthal/Jacobson experiment showed that teacher expectations were based on what they had been told about their students.
1. After testing children's abilities using standard IQ tests, researchers randomly classified 20 percent of the students as spurters. This was the basis for their report to teachers concerning which students would probably experience a learning spurt during the school year.
2. Those who had been labeled as "spurters" made more progress than other students simply because teachers expected them to and encouraged them more, another example of a self-fulfilling prophecy.

D. Teachers shaped the experiences the students had within the classroom.
1. George Farkas found students scoring the same on course matter may receive different grades: females get higher grades, as do Asian Americans.
2. Farkas used symbolic interactionism to understand this pattern. He noticed that some students signal that they are interested in what the teacher is teaching; teachers pick up these signals and reward those students with better grades.

VI. **Problems in U.S. Education — and Their Solutions**
A. A variety of factors have been identified as the major problems facing the U.S. educational system today. These problems include: mediocrity, violence, cheating, grade inflation and how it relates to social promotion and functional illiteracy, the influence of peer groups, and violence in schools.

B. Student achievement of the SAT sharply declined from the 1960s to the 1980s. Educators and Congress expressed concern. Schools raised their standards and the recovery in math has been excellent, but that has not been the case with the verbal scores. The SAT is now shorter and students are given more time to answer questions. The analogies and antonyms sections were dropped to make the verbal part easier.

    C.   It appears that grade inflation has become a widespread issue from high schools to the Ivy league. A result is functional illiteracy; high school students have difficulty with reading and writing.

    D.   Sociologists have found that peer groups are an incredibly important factor in how teens do in school. Tends who hang out with good students tend to do well; those who hang out with friends who do poorly do poorly themselves.

    E.   School violence and shootings are an issue for some schools, even though there is no trend toward greater school violence.

    F.   A number of solutions have been offered to address these problems: a secure learning environment; higher academic standards and expectations; and school choice and site-based management.

KEY TERMS
After studying the chapter, review the definition for each of the following terms.

correspondence principle: the sociological principle that schools correspond to (or reflect) the social structure of society (511)

credential society: the use of diplomas and degrees to determine who is eligible for jobs, even though the diploma or degree may be irrelevant to the actual work (506)

cultural transmission: in reference to education, the ways in which schools transmit a society's culture, especially its core values (506)

education: a formal system of teaching knowledge, values, and skills (500)

functional illiterate: a high school graduate who has difficulty with basic reading and math (518)

gatekeeping: the process by which education opens and closes doors of opportunity; another term for the *social placement* function of education (507)

grade inflation: higher grades given for the same work; a general rise in student grades without a corresponding increase in learning or test scores (518)

hidden curriculum: the unwritten goals of schools, such as obedience to authority and conformity to cultural norms (508)

latent functions: unintended beneficial consequences of people's actions (505)

mainstreaming: helping people to become part of the mainstream of society (507)

mandatory education laws: laws that require all children to attend school until a specified age or until they complete a minimum grade in school (501)

manifest functions: intended beneficial consequences of people's actions (505)

self-fulfilling prophecy: Robert Merton's term for an originally false assertion that becomes true simply because it was predicted (514)

social placement: a function of education—funneling people into a society's various positions (507)

social promotion: passing students to the next grade even though they have not mastered basic materials (518)

tracking: the sorting of students into different educational programs on the basis of real or perceived abilities (507)

KEY PEOPLE

Review the major theoretical contributions or findings of these people.

Samuel Bowles and Herbert Gintis: Bowles and Gintis used the term correspondence principle to refer to the ways in which schools reflect the social structure of society. Bowles also compared college attendance among the brightest and weakest students. Of the intellectually weakest students, 26 percent from affluent homes went to college compared to 6 percent from poorer homes. (511-512)

Anthony Carnevale and Stephen Rose: They confirmed the research conducted by Bowles. They found that regardless of personal abilities, children from more well-to-do families are not only more likely to go to college, but also to attend the more elite schools. (512)

James Coleman and Thomas Hoffer: A study of students in Catholic and public high schools by these two sociologists demonstrated that performance was based on setting higher standards for students rather than on individual ability. (521)

Randall Collins: Collins studied the credential society. (506)

Kingsley Davis and Wilbert Moore: They pioneered a view known as social placement: People are funneled into a societies various positions; rewards of high income and prestige are offered to motivate capable people to postpone gratification and to put up with years of rigorous education. (507)

Adrian Dove: A social worker in Watts who believes that the IQ test has bias so that children from certain social backgrounds will perform better than others. (511)

George Farkas: Farkas and a team of researchers investigated how teacher expectations affect student grades. They found that students signal teachers (and the teachers respond) that they are good students by being eager, cooperative and working hard. (514-515)

Harry Gracey: Gracey conducted a participant observation study of kindergarten and concluded that the purpose of kindergarten is to socialize students into the student role. He referred to kindergarten as a boot camp. (510)

Horace Mann: An educator from Massachusetts who proposed that "common schools," supported through taxes, be established throughout his state. (501)

Robert Merton: He coined the term, self-fulfilling prophecy. This is a false assumption of something that is going to happen, but then comes true simply because it was predicted. (514)

Talcott Parsons: Another functionalist who suggested that a function of schools is to funnel people into social positions. (507)

Ray Rist: This sociologist's classic study of an African American grade school uncovered some of the dynamics of educational tracking. (513)

Robert Rosenthal and Lenore Jacobson: These social psychologists conducted a study of teacher expectations and student performance and found that a self-fulfilling prophecy had taken place—when teachers were led to believe certain students were smart, they came to expect more of them, and the students gave more in return. (514-515)

STUDENT APPLICATION PROJECTS

This is your opportunity to apply the sociological perspective to the world around you. The projects in this section refer to material introduced in this chapter of your text. These projects help you apply the sociological perspective "down to your earth...down to your daily life."

1. Your text discusses research on tracking. What have you observed, what do you remember, and what do you still see, with regards to students being tracked? Were you "tracked" in your educational process? Explain. At the time, did you recognize that you were being tracked? In the long run, how do you think it affected your learning?

2. Your text discusses research by Farkas in which he examined the process by which teacher expectations affect grades. Do you think teachers' expectations in college affect grades? Has it happened to you? Explain and offer illustrations.

3. What do you think about distance learning education? List the positive and negative benefits of distance learning. Have you or someone you know ever taken a class via the internet? Briefly summarize the experience. Do you think it is possible to learn the same material via the internet as in a classroom experience? Explain. What do you think the future holds for distance education?

4. Do you think that violence is a problem in schools today? What are schools doing about this? What role do you think that media plays in portraying school violence?

SELF-TEST

MULTIPLE CHOICE QUESTIONS

1. In earlier societies: (500)
    a. there was no separate social institution called education.
    b. education was synonymous with acculturation.
    c. persons who already possessed certain skills taught them to others.
    d. all of the above.

2. Education is: (500)
    a. a formal system of teaching knowledge, values, and skills.
    b. the same as informal acculturation.
    c. very similar in countries throughout the world.
    d. all of the above.

3. Which of the following statements about education in the early years of our nation is *incorrect*? (500)
    a. The founders of our nation felt that formal education could help create a uniform national culture.
    b. The first thing that the founders of our nation did was create a comprehensive school system across all states.
    c. In the early years after the end of the American Revolution, the children of the rich attended private schools while the children of the poor received no formal education.
    d. It was believed that standardized texts would instill patriotism and teach the principles of representative democracy.

4. "Common schools," supported through taxes, were proposed by: (500)
    a. Thomas Jefferson.
    b. Noah Webster.
    c. Horace Mann.
    d. John Dewey.

5. Laws requiring school attendance up to a specified age or a minimum grade are: (501
    a. credential laws.
    b. mandatory education laws.
    c. compulsory education laws.
    d. none of the above.

6. In Japan, college admission is based on: (503)
    a. the ability of parents to pay the tuition.
    b. making a high score on a national test.
    c. being known by teachers as a "hard worker."
    d. the same procedures that prevail in the United States.

7. Since the collapse of the Soviet Union, which of the following has occurred? (504)
    a. There is a renewed interest in the humanities.
    b. Tens of thousands of teachers have lost their jobs.
    c. Teachers are allowed to encourage students to question and think for themselves.
    d. They have committed more money to education.

8. Which of the following statements about education in Egypt is *incorrect*? (504)
    a. Because education is free at all levels, the most talented children attend, regardless of parents' economic resources.
    b. The Egyptian constitution guarantees five years of free grade school for all children.
    c. The educational system consists of five years of grade school, three years of preparatory school, and three years of high school.
    d. Only 39 percent of women and 64 percent of men are literate.

9. Using diplomas to hire employees, even when they are irrelevant to the work, is: (506)
    a. a credential society.
    b. a certification mill.
    c. employer discretion in hiring.
    d. none of the above.

10. According to functionalists, all of the following are functions of education, *except*: (506-508)
    a. maintaining social inequality.
    b. transmitting cultural values.
    c. helping mold students into a more or less cohesive unit.
    d. teaching patriotism.

11. Which of the following is *not* one of the cultural values transmitted through the U.S. educational system? (506-507)
    a. individualism
    b. competition
    c. cooperation
    d. patriotism

12. _____ refers to educators incorporating students with disabilities into regular school activities. (507)
    a. mainstreaming
    b. disability rights
    c. enabling
    d. incorporation

13. _____ and _____ are two examples of gatekeeping. (508)
    a. credentialing, tracking
    b. mainstreaming, social placement
    c. cultural transmission of values, tracking
    d. social integration, mainstreaming

14. The hidden curriculum refers to: (508)
    a. the extra curriculum costs that are buried in school budgets.
    b. the lessons that teachers hide from the eyes of prying school boards.
    c. the unwritten rules of behavior and attitudes that are taught in school.
    d. all of the above.

15. IQ tests have been criticized because: (511)
    a. they are difficult to score.
    b. they are expensive to administer.
    c. they are often administered at the wrong point in a child's intellectual development.
    d. they are culturally biased.

16. Public schools are largely supported by: (511)
    a. state funding.
    b. federal funding.
    c. local property taxes.
    d. none of the above.

17. The ways in which schools correspond to, or reflect, the social structure of society is: (511)
    a. the reproduction of social class.
    b. the correspondence principle.
    c. the status quo quotient.
    d. the status maintenance process.

18. Research by Samuel Bowles on the connection between social class and college attendance showed that: (512)
    a. regardless of ability, students from affluent homes were more likely to go to college than students from poor homes.
    b. regardless of the family's social class, students with ability went on to college.
    c. among the brightest students, family background made no difference in terms of the student's decision to attend college.
    d. there were no social class differences among the weakest students in terms of their decision to go on to college.

19. All of the following examples are ways in which schools correspond to the needs of society *except*: (512)
    a. they encourage cooperation.
    b. unequal funding of schools exists.
    c. they enforce punctuality in attendance and homework.
    d. they promote patriotism.

20. Which sociologists view education as reproducing the social structure? (512)
    a. symbolic interactionists
    b. functionalists
    c. conflict theorists
    d. feminists

21. Which of the following is true regarding race-ethnicity and education? (513)
    a. Whites and Latinos are the most likely to attend college.
    b. Whites and African Americans are the most likely to attend private colleges.
    c. Native Americans are the most likely to attend two year colleges.
    d. Asian Americans are the most likely to attend 4-year colleges.

22. What did Rist's research demonstrate? (513)
    a. the ability of teachers to sort children accurately into ability groups
    b. the power of labels
    c. the importance of individual effort
    d. the cultural biases of the school system

23. The Rosenthal/Jacobson experiment tended to confirm which of these concepts? (514)
    a. cooling out
    b. cultural transmission
    c. acculturation
    d. self-fulfilling prophecy

24. Research by George Farkas focused on: (514-515)
    a. education of elite children.
    b. how teacher expectations affect a kindergarten class.
    c. how teacher expectations are influenced by students' alleged IQ scores.
    d. how teacher expectations affect students' grades.

25. When compared to scores from twenty to thirty years ago, today's student scores on tests such as the SAT: (516)
    a. are higher.
    b. are lower.
    c. have remained about the same.
    d. none of the above.

26. The practice of passing students from one grade to the next even though they have not mastered the basic materials is called: (518)
    a. age-based promotion.
    b. social promotion.
    c. expedient promotion.
    d. functional promotion.

27. High-school graduates who have difficulty with basic reading and math are known as: (518)
    a. "boneheads."
    b. functional literates.
    c. functional illiterates.
    d. underachievers.

28. Based on the statistics of shooting deaths that have occurred in U.S. schools, which of the following statements is *correct*? (519)
    a. There has been a dramatic increase in the number of shooting deaths over the last decade.
    b. The number of shooting deaths at the end of the 1990s was half what it was at the beginning of the decade.
    c. Girls are more likely than boys to be the targets of school shootings.
    d. Other types of homicides committed at school (stabbings, beatings, etc.) are just as common as shooting homicides.

29. Research by James Coleman and Thomas Hoffer, comparing student performance at Roman Catholic and public schools, found that: (521)
    a. students at public schools performed better because they had more resources available to them.
    b. students at public schools performed better because they were taught by better qualified teachers.
    c. students at Roman Catholic schools performed better because the teachers set higher standards for them to meet.
    d. students at Roman Catholic schools performed better because they had higher levels of faith.

30. What did Jaime Escalante do to improve the inner city school that was plagued with major problems? (522)
    a. He opened his students' minds to the possibility of success.
    b. Students needed to see education as a way out of the inner city.
    c. He changed the system of instruction.
    d. All of the above.

TRUE-FALSE QUESTIONS

1. _____In earlier societies, there was a separate social institution called education. (500)
2. _____By 1918, all American states had mandatory education laws. (501)
3. _____College graduation in the United States today is still less common than high school graduation was in 1910. (502)
4. _____Japanese schools teach the value of competition to their students. (501)
5. _____Since the breakup of the Soviet Union, Russia has allowed the establishment of private, religious, and even foreign-run schools. (504)
6. _____Because Egyptian education is free at all levels, including college, children of the wealthy are no more likely than children of the poor to get a college education. (504)
7. _____The United States is a credential society. (506)
8. _____Education's most obvious manifest function is to teach knowledge and skills. (506)
9. _____American schools discourage individualism and encourage teamwork. (506)
10. _____Students everywhere are taught that their country is the best country in the world. (506-507)

11. _____Over one half of students with disabilities now attend school in regular classrooms. (507)
12. _____Functional theorists believe that social placement is harmful to society. (508)
13. _____Matchmaking is a latent function of education. (508)
14. _____Functionalists emphasize the hidden curriculum in their analysis of U.S. education. (510)
15. _____In examining what occurs in the classroom, symbolic interactionists found that student performance tends to conform to teacher expectations, regardless of whether they are high or low. (511)
16. _____The correspondence principle states that schools correspond to the social structure of society. (511)
17. _____ African Americans are the group least likely to complete high school and go to college. (512)
18. _____George Farkas's research showed that teachers discriminate against females and some minorities because they do not fit their expectations of what a good student should be. (515)
19. _____In recent years, verbal scores on SATs have shown improvement, while math scores have continued to decline. (516)
20. _____Students perform better when they are expected to meet higher standards. (521)

FILL-IN-THE-BLANK QUESTIONS

1. In early societies, education was synonymous with _____. (500)
2. Horace Mann proposed the concept of _____ schools supported through taxes. (501)
3. Today, almost _____ of all undergraduates in the United States are enrolled in community colleges. (502)
4. A central sociological principal of education is that a nation's education reflects its _____. (501)
5. One result of Egypt's educational system is that _____ of Egyptian men are illiterate. (504)
6. Often what counts is not the learning, but the _____ of learning. (504)
7. Gatekeeping is often accomplished by _____. (508)
8. The unwritten goal of schools, such as teaching obedience to authority and conformity to cultural norms, is known as the _____. (510)
9. Harry Gacey concluded that kindergarten is a sort of _____ for education. (511)
10. _____ is the term for courses that are taught to students who are not physically present with their instructors. (516)
11. Sociologists' research suggests that the _____ is the most important factor on how teenagers do in school. (518)
12. _____ is higher grades given for the same work. (518)
13. Students perform better when they are expected to meet _____ standards. (519)
14. The proposal for improving schools that has received the most media attention is _____. (521)
15. _____ is controversial and resisted by teacher unions. (521)

MATCH THESE SOCIAL SCIENTISTS WITH THEIR CONTRIBUTIONS

_____	1.	Randall Collins	a. *gatekeeping sorts people on the basis of merit*
_____	2.	Bowles & Gintis	b. *teacher expectations and student performance*
_____	3.	Rosenthal & Jacobson	c. *function of education is to funnel into social positions*
_____	4.	Robert Merton	d. *correspondence principle*
_____	5.	Coleman & Hoffer	e. *self-fulfilling prophecy*
_____	6.	Harry Gracey	f. *IQ tests have social class bias*
_____	7.	Davis and Moore	g. *student performance linked to setting higher standards*
_____	8.	George Farkas	h. *students are rewarded for signals they send teachers*
_____	9.	Adrian Dove	i. *kindergarten as boot camp*
_____	10.	Talcott Parsons	j. *credential society*

ESSAY QUESTIONS

1. Explain the link between democracy, industrialization, and universal education.

2. Compare the educational systems of Japan, Russia, and Egypt and discuss what is meant by the statement that education reflects culture.

3. Select one of the three perspectives and design a research project to test the claims that perspective has about the nature of education.

4. In discussing solutions to educational problems, the author suggests that one direction in which schools should go is toward setting higher educational standards. Both the research by James Coleman and Thomas Hoffer, and the success of Jaime Escalante, support this. Discuss social factors that might explain why such a proposal has not been widely adopted by public schools across the country.

CHAPTER 18
RELIGION

CHAPTER SUMMARY

- The sociological study of religion involves the analysis of the relationship between society and religion to gain insight into the role of religion in people's lives. For Durkheim, the key elements of religion are beliefs separating the profane from the sacred, rituals, and a moral community.

- According to functionalists, religion meets basic human needs such as answering questions about ultimate meaning, providing emotional comfort, social solidarity, guidelines for everyday life, social control, adaptation, support for the government, and social change. Functional equivalents are groups or activities— other than religion—that provide these same functions. Functionalists also believe that religion has two main dysfunctions: religious persecution and war and terrorism.

- Symbolic interactionists focus on how religious symbols communicate meaning and how ritual and beliefs unite people into a community.

- Conflict theorists see religion as a conservative force that serves the needs of the ruling class by reflecting and reinforcing social inequality.

- Unlike Marx, who asserted that religion impedes social change by encouraging people to focus on the afterlife, Weber saw religion as a powerful force for social change. He analyzed how Protestantism gave rise to an ethic that stimulated "the spirit of capitalism." The result transformed society.

- The world's major religions include Judaism, Christianity, Islam, Hinduism, Buddhism, and Confucianism. As different religions have distinct teachings and practices, different groups within a religion contrast sharply with one another.

- Sociologists have identified cults, sects, churches, and ecclesia as distinct types of religious organizations. All religions begin as cults; although most ultimately fail, those that survive become sects. Both cults and sects represent belief systems that are at odds with the prevailing beliefs and values of the broader society. If a sect grows, and its members make peace with the rest of society, it changes into a church. Ecclesia, or state religions, are rare.

- Membership in religions in the United States varies by region, social class, and race-ethnicity. Religion in the United States is characterized by diversity, pluralism and freedom, competition and recruitment, commitment, tolerance, a fundamentalist revival, and the electronic church.

- The secularization of religion, a shift from spiritual concerns to concerns of "this world," is the force behind the dynamics of religious organization. As a cult or sect evolves into a church, its teachings are adapted to reflect the changing social status of its members; dissatisfied members break away to form new cults or sects.

- Even in countries where a concerted effort was made to eliminate it, religion has continued to thrive. Religion apparently will continue to exist as long as humanity does, in part because science is unable to answer some key questions such as whether God exists or not, the purpose of life, if there is an afterlife, and morality.

LEARNING OBJECTIVES
After reading Chapter 18, you should be able to:

1. Define religion and explain its essential elements. (526)
2. Describe the functions and dysfunctions of religion from the functionalist perspective. (527-530)
3. Know what is meant by functional equivalents of religion and provide examples. (529-530)
4. Describe the dysfunctions of religion and provide examples. (530)
5. Apply the symbolic interactions perspective to religious symbols, rituals, beliefs, and religious experience, and discuss how each of these help to establish and/or maintain communities of like-minded people. (530-533)
6. From the conflict perspective, discuss how religion supports the status quo, as well as reflects, reinforces, and legitimates social inequality. (533-534)
7. Summarize Max Weber's analysis of religion and the spirit of capitalism and explain its significance. (535-536)
8. Identify the major characteristics and key figures in founding the world's major religions. (536-541)
9. Define cult, sect, church, and ecclesia and describe the process by which some groups move from one category to another. (542-544)
10. Describe the three major patterns of adaptation that occur when religion and culture conflict with one another. (544)
11. Know how religious membership varies by social class (family income, education, occupational prestige) and race-ethnicity. (545-549)
12. Describe and discuss the major features of religious groups in the United States including diversity, pluralism and freedom, competition and recruitment, commitment, toleration, fundamentalist revival, and electronic church. (546-549)
13. Define secularization and distinguish between the secularization of religion and the secularization of culture. (549-551)
14. Discuss the future of religion and the questions that science cannot answer. (552)

CHAPTER OUTLINE

I. **What Is Religion?**
   A. Sociologists who do research on religion analyze the relationship between society and religion and study the role that religion plays in people's lives.
   B. According to Durham, religion is the beliefs and/or practices separating the profane from the sacred, uniting adherents into a moral community.

1. Sacred refers to aspects of life having to do with the supernatural that inspire awe, reverence, deep respect, or deep fear.
2. Profane refers to the ordinary aspects of everyday life.

C. Durham defined religion by three elements: (1) beliefs that some things are sacred (forbidden, set off from the profane); (2) practices (rituals) concerning things considered sacred; (3) a moral community (a church) resulting from a group's beliefs and practices.

II. The Functionalist Perspective

A. Religion performs certain functions: (1) answering questions about ultimate meaning (the purpose of life, why people suffer); (2) providing emotional comfort; (3) uniting believers into a community that shares values and perspectives; (4) providing guidelines for life; (5) controlling behavior; (6) helping people adapt to new environments; (7) providing support for the government; and (8) spearheading social change (as in the case of the civil rights movement in the 1960s).

B. A functional equivalent of religion is a substitute that serves the same functions; some are difficult to distinguish from a religion. Although the substitute may perform similar functions, its activities are not directed toward God, gods, or the supernatural. Examples include psychotherapy, humanism, transcendental meditation, or belonging to a political party.

C. War and terrorism, as well as religious persecution, are dysfunctions of religion.

III. The Symbolic Interactions Perspective

A. All religions use symbols to provide identity and social solidarity to members. For members, these are not ordinary symbols, but sacred symbols evoking awe and reverence, which become a condensed way of communicating with others.

B. Rituals are ceremonies or repetitive practices which unite people into a moral community by creating a feeling of closeness with God and unity with one another.

C. Symbols, including rituals, develop from beliefs. A belief may be vague ("God is") or specific ("God wants us to prostrate ourselves and face Mecca five times each day"). Religious beliefs not only include values (what is considered good and desirable) but also a cosmology (unified picture of the world).

D. Religious experience is a sudden awareness of the supernatural or a feeling of coming in contact with God. Some Protestants use the term "born again" to describe people who have undergone a religious experience.

E. Shared meanings that come through symbols, rituals, and beliefs unite people into a moral community, which is powerful. It provides the basis for mutual identity and establishes norms that govern the behavior of members. Not only are members bound together by shared beliefs and rituals, but they are also separated from those who do not share their symbolic world. Removal from the community is a serious concern for those whose identity is tied to that community.

IV. The Conflict Perspective

A. Conflict theorists are highly critical of religion. Karl Marx called religion the "opium of the people" because he believed that religion diverts the energies of the oppressed from changing their circumstances—the believers focus on the happiness they will have in the coming world rather than on their suffering in this world.

B. Religious teachings and practices reflect a society's inequalities. Gender inequalities are an example: when males completely dominated U.S. society, women's roles in churches and synagogues were limited to "feminine" activities, a condition which is beginning to change.

C. Religion legitimizes social inequality; it reflects the interests of those in power by teaching that the existing social arrangements of a society represent what God desires.

V. **Religion and the Spirit of Capitalism**

A. Weber saw religion as a force for social change, observing that European countries industrialized under capitalism. Thus religion held the key to modernization (transformation of traditional societies into industrial societies).

B. To explain this connection, Weber wrote *The Protestant Ethic and the Spirit of Capitalism;.* concluding that:

1. the spirit of capitalism (desire to accumulate capital as a duty, as an end in itself) was a radical departure from the past.

2. religion (including a Calvinistic belief in predestination and the need for reassurance as to one's fate) is the key to why the spirit of capitalism developed in Europe.

3. a change in religion (from Catholicism to Protestantism) led to a change in thought and behavior (the Protestant ethic), which resulted in the "spirit of capitalism."

C. Critics of Weber noted that he overlooked the lack of capitalism in Scotland (a Calvinist country) and the fact that the Industrial Revolutions originated in England, a non-Calvinist country.

D. Today the spirit of capitalism and the Protestant ethic are by no means limited to Protestants, becoming cultural traits that have spread throughout the world.

VI. **The World's Major Religions**

A. The origin of Judaism is traced to Abraham, who lived about 4,000 years ago in Mesopotamia.

1. It was the first religion based on monotheism, the belief in only one God. Prior to this, religions were based on polytheism, the belief that there are many gods.

2. Contemporary Judaism in the United States has three main branches: Orthodox (adheres to the laws espoused by Moses), Reform (more liberal, uses the vernacular in religious ceremonies, and has reduced much of the ritual); and Conservative (falling somewhere between Orthodox and Reform).

3. The history of Judaism is marked by conflict and persecution (anti-Semitism).

4. Central to Jewish teaching is the requirement to love God and do good deeds.

B. Christianity developed out of Judaism and is based on the belief that Christ is the Messiah that God promised the Jews.

1. During the first 1,000 years of Christianity, there was only one church organization, directed from Rome; during the eleventh century, Greek Orthodoxy was established.

2. In the Middle Ages, the Roman Catholic church, aligned with the political establishment, grew corrupt. The Reformation of the sixteenth century, led by Martin Luther, was a reaction to the Church's corruption.

3. The Reformation marked the beginning of a splintering of Christianity; today, there are about two billion Christians, divided into hundreds of groups.

C. Islam (whose followers are known as Muslims) began in the same part of the world as Judaism and Christianity; like the Jews, Muslims trace their ancestry to Abraham.

1. The founder, Muhammad, established a theocracy—a government based on God being the ruler, his laws the statutes of the land, and priests his earthly administrators.

2. After Muhammad's death, a struggle for control split Islam into the two branches that remain today: the Shi'ites, who are more conservative and inclined to fundamentalism (the belief that true religion is threatened by modernism and that faith as it was originally practiced should be restored) and the Sunni, who are generally more liberal.

3. It is the duty of each Muslim to make a pilgrimage to Mecca during his or her lifetime. The Muslims practice polygyny and can have up to four wives.

D. Hinduism, the chief religion of India, goes back about 4,000 years but has no specific founder or canonical scripture (texts thought to be inspired by God). Instead several books expound on the moral qualities people should strive to attain.

1. Hindus are polytheists (believe there are many gods). A central belief is karma, spiritual progress. They believe that there is no final judgment, but in reincarnation, a cycle of life, death, and rebirth.

2. Some Hindu practices, such as child marriage and suttee (cremating a widow along with her deceased husband) have been modified as a result of protest.

3. Every twelve years, the purifying washing in the Ganges Rives takes place. Millions of people participate.

E. About 600 B.C., Siddhartha Gautama founded Buddhism, which emphasizes self-denial and compassion.

1. During meditation he discovered the "four noble truths" which emphasize self-denial and compassion.

2. Buddhism is similar to Hinduism in that the final goal is to escape from reincarnation into the nonexistence of blissful peace.

3. Buddhism spread rapidly into many parts of Asia.

F. Confucius (China 551-479 B.C.) urged social reform and developed a system of morality based on peace, justice, and universal order.

1. The basic moral principle of Confucianism is to maintain *jen* (sympathy or concern for other humans) and to treat those who are subordinate to you as you would like to be treated by those superior to you.

2. Originally, Confucianism was atheistic; however, as the centuries passed, local gods were added to the teachings, and Confucius himself was declared a god.

VII. Types of Religious Groups
A. A cult is a new religion with few followers, which maintains teachings and practices that put it at odds with the dominant culture and religion.

1. All religions began as cults. Cults often begin with the appearance of a charismatic leader (exerting extraordinary appeal to a group of followers).
2. Christianity, the most popular religion in the world, began as a cult, as did Islam.
3. Each cult meets with rejection from society. The message given by the cult is seen as a threat to the dominant culture.
4. The cult demands intense commitment, and its followers confront a hostile world.
5. Although most cults ultimately fail because they are unable to attract a large enough following, some succeed and make history.

B. A sect is larger than a cult, but still feels substantial hostility from and toward society.
1. At the very least, members remain uncomfortable with many of the emphases of the dominant culture; nonmembers feel uncomfortable with sect members.
2. Sects are generally loosely organized; emphasize personal salvation (an emotional expression of one's relationship with God); and work toward recruitment of new members (evangelism).
3. If a sect grows, its members tend to become respectable in society, and the sect is changed into a church.

C. A church is a large, highly organized religious group with formal, sedate services and less emphasis on personal conversion. The religious group is highly bureaucratized (including national and international offices that give directions to local congregations). Most new members come from within the church (i.e. from children born to existing members), rather than from outside recruitment.

D. An ecclesia is a religious group so integrated into the dominant culture that it is difficult to tell where one begins and the other leaves off.
1. Ecclesia are also called state religions. The government and religion work together to try to shape the society.
2. There is no recruitment of members, for citizenship makes everyone a member. The majority of the society belongs to the religion in name only.
3. The Church of England, the Lutheran church in Sweden and Denmark, and Islam in Iran and Iraq are ecclesias.

E. Not all religions go through all stages. Although all religions began as cults, not all varieties of a religion have done so.
1. Some die out because they fail to attract members; some remain sects. Few become ecclesia.
2. A denomination is a "brand name" within a major religion (e.g., Methodist).

F. Three major patterns of adaptation occur when religion and the culture in which it is embedded find themselves in conflict.
1. Members of a religion may reject the dominant culture and withdraw from it socially, although they continue to live in the same geographic area.
2. A cult or sect rejects only specific elements of the prevailing culture.
3. The society rejects the religious group entirely and may even try to destroy it. The destruction of the Branch Davidians by the U.S. government is an example of this third pattern.

VIII. Religion in the United States

A. About 65 percent of Americans belong to a church or synagogue.

    1. Each religious group draws members from all social classes, although some are more likely to draw members from the top of the social class system and others from the bottom. The most top heavy are Episcopalians and Jews, the most bottom-heavy the Baptist and Evangelicals. People who change social class are also likely to change their denomination.

    2. All major religious groups in the United States draw from various racial and ethnic groups; however, people of Hispanic or Irish descent are more likely to be Roman Catholics, those of Greek origin belong to the Greek Orthodox Church, and African Americans are likely to be Protestants.

    3. Although many churches are integrated, there is still much segregation along racial lines. This is based on custom, not law.

B. Characteristics of religious groups in the United States:

    1. Diversity: With 300,000 congregations, there is no dominant religion in the U.S.

    2. Pluralism and freedom: No government interference with religion, although if officials feel threatened by a religious group, they may violate their hands-off policy.

    3. Competition: for believers from many religions.

    4. Commitment: Reflected in the high proportion of believers in God; about 44 percent report that they attend religious services each week. This commitment is backed up with generous financial support for religion and its charities.

    5. Toleration for religious beliefs other than one's own: Are reflected in the attitudes that religions have a right to exist as long as they do not brainwash or bother anyone and no one says which religion is the true religion. While each believer may be convinced about the truth of his or her religion, trying to convert others is a violation of individual dignity.

    6. Fundamentalist revival: Occurs because mainstream churches fail to meet basic religious needs of large numbers of people. As a result, mainstream churches are losing members while fundamentalists are gaining.

    7. The electronic church: Televangelists reach millions of viewers and raise millions of dollars.

    8. Religious groups now maintain home pages on the Internet, and discussion groups have formed around religion.

C. Secularization is the process by which worldly affairs replace spiritual interests.

    1. Secularization of religion is the replacement of a religion's other-worldly concerns with concerns about this world. It occurs when religion's influence is lessened (both on a society's institutions and on individuals). Secularization explains why Christian churches have splintered into so many groups: Changes in the social class of the members creates different needs, if the churches change they thereby fail to meet the needs of those whose life situation has not changed.

    2. Secularization of culture is the process whereby religion has less influence in society. Secularization is due to the spread of scientific thinking, industrialization, urbanization, and mass education that reflects modernization. Even though the culture has secularized, religious participation remains strong.

IX. The Future of Religion

A.   Prominent intellectuals once believed that science would replace religion. However, religion continues to thrive in the most advanced scientific nations.

B.   Religion has fundamental significance in people's lives.

C.   Science cannot answer questions about four concerns many people have: the existence of God, the purpose of life, morality, and the existence of an afterlife.

KEY TERMS

After studying the chapter, review the definition for each of the following terms.

animism: the belief that all objects in the world have spirits, some of which are dangerous and must be outwitted (537)

anti-Semitism: prejudice, discrimination, and persecution directed against Jews (537)

born again: a term describing Christians who have undergone a life-transforming religious experience so radical that they feel they have become new persons (532)

charisma: literally, an extraordinary gift from God; more commonly, an outstanding, "magnetic" personality (542)

charismatic leader: literally, someone to whom God has given a gift; more commonly, someone who exerts extraordinary appeal to a group of followers (542)

church: according to Durkheim, one of the three essential elements of religion—a moral community of believers (524); a second definition is the type of religious organization (528)—a large, highly organized group with formal, sedate worship services and little emphasis on personal conversion (526)

civil religion: Robert Bellah's term for religion that is such an established feature of a country's life that its history and social institutions become sanctified by being associated with God (529)

cosmology: teachings or ideas that provide a unified picture of the world (532)

cult: a new religion with few followers, whose teachings and practices put it at odds with the dominant culture and religion (542)

denomination: a "brand name" within a major religion, for example, Methodist or Baptist (544)

ecclesia: a religious group so integrated into the dominant culture that it is difficult to tell where one begins and the other leaves off; also called a *state religion* (543)

evangelism: an attempt to win converts (543)

fundamentalism: the belief that true religion is threatened by modernism and that the faith as it was originally practiced should be restored (538)

functional equivalent: in this context, a substitute that serves the same functions (or meets the same needs) as religion; for example, psychotherapy (529)

modernization: the transformation of traditional societies into industrial societies (535)

monotheism: the belief that there is only one God (537)

polytheism: the belief that there are many gods (537)

profane: Durkheim's term for common elements of everyday life (526)

Protestant ethic: Weber's term to describe the ideal of a self-denying, highly moral life, accompanied by hard work and frugality (535)

reincarnation: in Hinduism and Buddhism, the return of the soul (or self) after death in a different form (540)

religion: according to Durkheim, beliefs and practices that separate the profane from the sacred and unite its adherents into a moral community (526)

religious experience: a sudden awareness of the supernatural or a feeling of coming in contact with God (532)

rituals: ceremonies or repetitive practices; in this context, religious observances, or rites, often intended to evoke a sense of awe of the sacred (532)

sacred: Durkheim's term for things set apart or forbidden, that inspire fear, awe, reverence, or deep respect (526)

sect: a group larger than a cult that still feels substantial hostility from and toward society (543)

secular: belonging to the world and its affairs (549)

secularization of culture: the process by which a culture becomes less influenced by religion (551)

secularization of religion: the replacement of a religion's "otherworldly" concerns with concerns about "this world" (550)

spirit of capitalism: Weber's term for the desire to accumulate capital as a duty—not to spend it, but as an end in itself—and to constantly reinvest it (535)

state religion: a government-sponsored religion; also called ecclesia (529)

KEY PEOPLE
Review the major theoretical contributions or findings of these people.

Emile Durkheim: Durkheim investigated world religions and identified elements that are common to all religions, such as separation of sacred from profane, beliefs about what is sacred, practices surrounding the sacred, and a moral community. (526)

John Hostetler: Hostetler is known for his research and writings on the Amish. (533)

Benton Johnson: Johnson analyzed types of religious groups, such as cults, sects, churches, and ecclesia. (542)

William Kephart and William Zellner: These sociologists also investigated the Amish religion and way of life. (533)

Karl Marx: Marx was critical of religion, calling it the opium of the masses. (533-534)

Liston Pope: Another sociologist who studied types of religious groups. (542)

Lynda Powell: An epidemiologist that evaluated the research done on the effects of religion on health. (528)

Stanley Presser and Linda Stinson: They examined written reports of how people spent their Sundays. They concluded that about 30 percent or so attend church weekly. (547)

Ian Robertson: Robertson noted that there is a fundamental distinction between a religion and its functional equivalent; unlike the latter, the activities of a religion are directed toward God, gods, or some supernatural. (530)

Ernst Troeltsch: Yet another sociologist who is associated with types of religious groups from cults to eccelsia. (542)

Anthony Wallace: This anthropologist predicted that religion would eventually die out as a result of the increasing diffusion of scientific knowledge. (552)

Max Weber: Weber studied the link between Protestantism and the rise of capitalism and found that the ethic associated with Protestant denominations was compatible with the early needs of capitalism. (535-536)

STUDENT APPLICATION PROJECTS

This is your opportunity to apply the sociological perspective to the world around you. The projects in this section refer to material introduced in this chapter of your text. These projects help you apply the sociological perspective "down to your earth...down to your daily life."

1. What do you make of the scientific experiment on the power of prayer? Were you surprised? Using the knowledge gained in this chapter, develop an explanation for the findings.

2. Functionalists point out that most religions provide support for the government. List some ways you think Christianity supports the United States government? Do you think we come close to having a state or civil religion? Explain.

3. How has the United States culture been secularized? What do you think is causing this trend? Do you see this trend as positive or negative? Explain. What do you see as the future of religion in the United States? In the World?

4. Compare and contrast the major religions of the world. Are there any similarities? Why do you think that it is so important for religions to differentiate themselves from one another?

SELF-TEST

MULTIPLE CHOICE QUESTIONS

1. What was Durkheim's purpose in writing *The Elementary Forms of the Religious Life?* (526)
    a. He wanted to explain the development of Protestantism.
    b. He set to chart the history of world religions.
    c. He wanted to study the development of religion from sect to church.
    d. He wanted to identify elements common to all religions.

2. What did Durkheim mean by the word *profane*? (526)
    a. aspects of life having to do with the supernatural
    b. aspects of religion that are mysterious
    c. aspects of life that are part of everyday life
    d. aspects of religious worship

3. According to Durkheim, a church: (526)
    a. is a large, highly organized religious group.
    b. has little emphasis on personal conversion.
    c. is a group of believers with a set of beliefs and practices regarding the sacred.
    d. all of the above.

4. All of the following are functions of religion, *except:* (527-529)
    a. encouraging wars for holy causes.
    b. support for the government.
    c. social change.
    d. social control.

5. What did researchers discover about the effects of religion on health? (528)
    a. They discovered that there was little relationship.
    b. Prayer (or meditation) changes people's brain activity and improves their immune response.
    c. People who were hospitalized were more religious than the doctors realized.
    d. Regular prayer can cure many diseases.

6. War and religious persecution are: (530)
    a. manifest functions of religion.
    b. latent functions of religion.
    c. dysfunctions of religion.
    d. functional equivalents of religion.

7. A unified picture of the world, such as the belief in one God who is the creator of the universe, is called: (532)
   a. an ideology.
   b. a cosmology.
   c. a dogma.
   d. a religious creed.

8. What are Protestants referring to when they use the term *born again*? (532)
   a. reincarnation
   b. Christ's rebirth after his crucifixion
   c. a personal life-transforming religious experience
   d. finding salvation in the afterlife

9. Which of the following statements about the practice of *shunning* is *incorrect*? (533)
   a. Persons who are shunned are treated as if they do not exist.
   b. Family members are exempt from having to follow the practice when it involves one of their own.
   c. It is a serious matter for those whose identity is bound up in the community.
   d. The shunning occurs in all situations and at all times.

10. Religion is the opium of the people according to: (534)
    a. Max Weber.
    b. Emile Durkheim.
    c. Karl Marx.
    d. Charles Cooley.

11. An example of the use of religion to legitimize social inequalities is: (534)
    a. the divine right of kings.
    b. a declaration that the Pharaoh or Emperor is god or divine.
    c. the defense of slavery as being God's will.
    d. all of the above.

12. Weber believed that religion held the key to: (535)
    a. modernization.
    b. bureaucratization.
    c. institutionalization.
    d. socialization.

13. Weber analyzed how Protestantism gave rise to the Protestant Ethic, which stimulated what he called the _____. (535)
    a. Spirit of Capitalism
    b. secularization of religion
    c. secularization of culture
    d. ecclasia

14. Which major religion was the first to practice monotheism? (537)
    a. Judaism
    b. Christianity
    c. Islam
    d. Hinduism

15. The belief that all objects in the world have spirits is: (537)
    a. a central belief of Islam.
    b. referred to as animism.
    c. no longer accepted by people around the world.
    d. the same as monotheism.

16. What was an unanticipated outcome of the Reformation? (538)
    a. the splintering of Christianity
    b. the reunification of the Catholic Church
    c. the elimination of corruption in the Church
    d. the downgrading of women's status in the Church hierarchy

17. Which branch of Islam is more conservative and inclined to fundamentalism? (538)
    a. orthodox
    b. Sunni
    c. Shi'ite
    d. black Muslim

18. Polytheism is the belief: (537)
    a. that God is a woman.
    b. that there is only one God.
    c. that there are many gods.
    d. that God does not exist.

19. The religion with no specific founder is: (540)
    a. Islam.
    b. Hinduism.
    c. Buddhism.
    d. Confucianism.

20. Reincarnation: (540)
    a. is found only in Buddhism.
    b. is the return of the soul after death in the same form.
    c. is the return of the soul after death in a different form.
    d. none of the above.

21. All religions began as _____: (542)
    a. cults
    b. sects
    c. churches
    d. ecclasia

22. Although larger than a cult, a _____ still feels tension from society. (543)
    a. commune
    b. ecclesia
    c. sect
    d. church

23. Churches: (543)
    a. are highly bureaucratized.
    b. have more sedate worship services.
    c. gain new members from within, from children born to existing members.
    d. all of the above.

24. Which type of religious organization does not recruit new members? (543)
    a. cult
    b. sect
    c. church
    d. ecclesia

25. Which of the following groups has remained a sect: (543)
    a. Jewish people.
    b. Muslims.
    c. the Amish
    d. Hindus.

26. The Southern Baptist convention was formed in 1845 to: (545)
    a. organize freed slaves.
    b. defend the right to own slaves.
    c. defend prohibition.
    d. organize women for the right to vote.

27. Which of the following is *not* a feature of religious groups in the United States? (546-549)
    a. diversity of beliefs
    b. competition for members
    c. intolerance of differences
    d. commitment to beliefs

28. Secularization of religion occurs as a result of: (550)
    a. industrialization.
    b. urbanization.
    c. mass education.
    d. all of the above.

29. That religion has less impact on public affairs in the United States today is an example of: (551)
    a. secularization of religion.
    b. secularization of culture.
    c. a civil religion.
    d. an ecclesia.

30. Questions that science cannot answer include: (552)
    a. "is there a God?"
    b. "what is the purpose of life?"
    c. "what happens when a person dies?"
    d. all of the above.

TRUE-FALSE QUESTIONS

1. _____ The goal of the sociological study of religion is to determine which religions are most effective in peoples' lives. (526)
2. _____ According to Durkheim, all religions separate the sacred from the profane. (526)
3. _____ Functionalists believe that religion is universal because it meets basic human needs. (527-529)
4. _____ Psychotherapy is a functional equivalent of religion. (529)
5. _____ The terrorist attacks are an example of the dysfunctions of religion. (530)
6. _____ Being born again is a term frequently used to describe reincarnation by Hindus and Buddhists. (532)
7. _____ Shunning is practiced by the Sufi tribe. (533)
8. _____ Conflict theorists examine the relationship of religion to social inequalities, especially how religion reinforces a society's stratification system. (535)
9. _____ Emile Durkheim saw religion as a primary source of social change. (535)
10. _____ Contemporary Judaism in the United States comprises two main branches. (537)
11. _____ Fundamentalism is the belief that modernism threatens religion and that the faith as it was originally practiced should be restored. (538)
12. _____ Some Hindu practices have been modified as a consequence of social protest. (540)
13. _____ The basic moral principle of Confucianism is to maintain sympathy or concern for other humans. (541)
14. _____ Judaism, Christianity, and Islam are all polytheistic religions. (537)
15. _____ Unlike cults, sects do not stress evangelism. (542-543
16. _____ Islam in Iran and Iraq is an example of ecclesia. (543)
17. _____ Reform Judaism is a denomination. (544)
18. _____ Many religions around the world are associated with race and ethnicity. (546)

19. _____Many local ministers are very supportive of the electronic church because they are happy to see people who do not attend church hearing religious messages. (547-549)
20. _____Secularization of religion leads to a splintering of religious groups because some see it as a desertion of the group's fundamental beliefs. (550)

FILL-IN-THE-BLANK QUESTIONS

1. Sociologists do not seek to prove that one religion is _____ than another. (526)
2. According to Durkheim, church and _____ community were synonymous terms. (526)
3. Alcoholics Anonymous is a _____ equivalent of religion. (528)
4. A bar mitzvah is an example of a _____ practiced by Jews. (532)
5. A sudden awareness of the supernatural is known as a _____. (532)
6. When an offender is being ignored in all situations, they are being _____. (533)
7. Weber concluded that religion held the key to _____. (535)
8. The origin of Judaism is traced to _____. (536)
9. Today, _____ is the most popular religion in the world. (538)
10. The followers of Islam are known as _____. (538)
11. Hinduism can be traced back _____ thousand years. (539)
12. The central symbol of _____ is the eight-spoked wheel. (540)
13. All religions began as _____. (542)
14. Religion in the United States is stratified by _____. (545)
15. There is no doubt that religion will last as long as _____ lasts. (552)

MATCH THESE SOCIOLOGICAL CONCEPTS WITH THEIR DEFINITIONS

_____	1. denomination	a.	*an attempt to win converts*
_____	2. charisma	b.	*government-sponsored religion*
_____	3. civil religion	c.	*religious rites intended to evoke a sense of awe*
_____	4. evangelism	d.	*a "brand name" within a major religion*
_____	5. reincarnation	e.	*things set apart that inspire reverence or deep respect*
_____	6. polytheism	f.	*common elements of everyday life*
_____	7. rituals	g.	*return of the soul after death in a different form*
_____	8. sacred	h.	*an outstanding, magnetic personality*
_____	9. profane	i.	*the belief that there are many gods*
_____	10. ecclesia	j.	*a belief that a nation and its institutions are sanctified by God*

ESSAY QUESTIONS

1. Assume that you have been asked to make a presentation about religion to a group of people who have absolutely no idea what religion is. Prepare a speech in which you define religion and explain why it exists.

2. The functionalists point out the many functions of religion but also note how it has certain dysfunctions. Discuss both the functions and dysfunctions and then consider whether it is possible for religion to fulfill its functions without producing dysfunctions.

3. Discuss the process by which a religion matures from a cult into a church.

4. Consider why fundamentalist Christian churches in the United States are currently undergoing a revival.

5. Discuss the major patterns of adaptation that occur when religion and culture conflict with one another.

CHAPTER 19
MEDICINE AND HEALTH

CHAPTER SUMMARY

- Sociologists study medicine as a social institution; three of the primary characteristics of medicine as it is practiced in the United States include professionalization, bureaucracy, and the profit motive.

- The symbolic interactionists view health and illness as intimately related to cultural beliefs and practices; definitions of illness vary from one group to the next.

- Components of health include physical, mental, social, and spiritual. The functionalists study the sick role and the ways in which people are excused from normal responsibilities when they assume this role; in turn, they are obligated to get well in order to resume their responsibilities. The conflict perspective stresses that health care is one of the scarce resources over which groups compete. Globally, the best health care is available in the Most Industrialized Nations.

- Medicine in the United States has become a commodity, developing into the U.S.'s largest business enterprise. Due to public outcry, Medicaid and Medicare were established to assist the poor and the elderly.

- Americans are healthier than their ancestors were. Four of the leading causes of death in 1900 don't appear on today's list. However, diabetes and Alzheimer's disease didn't make the top ten in 1900, but they do now.

- The United States has a two-tire system of medical care in which the wealthy receive superior care and the poor inferior medical care.

- One major problem in U.S. health care is defensive medicine. This is when medical procedures are done for the physician's benefit, not for the benefit of the patient. The purpose of these tests is to protect doctors against possible lawsuits, but they end up adding huge amounts of money to the nation's medical bill. Other problems include depersonalization, medical incompetence, conflict of interest, medical fraud, sexism and racism, medicalization of society, and medically assisted suicide.

- HMOs and diagnosis-related groups are among the measures that have been taken to reduce medical costs. Other solutions include national health insurance, group care, pay-as-you-go programs, and rationing medical care.

- Major threats to health today include HIV/AIDS, obesity and skinniness, drugs, alcohol, and nicotine, disabling environments, and unethical experiments.

- Global travel has increased the risk of diseases occurring worldwide. So far, world health officials have been able to contain these diseases.

- Alternatives to the current health care system include individuals taking more responsibility for their health and a fundamental shift in the medical establishment toward "wellness", alternative, and preventive medicine.

LEARNING OBJECTIVES

After reading Chapter 19, you should be able to:

1. Understand the role of sociology in studying medicine. (558)
2. Use the symbolic interactionist perspective to explain how culture influences health and illness. (558)
3. Identify the four components of health. (558-559)
4. Know what is meant by the sick role and describe the social factors that can affect and/or influence people's claim to it. (560)
5. Explain how global stratification adversely affects the quality of medical care in the Least Industrialized Nations and how, for people who live in these nations, this is often a matter of life and death. (560-561)
6. Describe the process by which medicine was professionalized and monopolized in the United States, and discuss the consequences of that professionalization and monopolization. (562-564)
7. Discuss the changes in physical and mental health patterns in the United States over the past 100 years, and the consequences of those changes. (565)
8. Discuss the controversy in the U.S. over whether medical care is a right or a commodity. (565-566)
9. Identify the social inequalities in the American health care system. (566-567)
10. Describe the current problems in the American health care system including malpractice, medical incompetence, depersonalization, conflicts of interest, medical fraud, sexism and racism, the medicalization of society, and medically assisted suicide. Discuss some of the attempts to deal with these problems. (567-571)
11. Identify the factors that are contributing to the soaring costs of health care in the United States and evaluate the job that that HMOs and diagnosis-related-groups are doing to help reduce those costs. (573-574)
12. Discuss the pros and cons of national health insurance and rationing medical care. (573-574)
13. Describe the major threats to health in the United States and worldwide from HIV/AIDS; obesity; drugs; disabling environments; callous experiments; and the globalization of disease. (575-583)
14. Discuss alternatives to the way in which U.S. medicine is usually practiced. (583-584)
15. Examine health characteristics of health care around the world. (584)

CHAPTER OUTLINE

I. Sociology and the Study of Medicine and Health
   A. Medicine is a society's standard way of dealing with illness and injury. U.S. medicine is a profession, a bureaucracy, and a big business.

B. Sociologists study how medicine is influenced by ideals of professional self-regulation, the bureaucratic structure, and the profit motive; they also are interested in how illness and health are related to cultural beliefs, lifestyle, and social class.

II. The Symbolic Interactionist Perspective

A. Health is affected by cultural beliefs.
1. In Western culture a person who hears voices and sees visions might be locked up; in a tribal society, such an individual might be a shaman, the healing specialist who attempts to control the spirits thought to cause a disease or injury.
2. "Sickness" and "health" are not absolutes but a matter of definition. We are provided with guidelines to determine whether we are healthy or sick.

B. Expanding on the views of international health experts, the author of your text argues that health is a human condition measured by four components: physical, mental, social and spiritual. What makes someone healthy varies from culture to culture. Sociologists analyze the effects that people's ideas of health and illness have on their lives and even how people determine that they are sick.

III. The Functionalist Perspective

A. Functionalists point out that societies must set up ways to control sickness. They develop a system of medical care and make rules to keep too many people from "being sick."

B. The sick role is a social role that you are forced to play when you are not well.
1. It has four elements: (1) you are not held responsible for being sick, (2) you are exempt from normal responsibilities, (3) you don't like the role, and (4) you will get help so you can return to your usual routines. People who do not seek competent help are considered responsible for being sick and cannot claim sympathy from others.
2. Often there is ambiguity between the well role and the sick role because most situations are not as clear-cut as having a heart attack. A decision to claim the sick role typically is more of a social than a physical matter.
3. Parents and physicians are the primary gatekeepers, mediating between children's feelings of illness and the right to be released from responsibilities.
4. Gender is a significant factor in the sick role. Women are more willing than men to claim the sick role when they don't feel well. They go to doctors more frequently than men and they are hospitalized more often than men.

IV. The Conflict Perspective

A. The primary focus of conflict theorists is the struggle over scarce resources, including medical treatment.

B. One consequence of global domination by the Most Industrialized Nations is the international stratification of medical care.
1. The Least Industrialized Nations cannot afford the same lifesaving technology available in highly industrialized nations. Differences in life expectancy and infant mortality rates illustrate the consequences of global stratification.
2. Global stratification even changes the face of diseases. People living in the Least Industrialized Nations located in the tropics face illness and death from four

major sources: malaria, internal parasites, diarrhea, and malnutrition. People in the Most Industrialized Nations live longer, with the consequence that they face "luxury" diseases such as heart disease and cancer.

3. Many diseases that ravage populations of poor countries are controllable; the problem is having the funds to spend on public health. Generally, the money is spent by members of the elite on themselves.

C. In order to understand how medicine grew into the largest business in the United States, it is necessary to understand how medicine became professionalized.

1. In the 1700s, a person learned to be a physician by becoming an apprentice or simply hanging out a shingle to proclaim that he was a physician. During the 1800s, a few medical schools opened, and there was some licensing.

2. By 1906, the United States had 160 medical schools. The Carnegie Foundation funded Abraham Flexner to visit every medical school and make recommendations for change.

3. The Flexner Report resulted in the professionalization of medicine—the development of medicine into a field in which physicians undergo a rigorous education, claim an understanding of illness, regulate themselves, assert that they are performing a service for society, and take authority over clients.

4. Laws restricted medical licenses to graduates of approved schools; only graduates of these schools were eligible to be faculty members who trained the next generation of physicians. This select group of physicians gained control over U.S. medicine and set itself up as the medical establishment, either refusing to admit women and minorities to medical schools or placing severe enrollment limits on them. It wasn't until 1915 that the American Medical Association (AMA) allowed women members.

5. U.S. medicine always had a fee-for-service approach, but now it came under the physicians' control; they set their own fees and had no competition. Although the poor received services from some physicians and hospitals, many remained without medical care.

6. Until the 1960s, the medical establishment fought all proposals for government-funded medical treatment, including Medicare (government-sponsored medical insurance for the elderly) and Medicaid (government-paid medical care for the poor). Following the creation of these programs, physicians discovered how lucrative they were.

7. The medical establishment consists not only of physicians, but also of nurses, hospital personnel, pharmaceutical companies, pharmacists, manufacturers of medical technology, and corporations that own hospitals.

V. Historical Patterns of Health

A. Epidemiology is the study of the distribution of medical disorders throughout a population; it provides answers about patterns of health and illness over time.

B. There are different ways of determining the current state of physical health in the United States.

1. One way is to compare leading causes of death in 1900 to the present period. Four of the top ten causes of death in 1900 aren't even on the list today. Today's top two killers, heart disease and cancer, ranked fourth and eighth in 1900.

Diabetes and Alzheimer's disease didn't make the top ten in 1900, but currently they do.

    2.   Are Americans healthier today? If being healthier is measured by life expectancy, then Americans are healthier than their ancestors.

C.   When it comes to mental health, no rational basis for comparisons exists. Perhaps there were fewer mental health problems in the past; however, it is also possible that there is greater mental health today than in the past.

VI. Issues in Health Care

A.   A primary controversy in the United States is whether medical care is a right or a privilege. If it is a right, then all should have good access to it; if it is a privilege, then the rich will have access to one type of care and the poor another.

    1.   Today, the average person living in the United States spends $5,200 a year on health care, as compared to spending $150 a year in 1960.

    2.   Factors contributing to the increase in medical costs are the growing elderly population, the new, expensive technology, and more expensive malpractice insurance.

B.   Social class affects the incidence of illnesses and the quality of treatment.

    1.   The lower the social class, the higher is the proportion of serious mental problems. As compared with middle- and upper-class Americans, the poor have less job security, lower wages, more unpaid bills and insistent bill collectors, more divorce, greater vulnerability to crime, more alcoholism, and so on. Such conditions deal severe blows to their emotional well-being.

    2.   In general, few poor people have a personal physician and often wait in crowded public health clinics to receive care. When hospitalized, the poor are often admitted to understaffed, underfunded public hospitals, treated by rotation interns who do not know them and cannot follow up on their progress.

    3.   The U.S. has a two-tiered system of medical care in which the wealthy receive superior medical care and the poor inferior medical care.

C.   Prior to this century, doctors had four main treatments (purging, bleeding, blistering, and vomiting); today, science and technology have made advances, diagnoses are more accurate, and treatments are more effective.

    1.   At the same time, the number of malpractice suits has risen; patients hold doctors to a higher standard and are quick to sue if there is a mistake.

    2.   Physicians practice defensive medicine—that is, seeking consultations with colleagues and ordering additional lab tests—simply because a patient may sue. Defensive medicine greatly increases the cost of medicine.

D.   While medical mistakes are not everyday occurrences, they do happen.

    1.   Doctors correctly diagnose their patients' illnesses only 55 percent of the time.

    2.   The Institute of Medicine, a branch of the National Academy of Sciences, reports that each year between 44,000 and 98,000 Americans die due to mistakes in U.S. hospitals. A leading cause of death is cross-reactions of prescription drugs.

    3.   If death from medical errors were an official classification, it would rank as the sixth leading cause of death in the U.S.

    4.   There are various suggestions for reducing the number of needless deaths. One recommendation is that pharmacists accompany doctors as they make their

rounds. Another is to establish a federal Center for Patient Safety to investigate medical injuries and deaths.

E. Depersonalization is the practice of dealing with people as though they were cases and diseases, not individuals.

    1. Many patients get the impression that they are trapped by a cash machine with physicians watching the clock and calculating dollars while talking to the patient.

    2. Although students begin medical school wanting to "treat the whole person," as they progress through school, their feelings for patients are overpowered by the need to be efficient.

F. Physicians may encounter conflicts of interest in prescribing medications, referring patients to hospitals, pharmacies, or medical supply companies when they have a financial stake in the prescribed course of treatment.

G. Because of the high volume of health insurance claims that are filed on a daily basis (2 million Medicare claims daily), a large number of physicians, billing companies, and medical providers and suppliers make fraudulent claims, engaging in medical fraud.

H. Medicine is not immune to sexism and racism; there is evidence that women, men, and different racial-ethnic groups are treated differently by the medical establishment.

    1. Physicians do not take women's health complaints as seriously as they do men's.

I. Medicalization is the transformation of something into a matter to be treated by physicians. Examples include balding, weight, wrinkles, small breasts, and insomnia; yet there is nothing inherently medical in such conditions.

    1. Symbolic interactionists stress that medicalization is based on arbitrary definitions, part of a view of life that is bound to a specific historical period.

    2. Functionalists would stress how the medicalization of such issues is functional for the medical establishment since they can broaden their customer base. It also benefits patients who have someone to listen to their problems and are sometimes helped.

    3. Conflict sociologists assert that this process is another indication of the growing power of the medical establishment, and that as physicians medicalize more aspects of life, their power and profits increase.

J. With modern technology, machines can perform most bodily functions, even when the person's mind no longer works; this has created the question, "Who has the right to pull the plug?"

    1. Proponents or medically assisted suicides say that it allows people to die with dignity. Opponents say that is legalizes murder.

    2. Some people believe that physicians should practice euthanasia (mercy killing) and help patients die if they request death to relieve insufferable pain or to escape from an incurable disease ("assisted suicide"). Others believe that this should never occur or that euthanasia should be allowed only in specific circumstances.

    3. In Holland, in about 1000 cases, physicians kill their patients without the patients' express consent.

    4. Jack Kevorkian assisted 120 people commit suicide. Eventually, he was convicted of second degree murder and sentenced to 10 to 25 years in prison.

K. Medical costs in the United States have soared because of expensive technology, a growing elderly population, defensive medicine, and health care that operates as a commodity. Attempts are being made today to curb costs.

1. Health maintenance organizations (HMOs) represent a recent attempt to contain medical costs. HMOs are based on paying a predetermined fee to physicians to take care of the medical needs of subscribers. Although this arrangement may eliminate unnecessary procedures, it also creates pressures to reduce necessary medical treatment.

2. The federal government has classified all illnesses into 468 diagnostic-related groups and set the reimbursement amount for each. Hospitals make a profit only if they move patients through the system quickly. Although the average hospital stay has dropped, some patients are discharged before being fully ready to go home, and others are refused admittance because they might cost the hospital money instead of making it a profit.

3. One consequence of the desire to turn a profit on patient care is the practice of dumping, or sending unprofitable patients to public hospitals. With 44 million primarily poor Americans uninsured, pressure has grown for a national health insurance plan. Those in favor of national health care cite the social inequalities of medicine and the inadequacy of health care for the poor. Those opposed to national health insurance point to administrative concerns such as the vast amount of red tape that would be required.

4. One maverick solution that has been implemented is to replace individual consultation with group care. For example, eight or ten pregnant women may go in for their obstetrics check-up together. Other doctors refuse to treat patients who want to pay by insurance. They have a pay-as-you-go system in which patients pay by cash, credit card, or check.

5. The most controversial suggestion is to ration medical care.

VII. Threats to Health

A. Acquired immune deficiency syndrome (AIDS) is probably the most pressing health issue in the world today.

1. In the United States, AIDS has been transformed from a death sentence to a chronic disease that can be managed with expensive drugs. Globally, however, it is still out of control, with Africa the hardest hit region in the world.

2. The sub-Saharan region of Africa comprises 10 percent of the world's population, but has 60 percent of the world's HIV infections.

3. Its exact origin is unknown, although it is suspected that hunters who killed chimpanzees infected with a similar virus became infected through contact with the animals' blood.

4. It is transmitted through sexual contact and transfusions of contaminated blood. Patterns of transmission vary from one society to another.

5. AIDS hits men the hardest. However, in the United States, women account for a larger percentage of new cases each year. The risks vary by race and ethnicity due to factors such as rates of intravenous drug use and the use of condoms, not due to genetic factors.

6.   One of the most significant sociological aspects of AIDS is the stigma, which contributes to its spreading because people are afraid to be tested and stigmatized.

7.   Drugs have been found to slow the progress of AIDS, but there is no cure.

B.   Currently, 58 percent of Americans are overweight. We are the fattest nation on earth. People who are obese are more likely to have strokes, suffer heart attacks, diabetes, and cancer. The Centers for Disease Control recently found that being a little overweight can be good; it may reduce bad cholesterol.

C.   Alcohol and tobacco are the most frequently used drugs in the United States.

1.   Alcohol is the standard recreational drug in the United States. The average drinker in the United States consumes about 25 gallons of alcoholic beverages per year. Underage drinking is common, with drinking alcohol directly related to grade. College men and women are about equally likely to drink alcohol and smoke cigarettes.

2.   Of all drugs, nicotine is the most harmful to health. Smoking increases a person's risk of heart attack and causes progressive emphysema and several types of cancer. People continue to smoke despite the harmful health effects for two major reasons: addiction and advertising. In 2004, the tobacco industry introduced cigarettes spiked with candy flavors.

D.   A disabling environment is one that is harmful to health.

1.   Some occupations have high health risks which are evident (e.g., mining, riding bulls in a rodeo, and so on). In others, the risk becomes evident only after people have worked for years in what they thought was a safe occupation (e.g., laborers who worked with asbestos).

2.   Industrialization not only increased the world's standard of living, but it has also led to the greenhouse effect; a warming of the earth that may change the globe's climate, melt its polar ice caps, and flood the earth's coastal shores. Use of fluorocarbon gases is threatening the ozone shield (the protective layer of the earth's upper stratosphere that screens out a high proportion of the sun's ultraviolet rays). In humans, this high-intensity ultraviolet radiation causes skin cancer.

E.   At times, physicians and government officials have carried out research that has jeopardized the health and welfare of the individuals they are sworn to protect.

1.   One example of such research is the Tuskegee Syphilis Experiment. In this experiment, 399 African American men suffering from syphilis were left untreated for 40 years so that the Public Health Service could observe what happened.

2.   During the Cold War, the U.S. government conducted radiation experiments in which soldiers were ordered to march through an area just after an atomic bomb had been detonated. The purpose of this research was to determine if individuals could withstand fallout without any radiation equipment.

3.   In some instances, those in official positions believe that they can play God and determine who shall live and who shall die. The most expendable citizens, and therefore the ones who serve as subjects in such research, are the poor and the powerless. In order to protect ourselves against such a gross abuse of

professional positions, this research must be publicized and those who direct and carry out these experiments must be vigorously prosecuted.

F. Global travel has increased the number of diseases that are appearing worldwide. Antibiotics appear to be ineffective against many of them. So far, containment efforts have been successful.

VIII. The Search for Alternatives

A. Values and lifestyles have a major impact on health.

1. Within the same society, subcultural patterns and lifestyles produce specific patterns of health and illness. For example, although Nevada and Utah are adjacent states with similar levels of income, education, medical care, and other assets, the death rate is much higher in Nevada. This is because Utah is inhabited mostly by Mormons, who encourage conservative living and disapprove of the consumption of tobacco, alcohol, and caffeine.

2. Many of the threats to health are preventable. Individuals can exercise regularly, eat nutritious food, maintain sexual monogamy, and avoid smoking and alcohol abuse in order to prevent disease.

3. Instead of treatment, the U.S. medical establishment should have "wellness" as its goal. To achieve such a goal the medical establishment must make a fundamental change in its philosophy and see profitability in keeping patients well.

4. On a broader scale, there needs to be a systematic attempt to eliminate disabling environments and the use of harmful drugs.

B. Alternative medicine refers to nontraditional medicine typically imported from Asian cultures. Most Western doctors regard alternative medicine as a superstitious practice, but many U.S. patients have begun to demand alternative medicine and the U.S. medical establishment has started to accommodate those demands.

IX. Health Care in Global Perspective

A. The search for alternatives leads to an examination of health care in other nations.

1. Sweden has the most comprehensive health care system in the world, with all citizens and alien residents covered by health insurance financed by contributions from the state and employers. At the same time, it is very expensive and very inefficient.

2. In post-Soviet Russia the government owns all the health care facilities, all equipment, and determines how many students will attend the state-owned-and-operated medical schools. The physicians are not well trained and the overall health of the nation has been declining. Supplies and equipment are in short supply. Health care is free, but there are no choices in terms of physicians or facilities used.

3. Most Chinese see "barefoot doctors," people with a rudimentary knowledge of medicine. Chinese medicine relies on medicinal herbs and acupuncture. Today a system of private medical clinics is also developing. Bribery of medical personnel has become routine.

KEY TERMS
After studying the chapter, review the definition for each of the following terms.

alternative medicine: medical treatment other than that of standard Western medicine; often refers to practices that originate in Asia, but may also refer to taking vitamins not prescribed by a doctor (584)

defensive medicine: medical practices done not for the patient's benefit but in order to protect a physician from malpractice suits (567)

depersonalization: dealing with people as though they were objects; in the case of medical care, as though patients were merely cases and diseases, not people (569)

disabling environment: an environment that is harmful to health (581)

dumping: the practice of sending unprofitable patients to public hospitals (573)

epidemiology: the study of disease and disability patterns in a population (565)

euthanasia: mercy killing (572)

fee-for-service: payment to a physician to diagnose and treat the patient's medical problems (563)

health: a human condition measured by four components: physical, mental, social, and spiritual (558)

health maintenance organization (HMO): a health care organization that provides medical treatment to its members for a fixed annual cost (573)

medicalization: the transformation of something into a matter to be treated by physicians (571)

medicine: one of the major social institutions that sociologists study; a society's organized ways of dealing with sickness and injury (558)

professionalization of medicine: the development of medicine into a field in which education becomes rigorous, and in which physicians claim a theoretical understanding of illness, regulate themselves, claim to be doing a service to society (rather than just following self-interest), and take authority over clients (563)

shaman: the healing specialist of a preliterate tribe who attempts to control the spirits thought to cause a disease or injury; commonly called a witch doctor (558)

sick role: a social role that excuses people from normal obligations because they are sick or injured, while at the same time expecting them to seek competent help and cooperate in getting well (560)

two-tier system of medical care: a system in which the wealthy receive superior medical care and the poor inferior medical care (566)

KEY PEOPLE
Review the major theoretical contributions or findings of these people.

Jack Haas and William Shaffir: These sociologists did a participant observation of medical students and discovered that over the course of medical school their attitudes change from wanting to "treat the whole person" to needing to be efficient in treating the specific ailment. (569)

Talcott Parsons: Parsons was the first sociologist to analyze the sick role, pointing out that it has four elements: (1) not being responsible for your sickness, (2) being exempt from normal responsibilities, (3) not liking the role, and (4) seeking competent help in order to return to daily routines. (560)

STUDENT APPLICATION PROJECTS

This is your opportunity to apply the sociological perspective to the world around you. The projects in this section refer to material introduced in this chapter of your text. These projects help you apply the sociological perspective "down to your earth...down to your daily life."

1. What do you think about euthanasia? Do you think people have the right to decide when to die? Should doctors be able to assist them in this? Can you see a way this could be organized so that patients have rights and doctors are protected?

2. List the advantages and disadvantages of the Swedish, Russian, Chinese and U.S. health care systems. Which country would you want to receive medical treatment from if you were critically ill and poor? Explain. Which country would you want receive medical treatment from if you were critically ill and rich? Explain. What changes do you think need to take place to improve the current health care system in the United States?

3. What are your thoughts about the international black market for human body parts? Did you know that this existed and do you think that it should be illegal in other countries?

4. What do you consider to be the most important issue concerning health care in the U.S.? What do you think should be done to address this issue?

SELF-TEST

MULTIPLE CHOICE QUESTIONS

1. Sociologists focus on medicine as: (558)
   a. a profession.
   b. a bureaucracy.
   c. a business.
   d. all of the above.

2. A _____ is the healing specialist of a preliterate tribe who tries to control the spirits thought to cause a disease or injury. (558)
   a. soothsayer
   b. high priest
   c. shaman
   d. medicine man

3. As practiced in the U.S., the primary characteristics of the social institution of medicine include all of the following except: (558)
   a. personalization.
   b. professionalization.
   c. bureaucracy.
   d. profit motive.

4. How would a sick or injured person who can't fulfill normal role obligations be described? (560)
   a. a hypochondriac
   b. in the sick role
   c. deviant
   d. all of the above

5. The individual's claim to the sick role is legitimized primarily by: (560)
   a. demonstrating to others that he or she is ill.
   b. a doctor's excuse.
   c. employers, teachers, and sometimes parents.
   d. other workers or students who vouch for the fact that the individual is ill.

6. Why are women more likely than men to claim the sick role when they feel poorly? (560)
   a. They are generally not as healthy as men.
   b. They have more reasons to see a doctor than men, because of reproductive problems.
   c. They are socialized for greater dependency and self-disclosure.
   d. All of the above.

7. Which sociological perspective views health care as one of the scarce resources over which groups compete? (561)
   a. symbolic interactionism
   b. functionalism
   c. conflict theory
   d. feminism

8. Professionalization of medicine includes: (563)
   a. rigorous education.
   b. a theoretical understanding of illness.
   c. self-regulation.
   d. all of the above.

9. Which of the following statements about the medical monopoly is *incorrect*? (563)
   a. While doctors were able to control women's access to medical schools, they were never very effective in keeping other minorities out.
   b. The medical establishment was able to get laws passed to restrict medical licensing to graduates of approved schools.
   c. Because they operated as a monopoly, they were able to set themselves up as the most lucrative profession in the country, setting their own fees and controlling competition.
   d. The medical establishment was so powerful it was able to take childbirth away from the control of midwives.

10. Government-paid health care for the poor is: (566)
    a. Medicaid.
    b. Medicare.
    c. medical welfare.
    d. none of the above.

11. The study of disease and disability patterns in a population is called: (565)
    a. epidemiology.
    b. anatomy.
    c. biology.
    d. demography.

12. Today, the average American spends _____ a year on health care. (566)
    a. $150
    b. $1100
    c. $4500
    d. $5200

13. In the United States, medical care is: (566)
    a. a right.
    b. a commodity.
    c. socialized.
    d. none of the above.

14. According to the author of your text, why has the practice of defensive medicine grown in recent decades? (567)
    a. Doctors have found that they can provide the best care when they order a whole set of tests.
    b. The federal government requires such tests in order to protect patient interests.
    c. The insurance companies are willing to cover the costs of extensive tests.
    d. Doctors want to establish a paper trail to protect themself in the event they are sued by a disgruntled patient.

15. Which of the following statements about depersonalization is *incorrect*? (569)
    a. Tt is less common today because of all the reforms brought about by HMOs.
    b. It is the practice of dealing with people as though they were objects.
    c. It means treating patients as though they were merely cases and diseases.
    d. It occurs when an individual is treated as if he or she was not a person.

16. What underlies the sexism that continues to exist within medicine? (571)
    a. ignorance
    b. the fact that male doctors are not sensitive to women's needs
    c. continuing male dominance of medicine
    d. women's willingness to accept the status quo

17. _____ is the transformation of something into a matter to be treated by physicians. (571)
    a. sexism in medicine
    b. medicalization of society
    c. monopolization of medicine
    d. holistic medicine

18. The state of _____ passed a law allowing for medically assisted suicide. (571)
    a. Oregon
    b. California
    c. Florida
    d. Ohio

19. Which of these is *not* a reason why U.S. medical costs have risen dramatically? (573)
    a. Tests are performed for defensive rather than medical reasons.
    b. The size of the elderly population has increased.
    c. People want doctors to do unnecessary tests to assure themselves they are   healthy.
    d. Health care is seen as a commodity.

20. Sending unprofitable patients to public hospitals is known as: (573)
    a. turfing.
    b. sidewinding.
    c. dumping.
    d. discarding.

21. AIDS is known to be transmitted by: (577)
    a. casual contact between a carrier and a noncarrier in which bodily fluids are exchanged.
    b. exchange of blood and/or semen.
    c. airborne passage of the virus from carrier to non-carrier through coughing or sneezing.
    d. all of the above.

22. Which racial and/or ethnic group is at greater risk of contracting AIDS? (577)
    a. Whites
    b. African Americans
    c. Latinos
    d. Asian Americans

23. _____ is more life threatening to Americans than AIDS or alcohol abuse. (581)
    a. smoking
    b. obesity
    c. accidents
    d. SARS

24. Which of the following statements about smoking is *incorrect*? (580-581)
    a. Nicotine may be as addictive as heroin.
    b. The rate of cigarette smoking continues to climb, despite warnings about the dangers.
    c. The tobacco industry has a huge advertising budget to encourage people to smoke.
    d. When compared with nonsmokers, smokers are three times as likely to die before age 65.

25. An environment that is harmful to health is referred to as a(n): (581)
    a. disabling environment.
    b. health hazard.
    c. harmful setting.
    d. crippling environment.

26. The burning of carbon fuels has led to: (581)
    a. fossilization.
    b. global cooling.
    c. the greenhouse effect.
    d. glacial formation.

27. An example of physicians' and the government's callous disregard of people's health is: (581-582)
    a. the delay in providing open heart surgery for women patients.
    b. the Tuskegee syphilis experiment.
    c. the failure to curb advertising of tobacco products.
    d. all of the above.

28. To implement a national policy of "prevention, not intervention" would require: (583-584)
    a. a fundamental change in the philosophy of the medical establishment.
    b. a change in the public's attitudes towards medicine and health care.
    c. eliminating disabling environments and reducing the use of harmful drugs.
    d. all of the above.

29. Which of the following countries has the lowest infant mortality? (586)
    a. the former Soviet Union
    b. Sweden
    c. China
    d. the United States

30. *Barefoot doctors* provide much of the health care to the people of which nation? (585)
    a. China
    b. India
    c. Vietnam
    d. Korea

TRUE-FALSE QUESTIONS

1. _____ Health is not only a biological matter, but it is also intimately related to society. (558)
2. _____ People who don't seek competent help when they are sick are just behaving as expected, according to the social definition of the sick role. (560)
3. _____ There is little ambiguity between the well role and the sick role. (560)
4. _____ Men are more willing to claim the sick role when they don't feel well. (560)
5. _____ In the Least Industrialized Nations, few people live long enough to get cancer and heart disease. (561)
6. _____ Medical schools have existed since the 1700s in the United States. (563)
7. _____ The Flexner Report had a profound impact on American medicine. (563)
8. _____ The professionalization of medicine led directly to medicine becoming a monopoly. (563)
9. _____ Professionalization of medicine includes self-regulation of physicians. (563)
10. _____ An international black market exists for selling human body parts. (562)
11. _____ Women were allowed to be members of the American Medical Association in 1915 (563)
12. _____ People receive equal medical treatment regardless of social class. (566)
13. _____ Physicians practice defensive medicine to protect themselves from getting sued. (567)
14. _____ A functionalist would argue that the medicalization of society reflects the growing power of the medical establishment because the more physicians can medicalize human affairs, the greater their profits and power. (571)
15. _____ There is a lack of consensus about the practice of euthanasia. (572)
16. _____ The soaring cost of medical care can be explained by the fact that Americans are sicker than they used to be. (573)
17. _____ The most controversial suggestion for reducing medical costs is to adopt national health insurance. (574)

18. _____Today in the United States, AIDS is viewed as a chronic disease that can be controlled with medications. (577)
19. _____In general, people are very aware when they are working in a disabling environment, one that is harmful to their health. (581)
20. _____The most well known form of alternative medicine is acupuncture. (584)

FILL-IN-THE-BLANK QUESTIONS

1. We define health and illness according to our _____. (558)
2. Parents and physicians are the primary _____ to the sick role. (560)
3. Global _____ even helps determine what diseases we get. (561)
4. When medicine became a profession, it also became a _____. (562)
5. According to the conflict perspective, the struggle between doctors and midwives was really a _____ struggle. (564)
6. Diabetes and _____ now make the top ten list of causes of death in the U.S. (565)
7. A primary controversy in the United States is whether or not medical care is a _____ or a privilege. (566)
8. To protect themselves from malpractice suits, physicians practice _____ medicine. (568)
9. If the number of Americans killed by medical _____ were an official classification of death, it would rank as one of the top ten leading causes of death. (569)
10. To curb spiraling costs, the federal government has classified all illnesses into _____. (573)
11. The most controversial suggestion for how to reduce medical costs is to _____ medical care. (575)
12. In sub-Saharan Africa, _____ is the leading cause of death. (577)
13. _____ is the standard recreational drug of Americans. (579)
14. _____ is by far the most lethal of all recreational drugs. (580)
15. From the perspective of Western medical theory, _____ medicine does not make sense. (584)
16.

MATCH THESE SOCIOLOGICAL CONCEPTS WITH THEIR DEFINITIONS

_____	1. defensive medicine	a.	*a social role excusing the sick from normal obligation*
_____	2. alternative medicine	b.	*provides treatment to its members for a fixed cost*
_____	3. epidemiology	c.	*healing specialist in a preliterate tribe*
_____	4. euthanasia	d.	*transformation of something into a medical problem*
_____	5. depersonalization	e.	*organized ways of dealing with sickness*
_____	6. medicalization	f.	*study of disease patterns in a population*
_____	7. health maintenance organization	g.	*often refers to practices that originate in Asia*
_____	8. medicine	h.	*practices done to protect a physician from being sued*
_____	9. shaman	i.	*treating people as objects*
_____	10. sick role	j.	*mercy killing*

ESSAY QUESTIONS

1. Describe the elements of the sick role and identify variations in the pattern of claiming this role.

2. Discuss why medicine developed into a monopoly in this country and what the consequences of this development have been for the delivery of medical treatment.

3. Explain the pattern of the worldwide AIDS epidemic and suggest reasons why this threat to the health of the world's population has not been addressed more aggressively.

4. Define depersonalization and present evidence from the chapter as to its presence within medicine. Consider why it is present in a system that is supposed to care about the individual who is sick or injured.

5. Discuss and explain some of the threats to health, either in the United States or worldwide.

CHAPTER 20
POPULATION AND URBANIZATION

CHAPTER SUMMARY

- Demography is the study of the size, composition, growth, and distribution of human populations. Over 200 years ago, Thomas Malthus observed that populations grow geometrically while food supplies increase arithmetically; he argued that the population of the world would eventually outstrip its food supply. The debate between the New Malthusians and the anti-Malthusians continues today.

- Starvation occurs not because the earth produces too little food, but because particular places lack food. Droughts and wars are the main reasons for this. Starvation is due, therefore, to a maldistribution of food rather than overpopulation.

- People in the Least Industrialized Nations have large families because children are viewed as gifts from God, it costs little to rear them, and they represent parents' social security. To project population trends, demographers use three demographic variables: fertility, mortality, and migration. A nation's growth rate is also affected by variables like wars, famines, and changing economic and political conditions.

- Cities can only develop if there is an agricultural surplus; the primary impetus to the city development was the invention of the plow about 5,000 years ago. For much of human history cities were small, but after the Industrial Revolution cities grew quickly. Urbanization, the process by which an increasing proportion of a pop-ulation lives in cities, is so extensive today that some cities have become metropolises, and in some metropolises have merged to form a megalopolis. Today there are 19 megacities in the world (population of more than 10 million).

- Many urban patterns exist. There has been movement from the country to the city, from city to city, between and within cities, from cities to suburbs, and to smaller centers known as micropolises. There has also been a recent trend to retreating to rural areas.

- The primary models that have been proposed to explain how cities expand are the concentric-zone, sector, multiple-nuclei, and peripheral models. These models fail to account for medieval cities, many European cities, and those in the Least Industrialized Nations.

- Some people find a sense of community in cities; others find alienation. Herbert Gans identified five types of city dwellers: cosmopolites, singles, ethnic villagers, the deprived, and the trapped. An essential element in determining whether someone finds community or alienation in the city is that person's social networks. Noninvolvement is generally functional for urbanites, but it impedes giving help in emergencies.

- The decline of U.S. cities is due to forces such as disinvestment, suburbanization, and deindustrialization. Principles to guide future social policy are scale, livability, and social justice.

LEARNING OBJECTIVES

After reading Chapter 20, you should be able to:

1. Know what is meant by the Malthus theorem and state the major points and counterpoints in the debate between the New Malthusians and the Anti-Malthusians. (590)
2. Identify the primary causes of famines and starvation. (595-594)
3. Understand why people in the Least Industrialized Nations have so many children (596)
4. Discuss the implications of different rates of population growth. (597-598)
5. Describe the three demographic variables that are used in estimating population growth (598-600)
6. Explain problems in forecasting population growth. (600-602)
7. Trace the development of cities from ancient times through industrialization and the process of urbanization. (603-606)
8. Identify urban patterns in the United States and the return by some to rural areas. (606-609)
9. Describe and evaluate the four models of urban growth and the return to rural areas. (610-612)
10. Discuss how some people find a sense of community in cities while others become alienated. (612-614)
11. Describe the five types of urban dwellers identified by sociologist Herbert Gans. (615)
12. Talk about ways that people who live in cities can create a sense of intimacy. (616)
13. Explain why many urban dwellers follow a norm of noninvolvement and how this norm, may contribute to a dysfunctional diffusion of responsibility. (615-616)
14. Identify the primary problems of urban life today and discuss how suburbanization, disinvestment, and deindustrialization contribute to these problems. (617-618)
15. Evaluate current attempts to address urban problems in the United States and discuss the guiding principles for developing future policies to deal with these problems. (618-619)

CHAPTER OUTLINE

I. POPULATION IN GLOBAL PERSPECTIVE
   A. Demography is the study of size, composition, growth, and distribution of populations.

II. A Planet with No Space for Enjoying Life?
   A. Thomas Malthus wrote *An Essay on the Principle of Population* (1798) stating the Malthus theorem: population grows geometrically while food supply increases arithmetically; thus if births go unchecked, population will outstrip food supplies.
   B. New Malthusians believe Malthus was correct. The world population is following an exponential growth curve (where numbers increase in extraordinary proportions): 1800, one billion; 1930, two billion; 1960, three billion; 1975, four billion; 1987, five billion and 1999, six billion.

C. In the next twelve years, the world's population will increase as much as it did during the first 1800 years after the birth of Christ.

D. Anti-Malthusians believe that the three-stage process of population growth, known as the demographic transition, provides a model for the future.
   1. They cite the historical experiences of European countries over the last two centuries as an example.
   2. Stage 1 is characterized by a fairly stable population (high birth rates offset by high death rates); stage 2, by a "population explosion" (high birth rates and low death rates); and stage 3, by population stability (low birth rates and low death rates).
   3. They assert this transition will happen in the Least Industrialized Nations, which currently are in the second stage.

E. Who is correct? Only the future will prove the accuracy of either the projections of the New Malthusians or the Anti-Malthusians.
   1. The Least Industrialized Nations are currently in stage 2 of the demographic transition—their birth rates remain high while the death rates have dropped.
   2. There are signs that birth rates in the Least Industrialized nations are dropping, but the two sides greet this news differently. The New Malthusians say that the populations in the Least Industrialized Nations will continue to climb, only at a slower rate, while the Anti-Malthusians say that the slow rate is a sign that these nations are beginning to move into stage 3.
   3. Population shrinkage (a country's population is smaller because birth rate and immigration cannot replace those who die and emigrate) is now occurring in 65 nations, suggesting a fourth stage to the demographic transition.
   4. Some Anti-Malthusians predict a "demographic free fall." Eventually, the world's population will peak at 8 or 9 billion, and then begin to grow smaller.

F. Why are people starving?
   1. Anti-Malthusians note that the amount of food produced for each person in the world has increased: famines are not the result of too little food production, but from the maldistribution of existing food.
   2. The New Malthusians counter that the world's population continues to grow and the earth may not be able to continue to produce sufficient food.
   3. Famines have recently been concentrated in Africa. However, these famines are not due to too many people living on too little land; rather, they are due to drought, outmoded farming techniques and ongoing political instability that disrupt harvests and food distribution.
   4. Starvation in Africa is a result of the maldistribution of food rather than overpopulation.

III. Population Growth

A. Three reasons poor nations have so many children are (1) the status that parenthood provides; (2) the community supports this view; and (3) children are considered to be economic assets (the parents rely on the children to take care of them in their old age).
   1. The symbolic interactionist perspective stresses that we need to understand these patterns within the framework of the culture and society in which the behavior occurs.

2. The conflict perspective stresses that in the Least Industrialized Nations, men dominate women in all spheres of life, including that of reproduction. There is an emphasis on male virility and dominance, including the fathering of many children, as a means of achieving status in the community.

B. Demographers use population pyramids (graphic representations of a population, divided into age and sex) to illustrate a country's population dynamics.
1. Different population growth rates have different implications. Countries with rapid growth rates have to cope with increased numbers of people sharing resources; this can result in a declining standard of living.
2. A declining standard of living may result in political instability followed by severe repression by the government.

C. Estimated population growth is based on three demographic variables:
1. Fertility rate—measured by the number of children an average woman bears—is sometimes confused with fecundity—the number of children a woman theoretically can bear. To compute a country's fertility rate, demographers use crude birth rate (annual number of births per 1,000 people).
2. Middle Africa has the highest fertility rate and Macao and Hong Kong, the lowest fertility.
3. Mortality is measured by the crude death rate (number of deaths per 1,000 people). The highest death rates occur in Sierra Leone in Western Africa and the lowest, in Kuwait and United Arab Emirates.
4. Migration is measured by the net migration rate (difference between the number of immigrants moving in and emigrants moving out per 1,000 population). There are two types of migration: movement between regions within a country and movement between countries. "Push" factors make people want to leave where they are living (e.g., persecution, lack of economic opportunity); "pull" factors attract people (e.g., opportunities in the new locale) to a new location.
5. Around the world, the flow of migration is from the Least Industrialized Nations to the industrialized nations. The U.S. admits more immigrants each year than all the other nations of the world combined.
6. There is a debate as to whether immigrants are a net contributor or drain on our economy.

D. The growth rate equals births minus deaths plus net migration.
1. Economic changes, wars, famines, and plagues all make it difficult to forecast population growth. The primary unknown factor that influences a country's growth rate is its rate of industrialization—in every country that industrializes, the growth rate declines.
2. Some countries are concerned about underpopulation, and other countries, like China, are concerned about overpopulation and have had to institute policies to limit childbearing.
3. In every country that industrializes, the birth rate declines. Industrialization opens up economic opportunities, bit makes children more expensive.
4. Because of the difficulties in forecasting population growth, demographers formulate several predictions simultaneously, each depending on different assumptions.

IV. URBANIZATION

A. An introduction to what was once a garbage dump, now the district of El Tiro in Medellin, Colombia, provides a context for understanding urban life.

V. The Development of Cities

A. A city is a place in which a large number of people are permanently based and do not produce their own food. Small cities with massive defensive walls existed as far back as 10,000 years ago; cities on a larger scale originated about 3500 B.C. as a result of the development of more efficient agriculture and a food surplus. The key to the origin of cities is the development of more efficient agriculture.

B. The Industrial Revolution drew people to cities to work. Today, urbanization not only means that more people live in cities, but also that today's cities are larger; well over 300 of the world's cities contain at least one million people.

C. Urbanization is the process by which an increasing proportion of a population lives in cities. There are specific characteristics of cities, such as size and anonymity, that give them their unique urban flavor.

1. Metropolis refers to cities that grow so large that they exert influence over a region; the central city and surrounding smaller cities and suburbs are connected economically, politically, and socially.

2. Megalopolis refers to an overlapping area consisting of at least two metropolises and their many suburbs.

3. A megacity is a city of 10 million or more residents. Today there are 19 megacities and most are located in the Least Industrialized Nations.

D. In 1790, only about 5 percent of Americans lived in cities; by 1920, 50 percent of the U.S. population lived in urban areas; today, 79 percent of Americans live in urban areas.

1. The U.S. Census Bureau divided the country into 274 metropolitan statistical areas (MSAs), which consist of a central city of at least 50,000 people and the urbanized areas that are linked to it. About 60 percent of the entire U.S. population lives in just fifty or so MSAs.

2. As Americans migrate in search of work and better lifestyles, a two-way pattern of migration between regions appears. Today, six of the nine fastest-growing U.S. cities are in the West; the other three are in the South. Of the nine declining cities, all are in the Northeast.

3. As Americans migrate and businesses move to serve them, edge cities have developed (a clustering of service facilities and residential areas near highway intersections).

4. Gentrification, the movement of middle-class people into rundown areas of a city, is another major U.S. urban pattern. As a consequence of gentrification, the poor are often displaced from their neighborhoods. A common pattern is for the gentrifiers to be white and the displaced to be minorities.

5. Suburbanization is the movement from the city to the suburbs. The automobile served as the major impetus for suburbanization. Also, after racial integration occurred, many whites fled the cities.

6. The most recent trend is the development of micropolitan areas. A micropolis is a city of 10,000 to 50,000 residents that is not a suburb.

7. Some Americans are retreating to rural areas. Fears of urban crime and violence are "push" factors. The "pull" factors to these rural areas are safety, lower cost of living, and more living space.

VI. Models of Urban Growth

A. Robert Park coined the term "human ecology" to describe how people adapt to their environment (known as "urban ecology"); human ecologists have constructed four models that attempt to explain urban growth patterns:

B. Ernest W. Burgess proposed the concentric-zone model.
   1. The city consists of a series of zones emanating from its center, with each characterized by a different group of people and activity: zone 1 is the central business district; zone 2 is in transition, with deteriorating housing and rooming houses; zone 3 is an area to which thrifty workers have moved to escape the zone in transition while maintaining access to work; zone 4 is more expensive apartments, single-family dwellings, and exclusive areas where the wealthy live; and zone 5 is a commuter zone consisting of suburban areas or satellite cities that have developed around rapid transit routes.
   2. Burgess intended this model to represent the tendency for towns and cities to expand outward from the central business district.

C. Homer Hoyt proposed the sector model, which sees urban zones as wedge-shaped sectors radiating out from the center.
   1. A zone might contain a sector of working-class housing, another sector of expensive housing, a third of businesses, and so on, all competing with one another for the same land.
   2. In an invasion-succession cycle, poor immigrants move into a city, settling in the lowest-rent area available to them; as their numbers grow, they begin to encroach on adjacent areas. As the poor move closer to the middle class, the middle class leave, expanding the sector of lower-cost housing.

D. The multiple-nuclei model, developed by Chauncey Harris and Edward Ullman, views the city as comprised of multiple centers or nuclei, each of which focuses on a specialized activity (e.g., retail districts, automobile dealers, and others).

E. Chauncey Harris later developed the peripheral model of urban development to account for more recent changes in the use of urban space. In this model, people and services move away from the central city into the periphery; highways radiate out from the center and encourage this development along the edges of metropolitan areas.

F. These models tell only part of the story of how cities are constructed. They reflect both the time frame and geographical region of the cities that were most often studied. They cannot explain medieval cities or cities in other Most Industrialized or Least Industrialized Nations.

VII. City Life

A. Cities provide opportunities but also create problems. Humans have a need for community, which some people have a hard time finding in cities; they then experience alienation.

B. Louis Wirth argued that the city undermines kinship and neighborhood, which are the traditional bases of social control and social solidarity.
   1. Urban dwellers live in anonymity, their lives marked by segmented and superficial encounters that make them grow aloof from one another and indifferent to other people's problems.

C. The city can also be viewed as containing a series of smaller worlds, within which people find a sense of community or belonging.

D. Herbert Gans identified five types of people who live in the city.
   1. Cosmopolites—intellectuals and professionals; students, writers, and artists who live in the inner city to be near its conveniences and cultural benefits.
   2. Singles—young, unmarried people who come seeking jobs and entertainment.
   3. Ethnic villagers—live in tightly knit neighborhoods that resemble villages and small towns and are united by race and social class.
   4. The deprived—the very poor, emotionally disturbed, and handicapped who live in neighborhoods more like urban jungles than urban villages.
   5. The trapped—(1) those who could not afford to move when their neighborhood was invaded by another ethnic group, (2) downwardly mobile persons who have fallen from a higher social class, (3) elderly people who have drifted into the slums because they are not wanted elsewhere and are powerless to prevent their downward slide, and (4) alcoholics and drug addicts.

E. The city is divided into worlds that people come to know down to the smallest detail.
   1. City people create a sense of intimacy for themselves by personalizing their shopping (frequenting the same stores and restaurants becoming "regulars").
   2. Spectator sports also engender community identification. People maintain emotional allegiances to the team of the city in which they grew up even if they have moved to other parts of the country.

F. Urban dwellers are careful to protect themselves from the unwanted intrusions of strangers.
   1. They follow a norm of noninvolvement, such as using a newspaper or a Walkman to indicate inaccessibility for interaction, to avoid encounters with people they do not know.
   2. The more bystanders there are to an incident, the less likely people are to help because people's sense of responsibility becomes diffused.
   3. The norm of noninvolvement and the diffusion of responsibility may help urban dwellers get through everyday city life, but they are dysfunctional because people do not provide assistance to others.

VIII. Urban Problems and Social Policy

A. U.S. cities have declined due to suburbanization and disinvestment and deindustrializaton.
   1. As people have moved out of the city, so have the businesses and jobs.
   2. This shift has left people behind who had no choice but to live in the city. William Wilson notes that this has transformed the inner city into a ghetto: those left behind were trapped by poverty, unemployment, welfare dependency, and the victims of street crime.

3. The automobile has been a major fuel for suburbanization. This trend accelerated after the racial integration of schools in the 1950s and 1960s, as whites fled the cities.

4. Suburbanites, preferring that the city keep its problems to itself, fight movements to share suburbia's revenues with the city. However, the time may come when suburbanites may have to pay for their attitudes toward the city.

5. As suburbs age, they are becoming mirror images of the city, leading to a spiraling sense of insecurity, more middle-class flight, and a further reduction of property values.

B. As the cities tax base shrinks and services decline, neighborhoods deteriorate and banks began redlining.

1. Redlining occurs when banks draw a line on a map around problem areas and refused to make loans for housing and businesses located in these areas. This disinvestment pushes these areas into further decline.

2. The development of a global market has led to deindustrialization. Manufacturing firms have relocated from the inner city to areas where production costs are lower. As millions of urban manufacturing jobs were eliminated, inner-city economies were unable to provide alternative employment for poor residents, thereby locking them out of the economy.

C. Social policy usually takes one of two forms.

1. Urban renewal involves tearing down and rebuilding the buildings in an area. As a result of urban renewal, residents can no longer afford to live in the area and are displaced to adjacent areas.

2. Enterprise zones create economic incentives to encourage businesses to move into the area. Most businesses, however, refuse to move into high-crime areas.

3. If U.S. cities are to change, they must become top-agenda items of the U.S. government, with adequate resources in terms of money and human talents focused on overcoming urban woes.

4. William Flanagan suggests three guiding principles for working out specific solutions to urban problems: (1) regional and national planning is necessary; (2) growth needs to be channeled in such a way that makes city living attractive; and (3) social policy must be evaluated by its effects on people. Finally, unless the root causes of urban problems, such as poverty, poor schools, and lack of jobs, are addressed, solutions will only serve as band-aids that cover the real problems.

KEY TERMS
After studying the chapter, review the definition for each of the following terms.

alienation: used in several senses; in this context it refers to feelings of isolation, that you are not part of something or that no one cares about you (612)

basic demographic equation: growth rate equals births minus deaths plus net migration (600)

city: a place in which a large number of people are permanently based and do not produce their own food (603)

community: a place people identify with, where they sense that they belong and that others care what happens to them (614)

crude birth rate: the annual number of live births per 1,000 population (599)

crude death rate: the annual number of deaths per 1,000 population (599)

deindustrialization: industries moving out of a country or region (618)

demographic transition: a three-stage historical process of population growth; first, high birth rates and high death rates; second, high birth rates and low death rates; and third, low birth rates and low death rates; a fourth stage has begun to appear in the Most Industrialized Nations, as depicted in Figure 20.3 (592)

demographic variables: the three factors that influence population growth: fertility, mortality, and net migration (598)

demography: the study of the size, composition, growth, and distribution of human populations (590)

disinvestment: the withdrawal of investments by financial institutions, which seals the fate of an urban area (618)

enterprise zone: the use of economic incentives in a designated area with the intention of encouraging investment there (618)

edge city: a large clustering of service facilities and residential areas near highway intersections that provides a sense of place to people who live, shop, and work there (608)

exponential growth curve: a pattern of growth in which numbers double during approximately equal intervals, thus accelerating in the latter stages (590)

fecundity: the number of children that women are capable of bearing (598)

fertility rate: the number of children that the average woman bears (598)

gentrification: middle class people moving into a run-down area of a city, displacing the poor, buying and restoring homes (608)

growth rate: the net change in a population after adding births, subtracting deaths, and either adding or subtracting net migration (600)

human ecology: Robert Park's term for the relationship between people and their environment (such as land and structures); also known as *urban ecology* (610)

invasion-succession cycle: the process of one group of people displacing a group whose racial-ethnic or social class characteristics differ from their own (611)

Malthus theorem: an observation by Thomas Malthus that although the food supply increases only arithmetically (from 1 to 2 to 3 to 4 and so on), population grows geometrically (from 2 to 4 to 8 to 16 and so forth) (590)

megacity: a city of 10 million or more residents (606)

megalopolis: an urban area consisting of at least two metropolises and their many suburbs (606)

metropolis: a central city surrounded by smaller cities and their suburbs (606)

metropolitan statistical area (MSA): a central city and the urbanized counties adjacent to it (607)

net migration rate: the difference between the number of immigrants and emigrants per 1,000 population (599)

population pyramid: a graphic representation of a population, divided into age and sex (597)

population shrinkage: the process by which a country's population becomes smaller because its birth rate and immigration are too low to replace those who die or emigrate (593)

redlining: the officers of a financial institution deciding not to make loans in a particular area (618)

suburb: a community adjacent to a city (608)

suburbanization: the movement from the city to the suburbs (617)

urban renewal: the rehabilitation of a rundown area, which usually results in the displacement of the poor who are living in that area (618)

urbanization: the process by which an increasing proportion of a population live in cities (606)

zero population growth: a demographic condition in which women bear only enough children to reproduce the population (602)

KEY PEOPLE

State the major theoretical contributions or findings of these people.

Ernest Burgess: Burgess developed the concentric zone model of urban development. (610-611)

John Darley and Bibb Latané: These social psychologists found that people tend to remain uninvolved when they perceive there are others around who might become involved; they referred to this as the *diffusion of responsibility.* (616)

William Faunce: Writing about the far-reaching implications of exponential growth, this sociologist's views are consistent with the New Malthusians. (590)

William Flanagan: Flanagan has suggested three guiding principles for finding solutions to pressing urban problems: (1) use of regional planning, (2) awareness of human needs, and (3) equalizing the benefits as well as the impact of urban change. (619)

Herbert Gans: Gans studied urban neighborhoods, with the result that he documented the existence of community within cities and identified the several different types of urban dwellers that live there. (614)

Chauncey Harris and Edward Ullman: These two geographers developed the multiple-nuclei model of urban growth. Harris later introduced the peripheral model of urban growth to account for more recent developments. (611-612)

Homer Hoyt: Hoyt modified Burgess's model of urban growth with the development of the sector model. (611)

Thomas Malthus: Malthus was an economist who made dire predictions about the future of population growth. (590)

Steven Mosher: This anthropologist did field work in China and wrote about the ruthlessness with which the "one couple, one child" policy is enforced. (600)

Robert Park: Park coined the term "human ecology" to describe how people adapt to their environment. (610)

Julian Simon: Simon has argued that immigrants are a net contributor on the U.S. economy. (599)

William Wilson: Wilson observed that the net result of shifting population and resources from central cities to suburbs was the transformation of the cities into ghettos. (617)

Louis Wirth: Wirth wrote a classic essay, "Urbanism as a Way of Life," in which he argued that city life undermines kinship and neighborhood. (614)

STUDENT APPLICATION PROJECTS

This is your opportunity to apply the sociological perspective. The projects in this section refer to material introduced in this chapter of your text. These projects help you apply the sociological perspective "down to your earth...down to your daily life."

1. Think about your own family—your nuclear family, your extended family, and also several past generations of your family. How has your family illustrated some of the demographic patterns? Be as specific as you can. How has your family been affected by the major demographic factors of fertility, mortality, and migration?

2. Map out where you currently live, or where you have lived, in terms of one or more of the models of urban growth. Even if you live in "rural" area, which one of the models can you envision your "rural" area eventually becoming? Explain and illustrate.

3. List the ways your college campus is similar to living in a large urban environment. List the ways your college is different from living in a large urban environment. Why do many college students feel alienated and isolated? Explain. Do you think many college students follow a norm of noninvolvement? Why or why not? What steps could be taken to reduce alienation on college campuses? Explain.

4. Think about the future and what you think your community, the United States, and the world will be like. Identify positive changes that you see related to population and urbanization. Are there any concerns that you have related to how our society is changing?

SELF-TEST

MULTIPLE CHOICE QUESTIONS

1. Studying the size, composition, growth, and distribution of human population is known as: (590)
    a. population growth theory.
    b. growth specialists.
    c. demography.
    d. social development theory.

2. The proposition that the population grows geometrically while food supply increases arithmetically is known as the: (590)
    a. food surplus equation.
    b. Malthus theorem.
    c. exponential growth curve.
    d. demographic transition.

3. Which of the following statements is consistent with beliefs of the Anti-Malthusians? (592)
    a. People will blindly reproduce until there is no room left on earth.
    b. It is possible to project the world's current population growth into the indefinite future.
    c. Most people do not use intelligence and rational planning when it comes to having children.
    d. The demographic transition provides an accurate picture of what the future looks like.

4. The three-stage historical process of population growth is known as the: (592)
    a. demographic equation.
    b. demographic transition.
    c. exponential growth curve.
    d. implosion growth curve.

5. The process by which a country's population becomes smaller because its birth rate and immigration are too low to replace those who die and emigrate is: (593)
    a. population transfer.
    b. population annihilation.
    c. population shrinkage.
    d. population depletion.

6. Starvation occurs because: (594)
    a. there is not enough fertile land worldwide on which to grow food.
    b. some parts of the world lack food while other parts of the world produce more than they can consume.
    c. population is growing at a faster rate than the world's ability to produce food.
    d. people do not eat a well-balanced diet.

7. Why do people in the Least Industrialized Nations have so many children? (597)
   a. parenthood provides status
   b. children are considered to be an economic asset
   c. the community encourages people to have children
   d. all of the above

8. For conflict theorists, the explanation for why women in poor nations have so many children is that: (598)
   a. women derive special meaning from children.
   b. children's labor can be exploited by their parents.
   c. men control women's reproductive choices.
   d. women use sex as a means of control over men.

9. Mexico's current population will double in _____ years. (598)
   a. 18
   b. 37
   c. 58
   d. 78

10. To illustrate population dynamics, demographers use_____. (598)
    a. population growth charts
    b. population pyramids
    c. fertility rates
    d. demographic models

11. What are the factors that influence population growth called? (598)
    a. demographic variables
    b. demographic transitions
    c. demographic equations
    d. demographic constants

12. _____ refers to the number of children the average woman bears. (598)
    a. fertility rate
    b. fecundity
    c. crude birth rate
    d. real birth rate

13. The annual number of deaths per 1,000 population is the: (599)
    a. crude death rate.
    b. crude mortality rate.
    c. crude life expectancy rate.
    d. net death rate.

14. What factors might push someone to migrate? (599)
    a. poverty
    b. lack of religious and political freedom
    c. political persecution
    d. all of the above

15. Around the globe, the flow of migration is generally from: (599)
    a. most Industrialized Nations to Least Industrialized Nations
    b. one of the Least Industrialized Nation to another one.
    c. least Industrialized Nations to Industrializing Nations.
    d. least Industrialized Nations to Most Industrialized Nations.

16. According to your text, why is it difficult to forecast population growth? (600)
    a. government programs may encourage or discourage women from having children.
    b. government bureaus may be dishonest in reporting data.
    c. there is a lack of computer programs to deal with data adequately.
    d. births, deaths, and migration are human behaviors and thus impossible to predict.

17. China's practice of female infanticide is rooted in: (601)
    a. sexism.
    b. economics.
    c. traditions that go back centuries.
    d. all of the above.

18. The process by which an increasing proportion of a population lives in cities is: (602)
    a. suburbanization.
    b. gentrification.
    c. megalopolitanism.
    d. urbanization.

19. What does today's rapid urbanization mean? (602)
    a. More people live in cities.
    b. Today's cities are larger.
    c. By 2015, 564 of the world's cities will contain at least one million people.
    d. All of the above.

20. All are true about metropolitan statistical areas(MSA's) *except*: (606)
    a. there are 280 metropolitan statistical areas.
    b. MSA's consist of a central city of at least 50,000 people.
    c. about three of five Americans live in just fifty or so MSA's.
    d. an MSA consists of the urbanized counties adjacent to it.

21. What is a megacity? (606)
    a.   a city of 10 million or more residents
    b.   a city that is at the center of a megalopolis
    c.   a city with a multitude of problems
    d.   a central city of at least 50,000 people and the urbanized areas linked to it

22. Edge cities: (606)
    a.   consist of a clustering of shopping malls, hotels, office parks, and residential areas near the intersection of major highways.
    b.   overlap political boundaries and include parts of several cities or towns.
    c.   provide a sense of place to those who live there.
    d.   all of the above.

23. Who first proposed the concentric-zone model? (610)
    a.   Herbert Gans
    b.   Ernest Burgess
    c.   Robert Park
    d.   Homer Hoyt

24. When a new group of immigrants enter a city, they tend to settle in low-rent areas. As their numbers increase, those already living in the area begin to move out; their departure creates more low-cost housing for the immigrants. Sociologists refer to this process as: (601)
    a.   progressive population replacement.
    b.   reverse gentrification.
    c.   cycle of assimilation.
    d.   invasion-succession cycle.

25. The model that suggests that land use in cities is based on several centers, such as a clustering of restaurants or automobile dealerships is the: (612)
    a.   sector model.
    b.   concentric-zone model.
    c.   multiple-nuclei model.
    d.   commerce model.

26. Louis Wirth argued that city undermines: (614)
    a.   kinship and neighborhood.
    b.   economy and politics.
    c.   religion.
    d.   police.

27. According to Gans's typology, the trapped include: (614)
    a.   downwardly mobile persons.
    b.   elderly persons.
    c.   alcoholics and drug addicts.
    d.   all of the above.

28. The Kitty Genovese case in an example of: (615)
    a. ethnic villagers.
    b. cosmopolites.
    c. diffusion of responsibility.
    d. community.

29. What is suburbanization? (617)
    a. movement from the suburbs to edge cities
    b. movement from the city to the suburbs
    c. movement from rural areas to suburbs
    d. displacement of the poor by the relatively affluent who renovate the former's homes

30. Which principles of building community were identified by William Flanagan? (619)
    a. Regional and national planning is necessary
    b. Cities must be appealing and meet human needs
    c. Social policy must be evaluated
    d. All of the above

TRUE-FALSE QUESTIONS

1. _____ Thomas Malthus was a sociologist at the Univ. of Chicago in the 1920s. (590)
2. _____ The exponential growth curve is based on the idea that if growth doubles during approximately equal intervals of time, it accelerates in the latter stages. (590)
3. _____ The Anti-Malthusians believe that people breed like germs in a bucket. (592)
4. _____ There are two stages in the process of demographic transition. (592)
5. _____ The main reason why there is starvation is because there are too many people in the world today and too little food to feed them all. (593)
6. _____ The major reason why people in the Least Industrialized Nations have so many children is because they do not know how to prevent conception. (596)
7. _____ Population pyramids represent a population, divided into race, age, and sex. (598)
8. _____ Demographers study fertility, mortality, and migration to project population trends. (599)
9. _____ The fertility rate refers to the number of children that the average woman bears. (598)
10. _____ Migration rates do not affect the global population. (599)
11. _____ Julian Simon argues that immigrants costs exceed their contributions. (599)
12. _____ It is difficult for demographers to forecast population growth. (600)
13. _____ A megacity is a city of 5 million or more residents. (606)
14. _____ About 3 in 5 Americans live in fifty or so metropolitan statistical areas. (607)
15. _____ The concentric-zone model is based on the idea that cities expand from their central business district outward. (610)
16. _____ The multiple-nuclei model is the most accurate model of urban growth. (612)
17. _____ The world's cities are growing by one million people each week. (614)
18. _____ Sports teams often engender community identification in urban areas. (616)
19. _____ Upper-middle class residents live in gated communities to protect themselves form lower social classes. (616)

20. _____Urban renewal involves tearing down deteriorated buildings and replacing them with decent, affordable housing units. (618)

FILL-IN-THE-BLANK QUESTIONS

1. _____ is the observation that although the food supply increases arithmetically, the population grows geometrically. (590)
2. The_____ of 2004 can help us understand population growth. (596)
3. Conflict theorists point out that a declining standard of living often poses the threat of _____ instability.(598)
4. Three oil-rich countries of the world—Kuwait, Qatar, and United Arab Emirates—have the _____ death rate.(599)
5. Around the world, the flow of migration is from the Least Industrialized Nations to the _____ countries. (599)
6. To reduce the number of children, China has a _____ national policy. (601)
7. A demographic condition in which women bear only enough children to reproduce the population is _____. (602)
8. _____ refers to masses of people moving to cities and to these cities having a growing influence in society. (602)
9. An overlapping area consisting of at least two metropolises and their many suburbs is a _____. (606)
10. _____ is a city of 10,000 to 50,000 residents that is not a suburb. (609)
11. Harris and Ullman noted that some cities have several centers or _____. (611)
12. The urban growth model that portrays the impact of radial highways on the movement of people and services away from the central city to its outskirts is the _____ model. (611)
13. _____ is a sense of not belonging and a feeling that no one cares what happens to you. (612)
14. _____ are a city's students, intellectuals, professionals, musicians, artists, and entertainers. (615)
15. Darley and Latane uncovered, in their research that the more bystanders there are in a situation the _____ likely people are to offer help. (616)

MATCH THESE SOCIAL SCIENTISTS WITH THEIR CONTRIBUTIONS

_____	1. William Wilson	a. *transformation of cities into ghettos*
_____	2. Ernest Burgess	b. *human ecology*
_____	3. Herbert Gans	c. *concentric-zone model*
_____	4. Homer Hoyt	d. *urban villagers*
_____	5. Robert Park	e. *sector model*
_____	6. Julian Simon	f. *ruthless enforcement of China's one-child policy*
_____	7. Louis Wirth	g. *diffusion of responsibility*
_____	8. William Faunce	h. *immigrants contribute to U.S. economy*
_____	9. Darley / Latané	i. *alienation and urban life*
_____	10. Steven Mosher	j. *views consistent with the New Malthusians*

ESSAY QUESTIONS

1. State the positions of the New Malthusians and the Anti-Malthusians and discuss which view you think is more accurate, based on the information provided about each position.

2. Identify some of the population challenges that affect the Most Industrialized and the Least Industrialized Nations and provide explanations for these problems.

3. Identify the problems that are associated with forecasting population growth.

4. Discuss the five types of urban dwellers that Gans describes and how life in the city is different for each of these groups.

5. Discuss the factors that fueled suburbanization and consider the impact that this population shift had on cities.

CHAPTER 21
COLLECTIVE BEHAVIOR AND SOCIAL MOVEMENTS

CHAPTER SUMMARY

- Early theorists argued that individuals are transformed by crowds, losing all capacity for rationality. Terms such as "herd mentality," "collective mind," and "circular reaction" were developed to explain why people behaved as they did when in the midst of a crowd. According to Herbert Blumer, crowds go through five stages before they become an acting crowd: social unrest, an exciting event, milling, a common object of attention, and common impulses.

- Contemporary explanations emphasize the rationality of the crowd, the emergence of norms to govern behavior; collective behavior is seen as directed toward a goal, even if the behavior is cruel and destructive.

- Some of the major forms of collective behavior are lynchings, riots, panics, moral panics, mass hysteria, rumors, fads, fashions, and urban legends. Conditions of discontent and uncertainty provide fertile ground for collective behavior.

- Social movements usually involve more people, are more prolonged, are more organized, and focus on social change. Depending on whether their target is individuals or society and the amount of change desired is partial or complete, social movements can be classified as alterative, redemptive, reformative, or transformative. Some social movements have a global orientation and are known as transnational social movements. Metaformative social movements are a rare type of social movement.

- Tactics are chosen on the basis of a group's levels of membership, its publics, and its relationship to authority. Other factors that may be important are friendship, race-ethnicity, and size of town. Because the mass media are the gatekeepers, their favorable or unfavorable coverage greatly affects a social movement's choice of tactics.

- Mass society theory, relative deprivation theory, and ideological commitment theory all attempt to explain why people join social movements. Agent provocateurs are a unique type of participant in social movements.

- Social movements go through distinct stages. Resource mobilization theory accounts for why some social movements never get off the ground while others enjoy great success. To succeed, social movements must focus on broad concerns, which are generally deeply embedded in society and do not lend themselves to easy solutions.

LEARNING OBJECTIVES
After reading Chapter 21, you should be able to:

1. Discuss early explanations of collective behavior, focusing on how the crowd transforms the individual. (624-626)

2. Know the five stages that crowds go through before they become an acting crowd, as identified by Herbert Blumer. (625-626)

3. Understand contemporary views of collective behavior including the minimax strategy and emergent norms. (626-627)

4. Identify the five kinds of crowd participants, as pointed out by Ralph Turner and Lewis Killian. (627)

5. Discuss and provide examples of collective behavior including lynchings, riots, rumors, panics, moral panics, mass hysteria, fads, fashions, and urban legends. (627-636)

6. Describe what a social movement is and differentiate between proactive and reactive social movements. (636)

7. Identify and contrast the different types of social movements. (637-638)

8. Discuss the tactics that social movements employ and how and why these tactics are chosen. (638-639)

9. Describe the role that propaganda and the mass media play in helping to determine the effectiveness of social movements. (639-642)

10. Evaluate the different theories that explain why people are attracted to social movements, and the conditions that underlie their attraction. (642-645)

11. Discuss the special role of the agent provocateur in some social movements. (645)

12. Identify the five stages of social movements; talk about what social movements need to do in order to succeed; and explain why most social movements are unsuccessful. (646-647)

CHAPTER OUTLINE

I. **COLLECTIVE BEHAVIOR**
   A. Collective behavior is characterized by a group of people who bypass the usual norms governing their behavior and do something unusual. It is a broad term and covers a wide range of acts.

II. **Early Explanations: The Transformation of the Individual**
   A. In 1852, Charles Mackay concluded that when people were in crowds, they sometimes "went mad" and did "disgraceful and violent things"; just as a herd of cows will stampede, so too can people come under the control of a "herd mentality."
   B. Based on Mackay's idea, Gustave LeBon stressed that the individual is transformed by the crowd.
      1. In a crowd, people feel anonymous, not accountable for what they do; they develop feelings of invincibility, believing that together they can accomplish anything. A collective mind develops.
      2. They become highly suggestible; this paves the way for contagion, a kind of collective hypnosis, which releases the destructive instincts that society has so carefully repressed.
   C. To LeBon's analysis, Robert Park added the ideas of social unrest, which is transmitted from one individual to another, and circular reaction, the back-and-forth communication between the members of a crowd whereby a "collective impulse" is transmitted.

D. Synthesizing both LeBon's and Park's ideas, Herbert Blumer identified five stages that precede what he called an acting crowd.

1. A background condition of social unrest exists—when people's routine activities are thwarted or when they develop new needs that go unsatisfied.

2. An exciting event occurs—one so startling that people are preoccupied with it.

3. People engage in milling—the act of standing or walking around as they talk about the exciting event and a circular reaction sets in.

4. A common object of attention emerges—people's attention becomes riveted on some aspect of the event.

5. Stimulation of the common impulses occurs—people collectively agree about what they should do. Social contagion, described as a collective excitement passed from one person to another, becomes the mechanism that stimulates these common impulses. The end result is an acting crowd. Not all acting crowds are negative or destructive nor are they all serious.

III. The Contemporary View: The Rationality of the Crowd

A. Sociologists argue that beneath the surface, crowds are actually quite rational, taking deliberate steps to reach some goal and often acting in a cooperative manner.

B. Richard Berk pointed out that people use a minimax strategy (trying to minimize their costs and maximize their rewards) whether in small groups or in crowds; the fewer the costs and the greater the rewards that people anticipate, the more likely they are to carry out a particular act.

C. Ralph Turner and Lewis Killian noted that human behavior is regulated by the normative order—socially approved ways of doing things that make up our everyday life. However, when an extraordinary event occurs and existing norms do not cover the new situation, people develop new norms to deal with the problem (emergent norms).

1. There are five kinds of crowd participants: (1) the ego-involved, who feel a high personal stake in the event; (2) the concerned, who have a personal interest in the event but less than the ego-involved; (3) the insecure, who have little concern about the issue but have sought out the crowd because it gives them a sense of power and security; (4) the curious spectators, who are inquisitive and may cheer the crowd on even though they do not care about the issue; and (5) the exploiters, who do not care about the issue but use it for their own purposes (e.g., hawking food or T-shirts).

2. These participants have different points of view. Their contrasting attitudes, emotion, and motives help to set the crowd on a particular course of action. As a common mood for new norms emerges, activities that are "not OK" in everyday life may now seem "OK."

3. The concept of emerging norms is important because it points to a rational process as the essential component of collective behavior.

IV. Forms of Collective Behavior

A. Sociologists view collective behavior as they do other forms of behavior. They seek to understand the role that age, gender, race-ethnicity, and social class may play.

B. Riots are defined as violent crowd behavior aimed against people and property.

1. Frustration and anger at deprivation are usually at the root of a riot; the riot that broke out in Los Angeles after the verdict in the Rodney King trial is an example of this.

2. Beginning with a perception of being kept out of the mainstream society (limited to a meager education and denied jobs and justice), people's frustration builds to such a boiling point that it takes only a precipitating event to erupt in collective behavior.

3. It is not only the deprived who participate in the riots; others, who are not deprived but who still feel frustration at the underlying social conditions that place them at a disadvantage also get involved.

4. For some, riots are a handy event. It allows them to loot and participate in an event apart from their humdrum life.

5. The event that precipitates a riot is important, but so is the riot's general context.

C. Rumors thrive in conditions of ambiguity, functioning to fill in missing information.

1. Rumors are unverified information about some topic on interest. Most rumors are short-lived and arise in a situation of ambiguity, only to dissipate when they are replaced either by another rumor or by factual information. A few rumors have a long life because they hit a responsive chord (e.g., rumors of mass poisoning of soft drink products that spread to other many countries).

2. Three main factors in why people believe rumors are that they: (1) deal with a subject that is important to an individual, (2) replace ambiguity with some form of certainty, and (3) are attributed to a creditable source.

3. Rumors usually pass from one person to another, though they can originate from the mass media.

D. Panic, like the one that occurred following the broadcast of H. G. Wells's "War of the Worlds," is behavior that results when people become so fearful that they cannot function normally.

1. One explanation as to why people panic is because they are anxious about some social condition.

2. It is against the law to shout "Fire!" in a public building when no such danger exists. If people fear immediate death, they will lunge toward the nearest exit in a frantic effort to escape (e.g., the Beverly Hills Supper Club fire in Kentucky in 1977, in which 165 people died trying to get out of the two exits).

3. Sociologists who studied this panic found what others have discovered, that not everyone panics. Only 29 percent of the employees of the Beverly Hills Supper Club left when they learned of the fire. They extended their role to help customers, fought the fire, or searched for friends and relatives.

4. In some life threatening situations, a sense of order prevails. During the World Trade Center attack, many people helped injured friends and strangers.

E. Moral panics occur when large numbers of people become intensely concerned, even fearful, about some behavior that is perceived as a threat to morality; the threat is seen as enormous and hostility builds toward those thought responsible. They are often fueled by the mass media.

1. The most famous moral panic was the fear of witches in Europe between 1400 and 1650.

2. Moral panics are often fueled by the mass media and center around a sense of danger.

3. Moral panics are often fed by rumor, information for which there is no discernible source and which is usually unfounded.

4. Moral panics also thrive on uncertainty and anxiety.

F. A fad is a temporary pattern of behavior that catches people's attention, while fashion is a more enduring version of the same.

1. Very short, intense fads are called crazes. They appear suddenly and are gone quickly.

2. Fads come in many forms, and no one is immune to getting caught up in one. Some fads involve millions of people, die out quickly, and then make a comeback.

3. Fashion is a behavior pattern that catches people's attention, lasting longer than a fad. Most often thought of in terms of clothing fashions, it can also refer to hairstyles, home decorating, design and colors of buildings, and language.

G. Urban legends are stories with an ironic twist that sound realistic but are false. Jan Brunvand, who studied the transmission of urban legends, concluded that urban legends are passed on by people who think that the event really happened to someone such as a "friend of a friend"; the stories have strong appeal and gain credibility from naming specific people or local places. Urban legends are "modern morality stories," with each teaching a moral lesson about life; they are related to social change; and they are calculated to instill guilt and fear.

V. SOCIAL MOVEMENTS

A. Social movements consist of large numbers of people, who, organize to either promote or resist social change.

B. At the heart of social movements lie grievances and dissatisfactions. Proactive social movements promote social change because a current condition of society is intolerable. In contrast, reactive social movements resist changing conditions in society which they perceive as threatening.

C. To further their goals, people develop social movement organizations like the National Organization of Women or the Stop-ERA. They use attention-grabbing devices to recruit members and publicize grievances.

D. Mayer Zald suggests that a cultural crisis can give birth to a wave of social movements. According to Zald, when a society's institutions fail to keep up with social changes, many people's needs go unfulfilled, massive unrest follows, and social movements come into being to bridge the gap.

VI. Types and Tactics of Social Movements

A. Social movements can be classified into four broad categories according to the type and amount of social change they seek.

1. Two types seek to change people but differ in terms of the amount of change desired: alterative social movements seek to alter only particular aspects of people (e.g., the Women's Christian Temperance Union); while redemptive social movements seek to change people totally (e.g., a religious social movement such as fundamental Christianity that stresses conversion).

2. Two types of movements seek to change society but also differ in terms of the amount of change desired: reformative social movements seek to reform only one part of society (e.g., animal rights or the environment); transformative social movements seek to change the social order itself and replace it with their own version of the ideal society (e.g., revolutions in the American colonies, France, and Russia).

3. One of the more interesting types of transformative social movements is the millenarian movement, which is based on prophecies of a coming calamity. Cargo cults, a social movement in which South Pacific islanders destroyed their possessions in the anticipation that their ancestors would send items by ship, are an interesting example of millenarian movements.

4. Today, some social movements have a global orientation, committed to changing a specific condition throughout the world. They are called transnational (or new) social movements. The women's, environment, and animal rights movements are examples.

5. A rare type of social movement, metaformative social movements, also exists, with goals to change the social order itself of a entire civilization or entire world. We are witnessing another metaformative social movement, that of Islamic fundamentalism.

B. Tactics of social movements are best understood by examining levels of membership, publics they address, and their relationship to authorities.

1. Three levels of membership are (1) the inner core (the leadership that sets goals, timetables, and so on); (2) people committed to the goals of the movement, but not to the same degree as members of the inner core; and (3) people who are neither as committed nor as dependable. The chosen tactics depend on the predispositions and backgrounds of the inner core.

2. Publics are made up of a dispersed group of people who may have an interest in an issue. They can be described as sympathetic (sympathize with goals of movement but have no commitment to movement); hostile (keenly aware of group's goals and want the movement stopped); and people who are unaware of or indifferent toward the movement. In selecting tactics, the leadership considers these different types of publics.

3. The movement's relationship to the authorities is important in determining tactics: if authorities are hostile to a social movement, aggressive or even violent tactics are likely; if authorities are sympathetic, violence is not likely. If a social movement is institutionalized, accepted by the authorities, and given access to resources they control, the likelihood of violence is very low.

4. Other factors that can influence the choice of tactics include the nature of friendships, race, and even the size of towns.

C. In selecting tactics, leaders of social movements are aware of their effects on the mass media. Their goal is to influence public opinion about some issue.

1. Propaganda is a key to understanding social movements. Propaganda simply means the presentation of information in an attempt to influence people.

2. Propaganda, in the sense of organized attempts to influence public opinion, is a regular part of everyday life.

3. The mass media play a critical role in social movements. They have become, in effect, the gatekeepers to social movements. If those who control and work in the mass media are sympathetic to a "cause," it will receive sympathetic treatment. If the social movement goes against their own biases, it will either be ignored or receive unfavorable treatment.

VII. Why People Join Social Movements

A. In the mass society theory, William Kornhauser proposed that social movements offer a sense of belonging to people who have weak social ties.

1. Mass society, characterized as an industrialized, highly bureaucratized, impersonal society, makes many people feel isolated and, as a result, they are attracted to social movements because they offer a sense of belonging.

2. However, Doug McAdam (who studied those involved in civil rights movements) found that many who participate in social movements have strong family and community ties, and joined such movements to right wrongs and overcome injustice, not because of isolation. The most isolated (the homeless) generally do not join anything except food lines.

B. According to deprivation theory, people who are deprived of things deemed valuable in society, whether money, justice, status, or privilege, join social movements with the hope of redressing their grievances.

1. Absolute deprivation is people's actual negative condition; relative deprivation is what people think they should have relative to what others have or even compared with their own past or perceived future.

2. While the notion of absolute deprivation provides a beginning point for looking at why people join social movements, it is even more important to look at relative deprivation in trying to understand why people join social movements.

3. Improved conditions fuel human desires for even better conditions and thus can spark revolutions.

C. James Jasper and Dorothy Nelkin note that people join a particular social movement because of moral issues and an ideological commitment to the movement. It is the moral component, they argue, that is a primary reason for some people's involvement in social movements.

D. An agent provocateur is a special type of social movement participant.

1. An agent of the government or of a rival social movement, the agent provocateur's job is to spy on the leadership and sabotage their activities. Some are recruited from the membership itself, while others go underground and join the movement.

2. On occasion a police agent is converted to the social movement on which he or she is spying. Sociologist Gary Marx noted that this occurs because the agent, to be credible, must share at least some of the class, age, ethnic, racial, religious, or sexual characteristics of the group. This makes the agent more likely to sympathize with the movement's goals and to become disenchanted with the means being used to destroy the group.

3. Sometimes the agent provocateur will go to great lengths, even breaking the law, to push the social movement into illegal activities.

VIII. On the Success and Failure of Social Movements

    A.   Social movements have a life course—that is, they go through five stages as they grow and mature.

        1.   Initial unrest and agitation because people are upset about some social condition; leaders who verbalize people's feelings emerge at this point.

        2.   Resource mobilization by leaders of a relatively large number of people who demand that something be done about the problem; charismatic leaders emerge during this stage.

        3.   An organization emerges with a division of labor, a leadership who makes policy decisions, and a rank and file that actively supports the movement.

        4.   Institutionalization occurs as the movement becomes bureaucratized and leadership passes to career officials who may care more about their position in the organization than about the movement itself.

        5.   The organization declines, but there may be a possibility of resurgence. Some movements cease to exist; others become reinvigorated with new leadership from within or by coming into conflict with other social movements fighting for the opposite side of the issue (e.g., social movements relating to abortion).

    B.   Seldom do social movements actually solve problems. In order to mobilize sufficient resources to survive, they find it necessary to appeal to a broad constituency and, to do so they must focus on large-scale issues that are deeply embedded in society. Such broad problems do not lend themselves to easy or quick solutions.

    C.   Many social movements do vitally affect society. Some make valuable contributions to solving problems, for they highlight areas of society to be changed. Others become powerful forces for resisting the social change that its members consider undesirable.

    D.   Decline is not inevitable. New, more idealistic and committed leaders may emerge and reinvigorate the movement, or conflict between groups on opposing sides of an issue may continually invigorate each side and prevent the movement's decline.

KEY TERMS
After studying the chapter, review the definition for each of the following terms.

acting crowd: an excited group of people who move toward a goal (625)

agent provocateur: someone who joins a group in order to spy on it and to sabotage it by *provoking* its members to commit illegal acts (645)

alterative social movement: a social movement that seeks to alter only particular aspects of people (637)

cargo cult: a social movement in which South Pacific islanders destroyed their possessions in the anticipation that their ancestors would ship them new goods (637)

circular reaction: Robert Park's term for a back-and-forth communication between the members of a crowd whereby a "collective impulse" is transmitted (625)

collective behavior: extraordinary activities carried out by groups of people; includes lynchings, rumors, panics, urban legends, and fads and fashions (624)

collective mind: Gustave LeBon's term for the tendency of people in a crowd to feel, think, and act in extraordinary ways (624)

emergent norms: Ralph Turner and Lewis Killian's term for the idea that people develop new norms to cope with a new situation; used to explain crowd behavior (626)

fad: a temporary pattern of behavior that catches people's attention (634)

fashion: a pattern of behavior that catches people's attention and lasts longer than a fad (635)

mass hysteria: an imagined threat that causes physical symptoms among a large number of people (633)

mass society: industrialized, highly bureaucratized, impersonal society (642)

mass society theory: an explanation for why people participate in a social movement based on the assumption that the movement offers them a sense of belonging (642)

metaformative social movement: a social movement that has the goal to change the social order not just of a country or two, but of a civilization, or even the entire world (638)

millenarian social movement: a social movement based on the prophecy of coming social upheaval (637)

milling: a crowd standing or walking around as they talk excitedly about some event (626)

minimax strategy: Richard Berk's term for the effort people make to minimize their costs and maximize their rewards (626)

moral panic: a fear that grips a large number of people that some evil threatens the well-being of society, followed by hostility, sometimes violence, toward those thought responsible (634)

panic: the condition of being so fearful that one cannot function normally, and may even flee (630)

proactive social movement: a social movement that promotes some social change (636)

propaganda: in its broad sense, the presentation of information in the attempt to influence people; in its narrow sense, one-sided information used to try to influence people (642)

public: in this context, a dispersed group of people relevant to a social movement; the sympathetic and hostile public has an interest in the issues on which a social movement focuses; there is also an unaware or indifferent public (638)

public opinion: how people think about some issue (639)

reactive social movement: a social movement that resists some social change (636)

redemptive social movement: a social movement that seeks to change people totally, to redeem them (637)

reformative social movement: a social movement that seeks to change only particular aspects of society (637)

relative deprivation theory: in this context, the belief that people join social movements based on their evaluations of what they think they should have compared with what others have (644)

resource mobilization: a theory that social movements succeed or fail based on their ability to mobilize resources such as time, money, and people's skills (646)

riot: violent crowd behavior aimed against people and property (627)

role extension: the incorporation of additional activities into a role (633)

rumor: unfounded information spread among people (629)

social movement: a large group of people who are organized to promote or resist social change (636)

social movement organization: an organization to promote the goals of a social movement (636)

transformative social movement: a social movement that seeks to change society totally, to transform it (637)

transnational social movement: social movements with a new emphasis on some condition in the world, instead of on a condition in a specific country; also known as *new social movements* (637)

urban legend: a story with an ironic twist that sounds realistic but is false (635)

KEY PEOPLE
Review the major theoretical contributions or findings of these people.

William Banbridge: This sociologist found that some people did become frightened after the broadcast of "War of the Worlds" and a few even got into their cars and drove like maniacs, but most of the panic was an invention of the news media. (631)

Richard Berk: Berk developed the minimax strategy to explain collective behavior; it explains that people are more likely to act when costs are low and anticipated rewards high. (626)

Herbert Blumer: Blumer identified five stages that precede the emergence of an active crowd (an excited group that moves towards a goal). These are tension or unrest, an exciting event, milling, a common object of attention, and common impulses. (625)

Jan Brunvand: This folklorist studied urban legends and suggests they are modern morality stories. (635)

Hadley Cantril: This psychologist suggests that people panicked after hearing the famous "War of the Worlds" because of widespread anxiety about world conditions. (630)

James Jasper and Dorothy Nelkin: These sociologists argue that many become involved in social movements because of moral issues and an ideological commitment. (644)

Drue Johnston and Norris Johnson: These sociologists studied the behavior of employees during the Beverly Hills Supper Club fire and found that most continued to carry out their roles. (633)

William Kornhauser: Kornhauser proposed mass society theory to explain why people are attracted to social movements. He suggested that these movements fill a void in some people's lives by offering them a sense of belonging. (642)

Gustave LeBon: LeBon argued that a collective mind develops within a crowd, and people are swept away by any suggestion that is made. (624-625)

Alfred and Elizabeth Lee: These sociologists found that propaganda relies on seven basic techniques, which they labeled "tricks of the trade." (643)

Charles Mackay: Mackay was the first to study collective behavior; he suggested that a "herd mentality" takes over and explains the disgraceful things people do when in crowds. (624)

Gary Marx: This sociologist investigated the agent provocateur and found that some are converted to the movement because they share some of the same social characteristics as the movement's members. (645)

Doug McAdam: McAdam challenged the mass society theory on the basis of research findings related to people's decision to become involved in the civil rights struggle. He found they were well integrated into society rather than isolated from it, as mass society theory suggests. (642-644)

Clark McPhail: This sociologist studied the behavior of crowds, noting that the behavior of crowd participants is cooperative. (626)

Robert Park: Park suggested that social unrest is the result of the circular reaction of people in crowds. (625)

Victor Rodriguez: This sociologist suggests that minorities in the middle class might participate in riots when they feel frustrated with being treated as second-class citizens, even when they are employed and living stable lives. (628)

Ellen Scott: Scott studied the movement to stop rape and found that close friendships, race, and even size of town are important in determining tactics. (639)

Alexis de Tocqueville: This nineteenth century observer of social life noted that people organize collectively to improve their conditions when they are experiencing relative deprivation rather than absolute deprivation. Having experienced some improvement and being able to see better conditions ahead, they are motivated to work for change. (644)

Ralph Turner and Lewis Killian: These sociologists use the term "emergent norm" to explain the rules that emerge in collective behavior. They note that crowds have at least five kinds of participants: the ego-involved; the concerned; the insecure; the curious spectators; and the exploiters. (626-627)

Mayer Zald: This sociologist explained that social movements are like a rolling sea; during one period of time, a few may appear, but shortly afterward, a whole wave of them role in. He suggested that cultural crises give rise to social movements. (636)

STUDENT APPLICATION PROJECTS

This is your opportunity to apply the sociological perspective to the world around you. The projects in this section refer to material introduced in this chapter of your text. These projects help you apply the sociological perspective "down to your earth...down to your daily life."

1. Briefly list and explain an urban legend you have recently encountered. How do you know it is an urban legend? Explain. Search the internet for urban legend websites. List at least three. Do you think the internet is causing an increase in rumors, fads, fashions, and urban legends? Why or why not?

2. Have you or someone you know every participated in a craze? Briefly describe the situation. Why are people attracted to crazes? What role do the media and peer pressure play in encouraging crazes?

3. Choose an issue in society that you would like to change. How could you go about organizing a social movement around this issue? Be specific in your answer; define the type of movement, explain how you would recruit members, and discuss in detail how you would use propaganda. Overall, what would it take to make your social movement successful?

4. What fads and fashions are the current trends in society? What role do they play in society? How do you think that these got started? Do you participate in these fads or fashions? Why or why not?

SELF-TEST

MULTIPLE CHOICE QUESTIONS

1. Which of the following statements about Charles MacKay is *incorrect*? (624)
   a. He noticed that ordinary people did disgraceful things when in a crowd.
   b. He suggested that people have a "herd mentality" when in a crowd.
   c. He proposed that a collective mind develops once a group of people congregate.
   d. His work marked the beginnings of the field of collective behavior.

2. LeBon's term for the tendency of people in a crowd to feel, think, and act in extraordinary ways is: (624)
   a. social unrest.
   b. the "herd mentality."
   c. collective behavior.
   d. collective mind.

3. According to Park, which is most conductive to the emergence of collective behavior? (625)
   a. social alienation
   b. social apathy
   c. social unrest
   d. social cohesion

4. A crowd's back-and-forth communication whereby a collective impulse is transmitted is: (625)
   a. a circular reaction.
   b. milling.
   c. an acting crowd.
   d. a collective mind.

5. Acting crowd: (625)
   a. is a term coined by Herbert Blumer.
   b. is an excited group that collectively moves toward a goal.
   c. is the end result of the five stages of collective behavior.
   d. all of the above.

6. Richard Berk used the term "minimax strategy" to describe the tendency for: (626)
   a. crowds to operate with a minimum of strategy.
   b. for humans to minimize costs and maximize rewards.
   c. those in authority to maximize the costs of an action in order to minimize rewards.
   d. society to respond to even the most minimum of social movements.

7. The development of new norms to cope with a new situation is: (626)
   a. emergent norms.
   b. developmental norms.
   c. surfacing norms.
   d. none of the above.

8. According to Turner and Killian, which crowd participant's role is most important? (627)
   a. the ego-involved
   b. the concerned
   c. the curious spectators
   d. the exploiters

9. Which of the following are kinds of participants in crowds: (627)
   a. the ego-involved
   b. the insecure.
   c. the exploiters.
   d. all of the above.

10. Sociologists refer to unfounded information spread among people as: (629)
    a. hearsay.
    b. scuttlebutt.
    c. rumor.
    d. gossip.

11. Which of the following is true about rumors: (629)
    a. most last at least six months.
    b. they persist even when there is factual information.
    c. rumors can lead to the destruction of entire communities.
    d. most riots occur after a rumor has been spread.

12. Sociologists have found that when a disaster such as a fire occurs: (632)
    a. everyone panics.
    b. some people continue to perform their roles.
    c. people leave it to the police and firefighters to solve the problem.
    d. no one panics.

13. Which statement about moral panics is *incorrect*? (634)
    a. Moral panics occur when people are concerned about something viewed as immoral.
    b. Moral panics are generally based on an event that has been verified as true.
    c. Moral panics thrive on uncertainty and anxiety.
    d. Moral panics are fueled by the mass media.

14. A temporary pattern of behavior that catches people's attention is a: (635)
    a. panic.
    b. trend.
    c. fashion.
    d. fad.

15. Which of the following would be an example of a fashion? (635)
    a. the bungalow house
    b. mini skirts
    c. the use of the word "cool"
    d. all of the above

16. Social movements that seek to totally change people are: (637)
    a. alternative social movements.
    b. redemptive social movements.
    c. reformative social movements.
    d. transformative social movements.

17. A social movement that seeks to totally change society is a(n): (637)
    a. alterative social movement.
    b. redemptive social movement.
    c. reformative social movement.
    d. transformative social movement.

18. The Women's Christian Temperance Union is an example of which type of social movement? (637)
    a. alternative social movement
    b. redemptive social movement
    c. reformative social movement
    d. transformative social movement

19. A millenarian movement is a social movement: (637)
    a. in which South Pacific islanders destroyed all their possessions.
    b. that seeks to alter only particular aspects of people.
    c. based on the prophecy of coming social upheaval.
    d. that seeks to change individuals totally.

20. Today some social movements have a global orientation because many important issues today cross national boundaries. This new type of social movement is called a: (638)
    a. global social movement.
    b. multinational social movement.
    c. transnational social movement.
    d. worldwide social movement.

21. Levels of membership in social movements include: (638)
    a. the inner core.
    b. the committed.
    c. a wider circle of members.
    d. all of the above.

22. The public that social movements face can really be divided into: (639)
    a. supporters and opponents.
    b. informed supportive public, informed oppositional public, and uninformed mass.
    c. receptive audience, hostile audience, and disinterested mass.
    d. sympathetic public, hostile public, and disinterested people.

23. What factors influence a social movement's choice of tactics? (639)
    a. the predispositions and background of the inner core
    b. the movement's relationship to authorities
    c. the size of the town in which the movement is operating
    d. all of the above

24. How people think about some issue is: (639)
    a. irrelevant to most social scientists.
    b. public opinion.
    c. propaganda.
    d. mass-society theory.

25. Which statement about propaganda is *incorrect*? (642)
    a. Propaganda plays a key role in social movements.
    b. Propaganda generally involves negative images.
    c. Propaganda has become a regular and routine part of modern life.
    d. Propaganda is the presentation of information in an attempt to influence people.

26. The mass media: (642)
    a. are the gatekeepers of social movements.
    b. engage in biased reporting, controlled by people who have an agenda to get across.
    c. are sympathetic to some social movements, while ignoring others; it all depends on their individual biases.
    d. all of the above.

27. The Lees found that propaganda relies on seven basic techniques known as: (643)
    a. tricks of the trade.
    b. propaganda techniques.
    c. techniques of neutralization.
    d. none of the above.

28. According to mass society theory, social movements offer people: (642)
    a. a set of rules or guidelines to govern their behavior.
    b. an outlet for leisure activities.
    c. a sense of belonging.
    d. answers to basic questions concerning morality.

29. Which of the following statements about agent provocateurs is *incorrect*? (642)
    a. Some agent provocateurs are recruited from within the social movement itself, willing to betray their friends in the organization for the sake of payment.
    b. It is not surprising that the government or the other side will use agent provocateurs since the radical change advocated by some social movements poses a threat to the power elite.
    c. Despite any similarities, the agent provocateur may feel antagonistic toward the members of the social movement; this is a very effective strategy for undermining social movements because the agent provocateur is never tempted to switch sides and join the social movement.
    d. Sometimes agent provocateurs will go to great lengths in order to sabotage the group's efforts.

30. In order to turn a group of people who are upset about a social condition into a social movement, there must be: (646)
    a. agitation.
    b. resource mobilization.
    c. organization.
    d. institutionalization.

TRUE-FALSE QUESTIONS

1. _____Collective behavior is characterized by a group of people becoming emotionally aroused and engaging in extraordinary behavior. (624)
2. _____ Gustave LeBon's central idea was that the individual is transformed by the crowd. (624)
3. _____The term "circular reaction" refers to the process by which people become swept up in the crowd, reacting to any suggestion that is put forth. (625)
4. _____Herbert Blumer identified five stages of collective behavior. (625-626)
5. _____The term "acting crowd" is applied only to violent activities such as lynch mobs or people engaged in riots. (625)
6. _____Emergent norms refer to the development of new norms to cope with a new situation, especially among crowds. (626-627)
7. _____The event that precipitates a riot is less important than the riot's general context. (627-628)
8. _____People believe rumors because they replace ambiguity with some form of certainty. (629)
9. _____The fears that produce moral panics are generally out of proportion to any supposed danger. (634)

10. _____Urban legends are just another kind of rumor. (635)
11. _____A social movement that promotes some social change is known as a reactive social movement. (636)
12. _____A social movement based on the prophecy of coming social upheaval is known as a millenarian social movement. (637)
13. _____A social movement's relationship to authorities is significant in determining whether the tactics to be used are peaceful or violent. (639)
14. _____Propaganda and advertising are defined quite differently from one another. (642)
15. _____Deprivation theory and relative deprivation theory are identical perspectives. (644)
16. _____Moral shock is of little importance in motivating people to join a social movement. (644)
17. _____The role of the agent provocateur as a spy (on the leadership of a social movement) and to perhaps try to sabotage their activities is generally unsuccessful. (645)
18. _____Before resources can be mobilized, a social movement must become organized, and in some cases even institutionalized. (646)
19. _____In the final stage of a social movement, decline is certain. (647)
20. _____Social movements seldom actually solve problems. (647)
21.

FILL-IN-THE-BLANK QUESTIONS

1. Park used the term _____ to refer to the back and forth communication whereby a collective impulse is transmitted. (624)
2. An _____ is an excited group that moves toward a goal. (625)
3. After the verdict in the Rodney King Case was announced, there were _____ in major cities in the United States. (628)
4. Sociologists who have studied disaster situations have found that not everyone _____. (630)
5. _____ occur when large numbers of people become concerned, even fearful, about some behavior that they believe threatens morality. (634)
6. For about ten years, quality circles were _____. (635)
7. To further goals to make social change, people develop _____ organizations. (637)
8. Millenarian social movements are based on the _____ of coming calamity. (637)
9. The goal of _____ social movements is the change the entire world. (637)
10. If a social movement is _____, violence will not be directed toward the authorities. (639)
11. _____ relies on seven basic techniques known as "tricks of the trade". (643)
12. Kornhauser argued that people feel _____ and thus they join social movements. (642)
13. Some people join social movements because of _____ shock. (644)
14. _____ are agents of the government who join a group in order to spy on it. (645)
15. The fifth and final stage of a social movement is _____. (645)

MATCH THESE SOCIAL SCIENTISTS WITH THEIR CONTRIBUTIONS

_____	1. Charles Mackay	a. *emergent norm*
_____	2. William Kornhauser	b. *urban legends*
_____	3. Robert Park	c. *minimax strategy*
_____	4. Turner & Killian	d. *challenged mass society theory*
_____	5. Gustave LeBon	e. *mass society theory*
_____	6. Doug McAdam	f. *social unrest and circular reaction*
_____	7. Herbert Blumer	g. *studied movements to stop rape*
_____	8. Richard Berk	h. *collective mind*
_____	9. Jan Brunvand	i. *the acting crowd*
_____	10. Ellen Scott	j. *herd mentality*

ESSAY QUESTIONS

1. Compare and contrast the early explanations of collective behavior, as advanced by Charles Mackay, Gustave LeBon, Robert Park, and Herbert Blumer, with more contemporary explanations developed by Richard Berk, Ralph Turner, and Lewis Killian.

2. Develop an explanation as to why panics, rumors, and urban legends thrive in society.

3. Discuss the different theories about why people join social movements and consider how they could all be accurate.

4. Explain what propaganda is and why it is so important in the development of social movements.

5. Discuss the difference between fads and fashion and provide examples.

CHAPTER 22
SOCIAL CHANGE AND THE ENVIRONMENT

CHAPTER SUMMARY

- Social change, the alteration of culture and society over time, is a vital part of social life. Social change has included four social revolutions: (1) domestication, agriculture, industrialization, and information; (2) the change from *Gemeinschaft* to *Gesellschaft* societies; (3) capitalism and industrialization; and (4) modernization; and global stratification. Social movements indicate the cutting edges of social change.

- Theories of social change include evolutionary theories (both unilinear and multilinear); cyclical theories; and conflict theories. William Ogburn identified technology as the basis cause of social change. The processes of social change are invention, discovery, and diffusion. Cultural lag refers to the gap between changes in the symbolic culture in response to changes in technology.

- Technology is a driving force in social change, and it can shape an entire society by changing existing technology, social organization, ideology, values, and social relationships, as is evident when the impact that both the automobile and the computer have had on American society is analyzed. It is possibly that the changes in technology could perpetuate present inequalities nationally. It is possible that it will do the same on a global level.

- Social change has often had a negative impact on the natural environment. Today we face problems such as acid rain, global warming, and the greenhouse effect. Environmental problems are worldwide, brought about by industrial production and urbanization, the pressures of population growth, and inadequate environmental regulation. The world today is facing a basic conflict between the lust for profits through the exploitation of the world's resources and the need to produce a sustainable environment.

- A worldwide environmental movement has emerged, which seeks solutions in education, legislation, and political activism. Green parties are political parties which have emerged that focus on environmental concerns.

- Environmental sociology is the study of the relationship between human societies and the environment. It's goal is not to stop pollution or nuclear power, but rather to study the affects of humans on the physical environment and its affects on humans.

- If we are to survive, we must seek harmony between technology and the environment. It is essential that we reduce or eliminate the harm that technology does to the environment.

LEARNING OBJECTIVES
After reading Chapter 22, you should be able:

1. Describe the social transformation of society in terms of the four major social revolutions; the shift from *Gemeinschaft* to *Gesellschaft* societies; and the development of capitalism, industrialization and modernization. (652-653)
2. Discuss conflict, power, and global politics among nations, including discussion of the G-8. (654-655)
3. Identify and evaluate the different theories of social change, including cultural evolution, natural cycles, conflict theory, and William Ogburn's processes of invention, discovery, and diffusion. (656-659)
4. Define cultural lag and provide examples of it along with an evaluation of Ogburn's theory (658-659)
5. Explore the different ways that technological innovations are able to change society. (660-661)
6. Discuss the far reaching impact of the automobile on cities, farm life and villages, architecture, courtship and sexual norms, and women's roles. (661-663)
7. Discuss the far reaching impact that the computer has had on education, the workplace, business and finance, and national and global stratification. (664-666)
8. Describe how the globalization of capitalism contributes to environmental decay. (667-670)
9. Identify and compare the environmental problems of the Most Industrialized Nations, the Industrializing Nations, and the Least Industrialized Nations. (670-671)
10. Discuss the goals and activities of the environmental movement. (671)
11. Identify the main assumptions of environmental sociology. (672-673)
12. Suggest ways to achieve harmony between technology and the environment. (674)

CHAPTER OUTLINE

I. How Social Change Transforms Society

    A. Social change is a shift in the characteristics of culture and societies over time.

    B. There have been four social revolutions: the domestication of plants and animals, from which pastoral and horticultural societies arose; the invention of the plow, leading to agricultural societies; the industrial revolution, which produced industrial societies; and now the information revolution, resulting in postindustrial societies. Another type of society is emerging based on biotechnology.

    C. The shift from agricultural to industrial economic activity was accompanied by a change from *Gemeinschaft* (daily life centers on intimate and personal relationships) to *Gesellschaft* (people have fleeting, impersonal relationships) societies.

    D. Different sociologists have focused on different forces in order to explain the changes that took place in society at the time of the Industrial Revolution.

        1. Karl Marx identified capitalism as the basic reason behind the breakup of feudal (agricultural) societies. He focused his analysis on the means of production (factories, machinery, and tools): those who owned them dictated the conditions under which workers would work and live. This development set in motion antagonistic relationships between capitalists and workers that remain today.

2. Max Weber saw religion as the core reason for the development of capitalism: as a result of the Reformation, Protestants no longer felt assured that they were saved by virtue of church membership and concluded that God would show visible favor to the elect. This belief encouraged Protestants to work hard and be thrifty. An economic surplus resulted, stimulating industrialization.

3. Modernization (the change from agricultural to industrial societies) refers to the sweeping changes in societies brought about by the Industrial Revolution.

4. When technology changes, societies change. An example today would be how technology from the industrialized world is transforming traditional societies.

E. Social movements highlight the cutting edges of change in a society. Large numbers of people organize to demand, or resist, changes. With globalization, these issues increasingly cut across international boundaries.

F. A world system began to emerge in the sixteenth century; in the eighteenth and nineteenth centuries, capitalism and industrialization extended the economic and political ties among the world's nations.

1. Dependency theory asserts that because those nations that were not industrialized became dependent on those that had industrialized, they were unable to develop their own resources.

2. Today's information revolution, including the new bioeconomics, will have far-reaching consequences for global stratification. Those who make the fastest advances in these areas are destined to dominate in the coming generations.

3. The world's industrial giants (the United States, Canada, Great Britain, France, Germany, Italy, and Japan—the G-7) have decided how they will share the world's markets; by regulating global economic and industrial policy, they guarantee their own dominance, including continued access to cheap raw materials from the less industrialized nations.

4. Russia joined the G-7 and they are now known as the G-8.

5. The recent resurgence of ethnic conflicts threatens the global map drawn by the G-8.

6. If China follows the rules set forth by G-8, they may be incorporated into this exclusive group, which will then become the G-9.

II. Theories and Processes of Social Change

A. Theories that focus on cultural evolution are either unilinear or multilinear.

1. Unilinear theories assume that all societies follow the same path, evolving from simple to complex through uniform sequences; however, these theories have been discredited, and seeing one's own society as the top of the evolutionary ladder is now considered unacceptably ethnocentric.

2. Multilinear theories assume that different routes can lead to a similar stage of development; thus societies need not pass through the same sequence of stages to become industrialized.

3. Both unilinear and multilinear theories assume the idea that societies progress toward a higher state. However, because of the crises in Western culture today, this assumption has been cast aside and evolutionary theories have been rejected.

B. Theories of natural cycles examine great civilizations, not a particular society; they presume that societies are like organisms: they are born, reach adolescence, grow old, and die.

1. Toynbee proposed that civilization is initially able to meet challenges, yet when it becomes an empire, the ruling elite loses its capacity to keep the masses in line "by charm rather than by force," and the fabric of society is then ripped apart.

2. Oswald Spengler proposed that Western civilization was on the wane; some analysts think the crisis in Western civilization may indicate he was right.

C. Marx's conflict theory viewed social change as a dialectical process in which the following occurs:

1. A thesis (a current arrangement of power) contains its own antithesis (a contradiction or opposition), and the resulting struggle between the thesis and its antithesis leads to a synthesis (a new arrangement of power).

2. The history of a society is therefore a series of confrontations in which each ruling group creates the seeds of its own destruction (e.g., capitalism sets workers and capitalists on a collision course).

D. William Ogburn identified three processes of social change.

1. *Inventions* can be either material (computers) or social (capitalism); *discovery* is a new way of seeing things; and *diffusion* is the spread of an invention, discovery, or idea, from one area to another.

2. Ogburn coined the term "cultural lag" to describe the situation in which some elements of a culture adapt to an invention or discovery more rapidly than others. We are constantly trying to catch up with technology by adapting our customs and ways of life to meet its needs.

3. Ogburn has been criticized because of his view that technology controls almost all social change. People also take control over technology, developing the technology they need and selectively using existing technology. Both can happen; technology leads to social change, and social change leads to technology. In general, Ogburn stressed that the usual direction of change is for material culture (technology) to change first and the symbolic culture (people's ideas and ways of life) to follow.

III. How Technology Changes Society

A. Technology refers to both the tools used to accomplish tasks and to the skills or procedures to make and use those tools.

1. Technology is an artificial means of extending human abilities.

2. Although all human groups use technology, it is the chief characteristic of postindustrial societies because it greatly extends our abilities to analyze information, communicate, and travel.

3. While all human groups make and use technology, it is the chief characteristic of postindustrial societies. The new technologies of information, communication, and travel create new possibilities.

B. New technologies can reshape an entire society. Four ways in which technology can shape an entire society are:

1. Changes in social organization (e.g., introduction of factories changed the nature of work: people gathered in one place to do their work, were given specialized tasks, and became responsible for only part of an item, not the entire item).
2. Changes in ideology (e.g., the new technology that led to the factory stimulated new ideologies such as maximizing profits).
3. Changes in ostentatious consumption (e.g., if technology is limited to clubbing animals, then animal skins are valued; with technological change, Americans make sure that their trendy clothing labels are displayed. The emphasis on materialism depends on the state of technology).
4. Changes in social relationships (e.g., as men went to work in the factories, family relationships changed; as more women work outside the home, family relationships again are changing. However, new technology is now allowing many to work at home and this may strengthen families).

C. The automobile was one of the greatest inventions that shaped U.S. society.
1. The Model T was mass produced in 1908. As cars decreased in price, Americans found this more convenient than public transportation.
2. Farmers were able to travel in town where they found more variety of goods and had better access to medical care and education.
3. Commercial and home architecture changed as people needed a place to park their automobiles.
4. By the 1920s, the automobile was used extensively for dating and children were no longer under the watchful eye of their parents.
5. Women were able to drive as well as men and this removed them from the confines of the home. It allowed them to participate in areas of social life not connected to the home.

D. The computer is an example of how technology shapes our lives. Some people have reservations about our computerized society, fearing that government will be able to exert complete control over us.
1. Within the field of education, computers are transforming the way children from kindergarten through college learn. There is concern today about a digital divide in education, with wealthier school districts able to provide the latest technology to their students, while poor school districts are left behind.
2. Computers are altering the way we work, the types of social relationships we establish with co-workers, and even the location of work.
3. In the world of business and finance, computers have made national borders meaningless, as vast amounts of money are instantly transferred from one country to another.
4. The way wars are fought has also changed because of computers.

E. Computers shrink the world in terms of both time and space. With the information superhighway, homes and businesses are connected by a rapid flow of information.
1. Several million workers now work out of their home. This could be the beginning of a historical shift in which families are brought closer together.
2. The negative side of the technology is the increased surveillance of workers and depersonalization that occurs.
3. National borders have become meaningless as information can be transferred from one country to another.

4. On a national level, we may end up with information have-nots among inner-city and rural residents, thus perpetuating existing inequalities.
5. On a global level, the highly industrialized nations will control the information superhighway, thereby keeping the least industrialized nations in a perpetual pauper status.

IV. The Growth Machine versus the Earth
A. The globalization of capitalism underlies today's environmental decay.
   1. The Most Industrialized Nations continue to push for economic growth, the Industrialized Nations strive to achieve faster economic growth, and the Least Industrialized Nations, anxious to enter the race, push for even faster growth.
   2. If our goal is a sustainable environment, we must stop trashing the earth.
B. Industrialization led to a major assault on the environment. While it has been viewed as good for the nation's welfare, it has also contributed to today's environmental problems.
   1. The major polluters of the earth are the Most Industrialized Nations.
   2. Many of our problems today, including depletion of the ozone layer, acid rain, the greenhouse effect, and global warming, are associated with our dependence on fossil fuels.
   3. There is an abundant source of natural energy that would provide low-cost power and therefore help raise the living standards of humans across the globe. Better technology is needed to harness this energy supply. From a conflict perspective, such abundant sources of energy present a threat to the multinationals' energy monopoly. We cannot expect the practical development and widespread use of alternative sources of power until the multinationals have cornered the market on the technology that will harness them.
   4. Racial minorities and the poor are disproportionately exposed to air pollution, hazardous waste, pesticides, and the like. To deal with this issue, environmental justice groups have formed that fight to close polluting plants and block construction of polluting industries.
C. Environmental degradation is also a problem in the Industrializing and the Least Industrialized Nations, as these countries rushed into global industrial competition without the funds to purchase expensive pollution controls and few antipollution laws.
   1. Pollution was treated as a state secret in the former Soviet Union. With protest stifled, no environmental protection laws to inhibit pollution, and production quotas to be met, environmental pollution was rampant. Almost one-half of Russia's arable land is unsuitable for farming, air pollution in cities is ten times higher than that which is permitted in the United States, and half the tap water is unfit to drink. Pollution may be partially responsible for the drop in life expectancy.
   2. The combined pressures of population growth and almost nonexistent environmental regulations destined Least Industrialized Nations to become the earth's major source of pollution. Some companies in the Most Industrialized Nations use the Least Industrialized Nations as a garbage dump for hazardous wastes and for producing chemicals no longer tolerated in their own countries.

3. As tropical rain forests are cleared for lumber, farms, and pastures, the consequence may be the extinction of numerous plant and animal species. As the rain forests are destroyed, thousands of animal and plant species are extinguished.

D. Concern about the world's severe environmental problems has produced a worldwide social movement. Political parties, such as the green parties, are formed; their main concern is the environment. Activists in the environmental movement seek solutions in education, legislation, and political activism.

E. Environmental sociology examines the relationship between human societies and the environment. Its basic assumptions include (1) the physical environment is a significant variable in sociological investigation; (2) humans are but one species among many that are dependent on the environment; (3) because of intricate connections to nature, human actions have many unintended consequences; (4) the world is finite, so there are potential physical limits to economic growth; (5) economic expansion requires increased extraction of resources from the environment; (6) increased extraction of resources leads to ecological problems; (7) these ecological problems place restrictions on economic expansion; and (8) the state creates environmental problems by trying to create conditions for the profitable accumulation of capital. The goal is not to stop environmental problems but rather to study how humans affect the physical environment and how the physical environment affects human activities.

F. If we are to have a world that is worth passing on to the coming generations, we must seek harmony between technology and the natural environment. As a parallel to development of technologies, we must develop systems to reduce technology's harm to the environment, and mechanisms to enforce rules for the production, use, and disposal of technology.

KEY TERMS

After studying the chapter, review the definition of each of the following terms.

acid rain: rain containing sulfuric and nitric acid (burning fossil fuels releases sulfur dioxide and nitrogen oxide which become sulfuric and nitric acids when they react with moisture in the air) (668)

alienation: Marx's term for workers' lack of connection to the product of their labor; caused by their being assigned repetitive tasks on a small part of a product—this leads to a sense of powerlessness and normlessness; others use the term in the general sense of not feeling a part of something (660)

corporate welfare: the gifts or financial incentives (tax breaks, subsidies, and even land and stadiums) given to corporations in order to attract them to an area or induce them to remain (669)

cultural lag: Ogburn's term for human behavior lagging behind technological innovation (658)

dialectical process: (of history) each arrangement, or thesis, contains contradictions, or antitheses, which must be resolved; the new arrangement, or synthesis, contains its own contradictions, and so on (657)

diffusion: the spread of invention or discovery from one area to another; identified by William Ogburn as one of three processes of social change (658)

discovery: a new way of seeing reality; identified by William Ogburn as one of three processes of social change (658)

ecosabotage: actions taken to sabotage the efforts of people thought to be legally harming the environment (671)

environmental injustice: refers to the pollution of our environment affecting minorities and the poor the most (670)

environmental sociology: a specialty within sociology where the focus is the relationship between human societies and the environment (672)

global warming: an increase in the earth's temperature due to the greenhouse effect (669)

greenhouse effect: the buildup of carbon dioxide in the earth's atmosphere that allows light to enter but inhibits the release of heat; believed to cause global warming (668)

invention: the combination of existing elements and materials to form new ones; identified by William Ogburn as the first of three processes of social change (658)

modernization: the transformation of traditional societies into industrial societies (653)

postmodern society: another term for postindustrial society; its chief characteristic is the use of tools that extend the human abilities to gather and analyze information, to communicate, and to travel (660)

social change: the alteration of culture and societies over time (652)

sustainable environment: a world system that takes into account the limits of the environment, produces enough material goods for everyone's needs, and leaves a heritage of a sound environment for the next generation (668)

KEY PEOPLE

Review the major theoretical contributions or findings of these people.

James Flink: A historian who noted that the automobile changed women "from producers of food and clothing onto consumer of prepared foods and ready-made clothes." (661)

Karl Marx: He noted that capitalism set in motion an antagonistic relationship between capitalists and workers that remain today. Marx developed the theory of dialectical materialism. (657)

Lewis Henry Morgan: Morgan's theory of social development once dominated Western thought. He suggested that societies pass through three stages: savagery, barbarism, and civilization. (656)

William Ogburn: Ogburn identified three processes of social change: invention, discovery, and diffusion. He also coined the term "cultural lag" to describe a situation in which some elements of culture adapt to an invention or discovery more rapidly than others. (657-659)

Oswald Spengler: Spengler wrote *The Decline of the West* in which he proposed that Western civilization was declining. (656-657)

Arnold Toynbee: This historian suggested that each time a civilization successfully meets a challenge, oppositional forces are set up. Eventually, the oppositional forces are set loose and the fabric of society is ripped apart. (657)

Max Weber: Weber argued that capitalism grew out of the Protestant Reformation. (653)

STUDENT APPLICATION PROJECTS

This is your opportunity to apply the sociological perspective to the world around you. The projects in this section refer to material introduced in this chapter of your text. These projects help you apply the sociological perspective "down to your earth...down to your daily life."

1. In the last one hundred years, what technological invention do you think has had the greatest impact on the world? Why? In what ways did society change due to this technological invention? What technological invention has had the greatest impact on your everyday life? Explain? In what ways did you change due to this technology? Overall, how much of social change is due to technological change?

2. What are your views about technology's impact on our own and other societies? Do you think that technology helps or harms us? Do the Unabomber and the Luddites before him have a legitimate argument? Do you think that it is possible to control the impact of technology without having to go to such extreme measures? Why or why not?

3. What environmental problems most concern you? List them. In what ways do you actively strive to reduce these problems in your community? Explain. Do you think there can be harmony between technology and the environment? Explain.

4. What are your thoughts about the Defense Department's plan to "weaponize" space. Are you concerned about the use of technology to increase weaponry, and to spy on and fight enemies? How do you think that other nations will respond to this?

SELF-TEST

MULTIPLE CHOICE QUESTIONS

1. The alteration of culture and society over time is: (652)
    a. social transformation.
    b. social metamorphosis.
    c. social alternation.
    d. social change.

2. What does the author of your text identify as the fourth social revolution? (652)
    a. the invention of the steam engine
    b. the transformation from *Gemeinschaft* to *Gesellschaft*
    c. the invention of the microchip
    d. the development of capitalism

3. Weber identified _____ as the core reason for the development of capitalism. (653)
    a. religion
    b. industrialization
    c. politics
    d. none of the above

4. Which of the following statements about the second stage of the demographic transition is *incorrect*? (653)
    a. the population decreased
    b. it upset the balance of family and property
    c. it brought mass migration
    d. it brought hunger

5. What country is the newest member of the G-8? (654)
    a. Russia
    b. China
    c. Egypt
    d. Mexico

6. What country does the author note is a threat to the G-8? (655)
    a. Russia
    b. China
    c. Egypt
    d. Mexico

7. _____ theories assume that all societies follow the same path, evolving from simple to complex through uniform sequences. (656)
   a. cyclical
   b. uniformity
   c. unilinear evolution
   d. multilinear evolution

8. Today, evolutionary theories have been: (656)
   a. accepted because history has largely proven this perspective to be correct.
   b. rejected because the assumption of progress has been cast aside.
   c. neither rejected or accepted because these theories take into account the rich diversity of traditional cultures.
   d. none of the above.

9. Which of the following attempts to account for the rise of entire civilizations, not a particular society? (656)
   a. multilinear evolutionary theory
   b. cyclical theory
   c. conflict theory
   d. epoch theory

10. According to Karl Marx, each _____ sows the seeds of its own destruction. (657)
    a. thesis
    b. ruling class
    c. epoch
    d. exploited class

11. Capitalism, bureaucracy, and the corporation are all examples of: (657)
    a. social invention.
    b. cultural diffusion.
    c. evolution.
    d. conflict over power.

12. Ogburn called the process of change that involves new ways of seeing reality as: (658)
    a. invention.
    b. discovery.
    c. diffusion.
    d. exploration.

13. The situation in which some elements of a culture adapt to an invention or discovery more rapidly than others is: (658)
    a. cultural downtime.
    b. cultural lag.
    c. cultural delay.
    d. cultural drag.

14. Ogburn's analysis has been criticized because: (658)
    a. it is too narrow in focus, not suitable for explaining the transformation of industrial into postindustrial societies.
    b. it does not recognize the importance of technology for social change.
    c. it places too great an emphasis on technology as the source for almost all social change.
    d. it predicts that material culture will change in response to symbolic culture, when in fact it is symbolic culture that changes in response to material culture.

15. Technology refers to: (660)
    a. items that people use to accomplish a wide range of tasks.
    b. skills and procedures that are employed in the development and utilization of tools.
    c. tools ranging from combs or hairbrushes to computers and the Internet.
    d. all of the above.

16. According to Karl Marx, the changeover to the factory system produced: (660)
    a. rationality.
    b. alienation.
    c. efficiency.
    d. worker satisfaction.

17. The fact that as men were drawn out of their homes to work in factories, family relationships changed is an example of: (661)
    a. changes in social organizations produced by technology.
    b. changes in social relationships produced by technology.
    c. changes in ideologies produced by technology.
    d. none of the above.

18. Which of the following is *not* one of the ways that computers are transforming education? (665)
    a. they are making new areas of study available to students on-line.
    b. they are changing the way that students learn.
    c. they are increasing the opportunities for teachers and administrators to carry out surveillance on students.
    d. they are expanding the gap in educational opportunities between wealthy school districts and poor school districts.

19. Which of the following is *not* one of the ways computers transform the workplace? (665)
    a. changing the way in which we do work
    b. altering social relationships
    c. increasing social interactions
    d. reversing the location of where work is done

20. Which of the following will become a part of mainstream education? (666)
    a. telecommunication
    b. distance education
    c. teletransportation
    d. all of the above

21. One concern about the expansion of the information superhighway is: (666)
    a. interest in accessing it will outstrip capacity to carry so many users.
    b. social inequalities will become greater, both on a national and global basis.
    c. people will tie up the services with nonessential activities.
    d. people will become even more alienated as they relate more and more through their computers and less and less face to face.

22. Which of the following is true about Star Wars? (667)
    a. The Pentagon is building its own Internet.
    b. Robots are being used in Iraq.
    c. The Defense Department is planning to "weaponize space."
    d. All of the above.

23. According to the author of the text, which region of the world is considered the major polluter? (668)
    a. the most industrialized nations
    b. the industrializing nations
    c. the least industrialized nations
    d. the most and least industrialized nations

24. The consequence of burning fossil fuels is: (668)
    a. acid rain.
    b. the greenhouse effect.
    c. global warming.
    d. all of the above.

25. How do conflict theorists explain the energy shortage? (670)
    a. They note that the earth has a limited supply of energy, and that multinational corporations are rapidly depleting it.
    b. There is no reliable alternative to the internal combustion engine.
    c. They argue that multinational corporations are unwilling to develop alternative energy sources because it would threaten their monopoly over existing fossil fuels and cut into their profits.
    d. As a result of the past exploitation of natural resources by profit-hungry multinational corporations, there are no longer alternative energy resources that are reliable.

26. Which groups in U.S. society are disproportionately exposed to environmental hazards? (670)
    a. office workers and factory workers
    b. racial minorities and the poor
    c. farm workers and lumberjacks
    d. racial and ethnic groups

27. The major source of pollution in the future is likely to be: (671)
    a. the Least Industrialized Nations.
    b. the Industrializing Nations.
    c. the Most Industrialized Nations.
    d. none of the above.

28. Which of the following presents the greatest threat to the survival of numerous plant and animal species? (671)
    a. the continued burning of fossil fuels
    b. the dumping of toxic waste in the least industrialized nations
    c. the disappearance of the world's rain forests
    d. the greenhouse effect

29. Environmental sociology: (672)
    a. examines how the physical environment affects human activities.
    b. examines how human activities affect the physical environment.
    c. has eight main assumptions.
    d. all of the above.

30. What is the goal of environmental sociologists? (674)
    a. to stop pollution
    b. to do research on the mutual impact that individuals and environments have on one another
    c. to empower those who are disadvantaged by environmental threats so that the quality of their lives will be improved
    d. to lobby for alternatives to fossil fuels

TRUE-FALSE QUESTIONS

1. _____The rapid social change that the world is currently experiencing is a random event. (652)
2. _____Our lives today are being vitally affected by a third social revolution. (652)
3. _____Modernization is the change from agricultural to industrial societies. (653)
4. _____Capitalism and industrialization have brought the least industrialized nations to the second stage of the demographic transition. (653)
5. _____Russia is the newest member of the G-8. (654)
6. _____The assumption of evolutionary theories that all societies progress from a primitive state to a highly complex state has been proven. (656)

7. _____Cyclical theories assume that civilizations are like organisms. (656)
8. _____Some cyclical theories predict the decline of Western civilization. (656)
9. _____Invention, discovery, and diffusion are Ogburn's three processes of social change. (658)
10. _____Technology usually changes first, followed by culture. (658)
11. _____Technology is not a very powerful force for social change. (658)
12. _____Marx believed that the change to the factory system was a source of alienation. (660)
13. _____The automobile confined women to the home since only men drove. (663)
14. _____The use of computers in education will significantly reduce existing social inequalities between school districts. (665)
15. _____Computers create the possibility for increased surveillance of workers and depersonalization. (665)
16. _____Today's information revolution will perpetuate global stratification. (666)
17. _____A sustainable environment is one that takes into account the limits of the environment. (668)
18. _____The burning of fossil fuels releases sulfur dioxide and nitrogen oxide, which react with moisture in the air to become sulfuric and nitric acids, commonly known as acid rain. (668)
19. _____Green parties were formed in response to concerns about the environment. (669)
20. _____Environmental sociology examines the relationship between human societies and the environment. (666)
21.

FILL-IN-THE-BLANK QUESTIONS

1. The sweeping changes ushered in by industrialization are called _____. (652)
2. _____ societies are small, rural, and slow changing. (652)
3. According to Marx's view, each ruling group sows the seeds of its own _____. (657)
4. _____ coined the phrase cultural lag. (658)
5. All human groups make and use _____. (660)
6. _____ noted that technology also spurs ideology. (660)
7. Underlying today's environmental decay is the globalization of _____. (667)
8. The major polluters of the earth are the _____. (668)
9. Scientists are increasingly convinced that we face _____ warming. (669)
10. Conflict and unequal power have led to _____ with minorities and the poor being the ones who suffer the most from the effects of pollution. (670)
11. _____ welfare refers to handouts given to corporations. (670)
12. One result of the environmental movement has been the formation of _____ parties. (671)
13. As the rain forests disappear, so do the _____ tribes who live in them. (671)
14. _____ actions are taken to sabotage the efforts of people who are thought to be legally harming the environment. (671)
15. The goal of _____ sociology is to study how humans affect the physical environment and how the physical environment affects human activities. (672)

MATCH THESE SOCIOLOGICAL CONCEPTS WITH THEIR DEFINITIONS

	1. greenhouse effect	a.	*workers' lack of connection to the product of their labor*
	2. diffusion	b.	*human behavior lagging behind technological innovation*
	3. discovery	c.	*another term for post-industrial*
	4. invention	d.	*believed to cause global warming*
	5. global warming	e.	*spread of invention or discovery from one place to another*
	6. sustainable environment	f.	*process of change from traditional to contemporary society*
	7. alienation	g.	*a new way of seeing reality*
	8. cultural lag	h.	*combining existing elements to form new ones*
	9. modernization	i.	*increase in the earth's temperature*
	10. postmodern	j.	*takes the limits of the environment into account*

ESSAY QUESTIONS

1. The author of your text suggests that social movements reveal the cutting edge of change in a society or across the globe. In Chapter 21, you learned about different social movements and in this chapter there is discussion of the environmental movement. Discuss a specific social movement in terms of what it reveals about social change.

2. Discuss Ogburn's three processes of social change, provide examples to illustrate each, and evaluate the theory.

3. Choose a particular technology, such as the computer or another technology, and discuss the impact that it has had on U.S. society.

4. Discuss the role of the automobile in changing cities, architecture, courtship, and women's roles.

5. Consider whether it is possible for us to achieve a sustainable environment.

CHAPTER-BY-CHAPTER ANSWER KEY

CHAPTER 1

ANSWERS FOR THE MULTIPLE CHOICE QUESTIONS

1. **b** The sociological perspective is an approach to understanding human behavior by placing it within its broader social context.

2. **d** Sociologists consider occupation, income, education, gender, age, and race as dimensions of social location.

3. **d** All three statements reflect ways in which the social sciences are like the natural sciences. Both attempt to study and understand their subjects objectively; both attempt to undercover the relationships that create order in their respective worlds through controlled observation; and both are divided into many specialized fields.

4. **c** Generalization is one of the goals of scientific inquiry. It involves going beyond individual cases by making statements that apply to broader groups or situations.

5. **b** The Industrial Revolution, imperialism, and the development of the scientific method all contributed to the development of sociology. The fourth influence was the political revolutions in America and France — there was no political revolution in Britain at that time.

6. **d** Positivism is the application of the scientific approach to the social world.

7. **d** Of the four statements, the one that *best* reflects Herbert Spencer's views on charity is "The poor are the weakest members of society and if society intervenes to help them, it is interrupting the natural process of social evolution." While many contemporaries of Spencer's were appalled by his views, the wealthy industrialists found them attractive.

8. **b** The proletariat is the large group of workers who are exploited by the small group of capitalists who own the means of production, according to Karl Marx.

9. **a** Durkheim believed that social factors, patterns of behavior that characterize a social group, explain many types of behavior, including suicide rates.

10. **b** In his research on suicide rates, Durkheim found that individuals' integration into their social groups influences the overall patterns of suicide between groups. He called this concept *social integration.*

11. **c** Emile Durkheim's mail goal was to get sociology recognized as its own academic discipline.

12. **c** Max Weber's research on the rise of capitalism identified religious beliefs as the key.

13. **a** Weber wanted objectivity to be the hallmark of social research.

14. **c** Social facts and *Verstehen* go hand-in-hand. Social facts are patterns of behavior that characterize a social group. By applying *Verstehen*, your understanding of what it means to be human and to face various situations in life, you gain an understanding of people's behavior.

15. **b** The statement that, "Unlike the situation in Europe, many North American women found that there were few barriers and they were able to train in sociology and receive faculty appointments," is *incorrect.* In the early years of sociology, the situation of women in North America was similar to that of European women — they were largely excluded and their work ignored. As a result, many turned to social activism, especially working with the poor and immigrant groups. Many male sociologists who worked as professors denied female sociologists the title of sociologist, preferring to call them social workers.

16. **d** Jane Adams won the Nobel Prize for working on behalf of poor immigrants

17. **c** W. E. B. Du Bois was an African-American sociologist who wrote extensively on race relations. In both his personal and professional life, he experienced prejudice and discrimination. His commitment to racial equality led him to establish the NAACP.

18. **c** Sociologists who conduct research for government commissions or agencies investigating social problems are practicing applied sociology.

19. **b** Using objective, systematic observations is not an accurate description of theory.

20. **b** Symbolic interactionism is the theoretical perspective that views society as composed of symbols that people use to establish meaning, develop their views of the world, and communicate with one another.

21. **d** According to Robert Merton, an unintended consequence that can hurt a system's equilibrium is a latent dysfunction.

22. **d** Industrialization and urbanization have undermined the traditional purposes of the family, according to theorists using functional analysis.

23. **a** Karl Marx first asserted that conflict is inherent in all relations that have authority.

24. **b** Lewis Coser pointed out that conflict is more likely among people in close relationships.

25. **b** Conflict theorists might explain the high rate of divorce by looking at societies basic inequalities between males and females.

26. **a** Functionalists and conflict theorists focus on the macro level of sociological analysis.

27. **d** Since each theoretical perspective provides a different, often sharply contrasting picture of our world, no theory or level of analysis encompasses all of reality. By putting the contributions of each perspective and level of analysis together, we gain a more comprehensive picture of social life.

28. **c** The first phase of sociology in the United States stretched from the founding of the first departments of sociology in the last decade of the nineteenth century into the 1940s. This phase was characterized by an interest in using sociological knowledge to improve social life and change society.

29. **c** She studied job discrimination and found that having a prison record and race were significant factors in being offered a job.

30. **d** The author of your text suggests that *globalization*, the breaking down of national boundaries because of communication, trade and travel, is very likely going to transform sociology in the United States. As global issues intrude more into U.S. society, sociologists will have to broaden the scope and focus of their research.

ANSWERS FOR TRUE-FALSE QUESTIONS

1. *True.*
2. *True.*
3. *True.*
4. *True.*
5. *False.* Sociologists focus on external influences (people's experiences) instead of internal mechanisms, such as instincts.
6. *False.* Positivism refers to the application of the scientific method to study sociological phenomenon.
7. *True.*
8. *True.*
9. *True.*
10. *True.*
11. *False.* Weber agreed with much of what Marx wrote, but he strongly disagreed that economics is the central force in social change. Weber saw religion as playing that role.
12. *True.*
13. *True.*
14. *False.* Harriet Martineau's ground-breaking work on social life in Great Britain and the United States was largely ignored; she is remembered for her translations of Auguste Comte's work.
15. *True.*
16. *True.*
17. *False.* Although functionalists do believe the family has lost many of its traditional purposes, they do not believe they have all been lost. Some of the existing functions are presently under assault or are being eroded.

18. *False*. Some conflict theorists use this theory in much broader sense.
19. *False* Symbolic interactionism uses micro-level not macro-level analysis. Conflict uses macro-level.
20. *True.*

ANSWERS TO THE FILL-IN-THE-BLANK QUESTIONS
1. sociological perspective
2. social location
3. generalized
4. scientific method
5. problems
6. replication
7. functionalism
8. manifest
9. conflict
10. equal
11. marriage
12. macro
13. face to face interaction
14. analysis
15. Globalization

ANSWERS TO MATCH THESE SOCIAL SCIENTISTS WITH THEIR CONTRIBUTIONS
1. a Auguste Comte: *known as the father of sociology*
2. h Herbert Spencer: *developed concept of Social Darwinism, stated that societies evolve from lower to higher forms*
3. d Karl Marx: *argued that the engine of human history is class conflict between the "halves" and "have nots"*
4. i C. Wright Mills: *urged sociologists to go back to social reform*
5. c Emile Durkheim:*this person studied suicide and social isolation*
6. b Harriet Martineau: *wrote "Society in America" addressing American social life*
7. j Charles Horton Cooley: *founder of symbolic interactionism*
8. g W. E. B. Du Bois: *one of the founders of the NAACP*
9. e Max Weber: *argued that religion was the key force of social change and the rise of Capitalism*
10. f Jane Addams: *awarded the Nobel Prize for work establishing the Hull House*

GUIDELINES FOR ANSWERING THE ESSAY QUESTIONS
1. *Explain what the sociological perspective encompasses and then, using that perspective, discuss the forces that shaped the discipline of sociology.*

There are two parts to this question. First, you are asked to define the sociological perspective. As you define this, you would want to mention the idea of social location, perhaps by bringing into your essay C. Wright Mills' observations on the connection between biography and history. Another way to explain the perspective would be to contrast sociology with other disciplines, talking about what sociology is and what it isn't.

The second part of the essay involves discussing the forces that shaped sociology and its early followers. What you are being asked is to think about what was going on in the social world in the early nineteenth century that might have led to the birth of this new discipline. Referring back to the book, you would want to identify three: (1) the Industrial Revolution; (2) the political revolutions of America and France; (3) imperialism; and (4) the emergence of the scientific method. You would conclude by discussing how each of the early sociologists — Auguste Comte, Herbert Spencer, Karl Marx, Emile

Durkheim, and Max Weber — were influenced by these broader forces in making a contribution to sociology. You could also bring into the discussion some of the material on sexism in early sociology, noting how the ideas about the appropriate role for women in society functioned to exclude women like Harriet Martineau and Jane Addams from the discipline, or you could talk about the emergence of sociology in North America.

2. *Emile Durkheim studied European society at a time when it was undergoing major social upheaval as a result of the industrial revolution. In this first chapter, you are introduced to some of his major contributions — his work on suicide and his conclusions about social integration and anomie. Summarize what his contributions were and then consider how they are still useful for understanding social life today.*

You could begin by talking briefly about the research on suicide and how Durkheim analyzed how suicide rates varied for different types of social groups. You should also stress that Durkheim was trying to look beyond individual characteristics to locating social factors that underlie suicide; this was critically important to him as he tried to establish sociology as a separate academic discipline. In explaining this pattern, he identified *social integration*, or the degree to which individuals are tied to their social group, as a key social factor in explaining suicide. At that time, the connections between individuals and many traditional social groups were weakening, because of the growing individualism and impersonality of the emerging industrial society. Durkheim called for the creation of new social groups to stand between the state and the individual.

You then need to make the case as to why these concepts of social integration and anomie are still relevant. You should point out that the social conditions that Durkheim described still exist. If anything, the trends that he first identified have intensified. As examples, you could talk about how Durkheim's concepts could be applied to patterns of suicide among teenagers or the outbreaks of school violence in large, impersonal high schools.

3. *The textbook notes that Verstehen and social facts go hand in hand; explain how this is so. Assume that you have been asked to carry out research to find out more about why growing numbers of women and children are homeless and what particular problems they face. Discuss how you could use both Verstehen and social facts in your study.*

First, you would want to define what *Verstehen* and social facts are and how they are compatible in terms of arriving at a complete picture of a social pattern. Then you can argue that social facts would be most appropriate in trying to explain why growing numbers of women and children are homeless — you might look at the changing economic status of women in society, the increase in the number of female-headed households, and the decline in the amount of affordable housing. On the other hand, by applying *Verstehen*, you would be able to discover what particular problems they face, through face-to-face interviews at shelter sites you would be able to experience firsthand some of what they are experiencing.

4. *Explain why there has been a continuing tension between analyzing society and working toward reforming society since the very beginning of society.*

Referring to the work of such early sociologists as Auguste Comte and Emile Durkheim, you could begin by noting that sociology has had twin goals — the scientific study of society and the application of scientific knowledge to social reform — from its inception . When sociology was transplanted to the United States at the end of the nineteenth century, this society was undergoing significant changes, with industrialization, urbanization, and immigration among them. The earliest North American sociologists, like their European predecessors, defined the sociologist's role as both social scientist and social reformer. At the same time, the record suggests that the primary emphasis has generally been on the sociologist's work as social scientist. For example, women who had been trained as sociologists but then excluded from the universities, turned to social reform and were denied the title of sociologist; instead, they were called social workers by male sociologists working from within academic departments of universities.

At this point you could draw on material in the text about the development of North American sociology, as well as the discussion of the different phases it has passed through. From the 1920s through the early post–World War II era, the emphasis was on sociological research rather than social reform, as departments of sociology become more widely established (31-32). Sociologists like Talcott Parsons, whose work was primarily theoretical in nature, came to dominate the field. While the early part of this period was one of significant turmoil (with the Great Depression and World War II), at the end of this phase, social problems were largely "invisible," given the general prosperity of the immediate post–World War II era.

You could point out that people like C. Wright Mills kept the tradition of social reform alive during these years. And with the social upheavals of the 1950s and 1960s — the civil rights movement, the women's movement, and the anti-war movement but to name a few — the focus once again shifted back to social reform.

You could conclude by talking about applied sociology, a recent development that attempts to blend these two traditions. While it has gained legitimacy within the discipline, there are still those on both sides of this debate who reject applied sociology. For those whose emphasis is on pure sociology, it smacks of social reform, while for those who believe sociology should be working to reform society, it doesn't go far enough. The debate over the appropriate focus of sociological inquiry is unlikely to be resolved any time soon, because it reflects traditions that go back to the very origins of the discipline. Both sides can find ample support for their positions within the work and writings of earlier sociologists.

5. Explain what Weber meant when he said that sociology should be value free. Do you think this is possible? How do values play a role in determining the purpose and use of sociology?

When Weber said that sociology should be value free, he meant that a sociologist's values-beliefs about what is good or worthwhile in life and the way the world ought to be- should not affect his or her research. You could discuss that this is an ideal given that sociologists are also people and they are influenced by the values of the time in history in which they live. Values play a role in determining the research that will be conducted because values may drive interests that sociologists have to pursue one line of research of another.

CHAPTER 2

ANSWERS FOR MULTIPLE CHOICE QUESTIONS

1. **b** Sociologists would use the term "nonmaterial culture" to refer to a group's ways of thinking and doing, including language and other forms of interaction as nonmaterial culture.
2. **c** The value of individualism is not part of material culture.
3. **a** The one statement that is *not* true regarding culture is that "people generally are aware of the effects of their own culture."
4. **d** The disorientation that James Henslin experienced when he came into contact with the fundamentally different culture of Morocco is known as culture shock.
5. **c** An American who thinks citizens of another country are barbarians if they like to attend bullfights is demonstrating ethnocentrism.
6. **c** Robert Edgerton cautioned against blindly accepting other cultures on the basis of their cultures and values if those customs and values threaten the quality of people's lives. He advocated rating cultures according to their quality of life.
7. **d** Gestures can lead to misunderstandings and embarrassment when their meanings are not shared.
8. **a** It is possible for human experience to be cumulative and for people to share memories because of language.
9. **c** The example from Eviatar Zerubavel illustrates the Sapir-Whorf hypothesis, which suggests that language not only reflects a culture's way of thinking and perceiving the world, but also helps to shape thought and perception.
10. **c** Every group develops expectations about the right ways to reflect its values. These expectations are *norms*.
11. **c** A monetary reward, a prize, a hug, or a pat on the back are all examples of *positive sanctions*.
12. **d** Moral holidays like Mardi Gras often center on drunkenness and rowdiness. They are times when people can break the norms and not be sanctioned. Therefore, the correct answer is "All of the above."
13. **d** You have violated a folkway, norms related to everyday behavior that are not strictly enforced.
14. **a** Mores are essential to our core values and require conformity.
15. **c** The author of your text cites having sex with one's parents as an example of *taboos*, a norm that is so strongly ingrained that even the thought of its violation is greeted with revulsion.
16. **d** Subcultures are a world within a world; have values and related behaviors that distinguish its members from the dominant culture; and include occupational groups. Therefore, all of the above are correct.
17. **c** Sociologically speaking, the Hell's Angels are an example of counterculture.
18. **b** A sociologist would describe the United States as a pluralistic society because it is made up of many different groups.
19. **c** Romantic love is not a value identified by sociologist Robin Williams.
20. **c** Henslin suggests that a new value cluster, made up of the values of leisure, self-fulfillment, physical fitness, and youngness, is now emerging in the United States.
21. **a** Value contradictions occur when a value, such as the one that stresses group superiority, comes into direct conflict with other values, such as democracy and equality.
22. **d** The term *culture wars* refers to the contemporary clash in core values in U.S. society.
23. **b** Ideal culture reflects the values and norms that a people attempt to follow; it is the goals held out for them.
24. **b** . Discipline is *not* a cultural universal identified by George Murdock
25. **d** The perspective that views human behavior as the result of natural selection and considers biological characteristics to be the fundamental cause of human behavior is *sociobiology*.
26. **b** Edward Wilson believes human behavior is the result of natural selection.

27. **d** The printing press or the computer would be considered *new technologies*, because both had a significant impact on social life following their invention.
28. d Continuing to visit physicians and to rely on the judgment about diagnosis and treatment of illness, even when computer tests do a better job, is an example of cultural lag.
29. **c** The adoption of bagels, woks and hammocks by the United States illustrates the process of cultural diffusion.
30. **b** Exporting Coca Cola around the globe has produced cultural leveling.

ANSWERS FOR TRUE-FALSE QUESTIONS

1. *True.*
2. *False.* Culture has a great deal to do with our ideas of right and wrong. For example, folkways and mores have sanctions attached to them to encourage people to do the right thing.
3. *True.*
4. *True.*
5. *False.* The gesture of nodding the head up and down to indicate "yes" is not universal. In some societies this gesture means "no."
6. *False.* Humans could not plan future events without language to convey meanings of past, present, and future points in time.
7. *True.*
8. *False.* One society's folkways may be another society's mores.
9. *False.* Motorcycle enthusiasts who emphasize personal freedom and speed, while maintaining values of success, form part of a subculture, not a counterculture. Motorcycle gangs who commit crimes and use illegal drugs are an example of a counterculture.
10. *True.*
11. *True.*
12. *False.* Concern for the environment has not always been a core value in U.S. society. It is one of the emergent values that is now increasing in importance.
13. *False.* When values conflict with one another sociologists refer to it as value contradiction.
14. *True.*
15. *True.*
16. *True.*
17. *False.* He argues they are the same.
18. *False.* New technologies not only affect the material culture, but they have a profound impact on the nonmaterial culture, including the way people think and what they value.
19. *True.*
20. *True.*

ANSWERS TO THE FILL-IN-THE-BLANK QUESTIONS

1. material culture
2. culture shock
3. cultural relativism
4. symbol
5. Gestures
6. language
7. functionalism
8. folkway
9. Counterculture
10. Value cluster
11. value
12. real culture

13. new technology
14. cultural lag
15. cultural leveling

ANSWERS TO MATCH THESE SOCIAL SCIENTISTS WITH THEIR CONTRIBUTIONS

1.   f   Edward Sapir and Benjamin Whorf: *stated that language shapes reality*
2.   i   Robin Williams: *noted core values in U.S. society*
3.   c   George Murdock: *looked for cultural universals*
4.   a   Douglas Massey: *notes that Miami is becoming truly bilingual*
5.   h   Robert Edgerton: *criticized aspects of cultural relativism*
6.   g   Edward Wilson: *believed that natural selection produced human behavior*
7.   j   William Sumner: *developed the concept of ethnocentrism*
8.   d   Charles Darwin: *studied the principles of natural selection*
9.   b   William Ogburn: *introduced the concept of cultural lag*
10.   e   JoEllen Shively: *studied Native Americans' identification with Westerns*

GUIDELINES FOR ANSWERING THE ESSAY QUESTIONS

1.   *Explain cultural relativism and discuss both the advantages and disadvantages of practicing it.*

You would begin your essay by defining cultural relativism and explaining that it developed in reaction to ethnocentrism. The primary advantage of this approach to looking at other cultures is that we are able to appreciate another way of life without making judgments, thereby reducing the possibilities for conflict between cultures. The primary disadvantage is that it can be used to justify any cultural practice and especially those that endanger people's health, happiness, and survival. You could conclude with a reference to Robert Edgerton's proposed "quality of life" scale. .

2.   *As the author points out, the United States is a pluralistic society, made up of many different groups. Having read this chapter about culture, now discuss some of the things that are gained by living in such a society, as well as some of the problems that are created.*

The first thing to think about is how our national culture has been shaped by all of the different subcultures that exist within it You could consider both aspects of both material culture and nonmaterial culture that have been influenced by youth subculture, by ethnic and racial subcultures, and by occupational subcultures, to name but a few. At the same time, the presence of so many different subcultures creates the possibility for ethnocentrism and misunderstandings. Additionally, when the values of the subculture are too different from the mainstream culture, culture wars can develop.

3.   *Consider the degree to which the real culture of the United States falls short of the ideal culture. Provide concrete examples to support your essay.*

Your first step is to define what real and ideal culture mean. Then you would want to refer to the core values that are identified in the text as reflective of the ideal culture and discuss the ways in which Americans fall far short of upholding these values in their everyday. An interesting example of the difference between ideal and real culture would be the increasing value we place on leisure, and yet we are working more hours than ever before, or the value we place on physical fitness and yet we are more obese and less physically fit than ever.

4.   *Evaluate what is gained and lost as technology advances in society.*

One way to frame a response to this would be to identify a specific technology that has had a significant impact on our society and then to discuss both the gains and losses. For example, the automobile provided us with new opportunities for mobility, freeing us from the constraints of public transportation. The automobile created economic opportunities, as new industries and services opened up — car dealerships, gas stations, fast food restaurants, and malls are just a few examples. At the same time, automobiles have contributed to urban sprawl and the decline of downtown shopping areas. We have become more isolated as we travel around in our cars rather than meeting and traveling with others on public transportation. The use of automobiles has contributed to increased congestion and air pollution. Finally, you could make the argument that the automobile has contributed to cultural leveling within the U.S., as regional differences have disappeared under the spread of national businesses in malls and food chains.

5.   *Thinking about William Ogburn's term cultural lag, explain why college students still attend traditional classes in the classroom when the technology is available to take classes over the Internet.*

William Ogburn would call this a cultural lag. By this he meant that a group's material culture uses changes first, with the nonmaterial culture lagging behind. You could discuss that college students are still more comfortable taking a class in the classroom rather than taking the course online. It is possible that some students don't have a computer at home or don't have access to a computer and this would make it difficult, if not impossible, to take a course over the Internet. Some students might never want to take a course over the Internet because they have certain beliefs about what it means to be a student.

CHAPTER 3

ANSWERS FOR MULTIPLE CHOICE QUESTIONS

1. **b** Feral children supposedly were abandoned or lost by their parents and raised by animals.
2. **a** From the case of Isabelle, we can conclude that humans have no natural language.
3. **c** On the basis of studies involving institutionalized children, psychologists H.M. Skeels and H. B. Dye concluded that the absence of stimulating social interaction was the basic cause of low intelligence among these children, not some biological incapacity.
4. **d** Studies of isolated rhesus monkeys demonstrated that the monkeys were not able to adjust to monkey life, did not instinctively know how to enter into "monkey interaction" with other monkeys or how to engage in sexual intercourse.
5. **d** Forming opinions about others based on our self-concept is not an element of the looking-glass self.
6. **c** According to Mead's theory, during the play stage children pretend to take the roles of specific people.
7. **a** According to Mead, the "I" is the self as subject.
8. **d** According to Mead, all three, language, the mind, and the self, are products of society.
9. **d** According to Piaget, in the formal operational stage children are capable of abstract thinking.
10. **d** Using Piaget's theory, children likely to become "young philosophers," able to talk about abstract concepts, come to conclusions based on general principles, and use rules to solve abstract problems during the formal operational stage.
11. **a** Freud's term for the inborn drives for self-gratification is the id.
12. **b** According to Lawrence Kohlberg, when a young child like Larry tries very hard to be nice to his younger sister in order to please his mother, he is in the preconventional stage of moral development.
13. **d** Most people are unlikely to ever reach the postconventional stage, according to Kohlberg. This is the stage in which people reflect on abstract principles of right and wrong and judge a behavior according to these principles.
14. **c** From her early research, Carol Gilligan concluded that women are more likely than men to evaluate morality in terms of personal relationships. On the other hand, men use abstract principles, a code of ethics that defines what is right and wrong.
15. **b** Although people around the world may share emotions, because emotions are in part due to biology, the way they express them varies considerably, and this expression is learned through socialization. Therefore, the only statement that is *correct* is, "How we express emotions depends on our culture and our social location."
16. **c** According to this chapter, society sets up effective controls over our behavior by socializing us into self and emotions.
17. **b** The ways in which society sets children onto different courses for life purely because they are male or female is called gender socialization.
18. **d** Psychologists Susan Goldberg and Michael Lewis observed mothers with their six-month-old infants in a laboratory setting and concluded that the mothers unconsciously rewarded daughters for being passive and dependent.
19. **a** Research by Melissa Milkie indicates that young males actively used media images to help them understand what was expected of them as males in our society.
20. **c** According to Melvin Kohn, middle-class parents focus on developing their children's curiosity, self-expression, and self-control.
21. **b** Melvin Kohn suggests that the key to understanding social class differences in child rearing is the type of job the parents' have.
22. **a** Religion is a key component to life. It is not a substitute for what parents teach.
23. **b** The research on the impact that day care has demonstrated that the more hours per week a child spends in day care, the weaker the bond between mother and child.

24. **b** In schools the corridor curriculum exists in which students teach each other behavior that may not always be appropriate.

25. **d** In terms of children's peer groups and academic achievement, research by Patricia and Peter Adler suggests that for boys, to do well academically is to lose popularity, while for girls, getting good grades increases social standing.

26. **c** According to Michael Messner, sports encourage boys to develop instrumental relationships, that is, relationships based on how useful they are or on what you can get out of them.

27. **d** Resocialization occurs when a person takes a new job, joins a cult, or goes to boot camp.

28. **b** The statement that: "They are not very effective in stripping away people's personal freedom," is *incorrect.* In fact, total institutions are very effective in stripping away individuals' personal freedom because they are isolated from the public, they suppress preexisting statuses, they suppress cultural norms, and they closely supervise the entire lives of their residents.

29. **c** In adultolescence, or transitional adulthood, there is now the postponement of adult responsibilities.

30. **a** For women between the ages of 30-49 it is a time of juggling many roles.

ANSWERS FOR TRUE-FALSE QUESTIONS

1. *False.* Culture consists of material and non-material culture.
2. *False.* Studies of institutionalized children demonstrate that some of the characteristics that we take for granted as being "human" traits result not from basic instincts but rather from early close relations with other humans.
3. *False.* When frightened the monkeys ran to the comfort of the terry-cloth "mother."
4. *False.* George Herbert Meade developed the idea of the generalized other.
5. *True.*
6. *True.*
7. *False.* Socialization has a great deal to do with how we feel. Because different individuals' socialization differs, they will actually experience different emotions.
8. *True.*
9. *False.* Research indicates that parents let their sons roam farther from home than their daughters and that they subtly encourage them to participate in more rough-and-tumble play.
10. *False.* Advertising continues to reinforce gender stereotypes.
11. *False.* The first major agent of socialization to have a major impact on us is our family.
12. *True.*
13. *False.* It is a *manifest* function of education, not a *latent* function, to transmit skills and values appropriate for earning a living.
14. *True.*
15. *True.*
16. *True.*
17. *True.*
18. *False.* Divorce and losing jobs are common during the middle years.
19. *True.*
20. *True.*

ANSWERS TO THE FILL-IN-THE-BLANK QUESTIONS

1. language
2. monkeys
3. looking-glass self
4. take the role of other
5. generalized other
6. pre-operational stage

7. social class
8. religion
9. resocialization
10. degradatation ceremony
11. life course
12. adolescence
13. early middle years
14. 40
15. behavior

ANSWERS TO MATCH THESE SOCIAL SCIENTISTS WITH THEIR CONTRIBUTIONS

1. f Melvin Kohn: *found social class differences in child rearing*
2. e Erving Goffman: *studied total institutions*
3. c Melissa Milkie: *Studies adolescent boys' use of media images*
4. a Paul Ekman: *concluded that people everywhere experience six basic emotions*
5. i Jean Piaget: *discovered that there are four stages in cognitive development*
6. b Harry and Margaret Harlow: *conducted studies of isolated rhesus monkeys*
7. h H.M. Skeels and H.B. Dye: *studied institutionalized children*
8. j Lawrence Kohlberg: *studied the development of morality*
9. d Carol Gilligan: *studied gender differences in moral development*
10. g Colin Turnbull: *carried out research on the Ik of Uganda*

GUIDELINES FOR ANSWERING THE ESSAY QUESTIONS

1. *Explain what is necessary in order for us to develop into full human beings.*

You might want to begin by stating that in order for us to become full human beings, we need language and intimate social connections to others. You could draw on the information presented in the previous chapter as to what language enables us to do: grasp relationships to others, think in terms of a shared past and future, and make shared plans. Our knowledge of language, and our ability to use it, develops out of social interaction, as the evidence of those children raised in isolation demonstrates. Furthermore, we learn how to get along with others only through close personal experiences with others. The experience of Isabelle and the children raised in institutionalized settings confirms this.

The importance of social interaction and close social contact for our development is underscored by the work of a number of social psychologists. Mead and Piaget suggest that our mind and our ability to reason develop out of social interactions, while Kohlberg and Gilligan argue that our sense of right and wrong develop in the same way. Finally, even our expression of emotions comes out of our contact with others in our society.

2. *Why do sociologists argue that socialization is a process and not a product?*

Sociologists would argue that socialization is a process rather than a product because there is no end to socialization. It begins at birth and continues throughout one's life, whenever you take on a new role. Cooley was the first to note that we are continually modifying our sense of self depending on our reading of other's reactions to us. Mead's work on taking the role of the other in the development of the self also suggests that socialization is a process. Researchers have identified a series of stages through which we pass as we age; at each stage we are confronted by new demands and new challenges that need to be mastered.

3. *Having read about how the family, the media, and peers all influence our gender socialization, discuss why gender roles tend to remain unchanged from one generation to the next.*

You could begin your essay by defining gender socialization, the process of learning what is expected of us from society because we are born either male or female. You could then note that this socialization is so complete that, as adults, most of us act, think, and even feel according to our particular culture's guidelines of what is appropriate for our sex. We do not question the way in which gender roles are defined — we have come to see the way we behave as natural and normal. Consequently, when we have children, we set out to socialize them into the same set of gender roles. You could incorporate some discussion of the research by Susan Goldberg and Michael Lewis about child rearing, as well as the fact that children are generally provided with gender-appropriate toys and subject to different parental expectations.

The ways in which the media perpetuate traditional gender roles should also be noted. You could talk about gender stereotypes that show up in advertising, television, and video games. Include a reference to studies that show the more television people watch, the more they tend to have restrictive views about women's role in society. Milkie's research on peer groups also demonstrates how media images contribute to gender socialization; boys used the media images to discover who they are as males.

4.   *As the text points out, the stages of the life course are influenced by the biological clock, but they also reflect broader social factors. Identify the stages of the life course and indicate how social factors have contributed to the definition of each of these stages.*

You should begin your essay by noting that the stages of the life course are shaped by both biological and social factors. Begin with childhood (from birth to age 12) and talk about how this stage extends over the earliest years as our bodies and minds are developing; at the same time, our understanding of childhood has transformed by broader social factors like industrialization. The impact of social factors is even more apparent in the second stage, adolescence, which goes from ages 13 to 17. Biologically, our bodies are changing, but this stage is a total social invention, the result of the Industrial Revolution and the growing importance of education.

It used to be that most people immediately assumed adult responsibilities upon graduation from high school: jobs, marriages and children. However, a growing number of young people today are postponing this next step as they acquire the additional education and training called for in our modern world. Consequently, we are witnessing the birth of a new stage: young adulthood. By the end of their 20s, most people are ready to launch their careers and their families, which leads to the next stage, the middle years. But because this is such a long stage, spanning the years from 30 to 65, it is generally divided into two stages — early and later. Although the life expectancy of people in U.S. society has been extended, during the later middle years issues of health and mortality are important. As their own parents die, there is a fundamental shift in their orientation to life. This stage ends at 65, at a time when most people are retiring, or have retired.

The final stage is the older years, again divided into early and later. A few generations ago, when life expectancy ran to the late 60s or early 70s, this was a relatively short stage, characterized by preparations for one's own death. Today, because we enjoy longer lives, the early part of this stage is often experienced as an extension of the middle years. People are unlikely to see themselves as old and they continue to be socially active. As health declines, and friends and spouses die, they move into the final years.

5.   *Do you think that it is possible that society in the United States would ever be like that of the Ik? Please explain.*

You could start out by explaining who the Ik are. They are a group of nomadic people who were devastated by drought, hunger, and starvation. They then turned to extreme individualism in which selfishness, emotional numbness, and lack of caring for others became their norm. You could discuss ways in which our society expresses those same characteristics. If you look at the values that are promoted in the United States, they are individualism and competition. Hopefully, our society would never go to the extremes that they did. You could also look at natural disasters that we have faced as a nation and some of the rioting and looting that has happened when people are left to fend for themselves.

CHAPTER 4

ANSWERS FOR MULTIPLE CHOICE QUESTIONS

1. **a** Microsociology focuses on social interaction.
2. **d** Sociologists who study individuals would be using microsociology.
3. **a** As a budding sociologist who is interested in the best way to study different perceptions that different classes have of each other, you would use a macrosociological approach.
4. **c** "An individual's behaviors and attitudes are due to biology (one's race or sex, for instance) as much as it is due to his/her location in the social structure," is *incorrect*. As the author of your text points out, if you were to switch your social location, from being a college student to being a street person, you would still be the same person biologically, but because of the change, you would experience social life differently.
5. **d** Age is not part of the definition of social class.
6. **d** Sociologists use the term status to refer to the position that someone occupies.
7. **d** Positions you occupy are termed status set.
8. **a** A sociologist would use the term *ascribed status* to describe race, sex, and the social class of his or her parents.
9. **d** Once you finish your education, you will move into some kind of occupation or profession, perhaps one that is based on your educational training. This job or career you will eventually hold is considered an achieved status.
10. **c** Wedding rings, military uniforms, and clerical collars are all examples of status symbols.
11. **c** The *incorrect* statement is "Status symbols are always positive signs or people would not wear them." Some social statuses are negative, and therefore, so are their status symbols (e.g., prison clothing issued to inmates).
12. **c** Master statuses are both ascribed and achieved.
13. **a** Status inconsistency most likely occurs when a contradiction or mismatch between statuses exists. For example, a college professor is accorded relatively high prestige while at the same time is generally not very well-paid.
14. **d** The behaviors, obligations, and privileges attached to statuses are called roles.
15. **a** A group consists of people who interact with one another.
16. **a** Education would be considered a social institution and therefore is formally not informally structured.
17. **b** Conflict Theorists state that social institutions are controlled by an elite that uses them to its own advantage.
18. **d** "All of the above" is correct. Organic solidarity refers to a society with a highly specialized division of labor; whose members are interdependent on one another; and with a high degree of impersonal relationships.
19. **a** *Gemeinschaft* is the type of society in which everyone knows everyone else, people conform because they are very sensitive to the opinions of others and want to avoid being gossiped about, and people draw comfort from being part of an intimate group.
20. **b** The statement that "stereotypes are unlikely to be self-fulfilling" is *incorrect*. While stereotypes have no single, inevitable outcome, research by Mark Snyder found that college males immediately formed opinions about what women were like, based only on photographs. In subsequent telephone conversations, they adjusted the way they talked to fit their stereotype of the woman. In response, the woman responded in a way that was consistent with the stereotype.
21. **d** Public distance zone marks the impersonal or formal relationship.
22. **b** Goffman suggests that we go to *back stages* to be ourselves.
23. **d** Susan, both a full-time student and a full-time worker, finds herself experiencing role conflict when her boss asks her to work during the same hours that she is expected to be in class.

24. **a** If you have ever been in the situation described, of being torn between answering the professor's question or showing up your peers, then you have experienced role strain.

25. **b** The social setting, appearance, and manner are all sign-vehicles used by individuals for managing impressions.

26. **d** Background assumptions are common understandings of how the world works and doctors do not cut hair so this would violate the believe of the role of doctors.

27. **a** Harold Garfinkel encouraged his students to participate in experiments where they acted like they did not understand the basic rules of social life.

28. **b** they did research on vaginal examinations to better understand the social construction of reality.

29. **c** The Thomas theorem would fall within symbolic interactionism.

30. **d** Research on the Saints and the Roughnecks demonstrated that in order to fully understand what happened to the boys in the study William Chambliss needed to analyze both the social structure and the patterns of social interaction that characterized their lives.

ANSWERS FOR TRUE-FALSE QUESTIONS

1. *False.* Social structure has a large impact on the typical individual because it gives direction to and establishes limits on a person's behavior.

2. *True.*

3. *False.* Social class is a large number of people with similar amounts of income and education who work at jobs that are roughly comparable in prestige. Social status refers to the social position that a person occupies (mother, teacher, daughter, or wife). Thus, sociologists use the two terms quite differently.

4. *False.* Being a teenager is an example of an ascribed status.

5. *True.*

6. *False.* Being male or female is considered a master status.

7. *True.*

8. *False.* The amount and nature of control that a group has over you depends on the group. Some groups, like a stamp collecting club, don't have that much control over many aspects of our behavior, while other groups, like our family or friendship group, exert considerable control over a wide range of our behaviors.

9. *False.* Sociologists have identified at least nine basic social institutions in contemporary societies.

10. *True.*

11. *False.* Conflict theorists do not view social institutions as working harmoniously for the common good.

12. *False.* The Amish are an example of a *Gesellschaft* society.

13. *True.*

14. *True.*

15. *False.* Researchers have found that higher-status individuals tend to touch more, because they have more social power.

16. *False.* According to the dramaturgy, we use impression management in our front stages.

17. *False.* The same setting will often serve as both a back and a front stage. When you are alone in your car it is a back stage, but when you are driving around with friends it becomes a front stage.

18. *False.* Role strain, not role conflict, is defined as a conflict someone feels within a role. Role conflict is when the expectations of one role are incompatible with those of another role.

19. *True.* Studied nonobservance is a face-saving technique in which people give the impression that they are unaware of a flaw in someone's performance. Impression management describes people's efforts to control the impressions that others receive of them.

20. *True.*

ANSWERS TO FILL-IN-THE-BLANK QUESTIONS
1. Macrosociology
2. Social Interaction
3. structure
4. social Class
5. master
6. Roles
7. Functionalist
8. Social cohesion
9. Division of labor
10. Gesellschaft
11. four
12. Teamwork
13. face-saving behavior
14. ethnomethodology
15. consequences

ANSWERS TO MATCH THESE SOCIAL SCIENTISTS WITH THEIR CONTRIBUTIONS
1. b   James Henslin and Mae Biggs: *researched the social construction of reality regarding vaginal exams*
2. e   Ferdinand Tönnies: *described Gemeinschaft and Gesellschaft societies*
3. a   Erving Goffman: *developed dramaturgy*
4. j   Harold Garfinkel: *founder of ethnomethodology*
5. c   William Chambliss: *used macro and microsociology to study high school gangs.*
6. h   Edward Hall: *anthropologists who did research on personal space*
7. d   Elijah Anderson: *studied the lives on inner city residents*
8. f   Elliot Leibow: *studied street corner men*
9. i   Mark Snyder: *carried out research to discover whether or not stereotypes are self-fulfilling*
10. g   W. I. Thomas: *known for the statement, "If people define situations as real, they are real in their consequences."*

GUIDELINES FOR ANSWERING THE ESSAY QUESTIONS
1. *Choose a research topic and discuss how you approach this topic using both macrosociological and microsociological approaches.*

The way to answer this question is to first think of a topic. I've chosen the topic of labor unions. Remember that the macrosociological level focuses on the broad features of society. So from this level, I might research the role that unions play within the economy or the political system, what types of workers are organized into unions, the level of union organization among workers, or the level of union activity. Shifting to a microsociological level of analysis, I would want to look at what happens within unions or between unions and management in terms of social interaction. From this perspective, I might want to investigate the behavior of union members and leaders at a union meeting, or the behavior of union and management negotiators at a bargaining session. By combining both perspectives, I have achieved a much broader understanding of the role of unions within society.

2. *The concept of a social structure is often difficult to grasp. Yet the social structure is a central organizing feature of social life. Identify the ways in which it takes shape in our society and in our lives.*

You will want to begin with the definition of social structure as the framework for society that establishes the typical patterns for the society. Then you can identify the major components of it: culture, social class, social status, roles, groups and social institutions. It is these components that give social structure shape and substance. The rest of your essay would focus on discussing the contribution that each of these components makes to the overall social structure. You can conclude with the observation that when we are born into a society, we are immediately located within the social structure, based on the culture, the social class of our parents, and our ascribed statuses. As we grow and function within different groups and social institutions, we learn to perform roles that are consistent with our culture and our status. We may eventually acquire achieved statuses. All of this gives shape and meaning to our lives, which in turn gives shape and meaning to social life.

3. *Today we can see many examples of people wanting to recreate a simpler way of life. Using Tönnies' framework, analyze this tendency.*

You would want to begin by describing Tönnies' framework of *Gemeinshaft* and *Gesellschaft*, and discussing the characteristics of each. Using these concepts, you would indicate that individuals' search for community reflects a rejection of the ever-increasing impersonality and formality of modern society. In their actions, people are trying to re-create a social world where everyone knows each other within the context of intimate groups. Some sociologists have used the term "pseudo-*Gemeinshaft*" to describe the attractiveness of the past — people building colonial homes and decorating them with antiques.

4. *Assume that you have been asked to give a presentation to your sociology class on Goffman's dramaturgy approach. Describe what information you would want to include in such a presentation.*

You could begin by explaining how Goffman saw life as a drama that was acted out on a stage. This would lead you to making a distinction between front stage and back stage. You might even want to provide some examples. For instance, you are presenting on a front stage, but you practiced for this presentation in your bedroom without any audience. Because dramaturgy focuses on the performances we give when we assume different roles, you might also want to talk about the problems of role conflict and role strain and the fact that we tend to become the roles we play. An important contribution of Goffman's was his insights into impression management, so you would want to explain what that is and how it involves the use of three different types of sign-vehicles: social setting, appearance, and manner. Finally, you could conclude with his concept of teamwork, especially as it relates to face-saving behavior, and remember to include examples of all of these concepts as you proceed.

5. *Differentiate between role conflict, role exit, and role strain and give examples.*

Role conflict is a situation in which one status (role) conflicts with another. For example, a student who is also a mom and wife might feel conflict in trying to juggle and balance all of those roles. Role conflict involves conflict between roles while role strain involves conflict within the same role. If you are a good student who is prepared and knows the answers you may feel bad answering all of the questions when the teacher asks. You may feel that this makes the other students look bad. Role exit is leaving a role entirely. When people leave marriages or careers that they have been in for a long time, this is role exit. Some people feel that their identity is threatened because that role has been a part of their life for so long.

CHAPTER 5

ANSWERS FOR MULTIPLE CHOICE QUESTIONS

1. **b** A researcher interested in doing a macro level study would choose race relations as a topic. Waiting in public places, interactions between people on street corners, and meat packers at work are all topics that would interest a micro level researcher.

2. **d** "All of the above" is correct. Sociologists believe that research is necessary because common sense ideas may or may not be true; they want to move beyond guesswork; and researchers want to know what really is going on.

3. **c** Eight steps are involved in scientific research.

4. **c** Researchers review the literature in order to help them narrow down the problem by pinpointing particular areas to examine; to develop ideas about how to do their own research; and to determine whether the problem has been answered already. They are not trying to insure that their hypotheses are correct. That is why they will conduct the research.

5. **a** A relationship between or among variables is predicted by a hypothesis.

6. **b** Validity is important in the research process because the researcher wants to be sure that the operational definitions really measure what they are intended to measure.

7. **b** Reliability refers to the extent to which data produce consistent results.

8. **c** In analyzing data gathered by participant observation, a researcher is likely to choose qualitative analysis.

9. **d** All of the reasons stated in this question explain why computers are considered a valuable tool in quantitative analysis. They allow sociologists to analyze huge amounts of information and identify basic patterns; the software packages available for data analysis take much of the drudgery out of that work; and they make it possible for sociologists to try various statistical tests.

10. **c** Replication is the repetition of research in order to test its findings.

11. **a** Mean, median, and mode are ways to measure "average."

12. **a** Ethnomethodology is the study of how people use background assumptions to make sense of life and, thus, is a part of symbolic interactionism. Surveys, unobtrusive measures, and secondary analysis are research methods for gathering data.

13. **c** A sample is defined as the individuals intended to represent the population to be studied.

14. **c** If you had carried out the procedure described, you would have selected a stratified random sample, defined as specific subgroups of the population in which everyone in the subgroup has an equal chance of being included in the study.

15. **c** This situation reflects interviewer bias. The respondent may feel uncomfortable voicing his or her true opinions directly to another person, but would be willing to reveal them in an anonymous situation.

16. **b** A researcher might "load the dice" in designing a research project because of a vested interest in the outcome of the research. He or she may be hired by business firms and is thus motivated to find results that are consistent with the interests of the firm.

17. **b** Given the time and cost factors, you are most likely to choose to use self-administered questionnaires, because this method allows a larger number of people to be sampled at a relatively low cost.

18. **b** The advantage of structured interviews is that they are faster to administer and make it easier for answers to be coded.

19. **d** Problems that must be dealt with in conducting participant observation include the researcher's personal characteristics, developing rapport with respondents, and generalizability. Therefore, "All of the above" is the correct response.

20. **c** The analysis of data already collected by other researchers is secondary analysis.

21. **b** Sources such as newspapers, diaries, bank records, police reports, household accounts and immigration files are documents that provide useful information for investigating social life.

22. **c** In order to study patterns of alcohol consumption in different neighborhoods, you decide to go through the recycling bins in your town and count the number of beer cans, and wine and hard liquor bottles. This study would be using unobtrusive methods because you are making observations on people without their knowledge that they are being studied.

23. **a** A researcher who is trying to identify causal relationships is likely to use an experiment.

24. **b** In an experiment, the group not exposed to the independent variable in the study is the control group.

25. **a** The change in behavior that occurs when subjects know they are being studied is referred to as the Hawthorne effect.

26. **b** The simultaneous occurrence of alcohol and physical abuse is known as a correlation.

27. **c** Surveys are more likely to be used by researchers trained in quantitative techniques.

28. **d** All of the reasons help explain why it is important to consider gender when planning and conducting research. Gender is a significant factor in social life; the gender of the interviewer could possibly contribute to interviewer bias; and because men and women experience the social world differently, both need to be studied in order to gain a complete picture.

29. **d** "All of the above" is correct. Research ethics require openness; that a researcher not falsify results or plagiarize someone else's work; and that research subjects should not be harmed by the research.

30. **b** Research and theory are both essential for sociology, since research without theory is simply a collection of facts, and theory without research is empty and abstract.

ANSWERS FOR TRUE-FALSE QUESTIONS

1. *True.*
2. *True.*
3. *True.*
4. *False.* Sociologists do not place one above the other. Rather, they take great care to assure that both are achieved.
5. *True.*
6. *False.* Validity is important to insure that the operational definition measures what it was intended to measure.
7. *False.* Computers are valuable to researchers not because they store information efficiently, but because they reduce large amounts of data to basic patterns, they take the drudgery out of analyzing data, they can do different statistical tests easily, and they free the researcher up to do more interpretation of the data.
8. *True.*
9. *False.* In survey research, it is always desirable for respondents to express their own ideas.
10. *True.*
11. *True.*
12. *True.*
13. *False.* Secondary analysis and use of documents is not the same thing. The data used in secondary analysis is gathered by other researchers while documents may be anything from diaries to police records.
14. *False.* It is not always unethical to observe behavior in people when they do not know they are being studied. However, there are circumstances when the issue of ethics should be raised.
15. *True.*
16. *True.*
17. *True.*
18. *False.* Gender is an important factor in research, possibly contributing to interviewer bias, influencing the choice of research methods, and limiting generalizability.
19. *True.*

20. *False.* Scully and Marolla's research demonstrates that it is possible to do research that contributes to our body of sociological knowledge under less than ideal conditions.

ANSWERS TO THE FILL-IN-THE-BLANK QUESTIONS

1. hypothesis
2. analyze
3. population
4. three
5. random
6. neutral
7. rapport
8. unobtrusive measures
9. independent variable
10. survey
11. homeless
12. interviewer
13. Laud Humphreys
14. theory
15. common sense

ANSWERS TO MATCH THESE CONCEPTS WITH THEIR DEFINITIONS

1. b Hawthorne effect: *behavior change due to subject's awareness of being studied*
2. f population: *the target group to be studied*
3. h control group: *the group of subjects who are exposed to the independent variable*
4. c interviewer bias: *the interviewer's effect on respondents that leads to biased answers*
5. i replication: *repeating a study to see if the same results are obtained*
6. g secondary analysis: *the analysis of data already collected by other researchers*
7. e documents: *written sources of data*
8. j independent variable: *a factor that causes a change in another variable*
9. d operational definition: *the way in which a researcher measures a variable*
10. a unobtrusive measures: *the observation of people who don't know they are being studied*

GUIDELINES FOR ANSWERING THE ESSAY QUESTIONS

1. *Choose a topic and explain how you would go through the different steps in the research model.*

In order to answer this question, you must select a topic and then develop this from the beginning to the end of the research process, identifying all eight steps and explaining what tasks are carried out each step of the way. Your answer should make reference to variables, hypothesis, operational definitions, the different research methods, validity and reliability, different ways of analyzing the data, and replication.

2. *Discuss some of the things that can go wrong in the process of doing research and provide suggestions on how to overcome such problems.*

There are a number of problems that can arise if the researcher is not careful. Included would be: (1) deriving invalid and unreliable results because of inadequate operational definitions and inaccurate sampling procedures; (2) obtaining biased answers because biased questions were asked; (3) failing to establish rapport with research subjects because of personal qualities or characteristics; (4) failing to gain access to necessary documents because those who control the documents are unwilling to cooperate; and (5) failing to rule out possible spurious correlations. Each of these potential problems can be overcome if the researcher follows the steps in the research process carefully.

3. *The author of your text discusses six different research methods. Pick a research topic of interest to you and discuss how you might try to investigate this topic using these different methods. In your answer, consider how a particular method may or may not be suitable for the topic under consideration.*

To review, the different methods discussed in the text are (1) surveys; (2) participant observation; (3) secondary analysis; (4) documents; (5) unobtrusive measures; and (6) experiments. Your first step is to pick a potential research topic. Let's say you decide to research homeless women. You could do a survey, developing a questionnaire that would be either self-administered or completed through an interview. This would use either closed-ended or open-ended questions, or maybe a combination of both. You would need to discuss some of the problems that you might encounter in trying to define the homeless population or in attempting to draw a random sample. You could point out that while this method would allow you to sample a large number of people at a relatively low cost, you might have difficulties with rapport.

Using participant observation might be more suitable for the topic under consideration. You could spend time in a homeless shelter, getting to know the women who live there. Hopefully, over time you will have built some rapport with the clients and will be able to learn more about their lives and the reasons why they are homeless. You would want to make note that this method may make it difficult for you to generalize your findings.

As you proceed through the essay, you might consider the other methods. You could make an argument about using secondary analysis, documents, and unobtrusive measures. In all three instances, you would want to make note of how these could be used and the limitations that each presents. The only method you might find difficult to apply to this topic would be experiments.

Your conclusion would summarize what factors influence the researcher's choice of a method: available resources, degree of access to respondents, the purpose of the research, and the background of the researcher. You could also talk about the differences between quantitative and qualitative research.

4. *Explain why ethical guidelines are necessary when conducting social science research.*

Ethical guidelines are necessary for several reasons. First and foremost, the researcher is working with human subjects; there must be guidelines to protect these subjects from any undue physical or psychological harm. Secondly, the research is only valid and reliable if the subjects have honestly and accurately provided information to the researcher. For this reason, they must have confidence in the researcher and the research process; guidelines assure subjects that their identities will remain anonymous and their information will be confidential. Finally, an essential aspect of research is that it be shared with others in the research community and members of the wider society. Guidelines regarding falsification and plagiarism guarantee that all research will be carefully scrutinized, thereby assuring its validity and reliability.

5. *Discuss the relationship between research and theory and why commonsense is not enough.*

In this essay, you will want to begin with C. Wright Mills's observations about theory and research. He argued that research without theory is simply a collection of unrelated "facts," while theory without research is abstract and empty. Research tests theory and theory helps us explain unexpected or surprising findings. Both are essential for sociology, because both take us beyond common sense. Commonsense is not enough because problems and issues go well beyond what may sound logical. As sociologists do research, they often come up with surprising findings. You could conclude the essay by discussing the research by Scully and Marolla, which challenged common sense notions about rapists. They were not satisfied with the typical explanation that rapists were "sick." They found out that the motivating behavior in rape is power, not passion.

CHAPTER 6

ANSWERS FOR MULTIPLE CHOICE QUESTIONS

1. **d** People who have something in common and who believe that what they have in common is significant make up a group.
2. **b** The largest and most complex group that sociologists study is a society.
3. **c** Hunting and gathering societies consist of 25-40 members.
4. **a** Of all types of societies, the simplest is the hunting and gathering society.
5. **b** Pastoral societies are based on the pasturing of animals.
6. **d** "All of the above" is correct. The domestication revolution led to the human group becoming larger, the creation of a food surplus, and a more specialized division of labor.
7. **c** The society that emerged out of the invention of the plow was known as an agricultural society.
8. **d** "All of the above" is correct. Indicators of increasing equality include better housing, the abolition of slavery, and a move toward more representative political systems.
9. **a** Postindustrial society is based on information, services, and high technology.
10. **b** The United States was the first nation to have more than 50 percent of its work force employed in service industries; it was followed quickly by Japan, Australia, New Zealand, and Western Europe.
11. **d** "All of the above" is the correct answer. A *bioeconomic* society, in which the economy centers around the application of human genetics for medicine and plant genetics for the production of food, is associated with the identification of the double-helix structure of DNA and the decoding of the human genome in 2000. It may represent a new type of society or simply another aspect of postindustrial society.
12. **c** Emile Durkheim believed that small groups help prevent anomie, because, through their intimate relationships, they provide a sense of meaning and purpose to life.
13. **c** People who have similar characteristics are a category.
14. **c** An aggregate is a set of individuals who temporarily share the same physical space but do not see themselves as belonging together.
15. **a** Cooley saw that primary groups are essential to an individual's psychological well being.
16. **d** "All of the above" is correct. Secondary groups have members who are likely to interact on the basis of specific roles; are characteristic of industrial societies; and are essential to the functioning of contemporary societies.
17. **b** Groups that provide a sense of identification or belonging are referred to as in-groups.
18. **d** Because identification with a group generates not only a sense of belonging, but also loyalty and feelings of superiority, it can lead to rivalries with out-groups. Hence, the consequences of in-group membership can be all of the things mentioned: discrimination, hatred, and even killing.
19. **c** This would be her reference group. They are a group that you can compare yourself to and can provide you with standards even when you are not actually a member of the group.
20. **a** Sociologically speaking, the social ties radiating outward from the self, that link people together are social networks.
21. **b** Facebooking is a new, somewhat lazy, efficient way to meet friends that college students take part in via the Internet.
22. **d** "All of the above" is correct. Dyads are the most intense or intimate of human groups, require continuing active participation and commitment of both members, and are the most unstable of social groups.
23. **d** That the continuation of the triad depends on success of the arbitrator in settling disputes is *not* one of the characteristics of a triad; the other three are.
24. **c** A diffusion of responsibility occurs when a group is larger than a dyad and each member feels that someone else will act.
25. **c** An expressive leader increases harmony and minimizes conflict in a group.

26. **b** Research by Lippitt and White demonstrated that the authoritarian style of leader is most effective in emergency situations, and the laissez-faire style is generally ineffective. The one style that is best under most circumstances is the democratic style of leader.

27. **d** "All of the above" is correct. According to sociologists, leaders tend to have certain characteristics, including being more talking and able to express self-confidence, taller, and better-looking than others, and where they are sitting in a group.

28. **a** Of the 50 people that Solomon Asch tested, 25% stuck to their guns and always gave the right answer.

29. **c** The Milgram experiment demonstrates how strongly authority influences people.

30. **c** James Henslin suggests that the key to preventing groupthink is to guarantee that the results of social science research and the information that is gathered by media reporters is widely circulated among members of government decision-making bodies.

ANSWERS FOR TRUE-FALSE QUESTIONS

1. *True.*
2. *True.*
3. *False.* According to Elise Boulding, women's status fell rather than rose once metals were attached to plows. Plowing and the care of cows became associated with men, and their status rose even higher.
4. *False.* Industrial societies were brought about by the invention of the steam engine.
5. *True.*
6. *False.* The United States was the first country to have more than 50 percent of its work force employed in service industries.
7. *True.*
8. *True.*
9. *False.* Members of secondary, not primary, groups are likely to interact on the basis of specific roles.
10. *True.*
11. *True.*
12. *False.* A person does not have to belong to a group to use that group as a reference group.
13. *True.*
14. *True.*
15. *False.* Dyads are more intimate than any larger group because there are only two members of a dyad, but their smaller size also makes them *less* stable compared to larger groups.
16. *True.*
17. *True.*
18. *False.* Sociologically speaking, a leader does not have to be officially appointed or elected to be the "leader." A leader is someone who influences the behaviors of others.
19. *True.*
20. *True.*

ANSWERS TO THE FILL-IN-THE-BLANK QUESTIONS

1. society
2. Horticultural societies
3. anomie
4. family
5. in-group
6. reference
7. faction
8. electronic
9. coalition
10. task

11. authoritarian
12. six
13. increases, decreases
14. groupthink
15. tunnel

ANSWERS TO MATCH THESE SOCIAL SCIENTISTS WITH THEIR CONTRIBUTIONS
1. h Irving Janis: *groupthink*
2. c Georg Simmel: *dyads*
3. g Emile Durkheim: *small groups and anomie*
4. b Stanley Milgram: *obedience to authority*
5. i Solomon Asch: *conformity to peer pressure*
6. a Charles H. Cooley: *primary group*
7. j Robert K. Merton: *in-group prejudice leads to a double standard*
8. d Ronald Lippitt & Ralph White: *classic study on leadership styles*
9. f Elise Boulding: noted *womens' status changed with the invention of the plow*
10. e Lloyd Howells & Selwyn Becker: *leadership role influenced by seating in group*

GUIDELINES FOR ANSWERING THE ESSAY QUESTIONS
1. *After summarizing the fundamental social changes that resulted from each of the different social revolutions, evaluate the degree to which the new technology of the microchip is contributing to a similar level of fundamental change.*

You would want to begin by summarizing characteristics of the first three social revolutions. The first social revolution was the domestication of animals and plants. This created a more dependable food supply, thereby allowing groups to grow larger in size, develop a more varied division of labor and increase trade between communities; it also led to the emergence of social inequality. The second social revolution was the agricultural revolution. The use of the plow contributed to higher crop yields using less labor, so that more people were freed to pursue other activities. Cities grew and "culture" developed. Inequality becomes a permanent feature of society. The third social revolution was the invention of machines powered by fuels instead of animals. Productivity was further enhanced and social inequality was initially greater than before, although over time the amount of inequality began to diminish.

Having done that, you should turn your attention to the current transformation of industrial society into a postindustrial society and the role of the microchip. You could mention the impact that computers are having on our lives, including everything from communications to the way we work. The earlier transformations contributed to increased division of labor, changes in the level of inequality within society, and relations between social groups. Your conclusion is based on your evaluation of whether you think this transformation is as profound as the earlier ones.

2. *Durkheim was among the first sociologists to argue that small groups stand as a buffer between the individual and the larger society. The author of your text notes that secondary groups today have become essential to our welfare, yet they fail to satisfy our deep needs for intimate association. In this essay, consider how it is possible that they are essential for our welfare if they fail to satisfy essential human needs.*

The reason the author of your text claims that secondary groups are essential for our welfare has to do with the nature of industrial and postindustrial societies. These are societies with very large populations and a very complex division of labor. Given these changes in society, it is understandable why most of our activities are organized within secondary groups, since this type of group is defined as a large, relatively anonymous, formal organization devoted to a single interest or goal. Our daily lives would be chaotic and very unproductive without the work of secondary groups.

At the same time, just as Durkheim, concerned about how our individual needs would be met within a large, relatively anonymous society, believed that we form small (primary) groups to serve as a buffer between us and society, today we rely on this same type of group to serve as a buffer between us and the impersonality of the secondary group. Our essential human need for intimacy is provided by primary groups that tend to form within secondary groups. Without our friends at work and school and our families at home, our lives would be very alienating.

3. *Explain the three different leadership styles and suggest reasons why the democratic leader is the best style of leader for most situations.*

You would want to begin by identifying the three styles of leadership and listing the characteristics of each. Then you should evaluate how characteristics of a democratic leader, like holding group discussions, outlining the steps necessary to reach the goals, suggesting alternatives, and allowing the group members to work at their own pace, all contributed to the outcomes like greater friendliness, group-mindedness, and mutual respect, and ability to work without supervision. Finally, consider why those qualities and outcomes were judged to be the best under most circumstances.

4. *Explore the factors that influence the emergence of groupthink and consider strategies for minimizing the development of this collective tunnel vision.*

There are several factors you could discuss. First, you could bring in the findings of the Asch experiment about the influence of peer pressure in individual and group decision-making. You could also include some reference to the Milgram experiment about obedience to authority. There is also strong pressure on members of a group to think alike, since voicing opposition can be viewed as a sign of disloyalty; your role as a "team player" may even be questioned. Within groups, there is also a tendency to put aside moral judgments for the sake of the group.

The author of your text suggests that groupthink develops when leaders and members of groups are isolated and become cut off from information sources that do not fit with their own views. His suggestion is for leaders to have the widest possible access to research findings of social scientists and information freely gathered by media sources. You could also discuss how groupthink might be reduced by being sensitive to the size of the group and the nature of leadership — two factors that play a role in overall group dynamics.

5. *Discuss how the size of the group affects attitudes and behavior.*

You could start out by discussing the relationship between group size and what is known as the diffusion of responsibility. When someone feels a sense of responsibility and are part of a small group (dyad or triad), they are more likely to help others than when they are a part of a larger group. When they are a part of a larger group, they feel less personally responsible for others because they know that others are available to help out. When the group grows larger, it becomes more formal and loses its intimacy. All of the members can no longer feel close and know one another. When a group grows too large, it will break into smaller, more intimate groups.

CHAPTER 7

ANSWERS FOR MULTIPLE CHOICE QUESTIONS

1. **c** Rationality is the acceptance of rules, efficiency, and practical results as the right way to approach human affairs.
2. **a** The idea that the past is the best guide for the present is the traditional orientation.
3. **b** One of the major obstacles to industrialization was a traditional orientation to life that led people to resist change.
4. **c** According to Karl Marx, the force behind rationality replacing the traditional orientation to life was capitalism.
5. **d** "All of the above" is correct. According to Max Weber, capitalism is the investment of capital in the hopes of producing profits. It became an outlet for the excess money of Calvinists, as well as producing success for many that was then interpreted as a sign of God's approval.
6. **d** Because sociologists have not been able to determine whose views are most accurate, the two views still remain side by side.
7. **b** A secondary group designed to achieve explicit objectives is the sociological definition of a formal organization.
8. **b** In a bureaucracy, assignments flow downward, not upward, and accountability flows upward — not downward.
9. **c** In bureaucracies, the characteristic of impersonality is to be more concerned with the office rather than who holds than the person who holds that position.
10. **c** George Ritzer used the term "the McDonaldization of society" to refer to the increasing rationalization of daily living.
11. **b** The force behind "the McDonaldization of society" is the increased efficiency that contributes to lower prices.
12. **d** "All of the above" is correct because alienation, bureaucratic incompetence, and red tape are dysfunctions of bureaucracies.
13. **b** What Linda is feeling is referred to as alienation by sociologists.
14. **d** "All of the above" is correct because workers resist alienation by forming primary groups, praising each other and expressing sympathy when something goes wrong, and putting pictures and personal items in their work areas.
15. **c** According to your text, the alienated bureaucrat is not likely to do anything for the organization beyond what he or she is required to do.
16. **b** The Peter Principle states that each employee of a bureaucracy is promoted to his or her level of incompetence.
17. **c** Goal displacement occurs when an organization adopts new goals.
18. **d** The sociological significance of bureaucracy is that it represents a fundamental change in how people relate to one another.
19. **d** "All of the above" is correct. Voluntary associations are groups made up of volunteers who organize on the basis of some mutual interest. They include political parties, unions, professional associations, and churches, and they have been an important part of American life.
20. **a** Voluntary associations exist in the United States because they meet people's basic needs.
21. **d** David Sills identified four functions that some voluntary groups provide and that includes mediating between the government and the individual, provide training in organizational skills, and paving the way for social change.
22. **c** The tendency for organizations to be dominated by a small, self-perpetuating elite is called the iron law of oligarchy.
23. **a** According to Rosabeth Moss Kanter, in a large corporation the corporate culture contains hidden values.
24. **a** Pepsi is a company that has served as a positive example of diversity training.

25. **d** Humanizing a work setting refers to organizing a workplace in such a way that human potential is developed rather than impeded. Among the characteristics of more humane bureaucracies are the availability of opportunities on the basis of ability and contributions, a more equal distribution of power, and less rigid rules and more open decision making.

26. **d** Research on the costs and benefits of employer-financed day care demonstrates that such a benefit can save the employer money in terms of reducing employee turnover and absenteeism.

27. **a** Quality circles are an excellent example of a business fad.

28. **c** According to conflict theorists the interests of workers and owners are fundamentally opposed and, in the final analysis, workers are always exploited.

29. **d** "All of the above" is correct. Computers in the workplace have reduced drudgery of the work, could lead to more surveillance of workers by managers, and may be the first step toward a society in which every move a citizen makes is recorded.

30. **c** Despite the myth that all Japanese workers are guaranteed lifetime job security, today only about one-third of that country's work force actually finds it.

ANSWERS FOR TRUE-FALSE QUESTIONS

1. *True.*
2. *False.* Traditional orientation is *not* based on the idea that the present is the best guide for the future. It is based on the idea that the past is the best guide for the present.
3. *True.*
4. *False.* Max Weber did not believe that the growth of capitalism contributed to the rise of the Protestant ethic but, rather, that the rise of the Protestant ethic as a result of Calvinism contributed to the growth of capitalism.
5. *True.*
6. *False.* By definition, only secondary groups can be formal organizations. The text defines a formal organization as "a secondary group designed to achieve explicit objectives."
7. *True.*
8. *False.* Most colleges and universities do have written systems of accountability for faculty members. As Professor Henslin notes in the text, his institution requires faculty members to fill out reports indicating how they have spent their university-related time. These materials go to committees whose task it is to evaluate the relative performance of each faculty member. Other institutions utilize such things as student evaluations of faculty as part of an accountability package.
9. *True.*
10. *True.*
11. *True.*
12. *False.* It is difficult for workers to resist becoming alienated because of the nature of the organizational environment in which they work. According to Marx, alienation occurs because workers are cut off from the product of their own labor, which results in estrangement not only from the products but from their whole work environment.
13. *False.* The Peter Principle has not been proven to be true. If it were generally true, bureaucracies would be staffed entirely by incompetents, and none of these organizations could succeed. In reality, bureaucracies are remarkably successful.
14. *True.*
15. *True.*
16. *True.*
17. *True.*
18. *True.*
19. *True.*
20. *False.* The Japanese system works better in theory than in reality. For example, only about one third of Japanese workers find lifetime job security.

ANSWERS TO THE FILL-IN-THE-BLANK QUESTIONS

1. traditional
2. rationality
3. John Calvin
4. division
5. ideal
6. McDonaldization
7. Alienation
8. Peter Principle
9. mutual interest
10. iron law of oligarchy
11. hidden
12. work
13. confrontational
14. marriage
15. myths

ANSWERS TO MATCH THESE SOCIAL SCIENTISTS WITH THEIR CONTRIBUTIONS

1. h   Max Weber: *the rationalization of society*
2. a   Robert Michels: *the iron law of oligarchy*
3. j   William Ouchi: *the Japanese corporate model*
4. d   Karl Marx: *the exploitation of workers by capitalists*
5. g   Rosabeth Moss Kanter: *the hidden values in the corporate culture*
6. e   George Ritzer: *the McDonaldization of society*
7. b   Alexis de Tocqueville: *early observer of U.S. society who noted the presence of voluntary associations*
8. i   Fox & Arquitt: *problems of oligarchy in the VFW*
9. f   Gary Marx: *development of the "maximum-security" work place*
10. c   David Sills: *goal displacement in the March of Dimes*

GUIDELINES FOR ANSWERING THE ESSAY QUESTIONS

1. *Explain what sociologists mean by the expression "rationalization of society" and discuss why this change has occurred.*

The first step is to talk about the shift from a traditional orientation to life to one based on the widespread acceptance of rationality. You could explore what the traditional orientation is — relationships are long-term and based on custom and history, change is viewed with suspicion and comes very slowly, and people are evaluated on how well they fulfill their traditional roles. You could then introduce the characteristics of social life based on rationality — efficiency, impersonality, concerns over the bottom line, and the explicit measurement of outcomes.

Once you have established the differences between these two orientations and forms of social organization, you would then want to talk about how Marx and Weber each explained the shift. Although both believed that capitalism could not function without rational organization, they differed on the source of the change. For Marx, capitalism was the driving force behind these changes. When people discovered that they could produce more and generate higher profits by organizing work and the wider society around these principles, their views on life changed. On the other hand, Weber believed that religion, and religious beliefs, were behind the shift. He pointed to the Protestant Ethic, a combination of beliefs and values, as the source for the emergence of capitalism and rationalization.

2. *Explain "hidden values" within the workplace and why this continues in contemporary organizations.*

Rosabeth Moss Kanter stresses that the corporate culture contains "hidden values." These values create a self-fulfilling prophecy that affects people's corporate careers. For examples, workers are often hired who reflect the bosses' background. These people are then given better access to information, networking opportunities and "fast track" positions. These people are then more committed and perform better. They receive promotions since they are meeting the stereotype that the boss had of them to begin with. Those workers who may not fit the stereotype that they boss had, may not receive these opportunities. They may feel less committed the organization and
Not perform as well. They also then meet the boss's stereotype of them. These "hidden values" are very difficult to detect and stay below the surface. As such, the hidden corporate culture and stereotypes are likely to eventually give way, but very slowly.

3. *Define the iron law of oligarchy and discuss why this problem occurs in voluntary associations.*

You would begin by explaining that the iron law of oligarchy is the tendency within organizations for the leadership to become self-perpetuating. Although this problem occurs in all types of organizations, it is particularly evident in voluntary associations. A major reason for this is the nature of membership in this type of organization; it tends to be passive, varying in its degree of commitment to and involvement in the organization. The elite keep themselves in power by passing leadership positions from one member of the clique to another. If the leadership is not responsive to the membership, it runs the risk of being removed from office by a grassroots rebellion.

4. *This chapter provides discussion of strategies to humanize the work place. After identifying some of these strategies, consider the conflict perspective on these types of initiatives.*

Your essay should begin with a brief statement about what "humanizing the workplace" means. You could talk about how bureaucracies can contribute to alienation, and that this initiative is in response to that tendency toward dehumanization and alienation. From here, you would want to identify different strategies: quality circles, employee stock ownership plans, work teams, corporate day care, and even cooperatives. For each of these, you would provide a brief description of what aspect of dehumanization it is trying to address.

The second part of this essay is to consider the conflict perspective. Conflict theorists note that regardless of how the work is organized, the basic relationship between workers and owners is exploitative and confrontational. This is because they have conflicting interests: owners want to extract as much profit as they can so they exploit the workers and the workers want to find ways to resist the exploitation. That is the fundamental nature of capitalism, the "bottom line." Thus the conflict perspective sees such initiatives as just another way for the capitalists to exploit the workers.

5. *Evaluate whether the use of computer technology to control workers is an inevitable aspect of bureaucracy.*

You would want to begin by identifying the defining characteristics of bureaucracy — the presence of a hierarchy, a division of labor, written rules, written communications and records, and impersonality. You should then consider the ways in which computers are tied to these various characteristics. The computer's capacity to be accessed from remote sites means that managers can communicate with workers at any time and from any place and the workers' input on computers enable the managers to maintain records of their productivity (written communication and records); computers also promote impersonality. Your conclusion is to evaluate the degree to which such steps are inevitable.

CHAPTER 8

ANSWERS FOR MULTIPLE CHOICE QUESTIONS

1. **b** In sociology, the term deviance refers to all violations of social rules.
2. **b** Deviance is so often viewed as threatening because it undermines the predictability of social life that is established through the creation and observance of norms.
3. **c** Frowns, gossip, and crossing people off guest lists are examples of negative sanctions.
4. **c** Most negative sanctions are informal. At the same time, whether you consider the breaking of a norm simply an amusing matter that warrants no severe sanctions, or a serious infraction that does, depends on your perspective.
5. **c** The function of the stigma is to define or identify the person who violates the norm as deviant.
6. **a** A court martial in which the insignia of rank is publicly ripped off the uniforms of the officers found guilty is an example of degradation ceremonies.
7. **c** Differential association theory is based on the symbolic interactionist perspective.
8. **d** According to differential association theory, an individual becomes a deviant because he has learned to deviate from society's norms. In particular, family, friends, neighborhoods and even subcultures will teach him to either conform to or deviate from the norms.
9. **c** The idea that two control systems, inner controls and outer controls, work against our tendency toward deviance is called control theory.
10. **c** According to Travis Hirschi, it is our bonds to society that affects our inner controls; the stronger the bonds, the more effective are our controls. Bonds are based on attachments, commitments, involvements, and beliefs.
11. **c** All of the following are ways of neutralizing deviance: appeal to higher loyalties, denial of responsibility, and denial of injury and a victim. Denial of deviant labels is *not* one of the ways of neutralizing such behavior.
12. **b** William Chambliss's study of the Saints and Roughnecks suggests that people often live up to the labels that a community gives them.
13. **d** "All of the above" is correct. William Chambliss states that all of these are factors that influence whether people will be seen as deviant: social class, the visibility of offenders, and their styles of interaction.
14. **a** According to the functionalist perspective, deviance promotes social unity and social change.
15. **d** "All of the above" is the correct answer. Getting an education, then getting a good job and working hard, are all examples of what Merton meant by the term *institutionalized means*.
16. **d** Recidivism is not one of the responses to anomie identified by Merton.
17. **b** According to Merton's strain theory, people who drop out of the pursuit of success by abusing alcohol or drugs are retreatists.
18. **a** Steve's behavior reflects innovation. Steve is rejecting the institutionalized means, but wants to reach the cultural goal of wealth, so he finds a way to do it that is innovative.
19. **d** The illegitimate opportunity structures theory is based on the functionalist perspective.
20. **c** Crimes committed by people of respectable and high social status in the course of their occupations are called white-collar crimes.
21. **a** Corporate crime cost us as a society about $400/year.
22. **d** "All of the above" is correct. The marginal working class includes people with few skills, who hold low-paying, part-time, seasonal jobs, and who are the most desperate members of the working class.
23. **b** The United States has the largest percentage of its population in prison; it also has more people in prison than any other country.
24. **c** African Americans are disproportionately represented among the prison population of this country. They account for nearly one-half of all prisoners.

25. **b** The *correct* statement is that "about one-half of all recidivists have been convicted of a violent crime." There is no evidence that the "get-tough" policy has had a significant impact on lowering the rates of recidivism. Studies do show that individuals who have served time are likely to return to prison, but the statistic is that two-thirds will be rearrested within three years, not one year. Finally, approximately three-quarters of those in prison have served time before.

26. **b** Since the death penalty was reinstated in 1977, 37 percent of those executed have been African American.

27. **a** As a group, African Americans are more likely than other racial/ethnic groups to be victims of hate crimes.

28. **d** Hate crimes consist of all of the above.

29. **c** The medicalization of deviance refers to viewing deviance as a medical matter.

30. **d** With deviance inevitable, Henslin suggests that one measure of a society is how it treats its deviants.

ANSWERS FOR TRUE-FALSE QUESTIONS

1. *False.* What is deviant to some is not deviant to others. This principle holds true within a society as well as across cultures. Thus, acts perfectly acceptable in one culture may be considered deviant in another culture.

2. *False.* According to your text, a college student cheating on an exam and a mugger lurking on a dark street do have something in common: they are both engaged in deviant behavior, thus making them "deviants."

3. *True.*

4. *True.*

5. *False.* Sanctions can be either negative (a frown, a fine, a prison sentence) or positive (a smile, an award, a compliment). Negative sanctions are applied to behavior that violates the norm, while positive sanctions are applied to behavior that follows the norm.

6. *True.*

7. *True.*

8. *False.* Symbolic interactionists stress that we are not destined by our group memberships to think and act as our groups dictate; we are not prisoners of our socialization. Rather, we help produce our own orientations to life.

9. *True.*

10. *True.*

11. *True.*

12. *True.*

13. *False.* According to strain theory, everyone does not have an equal chance to get ahead in society because of structural factors in the society (e.g., racism, sexism, and social class) that may deny them access to the approved ways of achieving cultural goals. (212)

14. *True.*

15. *True.*

16. *False.* White-collar crime often is more costly than street crime. Examples include the plundering of the U.S. savings and loan industry and other "crimes in the suites."

17. *False.* Conflict theorists believe that the criminal justice system functions for the well-being of the capitalist class.

18. *True.*

19. *True.*

20. *False.* Official statistics are not always accurate counts of the crimes committed in our society. Both conflict theorists and symbolic interactionists believe that these statistics have bias built into them because of police discretion in arresting people, as well as many other factors.

ANSWERS TO THE FILL-IN-THE-BLANK QUESTIONS
1. deviance
2. negative
3. individual
4. outside
5. families
6. inner
7. neutralization
8. unity
9. accepts
10. anomie
11. white-collar
12. female
13. "Three Strikes and You're Out"
14. recidivism
15. problem

ANSWERS TO MATCH THESE SOCIAL SCIENTISTS WITH THEIR CONTRIBUTIONS
1. d Edwin Sutherland: *white collar crime*
2. a Robert Merton: *strain theory*
3. g Erving Goffman: *importance of stigma*
4. i Thomas Szasz: *myth of mental illness*
5. e Howard Becker: *definition of deviance*
6. f William Chambliss: *effects of labeling*
7. h Gresham Sykes and David Matza: *techniques of neutralization*
8. j Travis Hirschi: *inner controls*
9. c Harold Garfinkel: *degradation ceremonies*
10. b Mark Watson: *embracing the deviant label*

GUIDELINES FOR ANSWERING THE ESSAY QUESTIONS

1. *Discuss how the different sociological perspectives could be combined to provide a more complete picture of deviance.*

You would begin by identifying the strengths of each perspective. Symbolic interactionism focuses on group membership and interaction within and between groups, functionalism focuses on how deviance is a part of the social order, and conflict theory focuses on how social inequality affects definitions of and reactions to acts of deviance. An example of combining perspectives is reflected in the work of William Chambliss on the Saints and the Roughnecks; he looked at patterns of inequality and different interaction styles to explain the different treatment the two groups received. Another example would be Cloward and Ohlin's work on illegitimate opportunity structures; they added the concept of social class inequality to the notion of the strain between institutionalized means and cultural goals to explain patterns of lower class deviance.

2. *Explain how forms of deviance such as street gangs can be both functional and dysfunctional at the same time.*

You could begin your discussion by making reference to Durkheim's views on the functionality of deviance. In particular, the presence of street gangs may serve to affirm normative boundaries and to promote social unity, both within society and within the neighborhoods where gangs operate. Within this context, think about the dominant views we have of gang members and gang activity.

You would also want to make reference to Jankowski's research. Jankowski studied street gangs and discovered that gangs functioned within low-income neighborhoods as sources of employment (often the *only* source), recreation, and protection. In a few cases the gangs were involved in legitimate activities such as running small groceries and renovating and renting abandoned apartment buildings. All of these demonstrate the functional nature of gangs. At the same time, gangs generate most of their income through illegal activities, a dysfunctional aspect. Another dysfunctional aspect is the violence that accompanies gangs; violence that is not confined to gangs but often spills over into the neighborhood as a whole.

3. *Using any one of the different sociological perspectives, develop an explanation for why white-collar crime is generally treated as less serious crime in our society.*

First, you want to define what white-collar crime is. According to Edwin Sutherland, it is crime that people of respectable and high social status commit in the course of their occupations. You would then want to use the different perspectives to discuss why it is viewed as less serious than street crimes as a threat to our society. You could refer to labeling theory, especially the work of Sykes and Matza regarding techniques of neutralization. Given the nature of work and corporate life today, it is possible that not only do those responsible for the crimes not see themselves as deviant, but society as a whole does not see corporate employees as deviant. In addition, much of the crime that is committed is largely invisible and indirect — we may not even be aware that we have been victimized.

You could also write about the functionalist explanation for this type of crime. Specifically, you could begin with Merton's strain theory and then make reference to Cloward and Ohlin's discussion of illegitimate opportunity structures.

Perhaps it is easiest to apply conflict theory in trying to answer this question. White-collar crime is typically crime committed by those in power. As the conflict theorists point out, the law is an instrument of oppression. It does not operate impartially. It directs its energies against the violations of the law by the working class.

4. *Discuss the "get tough" policy that the United States has followed and how successful that has been.*

The United States has been following a get tough policy for about the last 20 years. One such example is the "three strikes and you're out" laws. This law gives a mandatory sentence, sometimes life imprisonment, for conviction of a third felony. While well intended, these laws have had unintended consequences. For example, a man was sentenced to 25 years for stealing a pizza. A man who stole nine videotapes from Kmart was sentenced to 50 years in prison without parole. The politicians in their haste to enact these laws did not limit the punishment to violent crimes. Also, they did not consider that some minor crimes are felonies. However, as a result of this as well as a few other changes, there has been a decline in crime. Judges have put more people in prison and reduced early releases of prisoners. Other sociologists disagree that these were the main reasons for the decrease in crime. Some believe that because of higher employment and a drop in drug use, the crime rate decreased.

5. *Obesity could be viewed as deviance because it is a condition that violates our cultural norms, regarding appearance. Develop an explanation for how this type of deviance is increasingly subject to medicalization.*

Your textbook has a discussion of how certain types of deviance have been medicalized —redefined so that they are viewed as external symptoms of internal disorders. Subsequently, they become medical matters and subject to the care of physicians. For a long time, overweight people were considered weak and unable to control their eating; it was a commonly held view that they were responsible for their condition. The standard treatment was for them to limit the intake of calories by going on a diet. In the last several years, a different view of obesity has begun to emerge. No longer is the individual viewed as responsible for his or her deviant behavior. Their excess weight (the external symptom) is due to some medical problem (internal disorder). Today it is increasingly common for obese people to be treated with medications or medical procedures.

CHAPTER 9

ANSWERS FOR MULTIPLE CHOICE QUESTIONS

1. **b** The division of large numbers of people into layers according to their relative power, property, and prestige is social stratification.

2. **b** Slavery is a form of social stratification in which some people own other people.

3. **d** "All of the above" is correct. Slavery in the United States started as indentured service. When enough indentured servants could not be recruited, individuals were imported from Africa and turned into slaves. An ideology of racism justified these actions by asserting that the slaves were inferior, and perhaps not even fully human. Slavery became inheritable because if one's parents were slaves, the child also was considered to be a slave.

4. **c** India is the best example of a caste system.

5. **b** Caste systems practice endogamy, marriage within the group, and prohibit intermarriage.

6. **d** "All of the above" is correct. The South African system of social stratification known as apartheid was a caste system that contained four different racial categories: Europeans (whites), Africans (blacks), Coloureds (mixed races), and Asians. It was enforced by law and was finally dismantled following decades of international pressure and protest.

7. **c** Under the estate system that existed in Europe during the Middle Ages, the clergy made up the *second estate.*

8. **a** Class systems are characterized by social mobility, either upward or downward.

9. **b** It is true that about 60 percent of the world's illiterate are females. Of the other statements, in every society women's earnings are lower than men's, gender is still an important basis for stratifying people, and gender cuts across all systems of stratification.

10. **b** Marx concluded that social class depends on the means of production.

11. **a** According to Max Weber, social class is determined by one's property, prestige, and power.

12. **d** According to the functionalist view, social stratification is not dysfunctional but an inevitable feature of social organization.

13. **d** Melvin Tumin's criticisms included the measurement problems (a), the reality that family background matters (b), and the dysfunctional aspects of stratification (c). The one statement that does not reflect his criticisms is "d." In fact, what Tumin noted was that functionalists place too great an emphasis on income and ignore the fact that some people are motivated to take jobs for reasons of status or power.

14. **a** A form of social stratification in which all positions are awarded on the basis of merit is called a meritocratic system.

15. **d** Gaetano Mosca argued that every society would be stratified by power.

16. **b** According to contemporary conflict theorists, the basis of social stratification is conflict over limited resources.

17. **a** According to Gerhard Lenski, the key to reconciling the different explanations for social stratification is whether a group has surpluses. The functionalists are correct when it comes to groups that do not accumulate any surplus, but once there is a surplus, groups compete with one another over who will control the extra; in these situations, conflict theory is more appropriate.

18. **d** "All of the above" is correct. The key to maintaining national stratification is having a strong police force and military to demand compliance, control of social institutions, and control of information.

19. **c** The British perpetuate their class system from one generation to the next by education.

20. **c** The system of stratification in the former Soviet Union was based on membership in the Communist Party; within the party there was also stratification, with most members at the bottom, some bureaucrats in the middle, and a small elite at the top.

21. **b** The former Soviet Union and its satellites in Eastern Europe would be placed among the Industrializing Nations of the world.

22. **a** It's true that most people live on less than $1000/year.
23. **c** The majority of the world's population lives in the Least Industrialized Nations; nearly 68 percent of the world's population lives in these nations, with the remaining 32 percent split evenly between the Most Industrialized and the Industrializing Nations.
24. **b** The colonialism of the United States usually involved planting corporate flags, thereby giving U.S. corporations ready access to the markets and raw materials of these colonies.
25. **d** According to Wallerstein these groups of interconnected nations exist: core nations that are rich and powerful; nations on the semiperiphery that have become highly dependent on trade with core nations; nations on the periphery that sell cash crops to the core nations; and the external area, including most of Africa and Asia, that has been left out of the development of capitalism and had few, if any, economic connections with the core nations.
26. **c** John Kenneth Galbraith used the culture of poverty theory to analyze global stratification.
27. **d** The reason sociologists generally reject the culture of poverty theory in trying to explain global stratification is because it places the blame for poverty on the poor nations themselves, rather than focusing on the international arrangements that benefit some at the expense of others.
28. **b** Neocolonialism refers to the economic policies of the Most Industrialized Nations that are designed to control the markets of the Least Industrialized Nations; they are able to set the prices they will charge for their manufactured goods and control the international markets where they purchase raw materials from the Least Industrialized Nations.
29. **d** "All of the above" is the correct answer. The reasons that the Least Industrialized Nations remain so poor is because their markets are controlled by the Most Industrialized Nations, who set prices and sell them goods on credit. The debt that they incur means that they will remain internal debtors, since their money must go to paying off the loans rather than developing their own infrastructure.
30. **b** With cheap telecommunications and the outsourcing of labor, workers in India and China are able to compete with their Western counterparts.

ANSWERS FOR TRUE-FALSE QUESTIONS

1. *False.* Your text notes that social stratification does not simply refer to individuals but rather to a way of ranking large groups of people into a hierarchy that shows their relative privileges.
2. *False.* Historically, slavery was based on defeat in battle, a criminal act, or a debt, but not some supposedly inherently inferior status such as race.
3. *True.*
4. *True.*
5. *True.*
6. *True.*
7. *True.*
8. *True.*
9. *True.*
10. *False.* Functionalists believe that society offers greater rewards for its more responsible, demanding, and accountable positions because society works better if its most qualified people hold its most important positions. From this standpoint, unique abilities would not be more important than the type of position held by the individual.
11. *False.* Some conflict theorists focus on conflicts that occur within the same social class.
12. *True.*
13. *False.* Gerhard Lenski felt that the functional view of stratification was most appropriate when studying societies that did not accumulate wealth.
14. *True.*
15. *False.* In maintaining stratification, elites find that technology, especially monitoring devices, is useful.
16. *True.*

17. *False.* Beginning more than 200 years ago, most industrialized nations pursued policies of colonialism in order to expand their economic markets and gain access to cheap raw materials; as a result of this strategy, many acquired colonies in the Middle East, Africa, Asia, and Central/South America.

18. *True.*

19. *False.* Most sociologists find imperialism, world systems and dependency theory preferable to an explanation based on the culture of poverty.

20. *True.*

ANSWERS TO THE FILL-IN-THE-BLANK QUESTIONS

1. Slavery
2. indentured
3. caste
4. husbands
5. gender
6. false consciousness
7. Most Industrialized Nation
8. ideology
9. Education
10. Colonialism
11. core
12. maquiladoras
13. culture
14. debt
15. elite

ANSWERS TO MATCH THESE SOCIAL SCIENTISTS WITH THEIR CONTRIBUTIONS

1. d   W.E. Du Bois: *false consciousness*
2. e   Kingsley Davis and Wilbert Moore: *the functionalist view on stratification*
3. f   Gaetano Mosca: *forerunner of the conflict view on stratification*
4. j   Immanuel Wallerstein: *world system theory*
5. i   Michael Harrington: *neocolonialism*
6. c   John Kenneth Galbraith: *stressed the culture of poverty*
7. h   Martha Huggins: *studied poverty in Brazil*
8. b   Melvin Tumin: *criticism of the functionalist view on stratification*
9. g   Gerhard Lenski: *synthesis of functionalist and conflict views*
10. a   Gerda Lerner: *women were the first to be enslaved by war*

GUIDELINES FOR ANSWERING THE ESSAY QUESTIONS

1. *Compare and contrast Marx's theory of stratification with Weber's theory. Discuss why Weber's is more widely accepted by sociologists.*

Your first task is to summarize these two perspectives, pointing out the similarities and the differences between the two. Then you would want to consider the advantages offered by Weber's theory. You could mention that Weber's concept of property (or wealth) was broadened to include *control* over decision-making and ownership; that prestige and power can both be based on factors other than wealth; and that the three dimensions are interrelated but can, and do, operate independently. Your conclusion should be that Weber's theory offers sociologists a more complete framework for understanding and analyzing systems of stratification.

2. *Using the different theories presented in this chapter, answer the question, "Why is stratification universal?"*

There are two competing views on why stratification is universal. You would begin by discussing the Davis and Moore thesis that stratification is functional for society. You would want to elaborate on their argument, pointing out that society has certain important positions that need to be filled by the most qualified people; to motivate the most talented to fill these positions, society offers them greater rewards. You could provide some examples — college professors, military generals, doctors.

The alternative explanation is offered by the conflict theorists. Begin by noting that groups compete for control over society's resources. The "winners" use their position to keep other groups weak, thereby maintaining their own position. For conflict theorists, this arrangement is inevitable, once society begins to produce a surplus. You could also bring in Mosa's argument about the need for leadership that comes with social organization and how leadership creates inequalities.

Your concluding paragraph could focus on Lenski and his efforts to reconcile these two views. Lenski focused on the level of social development and found that functionalism made sense in societies without any surplus resources, but once a surplus emerges, then conflict theory is better at explaining why stratification emerges and persists.

3. *Consider why ideology is a more effective way of maintaining stratification than brute force.*

You should begin by considering why it is even necessary to "maintain stratification." On the surface, the idea that some people get more than other people should produce widespread instability — after all, isn't it natural for those without to want to do whatever they can to take some away from those with? However, this doesn't often happen because the elites have a number of methods for maintaining stratification, ranging from ideology to force. Without question, the most effective is ideology. Once a system of beliefs develops and people accept the idea in their minds that a particular system of stratification is right or just, then they will go along with the status quo.

4. *Compare and contrast the three theories of global stratification.*

You can start out by identifying the three theories of global stratification. They are colonialism, world system theory, and the culture of poverty. The theory of colonialism stresses that the countries that industrialized got a jump start on the rest of the world. These countries were able to invade weaker countries and make them into colonies. These countries were then able to exploit the people and resources in the weaker countries thereby establishing dominance. Immanuel Wallerstein proposed another theory known as world system theory. His theory was also based on industrialization that led to four groups of nations. The core group was the group that industrialized first and they became rich and powerful. Other nations industrialized less or were left out of the development of capitalism altogether. Unlike the other two explanations, the claim of the third theory was that the cultures of the Least Industrialized Nations is what held them back. Kenneth Galbraith argued that some countries have a culture of poverty or that their religion encourages them to accept their situation. Most sociologists prefer the first two theories because the third explanation puts the blame on the victim.

CHAPTER 10

ANSWERS FOR MULTIPLE CHOICE QUESTIONS

1. **c** According to your text, most sociologists agree with Max Weber that social class is best defined by employing three dimensions of social class.

2. **c** In fact, 68 percent of the wealth in the United States is owned by only 10 percent of the nation's families; the richest 1 percent owns more that the bottom 90 percent combined.

3. **c** According to economist Paul Samuelson, if an income pyramid were made out of a child's blocks, most U.S. residents would be about 8 ft off of the ground.

4. **d** While it is true that the income distribution has not changed dramatically over the past 50 years, it is also true that the changes that have occurred have resulted in an increase in the percentage of income going to the top 20 percent of U.S. households and a decrease in the percentage going to the bottom 20 percent of households.

5. **c** Daniel Hellinger and Dennis Judd use the term *democratic façade* to describe the average citizen's belief that he/she exercises power when voting for Congressional representatives or the U.S. president.

6. **b** Mills used the term *power elite* to refer to those at the top of society who makes the important decisions.

7. **c** All of the following are true regarding jobs that have the most prestige: they pay more, require more education, and offer greater autonomy. They do not necessarily require special talent or skills.

8. **c** Gold discovered that the tenants did not like the fact that the janitors, as relatively low status workers, were earning more than themselves, so they reacted by being "snooty" to them.

9. **d** Wright responded to the criticism that Marx's categories were so broad that they did not accurately reflect the realities of people's lives by creating the concept of contradictory class location, which recognizes that some people can be members of more than one class simultaneously.

10. **b** Members of the upper-middle-class are the ones who owe their position to the achievement of a college and/or postgraduate degree.

11. **b** All of the following are characteristics of the working class: most are employed in relatively unskilled blue-collar and white-collar jobs; most hope to get ahead by achieving seniority on the job; and about thirty percent of the population belong to this class. However, most have *not* attended college for one or two years.

12. **d** All of the statements describe the situation of homeless people in our society today.

13. **c** According to your text, the typical mechanic in a Ford dealership would be in the working class.

14. **d** Differential risks of dying because the U.S. has a two-tiered system of medical care, social class differences in lifestyles, and unequal access to medical care all help explain the social class differences in death rates.

15. **b** It is actually the poor who experience higher levels of stress because they live with less job security and lower incomes; the rich have the resources to cope with life's challenges.

16. **c** According to Melvin Kohn lower-class parents are concerned that their children be conformists; they want them to obey conventional norms and authority figures while middle class parents encourage their children to be creative and independent.

17. **a** Members of the capitalist class tend to bypass public schools entirely, in favor of exclusive private schools.

18. **d** People in the working class are more likely to be more conservative on social issues and more liberal on economic issues.

19. **c** White-collar crimes committed by the more privileged classes are more likely to be dealt with outside the criminal justice system.

20. **c** Members of the lower classes are more likely to be robbed, burglarized, or murdered.

21. **d** The classes that benefit from technology are the capitalist and upper middle classes. For capitalists, technology enables them to integrate production globally and to increase profits. The

upper middle class benefits because they take a leading role in managing this new global economy; they also use the technology to advance in their chosen professions.

22. **d** A homeless person whose father was a physician has experienced downward mobility.

23. **c** Higgenbotham and Weber studied women professionals from working class backgrounds and found parental encouragement for postponing marriage and getting an education.

24. c He found that people actually experienced pain when moving up the social class ladder because they were caught between two worlds.

25. **d** The cost of upward mobility is being caught in two worlds and for African Americans especially troubling is the sense of leaving ones racial-ethnic group.

26. **c** The official measure of poverty, calculated to include those whose incomes equal less than three times a low-cost food budget, is the poverty line.

27. **c** In the United States, 11 percent of the elderly population live in poverty, compared to 13 percent for the total population.

28. **b** In trying to explain poverty, sociologists are most likely to stress features of the social structure that contribute to poverty rather than any individual characteristics.

29. **a** The reason most poor people do not defer gratification, giving up in the present for the sake of the future, is because they need whatever limited resources they have in order to simply survive.

30. **d** "All of the above" is correct. The Horatio Alger myth is beneficial to society, according to the functionalists, because it shifts the blame for failure away from the social system and onto the shoulders of the individual, thereby reducing pressures on the system. It also motivates people to try harder to succeed because "anything is possible."

ANSWERS FOR TRUE-FALSE QUESTIONS

1. *False.* While there is no one definition of social class on which all sociologists agree, most sociologists agree with Max Weber's conceptualization of social class as encompassing wealth, power and prestige.

2. *False.* Wealth and income are not the same; wealth includes both property and income.

3. *True.*

4. *True.*

5. *False.* Occupational prestige rankings are remarkably stable across countries and over time.

6. *True.*

7. *True.*

8. *True.*

9. *True.*

10. *True.*

11. *False.* The working poor, not the working class are functionally illiterate..

12. *True.*

13. *True.*

14. *True.*

15. *True.*

16. *True.*

17. *True.*

18. *False.* While it is true that there are more poor whites than there are poor minorities, the *rate* of poverty is much lower among the white population than minority populations. Only 11 percent of whites live below the poverty line, compared to 27 percent of Latinos and African Americans.

19. *False.* Research indicates that 59 percent of families studied lived in poverty for one year or less. Only 12 percent lived in poverty for five years or more.

20. *True.*

ANSWERS TO THE FILL-IN-THE-BLANK QUESTIONS

1. wealth
2. 10
3. power elite
4. Contradictory
5. 1
6. education
7. underclass
8. dying
9. divorce
10. economic, social
11. intergenerational mobility
12. poverty line
13. South
14. Feminization
15. reserve labor force

ANSWERS TO MATCH THESE SOCIAL SCIENTISTS WITH THEIR CONTRIBUTIONS

1. d Gerhard Lenski: *status inconsistency*
2. i Hellinger and Judd: *democratic facade*
3. e Erik Wright: *updated Marx's model*
4. j Gilbert & Kahl: *updated Weber's model*
5. f Daniel Moynihan: *childhood poverty and the breakdown of the family*
6. c Sennett & Cobb: *hidden costs of mobility*
7. b Elliot Liebow: *difficulty for street corner men to defer gratification*
8. h Higgenbotham & Weber: *women's patterns of social mobility*
9. g Steph Lawler: *upward mobility and British women*
10. a Ray Gold: *tenant reactions to janitors' higher status*

GUIDELINES FOR ANSWERING THE ESSAY QUESTIONS

1. *Identify the three dimensions of social class and discuss some of the consequences of social class.*

You could begin your essay by discussing how sociologists define wealth and income, power, and privilege. You might also talk about how each is unevenly distributed within American society. Finally, you should talk about the consequences of this uneven distribution in terms of physical and mental health, family life, education, religion, politics, crime and the criminal justice system, and access to new technology.

2. *Discuss why you think women have been largely ignored in studies of mobility.*

You would want to point out that most studies of mobility have focused on occupational mobility. Until quite recently, most women did not have continuous occupational careers because of the nature of traditional gender roles. They derived their status from their fathers and their husbands. Therefore, in studies of intergenerational mobility, they were excluded because they did not have work histories that spanned their lifetime. As women's roles have changed, so has researchers' awareness of them as research subjects. Also, because of structural changes in the economy, employment opportunities for women have opened up; this reflects structural mobility.

3. *Describe which groups are at greatest risk of poverty and then suggest ways in which poverty can be reduced by targeting these populations.*

You would want to begin by identifying those groups that are at greater risk — the rural poor, minorities, the undereducated, female heads of household, and children. You would then discuss specific ideas you have for overcoming some of the conditions that place these groups at greater risk; some possible programs would be improvements in education, including more funding for college and technical training, increases in minimum wage, increased number of jobs that pay a living wage, and more aggressive enforcement of anti-discrimination laws.

4. *Explore why individual explanation of poverty are easier for the average American to accept than structural explanations.*

When most Americans see or hear about poor people, their immediate response is that they are lazy and/or stupid. In trying to explain this response, you could refer back to the earlier discussion about American values, particularly the values of individualism and hard work. Given these values, it is understandable why people would draw this conclusion. Likewise, because we believe in the existence of a meritocracy, most people assume that they deserve the place they have earned in society. Therefore, if someone is poor, it must be because they don't deserve anything better.

You could also discuss the idea of the Horatio Alger myth. We grow up believing if we only work hard (a core value), we will be rewarded with success. Obviously, those who don't success haven't tried hard enough. Finally, you would want to point out that it is much easier to connect individual decisions to outcomes than it is to see broader social forces that are at work.

5. *Discuss the Horatio Alger myth and whether or not it is functional for society.*

The Horatio Alger myth was formed in the late 1800's. He was an author whose stories told of fictional boy heroes going from rags-to-riches. Many people still hold this believe today that if they really try hard enough, they can get ahead. It is a statistical impossibility to believe that most Americans, including minorities and the poor with have an average or better-than-average chance of getting ahead. You could discuss that functionalist would certainly say that this believe system is functional for society. It encourages people to compete for higher positions. It also places blame on the individual because if someone doesn't make it, it's their fault and they didn't try hard enough. It also helps to stabilize society since there is individual rather than societal blame. Therefore, since the social arrangements and structure within society are sufficient, it reduces pressure to change the system.

CHAPTER 11

ANSWERS FOR MULTIPLE CHOICE QUESTIONS

1. **a** Gender stratification cuts across all aspects of social life and all social classes and it refers to men's and women's unequal access to power, prestige, and property on the basis of their sex. It is *incorrect* to think that it is not a structured feature of society.

2. **b** The term "sex" refers to the biological characteristics that distinguish females and males.

3. **a** The *incorrect* statement is, "There is not a lot of variation in gender roles around the world." In fact, expectations associated with gender vary so greatly that some sociologists suggest we replace the terms *masculinity* and *femininity* with *masculinities* and *femininities*.

4. **c** All of the above" is correct. Patriarchy is a society in which men dominate women, it has existed throughout history, and it is universal.

5. **c** According to sociologists, if biology were the principal factor in human behavior, around the world we would find women to be one sort of person and men another.

6. **c** The study of Vietnam Veterans has led sociologists to slowly consider biological factors.

7. **c** Women represent the largest minority group in the U.S.

8. **a** The major theory of the origin of patriarchy points to the social consequences of human reproduction. In earlier times, life was short and many children needed to be born in order for the group to survive. Consequently, women were pregnant or nursing young children for much of their adult lives. As a result of these biologically driven activities, women were limited in terms of alternatives and assumed tasks associated with the home and child care and men took up tasks that required more strength or longer absences from home.

9. **a** What Murdock found was that there was nothing about biology that required men and women to be assigned different work; rather it was social attitudes.

10. **c** In regard to the prestige of work, greater prestige is given to male activities.

11. **b** The *incorrect* statement is the one that claims the U.S. leads the world in the number of women who hold public office. In fact, it is Norway, where 40 percent of the legislators are women; U.S. percentage is 10, which is typical for most nations.

12. **d** All of the answers are true about female circumcision.

13. **a** Women received the right to vote in 1920.

14. **d** All of the answers are correct. A "second wave" of protest and struggle against gender inequalities began in the 1960s when women began to compare their working conditions with those of men; it had as its goals everything from changing work roles to changing policies on violence against women.

15. **c** It is not yet clear if a "third wave" is emerging or not, but feminists point out that the values that currently underlie work and other social institutions — power, competition, emotional invulnerability, toughness, autonomy, and independence — represent "male" qualities. They need to be supplemented, if not replaced, with "female" values — cooperation, openness about vulnerability, gentleness, connection, and interdependence.

16. **b** Women were more likely to do because physicians did not take the chest pains of their female patients as seriously and waited longer to perform the surgery.

17. **c** Gender inequality in education is perpetuated by the use of sex to sort students into different academic disciplines.

18. **c** Researchers who have studied conversation patterns between men and women conclude that even in everyday conversation, the talk between a man and a woman reflects social inequality.

19. **c** The pay gap between men and women is found at all educational levels.

20. **c** The glass ceiling refers to the invisible barrier that keeps women from reaching the executive suite. Men who go into fields that are traditionally associated with women often encounter a glass escalator (they advance quickly) rather than a glass ceiling. (313)

21. **b** Of the four statements, the one that says, "Women do not seek out opportunities for advancement and do not spend enough time networking with powerful executives" is the only one that is *not* a reason why more women are not found in core corporate positions; all the rest represent valid reasons as to why women are underrepresented in top corporate offices.

22. **d** "All of the above" is the correct answer. The glass escalator is a term used by Christine Williams in her research on men employed in traditionally female occupations. It describes a situation in which men move up faster and is driven by the stereotype that because someone is a male, he is more capable.

23. **a** Conflict theorists believe that dividing workers by gender is another way that they capitalists can control them.

24. **d** Sexual harassment, rooted in the structure of the work place rather than individual relationships, involves a person in authority using the position to force unwanted sex on subordinates. Initially, it was seen as a women's issue, but today it is no longer exclusively a female problem. The only statement that is *incorrect* is that "male victims of sexual harassment receive more sympathy than female victims."

25. **d** Date rape is not an isolated event; most go unreported; and it is difficult to prosecute because of the pre-existing relationship.

26. **c** Women who are convicted of killing another person are more likely than men to be given probation for the murder.

27. **a** Rather than higher testosterone levels in males, feminists would point to the association of strength and virility with violence, males' frustration at their loss of power and status, and cultural traditions that are patriarchal as sources for gender violence.

28. **c** Women are reluctant to get involved in politics because the demands of political life are in conflict with the demands of their roles as wives and mothers.

29. **d** "All of the above" is correct.

30. **c** Increased female participation in decision-making processes of social institutions is most likely going to result in breaking down the stereotypes that lock both males and females into traditional gender activities.

ANSWERS FOR TRUE-FALSE QUESTIONS

1. *False.* Sex refers to biological characteristics that distinguish females and males. Gender refers to social characteristics that a society considers proper for its males and females.
2. *True.*
3. *False.* Patriarchy, or male dominance, appears to be universal.
4. *False.* Researchers have found a universal pattern of according male activities higher prestige than female activities.
5. *False.*
6. *False.* Female circumcision is still quite common in parts of Africa and Southeast Asia.
7. *True.*
8. *False.* In the second wave of the U.S. women's movement, both the liberal and the conservative factions of the movement had a radical wing.
9. *True.*
10. *False.* While women have made gains in terms of the proportion of degrees earned, and exceed men in earning Bachelor of Arts degrees, they still lag behind in postgraduate and professional degrees.
11. *True.*
12. *True.*
13. *False.* Men are more likely to interrupt a conversation and to control changes in topics than are women.
14. *True.*
15. *True.*

16. *False.* The "glass escalator" refers to the opportunities that men have to advance quickly in traditional female occupations.
17. *True.*
18. *False.* In the U.S., males kill at a rate several times that of females.
19. *True.*
20. *False.* There are several other factors that also contribute to women not holding public office: they are underrepresented in law and business, traditional recruiting grounds for public office; the demands of running for and holding public office often conflict with a woman's other role responsibilities; and they do not see themselves as a class in need of special representation.

ANSWERS TO THE FILL-IN-THE-BLANK QUESTIONS

1. master
2. group
3. Matriarchy
4. sex typed
5. Kuwait and United Arab Emirates
6. Feminism
7. conservative
8. men
9. masculinity
10. 50
11. 65
12. ceiling
13. escalator
14. power
15. Thirty-three

ANSWERS TO MATCH THESE SOCIAL SCIENTISTS WITH THEIR CONTRIBUTIONS

1.   j   Janet Chafetz: *studied the second wave of feminism in the 1960s*
2.   g   Alice Rossi: *women are better prepared biologically for "mothering" than are men*
3.   e   Giele and Lorber: *In the future, men and women will be more expressive of needs and emotions*
4.   b   Christine Williams: *men in nontraditional occupations often experience a glass escalator*
5.   h   Gerda Lerner: *patriarchy may have had different origins around the globe*
6.   a   Barbara Grosz: *experienced that female professors were taken less seriously than their male counterparts*
7.   i   Samuel Stouffer: *noted the devaluation of things associated with women among soldiers*
8.   c   Marvin Harris: *male dominance grew out of the greater strength that men had*
9.   f   Karen Horsfeld: *companies divide their workers along gender lines*
10. d   Douglas Foley: *study supports the view that things feminine are generally devalued*

GUIDELINES FOR ANSWERING THE ESSAY QUESTIONS

1.   *Summarize the sociobiology argument concerning behavioral differences between men and women. Explain which position most closely reflects your own: biological, sociological, or sociobiological.*

You would want to begin by stating how sociologists and biologists each explain the basis for differences in gendered behavior and then discuss how sociobiology tries to bridge the gap between these two disciplines' views. In discussing sociobiology you could refer to Alice Rossi's suggestion concerning the biological basis for mothering and the connection between biological predispositions and cultural norms. As further evidence of the relationship between biology and social forces, you could discuss the two studies cited in the text: the case of the young boy whose sex was changed and the study of Vietnam veterans. Your final task would be to state which view you think is most consistent with what you have learned about gender inequality and explain why.

2. *Compare and contrast the two waves of the feminist movement in this country by identifying the forces that contributed to both waves.*

You could begin by noting that both waves of the feminist movement were committed to ending gender stratification and both met with strong opposition from both males and females. In both cases, there were two different branches that emerged — a liberal and a conservative branch — and within these branches, there were radical wings. The major difference between the two had to do with goals. The first wave was characterized by rather narrow goals. The movement focused on winning the vote for women, while the second wave was broader and wanted to address issues ranging from changing work roles to changing policies on violence against women.

3. *Discuss gender tracking and how that perpetuates inequality in education and the workforce*

George Murdock found that in 324 societies around the world, activities are sex-typed. That is, every society associates certain activities with one sex or the other. You can discuss how this plays out both in the education system and in the workforce. It is important to note that this also plays out globally not just nationally. On a global level, two-thirds of the women in the world cannot read. In every nation, women average less pay than men. In the U.S., until 1832 women were not allowed to attend college with men. Gender tracking occurs in which degrees tend to follow gender, which reinforces male-female distinctions. Men earn degrees in "masculine" fields while women earn degrees in "feminine" fields. This continues in graduate school where women are less likely to complete doctorates. The affect of gender tracking then plays out in the work force where the average male college graduate can expect to earn more over the course of his lifetime as compared to the average female college graduate. You could also continue this discussion describing the research that has been done to discover why this difference persists.

4. *Discuss why women are so often the victims of violence.*

That women are often victims of violence is not only true in the United States, but globally. As your text points out, this has become a global human rights issue. Historically, women have been victims of foot binding (China), witch burning (Europe and the United States), and *suttee* (in India). Women around the globe continue to face the risk of rape, wife beating, female infanticide, and forced prostitution. In some areas of the world, young women are still being subjected to female genital mutilation.

In this country, women face the risk of becoming victims of rape, especially date rape, and of violence in the home. In trying to understand why this happens, you could use either symbolic interactionism or conflict theory. For symbolic interactionists, part of the explanation lies in the way in which our culture defines male and female roles. Men are expected to be strong and virile, while women are expected to be weak and submissive. Strength and virility are associated with violence, and both boys and girls learn this message as they grow up and are socialized into their respective gender roles.

For conflict theorists, the key lies in the changing nature of men's and women's roles in society. For the past century, women have slowly gained power and status in society. Because these are scarce and finite resources, women's gains translate into men's losses. For some men, the way to reassert their declining power and status is by becoming violent against women.

5. *As most of the legal barriers to women's full participation in society have been eliminated, it is commonly assumed that women have gained equality. Given what you have learned in this chapter, consider whether this is the case.*

Given the evidence that is presented throughout the chapter, it would be difficult to argue that women have gained equality. While they have made gains, as a group, they continue to be subordinate to men. In answering this question, you could talk about continuing gender inequality they face in education, both as students and teachers. There is still the problem of gender inequality in everyday life, including the devaluation of things feminine and the patterns of conversations.

Most significantly, there is the experience of women employed outside the home. You would want to discuss the continuing gap in pay that exists across all occupations and at all educational levels. There are the issues of the glass ceiling and the glass escalator, as well as the problem of sexual harassment.

Finally, you could explore the area of politics. While women have made gains, they are still far from equal in terms of their representation in public office. You could talk about the factors that contribute to this pattern and the hopeful signs that change is happening.

CHAPTER 12

<u>ANSWERS FOR MULTIPLE CHOICE QUESTIONS</u>
1.   **b**   Race is inherited physical characteristics that distinguish one group from another.
2.   **b**   People often confuse race and ethnicity because of the cultural differences people see and the way they define race.
3.   **a**   A minority group is discriminated against because of physical or cultural differences.
4.   **a**   The dominant group in a society almost always considers its position to be due to its own innate superiority.
5.   **d**   A group's sense of ethnic identity is affected by the amount of power the group has, the size of the group, and the degree to which the group's physical appearance differs from the mainstream. Those groups with a heightened sense of ethnic identity generally have little power, are small in size, and stand out because of physical differences.
6.   **c**   Tracing family lines would be an example of ethnic work.
7.   **a**   A society in which groups quietly blend into a sort of ethnic stew is the best description of a melting pot. Many experts thought the United States would become a melting pot, but this notion is challenged by the fact that more people have a renewed interest in ethnic background.
8.   **c**   Prejudice and discrimination appear to characterize every society.
9.   **d**   "All of the above" is correct. Prejudice is an attitude; it may be positive or negative, and it often is the basis for discrimination.
10. **b**   From his research on racist groups, Raphael Ezekiel concluded that the leaders of these groups take advantage of the masses' anxieties concerning economic insecurity and of their tendency to see the "Establishment" as the cause of economic problems. He discovered that they are likely to see that races represent fundamental categories, with race representing the essence of the person.
11. **d**   Discrimination that is woven into the fabric of society is refers to as institutional discrimination.
12. **a**   The negative treatment of one person by another on the basis of that person's characteristics is referred to as individual discrimination.
13. **d**   The research demonstrates that discrimination is built into the country's financial institutions; even when the credit histories were identical, African Americans and Latinos were 60 percent more likely to be rejected than whites.
14. **b**   For John Dollard, a psychologist, the source for prejudice was frustration. People who cannot strike out at the real source of their frustration look for someone on whom to blame their troubles.
15. **c**   The functionalists see prejudice as functional because it helps create solidarity within the group by fostering antagonisms directed against other groups; at the same time it can be dysfunctional because it has a negative impact on social relationships.
16. **d**   "All of the above" is correct. According to conflict theorists, prejudice benefits capitalists by splitting workers along racial or ethnic lines; contributes to the exploitation of workers, thus producing a split-labor market; and is a factor in keeping workers from demanding higher wages and better working conditions.
17. **a**   Symbolic interactionists stresses how labels create selective perception and self-fulfilling prophecies.
18. **d**   "All of the above" is correct. Genocide occurred when Hitler attempted to destroy all Jews, it is the systematic annihilation of a race or ethnic group, and it often requires the cooperation of ordinary citizens.
19. **b**   When a minority is expelled from a country or from a particular area of a country, the process is called direct population transfer.
20. **c**   A society's policy of exploiting a minority group, using social institutions to deny the minority access to the society's full benefits, is referred to as internal colonialism.
21. **d**   Segregation is the separation of racial or ethnic groups, thereby allowing the dominant group to maintain social distance from the minority and yet continue to exploit them economically.

22. **b** The process of being absorbed into the mainstream culture is assimilation.

23. **d** All of the above are true when trying to categorize into racial-ethnic groups.

24. **a** WASPs (which stands for White Anglo-Saxon Protestants whose ancestors came from England) were highly ethnocentric and viewed other immigrants as inferior. Because they were the ones who settled the colonies, they were able to take power and determine the national agenda, controlling the destiny of the nation. As white Europeans from other countries arrived in America, WASPs viewed them as inferior. Rather than being embraced by WASPs, they were typically greeted with negative stereotypes.

25. **a** According to your text, Latinos are distinguished from other ethnic minorities in the United States by the Spanish language.

26. **c** According to William Wilson, civil rights legislation created new opportunities for middle-class African Americans to move up the social class ladder.

27. **a** It is *incorrect* to say that the idea of reparations for the past injustices of slavery is widely accepted. There are many who are opposed, arguing that it is not a simple issue of white against black, and that most people living in this country today were not involved in any way with slavery and should not have to pay for past practices.

28. **c** While Asian Americans have been successful in this country, there are significant differences among Asian ethnic groups.

29. **a** The overarching issue for minorities is overcoming discrimination.

30. **b** Most immigrants who came over to the United States during the first wave of immigration were from Europe. In the current wave of immigration, immigrants are coming from a diversity of nations.

ANSWERS FOR TRUE-FALSE QUESTIONS

1. *False.* There is no general agreement as to how many races there are: the range is from two to thousands.
2. *False.* Race is physical characteristics; ethnicity is cultural.
3. *True.*
4. *False.* Groups are determined minority based on their relative power.
5. *True.*
6. *False.* Discrimination is an action, prejudice is an attitude.
7. *True.*
8. *True.*
9. *True*
10. *False.* Psychological theories of prejudice stress the authoritarian personality and frustration displaced toward scapegoats
11. *False.* In order to understand discrimination in the United States, it is necessary to explain the patterns of institutional discrimination.
12. *True.*
13. *True.*
14. *True.*
15. *False.* Conflict theorists, not functionalists, focus on the role of the capitalist class in exploiting racism and ethnic inequalities.
16. *True.*
17. *True.*
18. *True.*
19. *True.*
20. *False.* Affirmative action has been at the center of controversy for more than a decade.

ANSWERS TO THE FILL-IN-THE-BLANK QUESTIONS

1. homogenous
2. race
3. Minority groups
4. ethnic work
5. tossed salad
6. result
7. deliberate
8. age
9. Rwanda
10. Latinos
11. quadrupled
12. Asian Americans or Japanese
13. invisible minority
14. separatism
15. Proposition 209

ANSWERS TO MATCH THESE SOCIAL SCIENTISTS WITH THEIR CONTRIBUTIONS

1. d Theodor Adorno: *identified the authoritarian personality type*
2. f Ashley Doane: *identified four factors that affect an individual's sense of ethnic identity*
3. g John Dollard: *suggested that prejudice is the result of frustration*
4. j Raphael Ezekiel: *studied racism in neo-Nazis and the KKK organizations*
5. i Louis Wirth: *offered a sociological definition of minority group*
6. h Joe Feagin: *researched everyday racism*
7. a Donald Muir: *measured racial attitudes of white students*
8. b William Wilson: *argues that class is more important than race in explaining inequality*
9. e Charles Willie: *argues that race is still an important criterion for discrimination*
10. c W. I. Thomas: *observed that defining a situation as real, makes it real in its consequences*

GUIDELINES FOR ANSWERING THE ESSAY QUESTIONS

1. *Explain what the author means when he says that race is both a myth and a reality.*

You would begin by defining the concept of race. Then you would move on to talking about the myth of race, or how there is no universal agreement as to how many races there are and how a system of racial classification is more a reflection of the society in which one lives than any underlying biological bases. At the same time, race is a reality in terms of people's subjective feelings about race, the superiority of some and the inferiority of others. You should bring Thomas's observations into the essay; that is, if people believe something is real, then it is real in its consequences.

2. *Using the experiences of different racial and ethnic groups in the U.S., identify and discuss the six patterns of intergroup relations.*

The book identifies six different types of intergroup relations — genocide, population transfer, internal colonialism, segregation, assimilation, and multiculturalism. You could begin by mentioning how these are arranged along a continuum from rejection and inhumanity to acceptance and humanity. Then, as you define each pattern, bring into your discussion an example, or examples, from the history of the United States. For example, in discussing genocide you could mention the treatment of Native Americans by the U.S. military. For population transfer you could bring up the movement of Native Americans to reservations or the relocation of Japanese Americans to internment camps during World War II. In discussing internal colonialism you could mention the economic exploitation of Latino farmworkers. The example of segregation would be the Jim Crow South. The experiences of European immigrants would reflect assimilation. As the textbook notes, it is difficult to find an example of multiculturalism in the history of our nation; perhaps one example might be religious pluralism.

3. *Explore how both psychological and sociological theories can be used together to gain a deeper understanding of prejudice and discrimination.*

   Your essay should discuss how psychological theories provide us with a deeper understanding of individual behavior, while sociological theories provide insights into the societal framework of prejudice and discrimination. You could discuss the work of Theodor Adorno on the authoritarian personality or Dollard's work on individual frustration and the role of scapegoats. However, without an understanding of the social environment, this work is incomplete. Bridging the two perspectives is symbolic interactionism and the analysis of the role of labels, selective perception, and the self-fulfilling prophecy in maintaining prejudice. But you should also include in your essay some reference to the functionalist analysis and the work of Muzafer and Carolyn Sherif, as well as the conflict theorists and how the capitalist class exploits racial and ethnic strife to retain power and control in society.

4. *Discuss the difference between individual and institutional discrimination and give examples of both.*

   Individual discrimination is the negative treatment of one person by another based on the physical characteristics. The discrimination is between the two people. For example, it could be a student excluding another classmate from a project because of his/her race. Institutional discrimination is negative treatment of a minority group that is built into the social system. This is also called systemic discrimination. You could discuss institutional discrimination in the issuing of home mortgages and car loans. African Americans and Latinos were 60 percent more likely to have their loan rejected than whites. Also, institutional discrimination has been found in health care. Whites are more likely to receive preventive care services compared to blacks. This preferential treatment is given both by black and white doctors.

5. *What would have to change in our society in order for us to truly be a multicultural society?*

   Start by defining multiculturalism — the encouragement of racial and ethnic variation. In a pluralistic society, minority groups are able to maintain their separate identities, and still participate in their society's institutions. In a sense, minority groups no longer exist, since they would no longer be singled out for unequal treatment, nor would they regard themselves as objects of collective discrimination.

   Before we can claim to be a multicultural society, we would have to attack the racism that continues. While we have eliminated many of the most blatant forms of racism, there is still much to be done. As the chapter points out, minorities still face prejudice and discrimination in terms of banking practices, real estate transactions, health care, employment, and education. Much of today's discrimination is institutionalized, which makes it much harder to see and to fight.

CHAPTER 13

ANSWERS FOR MULTIPLE CHOICE QUESTIONS

1. **b** The Abkhasians are an interesting example regarding age because they live such long lives.
2. **b** In 2000, 12.4 percent of Americans were age 65 or older.
3. **b** The process by which older persons make up an increasing proportion of the United States population is referred to as the graying of America.
4. **c** The number of years an individual is likely to live is referred to as his/her life expectancy.
5. **c** Gender age refers to the relative value that a culture places on men's and women's ages.
6. **d** "All of the above" is correct. Factors that may spur people to apply the label of old to themselves include personal history or biography, cultural signals about when a person is old, and biological factors.
7. **c** A gerentocracy is a society run by the elderly. The Tiwi provide an example of this type of society.
8. **a** Symbolic interactionism states that industrialization brought mass education and mass production which eroded the meaning of aging and being elderly.
9. **b** It has been suggested that the Baby Boom generation will have a positive effect on U.S. social images of the elderly in the years to come, given the numbers and economic clout.
10. **d** All of the above are true.
11. **b** Some researchers believe that the process of disengagement begins during middle age.
12. **d** "All of the above" is correct. The mass media communicate messages that reflect the currently devalued status of the elderly. It also tells us what people over age 65 should be like and often treats the elderly in discourteous and unflattering terms.
13. **b** Activity theory assumes that the more activities elderly people engage in, the more they find life satisfying.
14. **d** Continuity theory, the idea that we use strategies we have developed over a lifetime to cope with changes in old age, has been criticized because it is too broad; it is a collection of loosely connected ideas; and it has no specific application to the elderly.
15. **b** Conflict theorists believe that retirement benefits are the result of a struggle between competing interest groups.
16. **a** The requirement that workers retire at age 65 was protested for many years by the elderly, who felt the decision should be voluntary and not mandatory. Finally, in 1986, Congress eliminated mandatory retirement at age 65.
17. **b** As the population of the United States grays, there is concern that the ratio of working people to retired people will become smaller, making it more difficult to support programs such as Social Security. This ratio is referred to as the dependency ratio.
18. **d** The first three are all problems currently associated with Social Security. The last is not. As your text points out, elderly poverty is actually lower than the overall rate of poverty in this country.
19. **b** The goal of the Gray Panthers, founded in the 1960s by Maggie Kuhn, is to encourage people of all ages to work for the welfare of both the old and the young.
20. **a** Isolation is a problem for many people over age 65, especially for women. This is because of differences in patterns of mortality between men and women. Because elderly women are more likely to live longer than their husbands, most elderly men are still living with their wives, and most elderly women are not.
21. **d** "All of the above" is correct. Nursing homes are very expensive, have residents who tend to be widowed or never married, and tend to strip away human dignity.
22. **d** 90 percent of nursing homes are understaffed.
23. **b** Researchers have found that elder abuse is fairly extensive.
24. **c** Most abusers are not paid health care staff, but family members who verbally and emotionally abuse, or financially exploit, their aged relatives. The *most* likely abuser is the spouse.

25. **b** A higher percent of elderly women are likely to be poor compared to elderly men.
26. **c** With industrialization, death was transformed into an event that is managed by professionals in hospitals. The result is that most of us have never seen anyone die. It is an event that is strange and alien to us.
27. **b** Karen Cerulo and Janet Ruane use the term *technological lifespace* to describe a form of existence that is neither life nor death — the brain is dead but the body lives on.
28. In preindustrial societies, the sick were taken care of at home.
29. **c** Conformity is not one of the 5 stages a person typically pass through on their way to dying, according to Elisabeth Kübler-Ross.
30. **c** A hospice is the term used to describe a place or services in one's home that provide a dying person with comfort and dignity. The hospice movement developed in response to the impersonality of dying in hospitals.

ANSWERS FOR TRUE-FALSE QUESTIONS
1. *True.*
2. *True.*
3. *True.*
4. *False.* Life expectancy refers to the number of years an individual can expect to live, while life span refers to the maximum length of life.
5. *True.*
6. *False.* A gerontocracy is a society (or some other group) run by the old.
7. *False.* In earlier times, because most people never reached old age, growing old was seen as an accomplishment. They were viewed as storehouses of knowledge about work skills and about how to live a long life. This view contrasts sharply with the more negative view our society has of old age today.
8. *True.*
9. *True.*
10. *True.*
11. *True.*
12. *True.*
13. *True.*
14. *True.*
15. *False.* Most researchers have found that the elderly are less isolated than stereotypes would lead us to believe.
16. *False.* Elderly women are likely to live longer and experience the loneliness of widowhood.
17. *True.*
18. *True.*
19. *False.* America's elderly are less likely than the average American to be living in poverty.
20. *False.* Denial is the first stage in the death process.

ANSWERS TO THE FILL-IN-THE-BLANK QUESTIONS
1. Abkhasians
2. Industrialized
3. Graying of America
4. Gender age
5. Ageism
6. age cohorts
7. More
8. broad
9. 65

10. 70
11. Gray Panthers
12 family members
13. less
14. acceptance
15. biomedical science

ANSWERS TO MATCH THESE SOCIAL SCIENTISTS WITH THEIR CONTRIBUTIONS
1.   h   Robert Butler: *coined "ageism" to refer to prejudice or discrimination based on age*
2.   g   Dorothy Jerrome: *criticized disengagement theory for its implicit bias against the old*
3.   f   E. Kübler-Ross: *suggested that facing death sets in motion a five-stage process*
4.   i   Cerulo & Ruane: *use the term "technological lifespace" for life sustained by technology*
5.   j   Cumming & Henry: *developed disengagement theory*
6.   b   Robertson & Minkler: *found no evidence that the elderly gained at children's expense*
7.   e   Pillemer & Suiter: *elder abuse and Alzheimer patients*
8.   c   Kinsella and Phillips: *In two decades half of the population of Italy and Japan will be older than 50s*
9.   a   Maggie Kuhn: *founder of the Gray Panthers*
10.   d   Charles Hart: *carried out anthropological studies of the Tiwi*

GUIDELINES FOR ANSWERING THE ESSAY QUESTIONS
1.   *Explain why sociologists say that aging is socially constructed.*
      You should begin your essay by explaining that "social construction of aging" means that there is nothing in the biological nature of aging that contributes to a particular set of attitudes either in the person who is aging or in others who surround him/her. Rather, attitudes toward aging develop out of society and are shaped by the particular context of the society. Consequently, attitudes will vary from one social group to another. You could also talk about how the Industrial Revolution and the emergence of industrial societies affected the size of the aged population, social attitudes about aging, and the role of the aged in society.
      In the context of this question it would be important to mention the symbolic interactionists' views on aging. In particular, you would want to discuss the fact that social factors influence individuals' perceptions about the aging process. These factors include biology, personal history, gender age, and timetables.

2.   *Choose one of the three different perspectives and discuss how that perspective approaches the subject of aging. Consider both the strengths and weaknesses of the perspective you choose.*
      In this question, you have the option of writing about symbolic interactionism, functionalism, or conflict theory. If you choose symbolic interactionism, you would want to talk about the process of labeling — both the cultural labels and factors that affect the individual's adoption of those labels. You would also want to bring up the concept of "ageism," the role of the media in defining images, and how the labels change over time. In particular, you could discuss how these labels changed with industrialization and how they are once again changing with the advent of a postindustrial society. The strength of this perspective is that it provides us with insights into the social nature of a biological process; a weakness would be that it does not consider the conflict that may surround the labeling process.
      If you choose to write about functionalism, remember that this perspective focuses on how the different parts of society work together. Two important theories associated with this perspective are disengagement theory and activity theory. Strengths might be the focus on adjustment and the smooth transitioning from one generation to the next. Weaknesses are tied to the theories; disengagement theory overlooks the possibility that the elderly disengage from one set of roles (work-related) but may engage in

another set of roles (friendship), while activity theory does not identify the key variables that underlie people's activities.

Finally, if you choose conflict theory, you would want to focus on the conflict that is generated between different age groups in society as they compete for scarce resources. As an example, you would want to discuss the controversy over social security, from its birth to the present time. A strength of this perspective is that it provides us with an understanding of why the elderly have reduced the level of poverty over time; a weakness might be that it tends to emphasize conflict to the extent that cooperation between generations is overlooked.

3. *Discuss the impact that industrialization and technology have had on aging as well as dying.*

You could begin the essay by talking about how technology and industrialization has brought improvements and new developments. You might want to refer to some of the discussion in this chapter on the cross-cultural variations in aging, such as with the Abkhasians, the Tiwi and Eskimo, or the Chinese. These were all preindustrial societies with various views on the elderly. To talk about the impact of industrialization, you should refer to the improvements in the quality of life and the changes in cultural views on aging. Finally, you would want to talk about how technology enables us to sustain life for longer periods, but that the quality of that life is often compromised.

4. *People who come here from other parts of the world are often very critical of families that place their elderly family members in nursing homes. Assume that a friend of yours who comes from another part of the world asks you about your family's decision to move your grandparent into a nursing home. Develop an explanation that draws on the material presented in this chapter.*

First, you should point out to your friend that most elderly are cared for by their families. It is only a small percentage of elderly who are in nursing homes at any one time. Also, those who are in nursing homes are generally there because they are very old and very likely do not have any family to care for them. Often, even when there is family to provide care, the elderly person is very ill; two-thirds of nursing home residents have memory loss or are disoriented.

You could also point out some of the broader changes that make it more difficult for families to provide care. Adult daughters or daughters-in-law are typically the ones who care for elderly parents. In the last few decades, more women are employed outside the home, which creates challenges for them if the elderly parent needs constant care. Also, families are more likely to be disrupted by divorce than in the past, which means there may not be a daughter-in-law who is available and the daughter may be a single mom who has to work to support her children.

Your friend should also know that being cared for in a nursing home does not necessarily mean that elderly family members are alienated from their children. One study found that the majority of residents of nursing homes reported good or improved relationships with adult children following their move to a nursing home. The researchers suggested that this was because having to provide care to an ailing parent can be extremely stressful. Once the parent is being cared for by professionals, the children are free to once again focus on the emotional needs of their parents.

5. *Discuss the five stages of death and what is being done to humanize the process of death and dying.*

You can review the five stages of the death process as described by psychologist Elizabeth Kubler-Ross. The first stage is denial – people have a difficult time believing they are going to die. The second stage is anger- they feel that their dying is unjust. In the third stage of negotiation- people start to bargain with God. The fourth stage is depression in which the death is grieved. The last stage is acceptance in which people come to terms with their impending death. Hospices have emerged as a way to humanize the dying process. Service is provided in the persons home for the purpose of giving comfort and dignity to the dying person. While medical needs are met, the hospice program is also concerned with the person's social and spiritual needs.

CHAPTER 14

ANSWERS FOR MULTIPLE CHOICE QUESTIONS

1. **b** An economy is a system of distributing goods and services.

2. **c** Hunting and gathering societies are characterized by a subsistence economy.

3. **b** In pastoral and horticultural economies a more dependable food supply led to the development of a surplus. This surplus was one of the most significant events in human history because it fundamentally altered people's basic relationships.

4. **d** Industrial economies are based on machines powered by fuels. Industrial economies also created a surplus unlike anything the world had seen, and these economies were based on the invention of the steam engine. Therefore, the *incorrect* statement is "A service sector developed and employed the majority of workers"; this is actually a characteristic of a *postindustrial society*.

5. **d** Thorstein Veblen used the term conspicuous consumption to describe the lavishly wasteful spending of goods in order to enhance social prestige.

6. **c** Postindustrial economies are characterized by a large surplus of goods; extensive trade among nations; and a "global village." While machines may still be powered by fuel, this is <u>not</u> a defining characteristic of this type of economy.

7. **c** The two forces that have combined to create this new society are biology and economics. Henslin identifies this new type as a *bioeconomic society*.

8. **d** In pastoral and horticultural societies since there was little surplus, bartering was a common medium of exchanging one item for another.

9. **a** Money was first used extensively in agricultural societies.

10. **c** The policy of only issuing as much paper money as there were gold reserves was known as the gold standard.

11. **a** The *gross domestic product* is the term used to describe the total goods and services produced by a nation.

12. **c** The debit card came into existence in the postindustrial economy.

13. **d** Private ownership of the means of production is an essential feature of capitalism.

14. **c** The possession of machines and factories by individuals, who decide what shall be produced, is referred to as private ownership of the means of production.

15. **b** An economic system characterized by the public ownership of the means of production, central planning, and the distribution of goods without a profit motive is socialism.

16. **b** According to Karl Marx, profits represent excess value that is extracted from workers. Because an item's value is derived from the work that goes into it, there can be no profit unless workers are paid less than the value of their labor.

17. **a** Advertising creates discontent by presenting images that are impossible to attain.

18. **b** Convergence theory states that capitalism and socialism will become more alike as they both develop industrially.

19. **a** Work binds us together, according to the functionalist perspective.

20. **b** As societies industrialize, they become based on organic solidarity.

21. **c** The joint ownership of a business enterprise, whose liabilities and obligations are separate from those of its owners, is a corporation.

22. **c** When stockholders are satisfied with the profits and their stock dividends, they generally just rubber-stamp whatever recommendations are made by management; a stockholders' revolt occurs when dissatisfaction with the overall level of performance leads to their refusal to approve management's recommendations.

23. **b** The statement that is *incorrect* is that "Relationships among members of the inner circle are always cooperative rather than competitive," since members often find themselves in competition with one another for business.

24. **a** Oligopoly is the control of an entire industry by several large companies.

25. **c** The elite who sit on the boards of directors of not just one but several companies are referred to as interlocking directorates.

26. **c** The fundamental changes in society that follow the movement of vast numbers of women from the home to the work force is referred to as the quiet revolution.

27. **c** The size of the underground economy (economic activity not reported to the government) runs about 10 percent of the regular economy.

28. **c** The *correct* statement regarding wages today is "The buying power of today's wages is actually less than it was 30 years ago." Inflation has whittled away the value of the increased dollars workers are paid.

29. **b** When compared to workers in Western Europe, U.S. workers have less leisure time. The trend toward more leisure was reversed in the 1960s. Only Japanese workers work more hours annually than workers in the U.S.

30. **c** According to conflict theory, low-level workers bear the brunt of technological change.

ANSWERS FOR TRUE-FALSE QUESTIONS

1. *False.* Pastoral and horticultural societies, not hunting and gathering societies, were the first economies to have a surplus.
2. *True.*
3. *False.* In agricultural societies people bartering for goods and services is a common practice.
4. *False.* Postindustrial economies, not industrial economies, are based on information processing and providing services.
5. *True.*
6. *True.*
7. *False.* Credit cards and debit cards are not the same thing. A credit card allows its owner to purchase goods but to be billed later. A debit card allows its owner to purchase against his or her bank account.
8. *True.*
9. *True.*
10. *True.*
11. *False.* According to convergence theory, socialist nations will gradually adopt features of capitalism and capitalist nations will adopt features of socialism to the point where a new, hybrid form will emerge.
12. *True.*
13. *True.*
14. *False.* The world's largest corporation is General Electric.
15. *False.* Oligopolies are formed when a small number of large companies operate within a single industry, dictating prices, setting the quality of their products, and protecting their markets.
16. *True.*
17. *False.* Researchers have found that female workers are more likely than male workers to be concerned with maintaining a balance between their work and family lives.
18. *True.*
19. *False.* Industrialization decreased the amount of leisure time workers had.
20. *True.*

ANSWERS TO THE FILL-IN-THE-BLANK QUESTIONS

1. plow
2. biology and economics
3. e-cash
4. welfare
5. monopoly

6. socialism
7. convergence theory
8. corporation
9. inner circle
10. Conflict
11. two
12. underground
13. undocumented workers
14. Telecommuting
15. Computer driven

ANSWERS TO MATCH THESE CONCEPTS WITH THEIR DEFINITIONS

1. e   barter: *direct exchange of one item for another*
2. j   democratic socialism: *a hybrid economic system in which capitalism is mixed with state ownership*
3. a   debit card: *purchases charged against bank account*
4. i   e-cash: *digital money stored on computers*
5. b   fiat money: *currency issued by a government and not backed by stored value*
6. h   market forces: *laws of supply and demand*
7. c   oligopoly: *the control of an industry by several large companies*
8. f   stored value: *backing of currency with goods that are held in reserve*
9. d   monopoly: *the control of an industry by a single company*
10. g   socialism: *public ownership of the means of production*

GUIDELINES FOR ANSWERING THE ESSAY QUESTIONS

1. *Discuss the advantages and disadvantages of both capitalism and socialism as ideologies and as economic systems.*

This is a difficult question to answer because it is laden with social values. In this country we have been taught that capitalism is good and socialism is bad. Nevertheless, you should try to approach this from as objective a position as possible. You would want to begin by discussing the advantages and disadvantages of capitalism. For advantages, you could mention the idea of private ownership and the pursuit of profits, the motivation among workers to work hard, and the vast array of goods that are available in the marketplace. Among the disadvantages you could note the possibility for monopoly, the creation of constant discontent through advertising, and the violation of certain basic human rights like freedom from poverty. Turning to socialism, you could note that advantages include production for the general welfare rather than individual enrichment and the distribution of goods and services according to need rather than ability to pay. Critics point out that socialism violates basic human rights such as individual freedom of decision and opportunity.

2. *Explain why functionalists believe that work is functional for society.*

The first point to make is that work is functional for society because without work, society would collapse. This has always been the case, regardless of the type of society. In the earliest hunting and gathering societies, the work people did was mostly hunting and gathering. If they did not do this, they would starve. As societies became larger and more complex, the nature of work changed, but it was still essential for the continuation of society for people to engage in it.

Beyond that, functionalists as far back as Emile Durkheim have stressed that it is work that binds us together in a social group. It was Durkheim who identified two bases for social solidarity. In preindustrial societies, people do similar work and directly share most aspects of life; he called the sense of unity that develops out of doing similar activities mechanical solidarity. As societies undergo change with industrialization, the kind of work people do also changes. A more specialized division of labor emerges, with the result that people may not feel the connection with one another that comes from doing similar work. However, people begin to realize that they are contributing to the welfare of others as they do their specialized tasks and others are contributing to their welfare. Durkheim called this interdependence that comes out of the more specialized division of labor, organic solidarity.

3. *Take the perspective of a conflict theorist and explain the goals of corporate leaders and the strategies they use to achieve these goals.*

The primary goal of corporate leaders is to make a profit for their corporation. There are a number of strategies they can use, or have used, in trying to achieve this goal. The first is the exploitation of workers. The corporation is interested in minimizing labor costs by hiring workers for the cheapest wage possible. In this country's past, that meant low wages and long working days. With the passage of minimum wage laws and regulated working hours, as well as the rise of unions, corporations sought business locations without these forces. In today's world, that means locating production facilities in the Least Industrialized Nations.

The conflict theorists also note that increasingly, these multinational corporations are headed by an inner circle, whose members are united by a mutual interest in preserving capitalism. They consult with high-level politicians in order to promote legislation that is favorable to big business. On a global level, they promote the ideology of capitalism and move capital from one nation to another in their search for greater and more immediate profits. You could also refer back to the discussion on neocolonialism in the chapter on global stratification for more information on the inner circle and local political elites.

Another strategy used by corporations is the attainment of monopoly control over an industry. In this way, they are able to set prices and make greater profits. As you now know from your reading, our government passed antimonopoly legislation in the wake of John D. Rockefeller's enormous success so it is very difficult for corporations to operate as a monopoly. Given this, they try for an oligopoly, where several large companies dominate a single industry. They can then divide up the market among themselves and dictate the quality and prices of their products. They can also use their combined power to cultivate political influence.

Finally, today corporate leaders are searching for merger partners globally. This not only reduces global competition but also enables them to dominate global markets. In the process, smaller competitors are driven out of business.

4. *Discuss what is meant by the underground economy and the extent to which it exists.*

The underground economy consists of the exchange of goods and services that are not reported to the government and escape taxation. These activities consist of legal and illegal activities. The largest source of illegal income is probably drug dealing. Billions of dollars flow from users to sellers each year. The million or so illegal immigrants who come to the U.S. each year are also a part of this underground economy. They work in restaurants, do housework, work in sweatshops, clean rooms in hotels, etc. The underground economy is estimated to be no less than 10 percent of the regular economy. It probably totals over $1 trillion a year.

5. *The chapter discusses several different economic trends that have been occurring in the second half of this century. Discuss the impact of each of the following: the movement of women into the economy, the underground economy, shrinking paychecks, changing patterns of work and leisure, and the emergence of the alternative office.*

The first development you will want to talk about is women's increased participation in the paid work force. This has transformed consumption patterns, relations at work, self-concepts, and relationships with significant others. The underground economy is another major force in our society today, generating about $1 trillion. What is significant is that its presence distorts official statistics on the nation's gross national product, income, and employment. It also means that the IRS loses more than $100 billion a year in taxes. The shrinking of workers' paychecks is connected to inflation —workers are finding that their buying power is less than it was 30 years ago. Finally, compared to a century ago, workers enjoy increased leisure, primarily because workers have organized and demanded greater leisure. At the same time, over the past 30 to 40 years, the trend toward greater leisure has been reversed, and workers today are working more than before.

CHAPTER 15

ANSWERS FOR MULTIPLE CHOICE QUESTIONS

1.   **d**   "All of the above" is correct. Power, as defined by Max Weber, is the ability to carry out one's will in spite of resistance from others; it is an inevitable part of everyday life.
2.   **b**   Governments, whether dictatorships or the elected forms, are examples of macropolitics.
3.   **b**   Coercion is the power people do not accept as just.
4.   **c**   Peter Berger considered violence to be the ultimate foundation of any political order.
5.   **b**   Revolutions are people's rejection of the government's claim to rule over them.
6.   **d**   "All of the above" is correct. Traditional authority, the hallmark of preliterate groups, is based on custom. With industrialization it declines, but does not totally disappear.
7.   **b**   Rational-legal authority comes from the position that someone holds. Because bureaucracies are based on written rules, rational-legal authority is sometimes called bureaucratic authority.
8.   **c**   Joan of Arc's authority to lead soldiers into battle is an example of charismatic authority. They followed her because they perceived that she was endowed by nature with exceptional qualities.
9.   **d**   "All of the above" is correct. John F. Kennedy was a rational-legal leader; was also a charismatic leader; and is an example of a leader who is difficult to classify in terms of ideal types.
10. **c**   The least stable type of authority is the charismatic.
11. **d**   "All of the above" would be the correct answer. Representative democracy is a form of democracy in which citizens elect public officials to represent them in government. It is considered by many to be the greatest gift the United States has given the world. At the time it was first conceived, it was considered revolutionary.
12. **b**   Universal citizenship is the principle that everyone has the same basic rights by virtue of being born in a country, or of immigrating to that country and becoming a naturalized citizen.
13. **b**   An individual who seizes power and imposes his will onto the people is a dictator.
14. **c**   A form of government that exerts almost total control is a totalitarian regime.
15. **a**   The United States has centrist parties.
16. **b**   The *incorrect* statement is the one that says, "members of Congress maintain strict party allegiances and will never cross party lines to vote for legislation proposed by a member of the other party."
17. **b**   European systems of democracy, in which seats in the national legislatures are divided according to the proportion of votes each party receives (proportional representation), encourage the formation of minority parties.
18. **b**   Studies of voting patterns in the United States show that voting varies by age, race/ethnicity, education, employment, income, and gender.
19. **d**   According to research by Portes and Rumbaut, immigrants initially organize politically along lines of race and ethnicity. Once they have achieved a certain level of political power, attaining political representation roughly equivalent to their numbers in the population, then social class becomes more significant than race and ethnicity.
20. **b**   In recent presidential elections, only about one-half of eligible voters actually cast a ballot.
21. **d**   "All of the above" is correct. Lobbyists are people paid to influence legislation on behalf of their clients; are employed by special-interest groups; and are a major force in American politics.
22. **b**   Functionalists believe that any one group is prevented from gaining control of the government because of the presence of checks and balances.
23. **a**   Functionalists suggest that political conflict is minimized as special-interest groups negotiate with one another and reach compromise.
24. **d**   Members of the power elite are drawn from all three arenas: the largest corporations, the armed services, and political office.
25. **c**   According to conflict theorists, the ruling class is made up of people whose backgrounds and orientations to life are so similar that they automatically share the same goals.

26. **a** War is armed conflict between nations or politically distinct groups. It is not necessarily universal nor is it chosen for dealing with disagreements by all societies at one time or another.

27. **a** A cultural tradition of war, an antagonistic situation in which two or more states confront incompatible objectives, and the presence of a "fuel" that heats the antagonistic situation to a boiling point are the three essential conditions of war identified by Nicholas Timasheff. The existence of a strong, well-armed military force was not one of the factors he identified as essential.

28. **d** The United States is the leading seller of arms in the world, followed by Great Britain and France.

29. **b** The characteristics of dehumanization include: emotional distance from others, following procedures, inability to resist pressure, and less personal responsibility.

30. **c** Since the United Nations operates a World Court they are striving to be the legislative body of the world.

ANSWERS FOR TRUE-FALSE QUESTIONS

1. *True.*
2. *False.* Authority, not coercion, refers to legitimate power.
3. *True.*
4. *True.* As societies industrialize, traditional authority is undermined; however, it never totally dies out. Parental authority provides an excellent example.
5. *True.*
6. *False.* It is because the authority of charismatic leaders is based on their personal ability to attract followers that they pose a threat to the established political system. They work outside the political structure and owe allegiance to nothing.
7. *True.*
8. *True.*
9. *False.* In early societies that were small in size there was no need for some form of political system because these societies operated more like an extended family with decisions being made as they became necessary.
10. *True.*
11. *True.*
12. *False.* The idea of universal citizenship caught on very slowly in the United States. Initially, it was believed that certain groups such as women, African Americans, Native Americans, Asian Americans and the poor should not be given the rights of citizenship.
13. *False.* The European system is based on proportional representation that encourages minority parties and the formation of noncentrist parties.
14. *True*
15. *False.* Most political action committees do not represent broad social interests but, rather, stand for narrow financial concerns, such as the dairy, oil, banking, and construction industries.
16. *True.*
17. *False.* Functionalists claim that no one group holds power in America; that the country's many competing interest groups balance each other.
18. *True.*
19. *False.* Because of technological advances in killing, the cost of war in terms of money spent and human lives lost has increased.
20. *True.*

ANSWERS TO THE FILL-IN-THE-BLANK QUESTIONS

1. Power
2. state
3. Traditional
4. charismatic

5. direct
6. Internet
7. Totalitarianism
8. proportional representation
9. apathy
10. special interest group
11. money
12. checks and balances
13. power elite
14. ruling class
15. Terrorism

ANSWERS TO MATCH THESE CONCEPTS WITH THEIR DEFINITIONS

1. i   anarchy: *lawlessness caused by the abuse or collapse of governmental authority*
2. e   charismatic authority: *authority based on an individual's outstanding traits*
3. h   democracy: *system of government in which authority derives from the people*
4. j   dictatorship: *government in which power is seized by an individual*
5. b   monarchy: *a form of government headed by a king or queen*
6. c   oligarchy: *a form of government where power is held by a small group of individuals*
7. d   citizenship: *birth and residence in a country imparts certain rights*
8. f   pluralism: *diffusion of power among many interest groups*
9. a   totalitarianism: *a form of government that exerts almost total control over people*
10. g   traditional authority: *authority based on customs*

GUIDELINES FOR ANSWERING THE ESSAY QUESTIONS

1. *Distinguish between macropolitics and micropolitics, explaining what each is and which perspectives are associated with each, and provide your own examples to illustrate each.*

You would begin by defining what each of these is — micropolitics is the exercise of power in everyday life, while macropolitics is the exercise of large-scale power over a large group. In general, symbolic interactionists focus more on micropolitics, because it is rooted in the social interactions that take place within social groups, although some conflict theorists could also take a micropolitical approach by focusing on the conflict that is generated by power inequalities. On the other hand, functionalists and conflict theorists are concerned with macropolitics, because they are concerned with the large-scale structures and patterns of a society. Finally, you would include some of your own examples of micropolitics (struggles between husbands and wives, parents and children) and macropolitics (struggles between political parties, between Congress and the President, between unions and elected officials).

2. *Compare and contrast the systems of democracy found in the United States and Europe and discuss how some of the problems associated with our system, such as voter apathy, the power of political action committees, and the concentration of power, are related to our system.*

For this essay you would want to point out that both systems are democratic, which means that the ultimate power resides in the people. Both are representative, rather than direct democracies, which means that citizens vote for representatives who actually make the decisions rather than the citizens themselves voting on each decision. Despite these similarities, the two systems have differences. You would want to mention the proportional representation of the European system versus the winner-takes-all outcomes of the American system, the encouragement of minority parties in the European system versus their discouragement in the American system, and the centrist parties of Europe versus the noncentrist parties of the United States.

Finally, you would want to consider how voter apathy, the power of political action committees, and the concentration of power are related to the specific features of the United States system. First, you might want to talk about how the winner-takes-all arrangement encourages the development of centrist parties which are forced to appeal to the middle of the voting population in order to receive the majority of the votes; because of this, many people come to feel that the political parties are too superficial and do not really represent their ideas or interests, so they decide to sit out the elections. The second problem, power of PACs, is also related to the particular feature of winner-takes-all systems. With so much riding on elections, candidates are pressured into spending excessive amounts of money in order to get their name and their message out to the voters. The cash requirements provide a perfect opportunity for PACs to donate and thereby influence not only the outcomes of elections but the voting behavior of the elected candidate. The final problem about the concentration of power is an outgrowth of the first two. You could go back to the discussion of the iron law of oligarchy and make the argument that the combination of voter apathy and the financial requirements of running for office produce a small elite that becomes committed to maintaining its power.

3. *Discuss the two major political parties in the United States. Explain differences and similarities.*

Even though numerous political parties had emerged after the United States was founded, two parties dominate. The Democrats are typically associated with the working class and the Republicans with wealthier people. They each represent different philosophical principles, but do appeal to a broad membership. It is difficult, for example, to discern the difference between a conservative Democrat and a liberal Republican. The extremes of each party are easier to distinguish. The strongly Democratic support legislation that transfers money from the richer to the poorer or that controls wages, working conditions, and competition. Strong Republicans would not be supportive of this legislation. They are similar in that both parties support fundamentals such as free public education; a strong military; freedom of religion, speech, and assembly; and capitalism.

4. *Discuss why wars happen.*

As the book states, war is not universal. Rather, it is simply one option that groups may choose when dealing with disagreements. As the record indicates, not all societies choose this option. At the same time, it would appear that war is rather common, both across history and in our own time. The question is then, *why*?

In trying to answer this, you would want to bring up the work of Nichoas Timasheff. He identified three essential conditions of war: (1) cultural traditions; (21) an antagonistic situation; (3) a fuel that heats the situation to a boiling point. You could also discuss the different fuels and the fact that leaders often see war as an opportunity to achieve certain objectives.

Finally, there is the whole issue of dehumanization. You could argue that just as experience in war can lead those who are fighting to see the enemy as less than human, a history or culture of warfare can contribute to an entire society viewing its enemies as less than fully human. In addition, as sociologist Tamotsu Shibutani stresses, dehumanization is aided by the tendency for prolonged conflicts to be transformed into struggles between good and evil. In our own history, many of the wars we have fought have been framed exactly this way. Wars exalt killing and those who fight and kill are often given metals to glorify their actions.

CHAPTER 16

ANSWERS FOR MULTIPLE CHOICE QUESTIONS

1. **a** Polyandry is a marriage in which a woman has more than one husband.
2. **d** A household is the term used to describe the people who occupy the same housing unit or other living quarters. A family that lives together in the same house would be considered a household, but unrelated people who live together are not considered a family.
3. **d** family of orientation is the one in which a person grows up.
4. **b** Endogamy is the practice of marrying within one's own group.
5. **a** In a matrilineal system, descent is figured only on the mother's side.
6. **c** Although the roots of authority with U.S. families is patriarchal, today a growing number of families are egalitarian, sharing authority between men and women.
7. **d** "All of the above" is correct. The incest taboo is rules specifying the degrees of kinship that prohibit sex or marriage; helps families avoid role confusion; and facilitates the socialization of children.
8. **b** According to functionalists, the family fulfills six essential functions in all societies.
9. **d** Conflict theorists focus on inequality in marriages, especially unequal power between husbands and wives.
10. **b** According to Arlie Hochschild, most men engage in the strategies of *playing dumb*, *waiting it out*, and *needs reduction*. The one that was not identified by her is *substitute labor*.
11. **c** According to research findings, men who earn less money than their wives feel most threatened by doing housework and consequently do the least.
12. **a** Research by Dutton and Aron found that love begins with a sexual attraction. This is followed by a cognitive awareness, as we attach a label to our feelings.
13. **c** The tendency of people with similar characteristics to marry one another is homogamy.
14. **b** Families of the same social class are likely to be similar, regardless of their race-ethnicity.
15. **b** In comparison with married couples, single mothers are much less likely to rely on the child's father for help.
16. **d** "None of the above" is correct. In regard to child rearing, Melvin Kohn concluded that parents of different social classes socialize their children differently. Working-class parents are more likely to use physical punishment than middle-class parents, who are more likely to withdraw privileges or affection.
17. **d** 42% of 24-29 year olds live with parents. Some live with them during college and some return after college.
18. **c** According to your text, a major concern of upper-class African American families is the family background of those whom their children marry.
19. **d** "All of the above" is correct. Machismo distinguishes Latino families from other groups; is an emphasis on male strength and dominance; and is seen in some Chicano families where the husband-father plays a strong role in his family.
20. **c** One of the ways in which Native American families differ from most U.S. families is in terms of the participation of elders in their children's families. They not only provide childcare, but also play an active role in teaching and disciplining the children.
21. **b** Since 1970, the number of children in the United States who live with both parents has dropped from 85 percent to 68 percent.
22. **d** The three major changes that characterize U.S. families today do not include an increase in inter-racial marriages.
23. **c** A family whose members were once part of other families is known as a blended family.
24. **c** In 2004, Massachusetts became the first state to legalize same-sex marriages.

25. **d** "All of the above" is correct. Cohabitation is the condition of living together as an unmarried couple, has increased ten times in the past 30 years, and has occurred before about sixty percent of all couples marry.
26. **d** The *sandwich generation* refers to people who find themselves caught between two generations, simultaneously responsible for the care of their children and their aging parents.
27. **d** All of the factors help to reduce the likelihood of divorce.
28. **c** The grandchildren whose grandparents had divorced were more likely to have marital discord in their own marriages.
29. **a** The growing numbers of women in the workforce are likely to continue to shift balance of marital power.
30. **d** According to the author of the text, all of the trends — increase in cohabitation, increase in age at first marriage, and parenting by grandparents are likely to continue into the next century.

ANSWERS FOR TRUE-FALSE QUESTIONS
1. *False.* Marriage and family are mechanisms for governing mate selection, reckoning descent, and establishing inheritance and authority.
2. *True.*
3. *False.* Laws of endogamy in the United States that prohibit interracial marriages have all been repealed.
4. *True.*
5. *True.*
6. *True.*
7. *False.* Arlie Hochschild concluded that women who worked the second shift are generally not happy about it but end up putting in the time because of the gendered division of labor.
8. *False.* According to Arlie Hochschild, one of the strategies used by some husbands to resist doing housework is "substitute offerings," or expressing appreciation to the wife for her being so organized that she can handle both work for wages and the second shift at home, when, instead, it would be better if he actually shared the work with her.
9. *True.*
10. *True.*
11. *False.* Marital satisfaction actually decreases after the birth of a child.
12. *True.*
13. *False.* Working class families are more likely to use physical punishment and middle class families to withdraw privileges or affection.
14. *False.* Women are more likely than men to face the problem of widowhood, not only because they live longer, but also because they are likely to have married older men.
15. *True.*
16. *True.*
17. *True.*
18. *False.* U.S. rate of births to unmarried women actually falls in the middle third among a group of ten industrialized nations for which there is accurate data. Sweden, Denmark, France, and Great Britain are higher, while Canada, Germany, Netherlands, Italy, and Japan are lower.
19. *True.*
20. *True.*

ANSWERS TO THE FILL-IN-THE-BLANK QUESTIONS
1. incest taboo
2. matriarchy
3. least
4. 95

5. Homogamy
6. Latino
7. fictive
8. poverty
9. Denmark
10. marriage
11. Commitment
12. grandparents
13. skipped generation
14. new chance
15. Incest

ANSWERS TO MATCH THESE SOCIAL SCIENTISTS WITH THEIR CONTRIBUTIONS
1. a   Judith Wallerstein: *divorce has long-term damaging effects*
2. f   Urie Bronfenbrenner: *children adjust better with a second adult around*
3. h   Andrew Cherlin: *noted lack of norms regarding remarriage*
4. b   Finkelhor & Yllo: *studied marital rape*
5. e   Mavis Hetherington: *75-80% of children of divorce will adjust well*
6. j   Arlie Hochschild: *identified the second shift*
7. i   Melvin Kohn: *studied social class differences in child-rearing*
8. c   Jankowiak and Fischer: *found that societies had the ideal of romantic love*
9. d   Diana Russell: *studied incest victims*
10. g   Bob Suzuki: *identified distinctive characteristics of Asian-American families*

GUIDELINES FOR ANSWERING THE ESSAY QUESTIONS
1. *Discuss whether the family still provides a useful function.*

   This is a rather straightforward question. You would want to refer to the functionalist explanation regarding the functions that the family performs.   These include (1) economic production, (2) socialization of children, (3) care of the sick and aged, (4) recreation, (5) sexual control, and (6) reproduction. Then, consider the degree to which families in this country still fulfill all of these functions. If they don't, which ones do they still do? Are there other institutions that could do the job as well? Given your answers to these questions, construct an argument as to the continued usefulness of the family.

2. *Discuss what factors contribute to successful marriages and to happy families.*

   You could discuss the research done by Jeanette and Robert Lauer. They interviews 351 couple who married for at least 15 years. 300 of the couples reported being happily married. They identified 8 factors that contributed to the success of their marriage. These were: (1) they think of their spouse as their best friend; (2) like their spouse as a person; (3) see marriage as a commitment; (4) believe marriage is sacred; (5) have similar aims and goals; (6) see spouse as more interesting over time; (7) want the relationship to succeed; and (8) laugh together. Sociologists have also found that those couples who get along with their in-laws and do enjoyable leisure activities are also happier. The research done on happy families shows the following to be important: (1) they spend a lot of time together; (2) express appreciation; (3) committed to each other's welfare; (4) talk and listen to one another; (5) are religious; and (6) deal with crisis positively.

3. *Identify the stages in the family life cycle, discussing what tasks are accomplished in each stage and what event marks that transition from one stage to the next.*

   You will want to discuss each of the several stages in sequence: love and courtship, marriage, childbirth, child rearing, the empty nest, and widowhood. For each stage, you should include the work that takes place and the events that mark the beginning and end of that stage. For example, the first stage is love and courtship. In our culture, this involves romantic love, with individuals being sexually attracted to one another and idealizing the other. Love actually has two components: one is emotion, related to feelings of sexual attraction, and the other is cognitive, attaching labels to our feelings. The stage begins with our meeting and being attracted to another person, and ends when we decide to get engaged to be married.

4. *Identify the trends among U.S. families today and explain the social forces that have contributed to each of them.*

This chapter identifies five trends in U.S. families: postponement of marriage, cohabitation, unmarried mothers, and the sandwich generation and elder care. You should take each trend in turn, identifying and explaining the pattern. For example, for the first half of the twentieth century, the age at first marriage steadily declined, so that by 1950, women married at about age 20. For the next 20 years, this figure remained unchanged. Then, beginning in 1970, the average age began to climb. In 2000, women are waiting until they are almost 26 to marry. Now that you have described the pattern, you need to try and explain it. Here's where you want to apply what you have learned previously about changing norms (Chapter 2). You can talk about how women's roles have changed tremendously since 1970 (see Chapter 11); these changes have affected women's lives and decisions on when to marry. You could also talk about attitudes about premarital sex, which began to change in the 1960s and 1970s. More liberal attitudes about premarital sex and cohabitation have also affected young people's decisions about when to marry. Research on changes in marriage and cohabitation supports this. Once you have described and analyzed this first trend, you would then go on to do the same with the other three trends.

5. *Discuss the impact that divorce has on family members — men, women and children.*

You would want to discuss each family role separately — children, wives and husbands. In your response, be sure to talk about the research on the impact on children, both short-term and long-term. In the short-term, this includes hostility, anxiety, nightmares, and poor school performance. In the long-term, it includes a loss of connection to parents, and difficulties forming intimate relations.

For spouses, there is anger, depression and anxiety following a divorce, but each also experiences unique problems related to their gender. For women, there is often a decrease in the standard of living, although the impact varies by social class. For men, there is a loss of connection to their children and the possible development of a series of families.

CHAPTER 17

ANSWERS FOR MULTIPLE CHOICE QUESTIONS

1. **d** "All of the above" is correct. In earlier societies there was no separate social institution called education; education was synonymous with acculturation; and people who already possessed certain skills taught them to others.

2. **a** Education is a formal system of teaching knowledge, values, and skills.

3. **b** The one statement that is *incorrect* is, "The first thing that the founders of our nation did was to create a comprehensive school system across all states." In fact, the system remained a hodgepodge of independent schools well into the 1800s.

4. **c** Horace Mann first proposed the idea of common schools, supported through taxes.

5. **b** Laws requiring all children to attend school until a specified age or until they complete a minimum grade in school are mandatory education laws.

6. **b** In Japan, college admission is based on making a high score on a national test.

7. **c** Since the collapse of the Soviet Union, the educational system is being reinvented. Private, religious and even foreign-run schools are allowed. More importantly, teachers are allowed to encourage students to question and to think for themselves.

8. **a** Despite the fact that education is free at all levels, including college, children of the wealthy are several times as likely as children of the nonwealthy to continue their education beyond the basics.

9. **a** The use of diplomas and degrees to determine who is eligible for jobs, even though the diploma or degree may be irrelevant to the actual work is known as a credential society.

10. **a** All of the following are manifest functions of education: transmitting cultural values; helping mold students into a more or less cohesive unit; and teaching patriotism. Helping to maintain social inequality is *not* one of the functions, according to the functionalists.

11. **c** Traditionally, the educational system in the United States has taught children the value of individualism, competition, and patriotism. Cooperation is less likely to be stressed.

12. **a** The policy that many schools now have of incorporating students with disabilities into regular school activities is called mainstreaming, or inclusion.

13. **a** Credentialing and tracking are two examples of gate keeping.

14. **c** The hidden curriculum refers to the unwritten rules of behavior and attitudes that are taught in school.

15. **d** IQ tests have been criticized because they are culturally biased. Children from middle-class and upper-class backgrounds are more familiar with the concepts used in the test. Minorities and the poor often score lower on these tests, which results in them being assigned less demanding courses.

16. **c** Public schools are largely supported by local property taxes.

17. **b** The correspondence principle is the ways in which schools correspond to, or reflect the social structure of society.

18. **a** Bowles found that regardless of ability, students from affluent homes were more likely to go on to college than were students from poor homes.

19. **a** Schools encourage competition rather than cooperation.

20. **c** The conflict perspective views education as reproducing the social structure.

21. **b** White and African Americans are the most likely to attend private colleges.

22. **b** Rist's research demonstrated the power of labels — the child's journey through school was essentially determined by the eighth day of kindergarten and was based on the teacher's somewhat biased assessment of their ability.

23. **d** The Rosenthal/Jacobson experiment tended to confirm the concept of a self-fulfilling prophecy.

24. **d** Research by George Farkas focused on how teacher expectations affect students' grades.

25. **b** When compared to scores of twenty to thirty years ago, today's scores on tests such as the SAT are lower.

26. **b** The practice of passing students from one grade to the next even though they have not mastered basic materials is called social promotion.

27. **c** High-school graduates who have difficulty with basic reading and math are known as functional illiterates.

28. **b** An examination of the statistics published on page 506 of your text would lead you to conclude that the number of shooting deaths in schools at the end of the 1990s was half what it had been at the beginning of the decade.

29. **c** Coleman and Hoffer found that students attending Roman Catholic schools out-performed students attending public schools. They attributed this to the fact that higher standards were set by teachers at the Roman Catholic schools.

30. **d** "All of the above" is the correct answer. Jaime Escalante did all of those things to improve the inner city school that he taught in.

ANSWERS FOR TRUE-FALSE QUESTIONS

1. *False.* In earlier societies there was no separate social institution called education.
2. *True.*
3. *False.* College graduation in the United States is now much more common than high school graduation was in 1910.
4. *False.* In Japanese schools the value of cooperation rather than competition is stressed.
5. *True.*
6. *False.* Despite the fact that Egyptian education is free at all levels, children of the wealthy are more likely to get an education.
7. *True.*
8. *True.*
9. *False.* American schools encourage, rather than discourage, individualism and although teamwork is encouraged, individuals are singled out for praise when the team does well.
10. *True.*
11. *True.*
12. *False.* Functional theorists believe that social placement is helpful, not harmful, to society because the process helps insure that the "best" people will acquire a good education and subsequently perform the most needed tasks of society.
13. *True.*
14. *False.* Conflict theorists, not functionalists, emphasize the hidden curriculum in their analysis of American education.
15. *True.*
16. *True.*
17. *False.* Latinos are the group least likely to complete high school and go to college.
18. *False.* According to Farkas's research females and Asian Americans got higher grades because they communicated to teachers through their demeanor and behavior that they were interested in what the teacher was teaching; they fit the teacher's idea of what a good student should be.
19. *False.* In recent years math scores have some improvement but verbal scores continue to be low.
20. *True.*

ANSWERS TO THE FILL-IN-THE-BLANK QUESTIONS

1. acculturation
2. common
3. half
4. culture
5. one-third
6. certification

7. tracking
8. hidden curriculum
9. boot camp
10. Distance learning
11. peer group
12. grade inflation
13. higher
14. vouchers
15. pay for performance

ANSWERS TO MATCH THESE SOCIAL SCIENTISTS WITH THEIR CONTRIBUTIONS
1. j Randall Collins: *credential society*
2. d Bowles and Gintis: *correspondence principle*
3. b Rosenthal and Jacobson: *teacher expectations and student performance*
4. e Robert Merton: *self-fulfilling prophecy*
5. g Coleman and Hoffer: *student performance linked to setting higher standards*
6. i Harry Gracey: *kindergarten as boot camp*
7. a Davis and Moore: *gatekeeping sorts people on the basis of merit*
8. h George Farkas: *students are rewarded for the signals they send teachers*
9. f Adrian Dove: *IQ tests have social class bias*
10. c Talcott Parsons: *function of education is to funnel into social positions*

GUIDELINES FOR ANSWERING THE ESSAY QUESTIONS
1. *Explain the link between democracy, industrialization and universal education.*

For this question, there are two strains of thought that need to be developed. The first is the link between democracy and universal education. Here you will want to talk about the need for voters who are knowledgeable about the issues and are capable of making sound decisions; it is necessary that they read and understand news that is published in newspapers. In addition, the political culture is maintained through the educational system, as children learn patriotism and the facts of the political process.

The second strain is to connect industrialization and universal education. Here you would want to talk about the need for an educated workforce that is able to read instructions and learn how to use increasingly more complex machines. The work force must also be able to move from job to job, learning new skills as the work requires. The most efficient way in which to train workers, both to have the specific skills needed for a particular job and the general skills needed to survive in a constantly changing workplace, is through universal education For these two reasons, universal education developed in the United States, as well as other industrialized nations.

2. *Compare the educational systems of Japan, Russia, and Egypt and discuss what is meant by the statement that education reflects culture.*

The education system is a reflection of the culture and economy of a country. The most industrialized nations tend to value education more and place higher standards on the level of education and insuring that their populace receives an education. In Japan, education is a top priority. Their core education and cultural values include solidarity within the group and team-work and this is reflected in how students are taught in schools. The children work together in groups and use the same textbook throughout the country. However, the contradiction lies in that college admission is highly competitive and only the top scorers on a national exam go on to college. Russia represents education in the industrializing nations. In Russia, they made sure that socialist values dominated the schools. Students were discouraged from any critical thinking. After the change to a more capitalistic system, teachers had to be re-trained and students taught how to be critical thinkers. Egypt represents education in the least industrialized nation. Many poor children do not receive any schooling as they stay home to work the land. There is little emphasis placed on formal schooling. As such, a significant portion of their population, especially women, are illiterate.

3. *Select one of the three perspectives and design a research project to test the claims of that perspective about the nature of education.*

In order to answer this question you must first choose one of the three perspectives For example, you might choose the conflict perspective and decide to do a research project on the relationship between ethnicity and individual educational achievement and goals. Your research will involve an analysis of student choices of curricula, their grades, retention rates, and graduation from a large racially/ethnically diverse high school. You have access to student records and you collect data on students in one class as this class moves through the high school. You will compare white students' records to those of African-American and Hispanic students in order to test whether the conflict theorists are correct in their assertion that the educational system reproduces the students' class background.

4. *In discussing solutions to educational problems, the author suggests that one direction schools should go is toward setting higher educational standards. Both the research by James Coleman and Thomas Hoffer, and the success of Jaime Escalante, support this. Discuss social factors that might explain why such a proposal has not been widely adopted by public schools across the country.*

In answering this question you will want to focus on obstacles to implementation. You could refer to some of the research on teacher expectations and student tracking to illustrate the status quo in the majority of schools.   Henslin notes that one of the biggest obstacles is bureaucracy itself, where ritual often replaces performance A routine becomes established and then difficult to change (refer to Chapter 7 for a complete discussion of bureaucracy). As the experience of Jaime Escalante demonstrated, it was only after he changed the system of instruction that student attitudes and performance changed.

CHAPTER 18

ANSWERS FOR MULTIPLE CHOICE QUESTIONS

1. **d** Durkheim wrote *The Elementary Forms of the Religious Life* in order to identify elements common to all religions.
2. **c** Durkheim was referring to aspects of life that are part of the ordinary, everyday life with the term *profane*.
3. **c** Durkheim used the word "church" in an unusual way to refer to a group of believers organized around a set of beliefs and practices regarding the sacred.
4. **a** All of the following are functions of religion: support for the government, social change, and social control. Encouraging wars for holy causes is a dysfunction of religion.
5. **b** In a review of the research, it was found that prayer (or meditation) changes people's brain activity and improves their immune response.
6. **c** War and religious persecution are dysfunctions of religion.
7. **b** A unified picture of the world, such as the belief in one God, creator of the universe, is called a cosmology.
8. **c** When some Protestants use the term *born again*, they are referring to a personal life-transforming religious experience.
9. **b** The *incorrect* statement is that "Family members are exempt from having to follow the practice when it involves one of their own." In fact, if the other family members want to remain in good standing in the congregation, they are expected to shun the person too.
10. **c** Marx felt that religion was like a drug and called it the opium of the people.
11. **d** "All of the above" is correct. These are all examples of the use of religion to legitimize social inequalities: the divine right of kings; a declaration that the Pharaoh or Emperor is god or divine; and the defense of slavery as being God's will.
12. **a** Weber believed that religion held the key to modernization.
13. **a** Weber analyzed how Protestantism gave rise to the Protestant Ethic, which stimulated what he called the Spirit of Capitalism.
14. **a** Judaism was the first major religion to practice monotheism.
15. **b** Some groups believe that all objects in the world have spirits. This is known as animism.
16. **a** An unanticipated outcome of the Reformation was the splintering of Christianity into separate branches.
17. **c** The Shi'ites are the branch of Islam that are more conservative and inclined to fundamentalism.
18. **c** Polytheism is the belief that there are many gods
19. **b** The religion with no specific founder is Hinduism.
20. **c** Reincarnation is the return of the soul after death in a different form.
21. **a** All religions began as cults.
22. **c** Although larger than a cult, a sect still feels tension from society.
23. **d** "All of the above" is correct. Churches are highly bureaucratized; have more sedate worship services; and gain new members from within, from children born to existing members.
24. **d** The answer is "ecclesia." In an ecclesia, there is no recruitment of members because all citizens are automatically members of the state religion, or ecclesia.
25. **c** The Amish have remained a sect.
26. **b** Convention was formed to defend the right to own slaves.
27. **c** Rather than intolerance of differences, religion in the United States is characterized by tolerance.
28. **d** "All of the above" is correct. Secularization of religion occurs as a result of industrialization, urbanization, and mass education.
29. **b** An example of secularization of culture is that the influence of religion on public affairs has lessened today.

30. **d** "All of the above" is correct. Questions that science cannot answer include: Is there a God? What is the purpose of life? What happens when a person dies?

ANSWERS FOR TRUE-FALSE QUESTIONS

1. *False.* The goal of the sociological study of religion is to analyze the relationship between society and religion and to gain insight into the role that religion plays in people's lives. It is not to determine which religions are most effective in people's lives.
2. *True.*
3. *True.*
4. *True.*
5. *True.*
6. *False.* Being born again is a term frequently used to describe Christians who have undergone a life-transforming religious experience so radical that they feel they have become new people. The term does not describe reincarnation by Hindus and Buddhists.
7. *False.* Shunning is practiced by the Amish.
8. *True.*
9. *False.* Max Weber saw religion as a primary source of social change.
10. *False.* Contemporary Judaism in the United States comprises three main branches: Orthodox, Reform, and Conservative.
11. *True.*
12. *True.*
13. *True.*
14. *False.* Judaism, Christianity, and Islam are all monotheistic religions
15. *False.* Both cults and sects stress evangelism, or the active recruitment of new members.
16. *True.*
17. *True.*
18. *True.*
19. *False.* Many local ministers view the electronic church as a competitor for the attention of their members and for money that could go to their own good causes. Thus, they are not supportive of the electronic church.
20. *True.*

ANSWERS TO THE FILL-IN-THE-BLANK QUESTIONS

1. better
2. moral
3. functional
4. ritual
5. religious experience
6. shunned
7. modernization
8. Abraham
9. Christianity
10. Muslims
11. four
12. Buddhism
13. cults
14. social class
15. humanity

ANSWERS TO MATCH THESE CONCEPTS WITH THEIR DEFINITIONS

1. d   denomination: *a "brand name" within a major religion*
2. h   charisma: *an outstanding, magnetic personality*
3. j   civil religion: *a belief that a nation and its institutions are sanctified by God*
4. a   evangelism: *an attempt to win converts*
5. g   reincarnation: *return of the soul after death in a different form*
6. i   polytheism: *a belief that there are many gods*
7. c   rituals: *religious rites that are intended to evoke a sense of awe*
8. e   sacred: *things set apart that inspire reverence or deep respect*
9. f   profane: *common elements of everyday life*
10. b   ecclesia: *government-sponsored religion*

GUIDELINES FOR ANSWERING THE ESSAY QUESTIONS

1. *Assume that you have been asked to make a presentation about religion to a group of people who have absolutely no idea what religion is. Prepare a speech in which you define religion and explain why it exists.*

For this question, your first task is to explain what religion is. To do this you might want to refer to Durkheim's work on the elementary forms of religious life, talking about the differences between the sacred and profane, the presence of beliefs, practices, and a moral community. Once you have done this, your next task is to discuss why religion exists. Here you could talk about either the functionalist perspective or the conflict perspective or both. If you choose to focus only on the functionalist view, you would want to talk about how religion meets basic human needs; you might also want to refer to the symbolic interactionist views on community. If you want to focus only on conflict theory, or add that to your discussion of functionalism, you would want to talk about how, for Marx, religion is like a drug that helps the oppressed forget about their exploitation at the hands of the capitalists. Furthermore, conflict theorists point out that capitalists use religion to legitimate social inequalities and maintain the status quo.

2. *The functionalists point out the many functions of religion, but also not that it has certain dysfunctions. Discuss both the functions and dysfunctions and then consider whether it is possible for religion to fulfill its functions without producing dysfunctions.*

At the end of the chapter, Henslin notes that people have four major concerns. These are (1) the existence of God, (2) the purpose of life, (3) the existence of an afterlife, and (4) morality. In his discussion of the functionalist perspective, Henslin outlines several important functions of religion that address these concerns. Religion provides answers to their questions about the ultimate meaning of life, which in turn comforts people. People find community among others who share their values and beliefs. Religion also sets out guidelines for everyday living — what we should and should not do, thereby setting limits and establishing morality. Having connections to a community and guidelines for living also help in adapting to new environments and social change.

Despite the fact that there are several major religions around the globe, people tend to see their religion as being the only true religion. This is understandable, given the nature of religion. At the same time, this orientation can produce dysfunctions. The author discusses two: (1) war and terrorism; and (2) religious persecution.

The final part of the essay is to consider whether religions can exist and be functional without producing dysfunctions. In answering this, you need to consider the nature of the world today. If contact between people of different religions could be minimized, these dysfunctions would not be problematic. However, today, people of different faiths are drawn even closer together today because of globalization. If we are to avoid the dysfunctional side of religion, a way needs to be found for everyone with different belief systems to live together in harmony. So far, we have few examples of this but can think of many examples of war and religious persecution.

3. *Discuss the process by which a religion matures from a cult into a church.*

This is a pretty straightforward question. All you are asked to do is to discuss the process by which a religion moves from cult to sect to church. You would want to talk about what each is, how they range along a continuum, and what events mark the shift from one type to the next.

4. *Consider why fundamentalist Christian churches in the United States are currently undergoing a revival.*

Begin by thinking about the nature of social life today. With the continuing rationalization of society (see Chapter 7 for more on rationalization), more and more of our interactions are impersonal and formal, taking place with strangers who are employed by bureaucracies. Consequently, people may feel disconnected from one another. Because we work more, we spend less time at home. We don't know their neighbors and often don't even have enough time for family and friends. Families aren't what they once were. As our society continues to change at a rather rapid pace, we feel that the old norms no longer apply, but are not sure what are the new norms are.

Now go back to the different sociological perspectives on religion. First there is the functionalist perspective. In response to the impersonality of our daily lives, religion provides connection and community. Religious teachings provide clear guidelines for everyday living, helping us find direction in the face of continuing social change. Henslin suggests that mainstream churches, which offer a more remote God and less emotional involvement, fail to meet basic religious needs of large numbers of Americans. In contrast, the different fundamentalist Christian churches, with their literal interpretation of the Bible, offer seekers comfort and direction

5. *Discuss the major patterns of adaptation that occur when religion and culture conflict with one another.*

You should identify the three patterns that occur when people find themselves in conflict between the religion and culture. The first pattern is that members of the religion may have as little to do as possible with nonmembers of their religion. They may withdraw into closed communities. In the second pattern, only certain aspects of the culture are rejected while others are acceptable. For example, some clothing that may be immodest is unacceptable, but other appropriate clothing is ok. This pattern has some mild tension associated with it that is resolved either by following the religion or by participating in the forbidden acts on the "sly." The last pattern is that the society rejects the religious group. They may even try to destroy it in extreme cases.

CHAPTER 19

ANSWERS FOR MULTIPLE CHOICE QUESTIONS

1. **d** Sociologists focus on medicine as a profession, a bureaucracy, and a business; therefore, "all of the above" would be the correct answer.

2. **c** The healing specialist of a preliterate tribe who attempts to control the spirits thought to cause a disease or injury is a shaman.

3. **a** As practiced in the U.S., the primary characteristics of the social institution of medicine do not include personalization.

4. **b** When a person is unable to fulfill their normal obligations because they are sick or injured, they are said to be in the sick role.

5. **b** The individual's claim to the sick role is legitimized primarily by a doctor's excuse.

6. **c** According to research, women are more likely than men to claim the sick role when they feel poorly because they are socialized for greater dependency and self-disclosure.

7. **c** According to conflict theorists, health care is one of the scarce resources over which groups compete.

8. **d** "All of the above" is correct. Professionalization of medicine included rigorous education, a theoretical understanding of illness, and self-regulation.

9. **a** The *incorrect* statement is that "While doctors were able to control women's access to medical schools, they were never very effective in keeping other minorities out." In fact, they were able to keep both women and minorities out of medical schools or to severely limit their enrollment.

10. **a** Government-paid health care for the poor is Medicaid.

11. **a** The study of disease and disability patterns in a population is called epidemiology.

12. **d** Today the average American spends $5200 annually; in 1960, the average was $150.

13. **b** Medical care is considered a commodity, not a right. It is available to those who can pay either privately, through insurance, or a government assisted program.

14. **d** Henslin suggests that the primary reason the practice of defensive medicine has grown is because it is in the doctors' best interest. They want to establish a paper trail to protect themselves in the event disgruntled patients sues them.

15. **a** Depersonalization is the practice of dealing with people as though they were objects, means treating patients as though they were merely cases and diseases, and occurs when an individual is treated as if he or she was not a person. The one statement that is *incorrect* is that "It is less common today because of all the reforms brought about by HMOs."

16. **c** The continuing male dominance of medicine is what lies at the heart of sexism in medicine. While the number of women who graduate from medical schools has increased dramatically, only one in four U.S. physicians is a woman.

17. **b** The transformation of something into a matter to be treated by physicians is referred to as medicalization.

18. **a** Oregon allows for medically assisted suicide.

19. **c** Medical costs have risen dramatically in the United States because of tests performed for defensive rather than medical reasons, an increase in the size of the elderly population, and because health care is seen as a commodity (and is operated for profit). People wanting doctors to do unnecessary tests to assure themselves they are healthy is *not* a factor in spiraling costs.

20. **c** Sending unprofitable patients to public hospitals is known as dumping.

21. **b** AIDS is known to be transmitted by exchange of blood and/or semen. The U.S. Centers for Disease Control and Prevention say that casual contact between a carrier and a noncarrier in which bodily fluids are exchanged will not result in the transmission of the virus.

22. **b** African Americans are at greater risk of contracting AIDS. The risk differences are related to social factors such as rates of IV drug use and the use of condoms.

23. **b** Obesity is more life threatening than AIDS or alcohol abuse.

24. **b** Rather than the rate of cigarette smoking increasing, it has in fact declined. In less than two decades, cigarette smoking has been cut in half among U.S. men and by a third among U.S. women.

25. **a** An environment that is harmful to health is referred to as a disabling environment.

26. **c** The burning of carbon fuels has led to the greenhouse effect.

27. **b** The Tuskegee syphilis experiment is an example of the callous disregard of people's health by physicians and the U.S. government.

28. **d** In order to implement a national policy of "prevention, not intervention" it would be necessary for the medical establishment, the general public, and businesses to work together to eliminate disabling environments and reduce the use of harmful drugs.

29. **b** Among the listed countries, the lowest infant mortality is in Sweden.

30. **a** "Barefoot doctors" provide much of the health care to the people of China.

ANSWERS FOR TRUE-FALSE QUESTIONS

1. *True.*

2. *False.* People who don't seek competent help when they are sick are not behaving according to the expectations of the sick role; in the sick role an individual is expected to seek help in order to get better and return to his/her normal routine. Someone who doesn't do this is denied the right to claim sympathy from others; they get the cold shoulder for wrongfully claiming the sick role.

3. *False.* There is often ambiguity between the well role and the sick role because the decision to claim the sick role is often more a social than a physical matter.

4. *False.* Women are more willing to claim the sick role when they don't feel well.

5. *True.*

6. *False.* Medical schools have existed since the 1800s, not the 1700s, in the United States; however, it was only after the Flexner Report in 1910 that the schools started to resemble the institutions we think of today as medical schools.

7. *True.*

8. *True.*

9. *True.*

10. *True.*

11. *True.*

12. *False.* There is a two-tiered system of medical care in which the wealthy receive superior treatment compared to the poor.

13. *True.*

14. *False.* It is not a functionalist but a conflict theorist who would argue that the medicalization of society reflects the growing power of the medical establishment because the more physicians can medicalize human affairs, the greater their profits and power.

15. *True.*

16. *False.* The soaring cost of medical care cannot be explained by the fact that Americans are sicker than they used to be. Sociological factors such as the increase in the elderly population, high-tech medicine with a large price tag, and the profit orientation of American medicine have contributed to soaring costs.

17. *False.* The most controversial suggestion for reducing medical costs today is the rationing of medical care, not the adoption of national health insurance.

18. *True.*

19. *False.* While the health risks of some occupations is evident (lumberjacks, rodeo riders, lion tamers), in many occupations, people do not become aware of the risks until years after they were exposed.

20. *True.*

ANSWERS TO THE FILL-IN-THE-BLANK QUESTIONS

1. culture
2. gatekeepers
3. stratification
4. monopoly
5. gender
6. Alzheimer's disease
7. right
8. defensive
9. error
10. diagnosis-related-groups
11. ration
12. AIDS
13. Alcohol
14. Nicotine
15. alternative

ANSWERS TO MATCH THESE CONCEPTS WITH THEIR DEFINITIONS

1. h defensive medicine: *practices done to protect a physician from suits*
2. g alternative medicine: *often refers to practices that originate in Asia*
3. f epidemiology: *the study of disease patterns in a population*
4. j euthanasia: *mercy killing*
5. i depersonalization: *dealing with people as objects*
6. d medicalization: *the transformation of something into a medical problem*
7. b health maintenance organization: *provides treatment to its members for a fixed cost*
8. e medicine: *organized ways of dealing with sickness*
9. c shaman: *the healing specialist of a preliterate tribe*
10. a sick role: *a social role excusing the sick from normal obligations*

GUIDELINES FOR ANSWERING THE ESSAY QUESTIONS

1. *Describe the elements of the sick role and identify variations in the pattern of claiming this role.*

You should acknowledge Talcott Parsons' contribution to our understanding of the sick role and his work in identifying the elements in that role. In terms of variations in claiming that role, the text talks about gender differences, but you could expand beyond this to talk about other variations within our society. For instance, children and old people have an easier time claiming this role than do adults because they are seen as more vulnerable and more dependent.

2. *Discuss why medicine developed into a monopoly in this country and what the consequences of this development have been for this development have been for the delivery of medical treatment.*

The key to the development of a medical monopoly was the professionalization of medicine. In the early 1900s, in reaction to the wide variations in medical training and practice, the Carnegie Foundation commissioned Abraham Flexner to investigate the state of medical education. He issued a report recommending that higher standards be set on the training of doctors and that training facilities in medical schools be significantly upgraded. As a result, doctors were increasingly subject to more rigorous education and licensing. In return, they were expected to regulate themselves and take control over their clients.

Given these changes, it was not long before doctors established a monopoly over the care of the sick and injured. In the interests of improved patient care, they were able to get laws passed that restricted medical licensing to graduates of approved schools. Given that only certain schools gained approval, they could control which philosophies of medicine were taught and who could acquire the education necessary to practice medicine. They were also able to set fees for services, and for more than half of the twentieth century, they were able to prevent any competition from government-funded medical care.

3. *Explain the pattern of the worldwide AIDS epidemic and suggest reasons why this threat to the health of the world's population has not been addressed more aggressively.*

You could immediately point out that the distribution of AIDS cases is not evenly balanced around the globe but heavily concentrated in Africa and South and Southeast Asia. Looking at AIDS globally, you would want to point out this maldistribution and note that those countries most directly affected have the least amount of money to spend. This reflects the global stratification of health care.

Looking at AIDS within the United States, you would want to point out that more than half of those with AIDS are members of minorities. Furthermore, the most common way in which to contract the disease is through behaviors that are stigmatized in our society — homosexual sex, promiscuous heterosexual sex, and IV drug users. You could point out that policy makers may have been slow to respond because of the character of those most directly affected by the epidemic.

4. *Define depersonalization and present evidence from the chapter as to its presence within medicine. Consider why it is present in a system that is supposed to care about the individual who is sick or injured.*

Begin with the definition; depersonalization is the practice of dealing with people as though they were cases and diseases, not individuals. Then you need to consider why this orientation exists. You could also talk about developments in the medical industry, such as the more than two million Medicare claims filed each day, the pressures to control costs, and the growing lack of confidence in doctors as reflected by increases in the number of malpractice suits. Finally, there are the examples of callous experiments. You could discuss how the Tuskegee Syphilis experiment and the Cold War nuclear experiments; to carry out such experiments on human subjects, doctors and medical researchers had to have seen them as less than fully human .

5. *Discuss a couple of threats to health either in the United States or worldwide.*

There are many threats to health that were identified in your textbook. HIV/AIDS is a serious health in the U.S. and most especially in Africa. You could also discuss obesity and skinniness or alcohol and nicotine. Many work in disabling environments. Industrialization is threatening our basic environment worldwide. The burning of carbon fuels has led to the greenhouse effect, a warming of the earth that may change its climate, melt the polar ice caps, and flood the earth's coastal shores. There have also been harmful medical experiments that have occurred throughout history that have been sanctioned by the U.S. government or other health officials. Lastly, you could choose to discuss the globalization of disease. As global travel has increased, so have the diseases that can be spread around the world.

CHAPTER 20

ANSWERS FOR MULTIPLE CHOICE QUESTIONS

1. **c** Studying the size, composition, growth, and distribution of human population is known as demography.
2. **b** The proposition that the population grows geometrically while food supply increases arithmetically is known as the Malthus theorem.
3. **d** Anti-Malthusians believe that the demographic transition, an explanation of the shift from high birth and death rates to low ones that occurred previously in Europe, is an accurate picture of what will happen in the future in the Least Industrialized Nations of the world.
4. **b** The three-stage historical process of population growth is the demographic transition.
5. **c** The process by which a country's population becomes smaller because its birth rate and immigration are too low to replace those who die and emigrate is population shrinkage.
6. **b** Starvation occurs not because there is not enough fertile land, there are too many people, or people are not eating a well-balanced diet. Rather, experts argue that it occurs because some parts of the world lack food while other parts of the world produce more than they can consume.
7. **d** "All of the above" is correct. People in the Least Industrialized Nations have so many children because parenthood provides status, children are considered to be an economic asset, and the community encourages people to have children.
8. **c** For conflict theorists, the reason women in poor nations have so many children is that men control women's reproductive choices.
9. **b** Mexico's current population will double in 37 years.
10. **b** population pyramids are used to illustrate population dynamics
11. **a** Factors that influence population growth (fertility, mortality, and net migration) are demographic variables.
12. **a** Fertility rate refers to the number of children that the average woman bears.
13. **a** The number of deaths per 1,000 population is the crude death rate.
14. **d** The factors pushing someone to emigrate include poverty, lack of religious and political freedoms, and political persecution.
15. **d** Around the globe, the flow of migration is from the Least Industrialized Nations to the Most Industrialized Nations. The United States is the world's number one choice of immigrants.
16. **a** According to your text, it is difficult to forecast population growth because of government programs that affect fertility.
17. **d** "All of the choices" is the correct option. In the first place, China's practice of female infanticide is rooted in sexism; there is a general preference for males over females. In terms of economics, males will support parents in their old age and are in a better position to take advantage of economic opportunities. Finally, there are traditions, such as the traditional expenses associated with marrying off a daughter, which go back centuries and also contribute to female infanticide.
18. **d** Urbanization is when an increasing proportion of a population lives in cities.
19. **d** "All of the above" is correct. Today's urbanization means that more people live in cities, today's cities are larger, and by 2015, 564 cities in the world will have over one million residents.
20. **a** There are 274 MSA's not 280.
21. **a** A megacity is a city of 10 million or more residents. Most megacities are located in the Least Industrialized Nations.
22. **d** "All of the above" is correct. Edge cities consist of a cluster of shopping malls, hotels, office parks, and residential areas near major highway intersections; overlap political boundaries and include parts of several cities or towns; and provide a sense of place to those living there.
23. **b** Ernest Burgess proposed the concentric-zone model.

24. **d** The pattern of a growing number of immigrants settling an area, with the consequence that those already living in the area move out because they are threatened by their presence is referred to as an invasion-succession cycle.
25. **c** The model that is based on the idea that land use in cities is based on several centers, such as a clustering of restaurants or automobile dealerships is the multiple-nuclei model.
26. **a** Louis Wirth argued that cities undermine kinship and neighborhood.
27. **d** "All of the above" is correct. According to Gans' typology, the trapped includes downwardly mobile persons, elderly persons, and alcoholics and drug addicts.
28. **c** The Kitty Genovese case in an example of diffusion of responsibility.
29. **b** Suburbanization is the movement from the city to the suburbs.
30. d William Flanagan identified all of the above answers.

ANSWERS FOR TRUE-FALSE QUESTIONS

1. *False.* Thomas Malthus was not a sociologist at the University of Chicago in the 1920s. He was an English economist who lived from 1766 to 1834.
2. *True.*
3. *False.* It is the New Malthusians, not the Anti-Malthusians, who believe that people breed like germs in a bucket.
4. *False.* There are three stages, not two, in the process of demographic transition, although some now recognize a fourth stage.
5. *False.* The main reason why there is starvation is because those countries that produce food surpluses have stable populations, while those with rapidly growing populations have food shortages
6. *False.* The major reason why people in poor countries have so many children is not necessarily because they do not know how to prevent conception. The reason is more sociological in nature, including the status that is conferred on women for producing children, as well as the need for children to take care of a person when she or he is old.
7. *False.* Population pyramids represent a population, divided into age and sex but not race.
8. *True.*
9. *True.*
10. *True.*
11. *False.* According to Julian Simon, immigrants to the United States contribute more to the country than the country expends on them. Such areas as talent and innovations cannot be measured simply in dollars.
12. *True.*
13. *False.* A megacity is a city of 10 million or more residents.
14. *True.*
15. *True.*
16. *False.* No one model is considered to be the most accurate because different cities develop and grow in different ways, especially if there are certain kinds of natural barriers such as rivers or mountains.
17. *True.*
18. *True.*
19. *True.*
20. *False.* Urban renewal involves the destruction of deteriorated buildings and the building of stadiums, high-rise condos, luxury hotels, and expensive shops.

ANSWERS TO THE FILL-IN-THE-BLANK QUESTIONS

1. Malthus theorem
2. Tsunami
3. political
4. lowest

5. industrialized
6. one couple, one child
7. zero population
8. Urbanization
9. megalopolis
10. micropolis
11. nuclei
12. peripheral
13. Alienation
14. Cosmopolites
15. less

ANSWERS TO MATCH THESE SOCIAL SCIENTISTS WITH THEIR CONTRIBUTIONS

1. a William Wilson: *transformation of cities into ghettos*
2. c Ernest Burgess: *concentric-zone model*
3. d Herbert Gans: *urban villagers*
4. e Homer Hoyt: *sector model*
5. b Robert Park: *human ecology*
6. h Julian Simon: *immigrants contribute to U.S. economy*
7. i Louis Wirth: *alienation and urban life*
8. j William Faunce: *views consistent with the New Malthusians*
9. g Darley & Latané: *diffusion of responsibility*
10. f Steven Mosher: *ruthless enforcement of on China's one child policy*

GUIDELINES FOR ANSWERING THE ESSAY QUESTIONS

1. *State the positions of the New Malthusians and the anti-Malthusians and discuss which view you think is more accurate, based on the information provided about each position.*

You should begin this essay by summarizing each side's arguments. For the New Malthusians you would want to include the idea of the exponential growth curve, while for the anti-Malthusians, you would want to refer to the concepts of the demographic transition and population shrinkage. For both, you would want to include some of the facts such as how world population growth does seem to reflect the exponential growth curve (New Malthusians), while the Least Industrialized Nations reflect the second stage of the demographic transition and the population of European countries is shrinking (anti-Malthusians). Finally, you need to draw conclusions about which view you think is more accurate.

2. *Identify some of the population challenges that affect the Most Industrialized and the Least Industrialized Nations and provide explanations for these.*

First, for some of the Most Industrialized Nations, populations are shrinking. Of the 42 nations of Europe, 40 are in this situation. As the author notes, they fill more coffins than cradles. The reason for this is a declining birth rate — couples are having fewer children and are not replacing themselves. A second challenge that the Most Industrialized Nations face is the migration of people from the Least Industrialized Nations. As immigrants move into these nations, there is some question about whether they contribute to the economy or are a drain. Regardless, as they immigrate, they create pressures on the receiving society to provide employment and services for them.

For the Least Industrialized Nations, the first challenge is how to feed people. People in many of these nations are starving because the country cannot produce enough food. In some cases, there is famine caused by drought, inefficient farming, and wars. In other cases, because of globalization, the major share of agricultural land is committed to producing crops for export rather than for indigenous consumption. A second challenge is to slow population growth. Some nations have successfully reduced the number of children a couple has, but the population continues to grow. The explanation lies in social and cultural factors. In these traditional societies, cultural values encourage couples to have large families, having children confers a status on the parents, and children will provide for parents in their old age. These factors are strong barriers to effective population control.

3. *Identify the problems that are associated with forecasting population growth.*

Your first step is to define the basic demographic equation — that is, the calculation used to project population growth. Then you need to identify problems that make the demographer's job more difficult. These would include natural phenomena (famines and plagues), economic factors (short-term booms and busts as well as longer-term industrialization), political factors (wars and government policy), and social factors (educational levels). In your essay you need to not only identify these, but also discuss the ways in which they make forecasting a challenge.

4. *Discuss the five types of urban dwellers that Gans describes and how life in the city is different for each of these groups.*

Gans discusses five groups that live in the city. Three of those groups live there by choice because of the opportunities and conveniences that the city offers. The cosmopolites are drawn to the city because of the conveniences and cultural benefits. The singles come to the city to seek jobs and entertainment. The ethnic villagers create their own close-knit neighborhoods in which they are united by race-ethnicity. The next two groups have little choice about where they live. The deprived are the poor and emotionally disturbed. Their neighborhoods are like urban jungles rather than urban villages. The trapped are those who have nowhere else to turn and cannot afford to move out. These include the unwanted elderly and drug and alcohol abusers.

5. *Discuss the factors that fueled suburbanization and consider the impact that this population shift had on cities.*

The trend in suburbanization began at in the early decades of the twentieth century, but really accelerated after World War II. One of the major factors in this shift of population from cities to surrounding communities was the automobile. As more cars were sold, and more highways were built, people had the means to live a distance from where they worked. The rate of suburbanization increased in the 1950s and 1960s, as racial integration of both city schools and neighborhoods increased. Driven by racism, many whites sought to escape these changes by moving to all-white suburbs.

The cities were deeply affected by this shift in population. As more people left, businesses and jobs soon followed. This contributed to a shrinking tax base, with the result that city governments found it harder to maintain city services. Banks began to redline certain deteriorating, and changing, neighborhoods; people in those neighborhoods found it harder to obtain loans for housing or business purposes. You might also point out how these population changes also contribute to the development of metropolises and megalopolises. This, in turn, leads to increased environmental problems like air pollution.

CHAPTER 21

ANSWERS FOR MULTIPLE CHOICE QUESTIONS

1. **c** The *incorrect* statement is that "He proposed that a collective mind develops once a group of people congregate." It was Gustave LeBon, not Charles Mackay, who suggested that the crowd develops a collective mind.

2. **d** Gustave LeBon's term for the tendencies of people in a crowd to feel, think, and act in extraordinary ways is collective mind.

3. **c** Social unrest is the condition most conducive to the emergence of collective behavior.

4. **a** A back-and-forth communication between the members of a crowd whereby a collective impulse is transmitted is a circular reaction.

5. **d** "All of the above" is correct. *Acting crowd* is a term coined by Herbert Blumer, is an excited group that collectively moves toward a goal, and is the end result of the five stages of collective behavior.

6. **b** Richard Berk used the term "minimax strategy" to describe the tendency for humans to minimize costs and maximize rewards. This is true regardless of whether an individual is deciding what card(s) to discard in a poker game or what store to loot in an urban riot.

7. **a** The development of new norms to cope with a new situation is emergent norms.

8. **a** The ego-involved has the most important role. Because this individual feels a personal stake in the unusual event, he/she may step forward to make suggestions about what should be done or will simply take action.

9. **d** The ego-involved, the insecure, and the exploiters, are all participants in a crowd.

10. **c** Sociologists refer to unfounded information spread among people as rumor.

11. **c** It doesn't occur often, but rumors can lead to the destruction of entire communities.

12. **b** Sociologists have found that when a disaster such as a fire occurs, some people continue to perform their roles.

13. **b** Moral panics are generally fed by rumor, information for which there is no discernible source and which is usually unfounded.

14. **d** A temporary pattern of behavior that catches people's attention is a fad.

15. **d** The bungalow house, the mini skirt, and the use of the word "cool" are all examples of fashion. We tend to think that the term fashion applies only to clothing, but it call also refer to furniture, hairstyles, and even the design and colors of buildings. Sociologist John Lofland points out that fashion also applies to language.

16. **b** Social movements that seek to change people totally are redemptive social movements.

17. **d** A social movement that seeks to change society totally is a transformative social movement.

18. **a** The Women's Christian Temperance Union, a powerful social movement in the late nineteenth and early twentieth centuries, is an example of an alterative social movement. Its goal was to alter the drinking behavior of individuals.

19. **c** A millenarian movement is based on the prophecy of coming social upheaval.

20. **c** This new type of social movement that has developed because many issues of concern today cross national boundaries is called a transnational social movement. Examples are the women's movement, labor movement, environmental movement, and the animal rights movement.

21. **d** "All of the above" is correct. Levels of membership in social movements include the inner core, the committed, and a wider circle of members.

22. **d** The public that social movements face can really be divided into sympathetic public, hostile public, and disinterested people.

23. **d** "All of the above" is correct. In deciding on what tactics to use, the inner core is influenced by its own predispositions and background, as well as its relationship to authorities. Research by Ellen Scott demonstrates that factors like friendship, race/ethnicity, and even the size of the town are important in determining tactics.

24. **b** How people think about some issue is public opinion.

25. **b** Although the term is often used to refer to a one-sided presentation of information that distorts reality, it is actually a neutral word.

26. **d** All of the answers are correct. The mass media are the gatekeepers to social movements; they engage in biased reporting, controlled and influenced by people who have an agenda to get across; and they are sympathetic to some social movements, while ignoring others; it all depends on their individual biases.

27. **a** The Lees found that propaganda relies on seven basic techniques known as "tricks of the trade"

28. **c** According to William Kornhauser's mass society theory, as societies become more industrialized, bureaucratized, and impersonal, members of such mass societies experience feelings of isolation. For them, social movements fill a void, because they offer them a sense of belonging.

29. **c** The *incorrect* statement is that "Despite any similarities, the agent provocateur may feel with members of the social movement, this is a very effective strategy for undermining social movements because the agent provocateur is never tempted to switch sides and join the social movement." In fact, it sometimes happens that agent provocateurs do convert to the social movement on which they are spying. Because of the similarities in their background, they are likely to sympathize with the group's goals and to become disenchanted with trying to harm the group. Additionally, as they try to position themselves at the center of the movement, they end up spending hours with the group's most committed members and may become friends.

30. **b** In order to turn a group of people who are upset about a social condition into a social movement, there must be resource mobilization. The resources that must be mobilized include time, money, people's skills, technologies such as direct mailings and fax machines, attention by the mass media, and even legitimacy among the public and authorities.

ANSWERS FOR TRUE-FALSE QUESTIONS

1. *True.*
2. *True.*
3. *False.* The term *circular reaction* refers to the back-and-forth communication that goes on; it can create a *collective impulse* that comes to dominate people in the crowd. This collective impulse, similar to the collective mind described by Gustave LeBon, leads people in the crowd to act on any suggestion that is put forth.
4. *True.*
5. *False.* The term acting crowd is not applied just to violent activities such as lynch mobs or people engaged in riots. It includes such diverse activities as food fights!
6. *True.*
7. *True.*
8. *True.*
9. *True.*
10. *False.* Urban legends are not just another kind of rumor. According to Jan Brunvand, they are passed on by people who think that the event happened to "a friend of a friend"; he sees them as modern morality stories, teaching us moral lessons about life.
11. *False.* A social movement that promotes some social change is known as a proactive social movement
12. *True.*
13. *True.*
14. *False.* Propaganda and advertising are not quite different from one another. In essence, advertising is a type of propaganda because it fits both the broad and the narrow definition of propaganda perfectly.
15. *False.* Deprivation theory and relative deprivation theory are not identical perspectives. Deprivation theory is based on the idea that people who are deprived of things deemed valuable in society join

social movements with the hope of redressing their grievances. Relative deprivation theory asserts that it is not people's actual negative conditions that matters but, rather, it is what people think they should have relative to what others have, or even compared with their own past or perceived future.

16. *False.* For some, moral shock, a sense of outrage at finding out what is really going on, is the motivating factor in deciding to join a social movement.

17. *False.* There is evidence that at times the agent provocateur has been able to push the social movement into illegal activity.

18. *False.* Resources mobilization precedes the organization and institutionalization of a social movement.

19. *False.* In the final stage of a social movement, decline is not always certain. Sometimes an emerging group with the same goals and new leadership will take over the "cause."

20. *True.*

ANSWERS TO THE FILL-IN-THE-BLANK QUESTIONS

1. circular reaction
2. acting crowd
3. riots
4. panics
5. Moral panics
6. fads
7. social movement
8. prophecies
9. metaformative
10. institutionalized
11. mass media
12. Propaganda
13. moral
14. Agent provocateur
15. decline

ANSWERS TO MATCH THESE SOCIAL SCIENTISTS WITH THEIR CONTRIBUTIONS

1. j Charles Mackay: *herd mentality*
2. e William Kornhauser: *mass society theory*
3. f Robert Park: *social unrest and circular reaction*
4. a Ralph Turner and Lewis Killian: *emergent norms*
5. h Gustave LeBon: *collective mind*
6. d Doug McAdam: *challenged mass society theory*
7. i Herbert Blumer: *the acting crowd*
8. c Richard Berk: *minimax strategy*
9. b Jan Brunvand: *urban legends*
10. g Ellen Scott: *studied movement to stop rape*

GUIDELINES FOR ANSWERING THE ESSAY QUESTIONS

1. *Compare and contrast the early explanations of collective behavior, as advanced by Charles Mackay, Gustave LeBon, Robert Park and Herbert Blumer, with more contemporary explanations developed by Richard Berk, Ralph Turner and Lewis Killian.*

You must first discuss the elements that these different theories have in common and then move on to the elements that separate them. First, they are all trying to explain why people act differently when they are swept up into a crowd of people. That is probably the single point on which there is agreement. The early explanations focused on the individual and how he or she was affected by forces outside themselves. Mackay talked about the herd, LeBon the collective mind, and Park the collective impulse. While Blumer developed a more systematic explanation, he also focused on events outside of the individual that impacted on his or her behavior. In contrast, the more contemporary explanations focus on the individual as a rational actor. Berk depicts humans as calculating, weighing the costs against the benefits before taking any action. Turner and Killian also see humans as rational; in their work they argue that people develop new norms when confronted with new and unfamiliar situations. They also suggest that there are different kinds of participants, with different motives for being involved.

2. *Develop an explanation as to why panics, rumors, and urban legends thrive in society.*

You could begin this essay by defining what each of these different forms of collective behavior is. A panic is when people are so fearful of something that they cannot function normally and may even flee. A rumor is information for which there is no discernible source and which is usually unfounded. An urban legend is a story with an ironic twist that sounds realistic but is false. What all three of these have in common is that they develop when people are anxious about changes that are occurring in their environment and where there is a certain degree of ambiguity.

One reason why these thrive in society is because of social change. In times of change, when the old, established and comfortable ways are disappearing, people are often susceptible to rumors and urban legends that restore some degree of certainty in their lives. Conditions of change can also produce fear of the unknown future in people, which leaves them open to panic when something unforeseen occurs.

3. *Discuss the different theories about why people join social movements and consider how they could all be accurate.*

The text presents three different theories about why most people get involved in social movements: mass society theory, deprivation theory, and ideological commitment theory. Each provides us with an understanding of why some people get involved, but no one theory explains why all people become involved in social movements. One theory may be more appropriate at explaining why some people get involved in some social movements but not others. By using all three, we come away with a better understanding of the process by which individuals are drawn into social movements. You might also want to tie this discussion to that of the different types of social movements and the different types of members. For example, those people at the core of the movement may be connected for moral or ideological reasons, while those further out, such as the committed or less committed, may be involved because they feel isolated or alienated by modern society. Finally, a small number of people become involved in order to spy on the movement and sabotage its activities. You should mention the special case of the agent provocateur.

4. *Explain what propaganda is and why it is so important in the development of social movements.*

Begin by referring to the resource mobilization theory of social movements. As sociologists have noted, a crucial factor in enabling a social movement to move beyond the first stage is resource mobilization — finding time, money, and skilled individuals for the movement, as well as gaining the attention of the mass media. There may be many people who are upset about a situation or condition, but they need to be mobilized. One of the primary ways in which this is accomplished is through propaganda.

Propaganda is simply the presentation of information in an attempt to influence people. In particular, the movement will want to use propaganda in order to attract members of the sympathetic public to its cause. It may also be important to try to reach members of the disinterested public with propaganda. Because these people do not care about the issue, or may even be unaware of the issue, propaganda can be a critically important tool in trying to win them to the cause.

The mass media is important to the social movement. Because of this, they are often referred to as the gatekeepers to the social movement. Depending on the type of connection to the media that develops, media propaganda will be sympathetic to or unfavorable toward the social movement. Either way, the success of the movement in getting its message across will hinge on the type of propaganda the media put forth.

5. *Discuss the difference between fads and fashion and provide examples.*

   A fad is a novel form of behavior that catches people's attention. It appears quickly and the media helps to spread the fad. Very short, intense fads are called crazes. Examples include beanie babies and the "Tickle Me Elmo" dolls. Organizations can also get caught up in fads. Quality circles at one time were a fad. Fads can involve millions of people and still die out quickly. Fads can affect child rearing, food, and diets. Fads that die out can make a comeback, such as the hula hoop. Fads that last are known as fashions. Fashions can be certain hairstyles, clothing or furniture. Fashion can also apply to common expressions. For example, "Awesome" in the 1980's, "Bad" in the 1990's and "Sweet" in the early 2000s.

CHAPTER 22

ANSWERS FOR MULTIPLE CHOICE QUESTIONS

1. **d** The shift in the characteristics of culture and society over time is social change.
2. **c** Henslin identifies the invention of the microchip as the fourth social revolution.
3. **a** Max Weber identified religion as the core reason for the development of capitalism.
4. **a** During the second stage of the demographic transition the population increased not decreased.
5. **a** Russia recently became part of the G-8.
6. **b** China
7. **c** Unilinear evolution theories assume that all societies follow the same path, evolving from simple to complex through uniform sequences.
8. **b** Today, evolutionary theories have been rejected because the assumption of progress has been cast aside.
9. **b** Cyclical theory attempts to account for the rise of entire civilizations, rather than a particular society.
10. **b** According to Karl Marx, each ruling class sows the seeds of its own destruction.
11. **a** Capitalism, bureaucracy, and the corporation are all examples of social invention.
12. **b** Ogburn called the process of change that involves new ways of seeing reality as discovery. The other two processes he identified were invention and diffusion.
13. **b** The situation in which some elements of a culture adapt to an invention or discovery more rapidly than others is cultural lag.
14. **c** Ogburn's analysis has been criticized because it places too great an emphasis on technology as the source for almost all social change. Technology and social change actually form a two-way street: technology leads to social change and social change leads to technology.
15. **d** All of the choices refer to technology; it includes items that people use to accomplish a wide range of tasks; the skills and procedures that are employed in the development and utilization of tools; and tools ranging from combs or hairbrushes to computers and the Internet.
16. **b** According to Karl Marx, the change to the factory system produced alienation.
17. **b** The fact that as men were drawn out of their homes to work in factories, family relationships changed is an example of how technology contributes to changes in social relationships.
18. **c** Henslin suggests that computers are providing students to study new subjects because they can access courses on-line. Computers are also changing the way students learn and widening the gap between wealthy and poor school districts. The one thing that he does not mention is that computers are increasing the opportunities for teachers and administrators to carry out surveillance against students.
19. **c** Henslin suggests that computers are altering social relationships, changing the way we do work, and reversing the location of where work is done – not increasing social interaction.
20. **b** distance education is becoming a mainstream part of the educational system.
21. **b** One concern about the expansion of the information superhighway is social inequalities will become greater, both on a national and global basis.
22. **d** All of the above answers are true. The Pentagon is building its own Internet, robots are being used in Iraq, and the Defense Department plans to "weaponize" space.
23. **a** While all regions of the world contribute to the world's environmental problems, the Most Industrialized Nations are considered the major polluters.
24. **d** Acid rain, the greenhouse effect, and global warming are all consequences of burning fossil fuels.
25. **c** Conflict theorists note that there is no energy shortage. Rather, they argue that multinational corporations are unwilling to develop alternative energy sources, because it would threaten their monopoly over existing fossil fuels and cut into their profits.
26. **b** Racial minorities and the poor are disproportionately exposed to environmental hazards.
27. **a** The major source of pollution is likely to become the Least Industrialized Nations.

28. **c** The disappearance of the world's rain forests presents the greatest threat to the survival of numerous plant and animal species.

29. **d** "All of the above" is correct. Environmental sociology examines how the physical environment affects human activities; how human activities affect the physical environment; and has eight main assumptions..

30. **b** The goal of environmental sociologists is to do research on the mutual impact that individuals and environments have on one another.

ANSWERS FOR TRUE-FALSE QUESTIONS

1. *False.* The rapid social change that the world is currently experiencing is not a random event. It is the result of fundamental forms unleashed many years ago.

2. *False.* Our lives today are being vitally affected by a *fourth*, not a third, social revolution. This revolution has been stimulated by the invention of the microchip.

3. *True.*

4. *True.*

5. *True.*

6. *False.* The assumption of evolutionary theories that all societies progress from a primitive state to a highly complex state has not been proven. With Western culture in crisis, it is no longer assumed that it holds the answers to human happiness; consequently, the assumption of progress has been cast aside and evolutionary theories have been rejected.

7. *True.*

8. *True.*

9. *True.*

10. *True.*

11. *False.* Technology is a very powerful force for social change because it alters the ways in which those tools are used.

12. *True.*

13. *False.* The automobile actually gave women freedom outside of the home.

14. *False.* The use of computers in education is likely to increase, rather than decrease, the social inequality between school districts, because poor districts will not be able to afford the hardware.

15. *True.*

16. *True.*

17. *True.*

18. *True.*

19. *True.*

20. *True.*

ANSWERS TO THE FILL-IN-THE-BLANK QUESTIONS

1. modernization

2. Gemeinschaft

3. destruction

4. William Ogburn

5. technology

6. Karl Marx

7. capitalism

8. Most Industrialized Nations

9. global

10. environmental injustice

11. Corporate

12. green

13. Indian
14. Ecosabotage
15. environmental

ANSWERS TO MATCH THESE CONCEPTS WITH THEIR DEFINITIONS
1.   d   greenhouse effect: *believed to cause global warming*
2.   e   diffusion: *spread of invention or discovery from one place to another*
3.   g   discovery: *a new way of seeing reality*
4.   h   invention: *combining existing elements to form new ones*
5.   i   global warming: *an increase in the earth's temperature*
6.   j   sustainable environment: *takes the limits of the environment into account*
7.   a   alienation: *workers' lack of connection to the product of their labor*
8.   b   cultural lag: *human behavior lagging behind technological innovation*
9.   f   modernization: *process of change from traditional to contemporary society*
10. c   postmodern: *another term for post-industrial*

GUIDELINES FOR ANSWERING THE ESSAY QUESTIONS
1.   *The author of your text suggests that social movements reveal the cutting edge of change in a society or across the globe. In Chapter 21, you learned about different social movements and in this chapter there is discussion of the environmental movement. Discuss a specific social movement in terms of what it reveals about social change.*

Let's use the discussion of abortion that is presented at the end of Chapter 21. The fact that there are opposing groups that have organized around this issue suggests that this is an extremely controversial one. The question you need to answer is, what does this suggest about our society and change? First, you need to consider the history of this struggle. Until 1973, abortions were illegal in this country. In the decade immediately preceding *Roe v. Wade*, a revitalized women's movement made abortion rights one of its issues. Bear in mind that this was a period in which our understanding of, and expectations about, women's role in society was changing. The Supreme Court ruling was considered a major victory for the champions of the pro-choice side.

In the aftermath of that decision, an opposing movement emerged. This prolife group was reacting not only to the decision by the Supreme Court, but also to the broader changes that were occurring in the context of women's roles. Many of the supporters of this view believe that if a woman becomes pregnant, it is her duty to have the child. They see women who advocate for the right to control their own reproductive rights as potential murderers — too self-centered to put the lives of their unborn child ahead of their own desires for school or career. If you stop and think about this, what they are reflecting is a traditional view of womanhood as wife and mother.

In most instances, it is possible to look beyond the surface arguments to see how a social movement is advocating or resisting a change in society. You just need to use your sociological imagination to do that.

2.   *Discuss Ogburn's three processes of social change, provide examples to illustrate each, and evaluate the theory.*

This is a fairly straightforward essay question. What you need to do is discuss each of Ogburn's processes — invention, discovery, and diffusion — and provide examples for each. Your conclusion would be an evaluation of the theory. How accurately do you think it explains the process of social change? Do you agree with the critics or do you think Ogburn is basically correct in his assumption that the material changes first and that the symbolic culture follows?

3.   *Choose a particular technology, such as the computer or another technology, and discuss what impact it has had on U.S. society.*

The author presents four different ways in which technology can transform society: changes in social organization, changes in ideology, transformation of values, and transformation of social relationships. The first part of your essay should include some discussion of these four. Then you would want to discuss how one particular technology affects these five different aspects of social life. The book provides information on computers but you could choose another one, such as the automobile, television, airplanes, and the telephone, to name a few significant ones. Remember to provide examples to illustrate each aspect.

4.   Discuss the role of the automobile in changing cities, architecture, courtship, and women's roles.

As your textbook notes, the automobile was the new technology within the last 100 years that had the greatest impact on social life. The automobile changed the shape of U.S. cities and stimulated urbanization. By the 1920s, Americans had begun to leave the city. Commercial architecture changed from the huge parking lots that surrounded shopping malls to the drive-up windows at banks and fast food restaurants. The architecture of homes also changed as garages were built to accommodate these automobiles. The automobile was used extensively for dating and removed children from the watchful eye of their parents. This invention may also lie at the heart of the changed role of women within society. It gave women the freedom to leave the confines of the home. They shopped for pre-made food and with the electric refrigerator, shopping became a weekly rather than daily activity. It changed the relationship women had with their spouses. Essentially, the automobile allowed women to participate in social life not connected with the home.

5.   *Consider whether it is possible for us to achieve a sustainable environment.*

Begin with a definition of a sustainable environment — a world system in which we use our physical environment to meet our needs without destroying humanity's future. As the author notes, we cannot continue to trash the earth, to rape the environment for the sake of profits. In this chapter, you have learned that much of the problem lies with industrialization and a capitalist economic system. For most of the industrialized world, the message has been "growth at any cost." And now, as the Industrializing Nations and the Least Industrialized Nations make an attempt to catch up with the Most Industrialized Nations, they too are forsaking the environment in the name of industrialization.

It is the goal of capitalism to produce in order to make a profit and this has two consequences for the environment. First, as capitalist enterprises seek new ways to lower costs, they are increasingly locating production facilities in countries with few environmental regulations, since having to comply with the environmental standards imposed by the Most Industrialized Nations often increases the cost of production and lowers the profit margin. Second, capitalist enterprises have got to sustain a market for their products so consumers have got to consume at a high level in order to maximize sales. We, like other industrialized nations, have become a disposable economy; the time before a product becomes obsolete has shrunk and we throw away our outdated products rather than recycle or reuse. This has produced enormous problems around garbage disposal.

The question then is, can we control the growth machine? Here's where you can use all the knowledge you have gained over the semester about stratification and inequality, as well as the power of social movements to bring about change. Consider the issues of capitalism, of global stratification, and other the global environmental movement as you frame your conclusions.

NOTES

NOTES

NOTES

NOTES

NOTES

NOTES

NOTES

NOTES

NOTES

NOTES

NOTES

NOTES

NOTES

NOTES

NOTES

NOTES

NOTES